VIATOR

Medieval and Renaissance Studies

VOLUME 3

VIATOR

MEDIEVAL AND RENAISSANCE STUDIES

Volume 3 (1972)

PUBLISHED UNDER THE AUSPICES OF
THE CENTER FOR MEDIEVAL AND RENAISSANCE STUDIES
UNIVERSITY OF CALIFORNIA, LOS ANGELES

UNIVERSITY OF CALIFORNIA PRESS
BERKELEY, LOS ANGELES, LONDON 1972

VIATOR
Medieval and Renaissance Studies

EDITOR

Lynn White, jr.

ASSISTANT EDITORS

H. A. Kelly   R. H. Rouse

BOARD OF EDITORS:

Milton V. Anastos	Gerhart B. Ladner
William Bowsky	Philip Levine
Robert Brentano	Lauro Martines
Carlo Cipolla	William Matthews
C. Warren Hollister	Ernest A. Moody
Charles Jones	Gilbert Reaney

† G. E. von Grunebaum

EDITORIAL CONSULTANTS:

Marshall Clagett	Robert M. Lumiansky
(*Institute for Advanced Study*)	(*Pennsylvania*)
Felix Gilbert	Millard Meiss
(*Institute for Advanced Study*)	(*Institute for Advanced Study*)
Sholomo D. Goitein	Johannes Quasten
(*Institute for Advanced Study*)	(*Catholic University of America*)
Paul Oskar Kristeller	Meyer Schapiro
(*Columbia*)	(*Columbia*)
Frederic C. Lane	Kenneth Setton
(*Johns Hopkins*)	(*Institute for Advanced Study*)
Robert S. Lopez	Joseph R. Strayer
(*Yale*)	(*Princeton*)
Edward Lowinsky	Brian Tierney
(*Chicago*)	(*Cornell*)

Manuscripts should be addressed to the Editor, the Center for Medieval and Renaissance Studies, University of California, Los Angeles, California 90024, U.S.A. *Viator* is open to contributions from all sources. Manuscripts should be typed entirely with double spacing, the footnotes being numbered consecutively and typed with double spacing on sheets following the text. Bibliographical references must be complete. All abbreviations, with the exception of AS (*Acta sanctorum*), PG and PL (J. P. Migne, *Patrologia graeca* and *Patrologia latina*), and MGH (*Monumenta Germaniae historica*), must be indicated in the notes of each article, with a minimum of punctuation. Texts, illustrations, maps, diagrams, musical examples, and the like, will be published when they are necessary to the documentation. Articles that have been, or soon will be, printed elsewhere in any language in substantially the same form are not acceptable. Contributors will receive gratis 75 offprints of their articles.

Inquiries concerning subscriptions should be addressed to the University of California Press, 2223 Fulton Street, Berkeley, California 94720, U.S.A.

University of California Press
Berkeley and Los Angeles, California
University of California Press, Ltd.
London, England
Copyright © 1972 by The Regents of the University of California
ISBN: 0-520-02145-2
Library of Congress Catalog Card Number: 71-111417

CONTENTS

THEOLOGICAL LEGITIMATION FOR INNOVATION
IN THE MIDDLE AGES

•

James S. Preus

Time was when the Middle Ages—at least its religious expression—evoked an image of serene and static harmony. The best symbol of medieval religion seemed to be the ethereal majesty of the Gothic cathedral, theology frozen in stone, or in the architectonic theology of Thomas Aquinas, poised on the frontier between passing time and coming eternity, between aspiring creation and transcendent Creator.

The undeniable "otherworldliness" of the medieval period makes it seem all the more remote from our own age. But that image has changed. More recently the real innovativeness, restlessness, and creativity of the Middle Ages has become more evident. Basic societal structures—church, university, city, nation-state—began pushing their way into shapes still recognizable. Long struggles waged between Church and Empire, between feudal and rising urban classes, between forces of ecclesiastical aggrandizement and apostolic renewal are now better understood. In the course of the Middle Ages, the Europe that is still with us began to take shape. Its Crusades sanctioned and mobilized those forces we now recognize under the names of imperialism and colonialism. Its universities arose to train the professional elites that society needed. Its nations began dividing and conquering the world. Its forms of religion lived on not only in monolithic Tridentine Catholicism but also in reformed, prophetic, and visionary movements.

For a historian of Christian thought, a most intriguing question is: What connection, if any, can be discovered between the Christian revelation and significant instances of medieval change and innovation? The West rose to a position of dominance in the world; unlike its Orthodox and Islamic neighbors, it came finally to place high value on change, creativity, innovativeness. Did Christian theology help this process along?

It is often assumed that Christianity functioned only on the side of order, as a cohesive, conservative and even retarding social force. This view is mistaken. The other side will be examined here: ways in which, for both good and ill, western Christians drew from deep resources of theology to justify fateful and even radical changes and innovations during the medieval period. Furthermore, some ideas developed during that time which, while showing no great immediate impact, reappear with considerable innovative power in later western history.

I find "innovation" itself difficult to define with precision. Obviously, there are many kinds and magnitudes. What I have in mind primarily are personal and social innovations—breaks in the customary way of conceiving the self and of doing things that result in the appearance of something new and relatively permanent: new patterns of individual behavior, new arrangements or structures of community and work, new institutions, new symbols of personal identity, new visions of the course history is taking. I look especially for things that affect more of society than just the Church. To be innovations, they must also be intentional, not merely broad, unpremeditated changes such as population growth or currency deflation.

One of the first factors that has to be recognized here is that medieval society in general placed a high premium upon stability and order; in the religious realm, innovation and heresy were practically synonymous. Both orthodox and heretical spokesmen—both the official representatives of the institutional church and their challengers—tended to agree on that point. We frequently find them accusing each other of "innovation."[1] Thus, we shall not expect to see innovations advertized when they appear. They often come in disguise, cloaked in the reassuring garb of ancient authority.

I am convinced that the Christian "Revelation" as understood in the West provided powerful resources for legitimating change. Change did not always have to fight against the deepest instincts of piety and religiousness. Neither, of course, did change always occur with the support of theological rationales. But there are certain basic assumptions that undergird the Christian system of symbols and ideas which were repeatedly invoked in the context of innovation.

One is tempted to begin hunting for ways of isolating and measuring the so-called "religious factor" in the complex phenomena of change—to try ferreting out some independent *causal* impact deriving from religious ideas and motivations in the innovative ventures of medieval men and women. Such is not my aim here. That kind of demonstration is difficult enough for contemporary sociologists of religion, even armed with questionnaires, statistics, and live interviews. Moreover, the assumption of a "religious factor" seems unduly to hypostatize religious ideas and motives as causal agents in history, ignoring the extent to which religious ideas are conditioned, if not determined, by the material conditions of existence.

[1] J. B. Russell, *Dissent and Reform in the Early Middle Ages* (Berkeley 1965) 19f. Paul Fournier, "The Roman Canonical Collections of the Period of Gregory VII," in *The Gregorian Epoch: Reformation, Revolution, Reaction?* Ed. Schafer Williams (Boston 1964) 20. Friedrich Heer, *The Intellectual History of Europe*, trans. J. Steinberg (Garden City 1968) 1.113.

Rather than get enmeshed in that kind of debate, I shall approach the problem from the more neutral angle of the notion of "legitimation," as defined by sociologists of knowledge and religion.[2]

This notion seems peculiarly useful because it does not demand the assumption that hidden causal connections exist between ideas and certain kinds of acts. We cannot penetrate the ultimate motivation of deeds done long ago, nor measure either the degree of autonomy or actual power of religious ideas. But we *can* study how medieval people brought theological ideas and arguments to bear in certain situations, and what theological and anthropological presuppositions were at work in their arguments. We can see in the surviving texts how they justified, before a generally Christian public, actions that seem to us innovative and significant in medieval history. Their written and spoken ideas show what they believed would be convincing and compelling justification for their actions within the overall framework of the medieval Christian universe. Thus, even though we do not presume to be uncovering the ultimate motivations, we can study ultimate justifications, and accepted norms, for action.

Legitimation involves more than haphazard rationalization. To be convincing, particular arguments need to fit into larger symbol systems, those socially constructed, legitimating worlds of symbol, myth, and story which locate all events "in a cohesive unity that includes past, present and future."[3] At several different levels of abstraction and generalization, every social system, and individual life within it, is supported by religious, mythic, or metaphysical symbols. By means of these symbols, which at their highest level develop a semi-independent life of their own, "the entire historic society and the entire biography of the individual are seen as events taking place within this universe," which is a symbolic totality.[4] Individual identity finds its "location" within this universe,[5] so that the symbolic structure not only sanctions institutions, but also shows the individual how to place and conduct himself acceptably within them. Men can hardly maintain themselves in isolation from such symbolic constructs without exposing themselves to the threat of psychic chaos and even terror.[6]

This perspective provides a helpful framework for understanding the Middle Ages, since in the West an exclusively "Christian universe" prevailed; the language of the Christian faith held a virtual monopoly on symbols of ulti-

[2] Peter L. Berger and Thomas Luckmann, *The Social Construction of Reality* (Garden City 1967) esp. 92-128.

[3] *Ibid.* 103.

[4] *Ibid.* 95f.

[5] *Ibid.* 98.

[6] *Ibid.* 102. Such a danger threatens those who in our time have entered into Charles Reich's "Consciousness III": see Peter Martin's review of Reich's *Greening of America* in *New York Times Book Review* (8 Nov. 1970) 3ff.

mate reality and value which legitimated the institutions, customs, and individual identities of the age.

If this analysis is accepted, a crucial question arises: did the medieval symbol system invariably lend itself to stability in the social order? In the sociological literature, the answer seems to be an almost unequivocal "yes." Little is said about whether, or how, symbolic universes might relate positively to social change. They seem by definition to call for stasis, for equilibrium, as the normal if not the ideal state of things. Despite recognition of their historical provenance, these systems are presented as though they were Platonic Ideas. It is allowed that they may become "problematical," and that the challenge of "deviance" has to be contended with. Meanwhile, in contrast to this model of stability, historians (not to mention most scientists, philosophers, and theologians) see some sort of process as the ultimate context of human existence. Hence, a sociological analysis of symbol systems which does not have more to say about change, process, or innovation seems less than adequate.

Moreover, when we examine western religious history, we see in the Middle Ages something more than occasional "deviance" beneath an unmoving umbrella of static symbols and theological ideas. We confront rather a system that at its deepest levels is intrinsically unstable. Medieval theology's vision of reality includes dynamic as well as stabilizing elements which could not be suppressed without denying universally accepted elements of the system—or "the Faith"—itself. Again and again, Christian symbols were employed to allow for, even demand, change. Medieval people of course, were not much interested in "change" per se, but rather in reform, renovation, perfection, and the like.

BASES OF SYMBOLIC INSTABILITY

I have made a study of some innovative moments and movements in medieval history, focusing on those in which theological reasoning was involved. From a variety of specific cases, I have tried to answer the question: what decisive elements of the Christian complex of ideas, images, myths, were brought to bear in the cause of change?

Abstracting and generalizing from specific cases (some of which will be discussed later on), I find three areas in which the inherent instability of western theology is apparent: in its views of man, history, and God. And although I cannot present a full-scale comparison here, I believe that understanding the West's grasp and use of these fundamentals, against the background of eastern Christian and Islamic thought, can contribute to our understanding of the contrast between the cultures—between the western tendency to move aggressively to ever more dynamic and innovative modes of cultural, social and political life, and the tendency of the two eastern cultures to reach a state of equilibrium, or even stagnation, during the medieval period.

Man.—An amazing phenomenon of western Christian thought is its seemingly inexhaustible capacity to generate new models for human identity. "New men" meet us time and again on our trek through that history. Behind this lies the medieval conviction that man is a *viator*. His earthly destiny is to be on his way somewhere. The critical presupposition of his pilgrimage is his radical fallenness—his primeval loss of the perfection embodied in him or intended for him by God. The medieval (and Reformation era) church was preoccupied with the idea of reform, and Gerhart Ladner has shown the anthropological basis for this holy restlessness in his study of the *Idea of Reform* in the patristic period. He shows that the notion of the renewal of God's image in fallen man is the central legitimating sanction for progress and reform as the basic human task on earth.[7]

Ladner notes that in the West (in contrast to the more cyclical view of eastern patristic theology) the idea of reform "is characterized by belief both in ineradicable terrestrial imperfection and in a relative perfectibility the extent of which is unforseeable."[8] The heart of western man is "restless," with Saint Augustine, till it finds its rest in God, the goal of its earthly striving.

For Augustine, the vital context of reform was a monastic and clerical one. It was based on an individualistic ideal of renewal of God's *imago* in men. But such men together constitute the coming "city of God," a company of elect men in whose lives the ultimate meaning of history is being played out. Augustine's ideal sanctioned the notion that life does not stand still, but must press forward relentlessly for realization of the eschatological goal destined for the people of God. The very other-worldliness (or rather, coming-worldliness) of Augustine's ideal fired an urge that could never be satisfied with the present state of affairs. Even his subordination of liberal and classical learning to Christian learning[9] gives an open-endedness to the educational enterprise that could yield unpredictable gains. Further, the goal of education was not simply accumulation of knowledge, but "change of life" —*mutatio vitae*—reformation to the image of God.[10]

This Augustinian idea was expanded by Gregory VII into an attempt to reform the whole *ecclesia*. In the age of Innocent III and Aquinas, the reform-idea was extended to the whole of Christianity, "to the political, socio-

---

[7] Gerhart B. Ladner, *The Idea of Reform: Its Impact on Christian Thought and Action in the Age of the Fathers*, rev. ed. (New York 1967) 62: "The idea of reform of man to the image and likeness of God became the inspiration of all reform movements in early and medieval Christianity."

[8] *Ibid.* 31.

[9] *Ibid.* 373f.

[10] *Ibid.* 374, 377.

economic, and cultural milieu of life, which the Church had helped to form and hoped to perfect."[11]

History.—Another decisive element contributing to the dynamism of western life was its conviction that the End of all things was not merely a return to the Beginning, and therefore that something decisive must happen in between, within history. Both a constitutive, normative past and the vision of a perfect, fulfilled future exerted great pressure on the present. Medieval reformers recognized above all that the time of the Incarnation, the constitutive moment of uniquely Christian history, was normative for individual, ecclesiastical, and social life. The most common theological rationale for religious change, both authorized (or official) and unauthorized, invoked the primitive norm of the Gospel—Christ, the apostolic community and its successors—against some disapproved present situation. Pope, popular prophet, and heretic alike would resort to similar argumentation along these lines. The formal similarity of these sorts of arguments should not be obscured by the fact that authorized reform or innovation, implemented by proper authority, is characterized in the textbooks as *"reformatio in melius,"* while its opponents, those who detect some illegitimate innovation—are labeled reactionaries; in contrast, meanwhile, unauthorized innovation is put down as heresy.[12]

The formal similarity of arguments appealing to the primitive New Testament norm (examples below) rests on the universal acknowledgment that Christianity has an authoritative cluster of events at its beginning. Against this unchallengeable standard the present state of affairs is always open to criticism. Hence, although innovation is considered heretical in most circles, heretics have no monopoly on innovation.

Besides this primitive norm, pressing in from the past, we discover a second normative mechanism intrinsic to the Christian conglomeration of symbols touching on the content and direction of history. This legitimating and critical mechanism seems at first glance just the opposite of the first: it appeals to norms from the future. Motifs from past and future are of course often mixed. Paradise, for example, is both a primitive and an eschatological symbol. Especially in Greek Christianity, the End and the Beginning

---

[11] *Ibid.* 424.

[12] Heresy, it should be noted, is not merely deviation in thought, although customarily treated as such among theologians. Rather, "the reference should be to religious doctrines which influenced numbers of people in all ranks of society to act in patterns outside contemporary orthodox Christian observance and to reject interpretation of doctrine by any authority but their own." Walter L. Wakefield and Austin P. Evans, *Heresies of the High Middle Ages; Selected Sources Translated and Edited* (New York 1969) 5.

[13] Ladner 63, 82, etc. This near-cyclical view should be contrasted to that of Augustine in the West, especially in his contention with Vincent of Lerins, who allowed for no development in Christian history, and considered Augustine to be an innovator: Ladner 410f.

are very close to being the same.[13] Visions of the future put forth by medieval prophets constantly echo primitive Gospel themes.[14]

But the crucial element of this appeal to the future is the idea that one must obey the call of a coming future age—a Third Age of the Holy Spirit —whose imperatives are so powerful as to override those of both past perfection and present official consensus.

The idea of a Third Age did not commend itself to the authorities, not being the kind of idea that underwrites institutional interest in stability. Although the medieval church never condemned such dispensationalism in any of its general councils, it did confront the problem at a higher symbolic level: in the doctrine of God as Trinity.

God.—We have seen how the instability of the medieval Christian symbol system was rooted in the myth of the Fall from Paradise, and its impact on the vision of man's earthly life. We have also sketched the tension in the religious understanding of history itself, with its norms weighing critically on the present from both past and future. Perhaps the most fundamental element of instability of all, however, lay embedded in the doctrine of the Trinity itself.

In a thirteenth-century dispute, we discover how the Church's official reading of this doctrine seems to have favored a domestication, a stabilizing of the Trinity in face of a rival and recurring interpretation that lent itself to change—even to revolution—in the name of an imminent future.

The ideological hero—or culprit, as one's judgment of the case may be— in this critical dispute was the humble monk of Calabria, Joachim of Flora (d. 1202).[15] As is well known, Joachim divided salvation history into three overlapping stages, or *status*. His theological authorization was an economic (i.e., dispensational) interpretation of the Trinity, which brought eschatology into an overlapping relationship with history. Each Divine Person presides over a stage in God's progressive education/redemption of the race; mankind eagerly anticipates the inbreaking of the third and final stage.

Such an interpretation of the Trinity stood in utter opposition to the reigning orthodoxy, although it had roots in the ancient church. The "economic" doctrine represented by some theologians of the pre-Constantinian church, with its eschatological, expectant thrust, was well suited to the outcast and often persecuted early Christian community. It gave a transcendent context of belonging, meaning, loyalty, and destiny amidst the confusion and disintegration of classical religion and culture.

---

[14] Joachim of Flora's vision of a new order of spiritual existence (discussed below) even makes an equation between *libertas spiritus* and *vita apostolica*, although his overall scheme suggests that the norms of the primitive Christian community are being surpassed; Marjorie Reeves, *The Influence of Prophecy in the Later Middle Ages: a Study of Joachimism* (Oxford 1969) 176f.

[15] Reeves *passim*.

But this doctrine was supplanted by one better suited to the building and stabilization of the established Church. For such a church, whether conceived along Byzantine imperial lines, or as the Augustinian city of God *in via*, neither Montanism nor chiliasm (which had a similar function) was appropriate.[16] Both "heresies" were definitively reinterpreted for the long pull by Saint Augustine. The 1000-year reign of Christ on earth, eagerly awaited by many earlier Christians, was reinterpreted by Augustine to refer to the present spiritual reign of Christ, already a reality in this, the age of the Christian Church.[17] His world view simply had no place for millenarianism.[18]

In his doctrine of the Trinity, which, insofar as its bearing on history was concerned, remained unchallenged in the West until Joachim, Augustine projected Unity as the fundamental and final reality of God. God is above all the *Deus incommutabilis*, far above time as well as above multiplicity.[19] Whereas the Cappadocian Fathers had used as their basic analogy to the Trinity three human beings (Peter, Paul, and John), Augustine referred to the individual human mind, or to aspects of individual things. Augustine pictures inner-Trinitarian relations in analogy to "the internal relations within a single person,"[20] since man's mind, as the seat of the *imago Dei*, still mirros the Holy Trinity (despite its fallenness). Moreover, one of Augustine's major contributions to the doctrine of the Trinity was the notion that "the Spirit is the unifying principle in the Godhead."[21]

The institutional function of this symbol already becomes evident in Augustine's confrontation with the schismatic Donatists, whose theology shows occasional Montanist motifs. He accuses them of breaking the bond of unity in the Church, which is charity—that *amor Dei* poured into our hearts by the Holy Spirit which makes Christians one in the Church. To act contrary to charity, Augustine insists, is to act contrary to God.[22] A striking analogy clarifies Augustine's point: "If a member is cut off from the body, does the spirit follow it? . . . So it is with a man separated from the Church. . . . The form is there, but except you be quickened within by the Holy Spirit, you

---

[16] Norman Cohn, "Medieval Millenarism: its Bearing on the Comparative Study of Millenarian Movements," in *Millennial Dreams in Action: Studies in Revolutionary Religious Movements*, ed. Sylvia L. Thrupp (New York 1970) 33.

[17] Augustine of Hippo, *The City of God* 20.6-17.

[18] Sylvia L. Thrupp, "Millennial Dreams in Action: a Report on the Conference Discussion," in Thrupp (n. 16 above) 20.

[19] Heer (n. 1 above) 1.123.

[20] Cyril C. Richardson, "The Enigma of the Trinity," in *A Companion to the Study of St. Augustine*, ed. R. W. Battenhouse (New York 1955) 247.

[21] *Ibid.* 245.

[22] Augustine of Hippo, "Homilies on I John," in *Later Works*, trans. John Burnaby, Library of Christian Classics 8 (Philadelphia 1955) 314.

glory in vain in the outward from."[23] Thus, as the principle of its organizational unity, Spirit-given charity is to the church what the Holy Spirit is to the Godhead: the bond of unity. And in both cases, unity is the reality which cannot be compromised at any cost.

When Joachim of Flora appeared, the prevailing doctrine of the Trinity retained that same stamp. As Peter Lombard has it in his *Sentences*—by A.D. 1200 the (de facto) official theological textbook at the University of Paris —God is depicted as a Supreme Being (*summa res*)[24] whose unity is hypostatized at an ontological level seemingly higher than that of the three persons. There is no trace of the three persons having successive missions in salvation history. Rather, the ever-repeated axiom of trinitarian theology is that of Augustine: the works of the Trinity are indivisible.[25]

Joachim singled out this doctrine of the Trinity for attack, detecting in it traces of "Sabellianism"—failure to do justice to the reality of the three Persons. In Joachim's view, God *is* three Persons, each distinct, whose unity is one of love—but a "social" sort of love analogous to that by which three human beings make up one people, or animals comprise one flock.

Whereas for Lombard (following Augustine), Unity transcends all differentiation, and God far transcends history, in Joachim's view the very essence of the Trinity cannot be thought of apart from its role in the history of salvation.[26] Above all, whereas Lombard's Trinity has no relation to time, Joachim's is the ultimate content and burden of human history, signifying and bearing in its own life the final meaning of time for mankind.

It is not surprising that the Fourth Lateran Council in 1215 came to Lombard's defense and condemned Joachim's trinitarian doctrine.[27] This event has not gotten much notice in the history of Christian thought. But from our perspective it takes on new significance. Here, two opposed ways of interpreting the very kernel of the Christian symbol system—its doctrine of God—are up for consideration and, aside from their merits as accurate readings of Scripture and tradition, set forth visions of ultimate reality which lead to very different versions of redemptive history and man's role in it, not to mention the different assessments of the permanency of the institutional church which they suggest.

It is possible that in singling out Joachim's doctrine for censure, Pope Innocent III and the council fathers recognized the subversive potential of Joachim's views. Of course any attack on Lombard at this point in history

---

[23] Augustine of Hippo, *Serm.* 268 c. 2, in *An Augustine Synthesis*, ed. Erich Przywara (New York 1958) 265.

[24] Peter Lombard, *Libri IV Sententiarum*, 1 *Sent.* d.5 c.1, ed. 2 (Quaracchi 1916) 1.44.

[25] See, for example, Reeves (n. 14 above) 179, citing Saint Bonaventura.

[26] Reeves 31.

[27] *Conciliorum Œcumenicorum Decreta* (COD), ed. Centro di Documentazione, Bologna (Freiburg im Breisgau 1962) 207-209.

would be inconvenient (although elements of his Christology had been attacked not long before, and successfully); it is also true that Innocent had studied under the Lombard at Paris. But this does not seem adequate to explain the emphatic manner in which the council sought to outlaw the Joachite doctrine, nor the prominent place (in the second article, immediately after the better-known one on transubstantiation) it received in the council's declarations. In addition, it may have been an intuition of the institutional rightness of Lombard's doctrine on one side, and the subversive implications of Joachim's on the other, which moved the council to act in this particular case. Unity and stability are overriding imperatives in institutions, and the council fathers already seem to have discerned that Joachim's doctrine was capable of undermining those values. For combined with its corollary of three ages, Joachim's trinitarian doctrine says that the Church is obsolescent, something that is to be surpassed.

The conciliar condemnation of Joachim's doctrine explicitly avoids condemning his person, and makes no mention of his doctrine of the three ages.[28] Neither, so far as we know, did Joachim's attack on Lombard (no longer extant) refer to it. There is some evidence, however, which allows us to read the condemnation not merely as a judgment on the merits of the two trinitarian doctrines taken *in abstracto*, nor merely as a protective reaction to preserve the good name of the Master of the Sentences.

In its constitution "On the error of the Abbot Joachim," the council—in the same paragraph and without transition—outlaws the Amalricians, named after a contemporary of Joachim, Amalric of Bena (d. 1206).[29] Amalric apparently taught a doctrine of the three *status* in history which is remarkably like Joachim's—an age that liberates Christians from the callings and constraints of the Second Age (of the Church) and justifies life in the Spirit under new personal models and new social and religious forms. Medieval accounts of the Amalricians accused them of teaching that:

> the Father has worked under certain forms in the Old Testament, to wit, those of the Law; the Son likewise has worked under certain forms, such as the Eucharist, baptism, and the other sacraments. Just as the forms of the Law fell away with the first coming of Christ, so now all the forms in which the Son has worked will fall, and the sacraments will come to an end, because the person of the Holy Spirit will clearly reveal himself in those in whom he is incarnated.[30]

---

[28] This doctrine, never condemned by a general council, was condemned by a provincial synod at Arles in 1263: Reeves 61.

[29] COD 209. The ambiguous state of the evidence regarding possible influence of Joachim's writings on Amalric is examined by M. W. Bloomfield and Marjorie Reeves, "The Penetration of Joachism into Northern Europe," *Speculum* 29 (1954) 783.

[30] Wakefield & Evans (n. 12 above) 260.

Although no unambiguous external evidence is available to connect the Amalricians to the writings of Joachim at this early date, the conciliar statement itself suggests that in its judgment, the Amalrician aberration was an example of the heretical—or rather "insane"[31]—results of a Joachimite doctrine of the Trinity. The three-ages idea, held in common, seems to explain why the condemnation of this particular sect was put into the article against Joachim rather than into the next paragraph "On heretics." In order to cut off at its very source that avenue of legitimation for radical religious innovation, the council condemned Joachim's brand of trinitarianism.

This concludes the examination of some fundamental presuppositions that are embedded in the inner recesses of Christian theology, and to which western Christians appealed as they tried to legitimate various sorts of innovation. In the following sections, we come to specific cases, acknowledging that historical actualities are never as neat as theoretical, systematized abstractions. We shall examine briefly innovative moments in medieval history which illustrate, first, appeal to the primitive norm, with its christological and apostolic criteria, then, instances of appeal to the norm from the future—the New Age of the Spirit. Under the first category we shall describe actions undertaken both by athorized (i.e. papal) parties and by people judged heretical; under the second, cases that are all considered more or less unacceptable by the established authorities.[32]

The character, magnitude, and impact of these actions as innovations obviously vary. The immediate impact of the Crusades upon Europe is much more obvious than that of the string of spiritual heresies that cropped up after about 1250; yet forms of the ideology on which the latter depended have also persisted to our own time. The innovativeness of the various movements cited can be briefly indicated as follows: the papal reform altered the relationship between papacy and empire in a permanent way; it created a class—almost a castle—of "new men" in the celibate clergy,[33] and created a whole new body of law to provide the legitimating juridical foundation for an autonomous church centralized in the papacy.[34] The Crusades marked Christian Europe's embrace of Holy War, and the integration of that notion into the framework of western symbolic and social structures.[35] The Crusades

---

[31] "Eius doctrina non tam haeretica censenda sit, quam insana"; COD 209.

[32] This classification of material differs slightly from my earlier, more systematic one (man, history, God); it works better for handling the specific historical cases. Yet the cases to be examined involve dependence upon and appeal to all three of those basic perspectives.

[33] Heer (n. 1 above) 106.

[34] The papal claims to be supported by this research enterprise were summed up in the *Dictatus papae*, ed. E. Caspar, *Das Register Gregors VII* (*Reg.*) 2.55a, MGH Epistolae selectae 2.1-2 (Berlin 1920) 202-208. Geoffrey Barraclough regards the *Dictatus* as a revolutionary manifesto: "The Invesiture Contest and the German Constitution," in Williams (n. 1 above) 56.

[35] Geoffrey Barraclough observes that total war as the West pursues it "is the linear

also sanctified the warlike habits of the nobility, creating the ecclesiastically blessed vocation of knighthood (another "new man"), and launching the first wave of European colonialism.[36] Moreover, the Crusades are the original instance of the western habit of going to war against the enemies of peace in order to end war.[37]

In the heresies to be noted, we find more or less radical alternatives to the medieval person's dependency on institutions (e.g., a willingness to break from the *ecclesia* outside of which there is no salvation), new ideals of personal identity (the *pauperes christi, boni homines, humiliati, homines intelligentiae, perfecti*, etc.),[38] cultic innovation (especially with baptism and eucharist) which makes ritually visible an altered self-understanding and a different set of norms for the relation between individuals and communities, and for the person's role in history.

Esoteric and abstract as the trinitarian decision of Lateran IV may be, it appears to be linked to lower and more popular levels of awareness through the dissemination of the writings of Joachim, and the radical actions of some of his followers of later generations.[39] In those popular movements we glimpse the connection between certain high-level scholastic debates, and the broad movements of popular religious and social life. The relevance of medieval theology to medieval life comes into clearer focus.

THE PRIMITIVE NORM

Papal Reform and Crusade.—In the theological language and rhetoric which he uses to legitimate his eleventh-century reform, Gregory VII appeals consistently to the principle of revitalizing primitive, neglected norms rooted ultimately in the earthly Jesus and the Apostles. The revelational basis

---

descendant of Holy War, as preached and practiced in the eleventh century." "Deus le Volt?" *New York Review of Books* (21 May 1970) 12 (citing E. Stillman and W. Pfaff, *The Politics of Hysteria* [New York 1965]).

[36] *A History of the Crusades*, ed. Kenneth M. Setton et al., 1 (Philadelphia 1958) 244f. J. A. Brundage, *The Crusades: a Documentary Survey* (Milwaukee 1962) 2.

[37] Jean Leclercq, François Vandenbroucke, and Louis Bouyer, *The Spirituality of the Middle Ages*, trans. the Benedictines of Holme Eden Abbey (London 1968) 131-133. According to the authors, the Crusade was to be "more than the result of an aggression complex, being in its way a war for peace, and as such the last of the wars, a war to end war."

[38] Wakefield & Evans (n. 12 above) observe that the Cathars never referred to themselves as "Perfect," a term used rather by their Catholic contemporaries and perpetuated in the histories. The Cathars themselves called those who had received the consolamentum *"boni homines."* 703 n. 6.

[39] Reeves (n. 14 above) 135: "One of Joachim's key ideas was the expectation of new orders of spiritual men sent 'ad vesperum huius saeculi,' i.e., in 'fine huius sexte etatis'. From the thirteenth to the sixteenth century, and even beyond, there were those who fastened on this conception of future spiritual orders and found in it the understanding of their own mission in the world."

of his reform was the desire to "restore the Christian community to its original likeness, to what Christ desired."[40] Ever since Tertullian, the argument that Jesus referred to himself as "the Truth," and not "Custom," provided a basis for criticism of the present situation and return to his standard.[41] Gregory's apologist Anselm of Lucca contended that centuries of evil custom could not turn injustice into justice.[42]

Gregory was extremely sensitive to charges of innovation,[43] and tried hard to forestall it, especially in his enterprising re-creation of canon law. He gathered all possible ancient authorities for his reform (or revolution). Barraclough comments: "Like all revolutionaries, he convinced himself that he was only restoring the old law."[44] And popes who followed him assiduously built on that same foundation.[45] The ancient norms became the disguise for the most far-reaching change.

The pope needed to channel to himself officially and personally all legitimate authority, so as to be able to act on behalf of the whole of Christendom. "Since the Papacy is the lever by which the Christian world ought to be uplifted, it is necessary to establish solidly this lever before putting it into action."[46] Gregory's invocation of christological symbols that would legitimate his claims includes the following: as vicar of Christ, he represents the one true emperor, and so claims exclusive right to the imperial insignia. He bids princes to kiss his foot. Christlike, he sends forth his legates, saying, "He that receiveth you, receiveth me." Deposing Henry IV, he invokes as his authority Saint Peter, and claims to be able to judge when a king is worthy to rule. He expressly asserts his right to implement new strategies (*nova consilia*) in defense of divine justice, which it is his duty to establish.[47] Going further, he claims authorization to make new laws if necessary.[48] In short, "rarely have the forces of heaven been summoned so directly and confidently to influence the minds and the behavior of men as they were by Gregory VII."[49]

[40] Russell (n. 1 above) 5.

[41] Ladner (n. 7 above) 138.

[42] Heer (n. 1 above) 1.103.

[43] K. J. Leyser, "The Polemics of the Papal Revolution," in *Trends in Medieval Political Thought*, ed. Beryl Smalley (Oxford 1965) 57.

[44] Barraclough (n. 34 above) 56.

[45] James A. Brundage, *Medieval Canon Law and the Crusader* (Madison 1969), traces the juridical development that legitimated the Crusades and provided laws for implementing them.

[46] Fournier (n. 1 above) 22.

[47] Leyser (n. 43 above) 59, quoting *Reg.* 2.45 (ed. Caspar) 184.

[48] Gerhart B. Ladner, "Two Gregorian Letters: On the Sources and Nature of Gregory VII's Reform Ideology," *Studi Gregoriani* 5 (1956) 236, citing the *Dictatus papae* no. 7, Reg. 2.55a (ed. Caspar) 203: "quod illi solo licet pro temporis necessitate novas leges condere."

[49] Leyser 56.

Objecting to the pope's deposition of the emperor, an opponent uses the same method: he invokes a more primitive source of authority than Saint Peter: "Christ alone, in unison with God, can give or take away dominion according to the Scriptures; but Hildebrand teaches that he himself has authority over kings and kingdoms, and can do that which, according to the Psalmist, can be done by God alone, who abases the one and elevates the other."[50]

Before the Crusades began under Urban II, Gregory had already proposed such an enterprise outside of Europe, and was instrumental in formulating the ideology of crusading as "all purpose Holy War."[51] As far as Gregory was concerned, a good ruler was one who used the office of the sword exclusively at the pope's behest. This ecclesiastical function was basis for the crusading knight's vocation. In Gregory's mind, all legitimate wars were holy wars fought under spiritual direction—a collapse of the classic Christian doctrine of the two swords.[52] It was assumed as a matter of course "that a holy war must necessarily be a just one."[53]

The Crusades themselves were legitimated by appeals to christological symbols. Part of the reason for this of course lies in the very nature of the Crusades, which were bent upon "liberating" (from Muslim rule) the land where Jesus had lived and died, and to which pilgrims had been coming from Europe for more than a century. Erdmann clearly has shown, however, that the essence of the Crusade was not its geographical goal, but its ecclesiastical initiation and direction.[54] This can be seen, for example, in Aquinas's listing of requirements to be met in order to qualify a military endeavor as a crusade: its destination does not belong to the official definition, but the ecclesiastical direction and aim do.[55]

The repeatedly sounded theme of the Crusade is the *imitatio Christi*: Saint Bonaventure, for example, writing near the end of the crusading era, says that following the example of Christ is the best reason for participation.[56] He repeats the appeal first made by Urban II, that one should "take up the cross" by joining the crusading armed forces.[57] In the formation of crusading rhetoric, taking up the cross had undergone a startling transformation in meaning: it meant now to participate in an armed pilgrimage—originally

---

[50] Barraclough (n. 34 above) 63.

[51] Brundage (n. 45 above) 193; Carl Erdmann, *Die Entstehung des Kreuzzugsgedankens* (Stuttgart 1935, repr. 1955) chaps. 5-7.

[52] Erdmann 148; cf. Brundage (n. 45 above) 193.

[53] Brundage (n. 45 above) 28.

[54] Erdmann vii, 306.

[55] Brundage (n. 45 above) 152 n. 49.

[56] *Ibid.* 140.

[57] Brundage (n. 36 above) 20.

a contradiction in terms.[58] The purpose was the relief of eastern Christendom, with the eventual reunification of the Christian Church under the papacy in view,[59] and the recapture of the "Holy Land"—itself a conceptual creation of the pilgrimage and Crusades.

The knight, fighting against the infidel in service of Christ and the pope, could achieve both forgiveness and martyrdom by armed combat and death, under the sign of the cross. "The soldier of Christ kills safely; he perishes even more safely," Saint Bernard exclaims.[60]

Ironically, the cross as symbol par excellence of the Crusade, in the form of a sewn-on patch, becomes the first military uniform in western history for those engaged in *expeditiones crucis*.[61] Guibert of Nogent recalls that Urban "instituted a sign well suited to so honorable a profession by making the figure of the cross, the stigma of the Lord's passion, the emblem of chivalry, or rather, what was to be the chivalry of God."[62] The lengths to which this co-optation of the cross-symbol could go is vividly illustrated in the spirited defence of the crusade by Peter of Troyes in a letter written about 1170 to the patriarch of Jerusalem: "You bear the sign of the cross on your heart [the pectoral cross] damnably if zeal for the Crucified One vanishes from your heart, and if you are afraid to defend the place of the crucifixion."[63] The goal of forcing safe passage for Christian pilgrims has escalated to the holding of captured territory. Honorable wearing of the symbol of his office for the Jerusalem patriarch now depends on his agreement with crusading policy.

The traditional *miles Christi*, formerly the ascetic engaged in spiritual combat which may entail martyrdom, now becomes the slayer of the infidel —or, if need be, of Christian enemies of the papacy.[64] And the *verbum crucis* —word of the cross—becomes an official technical term for preaching the Crusade, whether aimed against the Turk or against heretical Christians on European soil.[65] Approriate liturgical rites are instituted to complete the process of integrating the idea of holy war and holy knighthood into the

[58] Erdmann (n. 51 above) 306f.

[59] Erdmann 152; Setton (n. 36 above) 224; Steven Runciman, *A History of the Crusades*, 3 vols. (Cambridge 1951-54) 1.94.

[60] Bernard of Clairvaux, *De laude novae militiae* 3.4, *S. Bernardi Opera*, ed. J. Leclercq et al., 3 (Rome 1963) 217. Cf. Leclercq, Vandenbroucke, & Bouyer (n. 37 above) 133.

[61] Erdmann (n. 51 above) 318; Setton (n. 36 above) 233.

[62] Setton 248.

[63] J. Leclercq, "Gratien, Pierre de Troyes et la seconde Croisade," *Studia Gratiana* 2 (Bologna 1954) 593: "Dampnabiliter signum crucis geris in pectore si zelus crucifixi recessit a corde, si locum crucifixionis timueris, quod non opinor, defendere."

[64] Erdmann 185f., 313; Brundage (n. 45 above) 28.

[65] For example, Innocent III's preaching of the fifth Crusade at the Fourth Lateran Council, COD (n. 27 above) 244.

Christian universe of meaning and action.[66] The crusading knight's vocation
is glorified by Saint Bernard in his defence of the new semimonastic orders
of knights founded for the defence of Christians in the territory occupied
by crusaders in the Holy Land. This knight wields his sword as a *minister
Dei*.[67] "In the death of a pagan, let the Christian glory, for Christ is glorified;
in the death of the Christian, the liberality of the King appears, as the soldier
is led to his reward."[68]

Another dimension of appeal to ancient authority appears in the striking
use made by Bernard of the Old Testament promises of the liberation of
Zion made to Israel. Christian theologians had for centuries scored the Jews
for their "carnal" (i.e. literal) interpretation of such promises, but now Bernard
sees in them the legitimation for this brief era of Christian Zionism. At the
same time, he piously reminds his readers that such literal application to
the present situation should not diminish their hope for the spiritual goods
toward which true Christians aspire.[69]

All these invocations of biblical, primitive authorities were supplemented,
especially in popular preaching, by strong eschatological overtones that are
absent in the official documents.[70] In popular propaganda, the idea was
widespread that a decisive encounter between the forces of Christ (leader
of the crusading armies) and Antichrist was about to take place. The liberation of Jerusalem became a vital moment in the scenario of the Last Days.[71]

In contrast to some later movements dependent on the Joachimite pattern
of thought, we have seen how throughout the papal reform the pattern of
legitimation is almost exclusively christological: Christ as root of papal authority, as prime exemplar for life and action, Christ who is to come again
authorizes the reform and the Crusade. His reign, hidden under earthly
humility, is now soon to be realized in the triumph of the forces of righteousness—that is, of western Christendom—in the world.

The Holy Spirit, of whom we shall hear more later, hardly figures in all
of this complex of argumentation. Insofar as he is mentioned at all, the Spirit
fulfils a legitimating role related not to new historic ventures but to the papacy

---

[66] J. A. Brundage, "Cruce signari: The Rite for Taking the Cross in England," *Traditio* 22
(1966) 289-310.

[67] Bernard of Clairvaux (n. 60 above) 3.4.217.

[68] *Ibid.*

[69] *Ibid.* 3.6.218f.

[70] Runciman (n. 59 above) 1.115; Leclercq, Vandenbroucke, & Bouyer (n. 37 above) 132;
H. Hagenmeyer, *Peter der Eremite* (Leipzig 1879).

[71] Leclercq, Vandenbroucke, & Bouyer 131. The process of disillusionment with the
Crusades is traced by Runciman in "The Decline of the Crusading Idea," in *Storia del Me-
dioevo*, Relazioni del X Congresso Internazionale di Scienze Storiche 3, ed. G. C. Sansoni
(Florence 1955) 637-652. Cf. Palmer A. Throop, *Criticism of the Crusade: a Study of Public
Opinion and Crusade Propaganda* (Amsterdam 1940).

and the institutional church itself. Pope Gregory VII, in his campaign to concentrate the authority and power of Christendom in himself, seems to arrogate to himself the title of Saint Paul's spiritual man who is judged by no one.[72] Further reinforcing the authority of the church itself, the Spirit fulfills the role assigned by Saint Augustine: to provide that bond of charity which is the principle of unity in the Church just as in the Trinity the Spirit is the bond of the divine unity. Thus, the Spirit stands for and symbolizes the authority and the unity of the institutional church. Far from inaugurating a new dispensation, or having a "new" work of his own, the Spirit confirms the validity of the dispensation and work of Christ and the Apostles; he helps to guarantee its continuity, authority and unity. He does not press beyond the "Second Age," the Christian era under the lordship of Jesus Christ, but rather confirms its validity and lends divine authority to its offices and institutions.

The Authority of the "Vita Apostolica."—Not only for authorized ventures such as the papal reform and the Crusades, but also for independent and heretical movements that flourished during the same period, the *imitatio Christi* and the model of the *vita apostolica* provided the tools of symbolic legitimation for innovative extraclerical forms of religious life.[73] This appeal to the primitive Christian norm, concentrating on the imperatives of Christ and the description of the primitive church in chapter 4 of the book of Acts, is the most common (but not the only) basis for both dissent and reform throughout the Middle Ages, but is especially characteristic of twelfth-century movements.

The paradoxical character of this sort of appeal is as evident here as in the Gregorian reform: groups such as the Waldensians believed one must obey the command of Jesus to sell all and give to the poor. They could deny charges of innovation since their mandate was an ancient one. But at the same time, for the Church of the twelfth century to follow such an injunction would have required something like revolution.

Groups such as the Waldensians, Humiliati, Henricians, Arnoldists, and others who called for a return to the evangelical simplicity of the primitive church are early western manifestations of individuals and groups who have dared to exist outside the protective umbrella of institutionalized Christianity, if such a course proved necessary to fulfill their ideals. These dissenters

---

[72] *Dictatus papae*, no. 19, Reg. 2.55a (ed. Caspar) 206.

[73] Basic principles of the *vita apostolica* are given by Ernest W. McDonnell, "The Vita Apostolica: Diversity or Dissent," *Church History* 24 (1955) 15-31. Ladner (n. 7 above) 347 traces background in Augustine's thought. Wakefield & Evans (n. 12 above) summarize by referring to the model of the *vita* as "a key element in the transformation of twelfth-century religious orders, in the rise of associations of lay brothers, in the renewal of asceticism, in puritanism and religious enthusiasm. It brought forward new advocates of itinerant evangelism. It also led to new heresies"; 25.

take up new modes of life, form new communities (sometimes, as with Arnold of Brescia, allying themselves with revolutionary movements in the rising cities), set new models and ideals for individual identity (the apostolic life of poverty, penitence, communal life and unauthorized preaching of the gospel), and recast inherited sacramental rites to accord with their new grasp of Christian existence.

The stubborn intransigence with which they held to the express commands of Jesus and normative customs of the New Testament church are illustrated in this text of accusation against some of them:

> The Arnoldists, perfidious heretics . . . assert that it is nowhere read that Christ committed the care of His spouse, the Church, to dissolute and unchaste ministers, neither gave He them the power to perform the sacred mysteries, the keys of Heaven, or the power to bind and loose. As saith Gregory, only those who deal righteously and hold the faith and imitate the life of the Apostles have this power of the Apostles conferred on them.[74]

Like the Donatists of the ancient church, but now as a matter of general principle, they demand conformity between the Gospel norm and the contemporary Church. Not only are they willing to be separated from the church, but they authorize themselves to adapt and interpret what the Gospel says and means.

An important symbolic move is seen in the way that the Holy Spirit begins to be dislodged from his exclusive roles of authorizing the papacy, the institutional Church and the rights of clergy. Arnoldists and others, following the mandate of the New Testament, are now connecting the Spirit with the imposition of hands upon adults, rather than with infant baptism.[75] In so doing, they appear to be combining baptism with the rite that in the Catholic church authorizes a man to preach and make the sacraments, that is, ordination. The heretics are said to use the term *impositio manuum*— the technical term for orthodox ordination—for their own rite of baptism.[76] The implication is the "priesthood of all the baptized." Heer aptly describes the Cathar *consolamentum* as "baptism of the Spirit, confirmation, priestly ordination and the extreme unction, all in one."[77]

The Church could not regard such revisions with equanimity. It was all right to adopt apostolic life, but to assume apostolic office was intolerable arrogance.[78] That was a function on which the Church claimed a monopoly

---

[74] George W. Greenaway, *Arnold of Brescia* (London 1931) 94.
[75] *Ibid.*
[76] Wakefield & Evans (n. 12 above) 273.
[77] Heer (n. 1 above) 1.163.
[78] Wakefield & Evans 210.

in virtue of official succession from Christ. Only through sacramental ordination by superior ecclesiastical authority could the apostolic office be
conferred. It was on that issue that some men and women were willing to
defy Church authority and be excommunicated rather than to compromise
their understanding of the *vita apostolica*. Yielding on that same issue—
granting to the Church her traditional monopoly on the means of grace—
the preaching orders arose, and in sponsoring them the Church found a way
to direct the evangelical zeal of earnest Christians in authorized channels.[79]

THE NORM FROM THE FUTURE: THE NEW AGE OF THE SPIRIT

Legitimation for religiously innovative ventures takes a fresh and radical
turn about mid-thirteenth century under the aegis of a new (or rather revived
ancient) symbol: the vision of a Third Age, an age of the Spirit coming within history, succeeding the age of the Son and surpassing His works, going
even beyond the norms and ideals of primitive Chrisianity itself. This movement seems to be the first stage in western men's habit of envisioning the
future, and sometimes trying to help bring it about, on the basis of an imperative coming out of the future rather than out of the past.

The Joachimite doctrine of the Trinity examined above is the root-idea
here, and can be detected as the legitimating foundation of a long line of
prophets and movements, many of them heretical: Amalricians, Messalians,
some later Waldensians, Spiritual Franciscans, Beghards and Beguines, Brethren of the Free Spirit, Lollards, radical Hussites.[80]

The dispensational doctrine of the Trinity, with its correlative image of
God's three-fold time, is the most striking and powerful example of an integrated Christian symbol system which by its very nature undermines the
hierarchcial order of things established under the aegis of the New Law, the
dispensation of Christ—including his Church, his "vicar" the pope, and his
grace channeled through the clerical and sacramental system. It provides
the ideological basis for building something new as the old withers away in
its obsolescence. The *Deus incommutabilis*, high above the world, (the spatial, vertical metaphor is appropriate here), now enters as the God of time
—himself becomes the very *content* of time—a new kind of Christian time
which rushes toward its fulfillment, moving from the age of the Son to that
of the Spirit.

Here the inherent instability—indeed, the revolutionary possibilities—of
the Christian symbol system is clearest, and therefore also its problematic
character as a satifactory system for legitimating an institution which wishes
to remain forever stable and unchanging.

---

[79] *Ibid.* 36.
[80] Reeves (n. 14 above) fully documents this history up to the Reformation period.

The Spirit, whose special role is to usher in the final stage of history, which is about to begin (or has already begun to appear), makes permissible a forward leap ahead of the religious system in force. The reign of Christ in and through his Church is seen as mere preparation, parallel to that of the Old Testament dispensation, for the New Age. Like the Synagogue, the Church is to give way to something quite new.

Inspired by this vision of ultimate reality, some people spoke of the Spirit actually being incarnated in themselves. An inqusitor reports that almost all the Poor of Lyons "believed that God had formed men in bodies of clay and breathed life into them. The soul was thus considered to be the Holy Spirit and part of God."[81] Others adopted what they called liberty of the Spirit in opposition to the traditional monastic virtues of poverty, chastity, and obedience. The crucial point to notice, however, as we focus on the problem of authorization for innovation, is the manner in which this new sort of legitimating world-story was recognized to be incompatible with the more traditional appeal to the primitive norm of Christ and Gospel. This doctrine of the new age found a new source of authority altogether, a new location for legitimation, in men endowed with Spirit-given insight into the coming age, its gifts, promises, and imperatives. The Age of the Spirit was believed even now to be making its appearance in *homines intelliengtiae*—men of insight—who claimed, according to ecclesiastical records of their trials, to surpass in understanding even the Apostles themselves, and therefore also the acceptable procedure for establishing the literal and spiritual senses of Scripture.

"Again and again in Inquisitorial proceedings the claim to greater perfection than Christ and the Apostles was a major accusation" against heirs of the Joachimite system.[82] For example, in 1411 Bishop Pierre d'Ailly of Cambrai presided at Brussels over a trial of a sect which called its members "*homines intelligentiae.*" Among a host of miscellaneous deviations, the court was especially intent on their abjuration of the following claim:

> that the preaching and doctrine of the ancient fathers and doctors will cease, and new ones take their place, and that Scripture will be more clearly revealed than ever before, and that the Holy Spirit will illumine the human intellect more clearly than he had ever done before, *even in the Apostles*, because they had nothing but the outer shell, and that he will inaugurate a time in which is to be revealed that Law of the Holy Spirit, and spiritual liberty, and then the present law will cease.[83]

[81] Wakefield & Evans (n. 12 above) 52.

[82] Reeves 291

[83] *Corpus documentorum inquisitionis haereticae pravitatis neerlandicae*, ed. P. Fredericq, 1 (Ghent 1889) 273, italics mine. A similar claim is made in Lollard circles, according to Reeves 475.

According to Joachim of Flora, whose interpretation of history lies behind this claim, the third age actually had its beginnings with Benedict of Nursia and his monastic community. Thus, a concrete historical and human project is given eschatological significance. Joachim predicted that this new age would soon come to fruition (some of his disciples later calculated the date at 1260) in a new order of "spiritual men."[84] According to this system, it is as though the unfolding of God as three Persons generates the "unfolding" of man into new and unprecedented possibilities.

Joachim himself was no active revolutionary. He submitted his teaching to the judgment of the Church, and the Church honored his sanctity (even though rejecting his doctrine of the Trinity). As far as helping the New Age to be born, he was content to carry through a local monastic reform in southern Italy. He was not, however, interested merely in individual reform. "One's life must be changed," he wrote, "because the state of the world has to be changed."[85] His paradigmatic "new man" was the New Testament author of the book of Revelation: John. As exemplar of the man of the Third Age, this visionary and prophet supplants Peter, prototype and norm of the ecclesiastical organization man.[86]

In medieval times, the revolutionary implications of Joachim's doctrine were carried out most fully in Bohemia early in the fifteenth century, where the Taborites ventured "the first revolutionary society in Europe"[87]—a society that did not last, but which played a critical role in the establishment of a reformed church and society in that country. The Taborites' vision of the New Age combined themes social and religious, utopian and eschatological. "In that time," they said, "there will be no kingship or dominion on the earth, nor any subjection. All rents and dues will cease. No one will compel another to do anything, but all will be equal brothers and sisters."[88]

CONCLUSION

A great breadth of complex historical movement has been touched on in very brief, and necessarily superficial, scope. The basic argument has been

---

[84] Reeves 135ff.

[85] Heer (n. 1 above) 1.128; cf. Reeves 269. Herbert Grundmann, *Neue Forschungen über Joachim von Fiore* (Marburg 1950) 69-77, reviews the extended scholarly debate about Joachim's orthodoxy.

[86] Reeves 139. Heer projects this model of the replacement of ordained man by spiritual man as follows: "The man of the spirit, the spiritualist reformer, humanist scholar, and finally the enlightened gentleman of the eighteenth-century republic, were the later stages in the evolution of the *ecclesia spiritualis*. The status of the *Deus immutabilis* was replaced by the *processus* of the *Spiritus Sanctus*. Europe was on the move"; 1.129.

[87] Howard Kaminsky, "Chiliasm and the Hussite Revolution," in *Change in Medieval Society: Europe North of the Alps, 1050-1500*, ed. Sylvia L. Thrupp (New York 1964) 268.

[88] *Ibid.* 264.

that when certain kinds of change came about, religious sanctions were readily available to legitimate them; more than that, the western grasp of the meaning and import of the Revelation resisted stasis and encouraged an irrepressible striving for fulfillment. From the depths of its conceptual reservoir, theology yielded ideological resources to justify personal, social, and institutional actions ranging from reformist to revolutionary.

The most significant resources, as we have seen, were (1) the idea of radically fallen man *in via*, whose reformation is a life project, and which generated a succession of "new men" throughout our period. There was further (2) the imperative of forward movement in history, paradoxically prodded by a primitive norm that, though in itself statically conceived, could have revolutionary impact if applied seriously in times far removed from the original context. In addition, the idea of actual historical progression through ever-higher stages came to dramatic expression in the Joachite dispensationalism, rooted in (3) the very doctrine of God. This system of images and ideas indicated not merely a transcendent divine "Plan" plotted apart from personal decision and action, but one that called out certain elect men and women as a kind of avant-garde who should prepare the way for the coming time by venturing it in their own lives and opening it to others. This appears to me the beginning of European men's peculiar idea that they can have some effect on the course of history by acting on behalf of a future they envision. As Reeves comments, 'The full hope of a final and special flowering of human institutions within history could not be developed until all the possibilities of a third illumination in a third age of history had been grasped. Only the trinitarian structure of history as elaborated by Joachim could give the necessary framework."[89]

Obviously much innovation took place in the Middle Ages without explicit religious sanctions. Men often managed to find new ways of doing things without appealing to religious symbols for their justification. Urban communes reared their heads within a feudal order in whose preservation the Church had heavy economic and political stake, so that bishops were among the chief opponents of the rise of towns.[90] The Church fought the practice of taking interest, yet the financial requirements of an advanced papal bureaucracy led to development of the complex fiscal technique needed for modern society.[91] Technological change went on without any special religious accompaniment, although at a more fundamental level theological arguments and images were invoked late in the Middle Ages to pave the way for a society dominated by measured time and machines. This required an

---

[89] Reeves (n. 14 above) 299.

[90] Russell (n. 1 above) 233.

[91] John A. Yunck, "Economic Conservatism, Papal Finance, and the Medieval Satires on Rome," in Thrupp (n. 87 above) 77f., 82.

adjustment in basic values to give priority to virtues suited to new social and economic conditions.[92]

Glancing ahead, we see in the Reformation period both the primitive norm and the idea of a new age of the Spirit in operation. Seeking legitimate reform, men such as Luther appealed mainly to the primitive Church and its norms (especially as set forth in the Scriptures) in order to de-legitimate those specific doctrines and symbols that supported the medieval Church's exclusive religious claims. Meanwhile, in circles associated with the so-called Radical Reformation, the Joachite vision of a new age remained powerfully alive and disruptive. This tradition also fed into certain Renaissance aspirations for a new Golden Age, the *renovatio mundi*, as represented in men such as Guillaume Postel.[93] Postel combined a Joachite system of historical cycles with "a strikingly modern version of the idea of progress."[94] Significant is the way in which this tradition of thought was able to absorb and exult in the flood of innovations—new discoveries, inventions and intellectual styles —that characterized that critical period. Postel assigned eschatological significance not only to Renaissance progress in learning, geographical discoveries and printing, but even to the invention of artillery.[95]

There appears to be a large measure of futility in the long tradition of prophets and radicals that litter western history. Yet, in conceptualizing and venturing the future in their own lives, and despite disappointment and failure, these heirs of Joachim kept putting the challenge of their vision to the everyday world. The repeated failure of prophecy among those who were attracted to it did not kill it, but gave rise to revision—*re-vision*—and out of the continual discipline of vision and re-vision they may take some credit (and blame) for actually creating the future.[96]

Some examples that suggest the impact of images of the future upon the real future, and which invite further study, are the following. In 1516 Thomas More published his *Utopia*, and began a new (in Europe) way of thinking about alternatives to existing economic, social, and religious values and structures. The predominantely classical (rather than medieval) inspiration of this work shows most clearly in the fact that there is no *time* element what-

---

[92] Lynn White, jr., "The Iconography of *Temperantia* and the Virtuousness of Technology," in *Action and Conviction in Early Modern Europe*, ed. T. K. Rabb and J. E. Seigel (Princeton 1969) 197-219.

[93] William J. Bouwsma, *Concordia Mundi: The Career and Thought of Guillaume Postel* (Cambridge, Mass. 1957).

[94] *Ibid.* 282.

[95] *Ibid.* 271; cf. Reeves (n. 14 above) 507.

[96] Frederik L. Polak argues for the creative power of the eschatological or utopian image of the future which, "infusing . . . [man] with the foreknowledge of happiness and harmony to come, haunts him and challenges him to work for its realization. It is an unborn child seeking to be delivered and promising deliverance to man." "Utopia and Cultural Renewal," in *Utopias and Utopian Thought*, ed. Frank E. Manuel (Boston 1967) 287.

ever involved in this "vision." Utopia is purely a place, not a coming time, and thus foreign to the Augustinian or Joachite versions of a different world. After More, though, there reappeared among utopian thinkers the periodization of history in three ages (e.g., in Auguste Comte). Once again, as in medieval contexts such as that of the fifteenth-century Taborites, man's vision of a new world was attached to a timetable, and hence called for commitment and action. It finally inspired an international revolutionary movement in Marxism, which fused the utopian vision of a good place with a secularized version of the millenial idea of a fulfilled time within history— a time soon dawning for which man must work.[97]

Another intriguing connection between medieval future-oriented ventures and ideas and the modern world is suggested by Michael Walzer's study of the origins of radical politics, which he attributes to the dedicated Calvinist saints of prerevolutionary England. Walzer singles out as the three peculiar elements of radical politics the negative appraisal of an operating system, expression of discontent and aspiration, and organization for sustained political activity.[98] Now it is true, as he maintains, that these elements are found only in the postmedieval world—if one looks only at its politics. Very similar elements, nevertheless, can be detected already in certain medieval religious movements—particularly in the one singled out by Joachim as the harbinger of the Third Age: the Benedictines. Joachim understood that the future of religion rested in the communally organized reforming drive of monasticism, in its capacity to generate new orders of dedicated men drawn by the future and capable of organizing to embody it. More than that, Joachim loaded such movements with eschatological significance: not only the future of religion, but the future of the world, was somehow tied to these ascetic communities. Lacking the theocratic aspirations of the Puritans, the new orders sought to impose their high ideals mainly upon themselves. But Gregory VII had moved to impose them on the entire clergy. And later, in Geneva, John Calvin began to impose them on the world, if we may think of Geneva as a microcosm of a new world order under God's rule. Furthermore, such radical implications as Walzer derives from Calvinist thought come not so much from Calvin's conception of the political order, as such, as from his idea of a new order being established by the Word of God, which creates a new polity alongside that of the old order.[99]

Finally, I wish to indicate some brief comparisons to medieval Islam, which had its great creative period in the two centuries before the Christian Crusades

---

[97] In this light it is understandable that the two sixteenth-century figures most interesting to Marxist historians have been Thomas More and Thomas Müntzer.

[98] Michael Walzer, *The Revolution of the Saints* (Cambidge, Mass. 1965) 1.

[99] David Little, *Religion, Order and Law: a Study in Pre-Revolutionary England* (New York 1969), esp. chap. 3, "The New Order of John Calvin."

and then fell into a long period of stagnation. In light of my study, Islam does not appear to have had in its symbol system nearly the resources for justifying innovation which emerged in the western tradition. First of all, owing to its doctrine of the Trinity (especially the Holy Spirit), the intellectual and religious creativity of the West could never be suffocated by the authority of its Book. Despite efforts of ecclesiastical authorities either to confine the Spirit's authority to the Church's teaching office,[100] or to lock the Spirit into an orderly biblicism, as was done in the Reformation and after, the Spirit was invoked again and again to justify creative vision, innovation, and disruption.[101] In Islam, by contrast, the Koran gradually achieved almost the status of divinity, having attached to it the attributes of the Christian Logos and Spirit: eternity and uncreatedness.[102]

Lacking the Holy Spirit, Islam also lacks the companion element of a "new age" which can intrude onto the historical plane from the future. Its eschatology seems ever confined to the moment beyond history. In its doctrine of man in history, Islam had neither the doctrine of the fall nor a correlative vision of man's almost angelic destiny. The notion of man as *viator* in search of perfection in history thus did not function as a legitimating idea for progress.

In the authoritative words and life of its Prophet, Islam had a criterion formally similar to the Christian primitive norm, but it lacked Christianity's accompanying impulse, derived from its view of man in history, that "reform" was a constant imperative. Thus, the primitive norm tended to work in a conservative way. The "new men" of western history do not appear in the Muslim community. The highest ideal among Muslim mystics is a species of Gnostic or mystic perfection.[103] "Islam is eminently human in that it takes man for what he is, but it is not Humanist in that it is not in-

---

[100] See, for example, the case tried by D'Ailly and documented above, n. 83. The person on trial is asked to recant as follows: "Quod nullus potest sacram scripturam perfecte intelligere nisi Spiritus sanctus esset in eo, revoco tanquam falsam et erroneam; quia stat quod aliqui peccatores melius intelligunt sacram scripturam quam multi simplices habentes Spiritum sanctum et gratiam Spiritus sancti"; ed. Fredericq 274. This blocks the challenge to the authority of the teaching office of the Church by unauthorized Spirit-endowed interpreters of the Revelation.

[101] The Eastern Orthodox Church had developed a doctrine of the Trinity which, like that of Joachim, gave more emphasis to the threeness than the Augustinian-Western orthodoxy (see Vladimir Lossky, *The Mystical Theology of the Eastern Church* [London 1957] 56-64 for a critique of the trinitarian scheme represented by Lombard and Lateran IV). But this threeness was not construed dispensationally. The doctrine had been developed out of the hierarchical-ontological structure of Middle and Neo-Platonism, with its "vertical" subordinationism of the divine Triad eventually transformed into the Cappadocian doctrine of the consubstantial Trinity.

[102] Gustave E. von Grunebaum, *Medieval Islam: a Study in Cultural Orientation*, ed. 2 (Chicago 1953) 102.

[103] Von Grunebaum 138f., 141.

terested in the richest possible unfolding and evolving of man's potentialities, in that it never conceived of the forming of men as civilization's principal and most noble task."[104] If that assessment is at all accurate, key elements in the Islamic symbol system corresponding to the elements I have identified in the western tradition seemed to work against innovativeness in favor of stability, even stagnation.[105] The Muslim's world—very unlike that of the western Christian—was a world at rest.[106]

---

[104] Von Grunebaum 230. The "forming of men" was a central concern of medieval religion, despite the obvious fact that von Grunebaum's description does not correspond to medieval aspiration prior to its infusion with the ideals of renaissance humanism and ideas from later periods in Western history.

[105] Von Grunebaum 240-249.

[106] Von Grunebum 346

The Divinity School
Harvard University
Cambridge, Massachusetts, U.S.A.

THE ICONOGRAPHY AND THE DATE OF THE MOSAICS OF THE ROTUNDA OF HAGIOS GEORGIOS, THESSALONIKI

•

by W. Eugene Kleinbauer

This paper deals with one of the most important and artistically significant monuments of the Early Christian period: the Rotunda now known as Hagios Georgios at Thessaloniki. Organized in two parts, it will attempt to identify the correct meaning of the iconographic program of the decoration of the building and to date both the conversion of the pagan building into a Christian sanctuary and the execution of its extraordinary mosaic decoration to the middle or the third quarter of the fifth century, thereby casting aside the two currently accepted attributions of that decoration to the years 380-390 on the one hand and the early sixth century on the other.

THE ICONOGRAPHIC PROGRAM

It is here proposed that the three zones of mosaic decoration in the dome of the Rotunda depict the Second Coming of the Lord, the παρουσία τοῦ κυρίου or *adventus Domini*, which is the expectation of his messianic advent in glory

During 1969 parts of this study were read as public lectures on three occasions: the annual meeting of the College Art Association that was held at Boston; the regional conference of the Medieval Association of the Pacific that met at Riverside, California; and a lecture series sponsored by the Art History Graduate Students Association of the University of California at Los Angeles. I am indebted to the students who enrolled in my graduate seminar on the mosaics of Hagios Georgios that was held at UCLA in the winter quarter of 1969, especially Sister Catherine Bock, Mrs. Tina Lent, Mr. Steven Rhodes, and Mrs. Joan Starrels. Professors Ernst Kitzinger and Kurt Weitzmann were generous in reading drafts of this study and making valuable pointers and corrections. Many times have my colleagues Milton Anastos and Susan Downey offered me their wisdom and knowledge. The late Basil Laourdas, formerly director of the Balkan Institute at Thessaloniki, extended me many kindnesses and made it possible for me to obtain photographs of the mosaics in Hagios Georgios from Stergios Stergiopoulos of Photo Lykides at Thessaloniki. Miss Therese Christensen undertook the Herculean task of translating H. Torp's *Mosaikkene i St. Georg-Rotunden i Thessaloniki* for me. Finally, I must thank Michael Vickers of the Ashmolean Museum at Oxford for sharing with me the results of his research on Late Antique Thessaloniki.

at the end of this era to restore his kingdom, the earthly Jerusalem.[1] While in previous scholarship the thematic content of the mosaics has generally been identified as the Ascension of Christ, André Grabar has divined the correct meaning of the program.[2] As Grabar points out, the mosaics can not represent the Ascension of Christ, which is depicted in the semidome of the apse of the eastern sanctuary of the Rotunda. Although this fresco is a post-Iconoclastic work, there can not have been two images of the very same subject matter in the same building.[3] According to Grabar, the mosaics represent, from the crown to the springing of the dome, the Lord triumphant carried by four flying angels and accompanied by the phoenix, a ring of twenty-two figures, perhaps apostles and prophets, and the ideal Church in its celestial glory, in front of whose facades stand martyrs civilian and military. In our judgment Grabar adduces the wrong body of evidence to prove his identification of the ensemble, wrongly identifies the figures in the second zone of the dome, and is off the mark in his conception of the well-known frieze of martyrs. He adduces what he identifies as images of the Second Coming of Christ in the Vatican copy of the *Christian Topography* by Cosmas Indicopleustes (fig. 6) and the *Sacra parallela* by John of Damascus. The

---

[1] For the term Parousia in the New Testament and other Early Christian literature, see A. Oepke, in *Theologisches Wörterbuch zum Neuen Testament*, ed. G. Kittel, 5 (1957) 856 ff., s.v. παρουσία.

[2] A. Grabar, "A propos des mosaïques de la coupole de Saint-Georges, à Salonique," *Cahiers archéologiques* 17 (1967) 59ff. That the mosaics represent the Second Coming of the Lord has been briefly mentioned by F. Valentien, "Frühchristliche und frühmittelalterliche Voraussetzungen für eine Majestas-Darstellung des 12. Jahrhundert," in *Tortulae: Studien zu altchristlichen und byzantinischen Monumenten*, ed. W. N. Schumacher, *Römische Quartalschrift für christliche Altertumskunde und Kirchengeschichte*, (Rome 1966) 287f. That they represent the Ascension of Christ has been proposed by C. Ihm, *Die Programme der christlichen Apsismalerei von vierten Jahrhundert bis zur Mitte des achten Jahrhundert* (Wiesbaden 1960) 96 n. 4; K. Papadopoulos, *Die Wandmalerei des XI. Jahrhunderts in der Kirche Παναγία τῶν Χαλκέων in Thessaloniki* (Graz 1966) 22. In his *Mosaikkene i St. Georg-Rotunden i Thessaloniki* (Oslo 1963), H. Torp discusses the meaning of the program in the most general terms and fails to identify it specifically as the Second Coming of Christ. For the apse fresco in the Rotunda, see A. Xyngopoulos, "Ἡ τοιχογραφία τῆς Ἀναλήψεως ἐν τῇ ἁψῖδι τοῦ ἁγίου Γεωργίου τῆς Θεσσαλονίκης," *Archaiologike Ephemeris* 1938 (publ. 1941) 32ff. For other discussions of the iconography of the mosaics in the Rotunda, see nn. 56, 89 below.

[3] Similarity in the theological content of the Ascension and the Parousia of Christ has been pointed out by O. Demus, *Byzantine Mosaic Decoration* (London 1948) 19f. and analyzed in detail by B. Brenk, *Tradition und Neuerung in der christlichen Kunst des ersten Jahrtausends* (Vienna 1966) 55f., who develops a suggestion first made by O. Homburger, *Die Anfänge der Malerschule von Winchester im 10. Jahrhundert* (Leipzig 1912) 14, concerning the possible derivation of representations of the *adventus Domini* from those of the Ascension of Christ. See also Y. Christe, "La vision de Matthieu: origine et développement d'une image de la Seconde Parousie selon saint Matthieu," *Genava*, n.s. 16 (1968) 119ff.; 17 (1969) 59ff.; and n. 66 below.

Vatican manuscript copies the mid-sixth century *Christian Topography* of Cosmas Indicopleustes, as Grabar observes, and Weitzmann has shown that the *Sacra parallela* manuscript is based on early Christian sources. But the illumination in the Vatican manuscript represents not the Parousia of the Lord but a Christian topography of the cosmos, while that in the *Sacra parallela* probably depicts the Last Judgment (see below). As we hope to bring out in the following pages, better sources, textual as well as artistic, are at hand to identify the precise meaning of the program represented in the Rotunda. We hope to demonstrate that the theological advisors of the mosaic decoration drew upon various accounts of the Parousia and selectively integrated them into a unified program, in which liturgical elements were made to prevail over any narrative content. In this regard the importance of the mosaics as a forerunner in the Greek east of what has come to be known as the "classical system" of Middle Byzantine church decoration becomes at once apparent.

CHRIST AND HIS HOST

The longitudinal axis of the Rotunda points approximately 30 degrees south of east, but to facilitate discussion the walls and mosaics throughout this study will be referred to as north, south, east, and so forth.

The mosaics are arranged hierarchically in three concentric zones, extending from the summit of the dome to its springing and finally to the soffits of the barrel-vaulted passageways in the massive peripheral wall, whose decoration is part of the original program (figs. 1 and 3). The decoration in the dome is estimated to cover some 1850 square meters. The ambulatory and south vestibule that were appended to the Rotunda when it was converted into a church may initially have received mosaics, as perhaps did part of the exterior, but nothing is known of them.

The highest place in this scheme was reserved for the most important part of the program; there, in a medallion, a striding figure of Christ, his right foot advanced slightly, clad in a long himation and short billowing chiton, emerged from a shimmering silver background, a gem-encrusted gold cross staff held by his left hand, his right arm raised to the level of his head, the palm facing outward (fig. 3).[4] His head was encircled by a golden-gemmed nimbus, and his face was probably youthful and beardless, with his long hair combed and falling behind his shoulders, as can be gleaned from the preserved underdrawing and the representation in mosaic of the head of Christ in a medallion supported by a pair of angels in the pediment of the architectural

[4] Torp 34ff., fig. on 37. Similar underdrawings were found during the recent cleaning of the apse mosaic of Hosios David at Thessaloniki (M. Chatzidakis, in *Archaiologikon Deltion* 11 (1966) *Chronika*, 19 pls. 11-12).

facade in the northeast panel.[5] In other words, the figure of Christ seems to have resembled that shown in the apse mosaic of Hosios David at Thessaloniki with the exception of the standing pose. Of the executed figure in the Rotunda only parts of his nimbus, cross staff, and right hand survive; the remainder is lost and must be reconstructed from the preliminary drawing painted in black on the bare brickwork that was executed as a compositional tryout when the mosaicists began to work in the church.[6]

The silver medallion of Christ is surrounded by twenty-four eight-pointed stars, silver in color, which are regularly distributed on a night-blue band and which symbolize the starry sky, the celestial abode, whence he appears "coming on a cloud" (cf. Genesis 1.14).[7] The ring of fixed stars is surrounded, in turn, by a magnificent garland woven of evergreen and all the seasonal fruits and flowers, a traditional element in Early Christian art.[8] This garland is contained within a gold ring that is circumscribed by a number of narrow rainbow-colored bands forming the outer periphery of the central medallion.[9] Four gold-nimbed and proudly winged caryatidlike angels whose curly hair is held in place by white diadems effortlessly support the apparitional clipeus; portions of three of the angels survive. Thus the clipeus contains the figure of Christ Triumphant as the Lord of the World who advances from heaven, accompanied by the symbols of his victory over death, the gemmed nimbus and the $\sigma\tau\alpha\nu\varrho\grave{o}\varsigma$ $\nu\iota\varkappa o\pi o\iota\acute{o}\varsigma$.[10]

Such an iconography of the Christ figure is known from other works of the Early Christian period which in turn can be traced back to Roman Imperial art. Images of Christ shouldering the cross while treading on the beasts

---

[5] Torp 34, fig. on 29; Grabar figs. 2, 12.

[6] The figure of Christ that was executed in mosaic was reduced in length about ten per cent from that first sketched on the bare brickwork.

[7] See Origen, *In Gen. comm.* 3.5 (8.19 ed. Lommatzsch) and the discussion by L. Koep, *Das himmlische Buch in Antike und Christentum*, Theophaneia 8 (Bonn 1952) 42ff. Cyril of Jerusalem describes the appearance of stars at the time of the Second Coming as "like silver" (*Catechesis* 15.20; PG 33.898).

[8] Cf. G. M. A. Hanfmann, *The Season Sarcophagus in Dumbarton Oaks* (Cambridge, Mass. 1951). The best study of the wreath in Early Christian art is E. R. Goodenough, "The Crown of Victory in Judaism," *Art Bulletin* 28 (1946) 139ff. The multicolored band surrounding the Christ figure recalls Revelation IV, 3: "round the throne [of the Lord] was a rainbow, bright as an emerald."

[9] The gold ground of the enclosing wreath brings to mind the *aurum coronarium* of Constantine the Great and its antecedents (*Panegyrici latini*, 12, 25, 4). Consult T. Klauser, "Aurum Coronarium," *Mitteilungen des Deutschen archäologischen Instituts, Römische Abteilung* 59 (1944) 129ff.

[10] For the clipeus as an *imago mundi*, see H. P. L'Orange, *Studies on the Iconography of Cosmic Kingship in the Ancient World* (Oslo 1953) 90ff. For the idea of the cross staff, see J. Gagé, "$\Sigma\tau\alpha\nu\varrho\grave{o}\varsigma$ $\nu\iota\varkappa o\pi o\iota\acute{o}\varsigma$. La victoire impériale dans l'empire chrétien," *Revue d'histoire et de philosophie religieuses* 13 (1933) 370ff.; A. Alföldi, "Das Kreuzszepter Konstantins des Grossen," *Schweizer Münzblätter* 4 (1954) 81ff.

in the art of sixth-century Ravenna and the Carolingian period come to mind, for instance, the "god in uniform" trampling the beasts in the lunette mosaic of the vestibule of the Archiepiscopal Chapel at Ravenna,[11] as well as the central figure in the tympanum of the portal of the Palace of Theodoric which is represented in Sant'Apollinare Nuovo.[12] These depictions of Christ are known to derive from imperial images in Roman art.[13] In one of the wood panels of the doors of Santa Sabina at Rome a closer comparison is at hand: a youthful Christ figure with his right arm outstretched, the palm facing outward, while in his left he holds a scroll inscribed with a garbled rendering of the letters of the $IX\Theta YC$ acrostic (fig. 4).[14] In the visual manifestation of another eschatological Parousia, the apse mosaic of Saints Cosmas and Damian at Rome (526-530), the right arm of the Christ figure, in this instance bearded, is raised to the level of his nimbed head and, originally, the palm was open, all five fingers fully extended (fig. 8).[15] In the representation of the divinity of Christ in the apse mosaic of Saint Michele in Africisco at Ravenna, now in the Staatliche Museen at Berlin, the central figure is a youthful and nimbed Christ who holds in his right hand a gemmed cross staff, the *tropaion* of his victory, and in his left a codex inscribed with the words QUI VIDIT ME VIDIT ET PATREM and EGO ET PATER UNUM SUMUS (John 14.9 and 10.30).[16] While the iconography of the Christ figure

---

[11] J. Wilpert, *Die römischen Mosaiken und Malereien der kirchlichen Bauten vom 4.-13. Jahrhundert* 3 (Freiburg 1917) pl. 89; F. W. Deichmann, *Ravenna: Hauptstadt des spätantiken Abendlandes*, 1: *Geschichte und Monumente* (Wiesbaden 1969) 202ff.; E. H. Kantorowicz, "Gods in Uniform," *Proceedings of the American Philosophical Society* 105 (1961) 386f., fig. 40.

[12] Deichmann fig. 186; F. Gerke, *Spätantike und frühes Christentum* (Baden-Baden 1967) color pl. on 147.

[13] Kantorowicz (n. 11 above) 382ff.; A. Grabar, *L'Empereur dans l'art byzantin* (Paris 1936) 189ff., 237ff.

[14] E. H. Kantorowicz, "The 'King's Advent' and the Enigmatic Panels in the Doors of Santa Sabina," *Art Bulletin* 26 (1944) 223ff. For an interpretation of the acrostic, see F. J. Dölger, *IXΘYC: Das Fischsymbol in frühchristlicher Zeit* 1 (Rome 1910) 209ff.

[15] The present disposition of the fingers of the right hand is due to a restoration of 1879 (G. Matthiae, *SS. Cosma e Damiano e Teodoro* [Rome, 1948] pl. I). For the original arrangement of the fingers, see the pen drawing of the pontificate of Urban VIII which is reproduced by C. R. Morey, *Lost Mosaics and Frescoes of the Mediaeval Period* (Princeton 1915) 37 fig. 7. The mosaic shows the Lord descending from heaven to a region of the sky visible from the earth rather than to the earth itself. The biblical texts underlying the Christ figure are Revelation 1.7 ("Behold, He is coming with the clouds, and every eye will see Him") and Acts 1.11 ("This Jesus, who was taken up from you into heaven, will come in the same way as you saw Him go into heaven."). Cf. Matthew 24.30 and Mark 14.62. For an attempt to derive the iconography of the Christ figure with the phoenix from images of the *Traditio legis*, see C. Davis-Weyer, "Das Traditio-Legis-Bild und seine Nachfolge," *Münchner Jahrbuch der bildenden Kunst* ser. 3, 12 (1961) 7ff.

[16] Deichmann (n. 11 above) 221ff., figs. 211-217; G. Bovini, "S. Michele in Africisco di Ravenna," *Corsi di cultura sull'arte ravennate e bizantina* 16 (1969) 88ff.

in the Roman mosaic of Saints Cosmas and Damian derived from representations of the *Traditio legis*, the Ravennate work now in Berlin can be traced ultimately to images of the emperor being worshipped by his subjects.[17] A related origin may be postulated for the Christ figure in Hagios Georgios. The great right hand of this figure, raised calmly and erectly to the gaze of the spectator, may well derive from imperial images and specifically from the flat, frontal hand of *Sol invictus imperator* which appears in the third century A.D., an iconography that Christian art assimilated.[18]

A striking parallel to aspects of the thematic composition at the crown of the dome in the Rotunda is provided by the ceiling fresco attributed to the third century A.D. in the cubiculum of Clodius Hermes in the catacombs under San Sebastiano at Rome. This scene represents an unnimbed figure, wearing a purple chlamys, shouldering a scepter, his right arm outstretched with the hand open, hovering or ascending before a circle of ecstatic onlookers.[19] Perhaps a representation of the apotheosis of the deceased, this standing figure bears resemblance to the Christ figure at Thessaloniki and suggests that even the realm of Late Roman sepulchral art was penetrated by imperial religious imagery, the principal ultimate source of the iconography of the mosaics in the dome of the Rotunda.

Other analogies are found in a Roman pavement mosaic that is assigned to the second century A.D., in which the many-breasted Diana Ephesea is shown standing as the celestial Pantocrator in a crown "of life", the eagle of Jupiter hovering above her head, and the trees in the four diagonals signifying the seasonal changes.[20] Another is the representation of Jupiter Pantocrator in a sculpture in the Villa Albani at Rome, where the god is enthroned in a clipeus marked by the signs of the zodiac, with an eagle perched on it above the head of the central figure.[21] In Roman art almost any important figure could be provided with a zodiac frame to indicate celestial residence.

An association of Christ and of Christ-Logos with stars is known from Early Christian works and likewise derives from antique sources. The cross cen-

---

[17] Davis-Weyer 7ff.; Deichmann (n. 11 above) 223, who refers to scenes of acclamation on triumphal arches that survive from the period extending from the reign of Trajan to that of Constantine the Great.

[18] Consult the basic study by H. P. L'Orange, "Sol invictus imperator," *Symbolae Osloenses* 14 (1935) 86ff. Cf. A. Alföldi, "Insignien und Tracht der römischen Kaiser," *Mitteilungen des Deutschen archäologischen Instituts, Römische Abteilung*, 50 (1935) 107ff.

[19] F. Wirth, *Römische Wandmalerei* (Berlin 1934) 174, 190, pl. 50; A. Grabar, *Christian Iconography* (Princeton 1968) pl. 11. Kantorowicz (n. 11 above) 384 has identified the central figure as Christus Imperator, whereas T. Klauser excludes the possibility of a Christian interpretation of the paintings in the tomb (in *Jahrbuch für Antike und Christentum*, 10 [1967] 10).

[20] *Memoirs of the American Academy in Rome* 13 (1936) pl. 41, fig. 4; K. Lehmann, "The Dome of Heaven," *Art Bulletin* 25 (1945) 16 and fig. 47.

[21] L'Orange (n. 10 above) 92ff., fig. 67.

tered in a carpet of gold or gold and silver stars is an imagery common in the Latin West: for example, the mosaic of the central vault of the so-called Mausoleum of Galla Placidia at Ravenna, the semidome in the apse of the Archiepiscopal Chapel at Ravenna, and the dome of Santa Maria della Croce at Casaranello.[22] In a fresco in the Catacomb of Commodilla at Rome, Christ as Ruler of the Cosmos is represented as a nimbed, long-haired, and bearded bust figure, an alpha and omega to either side of his head and rays (?) and stars filling the ground of the composition.[23] In a pre-Iconoclastic icon at Mount Sinai a seated figure of Christ Emmanuel is surrounded by a starry background.[24] But the closest, and most meaningful, comparison to the association of Christ figure and stars is the abovementioned panel of the wooden doors of Santa Sabina at Rome, where images of the sun and moon as well as stars adorn the firmament between the figure of Christ and the three figures standing below (fig. 4).[25]

Such images derive from antique representations of deities and of emperors in celestial abodes. In the illustrated Codex Romanus of Virgil, attributed to the fifth or sixth century, one folio (234v) depicts a group of nimbed gods enthroned on a curved bench in a heavenly setting filled with an abundant number of stars.[26] The central god, Jupiter, holds a staff in his right hand, a globe in his left. Above the semicircular firmament in the upper corners of the illustration appear the globes of the sun and the moon. Related to such an imagery is a Roman pavement mosaic of the mid-first century A.D. which, as Karl Lehmann has shown, derives from the decoration of a ceiling painting: encircling the central medallion containing a bust of Minerva on a purple ground is a ring of disks of the sun and moon and stars on a blue ground.[27] This represents the goddess as the Pantocrator, the "supreme essence" (Lehmann). In Christian art, of course, the Lord would assume that role.

[22] F. W. Deichmann, *Frühchristliche Bauten und Mosaiken von Ravenna* (Baden-Baden, 1958) pl. 19 (gold stars) and pl. 219; Wilpert (n. 11 above) pl. 108; G. Bovini, "I mosaici di S. Maria della Croce di Casaranello," *Corsi di cultura sull'arte ravennate e bizantina* 11 (1964) 35ff., fig. 3 (gold and silver stars).

[23] Grabar (n. 19 above) fig. 81; idem, *Le premier art chrétien (200-395)* (Paris 1966) fig. 237 (color).

[24] G. and M. Soteriou, *Icones du Mont Sinai*, (Athens 1956) 1 pl. 8, 2.23ff.; Grabar (n. 19 above) fig. 287.

[25] Compare a poem in the Menologium of Basil II in the Vatican Library at Rome that was written ca. 1000: translated from the Greek by I. Ševčenko, in *Dumbarton Oaks Papers* 16 (1962) 272f., where references to other passages about star symbolism are cited.

[26] *Fragmenta et picturae Vergiliana codicis Vatic. lat. 3867*, Codices e Vaticanis selecti 2, ed. 2 (Rome 1930) fol. pl. 234v.; Grabar (n. 19 above) fig. 210; Brenk (n. 3 above) 60 fig. 13.

[27] Lehmann (n. 20 above) 5 fig. 8. Compare a stone relief from the holy of holies of the Temple of Bel at Palmyra, where a bust figure of Jupiter in a centrally placed hexagonal medallion is surrounded by either planetary gods or the Palmyrene pantheon of gods, while in the outer corners winged figures support the circuit of the firmament (H. Seyrig, in *Syria* 14 [1933] 258ff., fig. 5; a corrected drawing of this relief is published by Seyrig

The silver ground of the crowning medallion in the Rotunda is a dominant aesthetic feature by whose use the figure of Christ and his attributes are set apart from the surrounding gold ground. While there would seem to be a lack of specific meaning in the application of tesserae of this particular color, the silver ground signifies generally Christ as "the brightness of God's glory," "the Light of the World," or simply "light."[28] The analogy of light was sanctioned by the Church Fathers who used it to illustrate the various aspects of the relation of the Logos to the essence of God the Father, always with the qualification that light is an appearance only and has no real subsistence (*hypostasis*) of its own, that the "Son is a perfect subsistence inseparable from the Father's subsistence."[29] In the Gospel of Matthew and commentaries of the Second Coming it is said that Christ "will cover himself with light as with a garment," "for as the lightning comes from the east and shines as far as the west, so will be the coming of the son of man."[30] This notion long penetrated the Byzantine mind.[31]

Between the wings of the pair of angels on the western side of the top medallion, directly above the head of the figure of the Lord, are preserved the remnants of a blue phoenix bearing a crooked red feather, or worm, from the nimbed head of which radiate nine red rays (fig. 3). The lower half of the bird is lost, but Torp has identified the traces of the tryout drawing made on the bare masonry directly below its extant head and neck as the top of a palm tree, among whose branches the phoenix was perched, outwardly oriented.[32] What is the meaning of the phoenix in this context?[33] In the Greek

---

in his *Antiquités syriennes*, ser. 4 [Paris 1953] frontispiece, as pointed out to me by Professor Susan Downey).

[28] Hebrews 1.3; John 8.1; John 1.4, respectively. For the symbolism of *leukos* (usually translated as white), consult E. R. Goodenough, *Jewish Symbols in the Greco-Roman Period* 9 (New York, 1964) 165ff., where he points out that the term not only means bright or shining but is also used of the sun, light, ether, a "clear" voice, and a happy day.

[29] John of Damascus, *De Fide Orth.* 1.8 (PG 94.821), cited by H. A. Wolfson, *The Philosophy of the Church Fathers*, ed. 2 rev. (Cambridge, Mass. 1964) 1.301, 360, who discusses this analogy in connection with Early Christian thought about the generation of the Logos.

[30] Psalms 104.2 and Matthew 24.27. Cf. Cyril of Jerusalem, *Catechesis* 15.10 (PG 33.883). For Christ as the light of the world, see F. J. Dölger, *Sol salutis: Gebet und Gesang im christlichen Altertum* (Münster 1925) 158ff.

[31] In the ekphrasis of one of the domes of the Holy Apostles Church at Constantinople which he wrote between 1198 and 1203, Nikolaos Mesarites declared that

this hall (*stoa*), which can really be called the dome of Heaven since the Sun of Justice shines in it, the light which is above light, the Lord of Light, Christ . . .

("Nikolaos Mesarites: Description of the Church of the Holy Apostles at Constantinople," ed., trans. and comm. by G. Downey, *Transactions of the American Philosophical Society* n.s. 47 [1957] 870.) Also Lehmann (n. 20 above) 27.

[32] Torp (n. 2 above) 36f., fig. on 39.

[33] A connection between the phoenix and the palm tree is based on the freedom of interpretation of the word φοῖνιξ in the Septuagint (translated into Latin as either *phoenix* or

Physiologus, which was widely known among Early Christian writers, the bird is the image of the Savior.[34] Yet the animal acquired a more specific connotation. Tertullian elaborated on the many legends concerning the phoenix and pointed to the idea of the bird when adducing evidence of the resurrection of the body.[35] Later Cyril of Jerusalem would write that the phoenix was prepared by God the Father who knew of the lack of belief in the resurrection on the part of men who would seek proof of an animal clearly decayed that had risen again.[36] Thus the bird became a symbol of the Resurrection of Christ and of Christians in general. This is the meaning of the phoenix in the mosaics. The bird imparts an eschatological significance to the representation of the Parousia and provides one proof that the mosaics represent this theme rather than the Ascension of Christ. By its regeneration the legendary animal signifies the new age that is ushered in by the Parousia: "unica . . . vivit morte refecta sua."[37]

Because the bird existed only in legends, whose details vary widely, it lacked a firmly established iconography in pagan and Christian representations.[38] As a symbol of the resurrected Christ it occurs not altogether infrequently in the art of the pre-Iconoclastic period, though far more commonly in the Latin West than Greek East. A few examples will suffice. In an Early Christian sarcophagus in the Lateran Museum at Rome the cross of the Lord, on which is suspended a triumphal crown and a phoenix standing erect, is flanked by two soldiers sleeping and saints bringing the crowns of their martyrdom. This fragmentary sculpture suggests that such an iconography de-

---

palma). The literature on the phoenix legend is vast. For the ancient legends see J. Hubaux and M. Leroy, *Le mythe du phénix dans les littératures grecque et latine* Bibliothèque de la Faculté de philosophie et lettres de l'Université de Liège 82 (Liège 1939). For the bird in Christian thought consult E. H. Kantorowicz, *The King's Two Bodies* (Princeton 1957) 388ff.; M. F. McDonald, "Phoenix redivivus," *The Phoenix* 14 (1960) 187ff.; E. Dinkler-von Schubert, in *Die Religion in Geschichte und Gegenwart*, ed. 3, 5 (1961) 358ff.

[34] "ὁ γὰρ φοῖνιξ πρόσωπον τοῦ Σωτῆρος ἡμῶν λαμβάνει" (F. Lauchert, *Geschichte des Physiologus* [Strasbourg 1889] 237ff.).

[35] *De resurrectione mortuorum* 13.2 (*Corpus christianorum, series latina* 2.2.936). For the parallel idea of the eagle as an expression of the ascension to heaven, of the resurrection of the dead, of apotheosis, see L'Orange (n. 10 above) 69ff., *passim*.

[36] *Catechesis* 18.8 (PG 33.1025ff.).

[37] *Lactanti de ave phoenice* 32 (ed. Fitzpatrick, 42). See also the Leyden papyrus cited by P. Perdrizet, "La tunique liturgique historiée de Saqqara," *Monuments Piot* 34 (1934) 113, which reads: "I am the Phoenix, the sacred bird; I am the sun, whence the light comes;" and Eusebius, *Vita Constantini* 4.72.

[38] Compare the tunic of Saqqara, which is attributed to the second century A.D., where seven rays project beyond the circumference of the nimbed head of the phoenix (Perdrizet pl. VIII, below). A seven-rayed phoenix is also represented in an *emblema* in the mosaic pavement of the atrium of the south basilica of Aquileia (*La Basilica di Aquileia* [Bologna 1933] pl. L, 3).

rived from Roman triumphal imagery.[39] Comparisons much closer to the
iconography of the mosaics in the Rotunda are provided both by the rayed
phoenix placed directly above the monogram of the Lord which is enclosed
by a seasonal (?) wreath in the vault of the baptistery of San Giovanni in
Fonte in the cathedral of Naples, a mosaic whose dating is highly controver-
sial (early fifth century?),[40] and by the rayed phoenix perched atop the branches of a palm tree and looking toward the figure of Christ "coming on the
clouds," clad in a golden pallium, in the apse mosaic of Saints Cosmas and
Damian at Rome (fig. 8). Though the latter represents the coming of the
son of man incarnate, its iconographical sources can be traced back to Western images of the *Traditio legis* (see above), which is distinct from the iconography of the mosaics in the Rotunda. It is possible that imperial iconography influenced formally the representation of the Lord and the phoenix
in the Rotunda, and specifically images of the emperor triumphant surmounted
by the eagle, such as occurs on the northern flank of the southern pier of
the Arch of Galerius at Thessaloniki.[41]

The tête-à-tête arrangement of the phoenix and the Christ figure in the
Rotunda is exactly paralleled by the mosaics in the abovementioned dome
of the baptistry at Naples, where the phoenix faces east while the monogram
of the Lord is oriented to the west. In the Rotunda this is reversed.

In Hagios Georgios the new age of Christians is heralded by the inclusion
of yet another image: between the pair of angels on the northern side of the
central medallion, on the right side of the figure of the Lord, are preserved

[39] J. Wilpert, *I Sarcofagi cristiani antichi* (Rome 1929-1936) 1, pl. XVIII, 3; Grabar
(n. 19 above) 125, fig. 300.

[40] As in the Rotunda—if Torp is right in identifying that on which the mythical bird is
perched as a palm tree—the association of the phoenix with palms in Naples evokes paradise: Wilpert (n. 11 above) 1.130f., 3 pl. 29; J.-L. Maier, *Le Baptistère de Naples et ses
mosaïques*, Paradosis 19 (Fribourg 1964) and the important criticism of this study by T.
Klauser, in *Jahrbuch für Antike und Christentum* 8/9 (1965/66) 217ff. (where a dating of
about 500 A.D. is proposed). Cf. O. Perler, "Die Taufsymbolik der vier Jahreszeiten im
Baptisterium bei Kélibia," *Mullus: Festschrift Theodor Klauser, Jahrbuch für Antike und
Christentum, Ergänzungsband* 1 (Münster 1964) 286, who expresses doubt about the garland at Naples alluding to the seasons. Let it be observed that the phoenix stands on a
hillock directly in line with the head of the monogram of Christ, which is emphasized by
the hand of God coming through the canopy of heaven holding a jeweled crown above the
head of the monogram.

[41] W. F. Volbach, *Early Christian Art* (New York 1961) pl. 3; C. I. Makaronas ʽΗ ΚΑ-
ΜΑΡΑ, ΤΟ ΘΡΙΑΜΒΙΚΟ ΤΟΞΟ ΤΟΥ ΓΑΛΕΡΙΟΥ ΣΤΗ ΘΕΣΣΑΛΟΝΙΚΗ (Thessaloniki
1969) figs. 28-32). In Roman Imperial art the phoenix could signify the rejuvenation of
the world through a ruler, as revealed by coins dating as late as the fourth century (see
H. Mattingly, in *Numismatic Chronicle* ser. 5, 13 [1933] 187ff.), and as late as the sixth
century a renewal of happiness was proclaimed by the emperor through the imagery of
the phoenix (Corippus, *In laudem Iustini* 1.349, ed. Partsch, MGH Auctores antiquissimi
(Berlin 1879) 3.126).

the remnants of four rays that originally converged downward to some object, now destroyed, which was represented in the second concentric zone of the composition. From the remains of the drawing preserved on the brickwork at this place that Torp reports to have seen clearly, the lost object is to be identified as a cross with a crown of light. This drawing is of the greatest importance for an interpretation of the iconography of the mosaics. It is to be identified as the σταυϱὸς φωτοειδής, or luminous cross, which, as it descends from heaven to earth, precedes and announces the coming of the son of man.[42] Not a memorial of his Passion, the function served by the cross Christ shoulders in the medallion above, the luminous cross is a prophecy of the Parousia itself. At an early date the doctrine of the luminous cross had great eschatological significance and was expounded by many a Jewish and Christian writer, whose basic text was Matthew 24.30, in which the Second Advent is prophesied: "Then shall appear the sign (τὸ σημεῖον) of the son of man in heaven."[43] Cyril of Jerusalem declares that "the genuine and proper sign of Christ is the cross. The sign that precedes the king is a cross of light."[44] The doctrine was taken up by other writers time and again, and thus it was well known in the Greek East, and certainly at Thessaloniki.

In Early Christian art the glorious cross was frequently represented.[45] In the apse mosaic of Santa Pudenziana at Rome a large gemmed cross surrounded by the symbols of the four evangelists appears above the image of Christ enthroned with the twelve apostles in front of what may be identified as either the earthly Jerusalem or the heavenly Jerusalem. The cross is the sign of the coming of the victorious Lord who, shown before it, wears imperial garments and is seated on an imperial throne. Underlying the whole composition is clearly a Christian eschatological ideology.[46] A generation

---

[42] Torp (n. 2 above) 37. In this book Torp fails to investigate the meaning of the cross in the context of the program of the Rotunda's mosaics.

[43] ϰαὶ τότε φανήσεται τὸ σημεῖον τοῦ υἱοῦ τοῦ ἀνθρώπου ἐν οὐρανῷ. Compare Cyril of Jerusalem, Catechesis 15 de secundo Christi adventu 22 PG 33.900): Σημεῖον δὲ ἀληθὲς ἰδικὸν τοῦ Χριστοῦ ἐστιν ὁ σταυϱός. Φωτοειδοῦς σταυϱοῦ σημεῖον προάγει τὸν βασιλέα, δηλοῦν τὸν σταυϱωθέντα πϱότεϱον. On the luminous cross see E. Stommel, "Σημεῖον ἐϰπετάσεως," Römische Quartalschrift 48 (1953) 21ff., esp. 39ff.; J. Daniélou, Théologie du judéochristianisme (Tournai 1958) 290ff.; E. Dinkler, Das Apsismosaik von S. Apollinare in Classe (Cologne 1964) 78ff.; and the texts adduced by Kantorowicz (n. 14 above), 224ff. to buttress his identification of the scene in one of the panels of the wooden doors of Santa Sabina at Rome. The correctness of Kantorowicz's interpretation of the luminous cross in this scene is supported by the paper of E. Peterson, "La Croce e la preghiera verso oriente," Ephemerides liturgicae 59 (1945) 52ff.

[44] Catechesis 15.22 (PG 33.899f.); Kantorowicz (n. 14 above) 226 n. 120.

[45] Kantorowicz 227. E. Dinkler, "Das Kreuz als Siegeszeichen," Zeitschrift für Theologie und Kirche 62 (1965) 1ff., assembles a fairly complete catalogue of examples in pre-Iconoclastic art (that in Hagios Georgios was unknown to him).

[46] See now E. Dassmann, "Das Apsismosaik von S. Pudentiana in Rom, philosophische,

or two later the luminous cross as the precursor of the Parousia becomes more common, to wit the mosaic in the central vault of the so-called Mausoleum of Galla Placidia at Ravenna and one of the enigmatic panels of the wooden doors of Santa Sabina at Rome (fig. 4).[47] In the lower register of the latter work the figures of Peter and Paul reach up and grasp gently the cross within a circle that descends from heaven to earth. Above, the Lord himself appears from heaven.

We can not be sure of the exact form in which the luminous cross was manifested in Hagios Georgios, though Torp adduces the example of the cross in the mosaic of the bema vault of Hagia Sophia at Thessaloniki, an Iconoclastic or post-Iconoclastic work.[48] Another possibility is the luminous cross held by two angels in a scene that has been identified as a Last Judgment, integrating the Christ figure of a Second Coming with a group of apostolic witnesses, in the vault of the north chamber of funerary chapel of the church of Ayvali Kilise in Cappadocia. This church has been assigned to the years 913-920.[49] The traces of the rays projecting from the cross that Torp has reported bring to mind such Early Christian works as the mosaic in the vault of the presbytery of the Baptistery at Albenga, of the fifth century,[50] and the monogram of Christ on the triumphal arch of San Vitale at Ravenna, dedicated in 547.[51]

In these monuments and the texts on which they are based the glorious cross is described as appearing in the east, while in the Rotunda it was placed in the northern sector of the domical composition. No textual basis for this arrangement can be cited, for the position of the cross was dictated by other considerations. By its placement in the northern sector of the dome the sign of

---

imperiale und theologische Aspekte in einem Christusbild am Beginn des 5. Jahrhunderts," *Römische Quartalschrift* 65 (1970) 67ff.

[47] Toward the end of the fifth century the eschatological cross appears in the vault mosaic in the village church of Casaranello in Apulia, and in 549 it reappears, if Dinkler's interpretation is correct, as I believe it is, in the apse mosaic of Sant'Apollinare in Classe.

[48] Torp (n. 2 above) 37, fig. on 38. Owing to the absence of a technical examination of all the mosaics in this church, it is difficult to assign an exact date to the cross represented in the vault. The mosaics in the dome are generally dated ca. 886 (O. Wulff, in *Repertorium für Kunstwissenschaft* 23 [1900] 337ff.); n. 67 below.

[49] N. and M. Thierry, "Ayvali Kilise ou pigeonnier de Gülli Dere, église inédite de Cappadoce," *Cahiers archéologiques* 15 (1965) 97ff., esp. 131ff., figs. 24-27.

[50] Wilpert (n. 11 above) pl. 88, 1; V. Sciarretta, *Il Battistero di Albenga* (Ravenna 1966) figs. 9-10. Christ coming with the wreath of doves is an iconography unrelated to that of the Rotunda. For the meaning of such representations, see Kantorowicz (n. 14 above) 225; E. Stommel, in *Römische Quartalschrift* 48 (1953) 38ff. In a letter written by Paulinus of Nola to Sulpicius Severus at the very beginning of the fifth century the mosaic composition in the main apse of the episcopal church at Cimitile is described as featuring a rayed cross enclosed by a wreath: "crucem corona lucido cingit globo" (*Epistula* 32.10 — *Corpus scriptorum Christianorum latinorum* 29, ed. Hartel, 286).

[51] Deichmann (n. 22 above) pls. 311, 333.

the Lord could be immediately beheld by the bishop and his clergy as well as the faithful as they approached the mystery of the *naos* from the narthex and ambulatory at the southern flank of the converted Rotunda. Thus this prophecy of the Parousia provides one visual manifestation of the secondary, processional, or liturgical axis that characterizes the Rotunda and its decoration, the primary axis being defined by the placement of the Christ figure and the phoenix along the east-west axis of the sanctuary. A second visual indication of this secondary axis is supplied by the huge silver cross in the center of the gold carpet strewn with symbols of the Eucharist (?) which is placed in the soffit of the barrel-vaulted niche at the southern side of the massive peripheral wall, under which the worshipper would pass from the narthex and ambulatory in order to reach the center space. From this observation it appears that all the mosaics in the dome and passageways (nothing at all is known of the decoration of the ambulatory) belonged to a unified theological program. Moreover, the layout of such elements proves that mosaics are a singular original creation rather than a copy of a scene in an illuminated manuscript.

The compositional arrangement of the mosaics in the Mausoleum of Galla Placidia at Ravenna provides a close parallel to this interlocking of the primary and the secondary visual axes. As the spectator enters the Mausoleum from the north, where the building once adjoined the narthex of the Church of Santa Croce, he is confronted first by a cross in a medallion and then by the figure of Saint Lawrence marching triumphantly to his martyrdom, from right to left, or west to east, in the south lunette, while above, in the upper south wall of the center bay, a pair of unidentified apostles standing frontally gesture toward the east, thereby informing the spectator of a directional change in the iconographic program. As the spectator approaches the center of the Mausoleum, the two apostles flanking the window in the upper east wall of the center bay direct his glance upward and toward the large gold cross against the starry blue sky that is represented in the dome, this cross being placed along the major axis of the program, and corresponding in position to the triumphant Christ figure in the dome of the Rotunda.[52]

The precursor of the appearance of Christ at his Second Advent was witnessed not only by the faithful gathered in the church but also by the figures represented in the second and the third concentric zones of the composition. The figures of the second zone are completely destroyed except for small remnants of their garments, which were long white tunica and pallia, and their sandaled feet on a green ground (fig. 11).[53] Their number can not be precisely determined but has been estimated by Torp at from twenty-four

---

[52] *Ibid.* pls. 2-31.

[53] Torp (n. 2 above) 30ff. The circumference of this zone of the mosaics measures about 60 meters.

to thirty-six, their height at about three meters.[54] Since these figures were
taller than the martyrs in the frieze below (3 meters vs. 2.28-2.42 meters
in height), the composition was laid out according to the Late Antique convention of "inverted perspective" or "hierarchic scaling."[55] According to
Torp, the figures were arranged in groups of three. The preserved remnants
of the mosaic directly below the luminous cross disclose a figure that either
has come to an abrupt halt or is bowing in adoration of the cross. This figure
must have had a counterpart facing him, and thus both figures stood on the
secondary compositional axis of the program and directed the attention of
the beholder entering the church from the southern ambulatory to the luminous cross above. The other figures evidently stood in more upright poses,
facing the beholder, like the marytrs in the frieze below. As noted above,
the phoenix rested upon the top of what was perhaps a palm tree, suggesting
that the background of the second zone was occupied by other palm trees,
such as we find in the frieze of male and female martyrs in the nave mosaics
of Sant'Apollinare Nuovo at Ravenna and at the bottom of the mosaic in
the dome of Hagia Sophia at Thessaloniki, a work that may well have been
inspired by the mosaics in the Rotunda.

Whom did these missing figures represent? They can not be identified
from their number, which is unknown. But their garments suggest either
the twenty-four Elders of the Apocalypse or a host of angels. Gerke, among
others, has favored the first identification.[56] He reconstructs the second
zone of the mosaic decoration as a *communio sanctorum*, with the Elders
of the Apocalypse. For him, the top two zones of the decoration represent
an epiphany of the Pantocrator, the heavenly Church—he wrongly maintains
that at the summit of the dome the four flying angels support the throne
of the Logos—while the frieze of martyrs below represents the earthly Church.
Although we may take exception to Gerke's analysis of the entire iconogra-

[54] Grabar (n. 2 above) 59, has no grounds to assert that there were exactly twenty-two
pairs of feet in the second zone. He is apparently unaware of the contents of Torp's *Mosaikkene*.

[55] On "inverted perspective," see O. Wulff, "Die umgekehrte Perspektive und die Nie-
dersicht," *Kunstwissenschaftliche Beiträge August Schmarsow gewidmet* (Leipzig 1907) 1ff.;
W. Prinz, "Die umgekehrte Perspektive in der Architekturdarstellung des Mittelalters,"
Edwin Redslob zum 70. Geburtstag (Berlin 1955) 253ff.; M. S. Bunim, *Space in Medieval
Painting and the Forerunners of Perspective* (New York 1940) 7f., calls this arrangement
"hierarchic scaling." See n. 118 below.

[56] F. Gerke, *Spätantike und frühes Christentum* (Baden-Baden 1967) 171. E. Dyggve,
"Fouilles et recherches faites en 1939 et en 1952-53 à Thessaloniki," *Corsi di cultura sull'arte
ravennate e bizantina* 2 (1957) 83, identified the destroyed figures as apostles and patriarchs
in a paradisiac setting. In 1958 H. P. L'Orange spoke of the figures as "the first emanation
of the Logos in the crown, the Apostles, possibly also the Virgin Mary, eyewitnesses of
the Logos Incarnate on earth, and those who played the greatest part in God's revelation"
(L'Orange and P. J. Nordhagen, *Mosaics*, trans. A. E. Keep [London 1966] 21).

phic program, we should regard his identification of the missing figures as a hypothesis worthy of consideration.

That the Book of Revelation may well have played a role in the Early Christian art of Thessaloniki has recently been demonstrated by James Snyder in his study of the apse mosaic (of the second half of the fifth century?) in the church of Hosios David at Thessaloniki.[57] Snyder identifies the bearded figure seated in the rocky landscape to the right of the Lord in this composition as Saint John the Evangelist on Patmos, a New Testament witness to the *Maiestas domini* which corresponds to the Old Testament witness, probably Ezekiel, which stands in a cringing posture to the left of the Lord. Snyder contends that this iconography was based on a number of textual sources, among the most important of which was the Apocalypse of John, a book that was rarely accepted as canonical in the Greek East. If his identification is correct, then the likelihood that the figures in the second zone of the Rotunda's dome represent the Elders of the Apocalypse is increased.

But if more than twenty-four figures initially stood in the second zone —Torp suggests as many as thirty six—this identification would have to be discarded, unless it were assumed that other figures accompanied the twenty-four Elders, which is hardly plausible. An alternative identification, and one which we prefer, has a host of angels in the second zone, an identification that is supported by New Testament and biblical commentaries on the Second Coming, as well as artistic parallels, and even perhaps the original dedication of the Rotunda when it was transformed into a Christian Church.[58]

Drawing upon Hegesippus, Eusebius of Caesarea describes Christ and his kingdom at the time of their eschatological appearance as "neither of the world nor earthly, but heavenly and angelic."[59] The appearance of angels at the Parousia is described in the Gospel of Matthew and its numerous commentaries. Matthew (24.31-32) relates that after "all the tribes of the earth

[57] J. Snyder, "The Meaning of the 'Maiestas Domini' in Hosios David," *Byzantion* 37 (1967) 143-152. Cf. *idem*, "The Reconstruction of an Early Christian Cycle of Illustrations for the Book of Revelation—the Trier Apocalypse," *Vigiliae christianae* 18 (1964) 146ff.

[58] So Torp (n. 2 above) 33. That the converted Rotunda should be identified with the "holy sanctuary of the archangels" that is mentioned for the first time in a letter written by Theodore the Studite to Naukratios about the year 800, see G. I. Theocharides, "῾Ο ναὸς τῶν ᾿Ασωμάτων καὶ ἡ ROTONDA τοῦ ῾Αγίου Γεωργίου Θεσσαλονίκης," *Hellenika* 13 (1954) 24ff. The pertinent passage in the letter reads: ᾿Εκεῖσε γὰρ ἔφης, ἤτοι εἰς τὸν λεγόμενον τοῦ ᾿Αρχαγγέλου ἱερὸν δόμον τετύφθαι τὸν μάρτυρα [Euthymios] PG 99. 1097). While I find Theocharides' argument interesting, the fact remains that no evidence proves that this appellation is older than ca. 800. On this see my forthcoming paper cited in n. 111 below. For the conversion of the building into a mosque, see M. Kiel, "Notes on the History of Some Turkish Monuments in Thessaloniki and their Founders," *Balkan Studies* 11 (1970) 123ff.

[59] Eusebius, *Historia Ecclesiae* 3.20.4: ὡς οὐ κοσμικὴ μὲν οὐδ᾿ ἐπίγειος, ἐπουράνιος δὲ καὶ ἀγγελικὴ τυγχάνοι.

. . . will see the son of man coming on the clouds of heaven with power and great glory," "he will send out his angels with a loud trumpet call." In his fifteenth *Catechesis*, written about the year 348, Cyril of Jerusalem elaborates on the Gospel account by declaring that the "Lord will come down from heaven, not by himself, as he did before, but in company, escorted by thousands of angels."[60] A myriad of angels appearing at the Second Coming is implied in the account of the evangelist himself when he refers to the gathering together of the eagles (24.28: ἐκεῖ συναχθήσονται οἱ ἀετοί), which Saint John Chrysostom takes to mean "the multitude of the angels, of the martyrs, of all the saints."[61] In a sermon ascribed to Saint Augustine, the Second Coming of the Lord is announced by the bright triumphant standard carried on the shoulders of a host of angels, who precede the Lord.[62] These and other writings of the early centuries of our era clearly describe the appearance of angels at the Parousia, thereby lending support to our identification of the lost figures.

Our identification is also supported by works of the Early Christian period which represent the Parousia. The mid-sixth-century apse mosaic of Saint Michele in Africisco at Ravenna shows Michael and Gabriel flanking a standing figure of Christ victorious and proclaiming his divinity.[63] In the representation of the cosmic universe in the *Christian Topography* of Cosmas Indicopleustes, composed at Alexandria about the same time, eight ἄγγελοι ἐπουράνιοι stand upon the firmament under a figure of Christ enthroned (fig. 6).[64] Below these angels are the ἄνθρωποι ἐπίγιοι, the living people.

---

[60] *Catechesis* 15.10 (PG 33.883): ἐξ οὐρανῶν γὰρ ὁ Δεσπότης κατέρχεται. Οὐ μόνος ὡς πρὸ τούτου, ἀλλὰ πολλοστὸς, ὑπὸ μυριάδων ἀγγέλων δορυφορούμενος." Also other sections of this "lecture." This passage by Cyril, it should be noted, describes the son of man coming on the clouds, hence as He was seen ascending, that is, standing rather than seated.

[61] *In Matth. homil.* 76.3 (PG 58.697): Ὅπου τὸ πτῶμα, ἐκεῖ καὶ οἱ ἀετοί · τὸ πλῆθος τῶν ἀγγέλων, τῶν μαρτύρων, τῶν ἁγίων ἁπάντων δηλῶν. Cf. PG 56.287; 57.23f.

[62] *Sermo* 155 (PL 39.2051f.): "Ita Domino descendente de coelis praecedet exercitus angelorum, qui signum illud, id est triumphale vexillum, sublimibus humeris praeferentes divinum regis coelestis ingressum terris trementibus nuntiabunt" (cited by Kantorowicz [n. 14 above] 224 n. 107). See also a spurious sermon ascribed to John Chrysostom, the author of which writes that "before the Parousia of the Saviour (there appears) the royal standard, vulgarly called *signum* (which) foreruns the Parousia of Christ, glorified by angels" (cited *ibid.*, 225 n. 113; Dinkler (n. 43 above) 83f.).

[63] Deichmann (n. 11 above) 221ff. On groups of angels see J. Michl, "Engelkult," *Reallexikon für Antike und Christentum* 5 (1962), 169ff. For the praise of choirs of angels in the liturgies of the West and East, see J. A. Jungmann, *Missarum sollemnia*, ed. 5 (Vienna 1962) 2.159f.

[64] Known from the copy of the second half of the ninth century that is in the Biblioteca Vaticana, Rome, MS gr. 699 (C. Stornajalo, *Le miniature della Topografia cristiana di Cosma Indicopleuste* [Milan 1906] fol. pl. 89r). For the date of the original manuscript by Cosmas, see M. V. Anastos, "The Alexandrian Origin of the Christian Topography of Cosmas

While this image depicts not the Second Advent of Christ but the scheme of Cosmas's universe, it probably copies a scene of the Second Advent from an illustrated Acts of the Apostles (1.11). Moreover, its composition structured by horizontal bands resembles the arrangement of the mosaics in the Rotunda. There we find our missing figures placed above the standing martyrs, figures that surely rank higher in importance than the martyrs. That these figures represented angels is further confirmed by the white tunica and pallia in which they were clad, such garments being the ordinary costume of angels in Early Christian art, at least until the sixth century, when some angels begin to wear imperial and military garments.[65]

A full-page picture in the *Benedictional of Saint Ethelwold*, executed at Winchester between 963 and 984, provides a Western parallel to our composition (fig. 7). Preceding the benedictions for the Third Sunday in Advent, this miniature depicts not the Ascension but the Second Coming of Christ with a host of angels, being based on Mark 13.26-27: "And then they shall see the son of man coming in the clouds with great power and glory. And then shall he send his angels and shall gather together his elect." Christ is represented as standing and indeed moving downward "with great power and glory" in a titled mandorla of rayed light, holding a golden cross staff over his right shoulder and a gemmed book in his left hand. On the gold bands of the blue mantle over his right thigh the words "Rex regum et dominus dominantium" (from Revelations 19.16) are written in Carolingian minuscule. In the sky above there is a host of nimbed angels, three of whom carry instruments of the Passion. In our opinion this unusual picture copied a Carolingian model that, in turn, derived from an Early Christian prototype,

---

Indicopleustes," *Dumbarton Oaks Papers* 3 (1946) 73ff. Grabar is mistaken in identifying this miniature as a Parousia of Christ (n. 2 above, 64ff.). Rather, it is clearly an illustration of the scheme (τὸ σχῆμα) of the universe according to the author. For the relevant text by the Alexandrian, see *The Christian Topography*, trans. and ed. J. W. McCrindle (London 1897) 129. For the iconography, see B. Brenk, "Die Anfänge der byzantinischen Weltgerichtsdarstellung," *Byzantinische Zeitschrift* 57 (1964) 106 n. 2; and Ainalov (see below, n. 143) p. 40. Y. Christe, in *Cahiers archéologiques* 20 (1970) 241f., maintains that the eleventh-century copy of the Cosmas manuscript (Florence Laur. Plut. IX. 28, fol. 228v) stands closer to the prototype than the ninth-century copy in the Vatican. The picture by Cosmas did not directly influence the Parousia illustrated by John of Damascus in his *Sacra parallela*, Paris, Bibliothèque Nationale MS gr. 923, fol. 67v (Grabar [n. 13 above] pl. xxxviii.2; K. Weitzmann, *Die byzantinische Buchmalerei* [Berlin 1935] 80f., fig. 538). For the strong probability that this image of the ninth century copied a pre-Iconoclastic illuminated manuscript, see Weitzmann, "Die Illustration der Septuaginta," *Münchner Jahrbuch der bildenden Kunst* ser. 3, 3-4 (1952/53) 105ff., and a forthcoming publication on the *Sacra parallela* that Weitzmann has promised us. The iconography of the two images of these manuscripts inspired a fresco at Aght'amar (S. Der Nersessian, *Aght'amar, Church of the Holy Cross*, [Cambridge 1965] 47f. pl. 70).

[65] For the garments of angels, see T. Klauser, "Engel (in der Kunst)," *Reallexikon für Antike und Christentum* 5 (1962) 258ff.

representing not an Anastasis, as recently argued, but the Second Advent of Christ.[66]

Thus it seems the second zone of the mosaics in Hagios Georgios represented a host of angels, the messengers who were sent by Christ to glorify his luminous cross, thereby announcing his Parousia. Whether this host included other figures, such as the Virgin, cannot be determined.[67]

THE CALENDAR FRIEZE OF MARTYRS

The third zone is the best known and most fully preserved portion of the mosaic decoration of the Rotunda (figs. 1, 9 and 11). Originally it comprised eight rectangular panels, each measuring over six by eight meters, of which the panel above the entrance to the chancel of the converted building was destroyed sometime before the beginning of the nineteenth century.[68] Sep-

---

[66] Homburger (n. 3 above) 14 pl. I; F. Wormald, *The Benedictional of St. Ethelwold*, (London 1959) 20, pl. 3 (color); K. Weitzmann, "Various Aspects of Byzantine Influence on the Latin Countries from the Sixth to the Twelfth Century," *Dumbarton Oaks Papers* 20 (1966) 18f., fig. 33. Whereas Homburger believes that the figure of the Lord was "assimilated to the Christ of the Ascension," other authorities maintain that the Second Advent is represented. Both the place where the miniature was inserted in the text of the manuscript and the posture of the Christ figure in a mandorla that tilts downward prove the correctness of their identification. Weitzmann contends that the English artist copied a picture of an Anastasis in a Byzantine lectionary (e.g., *ibid.* fig. 34) and points to the close thematic bond between the figure of Christ raising Adam and his forefathers out of Hell and the Resurrection of the Elect on the Day of Judgment. While it is true that the Second Advent in Early Christian and early medieval art of the Latin West shows as a rule Christ enthroned, the standing Christ figure shouldering a cross in the mosaics in the Rotunda and the standing Christ figure in the wooden doors of Santa Sabina (see above) prove that this iconography had evolved in Early Christian art, the period of the archetype of the Winchester miniature. This is not to say that the latter was modeled on a monumental wall painting; such an iconography occurred in illuminated manuscripts, as I believe the so-called Ascension picture in the *Rabula Gospels* proves. Compare John Chrysostom, *De cruce et latrone* (PG 49.404).

[67] The figure of the Virgin may indeed have stood with the host of angels, which is suggested by such works as the fresco in the apse of Chapel VII at Bawit and the mosaic in the dome of Hagia Sophia at Thessaloniki. For the Bawit fresco (ca. 500 or later), the lower portion of which may illustrate Acts 1.15-16, see Ihm, (n. 2 above) 98 pl. 23, 1; Brenk (n. 3 above) 55ff. For Hagia Sophia, see, most recently, Robin S. Cormack, "Ninth Century Monumental Painting and Mosaic in Thessaloniki," Ph.D. dissertation (University of London 1968). See also n. 48 above.

[68] This panel was destroyed before 1806 when W. M. Leake visited the building and reported that "in one place they [the Turks] have supplied a fallen mosaic with a painting in imitation of it" (*Travels in Northern Greece* [London 1835] 3.240). I believe the number of panels in the mosaic frieze was dictated rather by formal considerations than by any symbolic connotations, such as an allusion to the theme of resurrection. Since no evidence of any pagan decoration in the dome has been reported, the surviving program is altogether of Christian inspiration.

arated from one another by borders of acanthus candelabra, the panels consist of resplendently bejeweled architectural vistas arranged in two stories that rise in front of a shimmering gold background, its glitter comparable to fresh fallen snow in the sunlight. The architecture is embellished with a plethora of motifs, including ciboria, fountains, candlesticks, *transennae*, curtains, gemmed crosses and books, lamps, votive crowns, chalices, and peacocks and other birds, as well as meander bands, peltae, and egg-and-dart mouldings.

In front of each facade two or three saints stand frontally in an orans position. All of them are unnimbed. They are arranged in the panels in a sophisticated manner, both visually and iconographically. In the panel facing the eastern chancel and in the two panels flanking the lost panel above the chancel itself there are three saints each. The other panels each contain two figures. Sixteen figures, wholly or partially preserved, still exist. The lost panel at the east formed in all probability a pendant to the western panel and hence showed three figures. Thus from the outset twenty saints occupied the whole frieze. All were male figures.

Each saint was identified by an inscription in Greek placed beside him (fig. 22). These inscriptions provide the name of the saint, his occupation, and the month of his feast day in the church calendar. Thirteen inscriptions are wholly or partially preserved. Numbering the panels from I to VIII, starting from the western panel and proceeding clockwise, they read as follows:[69]

Panel I	——, ——, ——
	Romanos, presbyter, ——
	Eukarpios, soldier, December
Panel II	——, ——, ——, (fig. 17)[70]
	Ananias, presbyter, January[71]
Panel III	Basiliskos, soldier, April
	Priskos, soldier, October (fig. 13)

[69] Until the final publication by L'Orange and Torp appears, consult the transcription of the inscriptions by L. Duchesne and C. Bayet, "Mission au mont Athos," *Archives des missions scientifiques et littéraires* ser. 3, 3 (1876) 517f. and J. Kurth, "Die Mosaikeninschriften von Salonik," *Mitteilungen des Deutschen archäologischen Instituts, Athenische Abteilung* 22 (1897) pl. XVI. J. Speiser has a study in press on the church inscriptions of Thessaloniki.

[70] E. Weigand, "Der Kalenderfries von Hagios Georgios in Thessalonike," *Byzantinische Zeitschrift* 39 (1939) 121, 122, identifies this saint as Aristarchos, basing his identification on the facsimile of inscriptions published by Kurth (n. 69 above). But Kurth specifically states that the character of the letters is so different from the other inscriptions that the name cannot be original but a subsequent addition, possibly by the Italian artist Rossi who painted the lost eastern panel in the late nineteenth century. Cf. Duchesne and Bayet (n. 69 above) 517; n. 68 above.

[71] Photograph of inscription in Torp (n. 2 above) fig. on 28.

Panel IV	Philippos, bishop, October
	Therinos, soldier, July
	Kyrillos, bishop, ——[72]
Panel V	(lost)
Panel VI	——, ——, ——
	Leon, soldier, June
	Philemon, flute-player, ——
Panel VII	Onesiphoros, soldier, August (fig. 9)
	Porphyrios, August (fig. 9)[73]
Panel VIII	——, ——, —— (figs. 11 and 15)[74]
	Damianos, physician, September (figs. 11 and 22)

The following observations may be made about these inscriptions. All parts of them are given in upper case letters and in the genitive case. While the names of the saints and the words *MHNI* (month) *IATPOY* (physician), and *XOPAYΛOY* (*choraulou* or flute-player) are spelled out in full, the other words are abbreviated. What looks like a Latin "S" occurs after the abbreviations of *CTPAT* (for *CTPATIΩTOY* or soldier), *EΠICK* (*EΠICKOΠOY* or bishop), *ΠPECB* (*ΠPECBYTEPOY* or presbyter), and all the names of the months. This must be a ligature for the letters *OY* or *IOY*. And whereas the civilian church officials are specified as either *ΠPECBYTEPOY* or *EΠIC-KOΠOY*, all of the soldier saints are identified as *CTPATIΩTOY*.

The station of each saint is further identified by his outer garment, either the chlamys or the phelonion. The chlamys is worn by Basiliskos, Priskos, Therinos, Leon, Onesiphoros, and Eukarpios and the unidentified saint next to him in the western panel (fig. 9). The other saints, including Porphyrios, whose occupation is unlisted, wear the phelonion (the medieval bell chasuble

---

[72] Although both Texier and Bayet failed to see this inscription, it is clearly visible today (Torp, fig. on 29). In 1897 Kurth (n. 69 above, pl. XVI) was able to read: *KYPIΛ(OY) EΠI (CKOΠOY) MH(NI)*.

[73] The omission of the occupation of Porphyrios from the inscription is puzzling.

[74] Without archeological justification, C. Texier and R. P. Pullan, *Byzantine Architecture* (London 1864) 138, 141, pl. XXXIII, restored the inscription of the figure as:

  KOCMOY
  IATPOY
  MHNICEΠ
  TEMBPI ⴳ

In his first published report on the Rotunda, Texier states clearly that the inscription of the figure had disappeared (*Description de l'Asie Mineure* [Paris 1849] 3.76), and this is confirmed by both Duchesne and Bayet (n. 69 above) 517 and Kurth (n. 69 above) 470 pl. XVI. But there can be no doubt that this is Kosmas, for (1) the first vertical stroke of the letter kappa in what was the first line of the inscription is visible today, and (2) the Index of Christian Art lists no examples of either of the two physician saints appearing alone. Early Christian art knows but one saint named Damianos, namely, the companion of the physician saint Kosmas. For Saint Kosmas the Poet, of the eighth century, see P·A. Underwood, in *Dumbarton Oaks Papers* 11 (1957) 179.

of the Latin West). Thus all the soldier saints are clad in the chlamys. This garment is worn over a sleeved and belted tunic ornamented with purple patches or *segmenta* below the waist, at the right shoulder, and at the knee. The *segmentum* sewn on the shoulder of the tunic of Onesiphoros, ordinarily an indication both of status and of the occasion of wearing, and identifying the wearer more fully than the cut and color of his garments, contains a standing figure with an upraised right arm and possibly a shield (a warrior? an emperor?).[75] The chlamys itself is a mantle extending to the ankles which hangs over the shoulders, worn so that the opening falls at the right side, leaving the right arm exposed. It is fastened at the right shoulder by a plain gold fibula outlined in red.[76] In color the chlamys of the soldier saints is either marble white or porphyry-violet, the latter worn only by Leon and Eukarpios,[77] and is decorated with two large purple insets or *tablia* (the ταβλίον πορφυροῦν), the one of the back being visible as a long narrow strip beneath the right elbow. The soldier martyrs thus appear dressed for an important festal occasion.[78] The outer garment worn by the other saints, the phelonion, is a round cloak, with an opening only for the head, and is worn over a sleeved white tunic extending to the ankles. The phelonion is a grey-white vestment on Damianos and his pendant (Kosmas) and also the unnamed saint occupying the panel with Ananias, whereas in all other instances, including Ananias, it is porphyry-violet, the same shade as the chlamys of Leon and Eukarpios. Yet all the garments glitter with silver tesserae strewn through their fabric, imparting a visual vitality and dramatic presence to the frieze of stationary figures.

The saints are disposed in the panels according to their station. To either side of the lost panel above the entrance to the bema a soldier saint stands

---

[75] Clearly visible in Volbach (n. 41 above) pl. 126. From the photographs of the mosaics at my disposal it seems that none of the other figures' *segmenta* feature such an image. For the *segmentum*, see R. Delbrueck, *Die Consulardiptychen und verwandte Denkmäler* (Berlin 1929) 38; R. MacMullen, "Some Pictures in Ammianus Marcellinus," *Art Bulletin* 46 (1964) 448ff.

[76] The chlamys held by a fibula at the shoulder reflects contemporary costume of soldiers as well as officials of the courts. Consult the evidence brilliantly marshalled by MacMullen 440 nn. 23-24.

[77] Since Late Imperial soldiers were distinguished by the different types or shades of dress from their officers and from other troops, the chlamys of Leon and Eukarpios perhaps points to a status higher than that of the other soldier martyrs. These martyrs are placed in panels stressing the primary (east-west) axis of the mosaic program. (But Therinos, the pendant of Leon in the northeast panel, wears a white chlamys.)

[78] For white uniforms worn by troops on festal occasions, see MacMullen (n. 75 above) 447. For the symbolism of such colored garments, see E. R. Goodenough, *Jewish Symbols in the Greco-Roman Period* 9 (New Haven 1964) 165ff. The Byzantine emperor is known to have worn white garments on special religious holidays, like Epiphany, Palm Sunday, and Easter Sunday: Constantine Porphyrogenetos, *De ceremoniis aulae byzantinae*, ed. I. Reiske (Bonn 1829) 1.1.24; 1.10.71f.; 1.25-27.142-148; 1.37.188-191.

between either two church officials or Philemon the flute-player and his
missing counterpart. Opposite the lost panel a deacon is flanked by a pair
of soldier martyrs (perhaps the disposition of the figures in the lost panel
itself). In the panel to the north of that appear two church officials, whereas
in that to the south there are the physician saint Damianos and his companion, who can only be the physician saint Kosmas, the two *anargyroi* always
appearing together in Early Christian art (fig. 11). Finally, in the two panels
placed along the processional, north-south axis stand two soldier saints (with
the curious exception of Porphyrios, who from his garment must be identified as a church official (fig. 9).

The subtle visual and ideological axes that are established by these placements extend vertically to the upper zones of the composition as well. The
Christ figure and the phoenix are aligned with the church official flanked
by soldier saints in the western panel, while the soldier saints standing to
either side of a huge gemmed cross in the northern and southern panels are
aligned with the luminous cross and the two figures beneath it in the northern
sector of the second concentric zone (fig. 1). Moreover, the primary axis,
that running from west to east, along which the Christ figure is placed, is
further emphasized by the inclusion of three figures in the western panel
and those above the entrance to the bema (and presumably in the lost panel
as well), the remaining panels containing but a pair of martyrs (to which
the four angels supporting the celestial medallion of Christ are aligned). Thus,
the composition, while arranged in three concentric zones, is united along
various vertical as well as horizontal and diagonal axes, extending from the
summit of the dome to the luminous cross, the two gemmed crosses and the
large gold cross against the silver ground in the soffit of the southern niche.
Even the arrangement of such motifs as the curtains, crosses, chalices, cen-
sers, and peacocks and other birds in the second stories of the architectural
vistas behind the martyrs conform to these directional lines. The whole
composition, a masterwork of carefully and subtly calculated systems of
antithetical placements, symmetries and asymmetries, rhythms and coun-
ter-rhythms, conveys an aesthetic and ecstatic vitality of imagery to the
beholder standing in the *naos*.

THE SELECTION OF THE MARTYRS

The martyrs identified by name in the great frieze are apparently not local
Thessalonikan saints but Christian heroes associated with sites throughout
the world of the pre-Constantinian church, as Edmund Weigand has demonstrated. From the early church calendars of Asia Minor, Syria, Egypt, and
Rome the following identifications of the martyrs can be tentatively posited. Ananias was a Christian priest martyred under Diocletian in Phoenicia; the inscription accompanying him identifies the month of his feast as
January, and both the *Hieronymian Martyrology* and the synaxary of Con-

stantinople record his feast on January 26 and January 27, respectively.[79] Philippos (with the month of October) is presumably the bishop of Heraclea in Thrace whose feast according to both the *Breviarium Syriacum* and the *Hieronymian Martyrology* was celebrated on October 10.[80] Though the month in his inscription is destroyed, Philemon *choraulos* is surely the flute-player who was a companion of Apollonios of Egypt.[81] Romanos was perhaps the native of Antioch in Syria who became a deacon at Caesarea in Palestine, his feast according to the *Hieronymian Martyrology* being celebrated on October 1.[82] Priskos is probably a martyr associated with the city of Tomi in the province of Scythia (fig. 13).[83] While no soldier saint named Onesiphoros is listed in any calendar, his pairing with Porphyrios suggests that they may be the companions of Saint Paul in Iconium (cf. 2 Timothy 19), whose feast was commemorated according to both the Greek synaxary and the *Breviarium Syriacum* on November 9, according to the *Hieronymian Martyrology* on September 6 (fig. 9).[84] (In the Latin West the feast of a saint named Porphyrios was celebrated in the month of August, the month inscribed in the mosaic.)[85] And Kosmas and Damianos are of course the well

[79] *Bibliotheca hagiographica graeca*, ed. 3 (Brussels 1957) 3.7: "Ananias pres. et milites septem mm. in Phoenicia sub Diocletiano"; *Bibliotheca hagiographica latina* (Brussels 1898-99) 66. Cf. Weigand (n. 10 above) 122; H. Delehaye, *Les origines du culte des martyrs*, ed. 2 (Brussels 1933) 231ff.

[80] Weigand (n. 70 above) 123f.

[81] *Bibliotheca hagiographica graeca*, 1.201; *Bibliotheca hagiographica latina* 989. See also PL 21.441f.; H. Delehaye, "Les martyrs de l'Égypte," *Analecta Bollandiana* 40 (1922) 115f. Philemon is recorded in fourth-century Latin sources (e.g., the *Martyrologium romanum*) as *choraulos*, under March 8, whereas in the Greek synaxary, which is of later date, he is indicated as *kitharistes*, under December 14. Both the Latin and Greek calendars derive their information from a common source of early times, and Weigand surmises that this source was a Greek-Egyptian synaxary: it may be noted that in the Coptic synaxary Philemon is inscribed with the date of Barmahât 7 = March 3 (*Bulletin de la Société d'archéologie copte* 17 [1963/64] 136).

[82] *Bibliotheca hagiographica graeca*, 1.226; Weigand (n. 70 above) 124 (listed in the Greek synaxary under November 18 as a deacon martyred under Diocletian).

[83] *In Thomis civitate Prisci Criscenti et Evagri* (ibid.). In the *Martyrologium romanum* under October 1 is inscribed: *Tomis in Ponto sanctorum martyrum Prisci, Crescenti et Evagri*, whereas the synaxary of Constantinople lists a soldier saint Priskos as one of the Forty Martyrs of Sebaste, whose feast was celebrated on March 9 (*Bibliotheca hagiographica graeca* 2.97f.; cf. *Bibliotheca hagiographica latina* 1009).

[84] *Bibliotheca hagiographica graeca* 1.216f., 3.56; Weigand (n. 70 above) 123. Onesiphoros and Porphyrios as companions of Saint Paul are mentioned in the Greek and Syriac calendars under November 9 and July 16, in the *Martyrologium romanum* under September 6. Bishop Porphyrios of Gaza (ca. 395-420), who was born at Thessaloniki, was remembered in the churches of both the East and West on February 26 (*Bibliotheca hagiographica graeca* 1.216f.; *Lexikon für Theologie und Kirche* 8 (1963) 619f.).

[85] PL 123.167f., 334. Cf. *Bibliotheca hagiographica latina*, Suppl. (1911) 258: *Porphyrius presb.* for May 4.

known *anargyroi* of Asia Minor whose *dies natalis* in the Latin West is said
to be September 27, the month accompanying the name of Damianos (fig.
22). In the Greek East at least three pairs of physician saints so named were
remembered, their feasts falling on July 1 and October 29, October 17, and
December 9.[86] (We shall return to Kosmas and Damianos when examining
the dating problem of the mosaics.) Our information about Basiliskos, Eukarpios, Kyrillos, Leon, and Therinos, however, is insufficient to ascertain
their origin with any assurance. Accordingly, it remains conceivable, though
we think unlikely, that at least some of them were local saints of Thessaloniki.[87] In sum, we know little about the identity of most of the saints, largely
because of the absence of the exact day of the month on which the feast of
each was commemorated.[88]

Thus several pressing questions arise as a matter of course. For instance,
the question of why these particular saints were selected for inclusion in the
frieze is puzzling and has not been answered thus far. For Weigand the
saints point to a universal church calendar. This hypothesis will be dealt
with below. Secondly, what is the iconographic relation between the frieze
of saints and the rest of the program? Weigand was unconcerned with the
top two concentric zones of the composition (he surely knew of the garland
at the summit of the dome but nothing of the Christ figure or the missing
second zone) and thus ignored this question. In his preliminary studies on
Hagios Georgios Torp has accepted Weigand's hypothesis of a universal
church calendar but has not tried to relate the great frieze to the rest of the
program.[89] And Grabar, who correctly divined that the program represents
the Second Advent of Christ—though not we believe for the right reasons
—has likewise disregarded the matter of the reasons for the selection of the
martyrs themselves.[90] As a matter of fact, the present state of published

[86] *Bibliotheca hagiographica graeca* 1.126-136; L. Deubner, *Kosmas und Damian* (Leipzig 1907); Weigand (n. 70 above) 126f.; G. Schreiber, "Kosmas und Damian," *Lexikon
für Theologie und Kirche* 6 (1961) 566f.; see below.

[87] Kyrillos, whose month is lacking, may be either the bishop saint of Gortyna on Crete
who was martyred in 304 (*Bibliotheca hagiographica graeca* 1.143), or a deacon of Heliopolis
(*ibid.* 3.45f.). See also the comments by Weigand (n. 70 above) 123f.; Delehaye (n. 79 above)
232. For the local saints of the city, consult T. L. F. Tafel, *De Thessalonica ejusque agro*
(Berlin 1839) 144ff.

[88] That which follows the *Apriliou* in the inscription identifying the martyr Basiliskos
is in all probability not a date but a squiggle that terminates the inscription; this is the only
inscription in the Rotunda's frieze of saints which spells out in full the name of the month
of the feast (Kurth [n. 69 above] pl. XVI no. 7).

[89] Torp (n. 2 above) 26. Cf. L'Orange and Nordhagen (n. 56 above) 22: "Thus the Logos
descends further, through the witnesses who shed their blood, to sacred vessels and shrines."
Also see n. 56 above.

[90] Grabar (n. 2 above) 59ff.

research on the frieze of martyrs has hardly surpassed Weigand's pioneering, and masterly, study of 1939.

Although our knowledge of the *cultus* of martyrs in Early Christianity is spotty and scanty, Weigand's hypothesis is simple yet ingenious. But is it correct? First of all, it may be observed that the saints are not arranged according to the system of any martyrology or menologium. Some months recur, others are absent. August, October, and (as we may supply for the inscription of Kosmas) September each occur twice, while February, March, May, and November (which may have existed in the missing inscriptions) are wanting. If a church calendar had been used by the mosaicists, that is to say, their theological advisors who devised the whole program, its order of saints could of course have been rearranged for formal or ideological reasons. And one of the principal entries of the church calendar, the day of the month, usually the *dies natalis* or *ta genethlia* on which the saint's feast was commemorated, is wanting in the mosaic inscriptions accompanying the figures. The listing of the months but not the days of the feasts brings to mind illustrated calendars of the labors of the months. The inclusion of the months of the feasts is to our knowledge unique in Christian art of the pre-Iconoclastic period. In the representation of martyrs in the Archiepiscopal Chapel and in Sant'Apollinare Nuovo at Ravenna, both of which Weigand believes were based on a church calendar, only the names of the saints are given, either abbreviated or in full.[91] Nevertheless, the omission of the day of the feasts notwithstanding, some calendar of Christian saints may be presumed to have exerted some influence on the planning of the program. The use of the word *MHNI* or month itself proves that (fig. 22).[92]

To return to the question of the universality of the saints: That the saints come from various parts of the Christian world has already been indicated. Ananias was martyred in Phoenicia; Philippos served as a bishop probably in Thrace; Priskos may have been a soldier saint of Scythia; Philemon was the companion of Apollonios in Egypt; and the cult of Kosmas and Damianos was commemorated in several centers in the Greek East and even in the Latin West at an early date (see below). And it seems that none were local saints of Thessaloniki. Thus they comprise a veritable pantheon of Christianity. For Weigand the represent a universal church calendar, transcending the interest of merely local history, and including heroes of Christendom in the East and West alike, possibly all of the pre-Nicene age. If correct, they

---

[91] Both buildings probably sheltered relics of the saints represented in their mosaics, though certain connections between the Milanese or Roman canon of the mass and the saints of Sant'Apollinare Nuovo would also seem to obtain: Deichmann (n. 11 above) 199f., 204.

[92] The use of the genitive case also points to a calendar. Compare the fragmentary marble *natales* calendar from Ostia: A. Stuiber, "Heidnische und christliche Gedächtniskalender," *Jahrbuch für Antike und Christentum* 3 (1960) 24ff.

stand as it were for all categories of men in all nations, like the chosen elect
of the Lord that He will assemble at the time of his Second Coming.

New Testament accounts of the Second Coming mention the appearance
of the elect of the Lord which have been gathered from the "four winds, from
one end of heaven to the other" (Matthew 24.31), "from the ends of the earth
to the ends of heaven" (Mark 13.26). According to John Chrysostom, the
elect comprise the "multitude of the angels, of the martyrs, of all the saints";
indeed, "the whole race of men will then be present."[93] Among the inhabi-
tants are the soldiers of the heavenly ruler ($\sigma\tau\rho\alpha\tau\iota\tilde{\omega}\tau\alpha\iota\ \beta\alpha\sigma\iota\lambda\acute{\epsilon}\omega\varsigma\ o\dot{v}\rho\alpha\nu\acute{\iota}ov$),
Christians as soldiers of the heavenly ruler.[94] Whence did the celestial army
and the martyrs come? Drawing upon the analogy of the imperial *adventus*,
John Chrysostom declares that when the Lord arrives at his Second Coming
the faithful shall go to meet Him in mid-air while the unjust have to remain
behind and await their judgment.[95] According to Cyril of Jerusalem, "many
bodies of the saints which slept arose, and came out of the graves after his
resurrection and went into the holy city ($\tau\grave{\eta}\nu\ \dot{\alpha}\gamma\acute{\iota}\alpha\nu\ \pi\acute{o}\lambda\iota\nu$) and appeared to
many."[96] The holy city itself is most splendid and embellished with the most
precious materials. For John Chrysostom it is a city of pure gold, "and more
precious than any gold," it outshines the glittering magnificence of royal
palaces, with "gates consisting of sapphires and pearls."[97] Such an imagery
is even more vividly described in Revelation 21, where the new Jerusalem
coming down out of heaven has a "radiance like a most rare jewel, like a
jasper, clear as crystal," its foundations adorned "with every jewel," each
of its twelve gates "made of a single pearl, and the street of the city was pure
gold color, transparent as glass."

So bejeweled and sumptuous do the architectural facades in the mosaics
appear that they would seem to square perfectly with these descriptions of
the celestial Jerusalem that will come down from heaven when the Lord
arrives at his Second Coming. They appear like a city of pure gold and precious gems, but do they represent the celestial Jerusalem? They are appointed with liturgical furnishings: chancel screens, ciboria, fountains, candlesticks, curtains, gemmed crosses, suspended lamps, votive crowns, chalices,
and closed gem-encrusted (Gospel?) books placed on altars (figs. 9 and 11).
Romanos the presbyter, the central figure in panel I, stands in front of a

[93] *In Matth. homil.* 76.3 (PG 58.697). Cf. Cyril of Jerusalem, *Catechesis* 15.24, 27 (PG
33.904, 909).

[94] John Chrysostom, *In Matth. homil.* 54 (PG 58.538). See the material gathered by
J. Kollwitz, *Oströmische Plastik der Theodosianischen Zeit* (Berlin 1941) 135ff.

[95] *In Epis. I ad Thessal.*, *Sermo* 8 (PG 62.440, adduced by Kantorowicz [n. 14 above]
225 n. 110).

[96] *Catechesis* 14.16 (PG 33.845).

[97] *In Matth. homil.* 1 (PG 57.23f.). Cf. the description in *Revelation* 21.18f.; *Ascension
of Isaiah* 4.14.

chancel area that calls to mind a solea or *schola cantorum*,[98] and the saints flanking the closed book on the altar in panels II and VIII are dressed in ecclesiastical garments as if participating in the drama of the liturgy. Since the liturgical furnishings are conspicuous features of the martyr panels, and since there is no reason for liturgical furnishings to appear in the new city that shall descend from heaven (cf. Revelation 21), the great frieze can not be identified with the celestial Jerusalem. Whereas in most representations of the Heavenly Jerusalem in Early Christian art the elect are shown standing inside of the city,[99] the saints in the mosaics stand in front of what must be interpreted as interior church facades. This interpretation is substantiated by comparison, say, with the main scene on the ivory casket from Pola that illustrates the liturgy taking place inside the martyrium of Saint Peter at Rome (fig. 12).[100] Moreover, this register of the mosaic decoration is sharply segregated from the upper two registers, whose locale is clearly celestial, by means of a projecting cornice illusionistically rendered in mosaic (figs. 9 and 11).[101] The iconographic function of this element is to distinguish the

[98] Hoddinott, *Early Byzantine Churches*, in *Macedonia and Southern Serbia* (London 1963), pl. 14 b; Grabar (n. 2 above) fig. 7. Grabar has quite correctly underscored the ideal liturgical character of these facades (Grabar 66ff.; *idem* (n. 102 below) 49f., 111f.). Cf. O. K. Werckmeister, *Der Deckel des Codex Aureus von St. Emmeram*, Studien zur Deutschen Kunstgeschichte 332 (Baden-Baden 1963) 35. I am grateful to Professor Werckmeister for helping me to clarify my thoughts on this aspect of the architectural facades. Torp (n. 2 above) 24 says that the panels are "reminiscent of the Heavenly Jerusalem . . . not only a palace but also a temple, a heavenly church," which Nordström, in *Byzantinische Zeitschrift* 59 (1966) 142 takes to mean that the panels represent the Heavenly Jerusalem itself. For J. Beckwith, *Early Christian and Byzantine Art* (Harmondsworth 1970) 14, "The mosaics of Hagios Giorgios (*sic*) express the glory of *Roma aeterna* in a new Christian guise and pay homage to Christ who is the true founder of the Holy City." Even if some of the architectural elements in the frieze of saints existed in real architecture, as posited by E. Alföldi-Rosenbaum, "External Mosaic Decoration on Late Antique Buildings," *Frühmittelalterliche Studien* 4 (1970) 1 ff., this does not mean that these panels directly copied actual architecture.

[99] For example, the third register of figures in the representation of the Second Coming in the *Sacra parallela* by John of Damascus (see n. 64 above); the group of figures shown inside the quadriporticus in the third-century (?) Tomb of the Aurelii at Rome (Grabar, *Le premier art* [n. 23 above] fig. 106, and [n. 19 above] 96, fig. 245).

[100] T. Buddensieg, "Le coffret en ivoire de Pola, Saint-Pierre et le Latran," *Cahiers archéologiques* 10 (1959) 157ff., fig. 47. See also an eleventh-century (?) ivory that depicts Saint Menas, a soldier saint, standing in front of an interior church facade (W. F. Volbach, *Elfenbeinarbeiten der Spätantike und des frühen Mittelalters* [Mainz 1952] 103, pl. 66, 242, where an Early Christian prototype is correctly surmised). In contrast, if the architecture behind the figures in the apse mosaic of Santa Pudenziana at Rome represents the Heavenly Jerusalem—it alludes to actual churches in the Holy Land—an exception to our observation is at hand; see n. 46 above.

[101] Torp (n. 2 above) fig. on 20; Texier and Pullan (n. 74 above) pl. XXXIV, fig. 2. A similar device, in marble, separated the first from the second story of the nave walls of Hagios Demetrios at Thessaloniki (*ibid.*, pls. XX-XXI, XXVI, fig. 4; G. and M. Soteriou, ʽΗ Βασιλικὴ τοῦ ῾Αγίου Δημητρίου Θεσσαλονίκης [Athens 1952] 2 pl. 2, a). It can

figures and setting of the upper registers from those of the frieze of saints. We also recall that the ground on which the destroyed figures stand in the second concentric zone was green, which is absent in the frieze of saints.

The locale of the frieze of saints is a celestial ecclesia, light filled and light emanating. Both the liturgical provisions of each of the panels—they are in fact present in all of them—and the pose of the saints point to this register forming a heavenly counterpart to the eucharistic rite that unfolds in the church itself.[102] These panels accord rather to the vision of heaven unfolding in Revelation 4, which describes the worship of God and his host in heaven, than to the fully restored Heavenly Jerusalem related so vividly in Revelation 21. In one of his Easter sermons Saint Augustine distinguishes the celestial church of the Lord from the ecclesia on earth: "Ibi est [Christus] in regno coelorum id est, in Ecclesia, qualis est isto tempore."[103] The liturgy that is celebrated by the church on earth may be interpreted as a participation in that worship that is offered to God by the angelic host and the saints in the heavenly *domus Dei*.[104] It is at once a symbolic representation of the past work of redemption and an anticipation of the Second Coming of Christ.[105] For the eucharistic rite embodies not only the Passion of Christ but also the final triumph of the church in the form of the restoration of the heavenly Jerusalem.[106] It is by reference to the liturgy that the mosaic panels of the

---

be traced back to Hellenistic painting: for instance, in the frescoed dome of a tholos at Kazanlik, where the principal frieze is separated from an upper frieze of shorter diameter by a cluster of four decorative string courses (C. Verdiani, "Original Hellenistic Paintings in a Thracian Tomb," *American Journal of Archaeology* 49 [1945] 402ff., figs. 7, 10-13).

[102] In this context the orant pose of the saints signifies not their resurrection by the Lord but either their participation in the eucharistic rite, as on the Pola casket (fig. 12), or their role as intercessors for the faithful, as in the case of the titular saint shown in the apse mosaic of Sant'Apollinare in Classe (Dinkler [n. 43 above] 72f., 101ff.). For orants in Early Christian art, see A. Grabar, *Martyrium* (Paris 1946) 2.24f., 48f., 105f., 292ff.; T. Klauser, in *Jahrbuch für Antike und Christentum* 2 (1959) 115ff.

[103] Augustine, *Sermo 251 in diebus Paschalibus* 22.4 (PL 38.1169). Cf. Cyril of Jerusalem, *Catechesis* 18.26 (PG 33.1047), where the earthly church presents the form and image of "Jerusalem which is above" (Galatians 4.26).

[104] See John Chrysostom, *De Sacerdotio* 6.4 (PG 48.681). In E. Peterson, *Das Buch von den Engeln* ed. 2 (Munich 1955) this and other scriptural and liturgical texts are adduced to support the thesis that the liturgy of the *ecclesia* on earth is a participation in the liturgy that is celebrated by angels and saints in heaven. In Gregory of Nazianzus's *Oratio de S. Theodoro* (PG 46.736ff.) the intercessory office of a saint—in this instance a military martyr—is explained: Theodoros both intercedes for mankind and worships the Lord with a choir of angels.

[105] Compare the evidence marshalled by O. von Simson, *Sacred Fortress* (Chicago 1948) 62, 97f., *passim*.

[106] See *The Liturgical Homilies of Narsai*, trans. R. H. Connolly, Texts and Studies 8 (Cambridge 1909) Homily 32 (D), 55f, 72f. By about 430 the Church of Rome celebrated Advent (see the material summarized by Kantorowicz [n. 14 above] 229 n. 135; cf. Dinkler [n. 43 above] 104f.). Whether the church of Thessaloniki celebrated it in the liturgy by

great frieze may be interpreted as a vision of the entry of the faithful into the sacred presence of the Lord and his celestial court; the panels illuminate the liturgy.[107]

An interpretation of the architectural vistas as liturgical facades returns us to the pressing question of why these particular saints were included in the great frieze. We have already proposed that one ground for their inclusion is their universality. But more than one principle of selection must have determined their inclusion. Universality alone can not be considered to have dictated it. Nor even would it seem to have been prescribed by any comparative popularity of the saints, for, so far as we know, they had, with the exception of the physician saints Kosmas and Damianos, no wide appeal in the Early Christian period; indeed these particular saints are obscure. But the fact that each is specifically identified by name and occupation points up his individual importance at the time of execution, hence the presumption that other principles of selection must have been operative.

A second ground for their inclusion is the strong likelihood that the converted Rotunda sheltered relics of these saints. For this the spade has brought evidence to light. Dyggve's excavations have disclosed the existence of two large crypts in the Galerian *exedrae* at the eastern and western extremities of the building that were directly accessible from its now destroyed ambulatories.[108] While no relics are reported to have been discovered in them, the crypts were constructed in all likelihood to house relics. And these relics may well have pertained to the saints depicted in the mosaic frieze. Moreover, relics could have been sheltered under the altar table in the apsed sanctuary—a small reliquary of common shape and undetermined dating was found by Dyggve under the floor of the chancel—or in the compartments

---

that date (which in our opinion is at least some twenty years before the mosaics of Hagios Georgios were executed) would depend on the extent of liturgical influence by the Church of Rome on Thessaloniki, which was under its ecclesiastical jurisdiction from the end of the fourth century (see below, n. 236).

[107] If this interpretation be correct, it may provide an explanation of the absence of the nimbus, the normal attribute of saints in Early Christian art from the fifth century on. The mosaic medallions in the soffits of the Archiepiscopal Chapel at Ravenna and the apse of the monastery church of Saint Catherine's on Mount Sinai contain unnimbed figures who are present as witnesses to the central action, an eschatological vision of the Lord in the one, the revelation of the divinity of the Lord in the other. For the lack of nimbi as a chronological index, a view to which I can not subscribe, see Weigand (n. 70 above) 136ff.

[108] E. Dyggve, "Compte rendu succinct des fouilles de Thessalonique 1939," *Rivista di archeologia cristiana* 17 (1940) 155, fig. 7; *idem*, "La région palatiale de Thessalonique," *Acta Congressus Madvigiani Hafniae MDMLIV* (*sic*) (Copenhagen 1958) 1.357, figs. 4, 7; Torp (n. 2 above) 9. E. Hébrard, "Les travaux du Service archéologique de l'Armée d'orient à l'Arc de Triomphe 'de Galère' et à l'église Saint-Georges de Salonique," *Bulletin de correspondance hellénique* 44 (1920) pl. III/IV had discovered the western crypt, Dyggve the eastern one.

in each of the massive piers marking off the central core of the building which are visible to this day.

The notion that the converted Rotunda preserved relics raises the question of whether from the outset the building functioned as a martyrium, possibly dedicated to Christ and the martyrs represented in the great frieze. That the Rotunda was converted to serve as a martyrium is suggested by the two large crypts at the extremities of the temenos that surrounded the complex, as well as the centralized plan of the Rotunda. According to Dyggve, the crypts were constructed when the site was pressed into service for the Christian cult. They were accessible by doorways in the peripheral wall enclosing the ambulatories of Hagios Georgios.

Centralized martyria are common in the Early Christian period, after the reign of Constantine the Great, and some of them were initially pagan edifices that were subsequently deconsecrated and rededicated to the Christian godhead (for example, the great Greek temples at Athens, the Hadrianic Pantheon at Rome).[109] The whole ensemble of Hagios Georgios at Thessaloniki brings to mind one of these martyria, namely the huge Rotunda of the Anastasis on Golgotha which was erected about the middle of the fourth century in the courtyard behind the basilica of the Holy Sepulcher.[110] As the rotunda in the Holy Land commemorated the Resurrection of Christ, the basileus of heaven, the Risen Sun, so the Rotunda in Macedonia commemorated the Second Coming of the Lord, the victorious ruler of heaven who shall return to this earth after his resurrection to restore his kingdom, the earthly Paradise, witnessed by the martyrs of the universal church.[111]

---

[109] For the Athenian temples, see A. Frantz, "From Paganism to Christianity in the Temples of Athens," *Dumbarton Oaks Papers* 19 (1965) 185ff. For the Pantheon, see R. Krautheimer, "Sancta Maria Rotonda," in *Arte del primo millennio*, ed. E. Arslan (Turin 1953) 21ff. (republished with a postscript by Krautheimer in his *Studies in Early Christian, Medieval, and Renaissance Art* [New York 1969] 107-114). For the problem in general, consult F. W. Deichmann, "Christianisierung II (der Monumente)," *Reallexikon für Antike und Christentum* 2 (1954) 1228ff.; and, of course, the monumental study by Grabar (n. 102) *passim* (with the important criticism by Krautheimer, in *Art Bulletin* 35 [1953] 57ff., repr. in his *Studies* 151-160).

[110] For the recent excavations: V. Corbo, "La basilica del S. Sepolcro a Gerusalemme," *Studi biblici franciscani, liber annuus*, 19 (1969) 65ff., with earlier bibliography.

[111] I suggest that an ideological connection may exist between the two rotundas, but I do not imply at all that the Rotunda at Thessaloniki was dedicated specifically to the Second Coming of Christ. See my "The Original Name and Function of Hagios Georgios at Thessaloniki," *Cahiers archéologiques* 21 (1971), in press. On the derivatives of the Anastasis, see the fundamental study by R. Krautheimer, "An Introduction to an 'Iconography of Mediaeval Architecture'," *Journal of the Warburg and Courtauld Institutes* 5 (1942) 1-33, repr. in his *Studies* (n. 109 above) 115-150. See also A. M. Ammann, "Le titre primitif de l'église de Saint-Georges à Salonique," *Orientalia christiana periodica* 22 (1956) 59ff.

As early as 1939 Dyggve published the seductive hypothesis that the converted Rotunda at Thessaloniki originally served as an imperial palace church.[112] His excavations proved beyond doubt that the edifice had been planned as an integral part of the Galerian palace. He adduced formal resemblances between the converted Rotunda and such imperial palace chapels as Charlemagne's octagon at Aachen, which derives from pre-Carolingian sources. His notion has gained a certain currency in contemporary scholarship, and has been accepted by Torp.[113] The hypothesis is especially attractive for the matter at hand in the light of André Grabar's fundamental discussion of palace churches and relics.[114]

But available evidence archeological and literary makes it difficult to accept Dyggve's hypothesis. The physical material that he unearthed at the site raises more questions concerning the function of Hagios Georgios than it settles. At issue is the fact that we cannot be certain that the Galerian ensemble was either still serving as an imperial residence when the Rotunda was transformed into a church or even intact at that time.[115] No reliable evidence is at hand to prove conclusively that the Galerian palace remained an imperial residence from its foundation to the time the Rotunda was transformed into a Christian edifice, nor can we assume that during this period the Rotunda remained an integral and functioning part of the palace. Hagios Georgios was physically separated from the residential quarters of the palace by one of the principal streets of the empire, the Via Egnatia, and during the Early Christian period the functional ties between the Rotunda and the palatial ensemble may have been severed.[116] Perhaps the Galerian ensemble

---

[112] E. Dyggve, "Kurzer, vorläufiger Bericht über die Ausgrabungen im Palastviertel von Thessaloniki, Frühjahr 1939," *Laureae Aquincenses memoriae Valentini Kuzsinszky dictatae, Dissertationes Pannonicae*, ser. 2 no. 2 (Leipzig 1941) 63ff.

[113] Torp (n. 2 above) 7 and *passim*. Cf. Krautheimer, *Early Christian and Byzantine Architecture* (Harmondsworth 1965) 54f.

[114] Grabar (n. 102 above) 1.559ff.

[115] Torp (n. 2 above) 80, maintains that "the palace was moved at a certain point in time (sixth century?) to the center of the city, where the later Byzantine emperors lived when they sojourned at Thessaloniki." The only evidence for this assertion which comes to mind is Radnoti's highly tentative attribution to the sixth century of some ceramic sherds found in the destroyed vestibule of the palace that was constructed to the south of the Arch of Galerius (as reported in Dyggve [n. 112 above] 68; *idem*, "Compte rendu" [n. 108 above] 152f., figs 3-4). We do know, for instance, that in 437 Valentinian III spent the winter months in the city (O. Seeck, *Regesten der Kaiser und Päpste für die Jahre 311 bis 476 n. Chr.* [Stuttgart 1919] 366). The Byzantine palace is known to have been situated in the hills to the north of the old city, near the present government house, but the date of its foundation in that location is unrecorded. Mr. Michael Vickers is currently investigating the problem of the survival of the Galerian palace: "A Note on the Byzantine Palace at Thessaloniki," *Annual of the British School . . . Athens* 66 (1971) 369 ff.

[116] See C. I. Makaronas, "Via Egnatia and Thessalonike," *Studies presented to David Moore Robinson* (Saint Louis 1951) 1.380-388.

became an episcopal palace and the Rotunda an episcopal palace church. Perhaps the Rotunda when rededicated to the Christian godhead became a martyrium. These questions should be held in abeyance.

THE THEATRICAL CHARACTER OF THE MARTYR FRIEZE

The architectural settings of the mosaics are presented not as enclosed interior spaces but as facades, through, behind, and even in which a dominating gold ground shimmers, thus fusing the facades with the background. Each facade rises from a podium in front of which the martyrs stand, facing the beholder. The facades are in two stories, with the lower story taller than the upper one. The types of the facades are the same, though the architecture is disposed in accordance with the major and minor visual and iconographic axes of the program, these axes being distinguished from one another by a carefully calculated employment of different details. Each story is divided into three parts, in which the center consists of a wide exedra or a *fastigium* (?) flanked by narrow side wings of open porticoes supporting open pavilions.[117] While these structures appear to be facades, they are conceived sculpturally, comprised of a complicated and rhythmically arranged sequence of projecting and receding *exedrae*, ciboria and domed pavilions, gemmed pilasters and spirally fluted columns that are embellished with a wealth of ornaments: *transennae*, small fountains, candlesticks, knotted silken curtains, jeweled crosses and books, chalices, lamps, suspended votive crowns, peacocks and other birds (partridges, pigeons, and ibises?). The architectural members are shown now in "worm's eye view," now in "bird's eye view," according to Late Antique conventions of perspective.[118] The martyrs stand before the facades on a platform, the front wall of which has niches alternating with pillars, presented consistently in "worm's eye view." By their number the martyrs reinforce the arrangement (but do not coincide with the axes) of the tripartite compositions: either three figures (panels I, IV, VI and probably V) or two figures, in which case they flank a ciborium placed on a podium and guard a huge cross in front of the ciborium (panels III and VII) or a closed gemmed book (gospel book?) on an altar table under the canopy of the ciborium (panels II and VIII; fig. 11).[119]

[117] For an identification of the central structure in Panels III and VII as a *fastigium*, see H. Torp, "Quelques remarques sur les mosaïques de l'église Saint-Georges à Thessalonique," Πεπραγμένα τοῦ Θ' Διεθνοῦς Βυζαντινολογικοῦ Συνεδρίου (Athens 1955) 1.495ff.; Grabar (n. 2 above) 69f.; E. B. Smith, *Architectural Symbolism of Imperial Rome and the Middle Ages* (Princeton 1956) 61f.

[118] Cf. E. Panofsky, "Die Perspektive als 'symbolische Form,'" *Bibliothek Warburg, Vorträge* (1924/25 [publ. 1927]) 310 n. 33; Bunim, *Space in Medieval Painting and the Forerunners of Perspective* (n. 55 above) 38ff.; and n. 55 above.

[119] The disposition of two soldier saints guarding a large gemmed cross can be traced

These panels resemble painted and marble *scaenae frontes* of the Roman Imperial theater.[120] While evolving from Hellenistic stage designs, the structure of the *scaenae frons* changed in appearance during the empire, becoming far more sculpturally conceived and sumptuously appointed. Resting upon a *pulpitum* the Roman *scaenae frons* was of two or three stories and normally contained curved and rectangular *exedrae* or niches, sometimes ringed with columns but always with a large central opening, or *regia*, flanked by side doors, or *hospitalia*, through which the actors could pass to present themselves to the audience. The stage scenery was decorated as a rule (at least in the theaters of the larger cities of the empire) with a considerable number of statues, bronze ornaments, carved friezes and parapets, painted scenery, masks, wreaths, garlands, and curtains. And the *proscenium* of the *pulpitum* contained niches and sometimes small pilasters.

The architectural settings of the mosaics bear a direct resemblance to the double-storied Roman *scaenae frons*.[121] Their triple divisions of graduated width are paralleled by the *regia* and the *hospitalia* enclosing a variety of fillings, with the central axis accented in form and content in both instances.[122] These openings are flanked by columns and pilasters set upon bases, and the friezes between the apertures are adorned by figures: mythological figures in the *scaenae frons* (for example, the Hadrianic theater at Corinth), pairs of swans confronting chalices in panels III and VII of the mosaics.[123] The entablatures especially of the upper stories of the facades are broken and consist of alternating triangular and curved pediments or projecting domed pavilions, as in some Roman theaters.[124] The luxurious adornment, golden and jeweled, calls to mind such scenography as the (admittedly exaggerated) report by Valerius Maximus (2.4.6): in 62 B.C. Antonius is said to have used silver, Petreius gold, and Q. Catulus ivory for the covering of the rear wall

---

back to early imperial iconography: Alföldi (n. 18 above) 128f., pl. 14, 1. For other Christian examples of such an arrangement, see Grabar (n. 102 above) pl. LI, 2-3.

[120] Consult M. Bieber, *The History of the Greek and Roman Theater*, ed. 2 (Princeton 1961) 167ff; A. M. G. Little, "A Roman Sourcebook for the Stage," *American Journal of Archaeology* 60 (1956) 27ff. A resemblance between the mosaics of the Rotunda and the *scaenae frons* has been noted by Weigand (n. 70 above) 141f.; Torp (n. 117 above) 495f.; Werckmeister (n. 98 above), 35.

[121] Early Christian authors themselves occasionally write of associations between the *scaenae frons* and heaven. For example, John Chrysostom, who had seen the theater at Antioch, metaphorically relates the facades of the tombs of the resurrected to the heavenly theater and to stage scenery (e. g., *In Epist. II ad Corin. homil.* 26.5 = PG 61.582; *In Matth. homil.* 1.8 = PG 57.24; *In Epist. ad Titum cap. 1 homil. 2* = PG 62.674).

[122] For example, compare Panels III and VII of the mosaics to the theater rebuilt by the emperor Hadrian at Merida in western Spain (Bieber [n. 120 above] 202f., figs. 680-684; Torp [n. 117 above] pl. 169, 1).

[123] Bieber 216.

[124] Compare the theater of Herodes Atticus at Athens (*ibid.* 211ff., fig. 715).

of the stage.[125] The statues, bronzes, and other ornaments of the *scaenae frons*
were transformed by the mosaicists into *transennae*, small fountains (the
Fountain of Life?), candlesticks, curtains, and other motifs.[126] The birds flanking the crosses and chalices that are perched on the roofs of the upper stories
of the facades resemble the acroteria of the painted Roman *scaenae frontes*.[127]
The front wall of the platform on which the facades stand is directly paralleled
by the Roman proscenium containing small niches.[128] The martyrs appear
like actors in dramatic poses who have moved downstage during a pageant
to salute the acclaiming spectators in the audience. Even in those panels
where two martyrs are positioned the central focal point, either a large gemmed
cross or a gemmed book on an altar table, assumes the role of a protagonist
whose identity is known to the Christian audience. The martyrs themselves
are personae likewise familiar to the spectators, identified by the inscriptions
accompanying them, so placed as to recall the rectangular sinkings for the
insertion of paintings on wood (to indicate the locale of the play enacted
before them) that flank the *regia* and the *hospitalia* of some *scaenae frontes*.[129]
The chlamys worn over the sleeved tunic by the soldier martyrs is a garment
that appeared on tragic actors and on heroes and fully armed warriors in
Roman mimes (fig. 10),[130] in which connection it should be recalled that the
theater and amphitheater served as vehicles for both the introduction and

---

[125] *Ibid.* 168.

[126] Curtains were used in both the Roman *scaenae frons* (the *siparia*) and the Christian
basilica; see *ibid.* 180; E. Bethe, "Die antiken Terenz-Illustrationen," *Jahrbuch des Deutschen archäologischen Instituts* 18 (1903) 107 figs. 5-7; A. M. Friend, Jr., "The Portraits
of the Evangelists in Greek and Latin Manuscripts," *Art Studies* 7 (1929) figs. 9, 13. The
small fountains in the lower side wings of Panels III and VII recall, as Grabar has noted,
the fountain in the mosaic of Theodora in San Vitale at Ravenna. While water basins
were built into the Roman theater (Bieber [n. 120 above] 210), it is possible that the fountains in the frieze of martyrs, who are shown as the elect resurrected in the heavenly *ecclesia*, refer to the theme of the *fons vitae* or *Fountain of Life*. This is suggested by the
poem *De ave phoenice* (n. 37 above), which in its allusions to Paradise and the resurrection
of the dead states that in the "far-off land" where the phoenix "lives renewed by her own
death . . . there is a fountain (*fons*) in the midst, the fountain of life they call it, crystal
clear, gently flowing, rich in its sweet waters" (verses 25-26), cited in the important study
by P. A. Underwood, "The Fountain of Life in Manuscripts of the Gospels," *Dumbarton
Oaks Papers* 5 (1950) 48.

[127] For instance, the well-known Fourth Style wall painting of Iphigenia in Tauris in
the House of Pinarius Cerialis at Pompeii (Bieber [n. 120 above] 231, fig. 774: also observe
here the use of *siparia*).

[128] *Ibid.* figs. 777-778 (painted *proscenia* of stages with victorious athletes).

[129] Compare the marble relief with the model of a stage in the Museo Nazionale Romano
delle Terme at Rome (*ibid.* 182 fig. 634). The vision of the city of God in Revelation 21.12,
may be recalled in this regard: on the twelve gates of its high walls are inscribed the names
of the tribes of the sons of Israel. For the use of the inscriptions in the mosaics, see below.

[130] *Ibid.* 232 fig. 775; 242 fig. 798.

the spread of fashions in the late empire.[131] The variety of the facial types and expressions, fully human yet structurally stylized by means of wide-open eyes and subtle asymmetrical dispositions if not makeup itself, brings to mind the tragic mask used in Roman plays (even though the faces lack the accentuated pathos and the abnormalities—like the huge open mouths —so common in such masks).[132] And the hairdos of some of the martyrs are unnatural in color—now reddish porphyry, now purplish-blue, now golden —as if dyed; replacing wigs on the stage after 100 B.C., Roman masks were painted in different colors, including gold. Whether they were worn on stage or during an *adventus* ceremony, both wigs and masks were used not so much to conceal the physiognomy of the wearer as to make him impressive in appearance and to focus attention on him.[133]

The frieze of martyrs thus seems indebted both to the painted or structural scenography of the Roman imperial theater and an actual stage production of a play. But no individual *scaenae frons* served as a prototype. As Friend has demonstrated apropos of the theatrical adaptation by Byzantine illuminators of evangelist "portraits," it is futile to search for sources in actual works of architecture.[134] Indeed an illustrated manuscript of a drama may have come into the workshop of the mosaicists, or they were familiar with stage productions.[135] But regardless of the medium of the prototypes the artists made individual borrowings that were judiciously selected and carefully reshuffled to accomodate the program of their work. The "idol madness" of the theater, such as pagan statues and mythological friezes, was eliminated,

[131] MacMullen (n. 75 above) 450, 453.

[132] K. Weitzmann has observed an influence of the tragic mask on pre-Iconoclastic art: "The Classical in Byzantine Art as a Mode of Individual Expression," in *Byzantine Art— An European Art. Lectures* (Athens 1966) 172; *idem*, "The Mosaic of St. Catherine's Monastery on Mount Sinai," *Proceedings of the American Philosophical Society* 110 (December 1966) 404. But I hasten to add that troops sometimes wore masks in parades in the Late Empire (Ammianus Marcellinus 16.10.2ff.), and an influence from this secular sphere I do not exclude.

[133] W. Beare, "Masks on the Roman Stage," *Classical Quarterly* 33 (1939) 139ff. For the purpose of wigs and masks, see M. P. Charlesworth, "Imperial Deportment," *Journal of Roman Studies* 37 (1947) 34ff. While from the pavement of the Rotunda the faces of the martyrs appear more human and natural than from the scaffold or closeup photographs, I would not maintain that the mosaicists took the distance between image and beholder into account while planning the decoration, as S. Kostof, *The Orthodox Baptistery of Ravenna* (New Haven 1965) 102, or Demus (n. 3 above) 30ff., would have it. For secure evidence that Byzantine wall mosaicists designed the proportions of images and possibly their visual impact on the beholder from the scaffold rather than the floor of a building, consult C. Mango and E. J. W. Hawkins, "The Apse Mosaics of St. Sophia at Istanbul," *Dumbarton Oaks Papers* 19 (1965) 117 n. 6.

[134] Friend (n. 126 above) 8.

[135] See K. Weitzmann, "Euripides Scenes in Byzantine Art," *Hesperia* 18 (1949) 159ff.

and a few conspicuously Christian motifs even introduced,[136] thereby evoking the tangible presence of ideal Christian sanctuaries conceived as liturgical facades in front of which appear the martyrs gathered by the Lord: *ut in theatrali scaena simulacrum quoddam insigne per aulaeum vel mimicam cavallationem subito putares emersum*.[137] The *tableaux vivants* are not terrestrial but otherworldly, heavenly, and cosmic, settings appropriate for the Second Coming of the Lord, the final and triumphal event in the cycle of Christian life.

The golden color of the frieze of martyrs and the eschatological ideology of the program identify the setting as a heavenly abode.[138] Some Pompeian murals of the Fourth Style whose backgrounds evoke the presence of a *scaenae frons* are populated by divinities, thus transforming the theatrical settings into celestial abodes. A mural in the House of Apollo at Pompeii shows three nimbed gods identified by Schefold as the sun god Apollo, Hesperus, and Venus, enthroned in front of a facade that is sculpturally articulated by a central niche enclosing a baldachin flanked by two projecting wings.[139] Even the whole composition of the mosaics in Hagios Georgios takes on a celestial appearance and may be likened to another feature of the Roman theater, the *velum* or painted canvas that was used as a sunshade over the auditorium. Our mosaics may be compared to decorated *vela*: as the emperor Nero appeared on a purple velum as the sun god in a chariot among golden stars gleaming all about him (Cassius Dio 43.6), so the figure at the summit of the mosaics appears as the triumphant Christian ruler standing in a heavenly clipeus of silver stars which is supported by four celestial angels against a golden ground.[140]

---

[136] Among the conspicuous Christian motifs is the bust of a youthful Christ figure in a clipeus or aureole held by two angels in the pediments of the *fastigium* (?) in Panels IV and VI (Hoddinott [n. 98 above] pl. 20, b; Grabar [n. 2 above] 69f., fig. 12). These pediments recall those *scaenae frontes* in the upper stories of whose *regia* images of the gods or emperors appeared (e.g., the theater at Orange). Cf. Bieber (n. 120 above) 170, *passim*. The confronted peacocks on the peaks of the roofs are probably symbols of celestial immortality, resurrection, incorruptibility, or eternal beatitude, referring to the immortality of the martyrs and their abode in the celestial *ecclesia*.

[137] Ammianus Marcellinus 26.6.15, describing the appearance of the usurper Procopius in A.D. 365

[138] Cf. II Chronicles 3.4-10; Revelation 21.18; Cyril of Alexandria, *Fragmenta in Canticum Canticorum* (PG 69.1279); Bede, *De templo Salomonis* 12 (PL 91.763). See further in J. Bodonyi, "Entstehung und Bedeutung des Goldgrundes in der spätantiken Bildkomposition," *Archeologiai Ertesitö* 46 (1932/33), reviewed by E. H. Gombrich, in *Kritische Berichte* 2/3, (1932/33) 65ff.; G. Haupt, *Die Farbensymbolik in der sakralen Kunst des abendländischen Mittelalters* (Dresden 1941) 65ff.; K. Wessel, "Farbensymbolik," *Reallexikon zur byzantinischen Kunst*, 12 (1969) 524ff.

[139] K. Schefold, *Pompejanische Malerei* (Basel 1952) 134 pl. 37; Torp (n. 117 above) 497 pl. 169 fig. 2.

[140] The earliest evidence of the appearance of an emperor as cosmocrator at the summit

THE IMPERIAL CHARACTER OF THE MOSAICS

While the facades represented in the mosaics appear to be based on the conventions of the Roman imperial *scaenae frons*, they were not necessarily originally intended to be thought of as such. As we know from such writings as Tertullian's *De spectaculis*, the early Church fathers denounced the theater not only as a place of immoral conduct but also for its idol madness and pagan religious associations. Only occasionally, as in the writings of John Chrysostom, do we find the theater and stage scenery metaphorically related to the facades of the tombs of those resurrected by the Lord.[141] One reason why theatrical settings occur not altogether infrequently in Early Christian, Byzantine, and early medieval art would seem to lie in the fact that artists associated them with the *Sacrum palatium*, as it was known to them. The *scaenae frons* was assimilated by Christian art presumably because artists saw in it an imperial palace tradition.[142]

The palace architecture of the Roman emperors is known to us from a variety of sources, archeological as well as literary, and bears out the contention that this aspect of imperial art influenced the course of development of Early Christian imagery. An important relic of painted palace architecture that resembles a *scaenae frons* was found in 1893 in a private, and possibly imperial, house on the Via de' Cerchi, built against the southern slope of the Palatine Hill at Rome.[143] Since the masonry of the walls is definitely Severan, the murals are dated about A.D. 200. These wall paintings show servants welcoming guests in front of a palatial facade placed against a yellowish (originally white?) ground. The servants are clad in contemporary costume: a short white tunic with purple *clavi* and long sleeves. The figure in the center of the preserved composition stands under a suspended garland in front of an open doorway. The architecture is not jeweled, and indeed the work is not of high quality, albeit important as a document of Severan mural painting. And these murals point to the influence of the *scaenae frons* on the evolution of imperial palace architecture.[144] Other works attesting to this influence,

---

of a heavenly dome is found in Lucanus, *De bello civili* 1.52-58. For the *adventus* of Nero, see A. Deissmann, *Licht vom Osten*, ed. 4 (Tübingen 1923) 318.

[141] See n. 121 above.

[142] So Smith (n. 117 above) 120ff.

[143] F. Wirth, *Römische Wandmalerei* (Berlin 1934) 125ff., pls. 29, 30, a, 31; G. Lugli, *Roma antica* (Rome 1946) 614ff.; color illustrations in *Papers of the British School at Rome* 8 (1916) pls. IIIff. This comparison with the mosaics in Hagios Georgios was first made by D. V. Ainalov, *Ellinisticheskie osnovy vizantiiskogo iskusstva*, (1900-1901), trans. by E. and S. Sobolevitch as *The Hellenistic Origins of Byzantine Art* (New Brunswick 1961) 203.

[144] Cf. the lost wall paintings of Nero's *domus aurea* at Rome (Wirth [n. 143 above] pl. 7, a) and the facade of the House of the Faun at Pompeii (Little [n. 120 above] pl. 24, fig. 17). A Christian parallel to our frieze of martyrs is provided by the recently discovered wall paintings in an upstairs room of a villa at Lullingstone in Kent which is tentatively as-

and especially that of the *aula regia* and *hospitalia* of the *scaenae frons* on the facades of imperial palaces, include the triple openings in the lower story of the facade shown on the *sestertius* of the seventeenth consulate of the emperor Domitian, which may possibly depict the west vestibule of the Domus Tiberiana at Rome,[145] and the facades shown on the Missorium of Theodosius at Madrid and of the courtyard of Diocletian's palace at Spalato and the PALATIUM of Theodoric in the nave mosaics of Sant'Apollinare Nuovo at Ravenna. By the age of Constantine the Great stage scenery had been assimilated by imperial palace architecture. The imperial *scaenae frons*, in turn, was presumably influenced by Hellenistic palace architecture. Vitruvius describes the *scaenae frons* in terms of a Hellenistic royal palace and the scenery of the tragic stage with "columns, *fastigia*, statues, and other objects suited to kings" (5.6.9: *deformantur columnis et fastigiis et signis reliquisque regalibus rebus*).

The imperial ceremonies that took place both within and without these palaces are known to have exerted some impact on the development of the liturgy in the Early Christian church.[146] Moreover, we have seen that the facades in the mosaic frieze of Hagios Georgios are equipped with liturgical furnishings and may be interpreted as an illustration of the liturgy unfolding on the stage of the church itself. As such the mosaics are the earliest preserved example of a Christian adaptation of the *scaenae frons* with its imperial associations.[147]

Not only the individual panels and their salient parts but also the whole hierarchic composition of the mosaics in the dome of Hagios Georgios relate to imperial iconography. The validity of comparing a representation of the Second Coming of the Lord to scenes of the emperor being acclaimed by his

---

cribed to ca. 350 and which shows seven orant figures wearing garments with pearl edgings and standing in the intercolumniations of a colonnade of red and blue columns and curtains (K. S. Painter, "The Lullingstone Wall-Plaster: An Aspect of Christianity in Roman Britain," *British Museum Quarterly* 33 [1969] 131-150).

[145] E. Nash, *Pictorial Dictionary of Ancient Rome*, ed. 2 (New York 1961) 1, fig. 452. See A. Boëthius, "The Reception Hall of the Roman Emperors," *Annual of the British School at Athens* 44 (1951) 25ff.; I. Lavin, The House of the Lord," *Art Bulletin* 44 (1962) 1ff. Morey, Torp, and others have adduced the rock-cut tombs at Petra in Transjordan as close comparisons to the architectural facades in the mosaics of the Rotunda (see M. A. Murray, *Petra, the Rock City of Edom* [London 1939] pls. 10, 12, 13, 16). The mosaics and these tombs would seem to derive from common, ultimate sources.

[146] As suggested in the important study by T. Mathews, "An Early Roman Chancel Arrangement and its Liturgical Functions," *Rivista di archeologia cristiana* 38 (1962) 73ff. See now *idem, The Early Churches of Constantinople: Architecture and Liturgy* (University Park 1971) 113 and *passim*.

[147] That the facades exhibit "eine Mischung von Formen des christlichen Bema und der *scaenae frons* der Römerzeit" has been asserted by E. Dyggve, "Über die freistehende Klerusbank," *Beiträge zur älteren europäischen Kulturgeschichte, Festschrift für Rudolf Egger* (Klagenfurt 1952) 1.49.

subjects is established by the author of a spurious sermon attributed to John Chrysostom, who recalls certain imperial images (βασιλικαὶ εἰκόνες) that were laid out in two registers. A crowd of imperial satellites is shown in one of the registers, the barbarians making obeisance to the victorious ruler in the other. Both the satellites and the captives worship the ruler. The author of the sermon declares that similar scenes will be seen at the Second Coming of the Lord, and specifically at the appearance of that "terrible and glorious sign" (φοβερὸν ἐκεῖνο καὶ ἔνδοξον σημεῖον), the cross.[148]

This passage calls to mind a well-known *ekphrasis* by Procopius, the prolific court historian of the emperor Justinian, of the mosaic decoration of the ceiling of the Chalkê of the Great Palace of Constantinople:

> On either side is war and battle, and many cities are captured, some in Italy, others in Libya. The emperor Justinian is winning victories through his general Belisarius, who returns to the emperor, with his whole army intact, and offers him spoils, both kinds and everything that is most prized among men. In the center stand the emperor and the empress Theodora, and they both look as if they were rejoicing and celebrating victories over the kings of the Vandals and of the Goths, who approach them like prisoners of war led to captivity. The Roman senate stands round them, all jubilant. This mood is expressed by the tesserae which take on a gay bloom on their faces. So they are proud and smile as they bestow on the emperor godlike honors because of the magnitude of his achievements.[149]

Attempts have been made to reconstruct this important work of imperial imagery, and two alternatives seem possible.[150] Whereas the military scenes were relegated to the ceilings of the adjacent chambers of the imperial vestibule (these are described by Procopius), the rulers and the senate were placed in its central vault. The location of the scene of Belisarius's victorious return with captives and spoils is dubious. The central vault featured either two or three concentric zones, with the emperor and the empress occupying the central medallion of the composition. Either the imperial couple was surrounded by a row of acclaiming senators or it occupied the medallion alone,

---

[148] PG 69.649f. This pertinent text is cited by Kantorowicz (n. 14 above) 225, who derives the comparison of the Parousia of the Lord to the *adventus* of a king in a city from a sermon attributed to Augustine (*Sermo* 155 = PL 39.2051f.). At the same time it should be noted that such metaphorical language was used in both the Latin West and the Greek East. Compare E. Kitzinger, "The Cult of Images in the Age before Iconoclasm," *Dumbarton Oaks Papers* 8 (1954) 99f., 124.

[149] *De aedificiis* 1.10.12-15, trans. by H. B. Dewing and G. Downey, Loeb Classical Library, 85ff. and by C. Mango, *The Brazen House*, Arkaeologisk-kunsthistoriske Meddedelser 4.4 (Copenhagen 1959) 32, who dates the mosaics of the Chalkê after A.D. 540.

[150] Mango, 32ff.; Grabar (n. 13 above) 81ff.

in which case the *togati* were placed in a second register and the army in the third register, and the three concentric circles were possibly of unequal height and not at all necessarily separated from one another by bands (as in the upper two zones of the mosaics of Hagios Georgios at Thessaloniki). Whether there were two or three registers—the second alternative would seem more likely—the composition was designed by the use of a principle of hierarchic grouping, as in Hagios Georgios, where the most important figure occupies the central medallion and the other figures are arranged in descending order according to rank.

Such a grouping of figures is rooted in imperial monuments in both the Latin West and the Greek East. For example, the decoration of one side of the carved pedestal of the triumphal column of the emperor Arcadius at Constantinople, as it is known to us from a set of anonymous drawings (the so-called *Freshfield Album*) that was executed about 1574, was organized in four superposed registers, with two angels carrying a wreath containing a cross in the top register, the emperors Arcadius and Honorius flanked by soldiers in the second, a row of acclaiming senators (?) in the third, and the captives and spoils of war in the fourth (fig. 5).[151] Both in form and content the mosaics of the central vault of the Chalkè are related to such a hierarchic principle.

Such a principle of compositional underlies religious imagery of the empire as well. We have already adduced a number of iconographic parallels to the mosaics which bear this out. At this point it is germane to point to yet another work that resembles both the formal conventions and the thematic display of the mosaics, namely the murals in the Temple of Zeus Theos at Dura Europos, which were painted during a single campaign circa A.D. 114-116 (fig. 2).[152] These frescoes decorated the north, south, and west walls of the *naos* of the temple, and showed on the rear wall a colossal figure of Zeus Theos being crowned by two victory figures and on the side walls his devotees making an oblation of fruits, incense, and wine. Dressed in the *paludamentum* and holding a golden spear, the nimbate figure of the god stood in front of a chariot and faced the beholder; he represents "the whole circle of the sky" of Herodotus and Strabo.[153] From the fragments of the

[151] E. M. Freshfield, "Notes on a Vellum Album . . . ," *Archaeologia* 72 (1922) 87ff.; K. Weitzmann, *The Joshua Roll* (Princeton 1948) 100ff.; Grabar (n. 13 above) 253ff.

[152] See F. E. Brown, "The Temple of Zeus Theos," in *The Excavations at Dura-Europos, Preliminary Reports 7-8* (New Haven 1939) 180ff., esp. 196ff., fig. 50. These murals are closely allied to the paintings in the *naos* of the Temple of the Palmyrene Gods at Dura (first half of the first century A.D.): see F. Cumont, *Fouilles de Doura-Europos (1922-1923)* (Paris 1926) 2 pls. XXV-LX. I am grateful to Professor Susan Downey for discussing this material with me.

[153] Herodotus 1.131; Strabo 15.13 (cited by Brown 196ff.). As Professor Downey has indicated to me, there is no evidence of Iranian gods at Dura; thus Brown's statement to that effect is in need of correction.

murals it seems that the color of the background of the rear wall was grey, perhaps a substitute for silver. Arranged in three superposed registers on the lateral walls the worshippers all stood frontally and isolated from each other and were identified by name by Greek inscriptions placed beside their heads. They included priests as well as private individuals of both sexes— possibly the family of the donor—and were placed against a deep yellow background, this color perhaps denoting gold. They were given portrait likenesses and wore showy garments adorned with jewels and purple *clavi*. Though not placed in a dome the compositional disposition of the murals and their meaning bear a direct resemblance to the mosaics in the dome of the Rotunda.[154]

A later work that belongs to the same tradition of Roman religious imagery is the ceiling fresco in the cubiculum of Clodius Hermes in the catacombs under San Sebastiano on the Via Appia at Rome, attributed to the late third century.[155] This mural shows a ring of ecstatic witnesses looking up to a striding figure clad in a purple chlamys and shouldering a scepter, his right arm outstretched with the hand open. While perhaps a representation of the apotheosis of the deceased (a Christian soldier?) rather than the Ascension of Christ, this painting, along with the murals of the Temple of Zeus Theos and related works, warns us not to accept blindly the derivation of our mosaics from the realm of pure imperial iconography, and certainly not to assume that they had to be executed on order of an emperor. Our mosaics are rooted in a matrix of both imperial and pagan religious imagery.

From such a representation as that on the base of the Column of Arcadius at Constantinople it is clear that by the beginning of the fifth century pagan religious imagery was being supplanted, at least in the Greek East, by Christian motifs: for instance, scenes of the libation of the emperor had by then disappeared from imperial monuments and winged victory figures had become angels bearing a wreath containing a cross. Even before the reign of Constantine the Great imperial iconography was beginning to be transformed into imagery acceptable to the Church.[156] And in the Greek East the ultimate manifestation of this transformation is found in what has come to be known as the classical system of mosaic decoration in the Middle Byzantine church. The mosaics in Hagios Georgios at Thessaloniki provide

---

[154] Compare also the triangular bronze relief whose scenes of the cult of Jupiter Dolichenus are arranged in five superposed horizontal registers (P. Merlat, *Répertoire des inscriptions et monuments figurés du culte de Jupiter Dolichenus* [Paris 1951] 134ff., pl. XIV); and a Roman floor mosaic from Carthage illustrating the months (R. Cagnat, in *Mémoires de la Société nationale des antiquaires de France* 57 [1896] 251f., pl. IV). For the ultimate antecedents in Egypt, see G. Daressy, "L'Égypte céleste," *Bulletin de l'Institut Français d'archéologie orientale* 12 (1916) 1ff.

[155] See n. 19 above.

[156] Gagé (n. 10 above) 370ff.; Grabar (n. 13 above).

one important forerunner of that system, and herein lies their great historical
importance, second only to their extraordinary artistic significance.[157]

THE DATING OF THE MOSAICS

Ever since they were first published by Texier and Pullan over one hundred
years ago, the mosaics have been dated to different points of time in the pre-
Iconoclastic period. A variety of opinions persisted until 1939, when the
distinguished classical archeologist and Byzantinist Edmund Weigand published an important paper on the mosaics in which they were attributed
to the years circa 515-530.[158] His case was erected on a firm superstructure,
the main supporting pillars of which have remained essentially undisturbed
to this day. In the same year as Weigand's paper appeared, the Danish archeologist, Ejnar Dyggve, accompanied by an international team of experts,
began to excavate the grounds of the imperial palace and Hagios Georgios
at Thessaloniki. This work was interrupted by World War II but was re-
sumed in 1952, when the Norwegian scholar Hjalmar Torp joined the team
as the member responsible for a cleaning and close technical examination
of the mosaics in the Rotunda. After four months of painstaking work Torp
contended that the mosaics were executed in a single campaign during the
reign of the emperor Theodosius the Great (379-395), and specifically in the
years circa 380-390, thus confirming an opinion held by Dyggve as early
as 1939 that the Rotunda of Galerius had been converted into a palace church
at the end of the fourth century.[159] Torp argued his attribution in both a
preliminary paper delivered at the Byzantine Congress held at Thessaloniki
in 1953 (and published in 1955) and a magnificently illustrated book written
in Norwegian that appeared in 1963.[160] Here, as evidently in the forthcoming

---

[157] For the Middle Byzantine system, see Demus (n. 3 above); Kostof (n. 133 above)
94ff., in particular 131.

[158] Weigand (n. 70 above) 116ff., with a survey of earlier opinions on the dating of the
mosaics.

[159] Dyggve (n. 112 above) 69, where the converted Rotunda is identified as a "palace
church" and dated "vielleicht in die Zeit Theodosius I." And in 1953 ("Recherches sur le
palais impérial," *Studia orientalia Ioanni Pedersen* [Copenhagen 1953] 68f.) he clearly states
that "en 1939 j'avais daté ces mosaïques de la fin du ıvᵉ siècle et ce jugement n'a pas du
être changé après les observations faites pour la première fois cette année [i.e., 1952/53, when
the scaffold was erected inside the Rotunda] dans de meilleurs conditions." See n. 232 below.

[160] Torp (n. 117 above) 489ff.; *idem* (n. 2 above) *passim*. Torp informed me in a letter
dated 20 February 1970 that, knowledge of my views about the dating notwithstanding,
he is as convinced as ever of the correctness of his attribution, which he shall publish with
full documentation in the forthcoming final report, coauthored by H. P. L'Orange. Meanwhile, consult L'Orange, "I mosaici della cupola di Hagios Georgios a Salonicco," *Corsi
di cultura sull'arte ravennate e bizantina* 17 (1970) 257-268, where a Theodosian dating
is attributed to the mosaics.

final report on the Rotunda, he rests his case primarily on a crucial technical observation about the relation of the tesserae to the masonry at the summit of the dome. Supported by stylistic observations but not a point-by-point rebuttal of Weigand's arguments (that may be made in the final report), his attribution has been accepted by nearly all modern specialists.

As the following analysis of the published evidence hopes to demonstrate, the attributions of both Weigand and Torp are wide of the mark. We intend to prove that the Galerian Rotunda was converted into a church and its mosaic decoration put up during a single campaign sometime in the third quarter of the fifth century.

Weigand ascribed the mosaics to the early sixth century by adducing the following body of evidence: the chlamys worn by the soldier saints; the contents of the inscriptions accompanying the saints; the universal church calendar which, it is conjectured, was used for the selection of the saints; related to that, the cult of the physician saints Kosmas and Damianos; and certain stylistic observations concerning the saints and the architectural sculpture at the site. Before assessing each of these points it is necessary to comment briefly on the nature of Weigand's method. Whenever attempting to date a monument, Weigand relied on both preserved monuments and monuments known from literary sources and inscriptions. If the earliest known example of a nimbed saint dates from about 450, this date would be accepted as a terminus post quem for all other nimbed saints, provided it is not contradicted by other evidence supplied by that monument. Weigand applied such a method not so much to internal stylistic evidence or formal qualities as to such external evidence as inscriptions, garment types, and attributes of saints. His outlook was essentially philological and archeological, his scholarship of the highest standards. Today, such an approach to the dating of Early Christian and Byzantine monuments finds little favor. Stylistic evidence is deemed far more crucial, partly because of the emphasis by specialists on stylistic phenomena in Renaissance and Baroque art and the impact their scholarship has had on other fields of art history, including Early Christian art. Be that as it may, it should be observed that Weigand's method is based on a fortuitous body of evidence that for the Early Christian period is insufficient for a demonstration of chronological limits. Nevertheless, the evidence adduced by Weigand to date the mosaics can not be dismissed out of hand; it must be reckoned with thoroughly.

GARMENTS

In the mosaic frieze the outer garments worn by the martyrs fall into two groups, with the chlamys worn by all the soldier saints, the phelonion by the other saints. These garments denote profession, as the inscriptions accompanying the figures prove. The question is whether they enable us to date the mosaics. For Weigand they do. He observes that the earliest dated example of a soldier saint clad in a chlamys is the figure of Saint Theodore in the apse mosaic of the church of Saints Cosmas and Damian at Rome, a work securely dated to the years 526-530 (fig. 8). After this time figures of soldier saints in Western art are almost always shown dressed in this garment.[161] But the single example of Saint Theodore is an insufficient ground for ascribing the mosaics of Hagios Georgios to the early sixth century. The figure occurs in the West, and indeed in a work that was conceivably influenced by an earlier, eastern prototype. In the art of the pre-Iconoclastic Greek East very few soldier saints are preserved, and none of them, with a couple of possible exceptions, antedate the sixth century.[162] But this does not mean that soldier saints or even soldier saints wearing the chlamys were not represented there at an earlier date. The chlamys was a garment of the highest distinction in the imperial wardrobe, being one of the primary symbols of imperial power.[163] It was also worn by various members of the court, in-

---

[161] Weigand (n. 70 above) 139f. Subsequent examples include St. Vitalis in his church at Ravenna, Saint Theodorus in the apse mosaic of San Teodoro in Palatino at Rome, Saints Primus and Felicianus in San Stefano Rotondo at Rome, the four soldier saints of Salona in the chapel of San Venanzio attached to the Lateran Baptistery at Rome, and the figure of Saint Menas on an ivory diptych in the British Museum at London (Volbach, [n. 100 above] 83 pl. 56, 182). See also M. L. Finaldi, "Il costume romano e i mosaici di Piazza Armerina," *Rivista dell'Istituto nazionale d'archeologia e storia dell'arte* 13/14 (1964/65) 226, fig. 18.

[162] Two fragments of terra cotta in the Benaki Museum at Athens which are attributed to ca. 400 show confronted horsemen wearing the chlamys and have been tentatively identified as Christian military saints (Kantorowicz [n. 11 above] 390ff., figs. 46-47). Kantorowicz believes that saints were dressed in military costume only ca. A.D. 400 at the earliest. A Christian *chlamydatus* that is identified as the physician saint Kosmas is attributed to the fifth century (*Handbook of the Dumbarton Oaks Collection* [Washington D.C. 1955] 104 no. 225). Professor Weitzmann has confirmed my suspicion that the identification of this figure as Kosmas is wrong (written communication); the figure holds a box on which the letters NOTA (= *notarius*) can be read. The figure of Saint Milix in the Catacomb of Pontianus at Rome wears a chlamys with a *tablion* (Grabar [n. 102 above] pl. LI, 3). The date of this work is uncertain; see G Ferrari, "Cimitero di Ponziano," *Enciclopedia cattolica* 9 (1952) 1754f. These examples suggest that the chlamys was indeed worn by military saints before the sixth century, and this opinion is borne out by some of the mosaics in the church of Hagios Demetrios at Thessaloniki (Soteriou [above, n. 101] 191ff., pls. 60-62), which may be dated as early as 475 (see my "Some Observations on the Dating of S. Demetrios in Thessaloniki," *Byzantion* 40 [1970] 36ff.) or ca. 500 (Robin S. Cormack, "The Mosaic Decoration of S. Demetrios, Thessaloniki: A Re-Examination in the Light of the Drawings of W. S. George," *Annual of the British School at Athens* 64 [1969] 17ff.). For a much later dating of these mosaics, see Kitzinger, "Byzantine Art in the Period between Justinian and Iconoclasm," *Berichte zum XI. internationalen Byzantinisten-Kongress München 1958* (Munich 1958) 21f.

[163] A general study of the chlamys in Late Antiquity and Early Christianity is lacking; but see Delbrueck (n. 15 above) 36ff.; Alföldi (n. 18 above) 105-110, 150ff.; P. Koukoules, Βυζαντινῶν Βίος καὶ Πολιτισμός (Athens 1949) 2.2, 5-59; G. P. Galavaris, "The Sym-

cluding the officers enlisted in the cadres of the imperial guards, who were allowed to be so uniformed by the end of the third century.[164] Since by the age of Constantine the Great regular soldiers of the army assumed both the whitish chlamys with purple inset or *tablion* and a tunic with colored insignia on it, such a garb on soldier saints could have been seen on monuments as early as the fourth century, an age well documented for its love of sumptuous fashions and excessive display.[165]

We have observed that the chlamys on Leon and Eukarpios is porphyry-violet and on the other soldier saints marble white, and that the *segmentum* sewn on the shoulder of the tunic of Onesiphoros contains a standing figure with an upraised arm, apparently unlike the *segmenta* of all the other soldier saints. Do the differences in color and the details of dress point to a specific dating? They should, for they give at once distinction between ranks and identity within a rank, matters of the utmost concern to the army in the later Roman Empire. But our corpus of monuments pagan and Christian depicting soldiers is far too meager to date the *chlamydati* on these grounds. In any event, we may be assured that the ornament and color of the chlamys and the size and position of the *tablion* of the soldier saints were deemed important at the time and, moreover, reflect contemporary customs and tastes in garments.[166]

The chlamys worn by the soldier saints in the Rotunda fails to establish a date. Likewise the phelonion cannot be used as a means of dating.[167] Moreover, its presence on all the nonmilitary saints in the Rotunda points up a distinction of importance between pre-Iconoclast and post-Iconoclast art of

---

bolism of the Imperial Costume as displayed on Byzantine Coins," *Museum Notes of the American Numismatic Society* 8 (1958) 99ff.; R. MacMullen, *Civilian and Soldier in the Later Roman Empire* (Cambridge 1963) 170ff., 179f.; *idem* (n. 75 above) 445ff.

[164] MacMullen, *Civilian and Soldier* 171, 179.

[165] By the late fourth century the uniforms of Roman soldiers were brighter and glittering, *auro colorumque micantia claritudine*, according to Ammianus Marcellinus 31.10.4. For uniforms decorated with silver, see R. MacMullen, "Imperial Bureaucrats in the Roman Provinces," *Harvard Studies in Classical Philology* 68 (1964) 315 n. 31, quoting Vegetius 4.37 and Herodian 4.7.3.

[166] Torp (n. 2 above) 83, asserts that the chlamys was simply adopted from the imperial wardrobe, a statement that reveals a misunderstanding of how common the wearing of the chlamys was in the later Roman Empire. And surely the appearance of the chlamys does not establish, as Torp intimates, imperial patronage of the decoration of Hagios Georgios. See n. 75 above.

[167] Cf. the figure of Saint Ambrosius shown in the mosaics of the chapel of San Vittore in Sant'Ambrogio at Milan (Volbach [n. 41 above] pl. 132); here, the same garments are worn by the figure of Saint Maternus. These mosaics are attributed to the late fifth century (E. Kitzinger, "Some Reflections on Portraiture in Byzantine Art," *Zbornik Radova* 8 [1963] 185ff.). Aside from some catacomb paintings, this is the earliest datable example known to us of a bishop saint shown wearing the paenula. From the sixth century there are numerous examples of bishop saints wearing the paenula.

the Greek East. In the Rotunda the phelonion is worn by bishops, presbyters, physicians, and the flute-player Philemon, without apparent regard to occupation or distinction in rank, whereas by the end of Iconoclasm, if not before, Byzantine artists almost always distinguish clearly and carefully the profession of saints by the type, shape, color, ornament, and accessories of their vestments, even if they are copying much earlier works of art.[168] In this "hierarchy through clothing" Byzantine art was strongly affected by its environment.[169]

Two notable peculiarities of the inscriptions accompanying the martyrs to which Weigand has drawn attention are the "figure eight" ligature of omicron upsilon and the derivation of the names of the months from the Julian calendar. According to Weigand, both features support a terminus post quem of the early sixth century. Of course, the use of inscriptions to identify individual figures or even entire scenes is one of the hallmarks of Early Christian and Byzantine art and can be traced back to Greco-Roman art.[170] But it must be pointed out that our knowledge of late Greek epigraphy is too fragmentary to make substantial use of the script for the determination of chronology. So far as we are able to glean, not even a relative chronology can be established by comparison of the inscriptions in the Rotunda with those in the apse mosaic of Hosios David or even those in the mosaics of Hagios Demetrios at Thessaloniki.

More important is the presence of a form of the "figure eight" ligature of omicron upsilon that usually looks like a Latin "S" (fig. 22). Weigand maintains that the omicron-upsilon ligature occurs for the first time only after about the year 500.[171] While in its true form the ȣ ligature seems to have become widespread only in the sixth century, there are a significant number of examples in the dated inscriptions of the fifth century, and one has been found in a text dated to the year 315.[172] An early form of the lig-

---

[168] Thus bishop saints are distinguished from priests, deacons, physicians, soldiers, imperial saints, monks and nuns, and virgins. There are a few notable exceptions to the rule in the art of the Macedonian dynasty, such as the *Joshua Roll* and a few figures (aside from some of the images of David) in the *Paris Psalter* (Bibl. Nat. MS gr. 139).

[169] R. S. Lopez, "The Silk Industry in the Byzantine Empire," *Speculum* 20 (1945) 20.

[170] One Roman example already cited in this study is the *naos* of the Temple of Zeus Theos at Dura Europos (fig. 2; see n. 152 above). Cf. F. Barišić "Grčki natpisi na monumentalnom živopisu" (The Greek Inscriptions in the Mural Painting of Byzantine Churches) *Zbornik Radova* 10 (1967) 47ff.

[171] Weigand (n. 70 above) 131ff. Cf. D. Levi, *Antioch Mosaic Pavements* (Princeton 1947) 627ff.

[172] G. Downey, as quoted in Marvin C. Ross, *Catalogue of the Byzantine and Early Mediaeval Antiquities in the Dumbarton Oaks Collection* (Washington D.C. 1962) 1.70.

ature occurs in the Flavian period.[173] At Thessaloniki itself one form of the ligature appears by the early third century A.D.[174] Some of these pre-sixth-century specimens show the V superimposed on the O without the two letters being really merged into a single loop.[175] Since some of these examples occur in publications where the arrangement and shape of letters are only approximated in printed type, it is impossible to refute Weigand conclusively. For that more photographs of inscriptions containing the omicron-upsilon ligature are needed. The use of ligatures could be dictated by considerations of the space available for an inscription or, as may be the case in Hagios Georgios, simply for calligraphic reasons. But regardless of the reason for their use, the ligatures fail to serve as an index of the chronology of the mosaics.

All the months of the feasts in the inscriptions accompanying the saints follow the names of the months in the Julian calendar rather than the Macedonian or other lunisolar calendars. For example, the feast of Damianos was commemorated *MHNI ΣΕΠΤΕΜ[ΒΡΙΩ]* (fig. 22). Does this fact enable us to date the mosaics? After surveying church inscriptions and the writings of historians in the pre-Iconoclastic period, Weigand concluded that the Julian calendar was adopted by the Christian church in the Greek East only in the early years of the reign of Justinian and in some provinces at yet a later date.[176] Although the history of the diffusion of the Julian reckoning has yet to be written, it is clear that some provinces, like Syria, whose Early Christian inscriptions Weigand discusses at length, adopted the Julian calendar only in the later sixth century. But Weigand has overlooked a large body of important evidence that proves that the central authorities in Constantinople were using the Julian calendar in imperial edicts and other official correspondence even before the dedication of the new capital in 330 A.D.; moreover, church officials of that city had adopted it no later than the reign of Theodosius II (408-450).[177] Even at the beginning of the reign of

---

[173] M. Avi-Yonah, "Abbreviations in Greek Inscriptions," *Quarterly of the Department of Antiquities in Palestine* 9 Suppl. (1940) 119, cited by G. Downey, in *Art Bulletin* 35 (1953) 144.

[174] C. Edson, "Cults of Thessalonica," *Harvard Theological Review*, 41 (1948) 154 no. 1, 193. Cf. *Die griechisch-christlichen Inschriften des Peloponnes*, ed. N. A. Bees (Athens 1941) 1.61 no. 31, 90 no. 42 (fourth- to fifth-century examples).

[175] As pointed out to me *in litteris* by Ernst Kitzinger.

[176] Weigand (n. 70 above) 133f. There is no comprehensive study of ancient calendars. For the Julian calendar, especially in the eastern provinces, see F. K. Ginzel, *Handbuch der mathematischen und technischen Chronologie* (Leipzig 1914) 3.7.294ff.; and E. J. Bickerman, *Chronology of the Ancient World* (London 1968) 47ff.

[177] Seeck (n. 115 above) 172ff., *passim*, for imperial edicts and other official correspondence, written in Latin; *ibid.* 343, where Bishop Atticos of Constantinople sends a transcript of the Nicaean creed to Bishop Bonifatius of Rome (26 November 419). Not all ecclesiastical correspondence from Constantinople during the fifth century was dated according to the Julian reckoning (*ibid.* 357, 359).

Theodosius the Great (ca. 380) the *Ecclesiastical History* written by Socrates
(who died at Constantinople in 439) uses the Roman names of the months,
taken from the Julian reckoning.[178] And of course the army, whose official
language was Latin, was familiar with the Julian calendar. Thus Weigand's
observation about the names of the months must be discarded, the absence
of any proof of the adoption of the Julian calendar by church officials at
Thessaloniki itself in the fourth and fifth centuries notwithstanding.[179] Concomitantly, this reassessment of the evidence fails to establish a new terminus post quem.

THE UNIVERSAL CHURCH CALENDAR

Weigand argues at length that the saints represented in the mosaic frieze
were selected from a universal church calendar, that is, a catalogue of the
names and *acta* of bishops, martyrs, church benefactors, ascetics, and others
without regard to local interest. He contends that such a calendar was compiled only toward 530, which he accepts as an approximate terminus ante
quem for the mosaic decoration. While this is perhaps the most persuasive
section of his study, we find ourselves unable to accept it.

In the first part of this paper we suggested that the saints depicted in the
mosaic frieze may have had something to do with relics that were sheltered
in the converted Rotunda. If this were in fact the case, then there is little
reason to assume that the saints were selected from a church calendar of
any kind. It is inconceivable that church officials at Thessaloniki would
have tried to obtain relics of saints that they found listed in a church calendar. Other reasons must explain how the relics came into their possession.

But more decisive is the fact that the universal church calendar may not
have been compiled as late as about 530, as Weigand supposed. The exact
time and place of the compilation of a truly universal church calendar has

[178] For example, *H. E.* 2. 47, Νοεμβρίου μηνός (PG 67.365). On Socrates, see B. Altaner,
Patrologie, ed. 7 (Freiburg 1966) 226f.

[179] Professor Charles Edson, the editor of the basic corpus of inscriptions of Thessaloniki (his *Inscriptiones Graecae*, 10.1.1 [Berlin 1970] has been announced), has kindly informed me by letter that he can not recall the Macedonian months appearing in any dated
monument from the city after about A.D. 300. While these inscriptions are found on pagan
and imperial monuments, there seems little doubt that the Julian reckoning had been
adopted at Thessaloniki by the fourth century. In the Christian monuments of Byzantine
Thessaloniki the Roman names of the months are used as a general rule (e.g., in Hagia Sophia and in Panagia Chalkeon). For other regions of Greece in the fourth and fifth centuries,
see *Die griechisch-christlichen Inschriften* (n. 174 above) 61 no. 31, 78 no. 36, 92 no. 43, 95
no. 44, 102 no. 149, 105 no. 50, all of which are attributed to this period. Two Greek mosaic
pavements depicting the months and inscribed with the Roman names of the months have
been attributed to the fifth century: H. Stern, *Le Calendrier de 354* (Paris 1953) 223f. (from
Tegea) and 221 (from Argos, cf. R. Ginouves, "La mosaïque des mois à Argos," *Bulletin
de correspondence hellenique* 81 [1957] 216ff.).

yet to be determined. The most general calendar of Early Christianity, the *Hieronymian Martyrology*, whose authorship is falsely ascribed to Saint Jerome, was made up sometime during the fifth century, probably between 430 and 450, in North Italy (Aquileia?).[180] The oldest copy of the *Hieronymianum* goes back to the eighth century and depends on a Gallican recension composed at Auxerre during the last decade of the sixth century. The archetype of the *Hieronymianum* has been reconstructed and shown to derive from a variety of sources: the *Deposito martyrum*, the *Depositio episcoporum* and other lists that were assembled by Dionysius Philocalus in 354; an African martyrology of which the fifth- or probably sixth-century calendar of the Church of Carthage represents a later recension; a general calendar of Eastern saints more complete and later in date than the *Breviarium syriacum*, which was composed at Nicomedia circa 362; and several local calendars of North Italy and Gaul. While the *Hieronymianum* contains a listing of Eastern saints that were added to it in the course of the fifth and sixth centuries, its emphasis is clearly on Western heroes of the faith. It can not have served as the prototype of the martyrs represented in the Rotunda's decoration, for many of these marytrs are absent from its original list. Moreover, the cultus of these martyrs is associated more with the eastern than the western provinces of the empire. If a general calendar was in fact used, it must have been of a different character.

The truly universal church calendar may have been compiled at Constantinople.[181] It is well known that the pre-Constantinian city was markedly lacking in Christian memories. After its foundation in A.D. 330 the city became the receptacle for the translation of a massive number of Christian relics, perhaps an instrument of an imperial policy to equate the "New Rome" with a "New Jerusalem." Such a translation was under way by the middle of the fourth century, when, for example, in the years 356 and 357, the bodies of Andrew, Luke, and Timothy were deposited in the Holy Apostles church.[182]

---

[180] See the critical edition by H. Delehaye, *Commentarius perpetuus in Martyrologium Hieronymianum ad recensionem H. Quentin = Acta sanctorum Novembris* 2 (Brussels 1931). For the history of the martyrology, see A. Ehrhard, *Überlieferung und Bestand der hagiographischen und homiletischen Literatur der griechischen Kirche*, Texte und Untersuchungen ... 50 (Leipzig 1938) 25ff.; R. Aigrain, *L'Hagiographie* (Paris 1953) 13ff.; Altaner (n. 178 above) 235f., with bibliography.

[181] Such an origin has been proposed by G. Dix, *The Shape of the Liturgy*, ed. 2 (Westminster 1945) 351 n. 1.

[182] For the translation of these relics, see Philostorgius *Epit.* 3.2 (PG 65. 480f.) and *Chronicon Paschale* ad ann. 356 and 357 (*ibid.* 93.783). Consult R. Krautheimer, "Zu Konstantins Apostelkirche in Konstantinopel," *Mullus: Festschrift Theodor Klauser, Jahrbuch für Antike und Christentum, Ergänzungsband* 1 (Münster 1964) 224ff. (= "On Constantine's Church of the Apostles in Constantinople," trans. C. L. Striker, in Krautheimer [n. 109 above] 27-34).

But whether the church officials of Constantinople had actually begun to compile a universal calendar of saints by this time remains an open question.[183]

For these reasons we discard Weigand's thesis concerning the universal church calendar, and the implications its presumption had for the dating of the mosaics. We find no connection at all between the decoration in Hagios Georgios and any calendar. Indeed, we must point out that not a single preserved monumental cycle of saints of the Early Christian period can be proved to have derived directly from a church calendar, illustrated or not.

THE CULT OF THE SAINTS

Doubt has already been cast upon Weigand's argument that the saints were selected from a universal church calendar, which he supposes came into being only after about 500 A.D. While this contention has been refuted, it would appear far more difficult to dismiss his demonstration that the cult of Kosmas and Damianos also indicates an early sixth century dating.

Of all the saints identified by name in the mosaics Kosmas and Damianos are the best known (figs. 11 and 15). The cult of these physician saints was widespread in Early Christianity in both the Greek East and Latin West. The Greek East distinguished at least three pairs of these *anargyroi*: (1) an Asiatic pair (the oldest known of the three pairs), whose feast was commemorated on November 1 and 25; (2) a pair from Rome who were stoned to death in the time of Carinus and whose feast was celebrated on July 1; (3) a pair from Aegae in Cilicia who were beheaded under Diocletian and Maximianus (according to some accounts along with their brothers Anthimos, Leon, and Euprepios) and whose feast fell on October 17.[184] It would seem that the Asiatic pair were martyred in the vicinity of Cyrrhos in Syria, where their tomb was witnessed early in the fifth century.[185] By the beginning of the

---

[183] Cf. H. Achelis, *Die Martyrologien* (Berlin 1900) 93ff., whose attribution to ca. 520-530, which Weigand accepted, is too late. The extant fragment of the *Gothic Calendar* is known to be a Visigothic document that was originally compiled at Constantinople (or in Thrace) toward the end of the fourth century: R. Loewe, "Der gotische Kalender," *Zeitschrift für deutsches Altertum* 59 (1922) 245ff. This document suggests that the orthodox church of Constantinople had begun to draw up a calendar of saints by the end of the fourth century. See also W. Lackner, "Westliche Heilige des 5. und 6. Jahrhunderts im Synaxarium ecclesiae Constantinopolitanae," *Jahrbuch der Österreichischen Byzantinistik* 19 (1970) 185-202.

[184] H. Delehaye, *Synaxarium ecclesiae Constantinopolitanae*: *Propylaeum ad acta sanctorum Novembris* (Brussels 1902) 185 and 294, 176 and 791, 144, respectively; *Bibliotheca hagiographica graeca* 1.126-136; Deubner (n. 86 above); Lucius, *Anfänge des Heiligenkults*, 256-260; F. Halkin, "Miracles des SS. Cosme et Damien," *Analecta Bollandiana* 53 (1935) 374ff.

[185] Deubner 82; P. Maas, in *Byzantinische Zeitschrift* 17 (1908) 604. Not mentioned in the *Breviarium syriacum*, composed ca. 370, the saints are referred to in a letter written by Bishop Theodoret of Cyrrhos about 432 (PG 84.747).

following century, their cult had reached Italy. Pope Symmachus (498-514) dedicated an oratory to their memory that was located near *S. Maria ad praesepe*.[186] This is the first clear evidence of their cult in the West. Some years later Pope Felix IV (526-530) converted the Templum Romuli and the Templum Urbis Romae in the Forum romanum into a grand church and on September 27 dedicated it in honor of the two saints.[187] This is the exact date of their feast in the Roman canon of the mass. While this date was inserted into the canon certainly no later than this time, it remains possible that September 27 was the date of dedication of the oratory erected under Symmachus.[188]

Weigand focuses attention on the fact that the Greek church had no feast for the two saints on September 27.[189] Since the month of September is given in the inscription of Damianos, and from the outset presumably in the lost inscription of Kosmas as well, and since this is the date when the feast of the two saints was celebrated in Italy, he deduces that the cult of these martyrs reached Thessaloniki from Rome, and no earlier than the episcopate of Symmachus. That their cult passed from Rome to Thessaloniki is further suggested by the fact that the church of Thessaloniki was under the ecclesiastical jurisdiction of the Church of Rome from 395 or 396 to 732 or 733.[190]

While Weigand's argument appears persuasive, we believe it can be discounted for the following reasons. It must be remembered that the inscription of Damianos provides not the day but only the month of his feast. This fails to prove that the cult of Kosmas and Damianos was commemorated at Thessaloniki on September 27. The feast could have been celebrated on another day of that month. Our earliest preserved sources for the cult of the two *martyres medici* stem from the post-Iconoclastic period.[191] Even though some are based on earlier sources now lost, they do not necessarily

---

[186] *Liber pontificalis* 53.9 (ed. L. Duchesne [Paris, 1955] 1.262): "Item ad sanctam Mariam oratorium sanctorum Cosmae et Damiani a fundamento construxit." Cf. Deubner (n. 86 above) 74.

[187] *Liber pontificalis* 56.1 (*ed. cit.* 279): "Felix . . . fecit basilicam sanctorum Cosmae et Damiani in urbe Roma, in loco qui appellatur via Sacra, iuxta templum urbis Romae." Cf. R. Krautheimer, *Corpus basilicarum christianarum Romae* (Vatican City 1937) 1.137ff.

[188] The saints are listed in the *Gelasian Sacramentary* (ca. 492-600). See J. Jungmann, *Missarum sollemnia*, ed. 5 (Vienna 1962) 2.220. The evidence does not seem to support the thesis of G. Schreiber, "Christlicher Orient und mittelalterliches Abendland," *Oriens christianus* 39 (1955) 72, that the names of the two saints were inserted into the Roman canon of the mass as early as the fourth century (see V. L. Kennedy, *The Saints of the Canon of the Mass*, ed. 2 [Vatican City, 1963] 145-148).

[189] Weigand (n. 70 above) 126-131.

[190] See n. 236 below.

[191] See n. 184 above. A monastery of Kosmas and Damianos stood in the upper part of Thessaloniki by the tenth century (O. Tafrali, *Topographie de Thessalonique* [Paris 1913] 195).

report all the miracles and dates of commemoration of the saints during the Early Christian period. Moreover, the fact that the church of Thessaloniki was accountable to the papacy does not mean that its martyrs had to be adopted from the Roman canon of the mass. Many of the saints identified by inscription in the mosaics derive from eastern Mediterranean sources.

These reservations are sufficient in our opinion to reject Weigand's most weighty single proof for an early sixth-century dating. But the cult of the two physician saints itself suggests an early fifth century terminus post quem. It is possible that the earliest known shrine in their honor was erected by Rabula, later a bishop of Edessa, at a site near Aleppo in Syria about the year 400.[192] By the reign of the emperor Theodosius II Proklos, patriarch of Constantinople (434-447), dedicated a martyrium in their memory in the Zeugma of the capital, and according to the work of the pseudo-Codinus, the Magister Paulinus, an appointee of Theodosius II, erected another shrine commemorating them in the same city.[193] The cult of Kosmas and Damianos thus reached Constantinople during the reign of Theodosius II. The day of the month on which their cult was commemorated at that time is unknown to us, but the month may possibly have been September. From Constantinople the cult may have passed to Thessaloniki and eventually to Italy. It suggests a terminus post quem not of 498 to 530 but of about 400, or much more probably, the second quarter of the fifth century, when it is known to have reached Constantinople from Syria.

STYLISTIC PHENOMENA

The formal characteristics of the mosaics which point most readily to their dating occur in the heads of the saints and angels as well as the three preserved decorative panels in the soffits of the radiating bays. The heads of the saints above all have been critically examined by Weigand, Torp, and others and dated from the fourth to the seventh century. But none has focused on *all* the heads as a cohesive group; each has singled out this or that head and tried to date it on grounds of its salient formal qualities, then at-

[192] For the panegyric of Rabula, see G. Bickell, *Ausgewählte Schriften der syrischen Kirchenväter Aphraates, Rabulas und Isaak v. Ninive aus dem Syrischen übersetzt* (Kempton 1874) 170. P. Maas, in *Byzantinische Zeitschrift* 17 (1908) 604, claims this is an unreliable source. In 457 Bishop Nonnos erected a martyrium at Edessa in honor of the two saints: L. Hallier, *Untersuchungen über die Edessenische Chronik. Texte und Untersuchungen zur Geschichte der altchristlichen Literatur* 9 (Leipzig 1892) 114; J. B. Segal, *Edessa, 'The Blessed City'* (Oxford 1970) 174, 184f.

[193] J. P. Richter, *Quellen der byzantinischen Kunstgeschichte* (Vienna 1897) 154; R. Janin, *La géographie ecclésiastique de l'empire byzantin*, 1: *Le siège de Constantinople et le patriarcat oecuménique*, 3: *Les églises et les monastères* (Paris 1953) 295f. For the alleged foundation by Paulinus, see *ibid.* 296f.; Richter, *Quellen* 150ff. Proklos served as bishop of Cyzicus before coming to Constantinople.

tributed that dating to the whole group. Thus one reason for a lack of a consensus on the question of dating is the failure of specialists to consider each of the heads as a member of a group—and technically no doubt at all exists that the saints were executed during a single working campaign.

When viewed as a group, the most striking characteristic of the saints is the variety of head types: heads purely en face and slightly turned; young and old; curly or tousled hair and straight or neatly combed hair, even one balding head (Philippos); clean-shaven and bearded; long beards and short beards; blonds, redheads, brunettes, even "bluebeards" and porphyry-colored coiffures.[194] The heads range in treatment from a soft and delicate modeling, somewhat impressionistically rendered, to a geometric simplification of facial features and vigorous schematism of line and color with little modeling. There are distinctions between types but not between actual individual physiognomic characteristics.[195] The saints thus represent a pantheon of types.

A more precise description of specific examples will clarify this observation and point to a correct dating of the mosaics. The head of the young soldier saint Priskos has a pliable oval shape and is sensitively modeled, with volume suggested by the technical device of a checkerboard pattern of alternately light and dark tesserae (fig. 13).[196] Its features are natural, except for the

[194] Torp (n. 2 above) 28, reports the colors of the hairdos of the saints are as follows: yellow-orange (Priskos); reddish porphyry (Porphyrios and Onesiphoros); porphyry, that is, red, orange, and violet, with some light marine blue (Basiliskos); yellowish (Philemon and Leon); grey, blue, and violet (Philippos, Kyrillos, Ananias, Kosmas, and Damianos). These reports differ somewhat from the colors seen in the copies of the heads which were made by the talented Greek artist Christos Lefakis, now on exhibit in the old Archeological Museum at Thessaloniki. Three of these copies have been published by A. Grabar, *Golden Age of Justinian*, trans. S. Gilbert and J. Emmons (New York 1967) figs. 137-139 (the artist wrongly identified as Father Lefakis). Were the differences in the colors of the hairdos intended to stress the variety of individual physiognomies of the saints rather than to imply iconographic meanings? Fair, red-haired soldiers, such as the fourth-century Frank Laniogaisus, served as *candidati* or personal bodyguards of the late Roman emperors (Hieronymus, *Vita S. Hilarionis* 22 = PL 23.40-41), which suggests to me that not all the colors of the hairdos of the saints in the mosaics are necessarily only visual qualities.

[195] Cf. Kitzinger (n. 167 above) 185ff. It should be observed that the heads of the angels at the summit of the dome of Hagios Georgios are presented not purely en face but turned to one side, as are Porphyrios and Onesiphoros (Torp [n. 2 above] pls. on 33, 35, 40).

[196] I can cite no exact parallels to this device (see the color plate of Ananias that was photographed by UNESCO under special lighting conditions at night; cited below, n. 199). The closest comparison known to me, the use of alternately light and dark tesserae placed in a single row, occurs in the apse mosaic of the Panagia Angeloktistos at Kiti on Cyprus (see J. Smirnoff, in *Vizantiiskii Vremennik* 4 [1897] 64; Grabar [n. 194 above] fig. 144). Two rows of checkerboard modeling occur in the forehead of the Christ figure in the heavily restored apse mosaic of S. Michele in Africisco at Ravenna (*Das ravennatische Mosaik in den Staatlichen Museen zu Berlin und seine Wiederherstellung* [Berlin 1953] fig. 16). The technique may be rooted in Late Antiquity: see the mosaic representing the Triumph of

low-set ears. As Torp has repeatedly emphasized, they coincide with those of the sculptures of the so-called Theodosian Renaissance of the Greek East, a misnomer now well rooted, of the late fourth and very beginning of the fifth century, the exact classical prototypes of which have never been correctly ascertained.[197] One typical example of these works—all are sculptures—is provided by the head of the marble statue from Aphrodisias of the young ruler Valentinian II, now at Istanbul (fig. 14).[198] Within the oval shape of the superbly carved head the features are fluidly and organically rendered, the expression dreamy and remote. The head is strikingly close— note even the low-set ears—but not identical to the Priskos, for in the latter, the transitions between the facial planes are not as soft and fluid, and the tesserae of the hair, comprised of alternately red and yellow-orange straight strands, create a graphic pattern of lines that is also apparent in the area of the eyes. But the correspondences between the two works outnumber the differences, so much so as to suggest contemporaneity. The statue of Valentinian II is attributed to circa 390, precisely the dating that Torp assigns to the mosaics.

But such a similarity between the mosaics and "Theodosian" sculptures does not pertain to some other figures. For example, the heads of Kosmas (fig. 15), Damianos, Ananias, and the unnamed saint accompanying the latter (fig. 17) differ markedly from the Priskos type.[199] Purely en face, they are not modeled but structurally conceived. Their features are tightly delineated, with asymmetries of form and color much in evidence. The heads

Poseidon and Amphitrite that was found near Constantine in Algeria (A. H. A. Delamare, *Exploration scientifique de l'Algérie* [Paris 1850] pls. 141-142).

[197] See, most recently, Kitzinger, "A Marble Relief of the Theodosian Period," *Dumbarton Oaks Papers* 14 (1960) 17ff.; J. Kollwitz, "Probleme der Theodosianischen Kunst Roms," *Rivista di archeologia cristiana*, 39 (1963) 191ff.

[198] Kollwitz (n. 94 above) 81ff.; Volbach (n. 41 above) pls. 50-51. For this very comparison, see Torp (n. 117 above) 492, pl. 166, figs. 1-2; *idem* (n. 2 above) 77, figs. on 78-79; H. P. L'Orange, "Der Subtile Stil. Eine Kunstströmung aus der Zeit um 400 nach Christus," *Antike Kunst* 4 (1961) 74, pl. 31, 6. The heads of Onesiphoros and Porphyrios belong to the Priskos group. Another type is represented by Philippos (Torp [n. 2 above] colorplate after the foreward and pl. on 31), which recalls the figure identified as Saint Paul in a marble relief at Dumbarton Oaks (Kitzinger [n. 197 above] fig. 14). This type recurs in later art: e.g., the head of Saint Andrew in one of the medallions that ring the apse mosaic of Saint Catherine's monastery on Mount Sinai.

[199] For good illustrations: Kosmas (L'Orange and Nordhagen [n. 56 above] pl. 47; Torp [n. 2 above] pl. on 53); Damianos (*Encyclopedia of World Art*, 9, pl. 62; Volbach [n. 41 above] pl. 125; no detail of the head has been published thus far); Ananias (*Greece, Byzantine Mosaics* [UNESCO 1959] pl. II, color); the companion of Ananias, our fig. 17 (S. Pelekanidis, *Gli affreschi paleocristiani ed i più antichi mosaici parietali di Salonicco* [Ravenna 1963] fig. 8; *Archaiologikon Deltion* 22 [1967] pl. 18, b). The style of this type of head has been defined with great precision by Ö. Demus, "Graphische Element in der spätantiken Plastik," *Tortulae* (n. 2 above) 77ff.

assume not oval but rectangular shapes; those of Kosmas and the unnamed companion of Ananias end in the triangle of a full beard. Because of these elongated proportions, the eyes are accentuated: wide open and staring intensely, they are encircled by strongly arched lines that fan out in rhythmic designs and create through color deep hollows. These arched lines converge to, but fail to merge with, the long rectangular shape of the nose; systematized, they are discontinuous rather than fluid. The facial planes defined by line and color are not integrated with but sharply segregated from each other. Structurally the faces are masks (see above), made of painted plaster segments juxtaposed. This approach to the human form shares nothing with the soft modeling and remote classicism of the Theodosian Renaissance, and indeed cannot be found in sculpture until the middle of the fifth century. The closest comparison to these three heads is provided by the so-called Eutropius from Ephesus, now in Vienna (fig. 16).[200] This white marble head has a narrow and elongated, almost rectangular shape, offset only by the puffed-out hair at the temples. Prismatically constructed, it consists of two intersecting circular shapes of different diameters, the larger shape formed by the hair, the smaller one by the jaw and clinging beard. The delineation of the facial features reinforces this geometric disposition. Dominating the long face are the large eyes with their arched eyelids and brows that follow each other in widening oscillations. The forehead is articulated by an asymmetric pattern of horizontal and vertical lines. Indeed, the whole face comprises different structural zones containing graphic patterns and produces a forceful, transcendental expression. The closest comparisons to this particular combination of geometric regularity, graphic linearity, and hypnotic expression are the heads of Kosmas, Damianos, Ananias, and his unnamed companion. In sculpture the Eutropius is among the earliest and finest examples of such stylistic phenomena.[201] It is dated in the third quarter of the

---

[200] Demus, 77ff; J. Inan and E. Rosenbaum, *Roman and Early Byzantine Portrait Sculpture in Asia Minor* (London 1966) 151 no. 194, pl. CLXXXI, 1-2, with bibliography.

[201] Inan and Rosenbaum 152; Demus (n. 199 above) 81, referring to a "Hierarchie von Wirkungsmitteln" evident in the mosaics that has replaced the "kontinuierliche Modellierung mit ihren stufenlosen Übergängen" (seen, e.g., in the nave mosaics of Santa Maria Maggiore at Rome). The colossal bronze statue of an emperor at Barletta represents the same matrix of features and must date, in my opinion, from the same period. The head of the soldier saint Therinos in Panel IV (Torp [n. 2 above] pl. on 59) may be compared to the head of a *chlamydatus* from Aphrodisias, attributed to the second quarter of the fifth century (Inan and Rosenbaum 179 no. 242, pls. CLXXVI, 1-2, CLXXVIII, 1). Similar types but a different style characterize the heads in the mosaic of the ambo of archbishop Alkison's Basilica B at Nikopolis in Greece (A. Xyngopoulos, "Αἱ δύο ψηφιδωταὶ προσωπογραφίαι τῆς Νικοπόλεως," *Archaiologikon Deltion* 22 [1967] 15ff., pls. 14-15), which are attributed to the beginning of the sixth century. A stylistic connection between these two heads and the martyrs in the Rotunda has been observed by W. F. Volbach, in *Byzanz und der christliche Osten*, Propyläen Kunstgeschichte 3 (Berlin 1968) 166.

fifth century, an attribution that is buttressed by a numerous class of portrait sculpture from Ephesus and other artistic centers of Asia Minor. Such a matrix of traits can not possibly have begun to evolve during the Theodosian Renaissance but only half a century later, and formally possibly under the influence of distinctions so characteristic of contemporary secular portraiture. And its appearance in the portrait sculpture of Asia Minor and the mosaics of the Rotunda at Thessaloniki points to Constantinople as the center of its origin.

Some analogies to the mosaic heads are also provided by the mosaic pavements of Antioch. In works executed at the same approximate time but in a far inferior quality we find both our so-called Theodosian types and our more abstract types. The former occur, for instance, in the hunters of the Megalopsychia mosaic from Yakto and a fragmentary nimbed head, identified by Doro Levi as a personification, but perhaps a portrait of a royal or aristocratic lady, from the upper level of the House of Ge and the Seasons at Antioch.[202] The latter is oval in shape and delicately shaded in light and dark tones that enhance the volume of the head. The reddish hair has waves in lighter tones and is gathered in a soft mass at the nape of the neck. This head, and those of the hunters, resemble Priskos, Onesiphoros, and Porphyrios in Hagios Georgios. To the more hieratic group comprised of Kosmas, Damianos, Ananias, and his unnamed companion belongs the personification of Megalopsychia (fig. 18).[203] Purely en face, this head has wide open eyes and a concentrated, almost severe expression. The modeling is less impressionistic than that of the nimbed head; the shadows tend to dematerialize the natural image. Moreover, like the garments of Kosmas and Damianos, the white tunic of Megalopsychia has soft undulations of cloth which are rendered in grey tones. This type is distinctly different in structure and expression from the first group of heads from Antioch, but all are securely dated in the third quarter of the fifth century.

The heads of the saints in Hagios Georgios represent not individualized likenesses but generalized types, a few Theodosian, others in structure and spiritual expression far different. The types that first emerged during the reign of Theodosius the Great survived into the second half of the fifth century and became part of the gallery of ideal "historical portraiture" of apostles and other saints that comes to the fore at that time and is, indeed, a hallmark of the art of the following century (for example, the Justinianic mosaics at Ravenna, Poreč, and Mount Sinai).[204] Kitzinger has correctly observed

[202] Levi (n. 171 above) 323ff., pls. LXXVII-LXXVIII and 346f., pl. LXXXII, a, respectively. Both mosaics are today in the Mosaic Museum at Antakya. For a color reproduction of one of the hunters in the Megalopsychia mosaic, see Grabar (n. 194 above) fig. 111. This pavement has a firm terminus post quem of 450-457.

[203] Levi (n. 171 above) 323ff., 575f., pl. LXXVI, b; Grabar (n. 194 above) fig. 109.

[204] I refer to the mosaic of Christ and the apostles in the chapel of Sant'Aquilino adja-

specific evidence of the survival of Theodosian art in works of the fifth century, its revival in Heraclian art of Constantinople early in the seventh century.[205] This point deserves emphasis. The types of the Theodosian Renaissance entered the stream of Hellenism that appears time and again in pre-Icono-clastic art. But they represent only one current in that stream. Another enters the stream at a later point. Its introduction is heralded by the structur-ally more developed heads of the saints in the Rotunda and the Eutropius group of portrait sculpture from Asia Minor. The stream flowed through different centers of the Greek East, Thessaloniki included.

Preserved in each of three barrel vaults of the radiating bays of Hagios Georgios is a mosaic panel, clearly coeval with the rest of the decoration, which also indicates a dating of about the middle of the fifth century at the earliest. The panel in the southern bay features an all-over carpet design, with a large gold cross centrally placed on a silver ground that is filled with birds wearing ribbons and pearled collars, eight-pointed stars in gold, baskets filled with loaves of bread (sacramental wafers?), and other elements, all of which are arranged in rows running at right angles to the axis of the gold cross and which face outward toward the border.[206] Its border contains blue and green four-petaled star motifs, whose ground gold creates a strong visual contrast to the silver ground of the enclosed carpet. The strong unframed centerpiece and the strong borders relate this mosaic to a development of compositions in the pavement mosaics at Antioch which begins in the second quarter of the fifth century and becomes widespread by mid-century.[207] Since

----

cent to San Lorenzo at Milan, which mosaic I believe dates from the second quarter of the fifth century (see my "Toward a Dating of San Lorenzo in Milan," *Arte lombarda* 13 [1968] 19 n. 110), as well as the mosaics in the Orthodox Baptistery at Ravenna. Both of these mosaic programs depict apostles rather than other saints, as in the Rotunda. See also the series of twenty-six marble heads of male saints brought to light by Martin Harrison at the site of the church of Saint Polyeuktos at Constantinople; these reliefs have been tenta-tively attributed by him to the second quarter of the fifth century (*Dumbarton Oaks Papers* 21 [1967] 277). While representing several distinct types, none embodies that brand of structural composition and emphatic linearism evident in the more advanced types in the Rotunda.

[205] Kitzinger (n. 197 above) 41f.; *idem* (n. 162 above) 4ff., fig. 5 (an ivory plaque in the Louvre) and figs. 4 and 6 (the Cypriote David plates of the early seventh century).

[206] Torp (n. 2 above) fig. on 21 (detail); Hoddinott (n. 98 above) pl. 20, c; Foto Mar-burg LA 1277/6. The ornamental mosaics are discussed briefly by Torp, 16ff., who, like Grabar in several studies, derives some of the motifs in this panel from Persian sources and discovers a royal symbolism in them.

[207] Cf. the "Striding Lion" pavement at Antioch (Levi (n. 171 above) 321ff., pl. LXXIV, a); the exquisite Phoenix mosaic—now in the Louvre—which cannot antedate the mid-fifth century (*ibid.* 351ff., pls LXXXIII, a, c, CXXXIV); and the Megalopsychia Hunt pave-ment in a *therma* at Serdjilla that is dated by an inscription to A.D. 473 (I. Lavin, "The Hunting Mosaics of Antioch and their Sources," *Dumbarton Oaks Papers* 17 [1963] 272, 274, fig. 142).

there is no reason to assume different lines of development for identical compositions in pavement mosaics and ceiling mosaics, the carpet in Hagios Georgios can be dated accordingly.

The mosaic panel in the vault of the western bay features a carpet of intersecting circles containing curvilinear squares and a border designed with a chain of alternating squares and circles (fig. 19).[208] In the carpet of intersecting circles the quatrefoils have in each leaf an inner decoration of a kind of maeander motif, red on blue. At the center of each curvilinear gold diamond is a silver disc, from which project four green arms. This treatment of the intersecting circle motif can be compared to some pavement mosaics from Antioch. The closest Antiochian parallel is provided by the border of a pavement from the House of the Sea Goddess.[209] The fillings of the intervals between the quatrefoils have enriched the geometric structure of its intersecting circles: central black crosslets in a light diamond bordered by dotted squares are inserted in the curvilinear squares, and the segments of the quatrefoils are filled with thin, black leaves. In his magisterial study of the floor mosaics of Antioch Doro Levi dates this pavement to the end of the fifth century, a dating that we believe should be moved back a couple of decades.[210] The last stage of the development of this motif at the Syrian capital is seen in an all-over pattern of intersecting circles in one of the fragmentary pavements from the House of the Rams' Heads (fig. 20).[211] Here rich visual effects have replaced clarity of geometric structure, the illusion of a three-dimensional space on a flat surface. Squares containing parallel zigzag lines fill each leaf, and a four-petaled flower on a white disc is inscribed in each black curvilinear square between the quatrefoils. The pictorial effect is richer than that of the panel in the Rotunda. Levi ascribes this mosaic to circa 500, which again may be a decade or more too late.

[208] Texier and Pullan (n. 74 above) pl. XXXIV, fig. 1; C. Diehl, M. le Tourneau, and H. Saladin, *Les monuments chrétiens de Salonique* (Paris 1918) 1.24, fig. 3; Hoddinott (n. 98 above) pl. 20, d. A simpler and much earlier mosaic pavement featuring interlaced circles containing inscribed diamonds has been found in the remains of the Galerian palace at Thessaloniki (*Archaiologikon Deltion* 19 [1964, publ. 1967] 2.3.329ff., pl. 374).

[209] Levi (n. 171 above) 477, 626, pl. CXXXIII, a. Compare also both a mosaic pavement from the peristyle of a villa at Jekmejeh (*ibid.* pl. XCIII, d) and a floor mosaic in a church at Khaldé in Lebanon, which is dated by its excavator to the mid-fifth century (M. H. Chéhab, *Mosaïques du Liban*, Bulletin du Musée de Beyrouth 14/15 [Paris 1957] 116, pl. LXV, 2).

[210] Levi's chronology (n. 171 above, 461, 574, 626) was influenced to some extent by his acceptance of Weigand's attribution of the Thessalonikan mosaics to the early sixth century.

[211] *Ibid.* 477f., pl. CXXXIII, d. Slightly earlier in date is an all-over carpet mosaic from the villa at Daphne (*ibid.* 397, pl. XCVI, e), where each of the interlacing white circles is inscribed with a red four-pointed star, with a square in the center and smaller squares in each of the four sections of the circle.

The gold border of the panel in Hagios Georgios also brings to mind some Antiochian pavements of the fifth century. It is decorated with a chain of alternating circles and squares, each of which contains an inscribed square or rectangle, circumscribed by silver lines. Shimmering blue or green birds and baskets with flowers and fruit fill the center of each of these compartments, and four similarly colored birds rim the periphery of the circular units. Thus the geometric structure is filled with organic elements. A pavement from the House of the Buffet Supper at Antioch shows a border of circles containing rosettes that alternate with regular diagonal squares filled with four-leaved flowers.[212] This specimen, correctly attributed by Levi to the second quarter of the fifth century, is somewhat simpler in design than that in Hagios Georgios. Closer in conception to the latter is a pavement from the Church of Prophets, Apostles, and Martyrs at Gerasa, which is dated by inscription to 464-465.[213] The border of this mosaic consists of a chain of alternating circles and elongated squares that are filled with colored rosettes and diamonds. During the fifth century the animals and floral motifs that appear in such geometric compartments begin to cause the clearly defined structural matrices embedded in flat, two-dimensional surfaces to disintegrate in favor of rich visual effects.[214] This trend is apparent at Antioch by the second quarter of the fifth century, before which time it is unlikely the related designs in the mosaics of Hagios Georgios could have been created.[215]

[212] Levi (n. 171 above) 460, 626, pl. CXXV, c.

[213] J. W. Crowfoot, *Churches at Jerash* (London 1931) pl. XIII, a; Carl H. Kraeling, ed., *Gerasa, City of the Decapolis* (New Haven 1938) pl. LXXIII.

[214] Levi (n. 171 above) 311f., pls. 124-126. Cf. E. Kitzinger, "Stylistic Developments in Pavement Mosaics in the Greek East from the Age of Constantine to the Age of Justinian," in *La mosaïque gréco-romaine*, Colloques internationaux du Centre National de la Recherche Scientifique, Paris 1963 (Paris 1965) 341ff., esp. 348f.

[215] The profuse use of gold and silver tesserae throughout the figures and ornaments as well as the backgrounds of the mosaics has been observed in these pages several times and emphasized as one of their salient formal qualities. I have also referred to the heavenly light that the gold ground denotes. But another question arises: does the exact manner in which these particular tesserae are employed provide a chronological index? For gold and silver tesserae not only create the light of the ground of the mosaic panels but also suffuse the figures and ornaments themselves, thereby transfiguring rather than intensifying, as it were, the natural. The mosaics of the Rotunda supply the earliest preserved example of such an employment of gold *and* silver tesserae (they also occur together in the apse mosaic of Hosios David at Thessaloniki which I believe cannot antedate the converted Rotunda's decoration). But they can not be dated on these grounds. With the exception of the mosaics in the soffits of the arcades of the Church of the Acheiropoietos at Thessaloniki, which are either slightly earlier than or roughly contemporary with the decoration in the Rotunda (see below), as well as the apse mosaic of Hosios David, which is somewhat later in date, no other mosaics from the pre-Justinianic period in the Greek East which contain gold and silver tesserae are extant. Quite possibly their employment is a feature that originated among the mosaicists working in Christian Thessaloniki. Moreover, we must fully recognize that such colored cubes presuppose technical innovations in the use of gold and silver

ARCHEOLOGICAL EVIDENCE

Torp's argument for a dating of about 380 to 390 A.D. depends on his assertion that the mosaics are exactly contemporary with the conversion of the Rotunda from a pagan building to a church, in other words, that the mosaic decoration was part of the major transformation of the edifice. This transformation included an enlargement of the original core by the addition of an outer ambulatory enclosed by a circular peripheral wall, an apsed sanctuary at the eastern end, and a narthex. Excavations undertaken by Dyggve at the site since 1939 have disclosed that the Rotunda was erected during the time of the ruler Galerius in the northeast sector of the precinct of the imperial palace.[216] The pagan Rotunda may not have been finished, for Dyggve maintains that the dome was "in all probability" left uncompleted when the emperor died in 311.[217] He reports that the masonry at the summit of the dome differs in character from that of the lower courses.[218] He also points to the existence of what he describes as a deep well found in the center of the Rotunda, the function of which would seem to be to siphon off rainwater coming in through the Galerian opaion.[219] About the masonry Torp is more explicit than Dyggve; he describes the masonry at the summit of the dome as identical in measurements and brick stamps to that of the apsed sanctuary of the building.[220] Completion of the Galerian dome is held to be contemporary with the erection of the apsed extension (and the now-destroyed ambulatory

---

foil, the exact origins of which have not been ascertained thus far. Until other early wall mosaics in eastern Mediterranean churches come to light, an unlikely eventuality, this feature of the Rotunda's decoration fails to contribute to the problem of dating.

[216] The sources referring to the palace as a Galerian foundation are late: (1) the *Acta of Saint Demetrios*: "Μαξιμιανός . . . ἐπὶ τὰς βασιλείους αὐλὰς ἐπανήρχετο" (PG 116. 1180); (2) the *Menologium of Basil II*: Μαξιμιανοῦ βασίλεια κτίζοντος ἐν Θεσσαλονίκῃ (PG 117.81). The attribution to Galerius as Augustus is further indicated by the scenes on the Arch of that ruler, which was erected on the Via Egnatia between the Rotunda and the residential quarter of the palace, and, as Dyggve's excavations have confirmed, by the exact axial alignment of the Rotunda with the palace complex, of which it must be viewed as an integral component unit. Cf. E. Oberhummer, in Pauly-Wissowa, *Real-Encyclopädie*, ser. 2, 6 (1937) 243ff., s.v. "Thessalonike"; Tafrali (n. 191 above) 130f.; H. von Schoenebeck, "Die Stadtplanung des römischen Thessalonike," *Bericht über den VI. internationalen Kongress für Archäologie Berlin 21.-26. August 1939* (Berlin 1940) 478ff.

[217] Dyggve, "Recherches sur le palais impérial," (n. 159 above) 62f.

[218] *Ibid.* 65.

[219] *Ibid.* 62f.: "Dans le haut, dans la coupole de la Rotunde, il y eut à l'origine *selon toute probabilité*, une ouverture ronde, un opaion. La présence d'un puits profond, placé à peu près au milieu de la salle centrale, semble appuyer *cette hypothesis* ainsi que le fait qu'on a pu constater que la partie supérieure de la coupole a été remaniée pendant la période chrétienne" (italics mine). In his last published report ("La région palatiale," [n. 108 above] 356), Dyggve reports that "on a trouvé au milieu de la salle un puits profond, chose qui laisserait supposer que la salle a eu à l'origine un opaion ouvert au sommet de la coupole."

[220] Torp (n. 117 above) 491. Cf. *idem* (n. 2 above) 11.

and narthex), hence with the conversion of the Galerian building into a Christian sanctuary. These observations would seem to preclude the possibility of a completed Galerian dome, the masonry of whose crown was reworked when the mosaic sheathing was about to be applied.

Having thus maintained that construction of the dome was finished only after the death of Galerius, the question of the time of its completion had to be answered. The measurements and stamps of the bricks found at the summit of the dome and in the apsed sanctuary are reported to be identical, hence coeval, and part of the same building operation of converting the Rotunda into a church. Since identical measurements and stamps characterize the bricks of the land walls and the Acheiropoietos basilica at Thessaloniki, it may be safely assumed that the enlarged Rotunda is contemporary with these other monuments. Although historical documentation of the foundation of the Acheiropoietos basilica is wanting (see below), the land walls are generally accepted as dating from the reign of Theodosius the Great. The conversion of the Rotunda is therefore to be dated to the late fourth century: in this important conclusion Dyggve and Torp concur fully.

But what of the mosaic decoration of the dome? To demonstrate that it was put up when the Rotunda was enlarged and transformed, Torp points to the evidence of the triple plaster rendering of the brick surfacing. Specifically, he refers to a considerable number of iron nails or clamps with large double-pronged flat heads, with a diameter of about 2 centimeters and a length of 10 to 15 centimeters, which were found embedded in the masonry of the summit of the dome.[221] These nails were inserted into the mortar interstices of the brick surface in order to reinforce the attachment of the first rendering of plaster.[222] This was standard procedure among mosaicists of the Greek East and Latin West alike and is no evidence of restoration work; similar devices have been found, for example, in the plaster renderings of the apse mosaic of the church of Saints Cosmas and Damian at Rome.[223] After a close examination of the mosaic remains in the dome, Torp deduced that the nails were driven into the mortar before it had hardened and solidified. This is his most crucial observation: "the mortar is smoothed around the nails, and a thin layer of lime placed on the mortar still adheres to the neck (cous) of the nails."[224] In other words, the way in which the layer of lime adhering

---

[221] Torp (n. 117 above) 491. In his later publication Torp refers to the discovery of two types of clamps in the masonry of the dome but fails to specify the differences between them: (n. 2 above) 45.

[222] Torp (n. 117 above) 491; idem (n. 2 above) fig. on 45. For the use of nails or clamps in Byzantine mosaic practice, see the excellent observations by P. A. Underwood, The Kariye Djami (New York 1966) 1.172ff., esp. 174.

[223] G. Matthiae (n. 15 above) 41.

[224] Torp (n. 117 above) 491; idem (n. 2 above) 80: "The large iron clamps which the mosaicists employed in order to keep the setting bed in place must have been inserted into

to the nails is preserved proves that the mortar of the brickwork at the crown of the dome was still soft and therefore had just been set. Since the third plaster rendering—that is, the setting bed and its tesserae—must be contemporary with the nails, and since Dyggve identified the masonry as Theodosian, the mosaic decoration was planned and executed at the time of the transformation of the Rotunda into a church: the mosaics were executed during the reign of Theodosius the Great.

Now if Dyggve is right in ascribing a Theodosian date to the masonry of the post-Galerian Rotunda, and Torp is right in his observation about the nails, then the mosaics can be dated with full assurance to the end of the fourth century. The stamped bricks mentioned by Torp would seem to confirm Dyggve's assertion that the Galerian dome featured an opaion that was subsequently filled in. From the excavations by Hébrard at the site in 1918 we know of two kinds of brick stamps, each with different dimensions and different unframed markings, the second and later group of which bear crosses.[225] That the first group of stamped bricks is Galerian was recently confirmed by Makaronas, who discovered bricks of identical dimensions and markings in the masonry of a huge niched octagonal building that he excavated in the southwest precinct of the imperial palace of Thessaloniki. This building exactly corresponds to the Rotunda in its overall size, orientation, and character of masonry.[226] Further indication of an unfinished Galerian dome in the Rotunda is provided by what appears to be a horizontal suture running around the circumference of the dome below the remnants of the four winged angels supporting the Christ medallion (fig. 1). This suture may mark the level to which construction of the original dome was carried and left in the year 311.[227]

---

the joints between the bricks of the dome simultaneously with the construction of this part of the dome."

[225] Hébrard (n. 108 above) 23, fig. 9 (Galerian) and 32, fig. 15 (post-Galerian). The earlier group bears striations created by the fingers of the brick workers. From his excavations Dyggve published only two broken brick stamps bearing fragmentary legends: (n. 112 above) pl. VI, no. 27. In 1745/48 J. B. Germain transcribed eight brick stamps from Hagios Georgios, two of which were subsequently published by Texier and Pullan (n. 74 above) fig. on 134 (post-Galerian group). See n. 260 below.

[226] C. I. Makaronas, "Τὸ ὀκτάγωνον τῆς Θεσσαλονικῆς," *Praktika* 1950 (publ. 1951) 309, fig. 6. For a plan of the building, see P. M. Petsas, "Χρονικὰ Ἀρχαιολογικὰ 1966-1967," *Makedonika* 9 (1969) 151ff. and pl. I. The bricks average 45 × 31 × 3.5-5.0 cm. (see fig. 4 on 307). Consult the important observations by J. B. Ward-Perkins, "Notes on the Structure and Building Methods of Early Byzantine Architecture," in *The Great Palace of the Byzantine Emperors, Second Report* (Edinburgh 1958) 88, pl. 33, E.

[227] Whereas the lower part of the dome, to a height of 7 meters, is a segment of a hemisphere based on a center located on the level of the springing line, the upper part has a different curvature, based on a center about 2 meters higher (A. Boëthius and J. B. Ward-Perkins, *Etruscan and Roman Architecture* [Harmondsworth 1970] 522ff.; cf. Torp [n. 2 above] fig. on 11).

That the Galerian dome originally featured an opaion can therefore be accepted with a reasonable degree of certainty. And lacking any new technical evidence with which to refute Torp, we must assume that the masonry and the mosaics at the summit of the dome are contemporaneous.[228] But a fundamental criticism of Dyggve and Torp's dating stems from their contention that the circuit walls of Thessaloniki were erected during the reign of the emperor Theodosius the Great.

The impressive land walls, extensive parts of which still stand on the ancient acropolis and to the west and east of the former center of the city, are almost universally accepted as one of the many architectural contributions that Theodosius the Great made throughout the eastern Mediterranean.[229] The walls were first attributed to him by Oreste Tafrali in an important monograph on the topography of Byzantine Thessaloniki which was published in 1913. This study includes the only extensive archeological survey of the land walls.[230] Tafrali based his dating on a carefully argued interpretation of an imperfect Greek inscription, in brick, high up on one of the towers in the upper stretch of the eastern walls above the Protestant cemetery, which the inscription faced. Today destroyed, the inscription was some nine meters in length, composed in verse, in two lines, and read:

. . . τείχεσιν ἀρρήκτοις Ὁρμίσδας ἐξετέλεσσε τήνδε πόλ(ιν) . . .

. . . with invincible walls Hormisdas provided this city. . .[231]

---

[228] So far Torp has published but one photograph to bear out his observation about the nails (n. 117 above, pl. 164, no. 3; cf. *idem* n. 2 above, fig. on 45). I find no reason to believe that the nails, which without doubt were inserted into the masonry only when the mosaicists had set to work, could have been driven into a hardened and dry mortar that then would have had to be reset in consequence of the disruption of the original joints. The first and the second plaster coats are each about 1.5 cm. thick, the setting bed 1.8 cm. (*ibid.* 44). Crushed brick occurs only in the first rendering, and the setting bed lacks chopped straw but may, according to Torp, contain marble dust and is surely of a finer consistency than the first and second coats. Hence the composition of the triple rendering conforms to what we know of other Early Christian mosaic preparations. The only exception to them would seem to be that the third, not the first, rendering is the thickest, though this may be explained by the location of the preparatory surfaces on the underside of a dome (cf. L'Orange and Nordhagen [n. 56 above] fig. on 56).

[229] Some of the architectural works undertaken during his reign are noted by Dyggve, "Recherches sur le palais" (n. 159 above) 65, n. 22 (not all of which, however, are correct attributions). See H. Grégoire and M. A. Kugener, *Marc le Diacre: Vie de Porphyre, Évêque de Gaza* (Paris 1930) lxivff. It must be emphasized that not a scrap of historical evidence intimates that Theodosius built or patronized a single monument at Thessaloniki.

[230] Tafrali (n. 191 above) 30ff.

[231] First published and transcribed (though incorrectly) by M. C. Ioannou Ἀστυγραφία τῆς Θεσσαλονίκης (Thessaloniki 1880) 12, 17. The verb ἐκτελέω, "to provide" or "to finish off," may mean that Hormisdas completed something that had been begun earlier. To my knowledge, no one has tried to date the inscription on the grounds of its epigraphy.

The city walls of Thessaloniki were provided (or finished off) by one Hormisdas, whose full identity may have been revealed by the lost portion of the
second verse of the inscription. Tafrali associated this Persian name with
Hormisdas junior, who served Theodosius the Great as military field commander of the imperial troops in Egypt after having apparently visited Thessaloniki in the year 380 when the emperor was residing there. In this survey of the historical sources Tafrali developed the documented connections
between the city and Theodosius, who, it is well known, made the city his
official residence in the years 379 and 380, during which period he was baptized by the local bishop Acholius, and who is especially remembered for the bru-
tish massacre that took place in the hippodrome in 390. These very facts,
it should be pointed out, also magnetically attracted Dyggve, who as early
as 1939, when he first undertook his preliminary excavations at the site of
the palace precinct, ascribed to this ruler not only the conversion of the Galerian Rotunda into a Christian sanctuary and palace church but also the
mosaic decoration of the Rotunda itself.[232]

Tafrali's interpretation of the all-important inscription raises several ob-
jections. First of all, our historical sources on pre-Iconoclastic Thessaloniki
are meager at best, and there may have been a Hormisdas associated with
the city of whom we are unaware.[233] For instance, our list of the names of
the *praefecti praetorio Illyrici* for the fifth and sixth centuries contains many
lacunae.[234] The walls were probably built before the reign of the emperor
Justinian, because the court historian Procopius is curiously silent about
this ruler erecting or repairing ramparts, or for that matter any building,
at Thessaloniki. Procopius's silence may be taken to mean that by the time
of Justinian the city had been fortified and required no repair work, an *argumentum ex silentio* suggesting a terminus ante quem for the construction
of the land walls. A firm terminus ante quem is established by an inscription
referring to repairs ordered by the local archbishop Eusebius late in the sixth

---

[232] In the initial report on his excavations at the site of Hagios Georgios, Dyggve first
broached the theory about the "Église du Palais" ("Compte rendu [n. 108 above] 155; "Ausgrabungen in Thessaloniki," *Gnomon* 17 [1941] 228ff.), and at the same time attributed this
"palace church" to about A.D. 400, *vielleicht in die Zeit Theodosius I* (n. 112 above, 69).
While in his first two reports he does not commit himself in print to a dating of the mosaics
(the scaffolding, after all, was not erected until the winter of 1952), he had dated them
from the beginning of his excavations to the end of the fourth century (see n. 159 above).

[233] Cf. O. Seeck, in Pauly-Wissowa, *Real-Encyclopädie* 8 (1913) 2410. According to Byzantine tradition, the imperial palace of Hormisdas (τὰ Ὁρμίσδου) at Constantinople, to
which Justinian adjoined the church of SS. Sergius and Bakchos between 527 and 548
(Procopius *De aed* I, iv, 1; I, x, 4) was named after the son of the Sapor who was exiled
from Persia in the reign of Constantine the Great and served as *magister militum* under
Julian. See R. Janin, *Constantinople byzantine*, ed. 2 (Paris 1964) 358f.; Mathews, *Early
Churches of Constantinople* (n. 146 above) 42ff.

[234] Cf. Seeck (n. 115 above) 473f.

century.[235] Thus it is chronologically possible that Pope Hormisdas (514-523) was the builder mentioned in the inscription once on the land walls. This seductive hypothesis, however, can easily be jettisoned. Although the pope exercised juridical authority over the ecclesiastical vicariate of Illyricum, through the bishop (and later archbishop) of Thessaloniki as vicar (*vicarius sedis apostolicae*), from 395 or 396 until 732 or 733, he lacked civil jurisdiction over the civil dioceses of Illyricum, Macedonia, and Dacia, which had been under the rule of the emperor in Constantinople from the end of the fourth century.[236] In the Roman Empire the construction and maintenance of all important public works were either sponsored by the emperor or required the approval of one of his appointed officials—the prefect, *vicarius*, or provincial governor; even when the emperor's assistance was not forthcoming, a situation common in many provinces after the early fifth century, the pope had no business erecting walls in Macedonia.[237] We therefore fully approve of Tafrali's rejection of Pope Hormisdas as the builder of the walls.

This observation raises a second query about Tafrali's identification of Hormisdas junior. Did this Hormisdas have the authority to erect such an important public work as the ramparts of Thessaloniki about the year 380? Ammianus Marcellinus, a contemporary witness, reports that this Hormisdas became proconsul under the usurper Procopius in the year 365.[238] The late Roman historian fails to mention the province, which is assumed to be Asia.[239] He does refer to the peculiar nature of the appointment by Procopius, *civilia more veterum et bella recturo*, that is a combination of civil and military

[235] Duchesne and Bayet (n. 69 above) 58 (republished in Tafrali [n. 191 above] 41). Eusebius was archbishop during the reign of the emperor Maurice (582-602). There is no evidence that either of the two emperors Zeno or Anastasius repaired the ramparts of Thessaloniki, though the latter may have ordered any necessary repairs during the Slavic incursions into the empire along its northern frontier at the beginning of the sixth century, at which time (that is, 507-512) he had the "Long Wall" (or Anastasian Wall) running from the Sea of Marmora to the Black Sea greatly strengthened (Evagrius, *H.E.* 3.38; Procopius of Gaza, *Panegyricus* 21; *Justiniani Novella* 26, pr., 535, as cited by A. A. Vasiliev, *Justin the First* [Cambridge, Mass. 1950] 307, n. 94, 355). We have no information about Thessaloniki during the barbarian invasion of 517 which devastated Macedonia and Thessaly (*Marcellinus Chronicon*, A.C. 517 = PL 51.393), and Vasiliev believes (354) that the city was spared during the crucial period of barbarian invasions and earthquakes in the fifth century and at the beginning of the sixth.

[236] For the *praefectura Illyrici*, see M. V. Anastos, "The Transfer of Illyricum, Calabria, and Sicily to the Jurisdiction of the Patriarchate of Constantinople in 732-33," *Studi bizantini e neoellenici* 9 (1957) 14ff., esp. 15 n. 2, for modern discussions of eastern Illyricum.

[237] Cf. *Codex Theodosianus* 15.1.1-32.

[238] Ammianus Marcellinus 26.8.12 (ed. Clark 1963): "Ormisdae regalis illius filio, potestatem proconsulis detulit [Procopius] et civilia more veterum et bella recturo"). Cf. Zosimus 4.8 (ed. Bonn, 181); Eunapius, *F.H.G.* (ed. Müller), 4.25 no. 27, 27 no. 35.

[239] Seeck (n. 233 above) 2410. Neither Ammianus nor Zosimus nor even Eunapius specifically identify the province as Asia.

functions that by the later fourth century would probably have been exceptional, because from the time of Constantine the Great such officials had been
shorn of their military functions.[240] So we may legitimately ask whether Hormisdas was still proconsul under Theodosius in the year 380, that is, whether
he remained in a position of high civil authority to which a contender to the
throne has nominated him some fifteen years earlier.[241] Hormisdas junior
presumably went to Thessaloniki in 380 to receive his command and orders
for leading the imperial troops to Egypt. There is no historical intimation
whatever of any civil activity on his part in the city itself.

A third objection to Tafrali's identification issues from the existence of
some large stepped marble blocks that were discovered in the eastern and
western stretches of the city walls. These blocks have been identified as
initially belonging to the local hippodrome, which was surely still standing
in the southeastern sector of the precinct of the Galerian palace as late as
the year 390, when the great Theodosian blood bath filled it.[242] If these blocks
were pilfered from the hippodrome, it is difficult to reconcile Hormisdas
junior erecting city walls in 380 with marble seats from the hippodrome that
was surely standing and presumably fully intact with its seats a full decade
later.

If the name mentioned in the inscription cannot be associated with either
the field commander of Theodosius the Great or Pope Hormisdas, can we
point to yet another Hormisdas? Two bishops by the name of Hormisdas
are known to have held office in Asia Minor about the middle of the fifth
century, but we find no justification for associating them with Thessaloniki.[243]
The only other Hormisdas of whom we have any knowledge is the man who
became *praefectus praetorio orientis* during the years 448 and early 449.[244]
That this Hormisdas erected the city walls of Thessaloniki was first proposed
by Harald Koethe in 1933 and has recently been accepted by Michael Vickers.[245]

---

[240] *Codex Theodosianus* 1.12.1ff.

[241] Zosimus 4.30.5 (ed. Bonn 208). I find no reason to assume, with Tafrali (n. 191 above)
39, that Hormisdas junior exercised the responsibilities entrusted to him by the usurper
Procopius in the year 365 (see above).

[242] Michael Vickers, "The Date of the Walls of Thessalonica," *Istanbul Arkeoloji Müze-
leri Yilligi* 15/16 (1969) 313-318. Cf. *idem*, "The Byzantine Sea Walls of Thessaloniki,"
Balkan Studies 11 (1971) 261-280.

[243] (1) Hormisdas, bishop of Philippopolis in the province of Arabia, who was present
at the Council of Chalcedon in 451 (M. Le Quien, *Oriens christianus* [Paris 1740] 2.862); (2)
Hormizes ('Ορμιζίω), bishop of Comanorum in Cappadocia about 460, perhaps the Hormisdas who in 457 joined the bishops of Armenia Secunda in a synodal letter to the emperor
Leo (*ibid.* 1.450 [misprinted 446]).

[244] Seeck (n. 115 above) 475 (16 Feb. 448-9 Jan. 449, not 3 April 450, as reported by Seeck
earlier [n. 233 above] 2410).

[245] H. Koethe, "Das Konstantinsmausoleum und verwandte Denkmäler," *Jahrbuch des
Deutschen archäologischen Instituts* 47 (1933) 197f.; Vickers, "The Date of the Walls of

This identification deserves careful attention. All we really know about this Hormisdas, who apparently derived his name from one of the fourth-century Persian generals, is that he seems to have enjoyed special favor from the emperor Theodosius II, who died in the year 450, after which time our historical sources are silent about the man.[246] The praetorian prefect of the East, who resided at Constantinople, was an imperial official higher in rank than the prefect of Illyricum, who resided at Thessaloniki.[247] He had a wide sphere of duties and responsibilities, among which were the construction and maintenance of public works. The cities themselves, however, were responsible for their own public buildings, including walls.[248] It is well known that the great land walls of Constantinople were erected in the year 413 under the auspices of Anthemius, *praefectus praetorio orientis*, and were repaired and strengthened by one of his successors, Constantine, in the year 447.[249] Also during the reign of Theodosius II, the city walls of Antioch were enlarged, but under the supervision of Antiochus Chuzon, who served as *praefectus praetorio per orientem* in 430-431.[250] We are uninformed whether there were appointees to the *praefectus praetorio* of Illyricum in the years 448 and early 449; a Theodoros held this post in 444, Salomo in 449.[251] If the prefecture of Illyricum was for some reason vacant in the years 448 and 449, the praetorian prefect of the East may have assumed its authority and decided to protect the vitally important city of the eastern Mediterranean by ordering

---

Thessalonica" (n. 242 above) 313ff. Koethe arrived at his identification of Hormisdas after a comparative analysis of preserved masonries and the brick stamps belonging to them, the only such published study of the city's monuments.

[246] Seeck (n. 115 above) 130, 140, 424.

[247] A letter addressed by Pope Hormisdas to the praetorian prefect of Illyricum in the year 519 suggests that the seat of the prefecture remained in Thessaloniki until the reign of Justinian: "Hormisda praefecto praetorio Thessalonicensi et ceteris illustribus a pari" (*Corpus scriptorum ecclesiasticorum latinorum* 35: *Epistulae imperatorum pontificum aliorum Avellana quae dicitur Collectio*, ed. O. Günther [Vienna 1895/1898] 601, no. 153).

[248] Jones, *The Later Roman Empire, 284-602* (London 1964) 2.449, 462, 736f.

[249] *Codex Theodosianus* 15.1.53 (4 April 413). See H. Lietzmann, *Die Landmauer von Konstantinopel*, Abhandlungen der Preussischen Akademie der Wissenschaften (Berlin 1929) 3ff., 27ff.

[250] The sources are unclear about whether this work was carried out on imperial initiative. Consult G. Downey, *A History of Antioch in Syria from Seleucus to the Arab Conquest* (Princeton 1961) 452f. Theodosius II also rebuilt the city walls of Anazarbus (M. Gough, "Anazarbus," *Anatolian Studies* 2 [1952] 98).

[251] Seeck (n. 115 above) 474. By April 449 Hormisdas was no longer praetorian prefect (*ibid.* 424). The last prefect before Hormisdas of whom we have any record was Theodorus (29 Nov. 444). After this study was completed Michael Vickers kindly informed me that the editors (A. H. M. Jones et al) of the forthcoming second volume of *The Prosopography of the Later Roman Empire* (Cambridge 1971ff.) identify our Hormisdas as *praefectus praetorio* of Illyricum in 448. (In 441-442 the prefecture of Illyricum was moved from Sirmium to Thessaloniki.)

the construction of ramparts. During the fourth decade of the fifth century bands of Huns were ravaging the northern frontier of the empire, and, although they signed two peace treaties, in the years 443 and 448, they may have been regarded by Theodosius II as posing a continual threat to its internal security.[252]

Nonetheless, this chain of events is too hypothetical in order to date the walls of Thessaloniki. Moreover, we cannot accept the possibility of Hormisdas as *praefectus praetorio orientis* having built the walls. But Vickers has entertained the idea that this Hormisdas may have erected the walls in some other capacity, either before he became prefect of the Orient in 448 or after he apparently left that office in 449;[253] a later date can be ruled out since this official seems to have passed from favor when Theodosius II died in 450.

Decisive for dating the walls, and hence the Rotunda, are the character of their masonry and the brick stamps. We shall see that the walls themselves are the rock on which Tafrali's identification of Hormisdas junior suffers shipwreck. Before analyzing this telltale evidence, it should be noted that Tafrali's monograph of 1913 is our only archeological survey of the land walls, and an incomplete one at that.[254] Since its publication a number of new inscriptions referring to the walls have come to light and been collected by Theocharides and others, and some brief reports on various stretches of the walls have appeared.[255] Moreover, a systematic investigation of preserved pre-Iconoclastic masonries in the city is lacking. Tafrali himself failed to capitalize on the potential stock of such an investment, even though he describes the masonry of the handful of Early Christian and Byzantine churches in the city.

Table 1 assembles some important data on the masonry of the Late Antique and Early Christian monuments that are preserved at Thessaloniki.[256] The rising walls of all these structures are built according to the same methods.

---

[252] E. A. Thompson, *Attila and the Huns* (Oxford 1948) 97f.; Jones (n. 248 above) 1.193f.; G. Moravčsik, *Byzantinoturcica* (Berlin 1958) 36ff. Although the Huns are said to have advanced to Thermopylae in the year 447, they did not approach Thessaloniki. See n. 235 above.

[253] Emending his paper "The Date of the Walls of Thessalonica" (n. 242 above). Vickers suggested this to me in correspondence dated 5 December 1969.

[254] The *magnum opus* of T. L. F. Tafel (n. 87 above) is still useful for its remarkable collection and appraisal of the sources relating to Thessaloniki until the tenth century.

[255] S. P. Kyriakides, "'Aπὸ τὴν ἱστορίαν τῶν τειχῶν τῆς Θεσσαλονίκης," 'Επιστημονικὴ 'Επετηρὶς τῆς Φιλοσοφικῆς Σχολῆς τοῦ Πανεπιστημίου Θεσσαλονίκης 3 (1939) 262ff.; A. Xyngopoulos, Συμβολαὶ εἰς τὴν τοπογραφίαν τῆς βυζαντινῆς Θεσσαλονίκης (Thessaloniki 1949); G. I. Theocharides, Τοπογραφία καὶ Πολιτικὴ ἱστορία τῆς Θεσσαλονίκης κατὰ τὸν ΙΔ' αἰῶνα (Thessaloniki 1959); idem, "'Άγνωστα τοπογραφικὰ τῆς Θεσσαλονίκης" Makedonika 5 (1961-1963) 1ff.

[256] Compare the data tabulated by Koethe (n. 245 above) 197.

They are constructed of alternating courses of mortared rubblework and brick bands, with the latter penetrating the entire depth of the walls. A course of bricks usually consists of four or five bands, which vary in height according to the thickness of the individual bricks and mortar beds. The stone employed in the rubblework is a brittle, dark green, schistlike rock that is found locally. The rubblework in the Late Antique walls is composed of two or three substantial layers of this stone and liberal amounts of mortar that have been built up, brought to a face, and leveled off into distinct successive layers, each about 35 centimeters high, that are demarcated by horizontal lines. No such formalized layers are evident in the walls of the Early Christian buildings.[257] The mortared rubblework neither possesses the physical properties of Roman concrete (*opus caementicium*), nor does it look like the Roman technique; it is not faced with bricks. In these respects the Thessalonikan walls resemble the walls of Early Christian monuments at Constantinople.[258]

Aside from the presence or absence of distinct formal layers of rubblework, the building methods of the Late Antique and Early Christian city are essentially the same. But the dimensions of the bricks and the thicknesses of the mortar beds vary and provide valuable indices to the relative chronology of these monuments. (The pointing of the mortar has generally disintegrated so much as to be of little use to us—I have observed careful pointing of the joints in the walls of the palace ensemble and the church of Hagios Demetrios—and the compositions of the mortars themselves have not yet been determined by laboratory examination.) Table 1 discloses that the Late Antique walls differ in significant respects from the Early Christian walls. For instance, the bricks are thinner in the Galerian works than in the city walls and the churches, and the mortar beds tend to average about one centimeter less. The proportion of brick to mortar is about 1:1—almost 1:1 in the land walls, the converted Rotunda, and the Acheiropoietos basilica, exactly 1:1 or slightly more in the peripheral walls of the church of Hagios Demetrios.[259] Moreover, our data reveal that the salient characteristics

[257] As pointed out by Ward-Perkins (n. 226 above) 88, pl. 33, E.

[258] See B. Meyer-Plath and A. M. Schneider, *Die Landmauer von Konstantinopel* (Berlin 1943) 21, on the differences between the Thessalonikan and the Constantinopolitan circuit walls.

[259] In Basilica A at Philippi, which is attributed to ca. A.D. 500, the mortar joints are as wide as the bricks (3 cm. rather than the 5.0 cm. thickness at Thessaloniki), while in Basilica B at Philippi, which is attributed to before the year 540, the bricks are thinner than the joints (4.0-4.5 cm. vs. 5.0-6.5 cm. at Thessaloniki); see P. Lemerle, *Philippe et la Macédoine orientale*, (Paris 1945) 1.395 (Basilica A), 489 (Basilica B). In the Church of the Virgin in the Chalkoprateia at Constantinople, ascribed to the mid-fifth century, the proportion of brick to mortar is 1:1 (W. Kleiss, "Neue Befunde zur Chalkopratenkirche in Istanbul," *Akten des 7. Internationalen Kongresses für christliche Archäologie, Trier 5-11 September 1965*, Studi di Antichità Cristiana 27 (Vatican City 1969) 587ff.

TABLE 1

Masonry Characteristics at Thessaloniki

Monument	Brick length (in cm.)	Brick thickness (in cm.)	Mortar joints (in cm.)	Source of Information	Illustrations of brick stamps
Arch of Galerius	38 x 25	3.3	—	K. F. Kinch, *L'Arc de triomphe de Salonique* (Paris 1890) 4.	
Rotunda: rising walls	39–45 x 30	3.5–5.0	3.5 (aver.) (4.0–5.0 in extreme cases)	personal observation	Hébrard, in *Bulletin de correspondence hellenique* 44 (1920) 23 figs. 9, 12, pl. V.
Rotunda: dome	39 x 26 (45 x 45)	2.0–2.5	—	Hébrard, in *Bulletin de correspondence hellenique* 44 (1920) 24.	
Palace of Galerius: octagonal building	45 x 31	3.5–5.0	3.5–4.0	personal observation	Makaronas, in *Makedonika* 2, 1941/52 (publ. 1953) 309 fig. 6.
Circuit walls (northeast of Tower of Hormisdas)	40 x 30	5.0	4.5	personal observation	Tafrali, *Topographie de Thessalonique* (Paris 1913) fig. on 76.

Acheiropoietos basilica	40 x 30-31	5.0	4.5-5.0[a]	personal observation	Tafrali, *Topographie de Thessalonique* (Paris 1913) fig. on 153.
Rotunda: original parts of eastern sanctuary	40 x 30[b]	5.0	4.5-5.0	personal observation	Tafrali, *Topographie de Thessalonique* (Paris 1913) fig. on 153; Hébrard, in *Bulletin de correspondence hellenique* 44 (1920) 32 fig. 15.
Rotunda: crown of dome	——	5.0	5.0		H. Torp, *Mosaikkene* (Oslo 1963) fig. on 45.
H. Demetrios: outer wall of north aisle	40 x 30	4.5-5.0	5.0[c]	personal observation	G. and M. Soteriou, Ἡ Βασιλικὴ τοῦ Ἁγίου Δημητρίου Θεσσαλονίκης 2 (Athens 1952) pl. 94.

[a] Mortar joints are lower at the east end of the peripheral south wall than at the east end of the peripheral north wall of the church; some are as thick as 6.0 cm. in the lowest courses.

[b] A course of five bricks measures about 46 cm., while in the Galerian parts of the building it measures 38 cm.

[c] Similar characteristics are found in the walls of the semicircular chapel at the west end of the outer north aisle, which is also in my opinion part of the original core of the present church; photographs taken of the church after the fire of 1917 suggest that the piers in the nave featured brickwork strikingly similar to that of these other original parts.

of the masonry of the circuit walls, the eastern sanctuary of the Rotunda, the Acheiropoietos church, and parts of the church of Hagios Demetrios are identical.[260] Since all these last-mentioned monuments have yielded identical brick stamps whose unframed monograms are quite distinct (⅄†Ⴄ⅄†) from those of the Galerian monuments, we may safely assume that they are approximately contemporaneous constructions.[261] This observation is of the greatest significance not only for the dating of the mosaic decoration in Hagios Georgios but also for the history of the topography of Early Christian Thessaloniki.

Although we can be certain of the approximate contemporaneity of these Early Christian monuments, we lack the necessary historical sources with which to establish firmly their exact dates of foundation. In fact, the chronology of the church of Hagios Demetrios is a matter of such considerable dispute that it requires a separate study. But the Acheiropoietos basilica can be dated with some precision on stylistic grounds, and this dating enables us to determine the time when the Rotunda was converted into a church and its mosaic decoration put up.

The present name of the Acheiropoietos basilica stems from the Late Byzantine period; the original patrocinium of the church may have been the Theotokos Hodegetria.[262] In plan the church is a basilica with nave arcades, galleries, and a tribelon leading from the inner of the two nartheces to the nave; an atrium preceded the exonarthex.[263] Its layout is closely paralleled

---

[260] The Galerian bricks in both the Rotunda and the octagonal edifice in the palace bear markings that are simple striations made by the fingers of the masons in the clay before it had hardened: Hébrard (n. 108 above) 23, figs. 9, 12, pl. V; Dyggve, "La région" (n. 108 above) 359, fig. 8; Makaronas, in *Makedonika* 2, 1941/52 (1953) 309, fig. 6. For the monograms from the church of Hagios Demetrios at Thessaloniki, see Soteriou (n. 101 above) 1.235, 2 pl. 94. As a class the Early Christian brick stamps of Thessaloniki differ from Constantinopolitan stamps, and the meaning of their markings remains a mystery (see C. A. Mango, "Byzantine Brick Stamps," *American Journal of Archaeology* 54 [1950] 19ff.).

[261] See my "Some Observations on the Dating of S. Demetrios in Thessaloniki," *Byzantion* 40 (1970) 36ff., which was written after the present study was completed.

[262] In two papers A. Xyngopoulos has argued that the place called *Kataphyge* in several texts is to be identified with the Church of the Acheiropoietos, which from the outset was dedicated in honor of the Theotokos Hodegetria: (n. 255 above), and *idem*, "Αἱ περὶ τοῦ ναοῦ τῆς Ἀχειροποιήτου Θεσσαλονίκης εἰδήσεις τοῦ Κωνσταντίνου Ἁρμενοπούλου," Πανηγυρ. Τόμος ἑξακοσιετηρίδη Ἁρμενοπούλου (Thessaloniki 1952) 1ff., on which see F. W. Deichmann, in *Byzantinische Zeitschrift* 45 (1952) 226. But it has been contended that the *Kataphyge* should be located to the west of the ancient agora of Thessaloniki, to the northwest of the Acheiropoietos basilica, and, specifically, near the Church of the Coppersmiths (P. Lemerle, in *Revue des études byzantines* 10 [1952] 206).

[263] As in Hagios Demetrios, the center of the west facade wall featured not an entrance but a triple-arcaded window. Consult the important observations by Krautheimer (n. 113 above) 74ff.; S. Pelekanides, Παλαιοχριστιανικὰ μνημεῖα Θεσσαλονίκης (Thessaloniki 1949) 9ff.

by the Church of the Baptist erected by John Studios at Constantinople, which is also a basilica with a tribelon and galleries, atrium, and two nartheces.[264] The primary distinctions in the two plans are the somewhat shorter proportions of the Constantinopolitan church and the use of architraves rather than arcades over the nave columns.[265] But these differences do not necessarily indicate anything of a chronological development. A second church bearing close similarity in plan to the Acheiropoietos church is Basilica A, identified as the cathedral, at Nea Anchialos in Thessaly.[266] Of these three churches only the Studios basilica is securely dated. It was consecrated in honor of the Baptist when John Studios was patrician in the year 463 and may have been begun as early as 454 when he served as *consul ordinarius*.[267] Basilica A at Nea Anchialos is attributed to about 470 but its exact date of construction can not be determined. The Church of the Acheiropoietos has been ascribed to various dates in the period from 431 to 500, but its architectural sculpture discloses construction in the third quarter of the fifth century, not much earlier than about the year 450.

The typology and style of its carved capitals prove this attribution. The twenty-four capitals of the ground-floor colonnades and the pair of the tribelon are of the type of the composite order known as Theodosian, an appellation first coined by Strzygowski which is a misnomer by now universally accepted.[268] These are the original capitals of the church and have never been moved. Rising from the leaf ornament on the collar at the foot of the bell of these capitals are two ranges of finely-toothed acanthus leaves, standing upright and curling over.[269] All but two of the capitals bear "double" leaves; one specimen in the narthex and one in the nave have single leaves below and double acanthus above. The channel of the echinus flanked by the volutes is covered by a wreath of standing palmettes. The flat edges of the diagonal volutes are decorated with leaf ornament and in three instances with birds, at least two of which (on different capitals) may be identified as eagles with closed wings. The astragal moulding below the palmettes is in a few instances ornamented with a string of pearllike motifs and in most instances is left plain. In the two capitals of the narthex the flat projecting

[264] Krautheimer (n. 113 above) 78f., pls. 21, B, 22, 326, n. 7, for further bibliography.

[265] The dimensions of the nave are 35.6 m. × 14.05m., those of the Studios basilica 25.22 m. × 12.73 m. (the length in both instances measured to the springing of the apse). Each nave terminates in an apse, semicircular in the Thessalonikan church, semicircular within and polygonal without in the Constantinopolitan church.

[266] G. A. Soteriou, "Αἱ χριστιανικαὶ Θῆβαι τῆς Θεσσαλίας" *Archaiologike Ephemeris* 1929 (1931) 19ff.

[267] The dating of the church has recently been reexamined by J. Kramer, *Skulpturen mit Adlerfiguren an Bauten des 5. Jahrhunderts n. Chr. in Konstantinopel* (Cologne 1968) 61f.

[268] J. Strzygowski, in *Byzantinische Zeitschrift* 1 (1892) 68. For the type and its development, see R. Kautzsch, *Kapitellstudien* (Berlin 1936) 115ff.

[269] Kautzsch, 133ff., pl. 26, nos. 431-432; Kramer (n. 267 above) 48f., figs. 20-23.

moulding that crowns the palmettes consists of pearllike ornamentation; this pair of capitals is the richest carved of the entire church. The "Theodosian" capitals bear impost blocks that in the nave are covered on the north and south faces by foliate decoration enclosing wreathed medallions and in the narthex with crosses. In the galleries the capitals are of the Ionic order, and their marble impost blocks bear large crosses, without leaves and tendrils.

The composite capitals of the nave and narthex of the Church of the Acheiropoietos are closely similar in type to the capitals of the narthex of the Studios basilica at Constantinople.[270] This observation deserves close attention. The collar of the bell is ornamented with thick palmettes worked à jour, with a cross placed in the center of the face. From this wreath rise two ranges of "double" acanthus leaves, deeply undercut, which curl over and hang. The palmettes in the channel between the volutes are placed in a row of alternate positions, and on the edges of the volutes there is either leafwork or a small winged eagle. In all four capitals of the narthex the astragal moulding is decorated with a string of "pearls." The capitals of the nave colonnades are of the same type but survive in poor condition.[271] Though the capitals of the galleries are no longer in situ, Krautheimer and Deichmann have argued, correctly we believe, that they were originally of the Ionic order and bore impost blocks covered with leaves and tendrils surrounding a cross; one example of such a capital now rests in the nave of the church.[272] Thus the impost blocks were more elaborate than those of the Acheiropoietos basilica, certainly no chronological index.

The capitals of the two churches consist of the same, Proconnesian marble and have closely related dimensions. Though in the Studios basilica the treatment of the "Theodosian" capitals is richer, the contrast of the white marble against the dark ground sharper than in the Acheiropoietos basilica, the same workshop in the Eastern capital executed both groups. That this was an imperial workshop can be deduced from the evidence of yet another capital carved there which was recently brought to light at the site of the great basilica at Lechaion in Corinth. This capital is also of the "Theodosian" type, with two ranges of fine-toothed double acanthus leaves, a row of standing palmettes between the volutes, and a small eagle on the flat edge of the volute.[273] Inscribed on the base of the capital are *ΝΕΣΤΟ* and *ΛΥΛΙ* (or

[270] Kautzsch (n. 268 above) 135f., pl. 27, no. 434; F. W. Deichmann, *Studien zur Architektur Konstantinopels* (Baden-Baden 1956) 69 ff., fig. 17; Kramer (n. 267 above) 39ff., figs. 8-10, 15, 16, 19.

[271] Kramer 66ff., figs. 17-18.

[272] Krautheimer, in *Art Bulletin* 26 (1939) 407, fig. 2; Deichmann (n. 270 above) 47, n. 152.

[273] Krautheimer (n. 113 above) pl. 36, A; Kramer (n. 267 above) 54f., figs. 25-27 (height, 67 cm.).

ΛΥΔΙ), abbreviations for Nestoros (*Νέστωρ*) and *aulikos*, respectively.[274] The capital has been assigned to the nave of the basilica, which from the evidence of some coins is ascribed to the third quarter of the fifth century.[275] Since the capital is of the same material and dimensions as the capitals in the Studios basilica and the Church of the Acheiropoietos, it was in all probability carved by the same generation of sculptors working in the same workshop. This workshop enjoyed imperial patronage, as can be inferred from the word *aulikou*.

Since the "Theodosian" capitals of the Studios basilica are in situ, and dated with certainty to the years just before 463 when the church was consecrated, the capitals of the Acheiropoietos basilica must be contemporary, that is executed by the same generation of sculptors in the same workshop at Constantinople. Though the Thessalonikan capitals of this type are somewhat simpler in treatment than the examples at the Studios basilica and at Corinth, they are not necessarily some years earlier in date. With a reasonable degree of certainty we therefore can attribute the capitals of the Acheiropoietos basilica to the period from about the late 440s to the early 470s, hence construction of the basilica itself to the very same period.

For the converted Rotunda and ramparts of the city this attribution is of the greatest importance. We have established that the character of the masonry and the stamped bricks of the Church of the Acheiropoietos, the ramparts, and the converted Rotunda prove contemporaneity. Since the Acheiropoietos basilica can be attributed to the third quarter of the fifth century, the other two monuments must date from the same time. Concomitantly, we are supplied with an approximate terminus post quem for the mosaic decoration of the Rotunda.

Such an attribution of the conversion of the Galerian Rotunda into a Christian *ecclesia* is not contradicted by the carved ornament that either has been excavated at the site or forms part of its present collection of architectural sculpture. Aside from a small amount of Galerian sculpture, the carved ornament at the site cannot antedate the middle of the fifth century. Of especial importance is the absence of any architectural sculpture that dates from the reign of Theodosius the Great. At the same time a warning must be issued. None of the post-Galerian sculpture is in situ and therefore does not necessarily belong to the converted Rotunda. This is the position taken

---

[274] As discussed by Kramer 56f.

[275] From the evidence of some coins the church foundation is ascribed by Pallas to 450-460 (*Archaiologikon Deltion* 17 [1961/62] *Χρονικά* 69ff., esp. 74). In a recent appraisal of the dating problem Pallas now ascribes the capitals to which we are referring to not before ca. 470 "auf Grund von anderen Kriterien" which are not detailed (*Byzantinische Zeitschrift* 63 [1970] 69f.). Pallas sees a prolonged period of construction of the church, but I think that the capitals could have been imported from Constantinople when the decision to build the huge basilica was made in 450-460.

by Torp, who discards all the architectural sculpture in the collection of
the Rotunda as evidence pointing to the time when the building was pressed
into service for the Christian cult.[276] But we believe that his position is un-
tenable. If we are allowed to assume that from the outset the (now destroyed)
ambulatory and entrance vestibule of the converted building featured carved
ornament, then it is quite possible that some of this sculpture remains at
the site. Quite clearly not all pieces in the collection today can be attributed
to its transformation into a church, and some certainly come from other
sites (for example, a capital from Hosios David at Thessaloniki). Hébrard's
excavations in 1918 revealed a number of Early Christian capitals, two of
which he published and illustrated as belonging to the converted building
(see below). These capitals may have been buried in the debris of Hagios
Georgios when its ambulatory and porch were destroyed at a subsequent
period (the modern floor level of the building is higher than both the Galerian
and Early Christian levels). That the pieces excavated by Hébrard, along
with some of the others at the site today, originally decorated the Early
Christian Rotunda may be further deduced from the fact that they form a
nucleus uniform in date. Thus we are less skeptical than Torp of their archeological value and believe they may shed light on the problem of the chronology of the site. As we shall now glean, none of the post-Galerian architectural sculpture at the site contradicts the dating proposed for the conversion
of the Rotunda by the evidence of the attribution of the Acheiropoietos basilica to circa 450-470s, and, let it be reiterated, none of it dates from the
end of the fourth century.

In the collection are two Corinthian capitals of the so-called leathercut
type, with a double row of fleshy leaves, drilled and sharply undercut, their
points separated by the dark shapes of triangular and quadrangular interstices.[277] A pair of capitals of the same type occurs in the narthex of Hagios
Demetrios at Thessaloniki and they have been dated by Kautzsch on stylistic
grounds to the years 480/510-525.[278] The type is known from other sites
in Greece, for instance, Basilica A at Nea Anchialos.[279] These parallels have
been collected by Kautzsch who shows that the leathercut capital appears
for the first time in the middle of the fifth century and survives until the
beginning of the sixth.

---

[276] Torp (n. 2 above) 12. According to Lemerle (n. 259 above) 1.407 n. 1, some of the
capitals at the Rotunda come from the district in Thessaloniki known as Vardar (at the
west end of the Late Antique city) and resemble some specimens at Basilica A at Philippi.

[277] Kautzsch (n. 268 above) 76, pl. 16, no. 230 (height of the better preserved example,
59 cm.).

[278] *Ibid.* 72ff., pl. 16, no. 225.

[279] *Ibid.* 76, no. 230. Also the capitals reused in the windows of the Church of the Holy
Apostles at Thessaloniki (*ibid.* 78, pl. 16, 235).

Another capital at Hagios Georgios is of the so-called Theodosian type that was discussed above in connection with the Acheiropoietos church (fig. 21).[280] The collar at the foot of the Corinthian bell is covered by a wreath of fleshy leaves (probably palmettes) on which the drill was used, and from the wreath rise two ranges of finely toothed acanthus leaves that curl over and droop. The channel between the volutes is covered by a belt of standing palmettes, and leafwork decorates the flat edges of the volutes. The abacus is carved like a ribbon of repeated leaves which is tied together and knotted in the center of each face. The treatment of this capital is so close to the capitals of the nave of the Acheiropoietos basilica as to suggest contemporaneity.[281]

The two pilaster capitals now in the chancel of the Rotunda can be attributed to the same period. One and perhaps both were excavated by Hébrard at the site in 1918 and thus may have decorated the converted building from the outset. The one published by the French archeologist is the larger of the pair and, though in fragmentary condition, is a "Theodosian" capital with two ranges of fleshy, "double" acanthus leaves, with the flat midrib of the leaves rising between finely toothed, pointed lobes.[282] The channel of the echinus between the volutes is ornamented with a row of palmettes in alternate standing positions above a decorated astragal moulding, an arrangement and treatment of light against dark strikingly close to the narthex capitals of the Studios church at Constantinople. The abacus was carved like a band with diagonal grooves pulled together as it were into a protruding boss at the center of the face, just as in the abaci of the "Theodosian" capital at the Rotunda (fig. 21) and the capitals of the Acheiropoietos basilica. The other pilaster capital in the Rotunda is smaller in size and far better preserved.[283] It resembles the fragmentary example except for the treatment of the belt of standing palmettes (all pointing upward) and the absence of an astragal. Both pilaster capitals are of Proconnesian marble and of the highest quality. Their closely similar relationship to the above-mentioned capitals in the Studios basilica indicates that they were imports from Constantinople and carved by the same workshop.[284] They can therefore be attributed to the generation working in the third quarter of the fifth

[280] First published by R. Farioli, "I capitelli paleocristiani e paleobizantini di Salonicco," *Corsi di cultura sull'arte ravennate e bizantina* 11 (1964) 152, fig. 3 (height, 65 cm.).

[281] See n. 274 above. Also a capital in the courtyard adjacent to the south flank of the church (Farioli, 154, fig. 4; height, 66 cm.).

[282] Hébrard (n. 108 above) 35, fig. 16; Kramer (n. 267 above) 72ff., pl. 30, right. Hébrard assigns the capital to the Rotunda at the time of its transformation.

[283] Kautzsch (n. 268 above) 136, pl. 27, no. 438; Kramer (n. 267 above) 73f., pl. 30, left (height, 50 cm.).

[284] For the Constantinopolitan export market, consult Deichmann (n. 270 above) 52, 173.

century, from as early as the end of the 440s to as late as the 470s. Of all the capitals now at the Rotunda these pilaster capitals are of the utmost importance because of the likelihood they were executed for the Rotunda when it was transformed into a church.

Yet another type of capital at the Rotunda likewise terminated a wall pilaster. This capital was excavated by Hébrard at the site and may also have decorated the converted building.[285] Its fleshy acanthus leaves appear windblown, leaning in the same oblique, almost horizontal direction. The broad flat midrib of the leaves is flanked by a series of drilled holes, and the lobes are deeply undercut. Windblown acanthus capitals virtually identical in morphology and style occur in the north and south arcades of Hagia Sophia at Thessaloniki and would seem to be contemporary.[286] Though Hagia Sophia is commonly ascribed to the early eighth century, its capitals are spoils and have been attributed by Kautzsch to the years 475-525.[287] The earliest known parallel to this treatment of the windblown acanthus is located in the church of Saint Simeon Stylites at Qalat-Siman in northern Syria, a grand martyrium that was probably erected in the decade(s) immediately following the death of the saint in 459.[288] The same type of capital, though carved in a different style, was found in the aisled tetraconch church excavated by Campbell in the village of Maǧaracik, a suburb of the ancient port city of Seleucia Pieria (modern Samandaǧ) near the present Syrian

[285] Hébrard (n. 108 above) 36, fig. 17; Kautzsch (n. 268 above) 145, no. 461. Another, better preserved windblown acanthus capital at the Rotunda (height, 52 cm.) has been published and dated at least half a century too early (about 400 instead of 450 or later): S. Pelekanides, in *Makedonika* 2, 1941-1952 (1953) 167ff., pl. Γ, above. I reject out of hand Pelekanides' implicit presupposition of a Darwinian development of typology from simple to complex, a development which is equated to a chronological progression from early to late.

[286] Kautzsch (n. 268 above) 141ff., pl. 28, nos. 457-458; M. Kalliga, *Die Hagia Sophia von Thessalonike* (Würzburg 1935) figs. 7-8.

[287] Kautzsch (n. 268 above) 143. For a recent appraisal of problems connected with Hagia Sophia, see Deichmann (n. 270 above) 50, n. 167; Krautheimer, *Early Christian and Byzantine Architecture*, 205ff. The ashlar and brick masonry to which Krautheimer refers occurs at the west and east flanks of the church and can not be part of the original, extant structure: the exposed portions of the encasement of the dome, which is surely part of the original structure, display courses of mortared rubblework leveled and held in place by brick bands, the very technique of the land walls, the converted Rotunda, the Acheiropoietos basilica, and Hagios Demetrios. A careful comparison of this masonry with that of the latter monuments might clarify the dating of the church. Kalliga (n. 286 above) 23, reports that the dimensions of the bricks of the original core vary but average 40 × 30 × 5 cm. (also 37.5 × 29 × 4.5 cm.; 36 × 30 cm.; 36 × 29 × 3.5 cm. [reused bricks]); however, he fails to indicate where he took his measurements. Still, a pre-eighth-century dating of Hagia Sophia is quite possible; the date of 475 to 525 proposed by Kautzsch, however, is clearly too early.

[288] Kautzsch (n. 268 above) 143, pl. 28, no. 460. Qalat-Siman was presumably built only after the death of the saint in the year 459 and may date as late as ca. 480/490.

border of Turkey, a building that was erected sometime in the third quarter of the fifth century.[289] The windblown acanthus capitals of Hagios Demetrios at Thessaloniki display the leaves in different directions and may date some years later.[290] The appearance of the windblown capital both at Thessaloniki and in Syria suggests the type originated at Constantinople.

This rapid survey of the architectural survey in the collection of Hagios Georgios has brought into prominence a group of carved capitals that is so closely related in materials, dimensions, typology, and style of carving to the capitals of the Acheiropoietos basilica and the Studios basilica as to be attributed to one generation of carvers working in the same imperial workshop. As we have seen, the capitals of the Acheiropoietos church can be dated by the Studios basilica, whose capitals had surely been finished by the year 463 when the church was consecrated. Thus we were able to date the Acheiropoietos church in the period from the last years of the 440s to the 470s. Since it has been demonstrated that the technique of construction and stamped bricks of the converted Rotunda are identical to those of the Acheiropoietos basilica, this monument may be dated with assurance to the very same time. This attribution is confirmed by the carved sculpture in the collection at Hagios Georgios, at least a few pieces of which may have adorned the building at the time of its transformation into a Christian church. But even if it is denied that any of this architectural sculpture ever belonged to the converted Rotunda, in which case all of its original carvings are presumably lost or unrecognized, contemporaneity with the Acheiropoietos basilica is still proved by the masonry and brick stamps. On this score we fully agree with Torp.

Our contention that the Christian Rotunda is roughly coeval with the Acheiropoietos church raises the question of the stylistic relationship, if any, between their respective mosaic decorations. Kitzinger has observed that the mosaics in the soffits of the arcades of the Acheiropoietos church contain motifs that seem to be derived from the mosaics of Hagios Georgios, though in somewhat garbled form.[291] We agree that there are such common

[289] *Antioch-on-the-Orontes* 3, ed. R. Stillwell (Princeton 1941) 157, pl. 33, nos. 74-75. For the dating of this important building see Krautheimer, *Early Christian and Byzantine Architecture*, 106.

[290] Kautzsch (n. 268 above) 146, pl. 29, no. 464. The large marble ambo now in the Archeological Museum at Istanbul, half of which was found at the main entrance of Hagios Georgios, the other half in the courtyard of Hagios Panteleimon a short distance west of the Arch of Galerius, may also date from the time when the Rotunda was converted into a Christian sanctuary. See A. Grabar, *Sculptures byzantines de Constantinople* (*IVe-Xe siècle*) (Paris 1963) 80ff. For good illustrations, see Volbach (n. 41 above) pls. 78-79; D. T. Rice, *The Art of Byzantium* (London 1959) pls. 46-47. The treatment of the acanthus of the terminating parapet resembles an unpublished carved frieze in the "sculpture garden" of the Rotunda and some of the carved impost blocks of the capitals of Hagios Demetrios at Thessaloniki, and the crisply carved acanthus capitals of the *Vierblatt* or "four-leaf"

motifs and would add that even such technical devices as the juxtaposition of alternately light and dark tesserae occur in both sets of decoration. For Kitzinger the mosaic decoration of the Acheiropoietos church "appears to presuppose" that of Hagios Georgios and points to a group of mosaics having been executed at a date subsequent to that of the decoration in Hagios Georgios, unless it were assumed that the mosaics in the first named monument were not an original part of the building. But in our opinion this mosaic decoration is an organic part of the original basilica. So far as we can determine, the mosaics in these churches are the products of two different mosaic workshops active at Thessaloniki at the same approximate time. That there were (at least) two workshops is suggested by the qualitative differences in the technique of the two sets of mosaics that are much in evidence. We find it conceivable that such a large and important city in the late empire as Thessaloniki had two or more workshops of mosaicists active at any given time, even that one may have influenced the devices and style of the other(s). Furthermore, it remains possible that the artists responsible for the mosaic decoration of Hagios Georgios were called from the capital, whereas the mosaicists working in the Acheiropoietos church were local craftsmen.[292] If the mosaic decoration of Hagios Georgios and the Acheiropoietos church was indeed put up at the same approximate time, the "certain connections between ornaments" in them that Kitzinger has detected may be explained by a common repertory of features upon which both groups of artists drew.

Unquestionably, Dyggve's dating of Hagios Georgios to the reign of Theodosius the Great is wide of the mark. The Galerian Rotunda became a Christian sanctuary sometime in the period from the end of the fifth decade to the eighth decade of the fifth century. Contemporaneously, the Acheiropoietos basilica and the city walls were erected, revealing a period of intense building activity in the city. The conversion of the Rotunda establishes a terminus post quem for the mosaic decoration, which proves Torp's attribution incorrect. Yet by accepting Torp's crucial observation concerning the exact contemporaneity of the tesserae and mortar at the summit of the dome at face value, and we can cite no technical evidence to contradict it, a secure terminus ante quem becomes available, thereby disproving Weigand's in-

---

type on the columns flanking the niches are close to a capital from Hosios David at Thessaloniki (Kautzsch [n. 268 above] 79, pl. 17, no. 239, first published by A. Xyngopoulos, in *Archaiologikon Deltion* 12, 1929 [1932], 154, fig. 14). Kautzsch dates this type of "four-leaf" capital to the second half of the fifth century, when Hosios David was in my opinion erected and decorated (cf. E. Weigand, in *Byzantinische Zeitschrift* 33 [1933] 211f.; and, more cautious, Krautheimer, *Early Christian and Byzantine Architecture*, 173, 339, n. 7).

[291] E. Kitzinger (n. 162 above) 23, n. 86. The connections await demonstration in published form (compare Hoddinott [n. 98 above] pls. 20, d. and 35, c).

[292] See n. 215 above. Kitzinger himself evaluates the mosaic decoration in Hagios Georgios as "pure imperial Constantinopolitan art" (n. 162 above, 22).

genious attribution to the early sixth century. If Koethe and Vicker's identification of Hormisdas is correct, the dating of the mosaics can be pinpointed
with even greater precision to the very end of the reign of the emperor Theodosius II, who died in the year 450. But even if Torp's observation should
prove mistaken, the mosaics can still be dated to the third quarter of the
fifth century on the grounds of the results of our analysis of their salient
iconographic and formal qualities.[293]

Department of Art
University of California
Los Angeles, California, U.S.A.

[293] After this study went to press I received an offprint from M. Vickers, "The Date of
the Mosaics of the Rotunda at Thessaloniki," *Papers of the British School at Rome* 38 (1970)
183ff., in which a mid-fifth-century dating is put forth. His evidence includes the brick
stamps, the marble pilaster capitals found by Hébrard, and the ambo now in Istanbul.
J. Kramer, "Attische Säulenbasen des 5. und 6. Jahrhunderts n. Chr.," *Bonner Jahrbücher* 70
(1970) 271ff., has examined column bases from the converted Rotunda, the Acheiropoietos
church, and St. John Studios at Constantinople and found their high profiles to be identical,
hence coeval. Pertinent remarks about the use of gold tesserae in Early Christian mosaics
(see n. 215 above) have been made by B. Brenk, "Early Gold Mosaics in Christian Art,"
Palette 38 (1972) 16ff. During gield work in 1972 I discovered parallels to the technical
device of checkerboard modeling in the Rotunda's mosaics (see n. 196 above) in the floor
mosaics of the tetraconch church at Ohrid, the basilica at Studenčišta, and the larger church
at Heraclea (Bitola); these Yugoslav churches are generally dated in the later fifth or early
sixth century and may depend on developments at Thessaloniki.

FIG. 1. Hagios Georgios, Thessaloniki: view of dome (Hirmer 581.1361)

FIG. 2. Temple of Zeus Theos, Dura Europos: reconstruction of paintings in naos (courtesy Yale University)

FIG. 3. Hagios Georgios, Thessaloniki: summit of dome (Photo Lykides)

FIG. 5. Column of Arcadius, Constantinople: anonymous drawing of 1574 of base (Freshfield Album) (after *Archaeologia . . . 1922*)

FIG. 4. Church of Santa Sabina, Rome: panel of wooden doors: Second Coming of Christ (Alinari)

FIG. 6. Cosmas Indicopleustes, *Christian Topography*: Cosmic Universe, copy in Vatican Library, Vat. gr. 699, fol 89r (courtesy Biblioteca Vaticana)

FIG. 7. *Benedictional of St. Ethelwold*: Second Coming of Christ (by courtesy of the Trustees of the British Museum)

FIG. 8. Church of Saints Cosmas and Damian, Rome: apse mosaic (Anderson)

FIG. 9. Hagios Georgios, Thessaloniki: Saints Onesiphoros and Porphyrios (Hirmer 581.1363)

FIG. 10. Triclinium House Reg. I, ins. 3, no. 25, Pompeii (after G. von Cube, pl. II)

FIG. 12. Pola Casket: interior of Old Saint Peter's, Rome (Gabinetto Fotografico Nazionale, series E, no. 51229)

FIG. 11. Hagios Georgios, Thessaloniki: Saints Kosmas and Damianos (Hirmer 581.1364)

FIG. 13. Hagios Georgios, Thessaloniki: Saint Pris-kos, detail (Photo Lykides)

FIG. 15. Hagios Georgios, Thessaloniki: Saint Kos-mas, detail (Photo Lykides)

FIG. 14. Statue of Valentinian II, marble from Aphrodisias (Istanbul, Archaeological Museum) (Hirmer 571.2485)

FIG. 16. Head of a man (so-called Eutropios), Vienna, Kunsthistorisches Museum (Hirmer 644. 2270)

FIG. 17. Hagios Georgios, Thessaloniki: unidentified saint accompanying Saint Ananias (Photo Lykides)

FIG. 19. Hagios Georgios, Thessaloniki: mosaic in barrel vault of western bay, detail (Photo Lykides)

FIG. 18. Megalopsychia floor mosaic, Antioch, detail of Megalopsychia (Antakya, Mosaic Museum) (courtesy Richard Stillwell)

FIG. 20. House of Rams' Heads, Antioch: floor mosaic, detail (courtesy Richard Stillwell)

FIG. 21. Hagios Georgios, Thessaloniki: "Theodosian" capital (author's photograph)

FIG. 22. Hagios Georgios, Thessaloniki: inscription in mosaic accompanying Saint Damianos (Photo Lykides)

ALFARABI AND AVICENNA
ON THE ACTIVE INTELLECT

•

by Herbert A. Davidson

The tale of the active intellect opens with a casual remark of Aristotle that
has exercized the commentators ever since. In his discussion of the human
intellect in the *De anima*, Aristotle describes the intellect as a "part of the
soul" which originally has "no nature" other than its potentiality for thinking, but subsequently can "become each thing."[1] Then he adds enigmati-
cally that as in every other realm, so in the realm of intellect, there must
exist a distinction between that which serves as matter and is potentially
all things, and that which is cause and agent ($\pi o \iota \eta \tau \iota \varkappa \acute{o} \nu$) by virtue of making
all things.[2] What Aristotle meant by these words is to this day moot, the
main issue being whether the intellect that *makes all things* is part of man
or rather a transcendent entity.[3] Even the key term $\nu o \tilde{\upsilon} \varsigma \ \pi o \iota \eta \tau \iota \varkappa \acute{o} \varsigma$ (translated variously as active intellect, active mind, active intelligence, active
reason, productive intellect, etc.) is not explicitly used by Aristotle and is
at best implied. Yet despite the brief and allusive character of his words,
the seed that Aristotle sowed flourished. D. Ross goes as far as to say that
"the famous doctrine of the active reason [is] perhaps the most obscure and
certainly the most discussed of all Aristotle's doctrines."[4]

The problem of the active intellect did not remain one of mere exegesis.
Even today, the line between philosophic commentary and philosophic speculation can be blurred, and that was especially so at the time when the role
of philosopher was indistinguishable from the role of historian of philosophy.
Textual interpretation with the object of determining what Aristotle meant
by his *active intellect* thus passed easily into philosophic inquiry with the
object of determining what sort of thing the active intellect really is. The
scales tip decisively in the latter direction in Avicenna (980-1037), the philosopher who brought the theory of the active intellect to its culmination.

---

[1] Aristotle, *De anima* 3.4.429a, 21-22; 429b, 6.
[2] *Ibid.* 5.430a, 10-15.
[3] Cf. R. Hicks's edition of Aristotle's *De anima* (Cambridge 1907) lxiv-lxix.
[4] Cf. Ross's edition of Aristotle's *Metaphysics* (Oxford 1924) 1.cxliii.

Avicenna construed the active intellect as an entity with an astonishingly wide range of functions, virtually the vicar of God on earth, responsible for all existence and all thought in the sublunar world. His theory presented both an opportunity and a challenge to philosophers and theologians alike. The achievement was clear, for Avicenna provided a unified explanation of a variety of natural phenomena and a scientific rationale for such religious beliefs as prophecy and immortality. But the challenge was no less obvious. Avicenna's explanation of natural phenomena—whether taken as an interpretation of Aristotle or as a theory in its own right—tested the credulity of philosophers. And while liberal theologians may have been pleased to have a scientific rationale for religious beliefs, conservative theologians could not but be vexed to find religious phenomena removed completely from the control of the deity and assigned to a lesser cosmic entity. Avicenna's theory consequently became a subject of debate for philosophers and theologians in the Islamic, Jewish, and Christian worlds.

Looking back from the vantage point of Avicenna it is easy to see how his theories could have grown out of similar but less developed and less consistent theories of Alfarabi (d. 950). When, however, we look back further, beyond Alfarabi, no immediate predecessor can be found. Still the tendencies that crystallize in both Alfarabi and Avicenna can be discovered in the Greek commentators on Aristotle and in Neoplatonic philosophy; some of them reappear in Arabic writers before Alfarabi. This probably does not mean that Alfarabi took material at his disposal and himself molded it into a general theory of the active intellect which was to be further developed by Avicenna. Alfarabi's treatment of this problem, as well as others, seems to be not an innovation but rather a summary of already familiar doctrines. Accordingly, his general account of the active intellect most likely came to him from a still unknown source, perhaps from the teachers whom he mentions but who remain for us mere names.

The first part of the present paper will deal with discussions in late Greek and early Arabic philosophy, not for their own sake, but only insofar as they illuminate the theory of active intellect in Alfarabi and Avicenna. The second and third parts deal with Alfarabi and Avicenna respectively. The late Greek works that will be considered here are: two paraphrases of Aristotle's *De anima* attributed to Alexander of Aphrodisias;[5] Themistius's paraphrase of the *De anima*;[6] a Greek commentary on the *De anima* attributed to John Philoponus;[7] a Latin translation of a different Greek commentary on *De*

---

[5] Alexander, *Scripta minora* 2.1 ed. I. Bruns (Berlin 1887) containing Alexander's *De anima* (1-100) and *De intellectu* (106-113). The authorship of the *De intellectu* has been questioned by some scholars.

[6] Themistius, *Commentaria in Aristotelem Graeca* (henceforth abbreviated as *CAG*) 5.3 (Berlin 1899).

[7] Philoponus, *CAG* 15 (Berlin 1897).

anima Bk. 3, also attributed to Philoponus;[8] Plotinus.[9] Of these, only the two works of Alexander and the commentary of Themistius are known to have been used directly by the medieval Arabs, in Arabic translation.[10] Plotinus was available in pseudepigraphous and anonymous paraphrases.

The Arabic works before Alfarabi to be considered here are: a paraphrase of the *De anima* attributed to Ḥunain ibn Isḥaq (d. 876); a fragment from a writer named Bakr al-Mawṣilî (ca. 900); the works of al-Kindi (ninth century); and a treatise *On the Soul*, of unknown date, attributed to Porphyry. For our purposes, the Arabic works preceding Alfarabi are less important than the late Greek philosophers, and of the latter, Alexander, Plotinus, and Themistius are the most significant.

A remark on terminology is in order. Greek and Arabic do not have separate terms for *intellect* and *intelligence*. However, a convention originating in the Latin middle ages distinguishes *intellect* from *intelligence*, applying the latter term to the incorporeal beings that in Aristotelian philosophy are assumed to govern the celestial spheres, and using the former term in other contexts. Since the convention seems to have become part of the idiom of the history of philosophy, the present paper will follow it. Thus *intellect* and *intelligence* will be distinguished here even though only a single Greek or Arabic word underlies the two terms.

I. Antecedents

Four separte issues within the doctrine of the active intellect may be distinguished: (A) The type of entity the active intellect is. (B) The manner in which it serves as a cause of human thought. (C) The manner in which it serves as a source of the existence of the whole or of part of our world. (D) The manner in which it causes certain religious phenomena.

A. The active intellect, the factor bringing the potential human intellect to actuality, is, it will appear, located by both Alfarabi and Avicenna outside of man at a definite spot in the universe: It is identified by them as the last of ten celestial intelligences, having functions relative to the sublunar world which are analogous to the functions of each of the celestial intelligences

---

[8] *Le commentaire de Jean Philopon sur le troisième livre du traité de l'âme d'Aristote*, ed M. Corte (Liège 1934).

[9] Plotinus, *Enneades*, ed. Henry-Schwyzer (Paris 1951-1959). Volume 2 contains a very useful English translation of the extant Arabic paraphrases of Plotinus.

[10] For the translation of Alexander, see below, nn. 54, 72. A fragment of the Arabic translation of Themistius has been discovered; cf. M. Lyons, "A Greek Ethical Treatise," *Oriens* 13 (1961) 35. Avicenna refers to both Alexander and Themistius; cf. *Arisṭû ʿinda al-ʿArab*, ed. A. Badawi (Cairo 1947) 88, 98, 114, 116, 120.

relative to the corresponding celestial sphere. This precise location of the active intellect cannot be discovered in any writer before Alfarabi, but there were transcendent interpretations of the active intellect, that is, interpretations identifying it as an incorporeal being and locating it some place in the universe above man.

The earliest known explicit[11] identification of the active intellect as a transcendent entity is made by Alexander of Aphrodisias, who connected Aristotle's statements concerning the active intellect in *De anima* Bk. 3 with the doctrine of *Metaphysics* Bk. 12, where Aristotle establishes a first, incorporeal, ever-thinking cause of the universe. The first cause of the universe, Alexander contends, is identical with the active intellect, the cause of the human intellect's passage from potentiality to actuality; in other words, the active intellect is identified with the deity.[12] Plotinus too, in effect, construed the active intellect as a transcendent entity, for his Universal Intellect, the second entity in the hierarchy of being, contains the functions of Aristotle's active intellect.[13] A third interpretation of the active intellect as—at least partly— a transcendent entity is given by Themistius. Among the evidence considered by Themistius was the analogy Aristotle drew between the active intellect and the phenomenon of light.[14] Since light is dispersed and enters the eyes of different individuals, Themistius reasoned, Aristotle's analogy must have been concerned with an aspect of the active intellect that enters the human intellect. But, Themistius also contends, just as light entering the eye must have an external source, so there must exist a transcendent source of the immanent aspect of the active intellect; and that transcendent source, also called "active intellect," was what Plato had in mind when he compared the Idea of the Good, the "cause of science and truth," with the sun, the cause of light.[15] Additional interpretations of the active intellect as a transcendent entity are to be found in the two commentaries on the *De anima* attributed to John Philoponus. Each of the commentaries lists four possible interpretations of the active intellect, and one interpretation in each list brings us closer than before to the position of Alfarabi and Avicenna. According to the Greek commentary attributed to Philoponus, a certain Marinus[16] construed the active intellect as "something daimonic (δαιμόνιον) or angelic."[17] According to a parallel statement in the Latin commentary

---

[11] Some scholars find an implicit identification of the active intellect as a transcendent entity in Aristotle, *De generatione animalium* 2.3.736b, 28; *Eudemian Ethics*, 1248a, 25.

[12] Alexander, *De anima* (n. 5 above) 89; cf. his *De intellectu*, 110 lines 1-3.

[13] Cf. A. Armstrong, *The Architecture of the Intelligible Universe in the Philosophy of Plotinus* (Cambridge 1940) 41.

[14] *De anima* 3.5.430a, 15-17.

[15] *CAG* 5.3.103. Cf. Plato, *Republic* 6.508.

[16] Perhaps identical with a student of Proclus by that name.

[17] *CAG* 15.535 line 5.

attributed to Philoponus, "some" thinkers construe the active intellect not as the deity, but "as a certain other intellect, inferior to Him, positioned close to our [intellect], which radiates upon our souls and perfects them."[18] Both of these interpretations, it will be noted, locate the active intellect near man, whereas Alexander, Plotinus, and Themistius locate it at the top of the hierarchy of being.

Very little is added by Arabic works before Alfarabi. In a paraphrase of the *De anima* attributed to Isḥaq ibn Ḥunain, the active intellect is referred to as the "actual intellect," and its functions are stated briefly without the slightest suggestion that it is an entity existing outside the human soul.[19] An obscure contemporary of Alfarabi named Bakr al-Mawṣilî argues against the position that the human intellect acquires knowledge through the intermediacy of an incorporeal being outside of man. He contends instead that the "principles" of thought, which are judgments concerning "the universal things," must be innate to the human intellect. To explain the way the principles of thought become known to man, Bakr al-Mawṣilî accepts Plato's theory of reminiscence.[20]

Al-Kindi offers at least two, perhaps contradictory, theories of the source of actual human thought. His brief treatise *On Intellect* construes the factor actualizing the human intellect as a transcendent thinking entity, called "first intellect" rather than *active intellect*, and described as the "cause" of all "intelligible thoughts and secondary intellects."[21] This treatise contains several echoes of Alexander,[22] and here al-Kindi could conceivably be reflecting Alexander's position that the active intellect is identical with the first cause of the universe, in other words, with the deity. More likely, though, by the term *first intellect* he means Universal Intellect, the second entity in the Neoplatonic hierarchy. A number of considerations support that interpretation. The Arabic paraphrase of Plotinus employs the term *first intellect* in the sense of Universal Intellect.[23] The Jewish philosopher Isaac Israeli (ca. 850-950) repeats the main points in al-Kindi's account of intellect,[24] but incorporates them into a Neoplatonic hierarchy of Creator-Intellect-Soul-Nature.[25] For Israeli, "first intellect" can only mean Universal Intellect, and since he is borrowing from al-Kindi, he must have understood al-Kindi

[18] *Commentaire* (n. 8 above) 30 line 19.

[19] *Talkhîṣ K. al-Nafs*, ed. A. Ahwani (Cairo 1950) app. 168.

[20] S. Pines, "La doctrine de l'intellect selon Bakr al-Mawṣilî," *Studi . . . in onore di. . Levi della Vida* (Rome 1956) 2.358-361.

[21] *Rasâ'il al-Kindî*, ed. M. Abu Rida (Cairo 1950) 1.356-357.

[22] Cf. E. Gilson, "Les sources gréco-arabes de l'Augustinisme avicennisant," *Archives d'histoire doctrinale et littéraire du moyen âge* 4 (1929) 23-27.

[23] Cf. n. 122 below.

[24] A. Altmann and S. Stern, *Isaac Israeli* (Oxford 1958) 35-38.

[25] *Ibid.* 46-47.

in that way. The Arabic text *On the Soul* attributed to Porphyry also employs the term "first intellect" in a Neoplatonic context and therefore also clearly in the sense of Universal Intellect.[26] The same usage appears too in a later philosopher, Ibn Gabirol,[27] and, in general, popular Neoplatonic literature used the term *active intellect* or *first intellect* for the Universal Intellect.[28] Further support for the Neoplatonic interpretation comes from a recently discovered passage in which al-Kindi gives separate definitions of "first cause" and "universal intellect" and in which he defines the latter as the "specificality of things," a description the treatise *On Intellect* applies to "first intellect."[29] Assuming that the newly discovered passage is genuine, we find *universal intellect* equivalent to *first intellect* and distinguished from *first cause*. Al-Kindi's universal intellect and first intellect could then hardly be anything but the second entity in the Neoplatonic hierarchy.

In a different work, al-Kindi reasons that since actual human thought consists in the union of the human intellect with the "species and genera of things," that is, with "the universals of things," those same universals must be the factor actualizing the human intellect.[30] Here al-Kindi gives no indication of the ontological status of universals. His wording resembles Bakr al-Mawṣilî's ("universals of things"—"universal things"), but his description of the human intellect as becoming unified with these universals would seem to exclude their being inborn, as Bakr al-Mawṣilî held. Al-Kindi could mean that the universals whereby the human intellect is actualized are contained in the transcendent first intellect. For, as seen in the previous paragraph, he describes first intellect as the "specificality of things," which seems to be equivalent to saying that it contains the "universals of things"; accordingly the statement that the "universals of things" actualize the human intellect could mean that they do so when communicated by first intellect to the human intellect. The harmonization, like all harmonizations, is tempting. However, since the passage in question contains no suggestion at all of a transcendent intellect, we should hesitate before introducing one. The universals in the passage may simply be concepts abstracted from physical objects or perhaps even abstract concepts contained in a Platonic world of

---

[26] W. Kutsch, Ein arabisches Bruchstück aus Porphyrios (?)," *Mélanges de l'Université St. Joseph* 31 (1954) 268.

[27] S. Ibn Gabirol, *Fons vitae*, ed. C. Baeumker (Münster 1892-1895) 5 §19.

[28] Cf. Long Version of the Theology of Aristotle, cited by P. Duhem, *Le système du monde*, 4 (Paris 1916) 398ff.; *Rasâ'il Ikhwân al-Ṣafâ'* (Beirut 1957) 3.386 chap. 41, Baṭalyusi, *ha-'Agullot ha-Ra'yoniyot*, ed. D. Kaufmann (Budapest 1880) 5; *K. Ma'ânî al-Nafs*, ed. I. Goldziher (Berlin 1907) 54; F. Rosenthal, "On the Knowledge of Plato's Philosophy," *Islamic Culture* 14 (1940) 399.

[29] Altmann + Stern (n. 24 above) 37-38, taken together with *Rasâ'il al-Kindî* (n. 21 above) 1.165.

[30] *Rasâ'il al-Kindî* 1.155.

Ideas. The character of al-Kindi's writings allows us to suppose that he advocated different theories at different times.[31]

We are thus left with two different theories stated by al-Kindi. According to one, the human intellect is led to actual thought by the transcendent first intellect, probably equivalent to the Neoplatonic Universal Intellect. According to the other, the human intellect is led to actuality by the "universals of things" with no further clarification. There is yet another passage in al-Kindi that could be pertinent here. He writes that the heavenly bodies are the "agent of [human] reason."[32] There, however, he probably means that the heavens generate the human rational soul with its potentiality for thought, not that the heavens bring the human rational soul to actual thought.

This survey shows that post-Aristotelian Greek philosophers who construed the cause of actual human thought as a transcendent entity identified it with the deity, with Plato's Idea of the Good—which may or may not be the same as the deity—, with the Universal Intellect, or with a supernal being located below the deity and close to man in the hierarchy of existence. Immanent interpretations of the active intellect in Greek philosophy were not mentioned here since they are not pertinent to our study. In Arabic philosophy prior to Alfarabi, some works propose a transcendent cause of actual human thought,[33] whereas others reject it,[34] and in al-Kindi alone one passage clearly recognizes a transcendent cause of human thought whereas another passage discusses the actualization of the human intellect without mentioning such an entity. Despite the various precedents for a transcendent interpretation of the active intellect, there is before Alfarabi no known statement to the effect that the chain of celestial intelligences ends in an entity linking the celestial realm with the sublunar world. Alfarabi was the first known writer to recognize such an entity, let alone identify it with Aristotle's active intellect.

B. The original moment in the theory of the active intellect was epistemological. In all nature, Aristotle reasoned, there are to be found both a material factor and a "causative, productive" factor; therefore, the soul also must contain two such factors, both an intellect with the characteristic of "becoming all things" and an intellect with the characteristic of "making all things," in other words, an intellect capable of receiving thought and an intellect capable of producing it.[35] Underlying this reasoning is the principle, established elsewhere by Aristotle, that when "what exists actually

[31] Cf. F. Rosenthal, "Al-Kindî and Ptolemy," *Studi. . . in onore di. . . Levi della Vida* (Rome 1956) 2.438, 446, 454-456.

[32] *Rasâ'il al-Kindî* (n. 21 above) 1.255.

[33] Cf. above, nn. 24, 26, 27, 28.

[34] Cf. above, at nn. 19, 20.

[35] *De anima* 3.5.430a, 10-15.

is generated from what exists potentially" it is "always by means of what [already] actually is [that thing]."[36] Aristotle's general justification for the existence of the active intellect became commonplace, but it does not explain just how the active intellect brings the human intellect to actuality.

In different works, it will appear, Alfarabi gives different explanations of the way in which the active intellect effects human knowledge. Sometimes he describes the active intellect simply as lighting up, as it were, the universal characteristics of physical objects and thereby enabling the human intellect to abstract universal concepts. In two works, however, he describes the active intellect as operating on the human intellect itself both at the beginning, and at subsequent stages of its development: The active intellect launches the human intellect on its way by presenting it with the first principles of thought, it subsequently presents the human intellect with the principles of the individual sciences, and, finally, if the human intellect reaches a perfect state called *acquired intellect*, the active intellect once again communicates with it. Avicenna describes the active intellect in yet another way as a sort of cosmic transmitter, continually transmitting all possible abstract thoughts, with those thoughts being received directly from the active intellect whenever the human intellect happens to be properly attuned. Antecedents for each of these descriptions of the active intellect are to be found in Greek and early Arabic sources.

Alexander of Aphrodisias calls the primitive state of the human intellect "potential" or "material" (ὑλικός) intellect,[37] and he describes it as being not a substance but only a "disposition" for thought.[38] When actualized, the human disposition for thought becomes what Alexander calls "intellect *in habitu*," a stage of intellect which is reached by the processes of actual thought, but which itself consists in the ability to think at will when that ability is not actually put to use. The stage of intellect *in habitu* is analogous to the craftsman when he is not working and to the "man of knowledge" when he is not thinking; it stands between the pure potentiality of the person who has not begun to learn, and the pure actuality of the man of knowledge engaged in thought or the craftsman engaged in his trade.[39] Since, Alexander contends, things "generated . . . by nature" must both contain a material factor and also be led to actuality by a productive factor bringing about "the generation of what the matter can receive"—so too "in the case of intellect," there must in addition to the material intellect, also be "a certain active intellect," which produces the stage of intellect *in habitu*.[40] Again:

[36] *Metaphysics* 9.8.1049b, 24-25.

[37] Alexander, *De anima* (n. 5 above) 81 lines 23-24.

[38] *Ibid.* 84 line 24.

[39] *Ibid.* 85-86; *De intellectu* 107. This sense of potentiality is Aristotelian; cf. *De anima* 2.5.417a, 22ff.

[40] Alexander, *De anima* 88.

"Whatever is . . . led from potentiality to actuality must be generated by something already actual," and consequently "there must exist an already actual active intellect" that gives "the hitherto potential intellect" the ability to "become actual and think."[41] This active intellect, as was already seen, is identified by Alexander with the first cause of the universe.[42]

The precise mode in which the active intellect acts upon the human intellect remains unclear in Alexander as in Aristotle,[43] but Alexander makes a number of suggestive statements. Alexander's *De intellectu* states that the active intellect "produces ($\dot{\varepsilon}\mu\pi o\iota\tilde{\omega}\nu$) . . . the intellectual *habitus* in" the material or potential intellect.[44] Both Alexander's *De anima* and his *De intellectu* state that human thought can have as its object not only forms abstracted from material objects but also incorporeal beings consisting in pure intellect.[45] More particularly, even the active intellect can be an object of human thought.[46] When describing that condition, Alexander uses such formulas as: "The active intellect . . . is generated in us from without,"[47] and "enters from without."[48] That is, since intellect, according to Aristotle, is identical with the form that it apprehends,[49] when the active intellect—which is pure form—becomes an object of human thought, it actually enters the human intellect.

We might expect that Alexander would allow the active intellect as an object of human thought only at the completion of human intellectual development.[50] After achieving intellectual knowledge of the physical universe, the human intellect would, it might be supposed, reach a point where it can have knowledge of the active intellect, the incorporeal first cause of the universe. However, in one passage of the *De intellectu*, where Alexander may in fact be representing views other than his own,[51] the active intellect is said to join the potential human intellect at the very beginning of its career. The active intellect "in us," Alexander writes, "is generated in" man by becoming an object of human thought, it "introduces the *habitus* [of thought] into the material [intellect]," and it thereby enables the human intellect to go

[41] *De intellectu* 110 lines 21-24.

[42] Above at n. 12.

[43] Cf. P. Moraux, *Alexandre d'Aphrodise* (Paris 1942) 72; P. Merlan, *Monopsychism, Mysticism, Metaconsciousness* (Hague 1963) 41.

[44] Alexander, *De intellectu* 107 line 33.

[45] Alexander, *De anima* 87-88; *De intellectu* 111 line 1.

[46] Alexander, *De anima* 89 line 21; *De intellectu* 111 lines 29-30.

[47] Alexander, *De anima* 90 line 19; *De intellectu* 113 line 24.

[48] *De intellectu* 110 line 24.

[49] Cf. n. 59 below.

[50] Such seems to be the implication of Alexander, *De anima* 89 line 21; 91 line 5; *De intellectu* 108 line 24; 109 lines 3-4.

[51] Cf. Moraux (n. 43 above) 143-149. There is no reason to suppose that Arabic readers could have realized that the passage does not represent Alexander's own view.

about its task of abstracting the forms of objects in the physical world.[52] In other words, the active intellect has to become an object of human thought before the intellect *in habitu* can appear and before the human intellect can think anything else. This account of the function of the active intellect is illustrated with the aid of the analogy Aristotle drew between the active intellect and light.[53] The analogy is developed in Alexander's *De intellectu* as follows: Just as light is both itself visible and also produces actual sight, so the intellect from without is both itself intellectually knowable and also makes intellectual thought possible in man.[54] In Alexander's version the analogy clearly implies that the active intellect must become known to the potential human intellect before anything else can be known, just as light must be visible before anything else can be seen. It is not at all clear what is meant by the active intellect's becoming an object of human thought at the very beginning of human intellectual development. Conceivably, that could mean receiving the principles of thought from the active intellect; the fundamental principles of thought would then make possible the appearance of the ability to think constituting the stage of intellect *in habitu*.

Besides the analogy of light, Aristotle introduced another signficant analogy by comparing the potential intellect with matter insofar as both have the characteristic of "becoming all things."[55] This analogy led Alexander to designate the potential intellect as *material intellect*,[56] and in a natural explication of the term he writes that in the process of thought the material intellect is receptive of form: "The material intellect is a certain disposition . . . for receiving forms";[57] that is to say, human thoughts are forms abstracted from physical objects which thereupon become forms of the material intellect. The stage of intellect *in habitu* is described by Alexander as a "form and perfection" of the material intellect.[58] This may mean both that the thoughts contributing to the appearance of intellect *in habitu* are forms received in the material intellect, and also that the intellect *in habitu*, as a higher stage of development, is itself the form of the material intellect. These statements are in the spirit of Aristotle.[59] The application of the dichotomy

[52] *De intellectu* 111 lines 21-32.

[53] *De anima* 3.5.430a, 15.

[54] *De intellectu* 111 lines 32-34. In the Arabic translation, the words "intellect from without" are translated "acquired intellect" and the words "itself intellectually knowable" are not rendered coherently. Cf. J. Finnegan, "Texte arabe du περὶ νοῦ d'Alexandre d'Aphrodise," *Mélanges de l'Université St. Joseph* 33 (1956) 194.

[55] *De anima* 3.5.430a, 10-15.

[56] N. 37 above.

[57] Alexander, *De anima* 84 lines 24-25; cf. 82 line 1.

[58] *Ibid.* 85 line 11.

[59] *De anima* 3.5.430a, 20; *Metaphysics* 12.7.1072b, 21; E. Zeller, *Die Philosophie der Griechen*, 2.2, ed. 4 (Leipzig 1921) 566-568.

of matter-form to intellect is given an extreme interpretation, however, in the commentary on the *Metaphysics* attributed to Alexander, where nothing less than the "divine intellect" is described "as a form of the human intellect."[60] The possible mystical implication of the statement has been noted by several scholars.[61] As an epistemological theory the statement simply says that the human intellect knows the active intellect in a way similar to that wherein it has intellectual knowledge of anything else, that is, by receiving in itself the form of the object of its knowledge. If the human intellect can indeed know the active intellect, as both Alexander's *De anima* and *De intellectu* allow,[62] then Alexander's commentary on the *Metaphysics* goes no further when it describes the active intellect as a "form" of the human intellect.

According to Alfarabi and Avicenna, the intellectual development of man can lead to a stage or state called *acquired intellect*.[63] In the Greek text of Alexander, the term *acquired intellect* is not conspicuous, appearing only once, as a synonym for intellect *in habitu*, that is, the human intellect after it acquires the ability to think.[64] A number of times, though, Alexander uses the expression "intellect from without," echoing a passage where Aristotle had described intellect as "entering [man] from without."[65] Alexander's *De anima* and *De intellectu* differ slightly in their use of the expression "intellect from without." Alexander's *De anima* calls any incorporeal form "intellect from without," since any such form is intellect by its very nature, with no need of being abstracted by the human intellect.[66] The *De intellectu*, on the other hand, mentions no incorporeal forms apart from the active intellect and designates the active intellect alone as intellect from without.[67]

In the Arabic translation of Alexander's works the expression "intellect from without" is generally rendered as "acquired intellect," sometimes even as "intellect acquired from without."[68] There is an added peculiarity in the Arabic translation, for it avoids the standard term "active (*faʿʿāl*) intellect" and instead uses the ambiguous term "acting (*fāʿil*) intellect." Accordingly, instead of using phrases such as "active, acquired intellect," which would show that *acquired intellect* is another term for the active intellect, the Arabic

---

[60] *CAG* 1 (Berlin 1891) 714.

[61] Cf. Moraux (n. 43 above) 103-104; Merlan 36-37.

[62] N. 46 above.

[63] On the problem of the *acquired intellect*, cf. F. Rahman, *Avicenna's Psychology* (Oxford 1952) 90-93; Finnegan (n. 54 above) 172-178; Merlan (n. 43 above) 14-15; and the references they give to earlier literature.

[64] Alexander, *De anima* (n. 5 above) 82 line 1.

[65] *De generatione animalium* 2.3.736b, 28.

[66] Alexander, *De anima* 90 line 22.

[67] *De intellectu* (n. 5 above) 108 line 22.

[68] Cf. Finnegan (n. 54 above) 172.

translation speaks of the "acting, acquired intellect,"[69] which leaves the nature of the acquired intellect obscure. Nevertheless, a fairly clear picture of the acquired intellect does come out of the Arabic translation. The acquired intellect, according to the Arabic, comes "from without,"[70] "exists actually,"[71] "by itself,"[72] and "by nature";[73] it "aids" the human intellect,[74] "establishes the *habitus* within the material intellect,"[75] and is the factor whereby the potential intellect is "led from potentiality to actuality";[76] it also is "generated in us from without,"[77] and "thought by us."[78] These descriptions show that the term *acquired intellect* designates a transcendent incorporeal entity and, in particular, the active intellect. The terms "acquired," and "acquired from without," however, indicate that this intellect is something belonging to man. The Arabic translator must have taken the expression "intellect from without" as designating the aspect of the active intellect—or any other incorporeal form—that enters the human intellect. Alexander did not in fact intend the phrase "intellect from without" in so strict a sense, and therefore the Arabic is reading something into the Greek text. Since, however, Alexander did recognize an aspect of the active intellect that enters man, the Arabic translation does not really misrepresent his thought. It merely gives a stricter interpretation to the expression "intellect from without," and a new sense to the term *acquired intellect*; also, simply by naming the aspect of the active intellect entering man, the translation draws additional attention to it.

For us, the significant points in Alexander's account of the epistemological function of the active intellect are the following: The active intellect causes the human intellect to develop by producing the stage of intellect *in habitu*. The active intellect does this, according to one passage, by entering the human intellect and providing it with an object of thought at the very beginning of human intellectual development. Intellectual thoughts, the stage of intellect *in habitu*, and even the active intellect when it becomes an object of human thought, are all called forms of the human intellect. In the Arabic

---

[69] *Ibid.* 186 line 5; 187 line 1. Alexander, *De intellectu* 109 line 5, describes intellect *in habitu* as "acting."

[70] Finnegan 191 line 4.

[71] *Ibid.* line 3.

[72] Hebrew translation—from the Arabic—of Alexander, *De anima* 90 lines 21-22; cf. Hebrew Ms. no. 894, Bibliothèque National, Paris.

[73] Finnegan (n. 54 above) 194 line 2.

[74] *Ibid.*

[75] *Ibid.* lines 5-6.

[76] *Ibid.* 191 line 2.

[77] *Ibid.* 186 line 6; 194 lines 4-5; Hebrew translation of Alexander's *De anima* 90 lines 19-20, as in n. 72.

[78] Hebrew translation of Alexander's *De anima* 89 line 23f., as in n. 72.

translation of Alexander, the aspect of the active intellect entering the human intellect is called *acquired intellect.*

In Plotinus the standard argument for the existence of the active intellect is employed as an argument for the existence of the Universal Intellect: There must exist an intellect that brings about actual thought in soul since "potentiality passes to actuality only through a cause that is in actuality similar to [what] the former [is in] potentiality."[79] By this argument the original text of Plotinus clearly means to establish the existence of Universal Intellect above Universal Soul, but the Arabic paraphrase of Plotinus does not make it clear whether Universal Soul or individual human souls are at issue. In the Arabic, therefore, the passage can be read as the standard proof for the existence of a transcendent intellect that leads the human soul to actual thought. This reading is completely in the spirit of Plotinus, for his Universal Intellect does contain the characteristics of Aristotle's active intellect;[80] and, indeed, as already noted, the Universal Intellect was recognized by medieval Neoplatonic writers as equivalent to the active intellect.[81]

According to Plotinus, part or all of human intellectual knowledge comes to the human rational soul from the Universal Intellect. When discussing the Platonic science of dialectic, which he describes as the "honored part of philosophy," Plotinus writes that Intellect gives dialectic its "clearest principles," and then dialectic operates on those principles until it "reaches perfect intellect."[82] Elsewhere he writes, in the language of the Arabic version: "The intellectual sciences, which are the true sciences, come only from Intellect to the rational soul."[83] The same is brought out with the aid of the already familiar dichotomy of matter-form. The soul is described by Plotinus as "analogous to matter," "receptive of form" from Intellect, and thus rendered perfect.[84] In the original the reference here is again clearly to Universal Soul rather than human soul, but Avicenna's comment on the Arabic paraphrase shows that by *soul* he at least understood precisely the human soul, and that by *intellect* he understood the "active intelligences."[85] Read in this manner Plotinus is describing the human rational soul as a kind of matter that is perfected and receives all of its intellectual knowledge through form

---

[79] *Enneades* (n. 9 above) 5.9.4; Arabic paraphrase in *Risâla fî al-ʿIlm al-Ilâhî*, ed. A. Badawi, in *Plotinus apud Arabes* (Cairo 1955) 168.

[80] N. 13 above.

[81] Nn. 27, 28 above.

[82] *Enneades* (n. 9 above) 1.3.5.

[83] *Risâla fî al-ilm al-Ilâhî* (n. 79 above) 169, paralleling *Enneades* 5.9.7.

[84] *Theology of Aristotle*, ed. F. Dieterici (Leipzig 1882) 106, paralleling *Enneades* 5.1.3.

[85] Cf. Avicenna's commentary on *Theology of Aristotle* in *Arisṭu ʿinda al-ʿArab* (n. 10 above) 72, trans. into French by G. Vajda, *Revue Thomiste* 51 (1951) 346-406. The Arabic pages are indicated in Vajda's translation.

coming to it from the realm of the incorporeal intelligences, specifically from the active intellect.

Intellectual thoughts (τὰ εἴδη) are, according to Plotinus, present in man in two ways. The highest level of the human soul is an offshoot of the Universal Intellect, and there intellectual thoughts are present "all together," that is, undifferentiated. At a lower level of the human soul, the level that is an offshoot of the Universal Soul, intellectual thoughts are present "unrolled and discrete, as it were."[86] The intellectual activity of the latter level is characterized as "cogitation and deliberation" (*fikr, rawiyya*; λογισμός), that is to say, the process of "seeking to discover wisdom," analogous to "training with a view towards a *habitus*" or "studying with a view towards knowledge"—as distinct from possessing wisdom without effort.[87] The "Creator,"[88] Intellect,[89] and even Universal Soul[90] are exempt from this striving. Since the rational soul must strive to attain intellectual knowledge and since it must receive its intellectual knowledge from the Universal Intellect, its thought is called "acquired intellect" (ʿaql muktasab; ἐπακτὸς νοῦς) by Plotinus,[91] in distinction from the intellectual activity of the Universal Intellect which is essential to Intellect and thus not acquired (*muktasab, mustafâd*).[92]

The general situation of the human soul is brought out by two suggestive metaphors, the metaphor of the two worlds and the metaphor of the mirror. The soul is described by Plotinus as standing between two worlds; it can either look up towards the world of Intellect, prefer to dwell there and enjoy the knowledge provided there; or else it can look down and sink into the physical world, thereby losing genuine knowledge.[93] Contained within the soul is a sort of mirror wherein images of Thought and Intellect are reflected when the soul succeeds in orienting itself properly.[94]

Plotinus's position will appear to be highly significant for Avicenna: Intellectual knowledge is radiated upon the properly oriented human intellect from Universal Intellect, Plotinus's version of Aristotle's active intellect. The relation of the soul to its thought is, as in Alexander, described as a relation of matter to form, but now all thought or the principles of thought are explicitly described as coming to the human soul directly from Universal

---

[86] *Enneades* 1.1.8.

[87] *Enneades* 4.4.12.

[88] *Theology of Aristotle* (n. 84 above) 168, paralleling *Enneades* (n. 9 above) 5.8.7. In the original the reference is to Universal Intellect, which is the "Maker" of the universe.

[89] *Theology of Aristotle* 107, paralleling *Enneades* 5.1.4.

[90] *Theology of Aristotle* 84 paralleling *Enneades* 4.8.8.

[91] *Al-Shaykh al-Yûnânî*, ed. F. Rosenthal, *Orientalia* 21 (1952) 480.

[92] *Theology of Aristotle* 51, paralleling *Enneades* 5.8.3.

[93] *Theology of Aristotle* 21-23, 79-80, paralleling *Enneades* 4.4.4; 4.8.7.

[94] *Enneades* 1.4.10.

Intellect. Cogitation and deliberation characterize the human intellect, but not the cosmic entities above it. Because thought is acquired by the human intellect from above, actual human thought is called acquired intellect.

Themistius provides yet another version of the mode in which the human intellect draws intellectual knowledge from the active intellect. On textual grounds he maintains that Aristotle's active intellect is something within the human soul.[95] but he also contends that the active intellect must exist as a single preexistent and eternal cause of thought for all men.[96] The two theses are harmonized by the suggestion that the active intellect is primarily one but, like light, breaks up in the different subjects receiving it.[97] The transcendent-immanent active intellect contains, according to Themistius, all thoughts simultaneously,[98] it penetrates and unites with the potential human intellect,[99] leads the potential intellect into actuality, and produces the intellect *in habitu*.[100] The active intellect is the cause making it possible for all men to grasp the "common notions," "first definitions," and "first axioms" of thought without being taught;[101] this may mean either that the immanent aspect of the active intellect brings the principles of thought to the human intellect directly from the transcendent aspect of the active intellect, or that the presence of the active intellect only enables the human intellect to discover those principles in sense perceptions entering from the physical world.

The analogy of light is used by Themistius to explain how the active intellect helps abstract forms from material objects and produce abstract thoughts. Light, he writes, acts upon the sense of sight in the seeing subject and upon colors in the object seen, rendering both actual. Analogously, the active intellect both leads the potential human intellect to actuality and also, as it were, illuminates potential objects of thought, rendering them actually intelligible to the human intellect; those potential objects of thought are impressions from the senses, mediated through the imaginative faculty and stored in the memory.[102] The active intellect works from within, joining

[95] *CAG* (n. 6 above) 5.3.103.

[96] *Ibid*. 102-103.

[97] *Ibid*. 103.

[98] *Ibid*. 100.

[99] *Ibid*. 99.

[100] *Ibid*. 98.

[101] *Ibid*. 103-104. Although Themistius criticized Alexander, there is a certain similarity between his position and the position stated by Alexander in the passage quoted above at nn. 52, 54. According to both, the active intellect must join the potential human intellect at the beginning of its development. The difference is that for Alexander, in the passage in question, the active intellect is merely the first human thought. In Themistius, however, the immanent active intellect is the motive and organizing factor at the beginning and throughout human intellectual activity.

[102] *CAG* 5.3.98-99.

the potential human intellect as an organizing factor, so that together they can construct a body of intellectual knowledge from the fund of impressions available to them.

The familiar analogy of matter and form also reappears in Themistius, who uses it to explain the relation of potential to active intellect: Each level of soul is a sort of material substratum for the next, the faculty of sense perception serving as matter for the imaginative faculty, the imagination serving as matter for the potential intellect, and that in turn serving as matter for the immanent active intellect. Whereas the intermediate stages are both matter and form from different points of view, the active intellect, which is the highest stage, is form in the "strict sense"; it is highest form, the "form of forms," and with it the process stops.[103]

In early Arabic philospohy, both al-Kindi's treatise *On Intellect* and the treatise *On the Soul* attributed to Porphyry assign the actualization of human thought to the direct action of a supernal cause upon the human intellect. Al-Kindi gives the standard argument for the existence of an agent that produces human thought: Whenever something has a certain characteristic potentially, it can only be actualized by something else already possessing the given characteristic actually.[104] In the treatise *On Intellect*, where al-Kindi establishes a transcendent first intellect as the cause of human thought, he writes that thought occurs when the human soul "makes contact" (*bâsharat*) with intellect, that is, with "forms" containing "neither matter nor imagination."[105] A few lines later it is explicitly the first intellect with which the rational soul makes contact. The result of this contact is "intellect acquired by the soul from the first intellect," the first intellect granting (*mufîd*) what the human soul acquires (*mustafîd*).[106] It is perfectly clear here that the human soul attains intellectual knowledge directly through contact with the first intellect, but it is not clear how that contact is made nor what part sense perception might play in the process. Isaac Israeli, who repeats al-Kindi's scheme of intellect, does not mention contact with first intellect, explaining instead that the human intellect becomes actualized through successive degrees of abstraction beginning from sense perception.[107]

The treatise *On the Soul* attributed to Porphyry does not articulate a complete theory of intellect, but it does describe thought as coming to man directly from a transcendent source. The treatise distinguishes "material intellect," that is, the potential human intellect, from "second, psychic (*nafsânî*) intellect" shown by the context to be a state of actual human intellect;[108] other

[103] *Ibid.* 100.
[104] *Rasâ'il al-Kindî* (n. 21 above) 155, 356.
[105] *Ibid.* 355-356.
[106] *Ibid.* 356.
[107] Altmann + Stern (n. 24 above) 36-37.
[108] Kutsch (n. 26 above) 268, §§ 3, 4.

writers use the term "second intellect" in a similar sense.[109] "Psychic intellect" is described as "identical with the [transcendent] first intellect when
they are in the upper world . . . whereas [second] psychic intellect is different from the other [transcendent intellect] when it appears in the body
through the medium of the soul."[110] An annoying change of terminology
occurs when human "intellect," with no further qualification, is said to come
"from . . . the intelligible world" and serve as "form" of the human soul.[111]
Since *intelligible world* is a Neoplatonic equivalent of *Universal Intellect*,[112]
the statement may be taken as follows: Actual human thought consists in
a form coming to the human soul from the universal first intellect, also called
intelligible world. When that form is in the universal first intellect the two
are identical; when the form is present in the human soul, it is distinct from
first intellect and is called second psychic intellect. The treatise *On the Soul*
also states that the material intellect can never think without the aid of the
estimative faculty (*wahm*), which is a physical faculty of the soul.[113] We can
connect this with the previous statements by understanding that the material
intellect contemplates perceptions coming to it from the physical world through
the physical faculties of the soul, and thereby prepares itself to receive actual
intellectual thought from the Universal Intellect.

C. Alfarabi and Avicenna not only construed the active intellect as the
agent producing knowledge in the human intellect, they also assigned it
functions in the causation and maintenance of the sublunar world. There
are again antecedents for their theories in Alexander and Plotinus.

Alexander, it was seen, identified Aristotle's active intellect as the first
cause of the universe.[114] Whereas Aristotle had presumed only to establish
a first cause of the *motion* of the universe,[115] Alexander understood the first
cause of motion to be the cause of the *existence* of the universe as well, and,
accordingly, he describes the active intellect as "cause and principle of the
existence of everything else."[116] Thus, for Alexander, the active intellect
combines two functions: It is the cause of actual human thought in addition
to being the ultimate cause of the existence of the entire universe outside
itself.

---

[109] *Rasâ'il al-Kindî* (n. 21 above) 354; Ibn Gabirol (n. 27 above) 5 § 34; Altmann +
Stern (n. 24 above) 36. Other senses of *second intellect* appear in the long version of the
Theology of Aristotle, ed. S. Stern, *Oriens* 13 (1961) 88, 91-92; Alfarabi, *Risâla fî al-ʿAql*,
ed. M. Bouyges (Beirut 1938) 19 line 10; 21 line 1.

[110] Kutsch (n. 26 above) 268, § 4.

[111] *Ibid.* § 2.

[112] E. Zeller, *Die Philosophie der Griechen* 3.2, ed. 5 (Leipzig 1923) 584-587.

[113] Kutsch (n. 26 above) 268, § 3.

[114] Above at n. 12.

[115] Cf. Zeller (n. 59 above) 379-381.

[116] Alexander, *De anima* (n. 5 above) 89 lines 9-10.

A similar combination of functions is spelled out in a more detailed manner in the concluding section of Alexander's *De intellectu*. Both the original Greek and the Arabic translation of this work raise a number of questions, the full discussion of which would lead too far afield, but basically the section in question examines and refutes a Stoic-inspired interpretation of the active intellect. According to that interpretation, the active intellect is a substance that penetrates the matter of the entire universe without ceasing to perform its own act of thinking. It governs the sublunar world either by itself or in conjunction with the movements of the heavenly bodies, through the process of combining and separating the materials from which natural objects are generated. It thereby is also the cause of the existence (*khâliq*; δεμιουργός) of the potential human intellect, which is generated whenever any portion of matter is mixed in such a way that it can serve as an instrument for thought. The potential human intellect is not merely brought to actuality by the divine active intellect; actual human thought is nothing other than the divine intellect's thinking through the human intellect.[117] Whether read incorrectly as Alexander's own position[118] or correctly as a Stoic position rejected by him, this section of the *De intellectu* provided medieval Arabic readers with another source assigning a double function to the active intellect: the production of all natural objects from the matter of the sublunar world—although not the production of matter itself; and the actualization of the human intellect. In addition, this section adds a significant explanation of the manner in which the potential human intellect is generated. It should be observed that in Alexander's statement of his own view, the cause of actual human thought is identified with the cause of the existence of the entire universe, matter as well as form, whereas in this Stoic account the cause of actual human thought is identified with the factor working within, and giving form to the matter of the sublunar world (and presumably to the matter of the rest of the universe as well).

In Plotinus too the entity bringing about actual human thought has the additional function of producing the existence of the universe below itself. Universal Intellect, the cause of intellectual activity in the soul,[119] is described in the formulation of the Arabic paraphrase of Plotinus, as "cause of what is beneath it,"[120] that is, the cause of the existence of both Universal Soul, and also the entire physical universe. Again: "[Universal] Intellect is all things, and all things are in it . . . they are in it as [in] their agent, whereas it is in them as cause."[121] "All things are in First Intellect; for the First Agent . . .

---

[117] *De intellectu* 112-113.

[118] Alexander's critique of the theory is not fully coherent in the Arabic translation.

[119] Above at nn. 82-85.

[120] *Theology of Aristotle* (n. 84 above) 145, paralleling *Enneades* (n. 9 above) 6.7.3.

[121] *Risâla fî al-'Ilm al-Ilâhî* (n. 79 above) 168 bottom, paralleling *Enneades* 5.9.6.

made . . . Intellect possessed of many forms and in each form He put all the things corresponding to that form."[122] In fact, for Plotinus, Universal Intellect is not the direct cause of the physical universe, but rather an incorporeal model of it,[123] as well as a distant agent insofar as it gives rise to Universal Soul, the immediate source of the existence and activity of the physical universe. It is Universal Soul, according to Plotinus, that in some way "engendered matter."[124] Then Universal Soul furnishes all form and life in matter.[125] As formulated in the Arabic version: "Soul emanates its power over this entire world, . . . nothing corporeal is free of the power of Soul, and each body obtains of the power and goodness of Soul in accordance with its ability to receive."[126] The first recipient of the goodness of Soul is "matter," and the "goodness" that Soul sends forth—according to the Arabic—is "form."[127] Inasmuch as matter is "solely a recipient," even the forms of the four elements must come "from another," that is, from Soul, which in turn receives its forms from Intellect.[128] In general, "each sense object obtains of the same goodness in accordance with its ability to receive."[129] Individual souls too descend upon this world from Universal Soul, with every living thing receiving as much of the power of Universal Soul as it is capable of.[130]

For Plotinus, Universal Intellect is thus a direct source of human intellectual thought as well as the model and distant cause of the existence of the entire physical universe. Universal Soul is the immediate emanating source of the matter of the universe and of all forms appearing in matter, ranging from the forms of the four elements to the human soul. Between them, Universal Intellect and Universal Soul are a direct source of human thought; they emanate all matter in the universe; they contain and emanate all forms appearing in matter; and thereby they produce the entire range of physical objects in the universe.

In al-Kindi there is no more than a suggestion of the combination of functions of the active intellect just met in Alexander and Plotinus. In one text, al-Kindi maintains that the heavens are the cause of generation and cor-

---

[122] *Theology of Aristotle* 142, paralleling *Enneades* 6.7.2.

[123] Cf. Armstrong (n. 13 above) 75.

[124] *Enneades* 1.8.14. Cf. Zeller (n. 112 above) 603-604.

[125] Cf. Zeller, *ibid.* 604.

[126] *Theology of Aristotle* 78, paralleling *Enneades* 4.8.6. Cf. Proclus, *Elements of Theology*, ed. E. Dodds, ed. 2 (Oxford 1963) Proposition 140, and Dodds's note.

[127] *Theology of Aristotle* 78, paralleling *Enneades* 4.8.6.

[128] *Risâla fî al-'Ilm al-Ilâhî* (n. 79 above) 168, paralleling Enneades 5.9.3.

[129] *Theology of Aristotle* 78-79, paralleling *Enneades* 4.8.6.

[130] *Enneades* 4.8.4; 4.9.2, with English translation of unpublished Arabic paraphrases. In Plotinus, individual souls are not completely separated from the Universal Soul; cf. Zeller (n. 112 above) 596-597; E. Brehier, *The Philosophy of Plotinus* (Chicago 1958) 66-68.

ruption in our lower world;[131] the cause of all life in this world;[132] more specifically, the "cause of [man's] being generated"; and finally "the agent of [human] reason,"[133] which presumably means that the heavens produce the potential human intellect. All the functions performed by the heavens are "assigned" to them by the creator.[134] Al-Kindi cannot mean, as Aristotle did, that the movements of the heavens are the cause of movement and generation in this world in a purely mechanical fashion,[135] for, he contends, it is insofar as they themselves possess life that the heavens "grant" (*mufīd*) life, and insofar as they are themselves rational that they "make us rational."[136] There is no attempt here by al-Kindi to connect these functions of the heavens with the function of actualizing the human intellect, assigned by him elsewhere to the "first intellect."

A different statement on the source of the human soul appears in a passage where al-Kindi describes the human soul not as coming from the heavens but as "of the substance of the creator," and as standing in the same relationship to the creator as the "light of the sun to the sun."[137] Some sort of combination of functions would result were one to venture the identification of the "creator" in this passage with the "first intellect," elsewhere described as the cause of actual thought.[138] However, that identification, though possible, was earlier shown to be unlikely.[139] At most we can safely say only that in general al-Kindi traces to higher realms such things as the actualization of the human intellect, the existence of the human rational soul, the existence of life in this world, the processes of generation and corruption. But he specifies the causes differently in different texts, assigning the actualization of the human intellect to "first intellect" and again to the "universals of things,"[140] and assigning the production of the human soul to the rational animate heavens and again to the Creator. The character of al-Kindi's writings constitute a presumption against, rather than in favor of, harmonizing his divergent statements.

D. In addition to the functions already mentioned, the theory of active intellect provided Alfarabi and Avicenna with a rationale for such religious

---

[131] *Rasā'il al-Kindī* (n. 21 above) 247.

[132] *Ibid.* 252.

[133] *Ibid.* 255.

[134] *Ibid.*

[135] Cf. Aristotle, *Metaphysics* 12.6.1071b, 9-17; *De generatione* 2.10.336a, 23ff. Cf. Alexander, *De anima* (n. 5 above) 24; *Quaestiones* 2.3; Zeller (n. 112 above) 827; Moraux (n. 43 above) 30-37.

[136] *Rasā'il al-Kindī* (n. 21 above) 252, 255.

[137] *Ibid.* 273.

[138] Above at n. 21.

[139] Above at nn. 23ff.

[140] Above at nn. 21, 30.

phenomena as human immortality, retribution, a quasi-mystical experience, prophecy, and miracles. In Greek and early Arabic philosophy we find antecedents for connecting the active intellect with two of these phenomena: human immortality and the quasi-mystical experience.[141]

One of Aristotle's enigmatic statements on intellect reads: "When separated, . . . it alone is immortal and eternal."[142] The subject of the sentence is not clear from the context, and can be either the active intellect construed as transcendent; the active intellect construed as immanent; or an actual state of the human intellect, if indeed such can be distinguished in Aristotle from the active intellect. Aristotle thus left the interpreters to their own devices.

Alexander contends that the human potential intellect is mortal since it is a faculty of the soul and when the soul perishes it too perishes. Nevertheless something in the human intellect can, according to Alexander, enjoy immortality. The key to his reasoning is Aristotle's conception of the act of thought. Actual intellect, Aristotle explained, consists in nothing but whatever thought the intellect happens to have; that is, the intellect is identical with its thought.[143] Thought originating in abstraction from physical objects, Alexander reasons, obviously cannot be self-subsistent since it exists only during the time when a given intellect is thinking it. As soon as it ceases to be the object of an intellect, a thought dependent on abstraction—as distinct from the thing from which it is abstracted—ceases to exist, and thus is shown to be subject to destruction by its very nature. But since, as Aristotle established, actual intellect consists in nothing other than its thought, actual human intellect, insofar as it consists in destructible thoughts, also is subject to destruction.[144] Consequently, immortality cannot be gained through thought abstracted from the physical realm.

However, Alexander contends, "if" besides intellectual thought abstracted from the physical realm there also exists intelligible thoughts that are actual and indestructible by virtue of themselves, and if, in addition, the human intellect can have them as its object, then insofar as the intellect is identical with something indestructible, it would also be indestructible. And, in fact, indestructible intelligible thoughts do exist according to Alexander. They are the incorporeal forms, which do not become objects of thought by being abstracted, but are such by their very nature.[145] They include, most specifically, the active intellect. Alexander contends that these incorporeal forms can become an object of human thought; and when that occurs the actual human intellect, being identical with something indestructible, is itself in-

---

[141] On miracles, cf. F. Rahman, *Prophecy in Islam* (London 1958) 45ff.
[142] *De anima* 3.5.430a, 22-23. Also cf. 408b, 29; 413a, 6; 429b, 5.
[143] Cf. n. 59 above.
[144] Alexander, *De anima* (n. 5 above) 90.
[145] *Ibid.* 87-88; *De intellectu* 108.

destructible.[146] According to the passage in *De intelletcu* stating that the active intellect is an object of human thought at the very beginning of human intellectual development,[147] an indestructible actual human thought would already exist at that early point. Immortality, Alexander insists, is restricted to the human *actual* intellect having an indestructible form as its object.[148] He explicitly denies immortality to the potential human intellect, to the "*habitus* whereby the potential human intellect thinks . . . this [incorporeal form]," and to the "intelligible concept (νόημα) qua intelligible concept."[149] There is a troublesome statement to the effect that the intellect *in habitu* can "become . . . identical" with incorporeal forms,[150] from which it would seem to follow that the intellect *in habitu* can, after all, attain immortality. However, it should be recalled, the intellect *in habitu* is not actual thought but the faculty whereby man can think at will.[151] Alexander accordingly may be taken as saying that no part of any human faculty is immortal, but when the intellect *in habitu* has an actual thought of an indestructible form, that thought alone remains immortal. The immortal actual thought in man, Alexander concludes, is the "intellect generated in us from without."[152] That is to say, the actual thought of an indestructible form does not exist independently—qua intelligible concept[153]—but only as identical with the form which is the object of thought. Thus hardly anything human and surely nothing individual can be said to characterize the human thoughts Alexander considered to be immortal. The Arabic translation, however, renders Alexander's *intellect from without* as *acquired intellect*,[154] and accordingly ascribes immortality to "the intellect that we acquire and that is generated in us";[155] in other words, the *acquired intellect* is immortal. The change in terminology entails a subtle change of emphasis, for the term *acquired intellect* suggests something human and not merely an incorporeal form that happens to be an object of human thought. And indeed, it will appear, Alfarabi states precisely that the human acquired intellect is immortal.

Incorporeal forms, Alexander further explains, do not exist merely as objects of thought; any such form must be an incorporeal intellect continually thinking itself and identical with the thought of itself.[156] If a human intellect

---

[146] Alexander, *De anima* 90.

[147] N. 52 above.

[148] Alexander, *De anima* 90 lines 14-17.

[149] *Ibid.* 91 lines 2-4.

[150] *Ibid.* 88 lines 5-6.

[151] Above at n. 39.

[152] Alexander, *De anima* 90 line 19.

[153] Cf. above at n. 149.

[154] N. 68 above.

[155] Hebrew translation of Alexander's *De anima* 90 line 19, as above, n. 72.

[156] Alexander, *De anima* (n. 5 above) 88 lines 1-2. Alexander reasons that incorporeal forms must be eternal actual objects of thought. Since the object of thought is identical

should have an incorporeal form as the object of its thought, it would become identical with the form and thus identical with the incorporeal intellect in which the form consists. In the instance where the object of the human intellect is the active intellect, it is only consistent for Alexander to state that the human intellect "becomes" the active intellect.[157] This sounds like the language of mystical experience: Since Alexander identifies the active intellect as the first cause of the universe,[158] he is saying in effect that man "becomes" the deity. The possible mystical moment in Alexander has been stressed by scholars.[159] But, it must be emphasized, union with the active intellect is understood by Alexander as a purely intellectual act, completely similar to the intellect's apprehending any other thought, and there is not the slightest suggestion of an ecstatic element in the experience.

For Themistius, too, human immortality is dependent on the active intellect. It is beyond question for Themistius that the nonrational parts of the human soul perish with the body,[160] whereas the active intellect in its transcendent aspect is an incorporeal, ever-actual being, and accordingly immortal.[161] The question of human immortality arises between these two areas and concerns the human potential intellect. The potential intellect is described by Themistius as "received"[162] by man, as "generated in us prior" to the active intellect and as a "precursor" of the active intellect.[163] The immanent aspect of the active intellect becomes "intertwined with"[164] the potential intellect, and each human "I" is a compound of potential and active intellect, the "essential me" coming from the latter.[165] The human potential intellect does attain immortality, by "sharing" the immortality of the active intellect.[166] Since, according to Themistius, the active intellect joins the human potential intellect at least by the time a man understands the first axioms of thought,[167] the human intellect presumably attains immortality from that early point. Thus for Themistius, too, human immortality is restricted to the intellect, with the rest of the soul being excluded, and immortality follows from a relationship with the active intellect. However, both that relationship and the resultant immortality are considered greater in Themistius

with the thinking subject (n. 59 above), incorporeal forms must also be eternal actual thinking subjects.

[157] *Ibid.* 89 lines 21-22.
[158] Above at n. 12.
[159] Moraux (n. 43 above) 104; Merlan (n. 43 above) 16ff.
[160] *CAG* (n. 6 above) 5.3.105, 106.
[161] *Ibid.* 99-100.
[162] *Ibid.* 104 line 14.
[163] *Ibid.* 105 line 30.
[164] *Ibid.* 98 line 22.
[165] *Ibid.* 100 lines 19, 32.
[166] *Ibid.* 104 lines 24ff.
[167] Above at n. 101.

than in Alexander. For according to Themistius, the active intellect enters the human intellect not merely as an object of thought, but as the productive factor, and what is immortal is not merely a thought identical with an incorporeal being, but the human potential intellect itself insofar as it is joined to, and perfected by the immanent active intellect.

Plotinus's statements on the immortality of the soul are not specifically pertinent to our study of Alfarabi and Avicenna, but among his statements of a mystical character at least one is of interest for us. Plotinus writes that when soul is present in the realm of Intellect it "becomes one with the object of its thought," which is Intellect, and "enters into unity with Intellect . . . [although] without being destroyed." As a result soul and intellect are "one" and yet remain "two."[168] The Arabic paraphrase here reads: "When the soul leaves this world and enters the higher world . . . it unites with [Intellect] without its essence perishing. . . . It is both intellectual thinker (ʿâqil) and intelligible thought (maʿqûl) . . . because of the intensity of its conjunction (ittiṣâl) with Intellect"; soul and Intellect are then "one thing, and two."[169] Elsewhere Plotinus advocated an ecstatic mysticism,[170] but the present passage is apparently still within the province of intellectual experience. Nevertheless the experience described by Plotinus goes far beyond the intellectual union with the active intellect described by Alexander, for the union of the soul with Universal Intellect is not here a routine intellectual act as in Alexander, but a climax in the life of the soul wherein it leaves this world and enters a higher realm of existence.

Impelled, perhaps, by the passage just quoted from Plotinus, al-Kindi also takes up the possibility of the union of the human soul with "first intellect." The human soul, he writes, becomes "actually intellectual" when it "makes contact with first intellect." At that point, "intelligible form unites with the soul . . . [and] *it and the intellect* are identical."[171] The italicized words are ambiguous, but the context shows the meaning to be that in the act of intellectual thought soul and first intellect become "identical." Al-Kindi qualifies the state of identity of soul and intellect through the following distinction: "Soul is both intellectual thinker (ʿâqil) and intelligible thought (maʿqûl). Consequently, intellect (ʿaql) and intelligible thought are identical from the viewpoint of the soul, whereas the intellect which is eternally actual . . . is not identical with what thinks it intellectually (ʿâqiluhu)." In an attempt to clarify this obscure statement, a marginal gloss or manuscript variant adds: "Thus from the viewpoint of first intellect, the intelligible

---

[168] *Enneades* (n. 9 above) 4.4.2.

[169] *Theology of Aristotle* (n. 84 above) 21.

[170] Cf. Zeller (n. 112 above) 666-671. Merlan (n. 43 above) 79-82 finds an ecstatic element even in union with Universal Intellect.

[171] *Rasâʾil al-Kindî* (n. 21 above) 356.

thought in the soul is not identical with first intellect."[172] Al-Kindi apparently means that whenever the rational soul thinks—and not merely at the climax of the development of the human soul—it has "intelligible form" as the object of its thought and becomes identical with intelligible form. But intelligible form is the same as—or part of—first intellect and thus the human soul can legitimately be described as having become "identical" with first intellect. Nevertheless, al-Kindi insists, the identity of soul and first intellect is acceptable only from the viewpoint of the soul, whereas from the viewpoint of first intellect, they remain distinct; this amounts to saying that soul and intellect are one yet remain two. Al-Kindi's statements thus are similar to those of Plotinus, sufficiently so for us to conjecture that he may have had the text of Plotinus in mind.

A most extreme statement of union with the supernal intellect appears in the treatise *On the Soul* attributed to Porphyry. Here it is insisted that the real man is intellect, and when the human intellect exists apart from the body and is present in the higher world, it is completely identical with first intellect.[173] The text distinguishes this complete identity from a lesser degree of union that fails to represent the situation of the human intellect in the upper world: the union of a thing with its form. The distinction is brought out through considering an analogy used in the Arabic paraphrase of Plotinus. There the soul had been compared to the air: Just as the air is the place occupied by the radiance of the sun, so the pure soul is a place occupied by the radiance of Intellect.[174] Seemingly in reaction to that analogy, the Porphyry text insists that the human intellect does not "unite with its form" in a manner similar to the "union of air with radiance"; the union is "purer."[175] That is to say, the human intellect does not combine with first intellect as something distinct, but rather becomes completely identical with first intellect.

Here we have seen that for both Alexander and Themistius, immortality is a result of a certain relationship between the human intellect and the active intellect: either having the active intellect as an object of human thought or having the active intellect "intertwined" with the human intellect. Alexander—and even Themistius—describes the relationship in language suggestive of a union of the human intellect with the divine active intellect. Plotinus makes something more of his version of the same intellectual experience, explicitly calling it union or conjunction, yet insisting that the soul does not thereby lose its identity. Al-Kindi, too, recognizes a union of the human intellect with "first intellect" and also insists that this union falls short of complete identification with the first intellect, at least from

---

[172] *Ibid.* 356-357.
[173] Kutsch (n. 26 above) 268, § 4.
[174] *Risâla fî al-'Ilm al-Ilâhî* (n. 79 above) 174, paralleling *Enneades* (n. 9 above) 5.3.9.
[175] As in n. 173.

the "viewpoint" of the latter. The text attributed to Porphyry, in contrast, insists that when the human intellect is united with first intellect, their identification is complete.

II. ALFARABI ON THE ACTIVE INTELLECT

Our discussion will be concerned primarily with four of Alfarabi's works containing more or less full discussions of the active intellect: *al-Madîna al-Fâḍila* and *al-Siyâsât al-Madaniyya*, which will be treated as representing one view, a work entitled *The Philosophy of Aristotle*, which suggests a second view, and the *Risâla fî al-ʿAql*, which represents yet another view.[176] Several works attributed to Alfarabi but containing views similar to Avicenna's are best omitted from our discussion since their authorship is doubtful.

A. *Al-Madîna al-Fâḍila* and *al-Siyâsât al-Madaniyya*. The universe as conceived by Alfarabi may be said to be constructed of bricks taken from Aristotle and mortar from Neoplatonic philosophy. Aristotle pictured the universe as consisting of a series of celestial spheres continually revolving around a stationary earth; and he inferred that those unceasing movements must depend on an incorporeal mover, that in fact very separate circular movement distinguishable within the heavens must have its own incorporeal mover, and that since the movements of all the heavenly bodies imply a total of fifty-five spheres and subspheres, the total number of incorporeal movers is "in all probability also fifty-five."[177] Both Alfarabi and Avicenna present a picture in which the number of spheres and movers is reduced to nine by ignoring the subspheres—epicyclical or eccentric—that medieval astronomy assumed in order to explain the full complexity of celestial motion. A slightly different reduction is known from Alexander.[178] The nine incorporeal movers, or intelligences as they are called in the Middle Ages, are the beings that move: the outer, diurnal sphere, which causes the daily motions of the heavens; the sphere of the fixed stars; and the seven planetary spheres, that is, the spheres containing the five planets known at the time, the sun, and the moon.[179]

Aristotle did not recognize any causal relationship in what might be called the vertical plane, that is, within the series of incorporeal movers; and in

---

[176] Cf. S. Pines, "Ibn Sina et l'auteur de la Risalat al-Fusus fi'l-Hikma," *Revue des études islamiques* 19 (1951) 121-124; Rahman (n. 141 above) 21. Their remarks apply to other works attributed to Alfarabi that are printed in the Hyderabad editions.

[177] *Metaphysics* 12.8.

[178] Zeller (n. 112 above) 827-828.

[179] *Al-Madîna al-Fâḍila* ed. F. Dieterici (Leiden 1895) 19; German translation by Dieterici, entitled *Der Musterstaat* (Leiden 1900), with indication of the pages of the original Arabic.

the horizontal plane, that is, from intelligence to corresponding sphere, he recognized only causality in motion, not in existence.[180] As the scheme reappears in Alfarabi, causal connections that were absent in Aristotle are supplied by the Neoplatonic doctrine of emanation. The deity standing at the head of the universe is conceived as the eternal emanating cause of the existence of the first intelligence. The first intelligence, in turn, is the eternal emanating cause of the existence of the second intelligence, the eternal emanating cause of the existence of the first sphere, and the eternal cause of the motion of that sphere. The second intelligence is similarly the cause of the third intelligence and of the existence and motion of the second sphere, with the process continuing down to the ninth intelligence which emanates and causes the motion of the ninth sphere, the sphere of the moon.[181] The Neoplatonic element in this account is not restricted to the general recognition of causal connections between the entities through a process of emanation. The grand Plotinian emanation scheme of: (a) One—(b) Intellect (νοῦς, ʿaql)—(c) Soul—(d) Material universe is reflected here at every step of the process. For (a) the deity, called by Alfarabi "the First," emanates (b) the first intelligence (νοῦς, ʿaql),[182] which in turn emanates (c) the soul[183] and (d) the body of the first sphere. The first intelligence initiates a similar series by emanating the second intelligence which in turn emanates the soul and body of the second sphere; and so forth.

Aristotle had no place for an incorporeal mover of the lower, sublunar world, since he recognized causality only in the realm of the motion of the universe, and the sublunar world in Aristotle's universe does not move as a whole. In the new scheme, however, since each intelligence is a cause of the existence of a further intelligence like itself, the ninth intelligence might be expected to emanate a tenth, which in turn would have characteristics similar to the intelligences above it. The scheme is in fact extended in that way by Alfarabi, who maintains that the ninth intelligence, which governs the sphere of the moon, emanates a tenth intelligence, identified by Alfarabi precisely with the active intellect of Aristotle's *De anima* Bk. 3.[184] Aristotle's active intellect is thus construed as a transcendent entity with a definite position in the overall structure of the universe. It is an added member to the series of celestial intelligences and a link between them and the sublunar world. None of the Greek commentators suggested just this identification of the active intellect, although several, as was seen, do offer transcendent interpretations, the closest being an anonymous view cited by Philoponus,

---

[180] Cf. Zeller (n. 59 above) 368ff.

[181] Cf. n. 179 above.

[182] It will be recalled that Arabic does not distinguish between *intellect* and *intelligence*.

[183] Alfarabi, unlike Avicenna, does not distinguish two phases in the emanation of the soul and body of the celestial spheres.

[184] *Mâdina* (n. 179 above) 19, 45; *al-Siyâsât al-Madaniyya*, ed. F. Najjar (Beirut 1964) 32.

according to which the active intellect is an "intellect inferior to [the Deity], positioned close to our [intellect]."[185] There are in all four features in the scheme of incorporeal intelligences that appear for the first time in Alfarabi. The number of celestial spheres and the intelligences governing them is now canonized at nine; each intelligence is deemed the cause of the existence of the succeeding intelligence and of its own sphere; to the series of incorporeal intelligences governing the celestial spheres, a tenth intellect-intelligence is now added; and the tenth intelligence is identified with the active intellect, whose existence had been inferred by Aristotle in *De anima* Bk. 3, as the cause of the actualization of the potential human intellect.

Each celestial intelligence, as already seen, emanates a celestial sphere consisting of a body and what Alfarabi once calls the soul of the sphere, and another time the intellect of the sphere;[186] in addition, the intelligence emanates the next intelligence in the series. The symmetry of the scheme leading to the assumption of a tenth intelligence might have been expected to lead Alfarabi to assign it functions analogous to all three functions performed by the other intelligences. He would then have construed the tenth intelligence or active intellect as the emanating cause of a body, soul, and intelligence, which could appropriately be the body of the sublunar world, and the souls and intellects existing in the world. For reasons about which we can only speculate, Alfarabi's *al-Madîna al-Fâḍila* and *al-Siyâsât al-Madaniyya* assign the active intellect only the function of actualizing the human intellect, whereas his *Risâla fî al-ʿAql* adds the function of emanating the natural forms of the sublunar world, including animal souls and the human soul with its potential human intellect. Only in Avicenna does the scheme appear in a completely consistent and symmetrical form, with the active intellect emanating the matter of the sublunar world as well as all natural forms, soul, and intellect in the world.

According to *al-Madîna al-Fâḍila* and *al-Siyâsât al-Madaniyya*, the heavens, not the active intellect, produce the body of the sublunar world and bring about the appearance of souls in this world, including the human soul with its potential intellect. The active intellect is responsible only for leading the potential human intellect to actuality, the same function it was assigned by Aristotle. The sublunar world, Alfarabi observes, contains features that are unchanging as well as those that vary, and both, he asserts, come from the heavens. Common to the entire sublunar world is an underlying, identical "prime matter." This Alfarabi describes as a necessary and eternal product (*yalzam*) of the "power" or "nature" communicated by the outer sphere to the spheres beneath it, causing the heavens to perform their daily motion from east to west. The uniform nature or power communicated by the outer

---

[185] Above at n. 18.
[186] Cf. *Siyâsât* (n. 184 above) 33–34, 53.

celestial spheres expresses itself—in an unexplained way—at the lowest stage of the universe by producing the matter of the sublunar world. Given their common prime matter, bodies in the sublunar world differ in their substances, and that difference, Alfarabi continues, in some way, "proceeds necessarily" from the difference in "substances" within the heavens. In addition, bodies in our world change, and their changes are explained as due to the movements of the heavens, the variations in the relative positions of the heavenly bodies, and other celestial changes. In sum, the source of all levels of existence in our world—mineral, plant, animal, and man—is the powers continually descending from the celestial region and their interactions with forces within the lower world, those forces themselves being ultimately dependent on powers descending from the heavens. Alfarabi states explicitly that even the generation of man is due to the interaction of celestial and natural forces, the active intellect having no part in it.[187] It is good Aristotelianism to understand the heavens to be the cause of generation and corruption in the lower world, and Aristotle even distinguished the effect of the uniform motion of the heavens from the effect of their variable motions.[188] No known source, however, describes the heavens as emanating the matter of this world.[189] Alfarabi not only advocates that doctrine here, but in other works assumes it to be the position of Aristotle's *De caelo*[190] and his *De generatione.*[191]

After the heavenly bodies have gone as far as they can by producing the highest grade of being that they are capable of, it becomes the task of the active intellect to complete the perfection of the sublunar world by leading the human intellect from potentiality to actuality.[192] In an abbreviation of the standard argument for the existence of the active intellect, more fully stated by Alfarabi elsewhere,[193] *al-Madîna al-Fâḍila* contends that the human potentiality for thought "cannot become actual intellect by itself"; it needs "an incorporeal actual intellect" to "cause it to pass from potentiality to actuality."[194] For this reason the forces descending from the heavens cannot bring about the final stage in the perfection of the sublunar world, and the existence of the active intellect must be assumed.[195] The active intellect "surveys" the efforts of the heavens, and whenever something in the sublunar world

[187] *Madîna* (n. 179 above) 27-29; *Siyâsât* (n. 184 above) 55ff.

[188] Cf. n. 135 above.

[189] It is perhaps implied in the material cited by Altmann + Stern (n. 24 above) 167-169.

[190] Alfarabi, *Philosophy of Aristotle*, ed. M. Mahdi (Beirut 1961) 99; English translation by Mahdi in *Alfarabi's Philosophy of Plato and Aristotle* (Glencoe 1962) 71ff., with pages of the original Arabic indicated.

[191] *Risâla fî al-ʿAql* (n. 109 above) 34.

[192] *Siyâsât* (n. 184 above) 71.

[193] *Philosophy of Aristotle* (n. 190 above) 127.

[194] *Madîna* (n. 179 above) 44; cf. above at nn. 35, 36, 40, 41, 79, 104.

[195] As far as I could see, Alfarabi does not explain why the ninth intelligence cannot perform this function.

has "to a certain degree attained perfection and separation from matter, [the active intellect] purifies it from matter . . . so that thing arrives at a degree close to the active intellect."[196]   In simpler words, once the forces of nature succeed in producing a member of the human species, it becomes the task of the active intellect to perfect the man's intellect.   In doing so, the active intellect exercises "providence" over man.[197]

The familiar metaphor of light is employed to explain the manner in which the active intellect operates.   The sun, Alfarabi writes, emits a light (*ḍaw'*) that does four things: It turns potential vision into actual sight; it makes potentially visible colors actually visible; it itself becomes visible to the eye; and it makes the sun visible to the eye.   Analogously—in the version of *al-Madîna al-Fâḍila*—the active intellect sends forth "something" similar to light which it imprints in the material intellect.   This "something" turns the material intellect into actual intellect, transforms potentially intelligible thoughts into actually intelligible thoughts, is itself known by the human intellect, and makes the active intellect known to the human intellect.[198]   There seem to be several echoes of Themistius here.   Themistius, it will be recalled, compared the transcendent active intellect to the sun, and the immanent aspect of the active intellect to the light emitted by the sun;[199] that distinction is paralleled by Alfarabi's distinction between the active intellect and the "something" it imprints on the material intellect.   Themistius also used the analogy of light to explain the operation of the intellect in actualizing both the potential intellect and potentially intelligible thoughts.[200]   Not Themistius, however, but Alexander used the analogy of light to establish the active intellect itself as an object of human thought.[201]

When the "something" analogous to light arrives in the human rational faculty, Alfarabi explains, a change takes place in the sense perceptions stored in the imaginative faculty,[202] those sense perceptions becoming "intelligible thoughts in the rational faculty."   The result is "the first intelligibles common to all men, such as [the principles] that the whole is greater than the part, and magnitudes equal to a single thing are equal to one another."[203]   For Themistius too, it will be recalled, the active intellect is the source of the first axioms of thought,[204] a similar view appeared in Plotinus,[205] and

[196] *Siyâsât* (n. 184 above) 55.

[197] *Ibid.* 32.

[198] *Madîna* (n. 179 above) 44-45; cf *Siyâsât* (n. 184 above) 35; nn. 14, 53, 54, 102 above.

[199] Above at n. 97.

[200] Above at n. 102.

[201] Above at n. 54.

[202] Cf. above at n. 102, and Aristotle, *De anima* 3.7.431b, 2.

[203] *Madîna* (n. 179 above) 45; cf. *Siyâsât* (n. 184 above) 71-72.

[204] Above at n. 101.

[205] Above at n. 82.

one passage in Alexander can plausibly be interpreted in the same way.[206]
The first intelligibles provided by the active intellect are to be understood
in a wide sense for, according to *al-Madîna al-Fâḍila*, they contain three
classes: "the principles of scientific geometry"; "the principles whereby one
can understand the noble and base in areas where man is to act"; "the principles used for learning about the states of . . . the primary existent things
and their degrees, for example, about the heavens, the first cause, the other
primary beings, and what . . . is generated from those primary beings."[207]
In other words, the emission from the active intellect transforms sensations in
the imaginative faculty of the soul into the principles of mathematical science,
the principles of the practical reason, and the principles of physics and metaphysics. Surprisingly, Alfarabi does not mention a class of logical principles.

The division of labor between the active intellect and man is drawn clearly
enough in *al-Madîna al-Fâḍila*: The active intellect produces the "first
intelligibles," and man "uses" them to construct a body of knowledge by
his own efforts, thereby attaining human perfection. This division of labor
is spelled out even more explicitly in the parallel account in *al-Siyâsât al-
Madaniyya*. There Alfarabi explains that the active intellect performs its
task in a way similar to that in which the heavens perform theirs. The heavens
do not perfect all parts of the sublunar world directly and by themselves.
Rather, things in the world are set in motion by powers descending from above
and these things operate on one another until they reach successively higher
levels of existence, through an interaction of their own efforts with the continually descending celestial powers.[208] Similarly, the active intellect does
not complete the perfection of the human intellect by itself. It rather initiates
the development of the human intellect and at later stages also contributes
necessary knowledge. The active intellect "first gives man a power or principle whereby he strives or can strive, by himself, towards whatever perfections
remain for him; this principle consists in the first notions (*ʿulûm*) and first
intelligibles that arrive in the rational part of the soul." A few lines later
Alfarabi reiterates that the "first items of knowledge (*maʿârif*) . . . arrive in
the rational part [of the soul] from the active intellect." Men differ in their
inborn ability "to receive" the common first intelligibles, ranging from those
who are unable to receive any, to those of sound innate ability who can receive all. Through the common intelligibles that all sound men do receive,
they "strive towards common matters and acts," presumably towards universal logical and ethical knowledge. Not only does the active intellect provide these initial "common" intelligibles, it subsequently provides "special"
intelligibles as well. Certain men have "special" (*khâṣṣ*) innate abilities to

---

[206] Above at n. 54.
[207] *Madîna* (n. 179 above) 45.
[208] *Siyâsât* (n. 184 above) 60ff.

receive "special" intelligibles, "whereby they strive" towards one or another "genus" of knowledge, and those special intelligibles, which are the principles of the several sciences, also come from the active intellect. Alfarabi adds a series of distinctions regarding the number of intelligibles different men are able to receive in each "genus," the differing innate abilities men have for using the principles of science, variations in the rapidity with which men draw inferences from the principles they are given, and variations in their ability to teach others. It is perfectly clear throughout that the active intellect first "gives" man the common principles of thought, subsequently gives ce tain men the principles of the individual sciences, and in each instance the individual man, "by himself," uses the principles received from the active intellect in order to "discover whatever can be apprehended by discovery (istinbât) in a given genus [of knowledge]."[209] Unlike al-Madîna al-Fâḍila, this account does not state that the emission from the active intellect transforms sense perceptions into the principles of thought; it simply states that the active intellect "gives" those principles. The discrepancy is small, however. The two accounts harmonize fairly well if, it is understood, the three classes of principles distinguished in al-Madîna al-Fâḍila are not given to man all at once, but the principles of physics and metaphysics, at least, are received only by a small number of men and only after they have received and developed more elementary intelligibles.

The body of knowledge constructed by man with the aid of the principles of thought and science contains deductions from those principles,[210] knowledge of the essences of things in the physical world, and knowledge of incorporeal beings. Like Alexander, Alfarabi distinguishes (a) incorporeal beings, which by their nature are actual intellect and actually intelligible, from (b) corporeal beings like "rocks and plants," which are only potentially intelligible.[211] By bringing about the passage of the human intellect from potentiality to actuality, the active intellect makes it possible for the human intellect to have both types as objects of its thought.[212] This presumably means that the human intellect obtains abstract concepts of things in the sublunar world with the aid of the tools provided by the active intellect, and it obtains thought of incorporeal beings, including the active intellect itself,[213] at the culmination of the intellectual development initiated by the active intellect. Thus the emission from the active intellect would be the immediate cause only of the principles of thought and science, but, in addition, would be the distant cause enabling the human intellect to have abstract concepts, in-

---

[209] Ibid. 71-72, 74-75.
[210] On the deductive character of science, cf. Philosophy of Aristotle (n. 190 above) 105. On the first principles of science, cf. 91-92, 127-128.
[211] Madîna (n. 179 above) 43; cf. above at n. 45.
[212] Madîna 44.
[213] Above at n. 198.

corporeal beings, and the active intellect, as objects of its thought. According to *al-Madîna al-Fâḍila*, it will be recalled, even the lightlike emission from the active intellect becomes an object of thought for the human intellect. Alfarabi does not explain how that occurs, and the statement is omitted in the parallel account in *al-Siyâsât al-Madaniyya*.

Not only does the active intellect provide the principles of human thought and human science, it also enters an especially close relationship with the culminating stage of the human intellect. Alfarabi distinguishes three stages of human intellect: (a) the human "disposition" for thought, also called "rational faculty," "material intellect," and "passive intellect";[214] (b) "actual intellect" also called "actual passive intellect"; (c) "acquired intellect."[215] The stage of acquired intellect is attained whenever a man "perfects his intellect with all intelligible thoughts."[216] When working out the comparison of the active intellect with the sun, Alfarabi described the faculty of vision as "acquiring" light from the sun.[217] By analogy, he could describe the light-like "something" imprinted in the human intellect as *acquired* from the active intellect. At most, however, the analogy would only justify his applying the term acquired intellect to human intellect consisting in knowledge of the principles of thought and science. It does not explain the usage of the term acquired intellect for the highest stage of intellect reached by the gifted man who, through his own efforts, develops the principles of thought into a knowledge of all human science. Alfarabi does not, in fact, explain why the highest grade of intellect should be called acquired intellect. His usage of the term, it should be noted, is quite different from the usage in the Arabic translation of Alexander and in Plotinus.[218]

Each stage of human intellect is described as serving as the "matter" of the succeeding level, and when the succeeding level does arrive, the two become "as one thing in the way that a compound of matter and form is one thing." When the stage of acquired intellect is finally reached and becomes the form of the prior stages, it in turn serves as matter for the active intellect, which—apparently immediately—joins the acquired intellect as its form.[219] Similar formulations were met in Alexander,[220] Plotinus,[221] and par-

---

[214] On the human *disposition* for thought, see above at n. 38. For *material* intellect, see above at n. 37. For the term *passive* intellect, see Aristotle, *De anima* 3.5.430a, 24-25; Themistius, *CAG* (n. 6 above) 5.3.101, 107; Simplicius, *CAG* 10 (Berlin 1882) 219.

[215] *Madîna* (n. 179 above) 58.

[216] *Ibid.* 57-58. In the *Risâla fî al-ʿAql* (n. 109 above), Alfarabi writes that at the stage of acquired intellect, man has "all" or "most" possible thoughts; below at n. 279.

[217] *Madîna* (n. 179 above) 44; *Siyâsât* (n. 184 above) 35.

[218] Above at nn. 68, 91.

[219] *Madîna* 58; *Siyâsât* 79.

[220] Above at nn. 58, 60.

[221] Above at n. 84.

ticularly Themistius, who described each successive level of the soul as the form of the prior.[222] None of those philosophers, however, presented a theory wherein the perfection of the human intellect consists in the active intellect's joining the highest stage of human intellect as its form.

Alfarabi describes the relationship of the active intellect to the acquired intellect in various ways: The active intellect serves as the form of the acquired intellect, it "enters" (*ḥalla*) the human subject possessing an acquired intellect, it sends forth an "emanation" on the human subject, rendering him a "philosopher and man of practical wisdom." The human soul thereby becomes "united" (*muttaḥid*) and "conjoined" (*ittaṣala*) with the active intellect, a description Alfarabi supports with the remark that "conjunction with the active intellect . . . was mentioned in the *De anima*."[223] The human acquired intellect is also described by Alfarabi as "reaching the degree" of the active intellect, or more precisely as being at the "closest degree" to the active intellect;[224] the latter description is intended as the more precise, since even when the human intellect reaches its highest level, "its degree is below that of the active intellect."[225] The terms *union* and *conjunction*, together with the denial that they imply actual identification with the transcendent intellect have been met in the Arabic paraphrase of Plotinus,[226] a work Alfarabi employed as a genuine work of Aristotle;[227] the denial of an actual identification of the human intellect with transcendent intellect has also been met in al-Kindi.[228] Alfarabi's statements on the union of the acquired intellect with the active intellect reveal not the slightest suggestion of an ecstatic or truly mystical experience.

At the stage of acquired intellect the human intellect becomes "similar to the incorporeal beings," for it is "free of matter," can "dispense with matter," and no longer "requires matter for its existence." Since immortality is simply the ability to exist independently of the body, immortality is thus a concomitant of the stage of acquired intellect. The acquired intellect enters the state of immateriality even before the body dies and "remains in that state perpetually," therein enjoying "supreme happiness."[229] It remains unclear whether immortality and the other attributes belong to acquired intellect as such, or whether they are due to its conjunction with the active intellect.

[222] Above at n. 103.

[223] *Madîna* 58-59; *Siyâsât* 79. On the man of practical wisdom, cf. Aristotle, *Nicomachean Ethics* 6.5; Alfarabi, *Fuṣûl al-Madanî*, ed. D. Dunlop (Cambridge 1961) § 36.

[224] *Siyâsât* (n. 184 above) 32, 35, 55.

[225] *Madîna* (n. 179 above) 46.

[226] Above at nn. 168, 169.

[227] *Alfarabi's Philosophische Abhandlungen*, ed. F. Dieterici (Leiden 1890) 31.

[228] Above at n. 172.

[229] *Madîna* (n. 179 above) 46, 64; *Siyâsât* (n. 184 above) 32, 35.

In any case, immortality is achieved before death, but only after man reaches the stage of acquired intellect.

Alfarabi generally is careful to speak of the human soul rather than merely the human intellect as immortal. He also explains that disembodied souls do not lose their individuality; they remain differentiated from one another since "dispositions for [receiving] souls follow the constitutions (mizâjât) of bodies,"[230] and once bodies differ, the souls following from them also differ. As additional souls enter the disembodied state, "each becomes conjoined with those similar in species, quantity and quality." The more souls enter a given group, the greater the pleasure of each, since each soul "has intellectual thought of itself and of [the souls that are] similar to itself, many times over."[231] There is undoubtedly some dissimulation on Alfarabi's part here. In a context not primarily concerned with immortality, he remarks that at its state of perfection the rational faculty separates from the other parts of the soul.[232] Thus not only is immortality a result of reaching the stage of acquired intellect, but in its state of immortality the acquired intellect leaves behind all other parts of the soul so that immortality is an affair of intellect exclusively. Nor would there seem to be any way disembodied acquired intellects can be differentiated from one another. Even when Alfarabi bases the differentiation of disembodied souls on their prior attachment to bodies, he insists almost in the same breath that disembodied souls are free of "all accidents affecting bodies insofar as they are bodies," and of every description of "body qua body" that might have been applicable to an embodied soul.[233] It is inconceivable that he had in mind some attribute of body that does *not* belong to body "qua body" and consequently remains applicable and differentiates souls—or, more accurately, acquired intellects—after death. For acquired intellects, which alone are immortal, consist in nothing except their thought, and they all, according to Alfarabi, have the same thought;[234] they could hardly be differentiated since incorporeal beings, it was understood, can be differentiated only if they differ in their essences,[235] and here we find immortal acquired intellects all with the same thought and the same essence. Apparently, therefore, Alfarabi accepted immortality only of the human acquired intellect with no differentiation between individual immortal acquired intellects, and his statements on the immortality of differentiated

---

[230] Cf. above at n. 117.
[231] *Madîna* 64-65; cf. *Siyâsât* 82.
[232] *Siyâsât* 42.
[233] *Madîna* 64.
[234] Above at n. 216.
[235] Cf. H. Wolfson, *Crescas' Critique of Aristotle* (Cambridge 1929) 665-666.

human souls were only intended to veil his real views from conservative religious readers.[236]

Human immortality thus results from the human intellect's being provided with the "first intelligibles" by the active intellect and then ultimately becoming an incorporeal substance conjoined with, yet inferior to the active intellect. Alexander and Themistius too ascribed a function to the active intellect in human immortality,[237] and in the Arabic translation of Alexander precisely the human acquired intellect is immortal.[238] Although the formulas are similar, however, the theories of immortality in those writers are quite different from Alfarabi's theory.[239] Alfarabi, though, does stand in the tradition of Aristotle, Alexander, and Themistius insofar as he restricts immortality to the human intellect, excluding the rest of the human soul.[240]

Until now the active intellect has been considered as operating only on the human intellect. There are, according to *al-Madîna al-Fâḍila*, also instances wherein the active intellect acts on the human imaginative faculty, thereby producing the phenomenon of prophecy. The imagination, Alfarabi explains, is the faculty of the soul standing immediately below, and serving the rational faculty. It is located in the heart, preserves sensations when the object of sensation is no longer present, and it separates and combines sensations in new ways,[241] thereby framing "figurative images" (*maḥâkât*). Dreams occur when the body is asleep and the imagination is not busy receiving sensations from the senses or supplying images to the intellect. Left to its own devices the imagination separates and recombines sensations at its pleasure, thereby producing the figurative images that constitute dreams. The condition of the body at the time may give the imagination direction; if, for example, there happens to be a preponderance of wetness in the body, the imagination may be led to frame a dream concerning water or swimming.[242]

Alfarabi recognizes two levels of prophets, the prophecy of each being constituted by an influence from the active intellect upon the imaginative faculty. The lower of the two levels is represented by men who have not

---

[236] Cf. S. Munk, *Mélanges de philosophie juive et arabe* (Paris 1857) 347; Rahman (n. 141 above) 23.

[237] Cf. above at nn. 152, 153, 166.

[238] Cf. above at n. 155.

[239] For Alexander, only the thought of the active intellect is immortal. For Themistius, the human intellect combines with the active intellect from the beginning of human intellectual activity, and from that point it is immortal.

[240] To the references in nn. 237 and 238, add n. 142 above.

[241] Cf. Aristotle, *De anima* 3.3.428a, 11; *Metaphysics* 9.10.1051b 1-5; Zeller (n. 59 above) 545-549.

[242] *Madîna* (n. 179 above) 35, 47-48. Related material is cited by Rahman (n. 141 above) 71 n. 22.

perfected their intellect, yet receive the influence of the active intellect in their imaginative faculty; the higher level is represented by men who have already reached the ultimate stage of acquired intellect and then receive a similar influence from the active intellect. The two levels thus parallel the two ways in which the active intellect plays a role in human intellectual development: as the initiator and as the culmination of that development. At both levels, the emanation from the active intellect gives the human imagination knowledge in two areas: knowledge of theoretical truths and future events.

Alfarabi describes prophecy at the lower level—the description in general also applying to the higher level—as follows: Since the imaginative faculty occupies, as it were, a position adjoining the human theoretical and practical reason, when the human reason receives the lightlike emission from the active intellect, it[243] "may emanate some of that [emission] on the imaginative faculty." As a result, the active intellect exercises an "action" on the imaginative faculty, with either a theoretical or practical effect, giving the imagination: (a) knowledge of intellectual truths that properly belong to the theoretical reason, or (b) knowledge of particular present and future events of the type properly falling within the ken of the practical reason. When theoretical knowledge is what the imaginative faculty receives through the influence of the active intellect, that knowledge must be recast since the imagination is a physical faculty capable of receiving only physical forms; the imagination recasts theoretical knowledge in figurative images appropriate to itself, thereby giving rise to "visions (kahânât) of divine matters." The other area of inspired knowledge through the imaginative faculty is described rather vaguely as knowledge of "particular sensibles" of the sort that the practical reason "performs by deliberation" (rawiyya).[244] The context, however, shows that the imagination is here assigned the function of predicting events. Unlike intelligible thoughts coming to the imagination, which, as was just seen, must be recast into a figurative form, information about particular present and future events already comes to the imagination as sensible images. Therefore, Alfarabi writes, the imagination is capable of receiving those images as they are, although it sometimes does recast them too into other figurative images. In either case, the result is a true dream or vision concerning practical matters; in the second case the dream or vision requires interpretation.[245]

Alfarabi does not explain just how the imagination acquires its knowledge of future events with the aid of the active intellect except for stating that

---

[243] The subject and structure of the sentence is ambiguous.
[244] *Madîna* 50-51.
[245] *Madîna* 51.

this knowledge is of the type the practical reason "performs by deliberation."[246] Deliberation generally was understood to be concerned with setting goals and planning the steps to achieve them.[247] Since every event is caused by a concatenation of prior events, the practical intellect starts with a desired future event, deliberates back from that event, seeking the series of causal steps necessary to bring it about, and finally determines the first step to be taken. In a similar but inverse way, Alfarabi seems to understand, deliberation can proceed forward from present circumstances through the ensuing series of causal steps to the prediction of events that will ultimately result. In prophecy the imagination makes such predictions, "without the mediacy of delibertation," that is to say, without laborious step-by-step reasoning. What makes prediction possible through the imaginative faculty is an "action" of the active intellect, and Alfarabi even describes the imagination as "receiving" knowledge of particular events from the active intellect.[248] Yet he could not consistently have held that the active intellect itself has knowledge of particular objects or events as such, since he accepted the Aristotelian epistomology, which excludes knowledge of particulars by any intellect.[249] The key to his view is perhaps to be found in a difficult statement in *al-Madîna al-Fâḍila*. The imagination, according to that statement, has knowledge of particular events "without the mediacy of deliberation, and consequently it [apparently: knowledge] results in these matters only after it has already been discovered through deliberation."[250] If the text is not corrupt, Alfarabi is saying that the imagination predicts future events only after a normal process of deliberation has drawn the necessary inferences. Thus the imagination would not really receive knowledge of particular events from the active intellect; rather the "action" of the active intellect, which comes to the imagination through the mediacy of the theoretical and practical reason,[251] gives the imagination inferences already drawn by the practical reason. This explanation obviously detracts a good deal from the value of prophecy.[252]

According to Alfarabi the imagination generally has access to the two areas of knowledge just discussed—knowledge of theoretical truths and of particular events—when the human subject is asleep, but there are rare instances where knowledge comes to the imagination when awake. In those

---

[246] *Ibid.*

[247] Aristotle, *Nicomachean Ethics* 6.5; Alfarabi (n. 223 above) §§ 6 (end), 35, 36; Zeller (n. 59 above) 651 n.

[248] *Madîna* (n. 179 above) 51.

[249] Zeller (n. 59 above) 210, 568.

[250] *Madîna* 51.

[251] See the beginning of the previous paragraph.

[252] In *Fuṣûl al-Madanî* (n. 223 above) § 89, Alfarabi makes it clear that this level of prophecy has little value.

instances, the imagination projects its vision of intellectual and particular matters out through the faculty of vision into the external world, and the subject then perceives them as if they were outside him. The result is "prophecy in divine matters," constituting "the most perfect degree to which the imaginative faculty can reach."[253]

Prophecy according to the foregoing account is accessible to anyone possessing a sufficiently strong imaginative faculty. A second, higher level of prophet, who enjoys what Alfarabi terms "revelation" (waḥy), is found exclusively among men who have passed through all the stages of human intellectual development, reached the level of "acquired intellect," and had the active intellect "enter" them.[254] At that point, the human soul is vouchsafed an emanation from the active intellect, the ultimate source of which, Alfarabi adds for the benefit of traditional readers, is the deity. The emanation enters the human intellect, rendering the recipient a "philosopher and man of practical wisdom,"[255] and then, should the imaginative faculty be properly prepared, the emanation descends to that faculty as well, rendering the recipient a "prophet and warner of future events"; that is to say, it gives his imagination the gift of predicting the future.[256] The other area of knowledge provided by prophecy is an imaginative depiction of theoretical truth, but the man who has reached the level of acquired intellect does not need prophecy to learn theoretical truths since he already has that knowledge in a purer form. Nevertheless the prophet at the stage of acquired intellect may employ the figurative depiction of theoretical truth for pedagogical ends. If he has certain specified gifts of leadership, he becomes a combination of prophet and philosopher-king, the only person qualified to govern the virtuous state. It is important for the philosopher-king to be able to reproduce the truths of metaphysics in a figurative form appropriate for the less intellectual members of his society, and this he can do through his inspired imagination. Most notably, the inspired imagination of the prophet frames the anthropomorphic descriptions of spiritual beings found in Scripture.[257]

To summarize: In the two works under consideration, Alfarabi identifies the active intellect of Aristotle's *De anima* as the last link in the series of ten incorporeal intelligences, with responsibilities only in the sublunar world. Its responsibilities, however, are limited. The heavens produce the matter of our world and the forces necessary for the generation of all natural sublunar beings including man, whereas the active intellect plays its providential role only in perfecting the human intellect. As a first step, the active in-

[253] *Madîna* 51-52.
[254] See above at n. 223.
[255] *Ibid.*
[256] *Madîna* (n. 179 above) 58-59; cf. *Siyâsât* (n. 184 above) 79-80.
[257] *Madîna* 58-59, 70; *Siyâsât* 85; cf. *Taḥṣîl al-Saʿâda* (Hyderabad 1927) 38, 44.

tellect radiates something analogous to light that provides the human intellect with the common principles of human knowledge and the principles
of the several human sciences.   Human intellectual perfection, consisting
in the possession of all possible intellectual knowledge, is reached through
human effort, which employs the principles provided by the active intellect.
At the final stage of perfection, called acquired intellect and attained by
philosophers, the human intellect becomes separated from the body and
lower parts of the soul. It makes contact with the active intellect, although
without becoming completely identical with it, and achieves supreme human
happiness and entrance into the state of immortality.   Two levels of prophet
are recognized in *al-Madîna al-Fâḍila*, both of them involving an emanation
from the active intellect upon the human imagination.   The lower level does
not require any specific degree of intellectual development.   Here the emission
from the active intellect affects the imagination, making possible a figurative
depiction of intellectual truths and knowledge of particular present and
future events.   The higher level of prophecy occurs at the stage of acquired
intellect when contact is made with the active intellect.   Then an emanation
from the active intellect flows through the human intellect onto the imaginative faculty again providing knowledge of particular future events and also
enabling the philosopher-king to teach philosophic truths in figurative images
comprehensible to the common people.

B. Alfarabi's *Philosophy of Aristotle*.   A different view from that just examined is suggested in Alfarabi's *Philosophy of Aristotle*, an ostensible summary of Aristotelian philosophy.   There Alfarabi repeats many of the points
made in the two works just discussed in regard to the epistemological functions
of the active intellect.[258]   He states that the heavens are the cause of the underlying matter of the sublunar world as well as of the four elements.[259]   But
he makes a significant departure regarding the cause of the existence of life
in the sublunar world.   The *Philosophy of Aristotle* distinguishes between
the cause of individual living beings and the cause of their species.   There
is no difficulty, Alfarabi writes, in determining the source of the soul of a
given individual living thing: The individual soul does not come from a higher
source but is engendered by its parents.[260]   Precisely this statement on the
generation of individual things never appears in *al-Madîna al-Fâḍila* and
al-Siyâsât al-Madaniyya; but the statement can be harmonized with the
position of those two works, where forces descending from the heavenly
bodies working together with forces within the sublunar world are described
as sufficient to explain the generation of the "elements, . . . minerals, plants,

[258] *Philosophy of Aristotle* (n. 190 above) 121, 125ff.
[259] *Ibid.* 99.
[260] *Ibid.* 129.

irrational animals, and the rational mind."[261]   After considering the cause
of individual souls, Alfarabi's *Philosophy of Aristotle* goes on to assert that
it is much more difficult to determine the cause of the form of each species
as a whole, for example, the cause of the entire species *man* or the species
donkey.   Four possibilities are suggested by Alfarabi: The cause of the species may be the celestial spheres, the souls of the spheres, the incorporeal
movers of the spheres, or the active intellect.   Although Alfarabi does
not decide between the four alternatives, the context excludes the possibility that the celestial spheres are the cause of the form of each species as
a whole.[262] This constitutes a distinct departure from *al-Madîna al-Fâḍila*
and *al-Siyâsât al-Madaniyya*.   There Alfarabi drew no distinction between
the cause of individual beings and the cause of species, and he recognized
only the forces of the celestial spheres together with forces within the sublunar
world as a cause of physical forms.   He did not suggest the possibility of a
role in the sublunar world for either incorporeal intelligences or the souls
of the spheres, and he restricted the function of the active intellect to perfecting the human intellect.   Now in the *Philosophy of Aristotle* he suggests
a different approach to the problem of causality in the lower world, assuming
an incorporeal cause of the existence of each species as a whole: either the
souls of the spheres, the celestial intelligences, or the active intellect.

C. The *Risâla fî al-ʿAql*.   Alfarabi's *Risâla fî al-ʿAql* explicitly assigns
a wider function to the active intellect in the production of the sublunar
world.   Like *al-Madîna al-Fâḍila* and *al-Siyâsât al-Madaniyya*, the *Risâla* i-
dentifies the active intellect of *De anima* 3.5 as the last member in the series of
incorporeal intelligences.   Alfarabi even offers an argument showing that the
active intellect cannot be the deity himself,[263] thereby in effect refuting Alexander's position,[264] although without mentioning Alexander; the argument differs
from the preserved Greek refutations of Alexander, which generally are based
on the text of Aristotle.[265] According to the *Risâla*, the heavens do not produce the sublunar world by themselves, but only in conjunction with the
active intellect.   "[Aristotle's] *De generatione*," Alfarabi writes, demonstrated
that the sublunar world in so far as it consists of "bodies" and "forces in
bodies" is a product of the "heavens."[266] Such, it will be recalled, was also
the position taken in *al-Madîna al-Fâḍila*, *al-Siyâsât al-Madaniyya* and

---

[261] *Siyâsât* (n. 184 above) 62.

[262] *Philosophy of Aristotle* 129-130.

[263] *Risâla fî al-ʿAql* (n. 109 above) 33.

[264] Cf. above at n. 12.

[265] Basically Alfarabi's argument is that the active intellect is not a self-sufficent cause
and therefore cannot be the deity.

[266] *Risâla* (n. 109 above) 33-34.

the *Philosophy of Aristotle*.[267] However, the "bodies" and "forces" provided by the heavens, Alfarabi now adds, serve only as "matters and substrata," upon which the active intellect operates. Contained within the active intellect are both the forms of the incorporeal beings above it, and the forms capable of appearing in the material world below it, the latter being present in the active intellect in an "undifferentiated" mode. The active intellect "gives matter the likes of what it contains in its own substance," that is to say, it emanates its forms on matter, and matter for its part receives forms from the active intellect in a "differentiated mode" appropriate to itself. All this, Alfarabi unexpectedly remarks, had been demonstrated by Aristotle in the *De anima*. The purpose served by the existence of matter is to allow the forms in the active intellect to manifest themselves, whereas those forms do manifest themselves in order to allow the active intellect to express its powers.[268]

The precise range of forms descending from the active intellect is not clearly defined in the *Risâla* and must be inferred. The heavens, as was just seen, are responsible for the appearance of "bodies" and "forces" in the sublunar world, which serve as the "matters and substrata" for the operations of the active intellect. Since the underlying prime matter of the sublunar world is not itself a body,[269] Alfarabi is asserting that the heavens are responsible not only for the existence of the matter of our world, but something more, most likely the four elements,[270] which are bodies and which serve as the material substratum for everything generated in the sublunar world. The heavens are also responsible for the "forces" in bodies, perhaps the qualities characterizing the four elements as well as motion within the sublunar world. If this is indeed the extent of the responsibility of the heavens, it would remain the task of the active intellect to produce everything beyond, that is, all forms existing in the sublunar world above the level of the elements, including all levels of soul. Alfarabi's *Philosophy of Aristotle* considered the possibility only of the active intellect's being the cause of each species as a whole, but not of individuals within each species.[271] Here, however, Alfarabi takes the position that the active intellect acts whenever it "finds the matter and substratum . . . prepared," and from the undifferentiated forms contained within itself, it produces the forms appearing in matter in a "differentiated mode."[272] This can only mean that the active intellect produces the forms of all species and individuals in the sublunar world. The

---

[267] Nn. 187, 259 above.

[268] *Risâla* (n. 109 above) 27-30. Cf. *Theology of Aristotle* (n. 84 above) 76, paralleling *Enneades* (n. 9 above) 4.8.6.

[269] Body consists of matter plus form.

[270] Cf. above at n. 259.

[271] Above at n. 262.

[272] *Risâla* (n. 109 above) 29, 33.

Risâla thus represents an adaptation of Plotinus's position, wherein the active intellect, rather than Plotinus's Universal Soul, continually emanates the forms of all natural objects in the sublunar world, and those forms actually appear whenever a portion of matter is ready to receive them.[273] The co-operation of the heavens and the active intellect in the production of the sublunar world also recalls the Stoic theory taken up at the end of Alexander's *De intellectu*.[274]

In regard to the epistemological functions of the active intellect, the *Risâla* again differs from *al-Madîna al-Fâḍila*, although to a less significant degree. The *Risâla* suggests that the potential human intellect is a "substance" rather than merely a "disposition in matter."[275] To illustrate the manner in which the active intellect brings the potential human intellect to actual thought, Alfarabi again employs the common analogy of light, explaining that the active intellect is analogous to the sun. It "gives" the potential human intellect "something" analogous to light, which serves as the "principle" whereby both the potential intellect and potentially intelligible thoughts become actual.[276] These formulas are virtually the same as those found in *al-Madîna al-Fâḍila* and *al-Siyâsât al-Madaniyya*.[277] Here in the *Risâla*, however, the lightlike emission from the active intellect is not described as producing the first principles of thought and science, for the "universal . . . necessary propositions" underlying all theoretical science are, according to the *Risâla*, present in the human intellect "by nature," and the principles of the practical intellect are learned from experience.[278] The effect of the lightlike emission from the active intellect is described here simply as enabling the human intellect to abstract the forms imbedded in material objects.

Beyond this, the *Risâla* does not differ from *al-Madîna al-Fâḍila* and *al-Siyâsât al-Madaniyya*, although it supplements them in a few points. The highest of the three levels of intellect is here too designated as acquired intellect and is reached once the human intellect possesses "all" or "most" of the intelligible thoughts that can be attained through abstraction. The stage of acquired intellect brings knowledge of incorporeal beings, and since incorporeal beings are actual objects of thought by their very nature, without having to undergo a process of abstraction, the acquired intellect knows, them simply by "encountering" (*ṣâdafa*) them.[279] In all actual human thought

---

[273] Cf. above at nn. 126-130.

[274] Cf. above at n. 117.

[275] *Risâla* 12, 22, 26-27; cf. above at n. 214.

[276] *Risâla* 27.

[277] Above at n. 198.

[278] *Risâla* (n. 109 above) 8-10. Similar statements in Alfarabi, *Fuṣûl* (n. 223 above) § 31; *Catalogo de las Ciencias*, ed. A. Palencia (Madrid 1953) Arabic part, 22.

[279] *Risâla* (n. 109 above) 20-22.

the intellect becomes joined with the form of the thing being thought.[280] Consequently the "substance" constituting the potential human intellect is described as a sort of "matter" vis-à-vis the degree of actual human intellect which is its "form," the latter too is like a "substratum and matter" vis-à-vis the acquired intellect which is "like [its] form," and when the acquired intellect has knowledge of incorporeal beings, they in turn are "like forms" of that level of the human intellect.[281] The *Risâla* does not explicitly mention union or conjunction with the active intellect, but union with the active intellect as well as with other incorporeal beings is implied in the statement that those beings can become the form of the acquired intellect. At the stage of acquired intellect "the substance of man or man in that wherein he becomes substantiated" are described as being as near as possible to the active intellect.[282] The phrase *that wherein man becomes substantiated* designates the acquired intellect, the crowning form wherein man achieves his final *substantiation*. Through this *substantiation* as an acquired intellect man gains "supreme happiness and the life to come" even before the death of the body, for the acquired intellect no longer needs its body or the nonrational parts of its soul either to think or to exist.[283] Immortality is thus again a concomitant of the stage of acquired intellect and is reached even before the death of the body. Prophecy is not mentioned in the *Risâla fî al-ʿAql*.

To summarize: The *Risâla* describes the epistemological function of the active intellect approximately as do *al-Madîna al-Fâḍila* and *al-Siyâsât al-Madaniyya* except that it recognizes a different source for the first principles of thought. The *Risâla* differs most significantly from the other two works by assigning the active intellect a role in the generation of natural beings in the sublunar world, the role of emanating the natural forms appearing in matter. Whereas *al-Madîna al-Fâḍila* and *al-Siyâsât al-Madaniyya* assign the active intellect only the original epistemological function it had in Aristotle, the *Risâla*, following the example of certain late Greek philosophers, particularly Plotinus, assigns the active intellect a function in the production of the sublunar world. Alfarabi's *Philosophy of Aristotle* seems to represent yet another position standing somewhere between the *Risâla* and the other two works.

D. Alfarabi's Commentary on the *Nicomachean Ethics*. All four of Alfarabi's works considered until now agree in recognizing the possibility of the active intellect's becoming an object of human thought, and they all construe human immortality as a concomitant of the stage of acquired intel-

---

[280] *Ibid.* 14-15.
[281] *Ibid.* 22.
[282] *Ibid.* 31; cf. 24.
[283] *Risâla* 31.

lect. But Alfarabi is reported to have repudiated his position on these points in his lost commentary on the *Nicomachean Ethics*.

According to Ibn Tufail, the "Commentary on the Ethics" differed from "*al-Siyâsât al-Madaniyya*"[284] by refusing to acknowledge the possibility of human happiness beyond this world and by branding claims of a hereafter as "raving and old wives' tales."[285] Thus it denied the thesis that the active intellect can bring the human intellect to immortality. Averroes provides somewhat more information, constrasting the position of Alfarabi's commentary on the *Nicomachean Ethics* with the position of his *Risâlâ fi al-'Aql*. The *Risâla*, as just seen, affirmed that incorporeal beings become the form of the human acquired intellect when they become objects of human thought, and precisely that, as Averroes understands Alfarabi, is the cause of human immortality.[286] But the commentary on the *Nicomachean Ethics*, Averroes reports, although it recognized the active intellect as the agent producing human thought, denied that any incorporeal being can become conjoined to the human intellect as its form thereby rendering the human intellect immortal. In denying the immortality of the human intellect, Averroes further explains, Alfarabi was consciously following Alexander, although, in fact, the reasoning he gives in no way does reflect Alexander.[287] Alfarabi's reasoning, still according to Averroes, rested on the principle that whatever is generated is necessarily subject to destruction:[288] Alfarabi concluded that since the human intellect is generated and not eternal in the past, it can by no means become eternal in the future.[289] Unless Averroes's report is a reconstruction based on Ibn Tufail's account, it provides a more detailed picture of the position taken in the Commentary on the *Nicomachean Ethics*. Alfarabi accepted the functions of the active intellect connected with the actualization of the human intellect, but denied that the human intellect can gain immortality by becoming conjoined to the active intellect or any other incorporeal being.

The reason why Alfarabi took variant positions in different texts can only be conjectured, but the tone of his writings is suggestive. *Al-Madîna al-Fâdila*, *al-Siyâsât al-Madaniyya*, the *Philosophy of Aristotle*, and the *Risâla fi al-'Aql* all read like matter-of-fact summaries of familiar positions —and yet the positions differ. It is therefore tempting to understand the differences as a result of Alfarabi's working from different oral and written

---

[284] And also from *al-Milla al-Fâdila*.

[285] *Ḥayy ibn Yaqẓân*, ed. A. Amin (Cairo 1952) 62; Munk (n. 236 above) 348.

[286] Alfarabi does not in fact explain immortality in this way; cf. above at n. 283.

[287] Cf. above at nn. 146ff.

[288] Aristotle, *De caelo* 1.10.279b 20; cf. below at n. 401.

[289] Averroes, *Commentarium magnum in Aristotelis De anima libros*, ed. F. Crawford (Cambridge 1953) 433, 485-486. Cf. Munk (n. 236 above) 348-349. M. Steinschneider, *Al-Farabi* (Saint Petersburg 1869) 98-99.

sources at different times; those sources could, perhaps, have come to him through the otherwise unknown teachers with whom he is reported to have studied.[290] The position of the Commentary on the *Nicomachean Ethics* would then have been taken by Alfarabi when his reading of Alexander finally convinced him of the impossibility of any true immortality of the human intellect.

III. AVICENNA ON THE ACTIVE INTELLECT

Like Alfarabi, Avicenna identifies the "active intellect governing our souls," that is to say, the active intellect of Aristotle's *De anima*, as the final link in the chain of incorporeal intelligences, connecting them with the sublunar world.[291] Inasmuch as each of the other celestial intelligences emanates the body of its sphere, the soul of its sphere, and an additional intelligence,[292] the symmetry of the system, as was noted earlier, would require assigning the active intellect three similar functions. That symmetry, which was not observed by Alfarabi, is now carried through by Avicenna, who even feels called upon to explain that the process of emanation could not continue ad infinitum.[293] The active intellect, as described by Avicenna, parallels the other incorporeal intelligences insofar as it is an emanating cause in three areas; it is the cause of (a) the matter of the sublunar world, (b) the forms appearing in matter, including the souls of all animate beings, and (c) the existence and actualization of the potential human intellect. In each instance, though, something aids the active intellect.

According to Alfarabi, it will be recalled, the celestial spheres by themselves are the cause of the existence of the matter of the sublunar world.[294] Avicenna follows Alfarabi in the un-Aristotelian position that the existence of matter in this world must have a cause, but he explicitly argues against taking the celestial spheres to be that cause. The point of departure for his reasoning is one of the central propositions in Aristotelian physics: Since the four sub-

---

[290] Cf. M. Meyerhof, Von Alexandrien nach Bagdad," *Sitzungsberichte der preussischen Akademie der Wissenschaften, Philosophisch-historische Klasse* 23 (Berlin 1930) 405ff.

[291] *Shifâ': Ilâhiyyât*, ed. G. Anawati and S. Zayed (Cairo 1960) 407; *Najât* (Cairo 1938) 278; *K. al-Ishârât wal-Tanbîhât*, ed. J. Forget (Leiden 1892) 174; French translation of *Ishârât* by A. Goichon (Beirut 1951) with pages of Forget's edition indicated; *K. al-Ḥudûd* ed., French trans. A. Goichon (Cairo 1963) Arabic part, 15-16; Gazali, *Maqâṣid al-Falâsifa*, (Cairo n.d.) 220, 302. A. Goichon, *La distinction de l'essence et de l'existence d'après Ibn Sina* (Paris 1937) 237, cites a minor work attributed to Avicenna, which identifies the active intellect with the intelligence of the sphere of the moon.

[292] *Shifâ': Ilâhiyyât* (n. 291 above) 406; *Najât* (n. 291 above) 277.

[293] *Shifâ': Ilâhiyyât* 407; *Najât*, 278. Avicenna seems to mean that the process cannot continue indefinitely because of the impossibility of an infinite series of causes and effects.

[294] Nn. 187, 259, 266 above.

lunar elements can be transformed into one another, each must consist of a material substratum common to all four plus the form peculiar to each.[295] An auxiliary factor in producing the single common substratum of all four elements, Avicenna concedes, is the characteristic common to all the celestial spheres, their uniform daily motion. But, he contends, the uniform motion of the spheres would in itself be insufficient to produce the common matter of the sublunar world. "A multiplicity of things agreeing in species and genus cannot, by themselves and without the participation of a unitary determining factor, be the cause of a substance which is the same and unitary in itself." The spheres, though belonging to a single species, are distinct beings, and consequently their common characteristic could not by itself produce the completely uniform prime matter of the sublunar world. Some other "unitary" being must serve as the governing factor, and that being can only be located in the realm of unitary "incorporeal intelligences"; "to be more precise, from the last of the intelligences, the one adjacent to us, there emanates, with the participation of the movements of the heavens, something containing the imprint of the forms of the lower world."[296] That is to say, prime matter, with its potentiality for receiving the forms of all natural objects in the sublunar world, emanates from the active intellect with the aid of the movements of the heavens. Just how the uniform movement of the heavens participates in the emanation of prime matter is not made clear by Avicenna—but indeed the entire concept of emanation has never been given a satisfactory explanation by the philosophers using it.

Whatever might be thought of Avicenna's reasoning, his argument is striking as reflecting a consistent method of establishing the existence of supernal beings: To the classic Aristotelian proof of the existence of the deity from *motion* in the universe, Avicenna added his well known proof from the distinction between necessary and possible *existence*. To Aristotle's inference of the existence of the celestial intelligences from the *motion* of the spheres, Avicenna added a proof inferring their existence from the *existence* of the spheres.[297] And now, to Aristotle's inference of the existence of the active intellect from what may be called the *motion* of the human intellect from potentiality to actuality, Avicenna again adds an inference from the *existence* of the matter of the sublunar world. In demonstrating the existence of the first cause of the universe, the celestial intelligences, and now the active

---

[295] Cf. Zeller (n. 59 above) 315ff.; Wolfson (n. 235 above) 572-573.

[296] *Shifâ'*: *Ilâhiyyât* (n. 291 above) 410; *Najât* (n. 291 above) 281; *Ishârât* (n. 291 above) 175. Gazali (n. 291 above) 221 establishes emanation of prime matter from the active intellect through the principle that one body cannot produce another body, and A. Goichon's French translation of *Ishârât* (n. 291 above) 431 n. 5, quotes Ṭûsî's commentary to the same effect.

[297] *Shifâ'*: *Ilâhiyyât* (n. 291 above) 407-408; *Najât* (n. 291 above) 278-279.

intellect, Avicenna thus consistently supplements Aristotelian proofs from motion with proofs from existence.

Not only matter but also the forms appearing in matter, Avicenna maintains, are emanated from the active intellect, which accordingly is called the "giver of forms."[298] The active intellect contains its forms in a unified, undifferentiated mode [299] and emanates them not through choice, but as an eternal and necessary expression of its being.[300] Here too the celestial spheres play a role, now more clearly defined: They are the factors predisposing matter to receive a given form from the active intellect to the exclusion of other forms.

At the bottom of the hierarchy of existence, the emanation of the active intellect produces the forms of the four elements: fire, air, water, and earth. Avicenna explicitly rejects a mechanical explanation according to which friction transforms the sublunar matter nearest the celestial spheres into fire, with the forms of the other three elements depending solely on their distance from that element.[301] The theory, he argues, would imply that each portion of prime matter first existed without the form of any of the four elements and then received a form by virtue of the location of the given portion of matter and the rapidity of its motion. But, Avicenna contends by way of refuting the theory, matter can never actually exist without possessing at least the form of an element,[302] and, further, matter has motion and a location in the sublunar world only by virtue of possessing an elemental form, not vice versa. The most reasonable explanation, he concludes, is that matter possesses the elemental forms from all eternity through the emanation of the active intellect. The active intellect, however, is an incorporeal, "unitary" being, and "a unitary [cause] produces only a unitary [effect] in a unitary [subject]." If, therefore, the active intellect acted upon undifferentiated matter, no differentiation of effect would be possible, and the form of one element as distinct from another could never appear. A "particularizing factor" (mukhaṣṣiṣ) must accordingly be assumed "to tip the scales" and "prepare" matter for receiving one form to the exclusion of another. The factors preparing matter to receive the forms of the four elements are influences emitted by the celestial spheres. For although themselves free of qualities, the spheres instill the four basic qualities—heat, cold, dryness, wetness—in matter,[303] and whenever a portion of matter is given the qualities predisposing it to receive the form of one of the four elements, it im-

---

[298] Shifâ': Ilâhiyyât 413; Najât 283.

[299] Cf. above at n. 268, below at n. 355.

[300] Shifâ': Ilâhiyyât 414-415; Najât 284.

[301] An explanation of this type is given by Alfarabi, Philosophy of Aristotle (n. 190 above) 104-105.

[302] That is to say, prime matter cannot exist solely with corporeal form. On corporeal form, see Wolfson (n. 235 above) 579ff.

[303] This seems inconsistent with the principle stated by Avicenna, below at n. 337.

mediately receives the appropriate form from the active intellect. Avicenna's interpretation is intended to explain both the fundamental differentiation of the elements from all eternity and also the changes of the elements into one another. He offers the following illustration: Water like the other elements has a latitude of qualities and can be heated to a certain extent without ceasing to be water. Eventually, though, a point is reached where heat "exceeds the bounds" appropriate to water. At that point the "relation" of the given portion of matter to the form of fire becomes stronger than its relation to its original form, and the water is transformed into fire. The new form comes from without, "emanated" from the active intellect.[304]

Forms above the level of the four elements are similarly emanated by the active intellect but Avicenna is not perfectly clear about precisely which are, and which are not emanated. He attributes to the emanation of the "giver of forms and powers," that is, the active intellect, the appearance of all "powers" and "characteristics" that cannot be explained by the constituent elements of a mixture, apparently including even tastes and odors.[305] He further maintains, as we shall see, that the forms of plants, animals, and man, emanate from the active intellect. When, however, considering the generation of mist and dry haze, the simplest compounds from the four elements, he gives a mechanical explanation, with no mention of a role for the active intellect.[306] A most comprehensive statement is made in Gazali's summary of Avicenna's philosophy where the four elements, mist and haze, metals, plants, animals, and man, are all described as receiving their forms from the emanation of the active intellect.[307]

The form that any given portion of matter does receive depends upon the mixture of the matter, and the better the blend, the more perfect the form. Up to a certain point in the hierarchy of existence, the complete contrariety of the unmixed elements "prevents them from receiving life."[308] The notion that matter, when insufficiently mixed, is *prevented* from receiving a new form may seem somewhat strange, but is consistent with Avicenna's viewpoint. Matter, he understands, has the potentiality of receiving all physical forms: It "contains the imprint of [all] forms of the lower world by way of affection, just as the [active] intellect . . . contains the imprint of forms by way of affecting."[309] When matter receives a new form, it simply receives actually what always belonged to it potentially; therefore the pro-

---

[304] *Shifâ'*: *Ilâhiyyât* (n. 291 above) 410-413, 436; *Najât* (n. 291 above) 150, 280-283, 299; *Shifâ'*: *Physical Sciences* 2-4, ed. M. Qassem (Cairo 1969) 190-191; *Ishârât* (n. 291 above) 175.

[305] *Shifâ'*: *Physical Sciences* 256-257.

[306] *Ibid.* 204; *Najât* (n. 291 above) 152ff. On 157 he mentions the generation of metals, but in too brief a way to infer whether or not he would assign a role to the active intellect.

[307] *Maqâṣid* (n. 291 above) 223.

[308] See n. 311.

[309] *Shifâ'*: *Ilâhiyyât* (n. 291 above) 410; *Najât* (n. 291 above) 281.

cess enabling matter to receive progressively higher and more inclusive forms
can be described not merely as a preparation of matter for those forms, but
more exactly as the removal of the factors that had prevented matter from
receiving what was rightfully its own.[310] The preventive factor is removed,
and a given portion of matter is prepared for receiving life, when the movements and influences of the heavens together with activity within the sublunar world "destroy" the contrary qualities in the portion of matter, so
that the constituent elements lose their separate identity and combine to
form a relatively homogeneous mixture. As the mixture approaches "the
mean that has no contrary," "resembling" the celestial bodies, which contain
no contrary qualities, just "to such a degree, [it] merits an animating faculty"
from the "governing incorporeal principle"; that is to say, depending upon
its degree of homogeneity, it receives the form of a plant or animal from the
emanation of the active intellect. At the upper limit, the mixture of a portion
of matter may go "as far as possible in approaching the mean and destroying
the contrary extremes," whereupon it "receives a substance similar, in a
certain way, to the incorporeal substance." In other words, when matter
reaches the highest possible degree of homogeneity, it receives the rational
human soul, which is an incorporeal substance in contradistinction to animal
and vegetable souls which consist only in an "animating faculty."[311] The
symmetry of the entire universe is reflected in man, for the relation of the
human body to the human soul is similar to the relation of "the celestial
substances" to what "they receive and are conjoined to," that is, their souls;
and the relation of the human soul to the active intellect is the same as the
relation of the soul of each sphere to the intelligence that is its cause.[312] Human body, human soul, and active intellect accordingly stand in the same
relationship as celestial sphere, soul of the sphere, and celestial intelligence.

From various passages in Avicenna, a set of arguments can be assembled
establishing that precisely the active intellect must be the cause of the existence of the human soul. The human body, he writes, cannot produce its
own soul, since a body does not act "insofar as it is a body . . . but only
through its powers." Nor can the powers of the body produce the human
soul, since they are corporeal, whereas the human soul—as Avicenna establishes elsewhere[313]—is incorporeal and cannot be produced by what stands
at a lower level of existence.[314] Elsewhere Avicenna considers and rejects

---

[310] Cf. *Shifā'*: *Physical Sciences* (n. 304 above) 259-260.

[311] *Shifā'*: *De anima*, ed. F. Rahman (London 1959) 261; *Najât* (n. 291 above) 191.

[312] Cf. *Shifā'*: *Ilâhiyyât* 401; *Najât* 273.

[313] Below at n. 399.

[314] *Shifā'*: *De anima* (n. 311 above) 228; *Najât* (n. 291 above) 185; Landauer, "Die Psychologie des Ibn Sina," *Zeitschrift der deutschen morgenländischen Geselschaft* (ZDMG) 29
(1876) 335ff. chap. 3. For the principle that the cause is at a higher level of existence than
the effect, see *Shifā'*: *Ilâhiyyât* (n. 291 above) 409; *Najât*, 280.

the suggestion that disembodied souls of past generations produce new souls.[315] In yet another passage he shows that the souls of the spheres cannot be the cause of the souls of the lower world since they operate only through their bodies and a "body cannot serve as an intermediary between one soul and another."[316] And in still another passage he shows that the first cause of the universe cannot be the cause of the existence of human souls and intellects, since it is a simple being, producing only a single effect whereas human souls and intellects are plural. Similarly, the celestial intelligences cannot be the cause producing human souls and intellects. Although the intelligences can produce a plurality of things, they cannot produce plurality within a single species, for that is possible only through divisible matter, whereas the intelligences operate on the bodies of the celestial spheres, which are not subject to division. Of all the supernal beings only the active intellect operates on the divisible matter of the sublunar world, and therefore it alone can produce a multiplicity of things within a single species.[317] These arguments for the existence of the active intellect supplement Avicenna's proof inferring the existence of the active intellect from the existence of matter and the four elements.[318] And insofar as Avicenna here establishes the existence of the active intellect from the *existence* rather than from the *actualization* of the human intellect, his reasoning parallels his other demonstrations of the existence of incorporeal entities from *existence*, rather than from *motion* in the universe.

Like Alfarabi in *al-Madîna al-Fâḍila* and *al-Siyâsât al-Madaniyya*, Avicenna thus connects the uniformity, diversity, and changes within the lower world to the uniformity, diversity, and changes within the heavens.[319] For Avicenna, however, the heavens are only an auxiliary cause. Like Alfarabi in the *Risâla fî al-ʿAql*, Avicenna assigns the active intellect the role of emanating the natural forms appearing in the sublunar world.[320] But Avicenna goes beyond that work too, for he understands the active intellect to be the cause of the matter as well as the forms of this world, his position being most similar to Plotinus's.[321] Avicenna's position on the epistemological

---

[315] *Mubâḥathât*, in *Ariṣṭû ʿinda al-ʿArab* (n. 10 above) 122, 194. Two reasons are given, the first of which I could not understand. The second consists essentially in showing that no particular dead soul can be designated as the cause of a particular living soul.

[316] *Shifâʾ*: *Ilâhiyyât* (n. 291 above) 407-408; *Najât* (n. 291 above) 278-279; *Ishârât* (n. 291 above) 172. This is really given as a proof that the soul of one sphere cannot be the cause of the next sphere or its soul.

[317] *Shifâʾ*: *Ilâhiyyât* 408-409; *Najât* 279-280. This is given as a proof that the celestial intelligences cannot be the cause of the human intellect.

[318] Above at n. 304.

[319] Cf. above at n. 187.

[320] Cf. above at n. 272.

[321] Cf. above at nn. 119ff.

function of the active intellect similarly goes beyond Alfarabi, and again strongly resembles the position of Plotinus.

The manner in which the active intellect produces actual human thought in Avicenna's system can only be understood against the background of his scheme of human intellect. By distinguishing three senses of potentiality illustrated by three stages in the process of learning to write, Avicenna arrives at a total of four levels of theoretical[322] human intellect: (a) "Material" intellect, the "unqualified potentiality" with which every human being is born, illustrated by the potentiality the infant has for eventually learning to write. (b) "Intellect *in habitu*," the "possible potentiality" the human intellect has after it has learned such "first intelligibles," as the propositions that "the whole is greater than the part" and "things equal to a single thing are equal to one another"; this is illustrated by the potentiality for writing possessed by the boy who knows the "letters." (c) "Actual intellect," the "perfect potentiality" reached when the "secondary intelligibles" have been added to the "first intelligibles," but with the proviso that the subject is not actually attending to his knowledge; this is illustrated by the potentiality for writing possessed by the master scribe at the time when he does not happen to be writing. (d) "Acquired intellect," not properly a further stage, but rather the state of "unqualified actuality" consisting in the presence of "intelligible thought" to which the intellect actually attends.[323] The scheme is obviously related to those of Alfarabi and Alexander. The examples Avicenna gives for the principles of thought contained potentially in the intellect *in habitu* are the same as those given by Alfarabi for the principles of thought provided by the active intellect,[324] and both authors agree in designating the highest degree of human intellect as *acquired intellect*, although Avicenna defines the term differently.[325] Avicenna's intellect *in habitu* and actual intellect are less and more perfect aspects of Alexander's single stage of intellect *in habitu*, which had also been defined as the ability to think at will as distinct from actual thought.[326] But there is only a partial similarity, between Avicenna's acquired intellect and the acquired intellect of the Arabic translation of Alexander. In both instances, acquired intellect is actual thought due directly to the active intellect. In the translation of Alexander, however, acquired intellect is the active intellect itself—or any other incorporeal form

[322] On the practical intellect, see below at n. 384.

[323] *Shifā'*: *De anima* (n. 311 above) 48-50; *Najāt* (n. 291 above) 160-161; *Ishārāt* (n. 291 above) 126; *K. al-Ḥudūd* (n. 291 above) 16.

[324] Cf. above at n. 203.

[325] Cf. above at nn. 215, 216.

[326] Cf. above at n. 39. Both aspects are implied in Alexander, *De anima* (n. 5 above) 85, 111. If *actual intellect* occurs only when a man has the potentiality for all thoughts, as is explicitly stated in *Ishārāt* 126, Avicenna has no term for the intermediate stage between intellect *in habitu* and actual intellect.

—insofar as it is an object of human thought.[327] In Avicenna, by contrast, acquired intellect is not the active intellect itself, but the result of an emanation from the active intellect; and it has as its object all possible human thoughts. Avicenna's usage is closer to Plotinus's where acquired intellect designates all intellectual thought in the soul, all such thought being acquired from the Universal Intellect.[328]

The active intellect, Avicenna maintains, is the cause of each of the four degrees of human intellect. As already seen, it is the cause of the existence of the material intellect insofar as it emanates a human soul upon any receptive portion of matter.[329] In addition it is the factor causing the material intellect to pass to the stage of intellect *in habitu*, the factor causing the latter to pass to the stage of actual intellect,[330] and the source of the actual thought constituting the state of acquired intellect.[331] One of the grounds for assigning these roles to the active intellect is the familiar principle: "Whatever passes from potentiality to actuality" does so "only through a cause that is actually [what the other is potentially]."[332] Since the rational faculty of the soul does pass from potentiality to actuality "there must be a cause that makes our souls pass from potentiality to actuality in respect to intelligible thoughts,"[333] and the cause is the "active intellect."[334] So much was commonplace,[335] but Avicenna sees new implications in the argument. When one thing causes another to pass to actuality, he reasons, it does so by "providing the actuality of the second."[336] Inasmuch as the actuality of intellect consists in the presence of intelligible thought, intelligible thoughts must be precisely what the active intellect provides the human intellect. But if the active intellect gives the human intellect intelligible thoughts, it must contain them itself[337] and "provide and imprint upon the soul the forms of intelligible thought from its own substance."[338] Thus the standard argument for the existence of the active intellect now not only establishes a cause of actual human thought, it also establishes the thesis that the cause must be the direct source of human thought, a thesis known to us from Plotinus and the early Arabic writers following him.[339]

---

[327] Cf. above at n. 68ff.

[328] Cf. above at n. 91.

[329] Above at n. 311.

[330] *Ishârât* (n. 291 above) 126-127.

[331] Cf. below at n. 351.

[332] *Shifâ': De anima* (n. 311 above) 234.

[333] Ibid.; *Fî Ithbât al-Nabuwwât*, ed. M. Marmura (Beirut 1968) 44.

[334] *Najât* (n. 291 above) 192; Gazali (n. 291 above) 302.

[335] Cf. above at nn. 35, 36, 40, 41, 79, 104, 194.

[336] *Najât* 197.

[337] This does not harmonize with Avicenna's statement above at n. 303.

[338] *Najât*, 192, with textual correction of Rahman (n. 63 above) 125.

[339] Above at nn. 82-85, 105, 106, 110.

Avicenna offers two additional proofs showing that the active intellect is the direct source of human thought. In an early work he contends that "experience" through the "senses" cannot be the source of either the principles of thought or the conclusions of demonstrations, for both those classes of propositions are necessary and universal whereas any judgment based on sense perception applies only to the particular instances perceived.[340] Universal judgments must therefore be "acquired" from outside the physical realm, "from a divine emanation . . . with which the rational soul is conjoined."[341]

A third proof of the thesis that the active intellect is the direct source of human thought takes its departure from an analysis of human memory. In Avicenna's mature philosophic works, five "internal senses" are distinguished within animal and human souls. All five are physical, operating through different parts of the brain, and two of the five have the functions of preserving the perceptions of others: The [retentive] imagination (khayâl; muṣawwira) preserves sensations received by the sensus communis, the internal coordinating faculty for the five external senses; and memory (ḥâfiẓa; dhâkira) preserves the perceptions of the estimative faculty (wahmiyya), the faculty that in sheep, for example, recognizes the wolf as dangerous and to be avoided.[342] To say a perception is forgotten, Avicenna explains, does not mean that it ceases to exist in the animal or human subject, for the perception remains, stored in the part of the brain serving either the retentive imagination or the memory. Forgetting is simply an instance of the soul's ceasing to attend to a given perception, and recollection is the soul's attending to it once again.

But, Avicenna contends, whereas this physiological theory satisfactorily explains memory of sense perceptions, it fails to explain memory of intellectual thoughts. Since intellectual thoughts, as he proves, are indivisible, they exist outside the realm of extension and can be neither present in a body nor known through a physical organ.[343] Consequently an intellectual thought cannot be stored any place in the human body during the time when it has been learned but is not actually attended to. Nor could it be present in the soul, since whatever is present in the soul is perforce known. When not attended to, Avicenna accordingly concludes, intellectual thought must exist outside the human soul and outside the physical realm. Avicenna rejects the Platonic theory of separately existing incorporeal forms, and by process

---

[340] This recalls Hume's critique of the principle of causality.

[341] Landauer, "Die Psychologie des Ibn Sînâ" (n. 314 above) 370-371.

[342] Shifâ': De anima (n. 311 above) 44-45; Najât (n. 291 above) 193. On the entire question, cf. H. Wolfson, "The Internal Senses," Harvard Theological Review 28 (1935) 95ff.; Rahman (n. 63 above) 81ff.

[343] Shifâ': De anima (n. 311 above) 209ff.; Najât (n. 291 above) 174ff.; Ishârât (n. 291 above) 130.

of elimination concludes that intellectual thoughts must exist in an incorporeal being from which they are emanated upon the human soul. Actually knowing them means entering a condition of "conjunction" (*ittiṣāl*) with the incorporeal entity—the active intellect—from which they emanate. When conjunction is established, an "intelligible form . . . emanates" upon the human intellect, "and this form is, in truth, the acquired intellect."[344] Learning an intellectual thought means establishing conjunction with the active intellect in such a way that the thought is emanated on the human intellect. Recalling the thought means reestablishing conjunction with the active intellect vis-à-vis the thought. And memory means the ability to reestablish that conjunction easily and at will.[345] It should be noted that whereas there is no justification in Alfarabi for designating the highest stage of human intellect as acquired intellect, the designation is fully appropriate as Avicenna uses it; for actual thought, he understands, is literally acquired from the active intellect. He even describes thought as "acquired from without," a phrase clearly echoing the Arabic translations of Alexander.[346]

The familiar analogy of light is also used by Avicenna in his explication of the way the active intellect serves as a direct source of human thought: The active intellect, he writes, resembles the sun. The sun is itself visible, its rays make potentially visible objects actually visible, and they render potential human sight actual. Analogously to the sun, which is "essentially visible," the active intellect is "essentially intelligible," and "from the active intellect a power emanates and proceeds to the potentially intelligible things in the imagination in order to render them actually intelligible and to render the potential intellect actual intellect."[347] This formulation is almost literally identical with Alfarabi's,[348] and like Alfarabi in the *Risāla fī al-ʿAql*, Avicenna explains that enlightenment by the active intellect produces all abstract concepts.[349] But, he adds, those abstract concepts really flow directly from the active intellect. "When the intellectual faculty gazes on particulars in the [retentive] imagination, and the light of the active intellect in us shines on them, . . . they become abstracted from matter and its concomitants and they become imprinted in the rational soul."[350] However, images are

---

[344] *Shifāʾ*: *De anima* (n. 311 above) 245-248; *Ishārāt* 129; Commentary on *De anima*, in *Arisṭū ʿinda al-ʿArab* (n. 10 above) 100-101; *Mubāḥathāt*, in the same volume 230-231; Commentary on the *Theology of Aristotle*, in the same volume 73; Rahman (n. 63 above) 117-120.

[345] *Shifāʾ*: *De anima* (n. 311 above) 247-248.

[346] *Ibid.* 50; *Najāt* (n. 291 above) 166; cf. *K. al-Ḥudūd* (n. 291 above), 13. Cf. above at n. 68.

[347] *Najāt* 193; cf. *Shifāʾ*: *De anima* (n. 311 above) 235.

[348] Above at n. 198.

[349] Above after n. 278.

[350] *Shifāʾ*: *De anima* (n. 311 above) 235; *Najāt* (n. 291 above) 193.

transformed into universal concepts "not in the sense that they are themselves transported from the [retentive] imagination to the intellect in us ... but in the sense that examining them prepares the soul for the abstract [concept] to emanate upon it from the active intellect." "The light of the active intellect enters into a kind of conjunction with the [forms in the imagination]," and the rational soul thereby "becomes disposed for the abstractions of those forms to be generated in it from the light of the active intellect."[351] Thus just as Avicenna rejects intellectual memory in the literal sense, so he rejects any true abstraction of universal concepts. Activity leading up to the ostensible act of abstraction does not bring about a real act of abstraction; rather examining the sensible forms stored in the retentive imagination makes possible the generation of corresponding abstract forms from the emanation of the active intellect.

Avicenna employs two additional analogies, a medical variation of the analogy of light and vision, and the analogy of the mirror known from Plotinus.[352] The preparation of the human intellect for receiving intellectual thought is compared by Avicenna to treatment of the eye; once treatment has made the eye healthy, the eye does not of course always see, yet it has the ability to see at will. Similarly, training the intellect means bringing it to the stage of actual intellect, from which it can receive thought from the active intellect at will.[353] The human intellect, once it does have the ability to think, is described as similar to a mirror; whenever it is turned towards the active intellect, a thought is reflected in it, but if it attends to other affairs it loses the reflection.[354]

Avicenna also discusses the emanation of thought from the active intellect without the aid of analogies. He begins by isolating the phenomenon of a person's being confident of his ability to answer a question even before having formulated the answer. This, Avicenna insists, is in no sense a state of potentiality, for the person answering the question is confident that he actually knows what he is going to say even before articulating it. The person must already possess knowledge in "a simple mode," which he then recasts in "another mode" as he articulates his knowledge. The simple mode belongs to what Avicenna here calls the "absolute intellectual faculty of the soul," which resembles the "active, celestial intelligences," inasmuch as it contains "no plurality whatsoever, and no sequence of one form after another." The absolute intellectual faculty is described as "in the soul" but "not the soul," and it apparently is identical with what Avicenna elsewhere calls the light

---

[351] *Shifā'*: *De anima* (n. 311 above) 235-236; cf. *Ishārāt* (n. 291 above) 129-130 *Mubāḥathāt* (n. 344 above) 205.

[352] Above at n. 94.

[353] *Shifā'*: *De anima* (n. 311 above) 247.

[354] *Ishārāt* (n. 291 above) 129.

of the active intellect "in us."[355] Acquiring a new thought, according to the present more precise analysis, involves two phases: first establishing conjunction with the active intellect and receiving "the intellect that is simple"; then having "differentiated forms emanate" from that simple intellect "upon the soul." Differentiation in sequences of concepts occurs only in the latter phase, for "differentiation pertains to the soul qua soul."[356] This recalls Plotinus's theory that the human soul contains intellectual thoughts at two levels, a higher level where thoughts are "all together," and a lower level where they are "unrolled and discrete, as it were."[357] The process of learning, according to the present passage in Avicenna, consists in developing a "perfect disposition"[358] both for entering conjunction with the active intellect and for differentiating separate thoughts. Rethinking a thought that has already been learned would accordingly consist in retracing the path through both phases. The person who is confident that he can answer a question before having articulated his answer has entered the first phase, and prior knowledge of the thought in question or of something similar makes him confident of being able to proceed to the second, the phase of differentiating the specific thought. When, however, a person is at one of the stages of potential intellect,[359] he has not even entered the first of the two phases.

Although Avicenna does not explicitly say so, he implies that the cogitative faculty of the soul is the medium for reaching both phases of thought. The cogitative faculty (*mufakkira*) is the human aspect of one of the five internal senses of the soul, the internal sense in question being "called the [compositive] imaginative [faculty] in reference to the animal soul, and the cogitative [faculty] in reference to the human soul."[360] This internal sense, whether in animal or man, is a physical faculty, for it operates through a part of the brain,[361] it involves "movement,"[362] and it ceases with the death of the body.[363] Its activity consists in "combining things in the [retentive] imagination with one another or separating them from one another."[364] Although the cogitative faculty is not itself an "intellectual faculty,"[365] nevertheless the differentiation of pure intellect into separate thoughts—the second

---

[355] Above, n. 350.

[356] *Shifā': De anima* (n. 311 above) 241-248.

[357] Above at n. 86.

[358] *Shifā': De anima* (n. 311 above) 247.

[359] Cf. above at n. 323.

[360] *Shifā': De anima* (n. 311 above) 45. Cf. above at n. 342.

[361] *Ibid.*

[362] *Ishārāt* (n. 291 above) 127; *Mubāḥathāt* (n. 344 above) 139.

[363] *Mubāḥathāt* 232 and *passim*.

[364] *Shifā': De anima* (n. 311 above) 45; *Najāt* (n. 291 above) 163. Cf. Aristotle, *Metaphysics* 6.4.1027b, 29-30; Wolfson (n. 342 above) 78.

[365] *Mubāḥathāt* (n. 344 above) 232.

of the two phases of thought—takes place according to Avicenna "through the mediacy of cogitation."[366] Avicenna further describes cogitation as preparing the rational faculty of the soul "for conjunction" with the active intellect[367] and for "receiving emanation";[368] this apparently means that cogitation prepares the way for the first phase of thought too. By virtue of being mediated through the cogitative faculty, differentiated knowledge is termed "cogitative," as well as "psychic" (nafsânî), as distinct from purely intellectual knowledge.[369] Plotinus, it will be recalled, also wrote that cogitation characterizes the rational soul.[370]

The cogitative faculty, as Avicenna explains its operation, combines and separates sense impressions stored within the soul, and presents such impressions as will permit the emanation of corresponding intelligible thoughts from the active intellect.[371] In so doing, cogitation makes it possible for the human intellect to receive abstract concepts including the "middle terms," which allow syllogisms to be framed and logical conclusions drawn; those middle terms are abstract concepts and consequently have to be received from the emanation of the active intellect.[372] Cogitation thereby helps to construct the entire body of human science, and to develop the human intellect: It starts with the first intelligibles potentially contained in the intellect in habitu, and then it seeks all the middle terms necessary for deducing the "secondary [intelligibles]," the body of propositions that are potentially contained in the stage of actual intellect.[373] In his collected notes, Avicenna considers the question "how error can occur" in reasoning if cogitation does nothing more than prepare the human intellect for receiving thought from the active intellect. His explanation is that "conjunction" with the active intellect is the source of abstract terms, but "combining" the terms is the task of the cogitative faculty which "sometimes does well, sometimes ill."[374] We thus have the following statements on the contribution cogitation makes to human thought: It prepares the way for conjunction with the active intellect; it mediates and differentiates the emanation of the active intellect; it presents sense impressions to the human intellect permitting the emanation of corresponding abstract concepts, including the middle terms of syllogisms; it combines terms into propositions and syllogisms; and yet it is a physical faculty and cannot itself contain intellectual thought.

---

[366] Shifâ': De anima (n. 311 above) 247.
[367] Mubâḥathât 199.
[368] Ibid. 232.
[369] Shifâ': De anima (n. 311 above) 243.
[370] Above at n. 87.
[371] Mubâḥathât 232.
[372] Ishârât (n. 291 above) 127; Mubâḥathât (n. 344) 199. Cf. above at n. 350.
[373] Ishârât 126; Mubâḥathât, 231. Cf. above at n. 323.
[374] Mubâḥathât 199. The two phases discussed above at n. 356 are implied here.

If we attempt to harmonize all these statements, the result must be more or less as follows: Cogitation prepares the human intellect for establishing conjunction with the active intellect as well as for differentiating separate thoughts, and it does so precisely by searching out appropriate sense perceptions and presenting them to the human intellect. The human intellect in some way scans the impressions presented to it and thereby breaks down the undifferentiated emanation into concepts and sequences of concepts. Errors in reasoning occur when cogitation presents sense impressions in ways that mislead the human intellect into articulating incorrect sequences.

Cogitation can be dispensed with by a fortunate few who have the gift of "insight" (*ḥads*),[375] the ability to do rapidly and with little or no effort what cogitation must labor to achieve.[376] It is described as a facility for establishing contact with the active intellect, resulting in the immediate presentation of the middle terms of syllogisms without recourse to the process of cogitation and without any "movement";[377] that is to say, it does not have to rummage in the retentive imagination for perceptions to prepare the intellect for the emanation of a thought. Insight is thus the ability to pass rapidly and unaided through both phases in the process of learning.[378] Elsewhere Avicenna describes insight somewhat differently as a "divine emanation and intellectual conjunction," rather than a facility for establishing conjunction; and through this emanation not only "the middle term" of a syllogism but also "the conclusion . . . occurs to mind without searching," such being the experience of "competent mathematicians."[379] Avicenna here advisedly stresses the ability of insight to bring knowledge of a complete syllogism, for if insight brought only the conclusion it would provide nothing more than a "report" and not scientific knowledge.[380] We shall see that the notion of insight is a key to Avicenna's theory of prophecy.

Reviewing the function of the active intellect in Avicenna's epistemology, we find it described as the direct source of: the first principles of thought bringing about the stage of intellect *in habitu*;[381] abstract concepts, including the middle terms of syllogisms; the deductions made from first principles

---

[375] In the Arabic translation of the *Organon*, ed. A. Badawi (Cairo 1948-1952) 2.406, we find the following translation of *Posterior Analytics* 1.34.89b, 10: "Quick wit (ἀγχίνοια; *dhakâ'*) is a faculty of hitting upon (εὐστοχία; *ḥusn ḥads*) the middle term [of a syllogism] instantaneously." Cf. Alfarabi, *Fuṣûl al-Madanî* (n. 223 above) § 46; *Shifa': De anima* (n. 311 above) 249; *Najât* (n. 291 above) 167.

[376] *Ishârât* (n. 291 above) 127.

[377] *Ibid.*; *Shifâ': De anima* (n. 311 above) 248; *Najât* 166-167; *Rasâ'il Ibn Sînâ* 2 (Istanbul, 1953) 3.

[378] Above at n. 356.

[379] *Mubâḥathât* (n. 344 above) 231.

[380] *Shifâ': De anima* (n. 311 above) 250; *Najât* (n. 291 above) 169-170.

[381] Landauer "Die Psychologie des Ibn Sînâ" (n. 314 above) 361, 371; *Fî Ithbât al-Nabuwwât* (n. 333 above) 44. I could not find this stated in the major works.

through those middle terms, bringing about the stage of actual intellect. Sense perception serves the human intellect by providing sense impressions and "empirical propositions,"[382] which the cogitative faculty then uses to mediate the emanation of the active intellect, but men of "insight" can do without the aid of the cogitative faculty and, perhaps, sense perception as well. One area of theoretical knowledge where the function of the active intellect is not clear, is thought of incorporeal beings including the active intellect itself. Avicenna writes that the human intellect can have those beings as an object of its thought[83] but he does not explain how that can occur, nor whether it can occur before or only after the death of the body. Knowledge of the principles of the practical intellect is explicitly excluded from the operation of the active intellect, for Avicenna follows Aristotle and Alfarabi's *Risâla fî al-ʿAql*—in contradistinction to *al-Madîna al-Fâ-ḍila* and *al-Siyâsât al-Madaniyya*—writing that the principles of the practical intellect are "commonly accepted views, traditions, opinions, and weak experiences."[384] In its general lines Avicenna's epistemology nicely parallels his theory of the emanation of natural forms upon the matter of the sublunar world. Just as all changes in a portion of matter prior to the appearance of a new form merely prepare the matter for the emanation of that form from the active intellect, so the activity of the soul prior to the appearance of an intellectual thought merely prepares the human intellect for the emanation of the form constituting the given thought.

Avicenna, as we have seen, speaks of a conjunction of the human intellect with the active intellect. In addition, he assigns the active intellect a role in human immortality and prophecy. Avicenna's exposition of these three subjects—conjunction, immortality, and prophecy—reveals a familiarity with Alfarabi, but differs from Alfarabi's exposition in significant ways.

There is, to begin, a fundamental difference between *acquired intellect* as defined by Avicenna and Alfarabi, inasmuch as Avicenna's *acquired intellect* does not designate a culminating stage of human intellect, but rather a state, the state of actual thought received from the emanation of the active intellect. For an unexplained reason, Avicenna sometimes restricts the term acquired intellect to the state of actual thought occurring precisely at the culmination of human intellectual development.[385] There seems, however, to be no intrinsic justification for him to withhold the term from all actual thought, inasmuch as he understands all actual thought to be acquired from the active intellect.

---

[382] *Shifâ': De anima* (n. 311 above) 222; *Najât* (n. 291 above) 182.

[383] *Mubâḥathât* (n. 344 above) 134, 135.

[384] *Shifâ': De anima* (n. 311 above) 46, cf. above at n. 278.

[385] *Ishârât* (n. 291 above) 126; *Shifâ': De anima* (n. 311 above) 248.

In both Alfarabi and Avicenna, the stage or state of acquired intellect involves a conjunction with the active intellect. In Alfarabi the connection was as follows: The culminating stage called acquired intellect results in an emanation from the active intellect and in what Alfarabi terms *conjunction* as well as *unification* with it; Alfarabi adds the proviso that the human intellect even then remains at a lower level than the active intellect itself.[386] In Avicenna, in contrast, the state of conjunction is not a supreme condition enjoyed exclusively by the perfect human intellect, but rather the normal condition of every act of human thought, for every such act consists in a "conjunction" with the active intellect, from which the human intellect acquires its thought.[387] Further, for Avicenna, conjunction with the active intellect is not the result of the state of acquired intellect, but rather its cause. Avicenna's conjunction does indeed have an analogue in Alfarabi: the reception of a sort of light from the active intellect, which brings man the principles of thought and science.[388] Alfarabi, however, did not use the terms acquired intellect, conjunction, and emanation, to describe the reception of that lightlike emission from the active intellect; perhaps he would have considered the overtones those terms had—from Alexander and Plotinus[389]—too lofty for application to the first groping steps of human thought. Possibly too, the overtones in the term acquired intellect are the reason for Avicenna's restricting the term to the state of actual human thought occurring precisely at the highest stage of human intellect.

Avicenna does not hesitate to speak of conjunction with the active intellect although, as our analysis has shown, he would have been more precise had he spoken of conjunction with the emanation of the active intellect.[390] But *unification* with the active intellect, by which Avicenna apparently means something more than conjunction,[391] is painstakingly rejected by him. Avicenna takes up an epistemological theory that construed each act of human thought as due to a unification of the human itellect with the active intellect. The theory in question held that "the active intellect causes our souls to pass from potentiality to actuality in respect to thought by uniting . . . with our souls, becoming a form of the soul, and becoming an acquired intellect in us." This theory is not identical with any we have met, but is

---

[386] Cf. above at nn. 223-225, 282.

[387] Above at n. 344.

[388] Cf. above at nn. 198ff.

[389] Cf. above at nn. 70-78, 169.

[390] Cf. above at nn. 355, 356.

[391] A. Goichon is of the same opinion; cf. her translation of the *Ishârât* (n. 291 above) 331 n. 5. In the passage cited in the next note, however, Avicenna uses *conjunction* as a synonym for unification.

very likely an interpretation of Alexander's position.[392] To refute the theory, Avicenna shows that the act of thought cannot consist in the human intellect's becoming identified with either the whole or a part of the active intellect. As long as the human intellect is in a body, he contends, it is incapable of thinking every possible human thought at once, for it always retains its potentiality for new thoughts. Accordingly, when "our soul is actualized in respect to a single intelligible thought," it cannot be united with the entire active intellect; if it were, by thinking a single thought it would obtain all knowledge contained in the active intellect, and that is absurd. Furthermore, the human intellect "cannot unite with part of the active intellect since the active intellect, an incorporeal being, has no parts." The human intellect consequently does not "acquire thought from the active intellect by uniting with it," but rather thought is produced by an "impression" (*athar*) coming from the active intellect.[393] That is to say, the human intellect does not become united with the active intellect but, as was seen earlier, receives an emanation from the active intellect from which it can differentiate only one thought at a time.

This conclusion would apply not only to ordinary souls, but even to souls possessed of a high degree of insight, for insight is not defined by Avicenna as union with the active intellect but rather as a "divine emanation and intellectual conjunction" by which "the revelation of the active intellect is received."[394] The conclusion also would seem to exclude unification—as distinct from conjunction—with the emanation of the active intellect; for if the human intellect were unified with that emanation, it should, by Avicenna's reasoning, receive all thought contained therein at once, and not merely single differentiated thoughts. And the conclusion applies as well to the instance where the active intellect itself is an object of human thought. Although in that instance, the human intellect necessarily receives the form of the active intellect, which should be nothing but the active intellect itself, Avicenna still denies that the active intellect really enters the human soul.[395] In general Avicenna demonstrates the absurdity in supposing that the human

---

[392] So J. Finnegan, "Al-Farabi et le περὶ νοῦ d'Alexandre," *Mélanges Louis Massignon* (Damascus 1957) 2.134-135. In this passage, Avicenna writes that *some* of those holding the position in question identified the active intellect as the deity (cf. above at n. 12), and that in general, the advocates of the position held that only the active intellect itself is immortal (cf. above at nn. 146, 153).

[393] Commentary on the *De anima* (n. 344 above) 92-93. On the continuing potentiality for new thoughts, cf. *Shifâ': De anima* (n. 311 above) 239, 241, 247.

[394] Above at n. 379; *Najât* 167.

[395] *Mubâḥathât* (n. 344 above) 135. Also cf. Avicenna's statement on thought of other incorporeal beings 134.

intellect becomes identical with what it thinks.[396] Thus Avicenna, like Plotinus, al-Kindi, and Alfarabi,[397] rejects the possibility of the human intellect's becoming identical with the entity that causes its thought. Conjunction with the emanation from the active intellect, thought of the active intellect itself, and thought of other incorporeal beings are, it should further be stressed, purely intellectual phenomena for Avicenna without any properly mystical element.[398]

Immortality of the human soul, for Avicenna as for Alfarabi, is dependent on the active intellect. Avicenna formulates his proofs of immortality differently in different works, but the various formulations can be organized into three main groups, which we can consider as three steps in a single overall demonstration. First, Avicenna proves that the human rational soul is an incorporeal substance, then that the destruction of the human soul is not a necessary consequence of the destruction of the body, and third, that an incorporeal substance cannot contain "the potentiality of being destroyed." Avicenna establishes the first step by contending that intellectual thought can be present only in an indivisible incorporeal subject, and since the human soul does receive intellectual thought, it must indeed be an incorporeal substance.[399] He establishes the second step through the thesis that the human soul is emanated by the active intellect upon a portion of matter ready to receive it. It follows, Avicenna explains, that the "mixture" of matter constituting the human body is only an "accidental cause of the soul," and the soul is not attached to the body as "an effect to its essential cause." The soul merely exists "with" the body. It is not generated "from" a body, but rather "from" the active intellect, the body determining only the "time" when a soul can appear. Since the soul is not dependent on the body for its existence, but only for the time of its appearance, the death of the body need not entail the death of the soul.[400] Avicenna completes his demonstration with the third step, contending that things are destroyed only if, by the side of the factor giving them actual existence, they contain an additional factor carrying the potentiality for destruction; that is to say, if in addition to their form they also contain matter. Since incorporeal substances do not contain the second of these two factors, they cannot be destroyed. And, Avicenna adds, the principle that whatever is generated is destroyed does not apply

---

[396] *Ishârât* (n. 291 above) 179-180; *Shifâ': De anima* (n. 311 above) 240. A different position is taken in the earlier work published by Landauer (n. 314 above) 364.

[397] Above at nn. 169, 172, 225.

[398] I understand such passages as *Ishârât* (n. 291 above) 204ff., as only a poetic formulation of Avicenna's epistemology.

[399] *Shifâ': De anima* (n. 311 above) 209ff.; Najât (n. 291 above) 174ff.; *Ishârât* (n. 291 above) 176ff.; Landauer "Die Psychologie des Ibn Sînâ" (n. 314 above) chap. 9.

[400] *Shifâ': De anima* (n. 311 above) 228-229; *Najât* (n. 291 above) 186, 192.

to them.[401] His conclusion, then, is that since the human soul is not affected by the destruction of the body, and since, being an incorporeal substance, it does not contain within itself the "potentiality of being destroyed," it must be indestructible. The nerve of the demonstration, it will be observed, is the thesis that the active intellect constitutes the human soul as an incorporeal substance.

Avicenna's theory of the generation of the human soul also serves to establish the individuality of immortal souls and to refute the belief in transmigration. Souls are differentiated from one another, according to Avicenna, inasmuch as a body must always exist as the occasion of the emanation of a soul from the active intellect, and that original differentiation carries over into the state of immortality.[402] A similar statement was made by Alfarabi, but lost its force inasmuch as Alfarabi's system could accomodate immortality solely of the intellect, not of the substance of the soul.[403] To refute the belief in transmigration, Avicenna contends that the belief would have to assume the entrance of transmigrating souls only into bodies fit to receive them. But whenever a portion of matter is capable of receiving a soul, it receives one automatically and necessarily from the active intellect. Consequently, Avicenna contends, the belief in transmigration would lead to the absurdity of two souls in one body: the transmigrating soul and the soul emanated by the active intellect.[404]

There is an essential difference between the role of the active intellect here in Avicenna's theory of immortality and its role in Alfarabi's theory. In Alfarabi immortality is a concomitant of the stage of acquired intellect, and the active intellect contributes in its role as a cause of human thought, by helping man reach that stage. Also, perhaps, immortality depends on the conjunction of the acquired intellect with the active intellect.[405] In Avicenna, however, the human intellect is immortal by its very nature, quite apart from its intellectual development. The active intellect therefore is a cause of immortality not by virtue of being a cause of human thought but more fundamentally, by virtue of being the cause of the existence of the human soul, and by constituting the human soul as an incorporeal substance. Still, even for Avicenna, thought supplied by the active intellect plays an important role, for although it does not render the soul immortal, it does determine the condition of the soul in its immortal state.

When considering the condition of disembodied human souls after death, Avicenna takes up the question whether and how intellectual thought can

[401] *Shifā'*: *De anima* 231-233; *Najāt* 187-189.
[402] *Shifā'*: *De anima* 225; *Najāt* 184; cf. *Mubāḥathāt* (n. 344 above) 223.
[403] Cf. above at nn. 230-236.
[404] *Shifā'*: *De anima* (n. 311 above) 233-234; *Najāt* (n. 291 above) 189; *Ishārāt* (n. 291 above) 196-197; *Risāla Aḍḥawiyya* (Cairo 1949) 91.
[405] Cf. above after n. 229.

be possible then. Since the rational soul depends upon sense perception and the cogitative faculty to prepare it for the emanation of the active intellect, intellectual thought might be assumed impossible after the destruction of the external and internal senses, including the cogitative faculty. Avicenna agrees that if a human soul fails to acquire intellectual knowledge during the life of the body it will be unable to acquire such knowledge in the life to come, for without sense perception and cogitation, it has no way of forming a disposition for receiving the emanation of the active intellect. He is vague about the amount of knowledge that must be gained in this world for the human intellect to be able to have any thought at all in the next. But he does make it clear that if the cogitative faculty—and, we may add, insight— produces a disposition sufficient for receiving that unspecified degree of emanation from the active intellect in the present world, then in the next world the soul will enter a permanent conjunction with the active intellect whereby all its knowledge will be permanently present.[406] Avicenna is more explicit about the soul possessing a disposition for receiving all possible knowledge: After such a disposition is attained, the intellect no longer needs its physical faculties and in fact is only distracted by them. "Once the soul is perfected and powerful, it isolates itself completely in its own activity, and the faculties of sense perception, [retentive] imagination, and the other bodily faculties, [merely] divert the soul from its [proper] act." Such is true even when the soul is still associated with a body, and no less so when it enters its disembodied state.[407] In the latter instance the soul becomes an "intellectual world paralleling the entire existing world"; it is "united with [the supernal world], is imprinted with its likeness, . . . enters into its company, and becomes of the same substance."[408]

Various grades of immortal souls are recognized by Avicenna. (a) Superlatively happy souls are those possessing the aforementioned perfect disposition whereby they can enter a complete perpetual conjunction with the active intellect,[409] But, Avicenna maintains, happiness (sa'āda) is also the lot of (b) souls possessing less than a perfect disposition for conjunction with the active intellect. He conjectures that the minimum amount of knowledge necessary for a minimum degree of happiness in the world to come is

[406] *Mubāḥathāt* (n. 344 above) 201-202, 209-210; *Rasā'il Ibn Sīnā* (n. 377 above) 3.

[407] *Shifā': De anima* (n. 311 above) 208, 223; *Najāt* (n. 291 above) 183; *Ishārāt* (n. 291 above) 176; Commentary on *Theology of Aristotle* (n. 344 above) 44; *Mubāḥathāt* (n. 344 above) 145-146, 210, 227-228, 231.

[408] *Shifā': Ilāhiyyāt* (n. 291 above) 425; *Najāt* (n. 291 above) 293. If Avicenna means that the human soul really becomes another substance, he would most plausibly mean that it becomes a pure intellect; cf. above at nn. 282, 355. But this interpretation does not seem consistent with Avicenna's views cited at nn. 399, 409, 418.

[409] *Shifā': Ilāhiyyāt* (n. 291 above) 425; *Najāt* (n. 291 above) 293; Landauer, "Die Psychologie des Ibn Sīnā" (n. 314) 371.

knowledge of all the basic theses of physical and metaphysical philosophy, with knowledge beyond that minimum bringing successively greater degrees of happiness.[410] (c) Some souls, Avicenna further writes, acquire enough knowledge in this world to recognize that true human happiness and perfection consists in intellectual thought, yet they know less than the minimum necessary to enjoy that happiness; in other words, they fail to learn the basic theses of physics and metaphysics. These souls suffer in the world to come for they desire to know more but cannot, since they no longer have the means to increase their disposition for conjunction with the active intellect.[411] It is unclear, however, whether they have no knowledge at all in the world to come, or whether they continue to possess whatever knowledge they did acquire, although without enjoying "happiness." It is also unclear whether even souls that do learn the basic theses of physics and metaphysics yet fall short of perfect knowledge lead only a bittersweet existence in the world to come, enjoying of course what they have, but still suffering pain for what they lack. Whether or not souls of this class have a minimal, unsatisfactory conjunction with the active intellect in the life to come, some souls, at least, do fail completely to "enter conjunction with an incorporeal being when separated from the human body."[412] Included among them are (d) completely ignorant souls that remain like a formless material substratum; these continue to exist, but their existence lacks all intellectual content.[413] Avicenna then unexpectedly writes that "a certain sort of ignorance" destroys certain souls.[414] He does not specify which do perish, but there seem to be none he could mean except souls lacking a sufficient disposition for any degree of conjunction with the active intellect. If Avicenna does mean that such souls perish, then his statement that ignorant souls continue to exist as an unrealized material substratum in the world to come would be just a euphemistic way of saying that their empty existence is, in fact, nonexistence. What is more astonishing about the present statement is its complete inconsistency with Avicenna's painstaking philosophic proofs of immortality. If it truly represents his considered position, then his position would turn out to be very similar to Alfarabi's.[415]

The distinctions drawn until now concern the intellectual content of the disembodied soul. According to Avicenna, the fate of the soul in the world to come is also affected by moral factors, for unfulfilled physical desires, like unfulfilled intellectual desires, cause the soul pain. Thus he describes

---

[410] *Shifā'*: *Ilāhiyyāt* (n. 291 above) 428-429; *Najāt* (n. 291 above) 295-296; *Ishārāt* (n. 291 above) 195; *Risāla Aḍḥawiyya* (n. 404 above) 120-121.

[411] *Ibid.*

[412] *Rasā'il Ibn Sīnā* (n. 377 above) 3.

[413] As in n. 410.

[414] *Ishārāt* (n. 291 above) 188.

[415] Above at nn. 236-240.

the ignorant good soul as leading a restful existence in the world to come, lacking all intellectual content since it has no intellectual thought, yet also suffering no pain. Sinful souls, however, which became encrusted with corporeal desires in the present world, suffer in the hereafter because of their inability to fulfill those desires. Avicenna offers hope for the last-mentioned souls—and perhaps for himself as well—for, he writes, their suffering can ultimately purify them and cease.[416] In a rationalization of traditional accounts of the hereafter, he also suggests a further way in which sinful souls may suffer, and in which simple souls may enjoy the physical pains and pleasures promised by religion: In their immortal state they may imagine pleasures, pains, and even the experiences of resurrection, as if in a very vivid dream.[417]

Several difficulties are raised by the foregoing statements on immortality. It is never made clear how much knowledge in the present world is necessary in order to establish conjunction with the active intellect in the next world. The statement to the effect that some souls perish is inconsistent with Avicenna's demonstration of immortality and with his statements concerning the survival of ignorant souls—classes (c) and (d)—in their disembodied state. And there is, as Avicenna himself recognizes, a difficulty in supposing that souls have physical desires or imagine anything in the world to come, for desire and imagination are functions requiring physical organs and should have no place in a disembodied soul. To bypass the last-mentioned problem, Avicenna suggests that the compositive imagination does after all survive despite its being a physical faculty, and again that the heavenly bodies may in some way supply disembodied souls with surrogate physical faculties.[418]

The active intellect is thus the cause of human immortality for Avicenna, insofar as it constitutes the human soul as an incorporeal substance. The state of the immortal soul depends upon its moral character and its disposition for conjunction with the active intellect. And there is a possibility that souls entering the immortal state without knowledge really have no existence there at all.

The active intellect is also the cause of prophecy. According to Alfarabi, it will be recalled, the lightlike emission from the active intellect can inspire the imaginative faculty of two types of men and thereby produce two levels of prophet: If the emission of the active intellect enters the imaginative faculty of a man who has not developed his intellect, it makes possible a figurative

---

[416] *Shifā'*: *Ilāhiyyāt* (n. 291 above) 427-428, 430-431; *Najāt* (n. 291 above) 295, 297; *Ishārāt* (n. 291 above) 195; *Mubāḥathāt* (n. 344 above) 202, 230; *Risāla Aḍḥawwiyya* (n. 404 above) 121.

[417] *Shifā'*: *Ilāhiyyāt* 431-432; *Najāt* 298; *Risāla Aḍḥawiyya* 125; cf. Hamlet's Soliloquy: "To sleep, perhaps to dream."

[418] *Shifā'*: *Ilāhiyyāt* 432; *Najāt* 298; *Ishārāt* 196; Commentary on the *Theology of Aristotle* (n. 344 above) 72; *Mubāḥathāt* (n. 344 above) 202; *Risāla Aḍḥawiyya* (n. 404 above) 125.

depiction of theoretical truth as well as knowledge of future events, this
constituting the lower grade of prophet. If the emanation of the active intellect enters the imaginative faculty of a man who has reached the stage
of acquired intellect, it has a like effect and thereby produces a higher grade
of prophet. In the second instance, the same emanation from the active
intellect also enters the acquired intellect of the recipient—before entering
his imaginative faculty—thereby rendering him a "philosopher and man of
practical wisdom."[419] It is not clear in Alfarabi why anyone at the stage of
acquired intellect should need an emanation from the active intellect to
render him a philosopher, since that stage is reached only by virtue of the
posesssion of all human science. In any case, the prophetic experience in
Alfarabi's account does not produce true theoretical knowledge. On the
one hand, Alfarabi applies the term prophecy only to the effect of the active
intellect on the imagination, which does not produce theoretical knowledge
but only a figurative depiction of it. On the other hand, when the same emanation of the active intellect that produces prophecy enters the intellectual
faculty of a man already possessed of theoretical knowledge, Alfarabi neither
designates that part of the phenomenon as prophetic nor, apparently, does
he understand that it adds to the knowledge of the recipient.

Avicenna departs radically from Alfarabi in maintaining that prophecy
does produce theoretical knowledge and in fact is the highest road thereto.
Insight, it will be recalled, is the ability to establish contact with the emanation of the active intellect without employing *cogitation*.[420] Not all individuals, Avicenna observes, possess the gift of insight to the same degree;
it varies both in its scope and speed. From that variability and from the
fact that individuals at the lower end of the spectrum completely lack the
gift, Avicenna extrapolates and infers that there "must" be men at the upper
end of the spectrum who have the gift in a superlative degree, that is to say,
men who enjoy insight in "all problems or most" and who can exercise their
gift in the "briefest time." The very highest degree of insight is called "holy
intellect" or "holy power" and it comprises the "highest" type of prophecy.
A man possessed of "holy intellect" is so firmly conjoined with the supernal
world that he "burns with insight, that is, with the reception of inspiration
from the active intellect" and as a result "the forms in the active intellect
regarding every subject are imprinted in him instantaneously or almost so."
If prophecy provided the conclusions of syllogisms without knowledge of
the syllogisms themselves, it would not give scientific knowledge.[421] The
insight of the prophet does, however, provide both the "middle terms" and

[419] Cf. above at nn. 243-257.
[420] Cf. above at nn. 375-380.
[421] Cf. Zeller (n. 59 above) 232.

the conclusions in "an ordered manner" and thus prophecy brings the fortunate recipient an instantaneous gift of scientific kowledge.[422]

In addition to this prophetic emanation upon the human intellect, which is not recognized and in fact consciously rejected by Alfarabi,[423] Avicenna also distinguishes what he calls "prophecy peculiar to the imaginative faculty." The latter includes a figurative representation of intellectual truth, as well as knowledge of future events, both familiar from Alfarabi, and Avicenna also presents a theory of projected prophetic visions similar to Alfarabi's theory.[424] On one point, however, Avicenna implicitly makes a correction. Alfarabi's statements concerning the prediction of future events failed to explain how the active intellect could have and communicate knowledge of them, seeing that such events would have to fall outside the scope of the active intellect which has only intellectual knowledge.[425] Avicenna avoids the difficulty by construing the souls of the spheres rather than the active intellect as the source of prophetic knowledge of the future. He writes that the souls of the spheres and the pure intellects above them—the deity, intelligences, and active intellect—all have knowledge of events, for all know the "primary" factors from which events in this world flow, those factors being the influences of the spheres, which prepare the matter of our world for the emanation of the active intellect. The manner in which the souls of the spheres know events differs, however, from that in which pure intellects know them. The knowledge possessed by pure intellectual substances is "universal" and does not extend to the particular aspect of things, whereas knowledge possessed by souls "is not purely intellectual," and does extend to particulars. Since the souls of the spheres are the immediate cause of the activity of the spheres, which are in turn the ultimate cause of events in the lower world, they have "particular" knowledge of the future eventualities "most likely to occur." That knowledge is communicated by the celestial souls to receptive human souls, which are thereby able to predict the future—or at least future probabilities.[426]

Thus Avicenna's theory of prophecy supplements Alfarabi's on one score and corrects it on another: Avicenna recognizes an intellectual type of prophecy absent in Alfarabi, thereby considerably augmenting the value of

---

[422] *Shifā'*: *De anima* (n. 311 above) 248-250; *Najāt* (n. 291 above) 167-168; *Ishārāt* (n. 291 above) 126-127; Landauer, "Die Psychologie des Ibn Sînâ" (n. 314 above) 365.

[423] N. 252 above.

[424] *Shifā'*: *De anima* (n. 311 above) 173, 249; *Najāt* (n. 291 above) 167; *Ishārāt* (n. 291 above) 215; *Aḥwāl al-Nafs*, ed. A. Ahwani (Cairo 1952) 120. Cf. above at nn. 243-253. According to Avicenna, the projection of visions takes place within the faculties of the soul, not in the external world as Alfarabi wrote. Cf. Rahman (n. 141 above) 38.

[425] Cf. above at n. 249.

[426] *Shifā'*: *De anima* (n. 311 above) 178-179; *Ilāhiyyāt* (n. 291 above) 436-438; *Najāt* (n. 291 above) 300-301; *Ishārāt* (n. 291 above) 210-211; *Aḥwāl al-Nafs* (n. 424 above) 114ff.

the prophetic experience. And he explains that prophetic knowledge of future events is communicated by the souls of the spheres rather than by the active intellect, thereby avoiding the objection that an intellectual substance could not communicate particular knowledge.

Conclusion. Avicenna's theory of the active intellect is more far-reaching and consistent than Alfarabi's. Avicenna construes the active intellect as the eternal cause of the matter of the sublunar world—with, however, the aid of the heavens. Given the matter of the sublunar world, the active intellect is the eternal cause of forms appearing in matter, ranging from the forms of the four elements to the incorporeal substance of the human soul— again with the aid of the heavens, which help prepare matter to receive one form to the exclusion of another. Whenever an incorporeal human soul is generated in the sublunar world, the active intellect enters in a new role. It is the cause of human thought, now with the aid of the lower faculties of the soul, which prepare the human intellect to receive one differentiated thought rather than another. By-products, as it were, of the active intellect's cosmological and epistemological functions are human immortality and prophecy. In its operation the active intellect is, as it were, an eternal cosmic transmitter, sending out an undifferentiated range of forms and thoughts, as well as the substratum that can receive them; forms and thoughts actually appear in this world whenever a portion of matter or a human mind is properly attuned for reception. Not only is Avicenna's position wider and more consistent, it is also more carefully supported with philosophic argumentation than Alfarabi's, which generally is simply asserted.

Avicenna's theory was highly influential both within the narrow circle of philosophers and beyond, both within Islamic literature and beyond it, in Jewish and Christian literature. The reactions, however, varied. There were those who accepted Avicenna's position, others who accepted only the epistemological part, yet others who rejected all or part for either philosophic or theological reasons, and perhaps most interestingly those who transferred the functions of the active intellect to the deity or to other entities of conservative theology.[427] I hope to examine this further history of the active intellect on another occasion.

[427] Judah Hallevi, *Cuzari* 5.20 (end); Averroes, *Tafsîr Mâ Ba'd al-Ṭabî'a* (Beirut 1938-1948) 1498; Maimonides, *Guide* 2.12; Gersonides, *Milḥamot ha-Shem* 1.6.11; 2.3; Goldziher *K. Ma'ânî al-Nafs* (n. 28 above) 42*-43*; Gilson (n. 22 above); I. Madkour, *La place d'al Fârâbî* (Paris 1934) 199-201; A. Wensinck, *La pensée de Ghazzâlî* (Paris 1940) 79ff.; A. Altmann, *Studies in Religious Philosophy and Mysticism* (Ithaca 1969) chap. 3.

Department of Near Eastern Languages
University of California
Los Angeles, California, U.S.A.

"LIBER MARII DE ELEMENTIS"
THE WORK OF A HITHERTO UNKNOWN
SALERNITAN MASTER?

•

by Rodney M. Thomson

The second volume of Manuscript Cotton Galba E. IV in the British Museum, written in England shortly before 1200, has long been known to scholars interested in the introduction of Greek and Arabic science into western Europe in the twelfth and thirteenth centuries. In 1924 C. H. Haskins commented upon the first four items of its contents,[1] of which three are treatises on the elements, the fourth a work on climate. All are anonymous except one, entitled *Liber Marii de elementis*. The identity of this Marius has, however, remained hidden until now. From internal evidence Haskins proposed a southern Italian or Sicilian origin for this group of treatises, characterizing them as belonging "to the epoch when Aristotelian science was coming in through Arabic channels but had not yet been fully absorbed."[2] The traditional sources, Seneca, Macrobius, Boethius, the Latin poets and Plato's *Timaeus* are quoted, as well as the new translations of Aristotle's *Physics*, *De caelo* and *Topics*, and the pseudo-Aristotelian *De elementis*.[3] More recently, R. C. Dales has studied and edited two of these works, both anonymous and dealing with the elements. One of them has proved to be a highly competent translation of the chapter *De elementis* from Nemesius's *De natura hominis*, a full version of which appears later in the manuscript in the well-known translation by Alfanus of Salerno.[4] The other treatise revealed features that led Dales to corroborate Haskins's suggestion of an Italian or Sicilian origin for it.[5] As for the work on climate, this proves to be a trans-

---

[1] C. H. Haskins, *Studies in the History of Medieval Science* (Cambridge, Mass. 1924) 93-95.
[2] *Ibid.* 95.
[3] *Ibid.* and R. C. Dales, "*Anonymi de elementis*; from a twelfth-century collection of scientific works in British Museum Cotton Galba E. IV," *Isis* 56 (1965) 174-189, esp. 175-179.
[4] R. C. Dales, "An unnoticed translation of the chapter *De elementis* from Nemesius' *De natura hominis*," *Medievalia et humanistica* 17 (1966) 13-19.
[5] Dales (n. 3 above).

lation of Hippocrates' *Liber de aere, aqua et regionibus*.[6] B. Lawn, in his monograph on the Salernitan questions, has also reiterated Haskins's dicta, noting in addition that other items in the manuscript, such as Alfanus's translation of Nemesius, point to a connection with the school at Salerno.[7] It is the purpose of this article to investigate further the date and provenance of the manuscript, and the origin of its contents, especially the *Liber Marii*. The results of this inquiry, it is hoped, will be found to have interesting implications for the history of Western science in the later twelfth century.

A full description of the manuscript is not available in print, and it will be convenient to give one here.[8] It is a large vellum codex of 58 folios, measuring 382 by 290 millimeters, written in two excellent hands, contemporary and very similar.[9] The first of these has provided the rubrics and colored initials throughout. This suggests that its copying must have been undertaken in one continuous operation, with little or no interval of time between the change of hands. Each separate item of contents opens with a fine painted initial, decorated with foliation exhibiting "Byzantine blossoms."[10] The second scribe, who begins by imitating the first, appears to have been the younger man, as his script, when he ceases to imitate, is narrower, less rounded and more vertical in ·emphasis, nearer the "Gothic" style. In contrast to the first scribe, who uses the ampersand, he employs the Tironian *et* invariably. There is also a perceptible recurve in his signs of abbreviation by contraction which is lacking in those by the first scribe. These hands resemble the "thorny" script originally practiced in the scriptorium of Christ Church, Canterbury, but which spread to other Benedictine houses in southeastern England during the twelfth century.[11] Could the manuscript be a product of the scriptorium at Bury Saint Edmunds abbey in Suffolk? Certainly it belonged to the library of that house by the later fourteenth century,

[6] L. Thorndike and P. Kibre, *A Catalogue of Incipits of Mediaeval Scientific Writings in Latin*, rev. ed., Mediaeval Academy of America Publ. 29 (Cambridge, Mass. 1963) 1249 (henceforward cited as TKI).

[7] B. Lawn, *The Salernitan Questions* (Oxford 1963) 66 (henceforward cited as LSQ). He also cites Constantine's translation of the pseudo-Galenic *De spermate*; but this is actually the genuinely Galenic *De semine*, just possibly translated by Constantine (TKI 1521).

[8] The description in J. Planta, *A Catalogue of the MSS in the Cottonian Library deposited in the British Museum*, 2 vols. (London 1802) 2.359, is inadequate and erroneous, omitting, inter alia, two items of contents. That given by Miss E. Parker, in her Ph. D. thesis, *The Scriptorium at Bury St. Edmunds in the 12th Century* (University of London 1965) 323, concentrates exclusively on the palaeography and decoration.

[9] Fols. 187-244 in the modern foliation, which numbers vols, 1 and 2 continuously. Miss Parker identifies only one hand.

[10] Parker (n. 8 above).

[11] *Ibid.*, and T. A. M. Bishop, "Notes on Cambridge MSS 1," *Transactions of the Cambridge Bibliographical Society* 1 (1949-1953) 438.

and many of the books produced there in the twelfth century are written in "Christ Church" script.[12] However, its foliated initials do not resemble contemporary Bury work.[13]

Haskins dated the manuscript to circa 1200, and Dales more recently to the last quarter of the twelfth century, most probably circa 1190-1200, both on palaeographical grounds.[14] Miss Parker, whose knowledge of the Bury scriptorium places her in a special position to judge, would date it anywhere in the second half of the twelfth century.[15] However, one work originally contained in part of the manuscript now lost, is known to have been composed in 1161,[16] and another item, also no longer extant, was written at about the same time.[17] Since the contents of the lost portion are of a similar character to those which are extant, it is probable that they were executed by the same hands, or at least contemporaneously. If this were the case, 1161 would be the terminus a quo for the copying of the whole manuscript. Moreover, if it be agreed that Gerard of Cremona began his work as a translator in 1175,[18] then this would be the terminus a quo for the extant portion, in which some of his translations are cited.[19] Indeed, even if it is conceded that he may have begun translating a decade or so earlier, one has still to allow for the dissemination of his works, and for the study of them by those authors who figure in our manuscript, and in whose treatises they are employed. Finally, it will be suggested shortly that the *Liber Marii* can hardly have been written much before circa 1175. With some confidence, then, it may be affirmed that the manuscript was written in southeastern England in the last quarter of the twelfth century.

By the late fourteenth century the book belonged to the Bury library, for at this time it received the library pressmark, ex libris, and table of contents, all inscribed by Henry of Kirkestede, a monk of that house who was *armarius* circa 1360-1380.[20] Kirkestede's inscription appears on the present

---

[12] Bishop (n. 11 above) and Parker (n. 8 above) 282-344, where upwards of a dozen Bury MSS of the twelfth century in hands of or resembling the "Christ Church" style are listed.

[13] Parker 323.

[14] Haskins (n. 1 above) 93 and n. 63; Dales (n. 3 above) 175.

[15] Parker (n. 8 above).

[16] Odo of Meung, *De virtutibus herbarum.* C. Singer, *From Magic to Science* (New York 1958 [repr. of 1928 ed.]) 188.

[17] Platearius (?), *De Simplici medicina.* Singer 189.

[18] A discussion of the propriety of this date is found in LSQ (n. 7 above) 61-62. In support of an earlier date, it is noteworthy that Hildegard of Bingen (d. 1179) makes use of some of Gerard's translations in her writings (Singer 235-236).

[19] Gerard's version of the *Topics* is cited in the *Anonymi de elementis* (Haskins [n. 1 above] and Dales [n. 3 above] 175).

[20] *Liber monachorum sancti eadmundi in quo continentur libri xxviiij. de medicina. de herbis pigme*[illegible]*ius.* Pressmark M. 21. On Kirkestede's dates and activities see

opening folio (187), which contains the beginning of the first anonymous treatise on the elements.[21] The likelihood is, therefore, that this was always the first item in the manuscript. Kirkestede notes that the total contents amounted to twenty-four books. After the Dissolution the manuscript found its way into the library of Dr. John Dee, whose catalogue shows that it then contained twenty-six items, of which only the first nine now remain.[22] Kirkestede's table of contents is almost totally obliterated, and in any case does not appear to have been very specific, so that no reason can be given for the variation of two books between his list and John Dee's. Probably Kirkestede has simply conflated some similar items. There is nothing in Dee's list which looks obviously added after Kirkestede's time, so that the contents as he gives them probably represent the original extent of what must have been a very large book. The extant portion is now bound after the fourteenth century Register of Henry of Eastry, prior of Christ Church, Canterbury, which forms Volume 1.

Here follows an annotated list of contents of Volume 2, together with the lost items listed in Dee's catalogue.

I. Extant items:

Fol. 187. The earlier part of an anonymous work on natural philosophy, dealing mainly with the four elements.[23] Ends imperfectly, due to loss of leaves. (Thorndike-Kibre Incipits [TKI] 1392; only MS.)

Fol. 190. *Liber Marii de elementis*. Beginning lacking, due to loss of leaves. Incipit: "[Natura] aque que est?" Explicit: "sit benedictus in secula seculorum Amen."

Fol. 200v. *De elementis*, a chapter from Nemesius's *De natura hominis*, in an anonymous translation.[24] (TKI 496; only MS.)

Fol. 201v. Hippocrates, *Liber de aere, aqua et regionibus*, given anonymously, in an unknown translation. (TKI 1249; many MSS, of which this is the earliest cited.)

Fol. 205. Nemesius, *De natura hominis*, translated by Alfanus of Salerno. (TKI 3; this MS om., one other given.)

Fol. 214. Adelard of Bath, *Dialogus*. (TKI 304, prologue; 865, text. Kirkestede, *Catalogus* [Cambridge U. L. Add. MS 3470] 39 gives same incipit and explicit as MS minus prologue.)

R. H. ROUSE, "*Bostonus Buriensis* and the author of the *Catalogus scriptorum ecclesiae*," *Speculum* 41 (1966) 471-499, esp. 480-494.

[21] No medieval foliation or signatures. Miss Parker's collation shows that the present opening quire consists of only 6 folios, as against the 8 of quires 2-7, but this is due to the loss of the two innermost folios.

[22] M. R. James, "List of MSS formerly owned by Dr John Dee," *Bibliographical Society Supplement* 1 (Oxford 1921) 29-30.

[23] Printed by Dales (n. 3 above).

[24] Printed by Dales (n. 4 above).

Fol. 228. *De phisionomia*; extracts from "Aristotle," "Loxus," "Palemon." (TKI 538; several MSS, one of the eleventh century.)

Fol. 233v. Galen, *De semine* in an early translation, ascribed in one fourteenth-century MS to Constantine the African. (TKI 1521; many MSS, of which this the earliest cited.)

Fol. 238v. Soranus, *Quaestiones medicinales*, ending imperfectly.[25] (TKI 860.)

II. Lost items:[26]

'*Constantini liber de Herbis.*'

Dioscorides, *De herbis femineis*. (Kirkestede, *Catalogus* 59, without incipit and explicit. As he mentions illustrations, his source might well have been Bodl. MS 130, made at Bury, eleventh-twelfth century. TKI 182 etc.)

Oribasius, *De herbarum virtutibus*. (TKI 6 etc.)

Odo de Meung, *Versus de virtutibus herbarum*, or *Macer*. (Kirkestede, *Catalogus* 107, as Macer, *De viribus herbarum*; inc. as in TKI 610.)

Isidore, *Etymologiae*.[27] (Kirkestede, *Catalogus* 147; incipit as TKI 435, and also explicit of complete work; but see preceding note.)

Constantine the African, *Liber de gradibus*. (Kirkestede, *Catalogus* 56, no incipit or explicit; TKI 11.)

'*Euphonis experimenta.*'

'*Adamarii experimenta.*'

'*Joh. Melancholici experimenta.*'

'*Experimenta abbatis.*'

'*Experimenta Wiscardi.*'

'*Experimenta Picoti.*'[28]

'*De urina mulieris.*' (Cf. TKI 116.)

A commentary on part of Hippocrates' *Epidimiarum*, entitled '*Expositio quintae incisionis epidemiarum Hippocratis.*'

'*Joh. Melancholici liber de substantia urinae.*'

Palladius, *De agricultura*. (Kirkestede, *Catalogus* 113; incipit as in TKI 1026, and also explicit of complete work.)

'*Liber de simplici medicina*'; Platearius?[29]

---

[25] Edited from this MS by V. Rose, *Anecdota graeca et graecolatina*, 2 vols. (Berlin 1864-1870) 2.243-274.

[26] Titles in inverted commas are as given in Dee's catalogue.

[27] LSQ (n. 7 above) 6 notes that book 4 of the *Etymologiae*, entitled *De medicina*, is often found separately in early medieval medical collections. Probably, therefore, this was the case here.

[28] This and the previous item bear Norman names; Picot was the name of a Norfolk family, but such a local name would seem strange in a collection of essentially Continental works.

[29] LSQ 30.

Of the above twenty-six items, about a dozen have some connection with southern Italy or Salerno. At least three or four, the translations of Alfanus and Constantine, are by Salernitan authors. The poem of Odo de Meung is based on works of Constantine,[30] and another five, the works of Nemesius, Soranus, Oribasius, Hippocrates, and Galen, were favorite texts of the medical school there.[31] If the *Liber de simplici medicina* is the work by Platearius, then it too is Salernitan.[32] Of the remaining items some are unidentified, and others were in common use all over twelfth-century Europe, so that they provide no clue as to the origin of the collection or collections from which the Cotton manuscript was copied. Its source was probably not a single manscript; the Norman names of Picot and Wiscard strike a jarring note amidst so many works that bear the stamp of an Italian origin. Again, the presence in the same manuscript of one full and one partial translation of Nemesius may be explained by the use of two or more separate sources. Nonetheless a large part, if not all, of the contents of the Cotton manuscript shows some connection with Salerno. But what of the four treatises that Haskins localized to southern Italy? If one of these could be shown to be Salernitan, this would make it more probable that all four were written there. This in turn would constitute a stronger case, while not amounting to direct proof, that the ultimate origin of the whole collection, or a large part of it, was Salernitan. In fact, one of these treatises, the *Liber Marii*, was almost certainly by a Salernitan author, as will now be demonstrated. Marius's work occupies folios 190-200 of the Cotton manuscript. Its beginning is lost, and the fact that the preceding treatise ends imperfectly on the opposite verso suggests that the two innermost folios of this, the first quire of the manuscript, are missing. This assumption is strengthened by the fact that this quire at present numbers six folios, whereas the next five quires each have eight. At the same time Marius's work probably occupied no more than one side of one of the two missing folios, namely the original verso opposite the present opening folio of his treatise, folio 190. This is suggested by the following line of reasoning. At the head of each double page of the treatise, the scribe has written *Liber Marii* on the left-hand verso, and *Liber i* or *ii* on the opposite recto. The only exception is folio 190, which is inscribed, more fully, *Liber primus*. The greater importance assigned by the scribe to this leaf surely indicates that it is the remaining half of the original opening double page of the work. This, of course, does not exclude the possibility of a preceding prologue.

The *Liber* is a dialogue between Master and Pupil in two books, the first dealing with the four elements, the second with their compounds. The Master

---

[30] Singer (n. 16 above). 188.
[31] LSQ 5, 18, and passim.
[32] *Ibid.* 30.

states that he has already written a work *De proficuo humano*[33] and promises another on the five senses.[34] Now in his well-known biobibliographic *Catalogus scriptorum ecclesiae*, "Boston of Bury," almost certainly identical with the above-mentioned Henry of Kirkestede,[35] notes *Marius Salernitanus* as the author of a work *De proficuo humano*.[36] Kirkestede does not give the incipit and explicit of this work, as he does whenever possible, nor does he indicate in which English libraries it might be found. This suggests second-hand knowledge, but the work is not to be found in any of Kirkestede's known sources, in particular the *Registrum Anglie de libris doctorum sive auctorum*.[37] In fact his source was probably the Cotton manuscript itself, which may have supplied him with other items in the *Catalogus*.[38] The now-missing leaf of the *De elementis*, if still in situ in Kirkestede's time, might well have provided him with the *Salernitanus*; certainly we know from his inscriptions that he was familiar with the manuscript. It does not necessarily detract from this argument that the *De elementis* itself does not figure in the *Catalogus*. Kirkestede's great work was never finished, and he frequently omits mention of books and treatises known to have been in the Bury library in his time, even if he used them as source material.

An earlier source seems to vindicate Kirkestede's description of Marius as a Salernitan. This is the necrology of the *Liber confratrum* belonging to the church of San Matteo di Salerno.[39] In a fragmentary calendar which it contains there appears the obit of one *Marius medicus* who died on 29 January in some year before 1217,[40] a date that would well suit the author of our treatise who was also obviously a *medicus*. They must surely be the same man. The likelihood of this is increased by the recent discovery of unacknowledged quotations from the *De elementis* in a work of Urso of Ca-

---

[33] Fol. 200ra.

[34] *Ibid.*

[35] Rouse (n. 20 above) 471-480. The *Catalogus* is extant only in a seventeenth-century transcript, Cambridge University Library Add. MS 3470.

[36] *Catalogus* 107.

[37] A catalogue of standard authors, their works, and the English libraries where these might be found, drawn up by the Franciscans between ca. 1250 and 1306. It is extant in three MSS, of which I have examined microfilms of the two best, Cambridge, Peterhouse 169, and Oxford, Bodl. Tanner 163.

[38] See the list of contents of the MS above. There are five *Catalogus* items of which the Cotton MS might possibly have been the source, although this cannot be proven.

[39] C. A. Garufi, *Necrologio del Liber confratrum di S. Matteo di Salerno* (Rome 1922).

[40] *Ibid.* 214. The calendar fragment, in one early thirteenth-century hand, with many later additions, extends from January to June of an unnamed year. On the basis of palaeography and the ferial numbers, Garufi worked out this year as either 1206 or 1217 (211). It must be the latter, since included in it is the obit of the well-known physician Maurus, who died in 1214 (216, 357).

labria, the great Salernitan physician who died in 1225.[41] From this we should expect Marius to be an older man than Urso, and this would fit in well with the pre-1217 date of *Marius medicus*'s death. Given this evidence, the character of his treatise, evidently a handbook for students, and the fact that in it he assumes the role of *magister*, it seems likely that Marius was a Master in the medical school at Salerno.[42]

Some attempt must now be made to date the composition of the *De elementis*. Firstly, the work can hardly have been written much before circa 1175, unless the author died at an exceptional age for a medieval man. The Urso quotations do not help much, since, with the possible exception of some fragments dated circa 1170, the earliest manuscripts of his works are dated circa 1200,[43] more or less contemporaneously with the Cotton Galba manuscript. Secondly, Marius had already written at least one other work before he came to compose the *De elementis* and had, as he testifies, traveled widely;[44] it is thus more likely to be the work of a mature than of a budding scholar. This in turn means that the transmission of the *De elementis* to England must have been relatively rapid, even if we give the Cotton manuscript its latest possible date of circa 1200. For the fact that it was written in England means, of course, that Marius's work had reached there already. It might be worth adding that the Cotton manuscript shows no sign of having been copied from a manuscript in Beneventan script, the script in which a Salernitan codex would have been written.[45] This may mean that it was copied from a northern European, perhaps yet another English manuscript; but this is to hazard too much.

Lawn has stated the Cotton manuscript to be the earliest piece of evidence for the presence of Salernitan-derived science in England, referring, of course, to the translations of Constantine and Alfanus contained in it.[46] At the same time, he does not doubt that such knowledge had begun to arrive at an earlier date,[47] and this has since been abundantly confirmed by the researches of

[41] Kindly communicated to me by Dr. R. C. Dales, who is currently preparing an edition of Marius's work. For Urso's dates, see LSQ (n. 7 above) 31-33.

[42] On the difference between *medicus*, any practicing physician, and *magister*, a teacher in the school at Salerno, see H. P. Bayon, "The Masters of Salerno and the origins of professional medical practice," *Science, Medicine and History; Essays in honour of Charles Singer*, ed. E. A. Underwood, 2 vols. (Oxford 1953) 1.203-219, esp. 207-210.

[43] LSQ 32 and n. 4.

[44] Fol. 199ra.

[45] Using the criteria listed by E. A. Lowe, *The Beneventan Script* (Oxford 1914) chap. 8.

[46] LSQ (n. 7 above) 66.

[47] *Ibid.* 58, 63. It was once thought—and sometimes still is—that the *Peri didaxeon*, a medical compilation drawing on the writings of the eleventh-century Salernitan physician Petrocellus, was written in Anglo-Saxon during the twelfth century (M. Löweneck, "*Peri didaxeon*; eine Sammlung von Rezepten in englischen Sprache aus dem 11-12 Jahrhundert nach einer HS des Britischen Museums," *Erlanger Beiträge zur englischen Philo-*

C. H. Talbot.[48] He notes Constantinian works at Westminster, Exeter, Battle, Bury, and Canterbury, a *Passionarius Galieni* at Norwich Priory, the *Experimenta archiepiscopi salernitani* (i.e. Alfanus) at Westminster, and an *Antidotarium Nicholai* at Durham, all in the earlier twelfth century.[49] The Bury books, three copies of Constantine's *Pantegni*,[50] appear in the earlier part of a composite twelfth-century library catalogue from that house,[51] dated by T. A. M. Bishop not long after circa 1150.[52] One of them is almost certainly to be identified with an extant copy written in the Bury scriptorium circa 1150.[53] At some time during his reign (1177-1194) Abbot Bartholomew of Peterborough presented the abbey library with a *Practica Bartholomei* "*cum pluribus aliis rebus in uno volumine.*"[54] Nor were such works found only in the more comprehensive libraries; at Lanercost Priory, about the turn of the twelfth and thirteenth centuries, a collection of Salernitan translations was copied, including works of Hippocrates, Galen, Johannitius, Theophilus, and Philaretus.[55] Dr. Talbot also notes a recipe from Constantine's *Liber graduum* quoted by John of Tilbury, one of Becket's *familia*, in about 1174, and a passage from Copho's *De febribus* utilized by Peter of Blois about the following year.[56] Nevertheless, in every case the works referred to are those of Salernitan physicians who flourished well before circa 1170, after which date a new kind of writing, distinguished by a more theoretical and philosophical approach, and using Arabic and Aristotelian sources,

---

logie 12 [1896], who edited the work; for a more recent repetition of this view, see Singer [n. 16 above] 148). However, the opinion of N. R. Ker must be authoritative: that the work is in early Middle English, and that the MS (Brit. Mus. Harl. 6258) must be dated after ca. 1200 (*Catalogue of MSS containing Anglo-Saxon* [Oxford 1957] xix). Cf., moreover, the statement of C. H. Talbot, that "the *Peri didaxeon* . . . is merely a part translation of a Petrocellus text available to the Anglo-Saxons in the ninth century . . . [and] . . . has no connection with Salerno." (*Medicine in Medieval England* [London 1967] 45.) Lawn himself convincingly demonstrates that Adelard of Bath did not, as is sometimes stated, draw on Salernitan writings in his *De eodem et diverso* and *Quaestiones naturales* (LSQ 20-30).

[48] Talbot (n. 48 above).

[49] *Ibid.* 46-47.

[50] That is, his translation of the *Theorica* or first part of the *Al-Malaki* of Ali ben Abbas, fl. tenth century (Haskins [n. 1 above] 131-132).

[51] Printed in M. R. James, *On the Abbey of St. Edmund at Bury 1: the Library*, Cambridge Antiquarian Soc. 8vo ser. 28 (1895) 23-32. See no. cxviii and previous unnumbered item.

[52] T. A. M. Bishop, "Notes on Cambridge MSS 2," *Transactions of the Cambridge Bibliographical Society* 2, (1954-1958), 185.

[53] Cambridge, Trinity Coll. 906. Parker (n. 8 above) 316.

[54] Talbot (n. 48 above) 47.

[55] *Ibid.* 46-47. This is the collection known later as the *articella* (42-43). Dr Talbot dates this MS tentatively to late in the twelfth century. Cf. N. R. Ker, *Medieval Libraries of Great Britain* ed. 2 (London 1964) 108.

[56] Talbot 47.

began at Salerno.[57] There has hitherto been found no evidence for the presence in England of the works of these later twelfth-century Salernitan writers such as Urso and Maurus until the next century.[58] Alexander Neckham is the first Englishman known to have employed typically Salernitan *quaestiones phisicales* based extensively on the works of Urso of Calabria, in his *De natura rerum*, circa 1215.[59] For actual English manuscripts of these later Salernitan works, Lawn is forced to draw on the mid-thirteenth and fourteenth centuries.[60]

It is in this respect that the Cotton manuscript is now shown to be of more interest than Lawn realized, since as well as the works of earlier Salernitan writers, it contains at least one later Salernitan treatise, possibly more, if we concede such an origin for the other three of Haskins's south Italian or Sicilian works. Certainly there is an inherent likelihood of a Salernitan provenance for the one identified as a translation from Nemesius, since his treatise was a standard text in the medical school there.[61] Marius's own work is in some ways representative of the new approach in Salernitan science, in its dialogue form, its comprehensive, philosophical emphasis, and its acquaintance, yet to be fully clarified, with Arabic and Aristotelian writings. At the same time, the work exhibits an impressive concern with observed facts and deliberately constructed experiments as the basis for reasoning about natural phenomena. The sophisticated distinction is continually drawn between arguments conceived *visibiliter, rationaliter,* or *per experimentum.*[62] In contrast, the medical interest of the work is marginal; its main emphasis is on chemistry. This might seem surprising in a treatise that we are trying to establish, in a brief compass, as typically Salernitan. A partial answer seems to be that Marius treated elsewhere of the more purely medical aspects of his study, in his *De proficuo humano,* and his work on the five senses, if it was ever completed. The *De elementis* may well represent only one facet of his interests.

The evidence of the Cotton manuscript is that this new type of Salernitan work was being transmitted to England from circa 1175 on, and soon after writing. It even seems permissible to conclude that, if a relatively obscure work like Marius's reached England so quickly, surely the same must have been true of the writings of his more important contemporaries, Urso and Maurus. Finally, the *De elementis,* inasmuch as it contains some typically Sa-

---

[57] *Ibid.* 42-44.

[58] LSQ (n. 7 above) 65-67.

[59] *Ibid.* 63.

[60] *Ibid.* 67 esp. n. 3 for the earliest known English MS (Brit. Mus. Add. 25031) to contain later Salernitan works.

[61] *Ibid.* 18.

[62] Fols. 192ra; 192v; 193vb; 196ra; 196vb, et al.

lernitan *quaestiones phisicales*,[63] seems to support Lawn's hypothesis that Alexander Neckham could have obtained his own knowledge of them in his native country.[64] More broadly, if it is agreed that Marius was, with a high degree of probability, a Salernitan Master, then the Cotton manuscript is evidence for a more rapid transmission of the new scientific learning across Europe than has hitherto been recognized.

[63] Cf. the *quaestiones* printed in LSQ 161-177, with those found in Marius, fol. 192vb; 199ra; 199va, *et al.*

[64] LSQ 64.

Department of History
University of Sydney
Sydney, New South Wales
Australia

MARIUS "ON THE ELEMENTS" AND THE TWELFTH-CENTURY SCIENCE OF MATTER

•

by Richard C. Dales

I

Very little is known about the study of matter in the twelfth century. Robert Multhauf, who has written the most comprehensive and satisfactory account of early chemistry[1] virtually ignores the period except for the translations that were made during that time, although he mentions the remarkable *De diversis artibus* of Theophilus.[2] During the past generation several writers have drawn attention to the subject,[3] and their suggestions have led a few contemporary scholars to explore the subject more fully.[4]

---

[1] Robert P. Multhauf, *The Origins of Chemistry* (New York 1966).

[2] Multhauf 157-158. On Theophilus see *Theophilus de diversis artibus*, ed. C. R. Dodwell (London 1961). Dodwell makes a strong case (xxxiii-xliv) for identifying Theophilus with Roger of Helmarshaven, a craftsman-monk of northwest Germany of the first half of the twelfth century.

[3] Alexandre Birkenmajer, "Le rôle joué par les medecins et les naturalistes dans la réception d'Aristote au xiie siècle," *La Pologne au VIe congrès international des sciences historiques, Oslo, 1928.* (Warsaw 1930) 1-15; Paul O. Kristeller, "The School at Salerno," *Bulletin of the History of Medicine* 17 (1945) 138-194, repr. in Kristeller, *Studies in Renaissance Thought and Letters* (Rome 1956) 495-551; Charles H. Haskins, *Studies in the History of Mediaeval Science* (Cambridge, Mass. 1924), repr. New York 1960, esp. 92-95. Avicennae *De congelatione et conglutinatione lapidum*, being sections of the *Kitab al-Shifa*, the Latin and Arabic texts, ed. and trans. E. J. Holmyard and D. C. Mandeville (Paris 1927).

[4] For example, Brian Lawn, *The Salernitan Questions* (Oxford 1963), and another study of the same subject to be published soon in the series *Auctores britannici medii aevi*; Joan Cadden, *De elementis: Earth, Water, Air, and Fire in the Twelfth and Thirteenth Centuries*, M. A. thesis, Columbia University 1968; Theodore Silverstein, "*Elementatum*: Its Appearance among the Twelfth-Century Cosmologists," *Mediaeval Studies* 16 (1954) 156-162, and "Guillaume de Conches and the Elements: *Homiomeria and organica*," *Mediaeval Studies*, 26 (1964) 163-167; Rodney M. Thomson, "*Liber Marii de elementis*: the work of a hitherto unknown Salernitan master," *Viator* 3 (1972) 179-189; James K. Otte, *Alfred of Sareshel's Commentary on the Metheora of Aristotle*, Ph.D. thesis, University of Southern California 1969; R. C. Dales, "Anonymi *De elementis*: From a Twelfth-Century Collection of Scientific Works in British Museum MS Cotton Galba E. IV," *Isis* 56 (1965) 174-189, and "An Unnoticed Translation of the Chapter De elementis from Nemesius' *De natura hominis*," *Medievalia et Humanistica* 17 (1966) 13-19.

But compared to the effort that has been expended on the Chartrain scientist-philosophers of the twelfth century, on Robert Grosseteste and his "school" in the thirteenth, and the mathematical physicists in the fourteenth, this may still be considered among the neglected topics in the history of medieval science.

A fuller investigation of twelfth-century studies of matter may well lead us to modify fairly drastically our characterization of twelfth-century science. It is generally described as naïve, lacking in rigor or in a coherent world view, painfully ad hoc in its explanations, dominated by magic and astrology, and as dependent for its advancement on the new translations from Greek and Arabic which appeared at an increasing rate throughout the century. A close examination of the texts dealing with the science of matter reveals that some of them do not fit this description. Outstanding among these is a book *On the Elements* by a certain Marius, probably but not certainly a Salernitan master.[5] This work was first noticed by Haskins,[6] who suggested that it would repay further study but who passed over it with a brief description. It is contained in a unique manuscript, British Museum, Cotton Galba E. IV, folios 190-200, written in an English hand of circa 1200, and probably copied from a north French manuscript that in turn would have been based on the south Italian original.[7] Thus the minimum number of manuscripts that must be posited to lie behind the only extant one already attests to a reasonably wide diffusion. Why then was it not used by later Latin writers?

In fact, it was. There are two twelfth-century works that pillaged much material from Marius,[8] and it would be unlikely if continued investigation did not turn up more of the same. We have hitherto been looking in the wrong places. Historians of chemistry turn to the alchemical works, to Michael Scot, Saint Albert, and Roger Bacon, and even to Saint Thomas for information about the development of Latin chemistry, while they and his-

[5] See Thomson (n. 4 above).

[6] Haskins (n. 3 above) 93-94.

[7] For the date of Cotton Galba E. IV see Dales, "Anonymi De elementis," 175 and Thomson 00, who also discusses the apparent fact that this manuscript was not copied directly from a Beneventan model. The most likely place for the intermediate manuscript to have been written is northern France, which had numerous connections with both Salerno and England during the twelfth century and where a twelfth-century manuscript plagiarizing Marius was written. See n. 8 below.

[8] Bibliothèque Nationale MS lat. 15015, fols. 200r-223v, late twelfth century, contains an anonymous work, largely on astronomy, which borrows considerable material from Marius. Using *De elementis* even more extensively is the anonymous *Compendiosus tractatus de philosophia et eius secretis* contained in Vatican MS Barb. lat. 283, fourteenth century, parts of which, fols. 61v-74r, Joan Cadden has edited in her M.A. thesis (see n. 3 above). She dates it early thirteenth century. I am indebted to Dr. Cadden for my knowledge of both these works.

torians in general have tended to overlook other kinds of writing which might provide a very different picture.

In the present essay I examine in detail Marius's *De elementis*, in the hope that it may lead to further studies of twelfth- and thirteenth-century chemical texts, and that it may point the way to a reevaluation of twelfth-century science in general and of the early history of western chemistry in particular.

II

De elementis is cast in the form of a dialogue between student and teacher. The characters of the two participants are developed to some degree, as is the relationship between them. The student is much more than a foil and frequently asks some very sharp questions, points out inconsistencies in the teacher's explanations, or refuses to accept an unsatisfactory answer. The style of the work is charming, sometimes striving for literary effect (and here the model seems to have been Calcidius), but often becoming conversational.

Its purpose is to investigate the material constitution and basic processes of the physical world, and in this it had no authoritative antique models. Robert Multhauf has pointed out[9] that the science of matter was not considered a separate and special area of investigation in Antiquity, but was peripheral to the main interests of all scientists and philosophers from Plato onward.[10] From this perspective, the subject matter alone of this treatise gives it the importance of a pioneer work. *De elementis* is characterized by its originality. The author had read other works that treated his subject, but none of these was adequate. He therefore found it necessary to choose among conflicting authorities, to fill in gaps in ancient accounts, and sometimes to strike out into unexplored territory.

Marius's work consists of two books, the first treating the simple elements, earth, water, air, and fire, and the second investigating the compound bodies that arise from them. The first two columns of the work are lost, and the extant portion begins with the student asking about the nature of water. One is struck immediately by the master's insistence on supporting every assertion by some sort of experimental evidence, ranging from appeals to everyday experience and "thought experiments" to experiments specifically contrived (and apparently performed) to test particular hypotheses, and by the rigor of his arguments. He observes closely and accurately over a

---

[9] Multhauf (n. 1 above) 11.

[10] Numerous authors, of course, had something to say about the topic, but their treatments were always fairly brief. Marius's treatise occupies 79 typed pages; it would be about 85 if the beginning were not lost.

wide range of phenomena. The investigation proceeds by the question-and-answer method, with the student and teacher sometimes exchanging roles. In order to provide a unifying framework for his treatise and perhaps also to connect it with the accepted authoritative learned tradition, Marius attempts to place all of his findings among Aristotle's ten categories: only the first four categories are found in the simple elements, the other six in compound bodies. Although the work is generally well planned and proceeds logically, it is interspersed with questions, sometimes of doubtful relevance, of the type common at Salerno.[11]

The heart of Marius's teaching is his doctrine of substance, which he calls "the key to the whole of philosophy". Its origin was God's creation. In itself it is three-dimensional extention, devoid of all qualities. In fact, during the first part of Book 1, Marius refers to it as "body" (*corpus*). It occupies place, is spherical, and is finite, for otherwise it could not be moved. Calcidius (speaking of matter—*hyle*—rather than substance) had posed the question of its finitude[12] but had concluded that it was infinite, since if it were terminated in space it would possess qualities, that is, number and figure. Marius is unwilling to accept the conclusion but argues unsuccessfully (or at least unclearly) that it could be both ways: finite, yet lacking all qualities. He argued that it could not be moved if it were infinite, and here his argument seems to owe something to Aristotle's *De caelo*,[13] although not directly. In language borrowed from Genesis, he has a god strongly resembling Plato's demiurge making an essentially Aristotelian universe in his summary of his teaching:

> In the beginning, God created a certain body, and He created it simple and devoid of any accident, but nevertheless a kind of thing which occupied a place, and He attributed quantity to it and circumscribed it by three dimensions; and it was capable of being moved, and behold, it received motion. But He also divided this same body into four parts, of which He completely heated up and dried out one, and from this He made fire; the second He also heated up and made completely wet—this was air. From the third, which He made completely cold as well as wet, He made water. The fourth was made cold and utterly dry—this is earth. There was therefore this one and simple substance for the four elements, much as a ball of wax is to the diverse forms made from it, one of a man, another of an ox, the third of a fish, and the fourth of a bird. For, just as, although

---

[11] This is also pointed out by Thompson (n. 4 above) 00. For examples of the questions, see Lawn (n. 4 above) 158-177.

[12] *Timaeus a Calcidio translatus commentarioque instructus*, ed. J. H. Waszink. *Plato latinus*, ed. R. Klibansky 4 (1962), Comm. 2 ch. 311.311.

[13] 1.3 (269b), 1.5 (271b-272a), 4.1 (308a).

the form of a man might be destroyed and the form of an ox take its place, or the form of an ox be replaced by that of a fish, or that of fish by that of a bird, or the other way around, nevertheless the wax will always be one thing; in the same way, although earth may be changed into water, water into air, and air into fire, and the other way around, nevertheless substance will always remain exactly the same. Also just as the forms that were in the wax will not be found existing by themselves but only in wax or in another body, similarly howsoever the qualities of the elements are changed or destroyed, you will never be able to find them apart from substance.[14]

This substance then is analogous to what will later be termed *forma corporeitatis* or *prima materia*, but it is not simply a metaphysical principle; it is the physical foundation of the three-dimensional universe—extended substance. It is imperceptible to sense and can only be known by reason. Nevertheless, through the qualities imposed upon its four parts by the Creator, it ultimately causes all the sensible qualities that we perceive.

These sensible qualities, thought of "all together at one time, as though they were one thing," constitute the "form" of each element; they cannot exist independently of substance (he does not say "matter"), but once joined to substance they can be perceived, and they make it possible to know substance by reason, even though it can never itself be sensed. This union of the formal parts, since it too can only be apprehended by reason, can be thought of in itself, and is not susceptible of corruption in thought, is also a kind of substance, and on the authority of Aristotle he calls it "secondary substance."

Marius describes both the "nature" and "property" of each element. Earth's nature is cold and dryness, its property is heaviness. Water's nature is cold

[14] In principio creavit Deus quoddam corpus, et creavit illud simplum, et omni accidente nudum, sed tale tamen, necnon occuparet locum, eique quantitatem attribuit, ac tribus dimensionibus circumscripsit; moveri quoque ipsum valuit, et ecce motum recipit. Sed et idem corpus in IIII partes divisit, quarum unam quidem omnino calefecit et siccavit, et inde ignem fecit; aliam quoque calefactam et omnino humiditatem fecit aerem. Quarta autem frigida facta est atque omnino sicca, hec est terra. Fuit igitur illa una ac simpla substantia ad IIII elementa, quod quedam cere massam ad IIII formas diversas ex eadem confectas, unam hominis, aliam bovis, terciam piscis, et quartam volucris. Quemadmodum enim, licet forma hominis deleatur, et fiat forma bovis, bovis vero forma piscis, et piscis forma volucris, et econverso, cera tamen semper una erit, ita licet terra mutetur in amnem, aqua in aerem, et aer in ignem, et econverso, substantia tamen prorsus eadem remanebit. Quemadmodum etiam forme que in cera erant non invenientur per se, nisi vel in cera vel in alio corpore ita et elementorum qualitates quoquomodo commutentur sive deleantur, sine substantia nequaquam poteris invenire. Fol. 192rb-va. Professor Marshall Clagett has pointed out to me the similarity between this and Saint Gregory of Nyssa's view (*De hominis opificio* 24; PG 44.211-214. See P. Duhem, *Le système du monde* II (Paris 1914) 429-431.

and moisture, its property is also heaviness. The nature of air is heat and
moisture, its property is "to rise upward". Fire's nature is heat and dryness,
and its property likewise is to rise upward. The tendency to move upward
or downward depends not on heat and cold, but rather on dryness and moisture.
The pure elements do not have colors, tastes, and odors; only composite
bodies do. Each element can be changed into the one contiguous to it by
an increase or decrease in one of the four qualities caused by the interaction
of mixed bodies. The element that receives the most interesting treatment
is fire, which is considered by Marius to be a stranger or visitor here among
us and consequently to need constant nourishment in order to maintain
itself in existence.[15] This nourishment he identifies as air, and to support
his contention he notes that nothing burns without first being vaporized
(that is, turned into air), and that if the supply of air is cut off, a flame goes
out.

There is no mention of the *"elementatum"* theory[16] in Marius's work, nor
is there any need for it in his scheme of things. His elements are not im-
material first principles, but the actual physical constituents of the universe.
The created things of the world all contain all four elements, and so no element ever actually exists in its pure state. However, everything that exists
derives its being and its characteristics from the exact proportion of each
of the four elements it contains.[17]

At the beginning of Book 2, Marius develops a quantitative theory showing
the various ways in which the four elements could be mixed, and presents
this schematically in tables. He begins with "just two elements at a time,
while we gain some practice and become more accustomed to this sort of
thing," and then goes on to specify the 145 possible mixtures of the four
elements, assuming that they can be mixed either in equal or unequal proportions; in the latter case there may be either more or less, or, if there were
more than two elements, there may be much, a moderate amount, or a small
amount of each element. Tables 1-3 reproduce his last three tables from
folios 195v-196r.

---

[15] He could have got this notion either from Aristotle, *De generatione et corruptione* 2.8
(335a) or Macrobius, *Saturnalia*, 7, 13, 3, ed. F. Eyssenhardt (Leipzig 1868) 444, but he
goes far beyond what either of these authors says.

[16] See Silverstein, *"Elementatum"* (n. 4 above).

[17] There is no claim here that Marius anticipated the law of definite proportions. He
does not discuss the question of whether they *can* only combine in certain proportions,
or whether there are infinite possibilities; he probably meant the latter. Nor does he seem
to think that a slight difference in the proportions would make any but a correspondingly
slight difference in the resulting compound.

TABLE 1
Twelve Species in Four Elements

Tabula ad alias XII species in IIII elementis, ubi duo de ipsis inter se sunt equalia, et alia duo inequalia et inter se et erga alia, que sunt equalia, sed est de equalibus mediocriter in compositione; de inequalibus vero, de altero magis quam de equalibus, de altero autem minus quam de equalibus.

Magis quam de equalibus	*Inequalia*		*Minus quam de equalibus*
	Equalia inter se		
Aqua	Ignis	Aer	Terra
Terra	Ignis	Aer	Aqua
Aer	Ignis	Aqua	Terra
Terra	Ignis	Aqua	Aer
Aer	Ignis	Terra	Aqua
Aqua	Ignis	Terra	Aer
Ignis	Aer	Aqua	Terra
Terra	Aer	Aqua	Ignis
Ignis	Aer	Terra	Aqua
Aqua	Aer	Terra	Ignis
Ignis	Aqua	Terra	Aer
Aer	Aqua	Terra	Ignis

TABLE 2
Twelve Species in Four Elements

Tabula ad tercias XII species in IIII elementis, duo de ipsis inter se sunt equalia, et alia duo inequalia et inter se et erga alia que sunt equalia, sed est de equalibus in compositione, de altero magis quam de suo inequali et de altero magisquam de equalibus, de equalibus vero minus quam de omnibus.

Inequalia		*Equalia*	
Magis quam de suo in equalibus	*Magis quam de inequalibus*	*inter se et est minus quam de inequalibus*	
Aqua	Terra	Ignis	Aer
Terra	Aqua	Ignis	Aer
Aer	Terra	Ignis	Aqua
Terra	Aer	Ignis	Aqua
Aer	Aqua	Ignis	Terra
Aqua	Aer	Ignis	Terra
Ignis	Terra	Aer	Aqua
Terra	Ignis	Aer	Aqua
Ignis	Aqua	Aer	Terra
Aqua	Ignis	Aer	Terra
Ignis	Aer	Aqua	Terra
Aer	Ignis	Aqua	Terra

TABLE 3

Twenty-four Species in Four Elements

Tabula ad XXIIII species, ubi in composito de IIII elementis, est inequale unumquodque ab alio; de secundo videlicet minus quam de primo, de tertio minus quam de secundo, de quarto minus quam de omnibus.			
Primum	*Secundum*	*Tercium*	*Quartum*
Ignis	Aer	Aqua	Terra
Ignis	Aer	Terra	Aqua
Ignis	Aqua	Aer	Terra
Ignis	Aqua	Terra	Aer
Ignis	Terra	Aer	Aqua
Ignis	Terra	Aqua	Aer
Aer	Aqua	Terra	Ignis
Aer	Aqua	Ignis	Terra
Aer	Terra	Aqua	Ignis
Aer	Terra	Ignis	Aqua
Aer	Ignis	Aqua	Terra
Aer	Ignis	Terra	Aqua
Aqua	Terra	Ignis	Aer
Aqua	Terra	Aer	Ignis
Aqua	Ignis	Terra	Aer
Aqua	Ignis	Aer	Terra
Aqua	Aer	Terra	Ignis
Aqua	Aer	Ignis	Terra
Terra	Ignis	Aer	Aqua
Terra	Ignis	Aqua	Aer
Terra	Aer	Ignis	Aqua
Terra	Aer	Aqua	Ignis
Terra	Aqua	Ignis	Aer
Terra	Aqua	Aer	Ignis

Of the 145 possible combinations, Marius says that "you will perceive some by a bodily sense, others you will understand only in your mind." Since everything that actually exists must be composed of all four elements, he must at least be excluding all combinations of fewer than four; whether or not he also means that some combinations of all four are only theoretically possible is not clear.

Marius also holds that any composite can be resolved into its constituent elements, and to illustrate his teaching he performs a qualitative analysis of milk:

> *Teacher*: If someone should give you some milk and ask you to which of the 145 kinds of mixture it was similar, what would you answer him?

Student: It is known immediately that milk is liquid, thick, and greasy—exceedingly liquid, somewhat less thick than liquid, but more so than it is greasy. And water is liquid, earth is thick, air is greasy. We cannot find fire in it visibly, but we can prove by experience that it is present, for man is warmed up as a result of drinking milk. Therefore it can truly be said that there is less of fire than of anything else in milk. And so I might answer that milk is similar to that kind of mixture in which there is much water, less earth, still less air, and least of all fire.

Teacher: You have answered correctly. But in order that you might understand the same thing better, I want you to divide that composite in the milk and separate each element from the others, for thus you will have a clearer and stronger argument.

Student: I wish you would show me how to do this.

Teacher: I shall gladly show you. But first answer a question. If someone now wished to tear down a certain house that had been built of wood, iron and stones, could the house revert to anything but wood, iron, and stones?

Student: Indeed, it would return to that which it was before it became a house.

Teacher: And if some one agitated milk, would not a greasy substance—that is, butter—appear on the top?

Student: Yes, it would.

Teacher: Then if he removes the greasy substance and puts what remains into a jar, and does to it what one does in making rosewater, you should know that fresh and potable water comes forth from it. But if he also burns the waste matter that remains in the bottom of the jar, it will turn into ashes, and thus earth.

Student: I see clearly that earth and water return from the milk; but concerning the greasy substance that you said was air, I do not understand that it is turned into air.

Teacher: Only air would nourish the fire; and that fire is nourished by it is visibly apparent to all.

Student: You have explained clearly about earth, water, and air. But how will you show fire to be in milk?

Teacher: Indeed, there is only a very small amount of fire in it, and for that reason it can be perceived only by reason. But it can be said to be present also, since that little bit of fire joins itself to other fire when the denser part of the mixture is burned.[18]

---

[18] M. Si ergo aliquis lac tibi afferret, et cui harum CXLV specierum simile esset inquireret, quid inde ei responderes?

D. Notum profecto est, lac esse liquidum, spissum, et pingue, liquidum quidem valde, spissum vero minusquam liquidum, sed plusquam pingue. Et liquidum est aqua, spissum

At this point, the student asks a key question: "How is it that there are in the world almost innumerable kinds of composite bodies, and yet you, in your analysis, have divided them into only 145 kinds?" But the teacher has a response: "If you multiply 145 kinds either by increasing or decreasing the parts, you will undoubtedly find them innumerable. There are only seven in which you cannot either diminish or increase the elements: one, the mixture of all four elements in which they are all equal; the six others, the mixtures of two elements at a time in which the two similarly are equal in the composite."[19]

The question now remains: In that way, if at all, do the elements persist in a compound?[20] For even though a compound may be resolved into its elements, it is clearly something other than a simple mixture of them. Aristotle

---

terra, pingue aer. Ignem vero in eo nequaquam possumus visibiliter invenire, sed possumus experimento approbare ipsum in eo esse, calefit enim homo ex lactis comestione. Vere igitur dici potest de igne minusquam de omnibus esse in lacte. Responderem itaque lac esse simile speciei illi, ubi magis est de aqua, minus de terra, minus etiam de aere, minimum vero omnium de igne.

M. Recte quidem responderes, sed ut idem melius intelliges, vellem in compositum lactis illud divideres, et elementa unumquodque ab alio separares, ita enim lucidius atque potentius argumentum haberes.

D. Volo illud quomodo faciam insinues.

M. Libenter utique ostendam, sed prius michi responde quod queram. Siquis modo diruere vellet domum quandam que ex lignis et ferro lapidibusque esset composita, nunquid redigi posset, nisi in ferrum, lapides atque ligna?

D. Profecto in id rediret, quod erat antequam domus fieret.

M. Si itaque aliquis lac moverit, nunquid non statim pinguendo, hoc est butirum superemineret?

D. Utique faceret.

M. Quod si emissa pinguedine quod remanet, in vas commiserit, ac sicut de aqua rosata fit de eo fecerit, scias quia dulcis inde atque potabilis aqua exibit. Si vero etiam fecam que in vasis fundo remanserit comburet, cinis quidem atque ita terra fiet.

D. De terra et aqua patenter video quod ex lacte redit; de pinguedine vero quam aerem esse dixisti, non intelligo quod aer fit.

M. Quippe nisi aer, nequaquam ignem dietaret, sed ignem inde dietari, cunctis visibiliter apparet.

D. Bene ostensum est de terra, aqua et aere; sed quomodo ostendes in lacte ignem esse?

M. Parum nempe est in eo de igne, quare et percipi non valet nisi ratione; sed et dici potest quoniam illud parum alii igni se adiunxit, in spissitudinis combustione. Fol. 196ra-rb.

[19] M. Si has CXLV species secundum partes sive crescendo sive decrescendo multiplices, innumerabiles eas proculdubio invenies. Septem tantum excipies, in quibus neque diminuere elementa neque augmentare multiplicando vales, unam quidem in IIII elementis in qua equalia sunt in composito cuncta elementa, sex vero reliquas in binis et binis, in quibus II similiter sunt in compositione equalia. Fol. 196rb.

[20] On the history of this problem, see H. H. Joachim, "Aristotle's Conception of Chemical Combination," *The Journal of Philology* 29 (1904) 72-86; Otto Apelt, "Die Shrift des Alexander von Aphrodisias über die Mischung," *Philologus* 45 (1886) 82-99; and Multhauf (n. 1 above) 122-123, 149-153.

had attempted a solution,[21] and it seems to me probable that Marius had some sort of second-hand knowledge of this. However, his own solution is much more thorough and more satisfactory. Aristotle had ignored the question of *how* the process from element to compound occurs, but had emphasized that the elements existed only potentially in a compound and that "only those agents are combinable which involve a contrary." He seems to have considered the resulting *mixis* (usually rendered *mixtio* in Latin) as simply the mean established among the contrarieties involved. Marius, utilizing the concepts of "temperament" and "complexion" from post-Aristotelian medical literature, as well as adapting Aristotle's doctrine of potentiality, gives a much more satisfactory explanation. When any two elements are combined, the similar qualities will reinforce each other, but the contrary qualities will each try to destroy the other and in the process each is altered from its own nature. This must occur before the compound is formed and is something more than the establishment of a mean between the qualities, as Aristotle had it. In introducing his discussion, Marius had pointed out:

> In a fruit composed of the four elements, none of them is found there actually, but only potentially. For if fire were actually in the fruit, that fruit would undoubtedly be found to be hot. If air were actually in the apple itself, the fire existing in it actually would destroy that air, and the fruit would not be durable. But we know that a fruit lasts for many months. If, however, water were actually in the fruit, it would either certainly flow out, or it would be turned into vapor by the force of the fire existing in it actually. And if earth were in the fruit actually, its own heaviness would clearly be the cause of its own destruction. Another argument: If the four elements were actually in the fruit, one of them would not be able to exist for an hour with another. For it has been established that fire flees from water, and conversely, as has been established above in this book. Therefore, it is clear that a fruit can only exist if each one of the elements in it were changed into something other than it was before it became a fruit.[22]

---

[21] *De generatione et corruptione* 1.10 (327b-328a) and 2.7 (334a).

[22] In pomo ex IIII[or] elementis composito, nullum illorum actu sed potentia reperitur. Si enim ignis in pomo actu esset, absque dubio calidum reperiretur. Si vero aer ipsi malo actu inesset, ignis in eo actu existens ipsum aerem pessundaret, pomumque durabile non esset. Sed multis mensibus pomum durare cernimus. Si autem aqua pomo actu inesset, vel certe deflueret, vel ob vim ignis in co actu existentis in vaporem redigeretur. Quod si terra pomo actu inesset, sua sine ambiguitate gravitas esset sibi causa ruine. Aluid argumentum: Si illa IIII elementa in pomo in actu essent, unum illorum vel una hora cum alio consistere nequiret. Ratum est enim ignem aquam fugare, et econverso, sicut in hoc libro superius explanatum est. Manifestum igitur est pomum consistere nequire, nisi unumquodque quod in eo est elementorum in aliud mutetur quam esset, priusquam pomum fieret. Fol. 197 va.

Rather, we have something occuring analogous to the modern notion of a chemical compound, with the result being actuality different from the elements, although made by and from them, its characteristics depending on the proportions of the elements that constitute the compound:

> But since fire would oppose water in the composition of an apple, fire operates on water and water undergoes its operation; also in the same way, water operates on fire, and fire undergoes the operation of water. And each of them tries to alter the other from its nature, since when fire operates on water it heats it up and dries it out; and conversely when water operates on fire, it imparts cold and moisture. And in the same way when air opposes earth in the composition of the fruit, both of them struggle to drive the other from their own nature, and each of them operates on the other and undergoes the operation of the other. When earth operates on air it bestows solidity and dryness on it; but when air operates on earth it makes it hot and moist. For this reason therefore there is made from the four elements another mixture, another temperament, and another complexion than existed before, since each one of them, from that state of actuality in which it existed earlier, is changed into something else. Nor will any of them be found in the fruit in that previous state of actuality, since each one is changed.[23]

The student then amplifies the author's meaning:

> I understand very clearly what you have said. For earlier I heard you affirming that when two contrary elements oppose each other, each of them seeks to alter the other from its own nature until it itself is altered from its own nature which previously existed actually. For example: When fire is joined potentially with a small amount of water so that there is not enough fire to turn away the water, nor so much water that it puts out the fire, each of them operates on the other and undergoes the operation of the other. For if fire operates on water, it lessens its thickness and moistness. But if water operates on fire, it diminishes the heat which was previously in it, and the dryness. And thus one fights against the other until

---

[23] Cum vero ignis in mali compositione aque obviet, ignis in aqua operatur, et aqua eius opera suscipit; aqua quoque eodem modo in igne operatur, et ignis aque opera suscipit. Unumquodque autem eorum aliud a natura sua removere nititur; quoniam cum ignis in aqua operatur, calefacit eam et siccat; et cum econverso aqua in igne operetur, ipsum frigidum humidumque reddit. Cumque eodem modo in pomi constitutione terre aer obviet, utrumque eorum alterum a natura sua propellere luctatur, et alterutrum in altero operatur et alterius suscipit opera. Cum enim terra in aere operetur ipsum gelidum aridumque reddit. Cum autem aer prius in terra operetur, illam calidam humidamque efficit. Hac itaque de causa ex illis IIIIᵒʳ elementis alia commixtio, alia contemperantia, aliaque complexio quam prius esset, efficitur, quoniam unumquodque eorum ex eo genere quod prius in actu erat, in aliud mutatur. Nec aliquod eorum in pomo eius generis cuius prius fuerat reperietur, cum unumquodque mutetur. Fol. 197 va-vb.

they come together, and from this a third thing is made, of which
it can truly be said that fire is not in it actually, but potentially;
and thus also water is not in it actually, but rather potentially.
Since if either one of them were in it actually, they would not come
together, nor would a third body be composed of them which is similar
to neither of them. But if that body were destroyed by force, each one
of the elements will again exist actually as before. And in this
manner I understand a fruit to be, and it consists of each one of the
four elements. Therefore, it can well be said that the fire which is
in the fruit was actually fire before it was in the composite apple.
But when the composite fruit was made of it, the fire was turned into
a different thing than it was before. And thus there is a different effect from it. And the other elements of which it consists behave in
the same way. For while the fruit endures, each one of the elements
of which it consists will be in it potentially. But when it rots or is
burned, each one of the elements will be removed and will exist actually, as they did before. But if it is eaten, it will change into a thing
of the same kind as the thing by which it was eaten. Also, each one
of those elements can be extracted per se, as we previously established
in the case of milk.[24]

Next, after a discussion of the nine complexions, Marius explains the formation of stones and metals. Noting that a goldsmith's pot becomes transparent and is changed to glass when subjected to great heat, he concludes that
all stones are formed this way in nature by heat enclosed in the interior of
the earth. Their differences result from the different kinds of earth from

---

[24] D. Quod dixisti optime intelligo. Audivi enim superius te affirmantem quod cum duo
elementa contraria sibi obviaverint, utrumque eorum aliud a natura sua removere laborat,
quousque a natura sua que prius in actu fuit removeatur. Verbi gratia: Quando ignis aque
pari addicione in potentia sic adiungitur quod ignis non pars tanta adsit que ad aque per-
duccionem sufficiat, neque aque tantum, quod ignem queat extinguere, utrumque eorum
in altero operatur et alterius opera suscipit. Nam si ignis in aqua operatur, et eius gelidi-
tatem minuit. Si vero in igne aqua operatur, caliditatem que pruis infuerat siccitatemque
aminuit. Sicque unum alii repugnat, donec illa conveniant, et ex eis res tertia efficiatur
que sane dici potest, quod ignis in eo non actu immo potentia est sicque etiam aqua non
actu verum potentia inest. Quoniam si quodlibet eorum in eo actu esset, non convenirent,
nec corpus tertium ex eis componeretur, quod nulli illorum simile est. Quod si corpus illud
vi defecerit, unumquodque elementorum ipsorum in actu sicut prius erit. Et hoc modo
predicto intelligo pomum esse et quodcumque de IIIIor constat elementis. Bene itaque dici
potest quod qui ignis pomo inest, prius in actu ignis fuit, quam ex eo compositum malum
esset. Cum vero compositum fuit ex eo pomum, ignis in rem alterius se generis transtulit
quam prius esset, sicque ex eo aliud effectum est. Et eodem ipso modo, se alia habent elementa ex quibus constat. Dum vero durabit pomum unumquodque elementorum ex quibus
constat in eo potentia erit. Si autem putridum ac combustum fuerit, unumquodque elementorum removebitur, ac in actu ut prius fuit existet. Si vero mansum fuerit, in rem eiusdem generis abibit, cuius res a qua comedetur fuerit. Elementorum quoque illorum unumquodque per se extrahi potest, sicut de lacte superius declaratum est. Fol. 197vb.

which they are made and from variations in the intensity of heat and the length of time the heat operates.

He then quickly describes the composition of the other minerals, using as examples sulphur, orpiment, petroleum, sal ammoniac, and mercury. This is preparatory to his discussion of metals, which he says (following the traditional doctrine) are compounded of sulphur and mercury. The metals differ from each other because of variations in the purity of the sulphur or mercury or both, and in the intensity and duration of the heat to which they are subjected in the earth's interior. He shows an intimate personal knowledge of the manipulation of minerals, metals, and other chemical substances, but not a trace of alchemy.

The next topic to be discussed in detail is the vegetable kingdom. After spending a long time proving that plants possess local motion as a result of their growth, he argues that the principle of growth of a plant is contained in the seed, from where it is distended into all the growing parts. There are four powers of this "viridal soul," the appetitive, the digestive, the retentive, and the expulsive. Growth takes place only as a result of increments of matter being changed into the nature of the plant and added to it. The seed "always grows until it reaches the limit set for it by these four powers, and then it makes innumerable plants completely similar to itself, just as each species of animal makes seed not dissimilar to itself."[25] Furthermore, a plant "will not stop growing so long as it is fertilized by the seed. That seed will grow similarly if it is saved by man until the proper time and then placed in the ground. . . . For God commanded and bestowed the power upon the viridal soul to be able to preserve its own kind always in its own form and seed. The only reason that man plants trees (instead of depending on wild ones) is so he might enjoy the convenience of the fruit more quickly: for they grow in the same way from seed, only it takes a little more time. If you had wandered through as many regions as I have traversed, you could have seen grapevines and trees of apples, oranges, and pears growing in the forest, which were not planted by man."[26]

---

[25] Semper quidem granum prefatum usque ad diffinitum seminant terminum crescit, et tunc semen facit gramina innumera sibi omnino consimilia, quemadmodum queque species animalis semen sibi ipsi non dissimile facit. Fol. 198vb.

[26] M. In superiori huius pagina voluminis, dominum in principio omnia ex IIII[or] creasse elementis memoraveram. Cum igitur ipsa elementa sub terra prope eius superficiem in tali complexione conveniant, unde aliquid componi, oporteat id quod tunc inde componitur crescit ac terram pulsat, seque in aerem exigit; ac si de semine prodiret et non desinit crescere quo ad fecundetur semine. Crescet similiter semen illud si ab hominibus reservatum apto tempore in terram iactetur primorum exemplo parentum ita de primis creaturis facientium. Nam deus precepit atque virtutem anime viridali contulit speciem suam semper in forma et semine suo posse reservare. Arborum autem plantatio non fit ob aliam causam, nisi ut homines fructuum commoda celerius capiant. Eodem enim modo de semine, etsi cum temporis dilatione, crescerunt. Quod si tot regiones quot ego perlustravi perer-

From this point on, the quality of the book declines. In the last few columns, Marius is depending completely on literary sources, which he has not subjected to the same rigorous criticism and experimental testing that characterized most of the work up to this point. In explaining the tastes, he says that he has found in a "philosophical book" a list of which elements cause which tastes, but he complains that his source does not tell him "how the elements come together to create these tastes," and he confesses to his student: "I do not have any lesson to show you this."[27]

The final subject of the book is the animal kingdom. It is quite brief and is confined mostly to investigating similarities and differences between animals and plants. His definition of an animal is "a thing which grows and declines, is mobile, and sensible."

Then, after putting off a number of his student's questions as inappropriate to the subject of his work, and telling us that he has already written a book *De humano proficuo* and intends to write another on the five senses, Marius ends his work with a proof that man is the most wonderful of God's creatures and with a praise of the Lord: "May He Who raised Himself above all the composite things of this world be blessed through all the ages."

III

Even in a work noted for its originality, it is important to ascertain the sources used by the author to trace the transmission of ideas, to see how old ideas are used in new ways, and to assist in dating the work. In this way likewise we can assess the relative importance in *De elementis* of the new translations of Greek and Arabic works as against the internal maturing and value changes in western Europe in the great intellectual advance that occurred between the twelfth and fourteenth centuries.

Marius's sources present quite a problem. One would expect him to have relied heavily on Calcidius's translation and commentary of the *Timaeus*. It is clear that he did know this work. He seems to have used it as a model of style, and he refutes Calcidius's argument that undifferentiated matter is infinite;[28] and there are other faint echoes of the *Timaeus* commentary in *De elementis*. But what is more remarkable is how little of this influential and prestigious work he accepted. He also knew Macrobius, both the *Sa-*

---

rares, malos, cinos, piros, vitesque silvestres, absque hominis plantatione in nemoribus crescentes vidisse potuisses. Fol. 199ra.

[27] Legi siquidem cuiusdam philosophi librum in quo saporum substantias et complexiones quales hec tabula declarabit inveni. Hoc modo esse saporum substantias et complexiones liber ille philosophicus refert, sed cum ego quomodo ipsa elementa ad hos procreandos sapores convenerunt ignorem, tuo documento ad hoc videndum indigeo." Fol. 199rb.

[28] See n. 12 above.

turnalia and *Commentary on the Dream of Scipio*. He took from the latter
the doctrine that matter never perishes and that all composite bodies can
be resolved into their elements,[29] and from the former the notion that fire
is in perpetual need of nourishment.[30]

Much more perplexing is the question of his knowledge of Aristotle. That
he knew the *Categories* is clear; he is at pains all the way through his book
to discover each of the categories in the elements and their compounds. But
he cites Aristotle a number of times and in one place mentions a specific
work—"sicut dicit Aristoteles in eo quem de elementis agit. Ait enim his
verbis"—and then proceeds to quote a lengthy section.[31] This verbatim
quotation makes it certain that no authentic work of Aristotle's is being
used here. There is a pseudo-Aristotelian work *De causis proprietatum elementorum* which was sometimes called *De elementis*, but this bears no similarity to Marius's quotation.[32] Other possibilities present themselves.
There was a considerable body of pseudo-Aristotelian literature in Latin
as well as Greek, but a comparison of Marius with Rose's edition[33] of this
literature fails to reveal any connection. The same is true of the pseudo-
Aristotelian *Problems*.[34] Faced then with several explicit citations, including
one long quotation of a work ascribed to Aristotle, and in view of our inability
to identify this with any known Aristotelian or pseudo-Aristotelian work,
we are forced to take the generally undesirable course of positing a book for

[29] Macrobii *Comm. in somnium Scipionis*, 2, 12, 12, ed. Eyssenhardt 615. This is also
contained in Constantine the African, *Pantegni*. Costantino l'Africano *L'Arte universale
della Medicina (Pantegni.)* Pt. 1, bk. 1, trans. Marco T. Malato and Umberto de Martini
(Rome 1961) 48.

[30] *Sat.* 7, 13, 3 (n. 15 above) 444; also contained, though less specifically, in Aristotle
Meteor. 4.7 (383) and *De longitudine et brevitate vitae* 5 (466a).

[31] Completa creatione firmamenti omniumque que ipsum in se comprehendit, movit
illud creator suus et mobile fuit. Ex motu vero firmamenti, pars illa predicti corporis,
simpli, et tamen VI partibus circumscripti, par inquam illa que ipsi firmamento iunctis-
sima fuit, moveri cepit et vehementer concalvit, atque ignis fuit. Pars vero alia que fuit
remotior paulisper, mota quidem est sed non adeo vehementer; quare et calefacta est, sed
nequaquam tam ardentem et ipsa est aer. Tercia autem quia multum fuit a firmamento
remota, neque mota est, neque calefacta, et ideo remansit frigida, et hec est aqua. Sed
et quarta quoniam omnino recessit, omnino immobilis extitit; quare et similiter frigida
remansit, et ea terra fuit. Fol. 192vb.

[32] Printed in *Aristotelis opera cum Averrois commentariis* 7 (Venice 1574, repr. Frankfurt
1962) 204v-220v. I have also used the following MSS: Vat., Borgh. 126, fols. 196r-200r,
Vat. lat. 718, fols. 19r-38v; Naples, Bibl. naz. VIII. E. 21, fols, 69r-74v, VIII. F. 12, fols.
390v-395v.

[33] *Aristoteles pseudepigraphicus*, ed. Valentin Rose (Leipzig 1863).

[34] *Die Übersetzung der pseudo-aristotelischen Problemata durch Bartholomaeus von Mes-
sana*, ed. R. Seligsohn (Berlin 1934); *Problemata inedita*, ed. Bussemaker (Paris 1857) in
Aristotelis *Opera omnia*, 5 vols. (Paris 1848-1874) 4.291-334; *Les Problèmes d'Aristote*,
trans. J. Barthélemy - St. Hilaire, 2 vols. (Paris 1891). See Lawn (n. 4 above) 12-14.

whose existence there is no other evidence. Let me present the reasons for this necessity.

Since, in the first sentence of Marius's quotation from Aristotle's work "on the elements", there is expressed a creation *ex nihilo* and there are only four rather than five elements, we may safely assume that this is not an authentic Aristotelian work. There is much genuine Aristotelian material incorporated in Marius's treatise, however, and even the quotation referred to above is quite similar to *Meteorology* 1.3 (341ᵃ) and 1.4 (341ᵇ), although expanded and somewhat altered. The assertion that Aristotle says that fire extends as far as the moon would refer to *Meteorology* 1.3 (340ᵇ). That oil and fat are "airy" could have come from *Meteorology* 4.7 (383ᵇ) or *De longitudine et brevitate vitae* 5 (466ᵃ). The terms of "the physicists," *de medio* and *ad medium* are from *De caelo* 1.3 (269ᵇ) ans 4.1 (308ᵃ). From the same work, 1.5 (271ᵇ-272ᵃ), are arguments similar to Marius's concerning the necessity of the spatial finitude of the universe if it is to be capable of motion. And the statement: "Colors sometimes deceive the sight, as Aristotle explains in his book," would be based on *Meteorology* 1.4 (346ᵇ), or possibly *De anima* 2.6 (418ᵃ) or 2.7 (419ᵃ).

There is another group of doctrines which may or may not have been based ultimately on an Aristotelian work. First among these is the explanation of how the elements persist in a compound, discussed by Aristotle especially in *De generatione et corruptione* 1.10 (327ᵇ). It would be difficult to determine with certainty whether Marius knew Aristotle's explanation and improved upon it or whether he was completely original in his own treatment. I lean toward the former. Marius's decomposition of milk into its elements may conceivably owe something to Aristotle's description of boiling and coagulating its "earth" by means of fig juice in *Meteorology* 4.7 (384ᵃ), although the possibility is slight. But there is a statement in *De caelo* 3.7 (305ᵇ) where Aristotle speaks of wax taking on the form of a sphere or a cube which may well have influenced Marius's doctrine of "substance". Aristotle usually mentions wax as analogous to matter in receiving the impressions of a seal (form), and in this he is followed by most medieval authors. This notion of it as corporeal extension capable of assuming various shapes rather than as an unqualified matrix capable only of receiving the reality of form from above or considered simply in its relation to form is crucial to Marius's thought and could very well have been suggested by Aristotle's remark. There is even one passing remark in *De sensu et sensato* 4 (441ᵇ) that may have suggested to Marius his table of proportions of the mixtures of the elements, but again this is only a possibility and no definite assertions can be made. Nor could this have been the "philosophical book" from which Marius drew his information on tastes. Aristotle's remarks are brief and do not give even the unsatisfactory information Marius says he got from his source.

At this point we might seem ready to conclude that Marius possessed at least Aristotle's *Meteorology, De caelo*, and *De generatione et corruptione*, probably in Gerard of Cremona's translation, or possibly in an even earlier Greek-Latin version. However, a close reading of Marius makes it clear that he could not possibly have known any of the "New Aristotle" at first hand. Even the closest correspondences between *De elementis* and Aristotle's works on natural philosophy are far from exact and appear to have been "filtered" through at least one intermediate source. And there are many discrepancies between Marius's view on a given subject and those of Aristotle. We must remember that Marius accepted Aristotle as a great authority. Consequently, when he differs from Aristotle and does not mention the difference, we may assume that he was ignorant of one. An essential part of Marius's teaching is that only bodies are capable of acting and being acted upon; qualities can be efficacious only insofar as they are attributes of bodies.[35] Aristotle, however, has the contrary qualities acting on each other, and the elements themselves play only a minor role in his thought, especially in the *Meteorology*. Marius also insists, over and over again, that every created thing contains all four elements in some proportion. Aristotle insists only that all substances are mixtures of the four elementary *qualities*,[36] and a little earlier in the same work he had said, somewhat inconsistently, that all substances are formed by earth and water.[37] Also, in his discussion of the formation of metals and other mineral substances, a very important section of *De elementis*, Marius seems to have been totally ignorant of Aristotle's teaching that they are formed "by vapors of smoky exhalations, developed within the earth's interior and brought by heat and dryness to their mineral condition."[38] Their treatments of liquefying (or "loosening", as Marius says) and congealing are also far apart. Marius holds fast to the doctrine that heat liquefies and cold congeals,[39] whereas Aristotle, observing much more closely, notices that many substances can be either liquefied or congealed by heat or cold, and that olive oil is congealed by both.[40] The conclusion seems inescapable then that Marius did not have direct access to any of Aristotle's works on natural philosophy.

The only solution to our problem which occurs to me is that there was a book available to Marius, ascribed to Aristotle and perhaps entitled *De elementis*, which was in fact based loosely on several Aristotelian works, at

[35] "Qualitas enim nichil operatur, sed opera sunt corporis, quod qualitati subicitur." Fol. 197ra.

[36] *Meteor.* 4.8 (384b).

[37] *Meteor.* 4.4. (382a).

[38] *Meteor.* 3.6 (378a-b).

[39] "Sed et idem visibiliter apparet in auro et argento atque omnibus metallis quibus ex calore mollicies, et ex frigiditate accedit duricies." Fols. 193vb-194ra.

[40] *Meteor.* 4.6-7 (383a-384a).

least *De caelo, Meteorology*, and *De generatione et corruptione*. It may well have been an Arabic work translated into Latin about the middle of the twelfth century, but this is pure speculation.[41]

If it could be established that Marius knew Avicenna, then the whole context of the question of his knowledge of Aristotle would be changed, since if he knew one of Gerard of Cremona's translations, he may well have known others too, and if he was late enough to have known Alfred of Sareshel's translation of *De mineralibus*, it is almost inconceivable that he was ignorant of Aristotle's natural philosophy. The first sentence of Book 2 suggests that Marius did know Avicenna or some other Arabic work on minerals.[42] There are also other things about *De elementis* which suggest a knowledge of Avicenna, namely Marius's antialchemical orientation and his explicit statement that species cannot be changed. Avicenna says the same thing in his *De mineralibus*,[43] generally attributed to Aristotle in the Middle Ages and one of the works I thought might have been meant by Aristotle *De elementis*. Marius also says that the only completely temperate part of man (who "has a more temperate complexion than any of the other animals and is the most handsomely formed creature of all of them") is his skin, a statement that also appears in Avicenna's *Canon medicinae*.[44] However, a closer examination makes it appear highly unlikely—and certainly beyond the possibility of proof—that Marius knew Avicenna. A naturalistic, antialchemical attitude was not unusual in the twelfth century, and we may assume that this was Marius's own and not derived from anyone, unless we can show otherwise that he knew Avicenna's works. But the remark about the temperate nature of man's skin, Galenic in origin, is also contained in Constantine the African's *Pantegni*,[45] which we know that Marius used. And although *De elementis* bears certain similarities in attitude and subject matter to Avicenna's *De mineralibus*, it is apparent that there is no direct relationship. The key test is a comparison of the accounts of the composition of metals in the two works.[46] Marius's account is fuller, adds the factor of the dura-

---

[41] This is in fact quite an accurate description of the ps.-Aristotelian *De causis proprietatum elementorum*, but as we have mentioned above, this work does not contain the appropriate information.

[42] "Iam igitur michi vellem dari argumenta, quod animalia atque\virentia et ea que vocant Sarraceni congelata ... composita sunt de IIIIor elementis cuncta." Fol. 194va.

[43] Avicennae *De congelatione et conglutinatione lapidum*, ed. E. J. Holmyard and D. C. Mandeville (Paris 1927) 40-42. Since the editors were contemptuous of Alfred Sareshel's Latin translation, they simply reproduced an inferior fourteenth-century manuscript. Therefore, I shall also give references to University of Paris MS 507, fols. 223v-224r.

[44] Lib. I. Fen I, doctrina 3 (Venice 1582) fol. 4ra and Lib. II, tract. I, cap. 1, fol. 91vE.

[45] *Pantegni* (n. 29 above) 54.

[46] *Marius* Fol. 198rb. *Avicenna* MS fol. 223v, ed. 52-53 (n. 43 above).

tion and intensity of the heat to which mercury and sulphur are subjected, and is in direct disagreement with Avicenna on the types of mercury and sulphur which compose the metals. We must therefore rule out that Marius knew Avicenna.

Another work that Marius may have been expected to know, especially if he was indeed a Salernitan master, was Nemesius of Emesa's *De natura hominis*. This work had been translated twice in its entirety, once by Alphanus of Salerno[47] in the eleventh century and once by Burgundio of Pisa[48] in the twelfth. The chapter on the elements had been translated independently in the twelfth century,[49] probably by a south Italian. However, Marius shows no knowledge whatsoever of this work. This is especially evident in his treatment of tastes, during which he refers to and complains about a "philosophical book" that he had used as well as an unspecified "Platonic book" which told how to create flavors artificially. Neither could have been Nemesius's.

It is also important to note once more that there is no trace of the "*elementatum*" theory in Marius's book. This doctrine, apparently originated by William of Conches, quickly found its way to Salerno where it was incorporated into the teaching of Urso and Maurus, the two leading Salernitan masters of the late twelfth century, and generally considered to be a Saler-

Gold: Pure mercury and pure sulphur heated for a long time.	Mercury and very pure and white sulphur and a subtle fiery virtue.
Silver: Pure mercury and a small amount of red sulphur heated for a short time.	Mercury and pure white sulphur.
Copper: Impure mercury and dirty and dense red sulphur, heated longer than gold at a very high temperature.	Good mercury and impure sulphur.
Iron: Mercury mixed with sulphur halfway between red and white, heated for a longer time than copper at a moderate temperature.	Corrupt, unclean, earthy mercury and impure sulphur.
Tin: Pure mercury and pure white sulphur heated for a short time.	Good mercury and corrupt sulphur.
Lead: Coarse mercury and coarse white sulphur mixed with just a little red.	Impure, heavy, clayey mercury and impure feeble and fetid sulphur.

Notice that both men assert that metals are composed of mercury and sulphur and give similar reasons: Marius fol. 198ra, Avicenna MS fol. 223v, ed. 52. This is commonly referred to as an "alchemical" doctrine, but while alchemists accepted it, it is certainly not restricted to them, as these two references prove.

[47] *Nemesii Episcopi* Premnon Physicon *sive ΠΕΡΙ ΦΥΣΕΩΣ ΑΝΘΡΩΠΟΥ. Liber a N. Alfano, Archiepiscopo Salerni in Latinum Translatum*, ed. C. Burkhard (Leipzig 1917).

[48] *Gregorii Nysseni (Nemesii Emeseni) περὶ φύσεως ἀνθρώπον liber a Burgundione in Latinum translatum*, ed. C. Burkhard, *Jahresberichte des k.k. Staats-gymnasiums* (Vienna 1891-1902).

[49] Dales, "An Unnoticed Translation" (n. 4 above).

nitan doctrine. As such, it was attacked as an absurdity of the "Salernitani pueri" by the anonymous author of a *Compendiosus tractatus de philosophia et eius secretis*.[50] This author also used much material from Marius's *De elementis*, including his table of the proportions of the elements in mixed bodies, so apparently he did not consider Marius to be a Salernitan. Whether Marius knew the *"elementatum"* theory and chose to ignore it or whether he was ignorant of it is not clear to me, but if he was indeed a writer of the late twelfth century or a Salernitan master or both, his ignorance of this doctrine would be very difficult to explain.

After having had to rule out so many books that one would hope Marius had known, we may now finally identify a book that he used extensively and beyond question. This is the *Pantegni* of Constantine the African,[51] a free translation of the *Kamil-As-Sinasa* of Ali Ibn al Abbas,[52] completed by Constantine at Montecassino sometime before 1087, the year of his death, and used as a textbook for medicine at Salerno from the middle of the twelfth century.[53] We have already mentioned the *Pantegni* as the source of Marius's statement that man is the most temperate of all animals and that only man's skin is completely temperate. Marius introduces this statement by a paraphrase of a sentence of Constantine in praise of man: "Homo unus idemque operatur omnia, et ideo racionalis est et intellectualis; quia quod facit intelligit, et racione discernit."[54] Much more extensive use of the *Pantegni* is evident in Marius's long discussion of the nine "complexions," one equal and eight unequal.[55] Although Constantine also discusses the four humors in this place, Marius does not mention them. He was also greatly indebted to Constantine in his treatment of the "viridal soul" in plants, especially the *virtus immutans* or *attractiva*,[56] which Marius expanded considerably. There are two other doctrines adopted by Marius which appear in the *Pantegni* but were also available in a number of other sources. These are that all composites can be resolved into their elements but that the elements themselves are never destroyed,[57] and that the four elements as we experience them are never pure, but each always contains an admixture of all the others.[58]

---

[50] Cadden (n. 4 above) 62.

[51] Ed. Malato and Martini (n. 29 above). For the rest, see the *Pantegni* in Isaac Judeus *Opera Omnia* (Lyon 1515) 1r-144r.

[52] The best recent study of Constantine is Boubaker ben Yahia, "Constantin l'Africain et l'école de Salerne," *Les Cahiers de Tunisie* 9 (1955) 49-59.

[53] Kristeller (n. 3 above) 154-155.

[54] *Pantegni* (n. 29 above) 52.

[55] *Ibid.* 51.

[56] *Ibid.* Theor. 4.2 and 3. Cited by Lawn (n. 4 above) 23.

[57] *Pantegni* 48.

[58] *Ibid.* 49.

This examination of Marius's sources sheds some light on the composition date of *De elementis*. There must still be some question as to whether Marius was a Salernitan master, but I am inclined to accept Thomson's arguments that he was such even though I have suggested some difficulties with this identification. Assuming then that he was a teacher at Salerno, let us try to fit him to what else is known about that school and its teachers.[59] The careers of Urso and Maurus have never been definitely dated, but they are usually assigned to the last quarter of the twelfth century and Urso may have lived on into the thirteenth.[60] But whenever one dates them, Marius was clearly earlier. Their knowledge of Aristotle is undeniable, and in addition to citing his works they were deeply influenced by his thought. Their works show a greater maturity as well as a more advanced (or at least more developed) teaching technique. They use a wider variety of sources and in every way give evidence of working in a later but related milieu.

How much earlier, then, shall we place Marius? Certainly not very much, for if Kristeller is correct Constantine's works were not used at Salerno until the mid-twelfth century.[61] Also, Marius's book is far from being a practical handbook of anything, and certainly not of medicine, as earlier Salernitan writings were. It is a work of philosophy, as were the other two books of his which he mentions. He would have been writing, then, after Constantine's works had reached Salerno from Montecassino, and after the school at Salerno had adopted philosophy as part of its curriculum, but before Aristotle's natural philosophy had been rediscovered and early enough that a dialogue based on the *Timaeus* was still considered a stylish way of presenting one's teaching; early enough too for some of the traditional "Salernitan questions" to have been included in a philosophical work. This would make a date of within ten years of 1160 seem most probable. One would have to explain a good deal to date it earlier than 1150 or later than 1170.

[59] Kristeller 143-163; From ca. 985 Salerno was renowned for the practical expertise of her physicians. From this time until mid-twelfth-century the writings associated with Salerno were practical handbooks of medicine. After the middle of the century, the writings of Constantine the African were used in medical instruction and "actual teaching . . . became increasingly broad and methodical." By about 1170 the commentary form was being employed and logic had become part of the curriculum. During the last quarter of the century Aristotle's natural philosophy was mastered.

[60] *Necrologia del Liber confratrum de S. Matteo de Salerno*, ed. C. A. Garufi (Rome 1922) cited by Cadden (n. 4 above) 24 and Kristeller (n. 3 above) 141. Dr. Wolfgang Stürner of the University of Stuttgart, who has just completed an edition of Urso's De commixtionibus elementorum, writes me that he is not convinced of the extent or accuracy of Urso's knowledge of Aristotle and sees it as being roughly on a par with that of Marius. Even granting this, I would hold that the far greater degree of sophistication in Urso's work indicates for him a later date.

[61] Kristeller 154-155.

IV

The innovative quality of much of *De elementis* has already been referred to. The characteristics it exhibits, as well as the doctrines it originates or modifies from antique works, are worthy of fuller treatment.

We have mentioned above the strong experimental tendency of the work. Consistently, except near the very end of the book, Marius buttresses all his points with references to sense experience. He places a wineskin, tied shut, below the surface of the water and notices the tendency of air to rise to its proper place. He separates the four elements out of milk. He tastes sal ammoniac to discover its "hot" nature. He carefully observes and accurately describes the behavior of the flame of a candle and of firebrands in proving that air is the nourishment of fire (neither of his possible sources, Macrobius or Aristotle, had said this; only that fire needed constant nourishment). He calls attention to the fact that the goldsmith's earthenware pot is turned to glass by intense heat, and from this he develops his theory of the formation of stones, holding that they are all kinds of glass. He notices the skin entering the tube when a physician places it on a patient's arm and sucks. He stops up the pipe of a bellows to test the corporeity and compressibility of air. He has not worked out the logical problems of induction from experience, as Grosseteste was to do, but he was a more able observer than the great bishop of Lincoln. Nor was he an inept logician. His arguments—with few exceptions—are of a high order. A description of all his experiments would take about twenty pages, but enough has been said to indicate that the experimental habit of mind and the close and accurate observation of nature are important characteristics of his work.

Allied to this type of mental outlook is Marius's primary interest in describing processes—in answering the question "how" a given effect is produced. And in four different places, this is made explicit: "But *how* do you say this is done?"[62] "I wish you would reveal to me *by what means* this is done."[63] "I do not know *how* it comes forth."[64] "But I do not know *how* the elements come together"[65] (to make the different tastes). Even disregarding these statements, it is this kind of question which he is concerned to answer through the book.

Marius was also disinclined to use technical language. Throughout the early part of his work, he refers to his first created stuff as "body." It is

---

[62] "Sed quomodo dicis hoc fieri?" Fol. 191vb.

[63] "Sed modo quo fiat, volo te michi aperire." Fol. 196vb.

[64] "Sed quomodo prodeat ignoro." Fol. 198va.

[65] "Cum ego quomodo ipsa elementa ad hos procreandos sapores convenerunt ignorem, tuo documento ad hoc videndum indigeo." Fol. 199rb.

only when he gets to his detailed investigation of it that he tells his student that he should have been calling it substance, but in order to make himself more easily understood he had referred to it as body. And the student replied: "I don't care much about the names, so long as I understand your meaning."[66] Of course, Marius has misunderstood Aristotle on this point, but the misunderstanding resulted in a significant innovation. The same may be said about this use of the terms "form" (which to him is a collection of qualities understood as "existing altogether as though they were one thing") and potency and act, of which he had only a feeble grasp. But if he had understood them in their strict Aristotelian meaning, he could not have produced his theory on the *mixtio*. And his ignorance of Avicenna and Aristotle prevented his becoming enmeshed in the problem of the remission of forms of the elements and the emergence of a new "substantial form" to account for the compound. Happily, he concentrated on the process.

Sometimes Marius seems to notice weaknesses in generally accepted doctrines, such as that cold arises from rest, and heat from motion. The student points out that if this is true, then either the original substance, being at rest, was not without qualities, since it would be cold; or that cold is not a quality. Marius answers this objection ingeniously: All things tend toward the center of the earth, but since this is a geometric point, none can actually occupy it. They are blocked by each other and forced to stop moving actually, although they still have a tendency to move. It is this, he says, which we inaccurately call "rest" and which gives rise to cold. The original state of rest gave rise to no quality.

In some twelfth-century scientific works, it is impossible to tell whether the author was Christian, Muslim, or Jew, or even without religion. There was a definite tendency among some twelfth-century authors to dissociate science and religion or to force religion to accommodate itself to the teachings of philosophy. At Chartres, William of Conches had struggled to reconcile Aristotle's assertion of the eternity of the world with the Christian doctrine of creation,[67] and one of Marius's contemporaries and perhaps fellow masters at Salerno, the anonymous author of another book on the elements, had asserted without reservation that the world was eternal and composed of atoms and the void.[68] Another south Italian of about the same time had suppressed all references to God or religion in his translation of the chapter on the elements from Nemesius's *De natura hominis*.[69] Marius, however,

---

[66] "Sive corpus appelles sive substantiam, non multo curo de nominibus cum sententiam intelligam." Fol. 191vb.

[67] *Glossae in libro De consolatione philosophiae Boethii*, 5, prosa 6, printed in J. M. Parent, *La doctrine de la création dans l'école de Chartres* (Paris 1938) 133-136.

[68] Dales, "Anonymi De elementis" (n. 4 above).

[69] Dales, "An Unnoticed Translation" (n. 4 above).

was patently and explicitly a Christian. He accepted the Christian doctrine of creation but understood it in a naturalistic way. He was clearly aware that there was some controversy about the matter, since he went out of his way to state his own views. He also refuted atomism, but his arguments were original rather than Aristotelian.

In spite of this, his attitude toward the universe is completely naturalistic and even mechanical. It is interesting to compare him with Adelard of Bath in this regard. In the *Natural Questions*, Adelard had explained the fact that water would not run out of a tube open at the bottom so long as the top was stopped by saying that "since the four elements make up this natural world, and they are joined together by a natural love in such a way that no one of them wishes to exist without the others, no place either is or can be empty of them."[70] Marius, in contrast, after showing by experiments that two bodies cannot occupy the same place, simply asserts that "you cannot empty a place of a given body without another body's immediately entering it."[71] The animism that had such a hold on even so naturalistic a thinker as Adelard is not to be found in Marius. On occasion during his treatise he had used metaphorical language, saying, for example, that fire flees from water, heat retreats into the earth's interior, and that contraries both flee from each other and seek to destroy each other. We might be inclined in any case to dismiss this as metaphor, since Marius is generally free from animistic notions. Fortunately he provides us with a specific statement on the subject. The student asks: "How can one quality so abhor another that it tries to demolish and destroy it, since a quality has no discretion, nor does it know what it ought to do?"[72] Marius answers that this is just a manner of speaking and gives as an example of what he means that the state of waking is the contrary of the state of sleeping, and that one may be said to flee as the other approaches.

Marius is also free of alchemical or magical notions. The crucial section here is the discussion of how metals are made. They are, he says, formed from sulphur and mercury of varying degrees of purity, cooked by varying degrees of heat for longer or shorter times by natural processes in the earth's interior. He never mentions the possibility of transmutation, although he

---

[70] "Cum enim huius mundi sensilis corpus quattuor elementa componant, ita ipsa naturali amore conserta sunt, ut cum nullum illorum sine alio existere velit, nullus locus ab eis vel vacuus sit, vel esse possit." *Die Quaestiones naturales des Adelard von Bath*, ed. Martin Müller. *Beiträge zur Geschichte der Philosophie und Theologie des Mittelalters*, 31.2 (Münster 1934) 54.

[71] "In hoc mundo non poteris quodam corpore vacuare locum illum, quin aliud statim subingrediatur in illum." Fol. 194rb.

[72] "Et quomodo potest qualitas una ita aliam abhorrere quod eam perdere nitatur ac delere cum nec discrecionem habeat aliqua qualitatum, nec scit quid debeat facere?" Fol. 197ra.

does show how sometimes colors may be altered. Nor will he allow any change
of species in nature. In a paragraph that sounds very much like a refutation
of magic, he says that only motion or rest can be added to plants. But

> the power of this motion cannot change one species into another,
> but only one quality into another. Green can become more red or yel-
> low, as we see in apples and pears, and acrid can become sweet, as
> is evident in grapes. But never can the plants be changed as a result
> of changes in their qualities. Therefore, nothing, by which something
> can be brought about different from an animal or plant, can be
> added to plants except sensible and transitive motion. And nothing
> can exist in the world except animals, vegetables, and minerals.[73]

Finally, we might investigate this twelfth-century scientist's view of man,
which according to the usage of some authors would qualify him as a Christian
humanist. There is nothing novel in it—in fact, it is made up of common-
places. But it places a very high value on man, and medieval men are frequently misrepresented on this point. To Marius, it is man's rational soul
that makes him the most excellent of animals, and because of this "he has
a more temperate complexion than that of any other animal, and he is the
most handsomely formed creature of them all." Marius sums up in these
words:

> Nothing is an animal that is not also composed of the four elements.
> Therefore, man is composed of the four elements. I also know that
> he is, in a certain way, similar to minerals, for if he is lifted up,
> he will fall to earth like a mineral; and after death he can be counted
> among the minerals. He is also similar to plants, for he grows like
> a plant. That he is an animal, no one denies. He is also similar
> to the angels, for he is rational like an angel. . . . Therefore he is
> called a small world by philosophers.[74]

[73] "Nam huius motus virtus non unam speciem in aliam sed unam qualitatem in aliam
transmutare valet. Viride quippe plerumque fit rubeum vel croceum ut in malis et piris
videmus; et acre dulce, sicut in racemis patet; numquam tamen per qualitatum mutationes
virentia possunt transmutari. Constat igitur virenti preter sensibilitatem et motum transi-
tivum nichil posse addi, unde aliquid ab animali et virenti diversum efficiatur. Constat
etiam nichil in mundo preter animalia et virentia et congelata posse existere. "Fol. 199vb.
[74] "Satis scio nullum esse animal quin etiam IIIIor componatur elementis. Homo igitur
ex IIIIor compositus est elementis. Scio quoque illum quodammodo esse congelatis si-
milem. Si enim sullevatur, ut congelatum in terra labitur. Post mortem vero inter congelata computari potest. Virentibus etiam similis est, crescit namque ut virentia. Animal
eum esse nullus abnegat. Angelis etiam similis est, racionalis namque est ut angelus. . . .
Ideoque a philosophis minor mundus nuncupatus est." Fol. 200rb.

V

In the twelfth century, the science of matter came to be recognized as a separate and very important area of investigation, and not just as an adjunct to other types of studies. Not only do we have Marius's book on the elements, but also the anonymous *De elementis* in the same manuscript, Urso's *De commixtionibus elementorum*, the anonymous *Compendiosus tractatus de philosophia*, and a renewed interest in those sections of ancient or Arabic works which dealt with matter.

The question of whether these works continued to be read and used is not so easy to answer in the present state of our knowledge. But there seems to be a continuous tradition reaching from around 1150 to the early thirteenth century.[75] It is possible that these works were displaced by Aristotle on the one hand and alchemy on the other, but we know enough now about the earlier tradition that we should not simply assume without further searching and study that such a displacement did occur. The only extant manuscript of the *Compendiosus tractatus* is, after all, of the fourteenth century, and this preserved a large part of Marius's work in summary form, including his tables of the elements. We should therefore question the assumption that modern chemistry grew out of medieval alchemy. There was a purely scientific study of matter flourishing alongside alchemy at least in the twelfth century, and we may find that this was more important in the later period than we have supposed.

There then remains the question of whether whatever excellence the twelfth century exhibited should be attributed solely to the translations of Greek and Arabic works,[76] which occupied so much of the scholarly energy of that century, or whether the translating activity itself was generated by a change in western attitudes and values. It seems fairly certain that there was a reciprocal influence, and I do not mean to disparage the enormous change wrought in the intellectual climate of Latin Europe as a result of the translations. But whether we draw our answer from a study of Adelard of Bath, Peter Abelard, William of Conches, Thierry of Chartres, or Marius, we are compelled to assert that the intellectual revival of western Europe came first and was an indigenous phenomenon, leading to a recovery of Antiquity and profiting greatly from this recovery. Marius did know some

---

[75] That is, from about Marius's time until the time of the *Compendiosus tractatus* and Alfred of Sareshel.

[76] Multhauf (n. 1 above) 146 speaks for the great majority of historians when he says: "The history of natural philosophy in Western Christendom really begins with the translations, during the period 1150-1250, of the works by Aristotle and his major Arabic commentators."

Aristotle—the Old Logic directly and portions of the natural philosophy apparently through an intermediate source. He also was in touch with Arabic science through the translations of Constantine the African and perhaps other sources that I have not identified. Even if it could be proved, however, that Marius possessed Aristotle's natural philosophy directly, it would still be true that he understood it only slightly, and that its most important consequence in the twelfth century was in being creatively misunderstood.

This brings us to a consideration of what *De elementis* tells us about the nature of twelfth-century science. First of all, there is a high degree of coherence both in Marius's world view and in his treatise. Marius's world consisted of the elements with their properties behaving according to the necessities of their natures and falling into the categories of animal, vegetable, or mineral. There was no room in his conception for spontaneity or caprice. The world of nature obeyed laws, and these laws were accessible to human reason. His presentation of this world does not consist of a string of ad hoc explanations, but rather of a carefully worked out, internally consistent, naturalistic scheme, one based on a careful and accurate observation of nature and handled with considerable dialectical skill. We conclude then that at least a part of twelfth-century science was far from being naïve, animistic, and ad hoc. It was also much more than a revival of Antiquity, important though this was. It was bold, original, imaginative, and daring. At its best, it was rigorous in its arguments and precise in its observations. The world that it investigated was regular and knowable, and man by virtue of his reason was the most wonderful of God's creatures.

Department of History
University of Southern California
Los Angeles, California, U.S.A.

THE DATE OF THE COMMENTARY ON CICERO'S "DE INVENTIONE" BY THIERRY OF CHARTRES (ca. 1095-1160?) AND THE CORNIFICIAN ATTACK ON THE LIBERAL ARTS

•

by J. O. Ward

The main purpose of this article is to fix an approximate date for Thierry of Chartres's commentary on the *De inventione* by placing it in the wider context of Thierry's career as a defender and teacher of the *artes liberales*. The task has involved a reassessment of Thierry's role in combatting the attempt to downgrade the value of the arts by those whom John of Salisbury called the followers of Cornificius. The chronology of the Cornifician attack on the arts, and its repulse, has been reexamined and related to the details of Thierry's own career. Finally, the relationship between the *De inventione* commentary with its illuminating personal outbursts, the so-called Cornifician Movement, and the educational career of Thierry himself is suggested. It is hoped that as a result, Thierry of Chartres will emerge as a more significant defender of the value of the liberal arts than has hitherto been recognized.

I

A thorough study of Thierry of Chartres as an educator has yet to be written. Such a study would undoubtedly show Thierry to have been one of the most wide-ranging and humanitarian scholars of his century. It would make of him, one suspects, a pioneer in that short age of confidence and discovery which preceded the great effort of analysis and digestion characteristic of the century and a half after his death. A considerable body of literature has already accumulated around Thierry and his scholarship, and a collected edition of his theological writings is eagerly awaited from the expert hands of Reverend N. Haring, who has so ably provided the scholar with similar definitive editions of the works of Clarenbald of Arras and Gilbert of Poitiers. The following pages are offered as a small contribution to the problem of assessing Thierry's achievement as a teacher of the *artes* in the first half of the twelfth century.

Thierry was admired as an incomparable master in the arts by a whole generation of students, from John of Salisbury to William of Tyre. Nevertheless, modern study of Thierry's teaching of the arts is remarkably hindered by a lack of materials. With the exception of the prologue to the *Heptateuchon*, and certain passages relating to the arts, and in particular the *quadrivium*, contained in his theological and scriptural works, the sole printed illustration of Thierry's writings on the arts is a forty-page fragment of his *De inventione* commentary, printed in a volume of 1834 with the daunting title (in Latin) of "A Critical History of the Latin Scholiasts." This fragment, published by a scholar who was convinced that the work was by an antique author, happens, in addition, to be the only printed illustration of any length of medieval commentation on the *Ad Herennium* and *De inventione*, two of the most popular textbooks of the Middle Ages. Whether Thierry wrote very widely on the arts is not at present known. The *De inventione* commentary and the *Heptateuchon* are the only two works within this category to have received much scholarly attention. In two respects, however, the full significance of these works for the study of Thierry's teaching of the arts has not been unraveled. In the first place, the Reverend Haring himself, reversing R. W. Hunt's decision in 1948, that the *De inventione* commentary was probably Thierry's earliest work, and a very innovatory one, condemned it as Thierry's last work and, in general, an exception to the rule that Thierry was "a keen thinker, an original writer and by no means a plagiarist." The value of the work as an indication of the originality of Thierry's study of the arts was thus apparently reduced. In the second place, scholars have shown a peculiar reluctance to elaborate the implications of John of Salisbury's assertion that when the "Cornifician" scholars had so lowered the prestige of the *artes* by their attacks and demands, the labors of Thierry and other scholars restored the arts to favor. I hope to demonstrate that there is no paradox here, that Thierry's *De inventione* commentary is a worthy example of his enlightened teaching of the arts, and that John of Salisbury may not be wrong in supposing that Thierry played a considerable role in a "revival" of the arts at some point in the first half of the twelfth century.[1]

---

[1] The editions of the works of Gilbert and Clarenbald referred to in the first paragraph of section I are: N. Haring, ed., *Life and Works of Clarembald of Arras*, Pontifical Institute Studies and Texts 10 (Toronto 1965) henceforth cited as Haring, *Clarembald*; *The Commentaries on Boethius by Gilbert of Poitiers*, Pontifical Institute Studies and Texts 13 (Toronto 1966). The *Heptateuchon* prologue has been edited in two places: E. Jeauneau, "Le *Prologus* in Eptateuchon de Thierry de Chartres," *Mediaeval Studies* (henceforth *Med. St.*) 16 (1954) 174; Jeauneau, "Note sur l'école de Chartres," *Studi medievali* (henceforth *St. Med.*) ser. 3, 5 (1964) 854-855. For Thierry's views on the study of the *quadrivium*, see the *De sex dierum operibus*, ed. N. Haring, "The Creation and Creator of the World according to Thierry of Chartres and Clarenbaldus of Arras," *Archives d'histoire doctrinale et littéraire du moyen âge* (henceforth, *Archives*) 22 (1955) 194 etc. On the possibility that

II

The "Cornifician" attack on the arts during the first half of the twelfth century is too complex a development to outline in any detail here. The essence

---

Thierry wrote other works on the *artes*, see n. 46 below. The fragment from the *De inventione* commentary was edited by W. H. D. Suringar, *Historia critica scholiastarum latinorum* (Leyden 1834) 213-252. Until the part-publication of Mary Dickey's 1954 thesis, in 1968, this fragment was virtually the only printed illustration of any consequence of medieval commentation on the *De inventione* and *Ad Herennium*. See n. 99 below. A portion of the fragment has been reedited by the Reverend Haring, "Thierry of Chartres and Dominicus Gundissalinus," *Med. St.* 26 (1964) 271-286. The description of Thierry's commentary quoted in the text is from 271. For R. W. Hunt's 1948 article, see n. 76 below. On Thierry's Life and works, see M. Manitius, *Geschichte der lateinischen Literatur des Mittelalters*, 3 (Munich 1931) 198-202; E. Jeauneau, "Mathématiques et trinité chez Thierry de Chartres," *Actes du 2ᵉ congrès internationale de philosophie médiévale, Cologne 31 Aug.-6 Sept., 1961* (Berlin 1963) 289-295; "Un réprésentant du platonisme au XIIᵉ siècle, Maître Thierry de Chartres," *Mémoires de la Société archéologique d'Eure-et-Loir,* 20 (1954) 1-10; "Simples notes sur la cosmogonie de Thierry de Chartres," *Sophia* 23 (1955) 172-183; B. Widmer, "Thierry von Chartres, ein Gelehrtenschicksal des 12 Jahrhunderts," *Historisches Zeitschrift*, 200 (1965) 552ff. The following references contain occasional information: André Vernet in *Bulletin de la Société Nationale des antiquaires de France*, 1950-1951 (Paris 1954) 38-39, and 1952-1953 (Paris 1955) 52-53; Wattenbach in *Sitzungsberichte der Königlichen preussischen Akademie der Wissenschaften zu Berlin* (1895) 123-157; Duhem in *Revue des sciences philosophiques et théologiques* 3 (1909) 525; R. Palacz in *Bulletin de la Société internationale pour l'étude de la philosophie médiévale* (1962-1963) 198. R. W. Southern, "Humanism and the School of Chartres," in *Medieval Humanism and Other Studies* (Oxford 1970) 61ff. provides a brief sketch of the career and works of scholars traditionally associated with Chartres. Southern's attempt to "dismantle" the "school of Chartres" is no more convincing than the attempt by Clerval and Poole to "assemble" it a century ago. One must beware the tendency to overdo hindsight: the school of Chartres was certainly outmoded by the second half of the twelfth century, but whether 1120 or 1150 was the decisive date in the decline of the school is hard to say. Certainly the interests of Bernard of Chartres, William of Conches, and even, in part, Thierry himself (literature, natural philosophy) do not necessarily suggest Paris, with its pronounced dialectical concentration. H. Schipperges ("Die Schulen von Chartres unter dem Einfluss des Arabismus," *Sudhoffs Archiv für Geschichte der Medezin und der Naturwissenschaften* [1956]) linked Chartres in particular with the influx of Arabic, pseudo-Arabic, and Greek scientific knowledge from the East, in view of Thierry's relations with Hermann the Dalmatian and Bernard Silvester, and in view of the content of William's *De philosophia mundi*; B. Lawn, in a recent masterly study (*The Salernitan Questions* [Oxford 1963] 50ff.) saw no reason to disagree. Southern (70 n. 1) says Clerval was mistaken in seeing Thierry's name in charters issued by Chartres Cathedral 1119-1124. This I cannot verify. However, in attempting to disassociate William of Conches from Chartres, Southern ignores Jeauneau's (admittedly not especially convincing) evidence in *Recherches de théologie ancienne et médiévale* (henceforth *RTAM*) 27 (1960) 230ff., and posits the difficult hypothesis that John of Salisbury returned to Mont Sainte Geneviève at the end of his three years with William of Conches, in 1141 (73). In fact John did not return to the Mont until the conclusion of his twelve years of study, as he expressly

of the attack is contained, I believe, in a number of important passages from the following texts: William of Conches's *De philosophia mundi, Dragmaticon* (or *Dialogus de substantiis physicis*), glosses on Priscian's *Institutes of Grammar*, on Plato's *Timaeus*, and on Boethius's *De consolatione philosophiae*; Hugh of Saint Victor's *Didascalicon*; Robert of Melun's *Sententiae*; Thierry of Chartres's Commentary on the *De inventione*; the anonymous Goliardic poem known as the *Metamorphosis Goliae*, and, finally, the *Metalogicon, Policraticus* and larger *Entheticus* of John of Salisbury.[2]

---

tells us at the end of *Metalogicon* 2.10. Against Southern's contention (76) that after the death of Bernard of Chartres, the Cathedral School was of no more than local importance, it is worth noting that Thierry donated to the Cathedral, on his death (in a monastery) 55 volumes, including the *Heptateuchon* and *Codex Justinianus* (Poole, *Studies in Chronology and History* 243; J. A. Clerval, *Les écoles de Chartres au moyen-âge* (Chartres 1895) 172). Would Thierry have made this donation if the Chartres Cathedral School was of little account?

Under the supervision of Dr. Pinborg, Karin Margarita Fredborg, of the University of Copenhagen's *Institut for Graesk og Latinsk Middelalderfilologi*, has recently completed an M. A. thesis (in Danish) on the theory, practice, methods and aims of the School of Chartres in the first half of the twelfth century. In this thesis, it appears, Thierry's *De inventione* commentary was subjected to considerable scrutiny. Karin Fredborg is now preparing an edition of Thierry's *De inventione* and *Ad Herennium* commentaries, has already at the printers an article detailing her views on the school of Chartres, to appear in the *Cahiers de l'Institut du moyen-âge grec et latin de Copenhague*, and has been most generous to me with letters and advice. To her I owe the impetus which lead to the writing of Appendix B below. All scholars interested in the figure of Thierry of Chartres and his school must await with interest the full publication of Fredborg's work.

[2] The passages in detail are:

William of Conches, *De philosophia mundi*, 1 *praef.*, 3 *praef.*, 4.36-38 (PL 172.43A, 75, 100A etc.)

— , *Dragmaticon*, or *Dialogus de substantiis physicis*, ed. Gul. Gratarolus (Strasbourg 1567) 1, 2, 7, 35, 63, 157, 211-212, etc.

— , *Glosses on Priscian*; cf. E. Jeauneau, "Deux rédactions des gloses de Guillaume de Conches sur Priscien," *RTAM* 27 (1960) 221, 223-224, 233-234 etc.

— , *Glosses on the Timaeus*; cf. the article cited above 220, 221 n. 30 and now *Guillaume de Conches, Glosae super Platonem*, ed. E. Jeauneau (Paris 1965) 57, 224.

— , *Glosses on Boethius' De consolatione philosophiae*. Cf. C. Jourdain, "Des commentaires inédits de Guillaume de Conches et de Nicholas Triveth sur 'La consolation de la philosophie de Boèce," *Notices et extraits des manuscrits de la Bibliothèque Impériale*, 20 (1862) 51, and *RTAM* 27 (1960) 219.

Hugh of Saint Victor, *Didascalicon*, preface and 3.3.13.

Robert of Melun, *Sententiae*, ed. R. Martin, *Œuvres de Robert de Melun*, 1 (Louvain 1932) 4, 6-9, 14-16, 19. See D. E. Luscombe, *The School of Peter Abelard* (Cambridge 1969) chap. 12.

Thierry of Chartres, the two personal expostulations printed by Paul Thomas from the commentary on the *De inventione*, in *Mélanges Graux* (Paris 1884) 41-45.

The *Metamorphosis Goliae* has been edited by R. B. C. Huygens, *St. Med.* ser. 3, 3 (1962) 764-772. The poem implicitly attacks the *disertissimi* of the *De inventione* commentators, the *insipientes* of John of Salisbury, and the *De inventione* itself (1.3.4), who divorce *sapientia* and *eloquentia* (*De inventione* 1.1.1) by neglecting the goal to which all skill in the

As John of Salisbury presents it, the "Cornifician Movement" seems to have foreshadowed the popularity of law, medicine, and dialectic that became so characteristic a feature of the later twelfth-century Parisian scholastic scene.[3] To the followers of Cornificius, perhaps the first generation

arts should be directed (a goal to be ascertained partly by a study of the "extrinsic" aspects of the art), concentrating instead on empty verbal sophistry.

John of Salisbury, *Metalogicon, passim,* but esp. 1.3; the larger *Entheticus* (PL 199) and the *Policraticus,* esp. 7.9 and 12. See Brian P. Hendley, "John of Salisbury's Defence of the *Trivium,*" *Actes du Quatrième congrès internationale de la philosophie médiévale, Montréal, 27 August-2 Sept. 1967* henceforth cited as *Actes*; Montreal 1969 753ff.; L. M. De Rijk, *Logica modernorum* 2.1 (Assen 1967) 215ff. On Abelard and the "Cornifician Movement," see M. M. McLaughlin, "Abelard's Conceptions of the Liberal Arts and Philosophy," *Actes* 523ff. On *Cornificius . . . loquacitatis,* see Peter of Blois, PL 207.290-291.

[3] See the references cited below, n. 115. I have sketched in outline the context of the "Cornifician crisis" in "Educational Crisis and the Genesis of Universities in Medieval Europe," *Teaching History* 3 (N.S.W., Australia 1969) 5-18. The exact sociological and educational nature and significance of the "Cornifician Movement," however, as it is described in the texts cited in n. 2 above, has not yet been adequately set out in detail. The name Cornificius refers to a detractor of Vergil and the liberal arts mentioned in Donatus's *Life of Vergil:* D. D. McGarry, trans., *The Metalogicon of John of Salisbury,* (Berkeley 1962) xxi. The personage whom John intends to conceal under the pseudonym is a mystery. See C. C. J. Webb, *John of Salisbury* (London 1932) 18-19; H. Liebeschütz, *Medieval Humanism in the Life and Writings of John of Salisbury* (London 1950) 90ff. and 118, and on the circumstances surrounding John's conflict and disillusion with Henry II's government 11-22; C. Prantl, *Geschichte der Logik im Abendlande,* 2.230; R. L. Poole, *Studies in Chronology and History,* ed. A. L. Poole (Oxford 1934) 244; M. Grabmann, *Die Geschichte der scholastischen Methode* (Graz 1911, repr. 1957) 2.114f.; H. Brinkmann, *Zeitschrift für deutsches Altertum und deutsche Literatur* (henceforth, ZFDA) 62 (1925) 32; Clerval (n. 1 above) 227; L. Levillain in *Le moyen âge* (1895) 115-116. Prantl identified Cornificius with the monk Reginaldus of *Metamorphosis Goliae* line 201. De Rijk follows Mandonnet and identifies the Parisian logician Gualo (fl. ca. 1115-1130) with Cornificius (see *Vivarium* [1966] 4-8, *Actes* 524, 795, and references there to de Bruyne, Grabmann, and McKeon). From internal evidence provided by the *Metalogicon* and *Policraticus* it seems that John's thorough literary education and the political-ecclesiastical conclusions he drew from it, had by 1159 come under attack from Henry II and the courtiers opposed to the primacy of ecclesiastical influence in the state. Liebeschütz supposes, too, that a conflict developed between humanistic studies and administrative experience as the proper training for an official career. John, urged on by his friends (*Metalogicon,* prologue) composed the *Metalogicon* to vindicate his educational stance. John implies that Cornificius was in religious orders, and perhaps a monk (*Met.* 1.2. PL 199.827D). But to support the contention that Cornificius has definite secular and political connections, John appears to say in one place that his opponent had entered *vulgi professiones* (*Met.* 1.4, PL 199.831C). Pseudonyms like *Lanvinus* or *Gnatho* appear in profusion in John's *Entheticus* and *Policraticus.* Even Gilbert of Poitiers, at one point calls his opponents *Fennii* and *Praeconii temporum nostrorum.* The MSS (J. R. O'Donnell, ed., *Nine Medieval Thinkers,* [Toronto 1955] 27) have *Pachomii, Paconii, Praconii (Pacuvius* or *Pachomius*) and either *Ennii* or *Fannii (Fannius* was a vain poetaster in the time of Horace, cf. Pauly-Wissowa, *Real-Encyclopädie* 6 (1909) col. 1987) would appear to be acceptable for *Fennii.* John of Salisbury (*Policraticus* 7.9, PL 199.651B)

of tertiary-trained "job-hunters" in the modern sense, these studies lead to the kind of immediate success in debate and business which made a mockery of the insistence on a balanced education in the *trivium* and *quadrivium* by the older or more conscientious masters of the first half of the twelfth century. Since they set themselves a more limited educational goal than the academic theologians and scholars of the time, the "Cornificians" found the stress on grammar and rhetoric in the contemporary curriculum a time-consuming and tedious exercise. Grammar, insofar as it was a necessary art, would come naturally to the student, they argued, and the customary reasons for the study of rhetoric, its utility in law, dialectic, and document composition, had lost their relevance in view of the burgeoning study of *dictamen* in the twelfth century, and the emergence of law and dialectic from the aegis of rhetoric as independent studies in their own right.

Having described the nature of the "Cornician" attack on the arts, John proceeds to explain that

> Others, who were [real] lovers of letters, set themselves to coun-
> teract the [Cornician] error. Among the latter were Master Thierry,
> a very assiduous investigator of the arts, William of Conches, the
> most accomplished grammarian since Bernard of Chartres and the
> Peripatetic from Pallet, who won such distinction in logic over all
> his contemporaries, that it was thought that he alone really under-
> stood Aristotle. They themselves became [temporarily] insane while
> combating insanity, and for quite a time floundered in error while
> trying to correct it. The fog, however, was soon dispelled. Thanks
> to the work and diligence of these masters, the arts regained their
> own, and were reinforced in their pristine seat of honour.

Scholars whom the Cornificians attacked included, John continues, Anselm and Ralph of Laon, Alberic of Rheims, Simon of Paris, William of Champeaux, Hugh of Saint Victor (who was to some extent immune from attack because of his religious habit) and Robert Pullen.

---

describes the "Cornician" logic-choppers as "illos qui altius praeconantur, quos auditorum multitudo circumstrepit," suggesting that *Praeconii* may be what Gilbert had in mind. Thierry of Chartres in his *De inventione* commentary had called his detractors *histriones* (Thomas [n. 2 above] 42). The most famous pseudonym of the twelfth and thirteenth cen-turies, however, is perhaps the figure of the poet Golias, whose identity (if any) is also a mystery. On the sociological context cf. Classen, *Arch. f. Kulturgesch.* 48 (1966) 155ff.

G. Misch, "Studien zur Geschichte der Autobiographie, 5: Johann von Salisbury und das Problem des mittelalterlichen Humanismus," *Nachrichten der Akademie der Wissenschaften in Göttingen*, 1, Phil.-Hist. Klasse, 6 (1960) 297, professes to see in the "Cornician Move-ment" "ein Schattenbild der sozialen Differenzierung . . . die damals sich ausbilden begann." See also P. Delhaye, "L'organisation scolaire au XIIᵉ siècle," *Traditio* 5 (1947) 264.

Later in the *Metalogicon* John writes:

> My own instructors in grammar, William of Conches and Richard,
> who is known as "The Bishop," a good man both in life and conver-
> sation, who now holds the office of Archdeacon of Coutances, for-
> merly used Bernard [of Chartres's] method in training their disciples.
> But later, when popular opinion veered away from the truth, when
> men preferred to seem rather than to be philosophers, and when
> professors of the arts were promising to impart the whole of philo-
> sophy in less than three or even two years, William and Richard were
> overwhelmed by the onslaught of the mob and retired. Since then,
> less time and attention have been given to the study of grammar.[4]

Simply put, the problem to be discussed in the following pages is twofold:
how can these developments be placed in precise chronological perspective,
and how do the known facts of Thierry's career and writings relate to his
role in them?

A basis for our understanding of the chronological development of the
"Cornifician Movement" can be laid by considering the dates of the important
texts describing it.

The date of the *Metalogicon* itself, and the teaching career of Robert of
Melun (ca. 1137-1163) are too well known to require elaboration. The *Metamorphosis Goliae* was probably written between 1150 and 1155.[5] William

---

[4] *Metalogicon* 1.5 (McGarry [n. 3 above] 21) and 1.24 (*ibid.* 71).

[5] The poem must have been written after 1140, the trial at Sens, but need not have been
completed before the death of Abelard (1142) as Hauréau thought in 1876. See *Mémoires
de l'Académie des inscriptions et belles-lettres* (MAIBL) 28 (1876) 224, and Denifle in *Archiv für Literatur- und Kirchengeschichte des Mittelalters* 1 (1885) 605. The poet is imagining
a heavenly situation, and, as Brinkmann has shown, the reference to Abelard in stanza 54
forces us to date the poem twenty years before 1140 if we interpret the stanza literally,
or at any time after 1140, if we accept the requirements of the dream situation. Since the
first alternative is improbable, we are left with the second (ZFDA 62 (1925) 32-33). The
mention of Mainerius in the poem suggests a date considerably later than 1142. Mainerius
would have been very new to the ranks of the *magistri* in 1142. See Denifle and Chatelain,
Chartularium Universitatis Parisiensis 1 (1889) 7 note to no. 6; Poole (n. 3 above) 246, Luscombe (n. 2 above) 55. The list of *magistri* in the poem approaches far more closely the
list given by William of Tyre (R. B. C. Huygens, "Guillaume de Tyr, étudiant: un chapitre
[19.12] de son *Historia* retrouvé," *Latomus* 21 [1962] 811ff.), than it does the list given by
John of Salisbury, *Metalogicon* 2.10, as the following summary should make clear:
masters common to both John and the *Metamorphosis Goliae*:   6.
masters common to both John and William: 4.
masters common to the *Metamorphosis Goliae* and William: 8.
John mentions 12 masters who taught him, the *Metamorphosis Goliae* mentions 13 (one
of whom is the monk Reginald), and William mentions 16, one of whom, William of Soissons, was a student of John's. William's studies took place in the fifties (cf. Huygens 819),
and I would therefore place the *Metamorphosis Goliae* nearer the middle fifties than 1142
(cf. Luscombe 55).

of Conches's *De philosophia mundi* (the original version), his commentary on the *Timaeus* and the commentary on the *De consolatione philosophiae* of Boethius, may all, it appears, be dated to the period 1120-1130. According to the *Dragmaticon*, probably written shortly after 1144,[6] the first version of the *Philosophia* was written "in juventute."[7] The glosses on Priscian were also first written "in youth."[8] In view of the fact that the *Philosophia* anticipates the glosses on Priscian, we may place its composition before that of the glosses.[9]

When was William a "youth"? In the *Dragmaticon* he says that he has been teaching for "twenty years and more,"[10] that is to say, from approximately 1120 onwards. If "Magister G" in a letter written before 1116 is, in fact, William, then his teaching career will have begun even earlier than this.[11] This supposition is to some extent strengthened by the fact that William is prepared to call himself "an old man" in the forties and fifties of the century: the second version of the glosses on Priscian was produced, he tells us, "in nostra senectute."[12]

The probable date of Hugh of Saint Victor's *Didascalicon* is circa 1127.[13] It would thus appear that the *artes* were under fire from the Cornificians (the *garciones* of the texts?) from the 1120's onwards, and perhaps even earlier.

---

[6] Poole (n. 3 above) 238; E. Jeauneau, *Glosae super Platonem* (n. 2 above) 9-10; Lawn (n. 1 above) 51, citing T. Gregory, *Anima mundi*, on the date of the *De philosophia*, and 54, offering 1122-1127 as the date; 55, 1146-1149 as the date of the *Dragmaticon*, citing Gregory again.

[7] R. L. Poole, *Illustrations of the History of Medieval Thought and Learning*, ed. 2 (London 1920, repr. N. Y. 1960) 302.

[8] Jeauneau, RTAM (n. 1 above) 243.

[9] Cf. William of Conches, *De philosophia mundi* (n. 2 above) 4.41.

[10] Poole (n. 7 above) 300.

[11] Letter 23 of the Chartres Letter Book. Cf. L. Merlet, "Lettres d'Ives de Chartres et d'autre personnages de son temps, 1081-1130," *Bibliothèque de l'École des chartes* (BEC) 16 (1854-1855) 463; Poole (n. 3 above) 225-228.

[12] William died after 1154. See Jeauneau, *Glosae* (n. 2 above) 10, Poole (n. 7 above) 111 n. 25, Jeauneau, RTAM (n. 1 above) 244. In general on the dating of William's works, see Poole (n. 7 above) 298-304 and M. Grabmann, "Handschriftsliche Forschungen und Mitteilungen zum Schrifttum des W. von Conches," *Sitzungsberichte bayrischen Akademie der Wissenschaft, phil-hist. Kl.* 10 (1935) 4-25. In his glosses on Boethius, William speaks of intended commentaries on Macrobius and Martianus Capella: cf. E. Jeauneau in *St. Med.* (n. 1 above) 840f. and in "Gloses de Guillaume de Conches sur Macrobe, note sur les manuscrits," *Archives* 27 (1960) 17-28. Grabmann's conclusions on the date of the *Summa philosophiae* ("Handschriftsliche" 7-10) are no longer relevant, since the work is not thought to have been written by William (cf. T. Gregory in *Giornale critico della filosofia italiana* [1951] 119ff.). Taylor would date the glosses on Boethius to 1120-1125. The early version of the commentary on Plato, he thinks, is pre-1125, and the *Philosophia* he considers to have been written 1125-1130 (Hugh of Saint Victor, *Didascalicon*, trans. J. Taylor [New York 1961] 8, 162).

[13] Taylor, 3, 162.

This is in accord with the evidence of the *Metalogicon*. Not only does John describe Cornificius as, by 1159, an old man, but he tells us that the followers of the renegade had spent, by 1159, not just ten or twenty years in their misbegotten pursuits, but a whole lifetime. When the arts regained their popularity, as a result of the untiring efforts of the humanists, Cornificius was even then a *senex insulsus*. Nor was he the first of his breed: he had learned his evil trade from his own masters, who must themselves have been "tainted."[14] If John's words are to be taken literally, the beginnings of the Cornifician movement must be taken back to the first years of the twelfth century, if not earlier.

Nevertheless, it seems that Cornifician tendencies were very manifest at Paris in the 1130s. When John himself went to school at Mont Sainte-Geneviève, in the late thirties, an exclusive preoccupation with dialectic was noticeable. After two years at the Mount, John writes of himself as he does of the Cornifician scholars.[15] William of Soissons, John's own student, con-

---

[14] *Metalogicon* 1.5, PL 199.832C; 1.3, 830A; 2.7 *init.*; 1.3, 828D.

[15] *Metalogicon* 2.10, PL 199.868A. The Cornificians, writes John elsewhere, debate tiny, useless points of argument *ad infinitum*, "multitudine verborum," "multis cavillationibus," "sine fructu sensuum," seeking verbal ornament rather than truth, fleeing the "difficultas rerum" (*res* being opposed to *verbum*), "pondere rei vacui," "determinata multiplicate sermonis," judging words to be wisdom, and forever relying upon the *sermo rotundus*, the opposite of *sermo frequens* (speech disciplined by *usus* and *exercitio*). Thierry himself has this to say of such "philosophers": "Scolasticae disputationis histriones inanium verborum pugnis armati, tales quidem mea castra sequuntur" (preface to the *De inventione* commentary). The "humanists" never tire of railing at dialectical excesses, as the language used in the following passages (selected more or less at random) should indicate: William of Conches, *Dragmaticon* 2, 80-81 (cf. Poole [n. 7 above] 313), *De philosophia mundi* 1 *praef.*, PL 172.43A ("id etiam est gladium semper acuere, sed nunquam in proelio percutere"), 2 *praef.* (Poole *ibid.* 312); John of Salisbury, *Policraticus* 7.9, PL 199.655A, 653D, J. B. Pike trans. (Minneapolis 1938) 244; 7.12 generally and esp. Pike 258, 260-261, PL 119.662A-C and 664C; *Metalogicon* 1.3, PL 199.828C; 2.6 (compare John's opposition to the stress on definition with William of Conches, Jeauneau RTAM [n. 1 above] 218, where William states that he plans to supplement Priscian by providing proper attention to definitions); 2.7-9 (McGarry [n. 3 above] 93); 2.10, PL 199. 867D; 2.15, 17-19 *fin.*; 4.3 (*intricatione verborum*, PL 199.917D); 4.23, 26, 29; *Metamorphosis Goliae* stanza 23; John's *Entheticus* (PL 199) lines 22, 68, 79, 90-91, 152, 160, 174 (*sermo frequens: usus* and *exercitio*, have, of course, to be in moderation and guided by reason, cf. *Metalogicon* 2.8, *init.*), 182, and the smaller *Entheticus*, trans. Pike 420, ed. Webb 6, line 24. John's *sermo rotundus* (the speech of *aulicus . . . noster*) has elements of the classical *urbanus, lepidus, venustus, dicax, facetus*, as opposed to *rusticus*, with this difference that whereas late republican Romans admired verbal sophistication, honest medieval Christians had learned to suspect it, as not necessarily consonant with truth or simplicity. Cf. Lewis and Short, *A Latin Dictionary* s.v. *rotundus* (II.B), Quintilian *Institutiones* 2.8.4, Tacitus *Dialogus de oratoribus* 18, Horace *Ep.* 1.15.27, *Sat.* 1.4.90, 2.6.80 (*the urbanus et rusticus mus* fable), Catullus *Carmina* 1.1, 10.4, 12.8. 16.7, 22.2 and 9, 39.8 and 10, 57.4 etc., John of Garland, *Morale scolarium*, ed. Paetow (Berkeley 1927) 188-189, Geoffrey of Vinsauf *Poetria nova* 124, ed. E. Faral,

forms to norms elsewhere described as Cornifician.[16] Alberic of Paris and
Robert of Melun, John's two professors at the Mount, do not emerge unscathed:
both would have been outstanding scholars "si de magno litterarum nitentur fundamento, si tantum institissent vestigiis majorum, quantum suis applaudebant inventis."[17] Both were preeminently dialecticians and, John admits, possessed keen minds.[18] Alberic later departed for Bologna, in accordance with the Cornifician pattern that John has already described.[19] Adam
of the Little Bridge is another noted scholar of the day to have fallen, in
John's opinion at least, under a "Cornifician" cloud.[20] All these scholars
enjoyed long teaching careers. William of Tyre studied under them in the

---

Les arts poétiques du XIIe et XIIIe siècle (Bibliothèque de l'École des hautes études, fasc.
238) 201, and John's Entheticus lines 141, 143, 152.

[16] Metalogicon 2.10, PL 199.868CD, and compare, in addition to the references given
in n.15 above, Metalogicon 3 prol., McGarry 13, 15, 16, 144-145; PL 199.864C, Poole (n. 7
above) 193.

[17] Metalogicon 2.10, PL 199.867D. Lack of fundamental literary training, and a tendency
to deride the achievements of past scholars in favor of modern "novelties" are three important characteristics of "Cornifician" scholars. See the texts cited at the beginning of
this paper, on the nature of the "Cornifician" attack on the arts. Detailed illustration of
these themes must await another occasion.

[18] PL 199.867C. Cf. Delhaye, Le Microcosmus de Godefroy de St. Victor (1951) 185.

[19] Metalogicon 1.4, where some Cornifician scholars depart to Montpellier or Salerno to
become as poor doctors as they had been philosophers. On Alberic and Robert, see Luscombe (n. 2 above) 52, 90; De Rijk, Vivarium 4 (1966) 4ff, and Logica modernorum (n. 2
above) 2.1.209ff., 281, 287ff.; John of Salisbury, Epistola 183, PL 199.186A ("laudis avarus
erat," etc.); Metamorphosis Goliae, lines 193, 205 (with Poole [n. 3 above] 244ff.). Compare
Metamorphosis Goliae line 196 with Entheticus line 54 and cf. too Entheticus lines 55ff.
Alberic's departure to Bologna indicates the absence of adequate legal instruction at Paris
at the time. John does not mention law, yet William of Tyre studied it (Huygens [n. 5
above] 823). By the student days of Gerald of Wales, legal studies at Paris were well entrenched. Thierry of Chartres left a number of legal text books to the Cathedral of Chartres at his death (Hauréau, "Bernard de Chartres et Thierry de Chartres," Comptes rendus
des séances de l'année 1872, de l'AIBL., ser. 3, 1[1873] 82, and Haring, Clarembald [n. 1 above]
26 n. 22), but the younger magister Ivo of Chartres is reputed to have abhorred the study
of the subject. What was the fate of legal studies at Chartres after the death of Bishop
Ivo, early in the century?

[20] On Adam see Metalogicon 4.3, 2.10, PL 199.868C. Attention to the works of Aristotle
did not apparently (Metalogicon 2.7, McGarry [n. 3 above] 89) absolve a scholar from "Cornificianism." See also Entheticus 49ff. (PL 199.966); John may well have changed his
opinion of Adam: in Metalogicon 2.10 he can clearly find much of merit in the man. Adam,
a novus auctor in arte, suffers, says John "ex desipientia vel invidentia vani." On insipientia
as a Cornifician characteristic, cf. Metalogicon 1.5 (PL 199.832B), Entheticus line 66,
Dragmaticon 3, 63, 158. Adam's Ars disserendi has been published by L. Minio-Paluello in Twelfth-Century Logic. Texts, and Studies, 1: Adam Balsamiensis Parvipontani, Ars
disserendi (Dialectica Alexandri) (Rome 1956); cf. also Minio-Paluello's article in Mediaeval
and Renaissance Studies (henceforth MRS) 3 (1954) 116-69. See too De Rijk (n. 2 above)
2.1.206ff.

1150s.[21] When John returned to the Mount, at the end of his twelve years of study, he found it confirmed in the academic characteristics that had partly converted him in his early years of study. Of these, the chief was an overwhelming devotion to dialectic, as an end in itself.

At Chartres, it may be inferred, the flood tide of the Cornician movement occurred during the chancellorship of Gilbert of Poitiers (1126-1138).[22] Apart from John of Salisbury's direct reference to Gilbert and the Cornician scholars (*Metalogicon* 1.5), a curious anecdote has come down to us illustrating the self-confidence of the Cornician *garcio*. A certain Master Albricus, a Master Garnerus Gramaticus and many others had entered the school of Gilbert of Poitiers. "One day Master Garnerus had said to the master: 'Answer that, Master Gilbert Porreta.' The lord teacher turned on him with disgust: 'Garcio,' he said, 'do you not know that an adjective ought to be put before the noun? Thus you should have said "Porreta Gilbert." You have made an error and you will suffer for it,' With that he had him lashed soundly."[23] It would be fanciful to hang very much on this anecdote, but if it does refer to Gilbert's teaching at Chartres, it may be that, in the case of Master Albricus at least, if he is to be identified with the teacher of John of Salisbury, a period of broad study in the *trivium* at Chartres ended in an impatient departure to the dialectical schools of the Mount, in a manner appropriate to a scholar infected with Cornician distemper.

Grammar, it seems, was an exception to the general revival of the arts effected by the labors of the humanists. After the retirement of William

---

[21] Huygens (n. 5 above) 822ff. It is a common complaint in the anti-Cornician writings of the day, that the *novi doctores* enjoyed great popularity: *Entheticus*, line 53; William of Conches's *De philosophia mundi* 2. praef. (*nihil de multitudine*); *Metalogicon* 2.6 (PL 199.862B, "tantus undique est cursus populorum"); Bernard of Clairvaux, *De conversione ad clericos*, PL 182.853D (ed. and trans. W. Williams [London 1938] 53, 97), "curritur passim ad sacros ordines." Cf. also William of Conches's remarks, *Dragmaticon* 1, 35, 63, 211. Thierry too, speaks of a *vulgus* (Thomas [n. 2 above] 42).

[22] John of Salisbury's statement that the followers of Cornificius entered the monastic orders (*Metalogicon* 1.4, McGarry 17) can be amply documented in the sources. In many cases the language of polemic used against the Cornician scholars and the monks is identical. In this context, it is interesting to learn that Chartres was much plagued in the first half of the century by these "sham" monks. The subject is too extensive to document here, but see J. Leclercq, "Le poème de Payen Bolotin contre les faux ermites." *Revue bénédictine* 68 (1958) 52-86, Clerval (n. 1 above) 215, and *Histoire littéraire de la France* 11.3. On the career of Gilbert of Poitiers to ca. 1124, when he appears as a canon at Chartres, see N. Haring, "Zur Geschichte der Schulen von Poitiers im 12 J/h.," *Archiv für Kulturgeschichte* 47 (1965) 25. Clerval's assertion that Gilbert established a school at Poitiers after Anselm of Laon's death in 1117 is without foundation (Clerval [n. 1 above] 164, Poole [n. 3 above] 228, Haring *art. cit.* 25 n. 9).

[23] See Jeauneau, RTAM (n. 1 above) 220; R. W. Hunt in MRS 2.42; Luscombe (n. 2 above) 55-56. The word *garcio* appears frequently in the texts to describe a scholar of the "Cornician" type.

of Conches and Richard the Bishop, John states: "Exinde autem, minus temporis et diligentiae, in grammaticae studio impensum est."[24] When did the attacks of the Cornifician scholars cause the retirement of these grammarians? Precision in this and related problems raised by the passages quoted from the *Metalogicon* at the beginning of this study, cannot be attempted without a clarification of John of Salisbury's movements as a student in Paris and Chartres during the late thirties and early forties of the century. The following remarks are offered as a speculative contribution to this much-discussed, yet still perplexing topic.

Three fixed dates are usually cited. In the first place, John tells us that he went to Gaul in the year after the death of Henry I, that is, some time in 1136.[25] In the second place, we know that Gilbert of Poitiers took up the bishopric of that city after July 1142.[26] In the third place, at the beginning of the prologue to Book 3 of the *Metalogicon*, John tells us that almost twenty years had elapsed since he departed from the schools of the logicians (at the Mount, or Paris generally). This prologue was probably composed in the late spring or early summer of 1159; John would thus appear to have left the Mount, or Paris generally, in May 1139 or thereabouts.[27]

Two years after his arrival in France, John, with the help of his instructors, took stock of his situation: "metiens vires meas, bona praeceptorum meorum gratia."[28] This reassessment of his position seems to have occupied part or all of the period from the summer of 1138 to the spring of 1139. At that point John began a period of study under William of Conches which lasted *triennio*, that is, from about May 1139 to the early months of 1142, or a little earlier if the expression *triennium* was not intended to imply three

---

[24] *Metalogicon* 1.24, PL 199.856 AB.

[26] Poole (n. 3 above) 223; Delhaye (n. 3 above) 261ff; P. Gennrich in *Zeitschrift für Kirchengeschichte* 13 (1892) 544.

[26] Poole (n. 3 above) 237.

[27] Our dating of *Metalogikon* Prologue to Book 3 is a little less sure since Constable demolished Poole's belief that John of Salisbury's fifth trip to Rome took place Dec. 1158-May 1159. For my present purposes, however, the date of composition for the *Metalogikon* is firmly enough fixed. See Poole (n. 3 above) 268-269, *Historia Pontificalis*, ed. Poole (Oxford 1927) lxxiii, Liebeschütz (n. 3 above) 11-22, McGarry (n. 3 above) xix n. 26, G. Constable "The alleged disgrace of John of Salisbury in 1159," *English Historical Review* 69 (1954) 73f., *The Letters of John of Salisbury* (ed. Millor, Butler, and Brooke), vol. 1 (London 1955) xiv-xv. On the likelihood that the *Metalogicon* was compiled during 1159, whilst the *Policraticus* was based on material collected over previous years, see Liebeschütz 13-15. In the introduction to his *Policraticus*, John informs his readers that he has been busy with the frivolities of courtiers for twelve years (i.e. since leaving Paris, 1147/1148), during which time he has had little pause for philosophical reflection (Poole, *Historia Pontificalis* lxxii, Liebeschütz 16).

[28] *Metalogicon* 2.10, PL 199.867C, *sic ferme toto biennio*, 868A *toto . . . biennio*. *Metalogicon* prol. to 3 refers either to this development, or to the slightly later departure (?) from Paris (?) to William of Conches.

full calendar years. *Postmodum*, after the three years spent with William, John reviewed the *quadrivium* and rhetoric with Richard the Bishop. He had studied a little of each previously with Thierry and Hardewin. While engaged in these studies, he had taken on some teaching because "I lacked the help of friends and relatives." In the course of this, John instructed William of Soissons and had recourse to Adam of the Little Bridge. After a digression on William's logical reasoning, John rather confusingly resumes the thread of his narrative with the statement that his pinched finances, the entreaties of his associates, and the advice of his friends (whom he now, apparently, possessed) "extracted" him from the occasional teaching and learning in which he had been engaged, and advised that he pursue the *officium docentis*. Returned thus, after the three years with William, he met with (or discovered again: *reperi*) Gilbert of Poitiers and embarked on a course of theological instruction.[29]

There are, as has long been recognized, many problems involved in this summary. Where did John reassess his position, at the Mount, or Paris? Where and when did John first study under Thierry? Where did he study under Richard and William? Where did he meet Adam and instruct William of Soissons? What evidence is there that he left Paris or its environs at any stage? From where or from what did John's friends "extract" him when they urged that he seek the *officium docentis*, from Chartres, from Paris, from the Mount, or from his previous mode of living? To what does the second reference to a three year period refer (PL 199.868D)? It cannot be additional to the three years with William of Conches, because that would bring us far beyond the date at which Gilbert of Poitiers left Paris (1142). If, however, it is to be identified with the three years at the feet of William (as seem likely) why does John so suddenly recapitulate and confuse his narrative? When did he take in pupils, after leaving the Mount in 1138/39 or after his three years with William of Conches? Why do his friends now advise him to take up teaching when one page earlier he had undertaken teaching because he "lacked the help of friends and relatives?" Is there a formal distinction to be understood between casual teaching and a course of instruction that might lead to an official *licentia docendi*?[30] If so, how can the immediately ensuing reference to a three year period be the three years

---

[29] *Metalogicon* 2.10, PL 199.868D: "Unde nec amici machina impellente urgeri potui, ut credam ex uno impossibili omnia impossibilia provenire. Extraxerunt me hinc rei familiaris angustia, sociorum petitio, ei consilium amicorum, ut officium docentis aggrederer. Parui. Reversus itaque in fine triennii reperi magistrum Gilbertum, ipsumque audivi in logicis et divinis." Compare Otto of Freising, *Gesta Frederici*, trans. C. C. Mierow (1953) 2.28, writing of Arnold of Brescia in Zürich, "officium doctoris assumens perniciosum dogma aliquot diebus seminavit." On *reperi* see Poole (n. 7 above) 181 n. 6.

[30] As Poole (n. 3 above, 224) seems to suppose.

with William of Conches which occurred before John's resolve to regularize his course of learning and his educational ambitions?

It seems clear from John's language that he did leave either Paris or the Mount in 1139. When he wishes to indicate that he "became the disciple" of a scholar, without leaving his current geographical position, he makes use of words or phrases of the following kind: *adhaesi, praeceptoribus usus sum, audivi, me excepit*.[31] On three occasions, however, in the course of the auto-biographical chapter of the *Metalogicon*, John uses obviously spatial expressions: *contuli me ad Peripateticum*, when it is clear that he has made a journey from England; *me ad Grammaticum de Conchis transtuli*, and *postmodum vero Ricardum . . . secutus sum*.[32] This last expression may not indeed involve the notion of travel, but it differs slightly from John's usual expressions of adherence to a master. Again, if the *reversus itaque* of the later recapitulation (PL 199.868D) refers to a return from Chartres, the view that *secutus sum* at this point involves spatial movement is strengthened.

Since John, on his own admission, does not return to the Mont Sainte Geneviève, until the end of his twelve-year period of study, it cannot be asserted that he went from the Mount to Paris in 1139 and returned there three years later. It is more likely, in fact, that he left the Mount in early (?) 1138, transferred to Paris (which could be "the workshop and gymnasium of the logicians" of the prologue of *Metalogicon* 3 as easily as Mont Sainte Geneviève), reassessed his position and consulted his instructors, discovered that life in the capital was expensive, and betook himself to William of Conches who was teaching outside Paris, presumably at Chartres. John's language implies that the decision to study with William was not above criticism: "I then transferred, after deliberation and consultation and with the approval of my instructors, to the grammarian of Conches. I studied under the latter for three years, during which time I learned much. Nor will I ever regret the time thus spent" (*Metalogicon* 2.10, trans. McGarry 97).

Early in 1142, it seems most reasonable to conjecture, John must have left Chartres to review his studies with Richard the Bishop at Paris. This follows from the assumption that John's period of study with Richard seems to have coincided with his performance of the *officium docentis*, his tutoring of William of Soissons and his occasional resort to Adam of the Little Bridge. Both the latter scholars are more likely to have lived at Paris rather than Chartres during these years. John may have met Richard at Chartres.[33]

---

[31] PL 199.867CD, 868D, 869A.

[32] *Ibid.* 867B, 868B.

[33] Otto of Freising, (n. 29 above). 1.53(51), 89, records that Adam was made a canon of Notre Dame before 1147. John's statement in *Metalogicon* I.24 that Richard was one of his teachers, with William of Conches, and used Bernard of Chartres's teaching methods, is the only evidence linking Richard with Chartres, unless one is disposed to accept that

He does not say that he had grammar from Richard in *Metalogicon* 2.10, but Richard was clearly one of his preceptors in the art (*Metalogicon* 1.24). Richard may have been compelled to cease his instruction at Chartres because of pressure from the Cornifician scholars; he might then have departed for Paris, followed by John, who undertook further instruction from him.

----

the cleric Richard in letter 24, BEC (n. 11 above) 464, is the student who later came to be called Richard the Bishop. In this case, the latter scholar would appear to have had his early education at Chartres.

Poole (n. 7 above) 180-181, Levillain (n. 3 above) 114, C. Schaarschmidt (*Johannes Saresberiensis, nach Leben und Studien, Schriften und Philosophie* [Leipzig 1862] 22f.), and G. Misch (n. 3 above) 265, feel that John of Salisbury *did* study at Chartres with William. Clerval (n. 1 above) 180-181 and Delhaye (n. 3 above) 262 n. 41, cannot decide. Poole (n. 3 above) 237-239 and Jeauneau, RTAM (n. 1 above) 230ff. sum up the evidence linking William of Conches and Chartres. It is a tenuous case, but Southern (cf. n. 1 above) cannot put up any stronger arguments to the contrary. A small point may help suggest John's absence from Paris 1139-1141. During this period Arnold of Brescia seems to have been a student of Abelard's (*Historia Pontificalis* 31, ed. Chibnall [1956] 63, ed. Poole lxi). In the *Metalogicon*, John does not seem to have been aware that Abelard was teaching at or in the environs of Paris at this time, for he mentions that Abelard left Mont Sainte Geneviève in 1137 (*Metalogicon* 2.10, Poole, *loc. cit.* Klibansky, MRS 5.16, thinks that Abelard was actually at some distance from Paris and the Mont in the months preceding the trial of Sens). On another point too, it is possible that John was not fully aware of Arnold's career. Otto of Freising (n. 29 above) 2.28.143-144, and W. Williams, *St. Bernard of Clairvaux* (Manchester 1935) 320-322 place Abelard's period as a teacher of Arnold between the years 1115 and 1120 (by implication; see G. Greenaway, *Arnold of Brescia* [Cambridge 1931] 41-42). If this is so (and Otto's account of Arnold's career is not above suspicion on a number of counts, see Luscombe [n. 2 above] 27), then John's acquaintance with Arnold cannot have been extensive, although both were students in Paris at the same time, and one at least, was something of a celebrity. If we suppose that John was not in Paris or its environs at this period (ca. 1139/1140), and did not have any personal contact with Arnold, or his fellow students, then it becomes more explicable that he makes no reference to such an early period of study with Abelard, on Arnold's part, and does not mention Arnold's religious status at Brescia before he returned from Paris (ca. 1120) and became a canon regular and abbot. John's familiarity with Arnold's career does not extend much earlier than the 1130s. A second, but far less plausible explanation is that since Abelard and Arnold were, in 1139/1140, presumably at Mont Sainte Geneviève (*apud Sanctum Hilarium?*), John, on the Île de la Cité, would have been out of contact with them both. See Luscombe (n. 2 above), 105.

Poole (n. 7 above, 180-183) appears to have thought that John spent only part of his *triennium* with William of Conches at Chartres. After a period of study with William, Poole argued, John, still at Chartres, transferred to Richard (and Hardewin?) with whom he entered on a course of instruction in the *quadrivium*. Poverty intervened and John returned to Paris to study theology with Gilbert of Poitiers and pursue the *licentiam docendi*. This interpretation has the advantage of harmonizing with *Metalogicon* 1.24 where Richard and William are described in tandem as John's masters in grammar (implying that he studied under them together, or in succession at the same school). John, however, explicitly states that he studied with William for a *triennium*, at the end of which he returned to Paris. Nor is it clear that John's studies with Richard are to be disassociated in time and place from his teaching of William of Soissons and his recourse to Adam of the Little Bridge.

Did John also study under Thierry at Chartres? It is not necessary to suppose so. Between mid-1138 and spring 1139, as has been mentioned, John reviewed his academic studies. From his remarks at that point it could be concluded that he had hitherto studied only dialectic. After two years at the Mount, it seems probable that he came across a friend or scholar who pointed out to him that he had no sure foundation in the arts. In the few months between his departure from the Mount and his removal to Chartres, he could well have attempted to gather together the elements of a broader instruction in the *trivium* (and *quadrivium*?). In the course of these studies, John may well have discovered Thierry, who instructed him a little (*tenuiter*, PL 199.868B) in rhetoric and other matters. Thierry no doubt suggested that he undertake fuller study of the arts at Chartres itself, and perhaps even gave him letters of introduction to William. This would be the *bona gratia* of his teachers to which John refers.

Two considerations remain, one casting doubt upon the sequence of events presented so far, the other strengthening it. If, as I am assuming, the second reference to a three-year period of study is in the nature of a recapitulation and refers to John's sojourn at Chartres, we are required to believe that in addition to undertaking a review of the arts with Richard, teaching William of Soissons, and discussing knotty problems with Adam of the Little Bridge, John also fitted in a month or two with Gilbert of Poitiers whose disciple he became "in dialectical and theological subjects". Does John qualify the nature of Gilbert's instruction because he has already explained to us that he was Richard's disciple in the arts? Or did John return from Chartres, enroll with Gilbert (spurred on by his friends who felt that the arts ought not be dallied over), and then undertake his period of study with Richard, moving later to Robert Pullen and Simon of Poissy? It is probably impossible to say. At this point John's narrative is undeniably weak.

The second consideration is as follows. John creates the impression that he made little use of Thierry's talents as an instructor. He mentions, vaguely, "previous studies with Master Theodoric," and in this connection a little instruction in rhetoric, but does not list him as an important teacher and essays no description either of his teaching or his personality (although it could be inferred from *Metalogicon* 4.24 that John had had some instruction in logic from Thierry which he felt worthy of a sentence or two by way of description). In general, however, Thierry ranks with Hardewin as the least notable of the instructors mentioned in *Metalogicon* 2.10, despite the fact that he appears in *Metalogicon* 1.5 in the forefront of scholars as "a very assiduous investigator of the arts." Why does John give no personal insight into the teaching of the scholar whose views come closest to his own? I can only suggest the following explanation: the only opportunity John had to sample Thierry's instruction was the short period of "reassessment" in 1138-1139. By the time John had returned from Chartres, Thierry must have

been on the point of setting out for that city from Paris. John's decision
in 1139 to study grammar with William of Conches is not difficult to explain:
Thierry put grammar first and foremost among the arts in his *Heptateuchon*
and no doubt considered William to be a better instructor in the art than
himself. By the time John was ready to pursue the arts further, Thierry
was not on hand, because John was at Chartres whilst he had remained at
Paris, and when John returned to Paris, Thierry's mind, as we shall see, lay
elsewhere.

It should be noted, however, that this reasoning does not unconditionally
support the notion that John studied with William at Chartres rather than
Paris: if Thierry felt William to be the better instructor in grammar, and
if John studied only grammar and the *auctores* with William for three years
on the advice of both William and Thierry, then it is unlikely, even if all
scholars had been located at Paris, that either Thierry or William would
have seen fit to interrupt the grammatical studies John had undertaken.
To have done so would have been to cut short John's acquisition of the literary *fundamentum* so essential in the eyes of those scholars associated with
the school of Chartres. It is not, of course, impossible that John studied
grammar with William in Paris for three years and undertook a little instruction in the other *artes* with Thierry, but such a supposition, as will be
evident, fits the requirements of the sources less comfortably than the view
that John studied with William at Chartres while Thierry remained at Paris.

Why did John not stay on at Chartres at the end of his three years with
William? He may have been anxious to press ahead with his theological
career or he may have been primarily concerned in his trivial studies with
logic, but it may also be that Chartres at the time was undergoing a crisis
that affected the credit of its teaching. Towards the end of John's period
of study with him, William may have adapted his teaching to accommodate
Cornifician criticisms, as John hints in *Metalogicon* 1.5. The "revival" of
the arts that followed the temporary concessions of the greater scholars,
may be associated with the return of Thierry to Chartres, shortly after John
(and Richard?) had set out for Paris, the designing of the liberal arts tympanum of the west facade, the Royal Portal, of the Cathedral of Notre Dame,
and the *Heptateuchon*, the "abbreviated" arts course so much desired by
the *garciones*. The implications of this suggestion will be taken up below.

R. L. Poole long ago maintained that the *cesserunt* of *Metalogicon* 1.24
meant that William and Richard "gave up" their teaching when overwhelmed
by the Cornifician onslaught.[34] This is not a necessary inference. The meaning could equally be that William and Richard "yielded" and adapted their
teaching to the new demands. Certainly John does not say that William
and Richard used Bernard of Chartres's methods exclusively, right up to

---

[34] Poole (n. 7 above) Appendix 7. See Clerval (n. 1 above) 183.

the point at which they stopped teaching. He simply says that at one time (*aliquandiu*) they followed Bernard's methods. An interesting passage from the second version of William's glosses on Priscian throws some light on the problem. A translation of the text printed by Jeauneau[35] might run thus:

> The first masters, loving their pupils with the affection of a father, composed for them certain writings; because a master cannot always be present to help a student out in his studies, these writings were intended to convey to the student what the master might have said had he been present. Other masters too were at liberty to consult these writings. For no one ought to write glosses simply for his own use. He ought to write them for the use of others. But we wretched masters of today, what is there for us to say *in districto examine*? We confuse our lectures with verbal novelty, or we adopt unusual arrangement of material, with the result that our pupils understand little or nothing. Nothing we write profits them; what we write we set down obscurely, with the result that we retain around us only the insignificant few (*parvi*) for the display of our pomp. Two evils arise from this. Sometimes (*aliquando*), on account of the obscurity of our teaching (*doctrina*), the pupils view the arts with hatred. Certain of them, in whom there may be detected an innate love of learning, acquire understanding slowly and with great difficulty. Swiftly and without difficulty would they learn if we were only to lecture and write out of love for them (*diligenter*).[36]

[35] Jeauneau (n. 1 above) 224.

[36] The passage presents a crux, the meaning of *in districto examine*. The phrase is used in a letter of Abbot Guibert of Gembloux, *Ep.* 16, PL 211.1305A (I owe thanks to the Reverend N. Haring for the reference), where it seems to mean "careful consideration, examination." Interpreted along these lines, William's meaning may be: "What are we wretched masters to say in our explication of the text, when we only confuse?" *Examen*, however, can also mean a crowd or throng (so Livy, Horace) and if *districtus* is to imply "hounded, delimited" (cf. Ducange *s.v.* and the use of the word in J. A. Giles, *Opera omnia Petri Blesensis* 2 [London 1847] c; cf. also Knowles, *The Historian and Character, and Other Essays* [Cambridge 1963] 51, where Anselm describes Cluniac liturgy as *ordo districtus*; cf. also Geoffrey of Auxerre, ed. Haring, *Analecta cisterciensia* 22 [1966] 76 [5 sect. 43], where the pope gives strict instructions that Gilbert of Poitiers's works not be read before Rome had censored them: *districte precipiens*), the meaning may be: "What are we masters to say, with our classes so reduced in numbers?" (and, therefore, with our opportunities for display [another meaning of *examen*] also reduced?). Compare William's pessimism in this passage with regard to the profit a student may expect from his lectures, with the optimism of such passages as *Dragmaticon* 3, 98 ("proficere possent"), *De philosophia mundi* 1, *praef.* PL 172. 43A ("proficiamus"). Compare also the emphasis on the obscurity of "modern" lectures, with intricacy and obscurity as a Cornifician "vice": *Metalogicon* 2.17 (*fin.*), 4.3; *Dragmaticon* 80-81, 210 (Poole [n. 7 above] 300, "vixque intellecta propriis et apertis verbis explicare valeo"); Thomas (n. 2 above) 43, where Thierry of Chartres's critics say that "eum legere provectis ut novos detineat vel potius corrumpat," and that he "longas interpretationes inculcat." William of Conches also speaks of the *tardi* and *hebetes* going home

I am not sufficiently acquainted with the study of grammar in the twelfth century to know whether this passage must be read in the light of the "new" grammar discussed by William in the *Philosophia*;[37] it seems reasonable, however, to suppose that William is speaking of a general educational situation. His remarks may be compared with those he gave voice to in the twenties of the twelfth century.[38] At that time William advised against "withdrawing" one's teaching because of envy or the fear that others might become one's equals. He stated that he took no pleasure in the views of the multitude, but only in the probity of the few. Are we to suppose, therefore, that William, by the time of the composition of the second version of the glosses on Priscian, had altered his views and "courted the multitude," only to learn that this not only deterred the majority but positively hindered the minority who might really have profited from the thorough, old-style education? Thierry of Chartres, it must be remembered, complained in the preface to his *De inventione* commentary[39] that "we masters will be left alone in the schools unless we flatter the multitude and trap them into listening. This I will not do, for by the God of Truth, I have prostituted my wares before many, but won the favor of only a few. To these latter, however, I have contracted my counsel so that I might exclude the profane crowd and butting rabble." Were Thierry and William two of the greater scholars of whom John writes that "insipientes itaque facti sunt, dum insipientiae resistebant?"[40] Did William "succumb" to the Cornificians during the period in which John studied under him, "recover" sufficiently to revise his Priscian glosses early in the 1140s, and retire into the service of Geoffrey of Anjou sometime between the years 1144 and 1149 in order, among other things, to rescue his theological integrity by revising his *Philosophia*?

to their parents with their books full of interlinear glosses (? *cum amplis interlineis*, Poole [n. 7 above] 193). This may be the species of confused, shaggy glosses of which William speaks in the passage under discussion, which John of Salisbury derides in *Metalogicon* 2.7 (PL 199.864C) and Robert of Melun condemns: "textu et serie legendorum librorum postpositis, totam lectionis operam in studio glosularum expendunt," "glosularum recitatores malunt haberi quam ipsius textus in veritate doctores fieri" (Robert of Melun, *Œuvres* [n. 2 above] 9, 16).

[37] Jeauneau, RTAM (n. 1 above) 218, De Rijk in *Actes* (n. 3 above) 150 and *Logica Modernorum* (n. 2 above) 2.1.97ff., 109ff.

[38] Cf. n. 36 above and the preface to the *De philos. mundi* bk. 2.

[39] Thomas (n. 2 above) 41-42; the passage is partially translated in Haring, *Med. St.* (n. 1 above) 277; a French version is to be found in Clerval (n. 1 above) 211-212.

[40] *Metalogicon* 1.5, PL 199.832B. On *insipientia*, cf. n. 20 above, and "insipientes et quaedam Dei sunt non sapientes," *Electio Hugonis*, ed. T. Arnold, *Memorials of St. Edmunds Abbey*, Rolls Series, 3 vols., (1890-1895) 2.50, and R. M. Thomson (trans.), *The Electio Hugonis*, M. A. thesis Melbourne (1969) 40. This translation with a new text is to appear in the *Oxford Medieval Texts* series. Cf. also n. 2 above.

No definite answers can be given to these questions, but they will serve as a transition to the proper subject of this investigation, Thierry of Chartres and the date of the protest recorded in the introduction to his commentary on the *De inventione*.

III

Of all the scholars of the twelfth century, Thierry of Chartres would appear to have been the one most concerned with the study of the seven liberal arts as the essential preliminary step to complete wisdom. John of Salisbury recalls him only as a most assiduous investigator of the arts.[41] From the details furnished by the recently discovered autobiographical chapter from William of Tyre's *History of Deeds done beyond the Seas* it seems that the chief *magistri* in the *trivium* at Paris in the 1150s were all trained by Thierry.[42] His *Epitaphium* recalls him as skilled in the Latin tongue,[43] a worthy successor of Aristotle, a theorist on the creation, a logician of the first order, an expounder of Plato, and a teacher of the *trivium* and *quadrivium*.[44] His concern for the *artes* is sufficiently evinced for us today by his *Heptateuchon*, a compilation that brings to a most unusual and distinctive conclusion a series of *compendia* designed to facilitate the study of the arts.[45] Clerval believed that the composition of this handbook occupied some twelve years of Thierry's life. The commentary on the *De inventione*, a recently identified commentary on the *Ad Herennium*, and the possibility of his having commented Martianus Capella's *De nuptiis* and Boethius's *De arithmetica* further our understanding of Thierry's devotion to the arts.[46] There is ample evidence

---

[41] *Metalogicon* 1.5.

[42] Huygens (n. 5 above) 822.

[43] Cf. *Metamorphosis Goliae* line 190.

[44] A. Vernet, "Une epitaphe inédite de Thierry de Chartres," *Recueil de travaux offert a M. Clovis Brunel*, 2.669-670. For Thierry's importance as an Aristotelian scholar, see J. A. Clerval, "L'enseignement des arts libéraux à Chartres et à Paris dans la première moitié du XIIᵉ siècle d'après l'*Heptateucon* de Thierry de Chartres," *Congrès scientifique international des catholiques tenu à Paris du 8 au 13 Avril, 1888*, 2 (Paris 1888) 286ff.

[45] See *Actes* (n. 2 above) 124.

[46] Thomas (n. 2 above); Jeauneau, "Note sur l'école" (n. 1 above) 830ff.; Klibansky, in M. Clagett *et al.*, ed. 1, *Twelfth Century Europe and the Foundations of Modern Society* (Madison 1961) 5. The Reverend Haring, *Archives* 27 (1960) 76 mentions a reference in the *Quae sit* lectures on Boethius's *De trinitate*, to a possible gloss on logic ("sed in logica de hoc satis diximus," ed. Haring, *Archives* 25 [1958] 4.44.148). K. M. Fredborg (see below) refers to a passage in the *De inventione* commentary long ago printed by Paul Thomas (n. 2 above) 43, MS Brussels Bib. Roy. 10057-62 fol. 9rb, in which Thierry has Envy defaming his teaching by spreading false rumors. "Among people who know Thierry's true worth (the passage continues), Rumor is silent, and if by chance in such company she makes mention of Thierry's name, she at once switches to another story. In the schools, though,

that Thierry made use of a knowledge of the *quadrivium* in his theological and scriptural writings.[47] He has been credited by reputable scholars with the general design of the liberal arts portal on the west facade of Chartres Cathderal.[48] It is only to be expected, therefore, that if the arts, as John of Salisbury says, enjoyed a revival of popularity after the onslaught of the Cornifician scholars, Thierry would have played an important part in it. What was the nature of Thierry's contribution to the renewed prestige of the arts? The question requires a résumé of Thierry's teaching career.

It may be inferred with some probability that Thierry was not teaching when Gilbert studied under Bernard of Chartres (before 1117).[49] At this point it appears that Chartres Cathedral supported only one *magister*, and this was clearly Thierry's brother Bernard. Had Thierry been a teacher at the time, it is reasonable to expect that he would have appeared as one of Gilbert's teachers. One of the letters in the Chartres Letter Book asks news of the "brother of *Magister* B." If this is Bernard, then it may be that Thierry, before 1116 or 1117, was a student at Chartres. Since the *Terricus quidam scolarum magister* who appears at the Council of Soissons in 1121 in Abelard's defence is probably Thierry,[50] it is reasonable to suppose that after Bernard's elevation to the Chartres Cathedral chancellorship following

and gatherings of scholars, she changes minds in order to spread the idea that he is ignorant. She agrees that he can lecture on Plato (or "knows much of Plato"), in order to give credibility to her assertion that he knows no rhetoric. Rhetoric and grammar she allows him but uses this as an argument to deny him any dialectical skill. If she concedes him dialectic (as many insist), she defames his improper habits, his negligence in study, his obscure glosses." This fairly free, but I hope accurate, translation should make clear that Thierry taught "Plato" (Fredborg thinks this may refer to the *De septem diebus Genesis* commentary, ed. Haring, *Archives* [n. 1 above] 184ff., or the Martianus Capella glosses, though it could simply mean that he gave lectures on Plato's *Timaeus*), grammar, dialectic, rhetoric, but it is not necessary to suppose, except where other evidence is explicit, that he published glosses on these subjects. The *Heptateuchon* is, by itself, sufficient evidence of Thierry's interest in and teaching of these subjects. There would, in fact, be nothing unusual in the possibility that Thierry at some stage in his life turned his attention to the teaching of all the arts, Platonism, theology, and even biblical exegesis. That Thierry published a set of glosses on the *Ad Herennium* is possible from later quotations of his work on this text (Fredborg points to M. Wisén, *De scholiis rhetorices ad Herennium, codice Holmiensi traditis* . . . [MS Va 10], [Uppsala 1905] 56, and see Joseph Martin's edition of Grillius's commentary xvi-xxi: *Grillius, Ein Beitrag zur Geschichte der Rhetorik* [Paderborn 1927]). Karin Fredborg, to whom I am indebted for much of the content of this note, has informed me by letter that she has identified the *Ad Herennium* commentary in MS Berlin Deutsche Staatsbibl. lat. oct. 161 fols. 36vb-75vb as Thierry's. In my own research I had already noted that this commentary began with the same *Circa artem incipit* that appears in the *De inventione* commentary; I have not, however, had an opportunity of inspecting the manuscript.

[47] Cf. n. 1 above.

[48] Cf. n. 68 below.

[49] Cf. Otto of Freising (n. 29 above) 1.52; 88; Poole (n. 3 above) 228-229.

[50] Luscombe (n. 2 above) 57.

the death of Vulgrin in 1119, Thierry became a *magister* in the Cathedral School. If the tradition that Thierry gave some form of instruction to Abelard in the *quadrivium* has any substance to it, the most likely periods during which the instruction may have taken place would seem to be these: before 1119, in which case Thierry would perhaps have offered the lessons in his capacity as an especially capable student of the *quadrivium*, rather than as a *magister*; between 1119 and 1121; between Abelard's departure from Saint Gildas de Rhuys and his arrival at the Mount; some time in the course of his teaching at the Mount, in the late thirties of the century.[51]

References to Thierry in the twenties are few. He may have taught at Chartres and around the same time it appears that he held unorthodox views on God, and was counted, with his brother, as one of the most distinguished masters of the day. A few years later, the two brothers struck a contemporary as "most learned men." Henceforth, Thierry's brother drops out of the picture, whilst Thierry himself lives on for at least another thirty years, perhaps more. These thirty years represent Thierry's heyday.[52]

---

[51] See BEC (n. 11 above) 460, letter 18. Letter 19, 461, as interpreted by Poole (n. 3 above) 228, would also indicate that Bernard was the *magister* prior to the death of Chancellor Vulgrin (229) in 1119. Bernard is mentioned as *magister* in 1114, 1115, 1118, 1119 (Clerval [n. 1 above] 160), and as chancellor for some period between 1119 and 1124 (*ibid.*). In 1126, and perhaps a little earlier, Gilbert appears as chancellor (*ibid.*). Hauréau's conjecture that Thierry was chancellor in 1122 seems thus to be without evidence (*Mém.* AIBL 31.2 [1884] 80; Haring, *Clarembald* [n. 1 above] 23; Poole [n. 3 above] 242). Poole (228) seems to imply that the cathedral school at Chartres in this period had only one *magister* to assist the chancellor; Clerval 145. On Abelard's studies under Thierry, see Poole (n. 7 above) 314-317; Klibansky (n. 46 above) 12; Luscombe (n. 2 above) 58. De Rijk, *Logica modernorum* (n. 2 above) 2.1.287 discusses the chronology of Abelard's life 1132-1136.

[52] According to Thierry himself (Thomas [n. 2 above] 42), his opponents were accustomed to label him "necromanticum vel haereticum." A more explicit reference to Thierry's theological beliefs, assuming that the *duos fratres* are, as is usually supposed, Thierry and Bernard, is Abelard, *Theologia "scholarium"* 4, PL 178.1286AB. The date of this recension of the *Theologia* is usually given as 1123-1124 (Sikes, *Peter Abailard* [1932] 266; Gilson, *History of Christian Philosophy in the Middle Ages* [New York, 1955] 162) although the work itself was being revised as late as 1139-1140. See E. F. Little, "The Status of Current Research on Abelard," *Actes* (n. 2 above) 1119ff.; Klibansky, "Peter Abelard and Bernard of Clairvaux," MRS (1961) 19, with references there cited. On Thierry's theological views cf. also Haring, *Archives* (n. 1 above) 138) on the alleged letter of Walter of Mortagne to Thierry. Haring (165ff.) characterizes Thierry's views on Genesis as "bold rationalism." The second reference alluded to in the text of the article is Otto of Freising (n. 29 above) 1.49 (47) 83. The passage was written ca. 1157, but it recalls Otto's student days ("quales . . . *fuerunt*"). Otto appears to have studied in Paris in the late twenties and perhaps the early thirties of the twelfth century (Hauréau [n. 51 above] 88; Hofmeister, *Neues Archiv* 37 (1912) 125ff.; Otto's *Two Cities*, trans. C. C. Mierow 11-12; cf. also Hauréau, *Comptes rendus* [n. 19 above] 82). Both Abelard and Otto mention Thierry last, implying, perhaps, that he was the younger brother. Since the relationship between Bernard and Thierry is still in some respects unclear, it has been thought desirable to relegate a full review of the subject to an appendix (A).

From the autobiographical chapter of William of Tyre's *History*, it appears that Thierry taught Peter Helias, at some time, presumably before Peter himself taught John (after 1142, *Metalogicon* 2.10). Master Ivo of Chartres may also have studied under Thierry at approximately the same time.[53] In the mid-thirties Thierry was teaching rhetoric and logic to Adalbert II of Mainz.[54] Clarenbaldus also heard Thierry's lectures, probably in the thirties since he also studied under Hugh of Saint Victor (d. 1141).[55] Hermann the Dalmatian, a student of the *quadrivium*, may also be added to the list of Thierry's disciples in the thirties.[56]

While this catalogue of students would suggest that Thierry, as seems to have been thought proper for the *magister* in a cathedral school,[57] concentrated on the teaching of the *artes*, he appears also to have found time for the composition of two treatises on Boethius's *De trinitate*. One has come down to us as a formal commentary, the other appears to be lecture notes made by one of Thierry's students.[58] The first work contains an attack on Thierry's theological opponents, who are described as *imperiti*, a word suggestive of the alleged attributes of the Cornifician scholars of the time.[59]

The evidence at our disposal suggests that Thierry taught in Paris during the thirties. How long he had been there is not known. On two occasions Thierry is described as "Chancellor and Archdeacon of Chartres" and he appears to have held the archdeaconry of Dreux sometime between 1125 and 1142; in 1155 the same archdeaconry has another occupant. In 1138 the chancellorship at Chartres had probably become vacant. There is a shadowy "Guido cancellarii" for 1139, and a certain "Ernaldus" appears as chan-

---

[53] Huygens (n. 5 above) 822 lines 9-20.

[54] Cf. Poole (n. 3 above) 243; Vernet (n. 44 above) 661; Hofmeister (n. 52 above) 133, 135. The *Vita Adalberti* describes Thierry as "orator et rhetor et artis amator grammaticae, logicae, vitam ducendo pudice." Under Thierry, Adalbert "read rhetorical flowers and varied colors, laboring to be considered a grammarian and to become a logician"; Haring, *Clarembald* (n. 1 above) 24.

[55] Poole (n. 7 above) 321; Haring, *Clarembald* 25 and *Med. St.* (1964) 271. Clarenbald may well have studied the *De inventione* with Thierry: he appears to have had a considerable knowledge of the text: Haring, *Clarembald* 175.90, quoting the *De inventione* (1.26.37-38) on *tempus* and *occasionem*. All indications suggest, therefore, that before 1140 Thierry's teaching of rhetoric attracted the leading students of the day: Adalbert, Clarenbald, Peter Helias, John of Salisbury and others. Poole (n. 7 above) 320 considers that Clarenbald died in 1160.

[56] Vernet (n. 44 above) 661.

[57] Clerval (n. 1 above) 145, the chancellor specializing in theology.

[58] The *librum hunc*, or *commentum*, ed. Haring, *Archives* (1960) 65ff. (74 for date), and the *quae sit*, or *lectiones*, ed. Haring, *Archives* (1958) 113ff. (121-122 for date). See Appendix B for further discussion of date and authorship of these commentaries.

[59] *Archives* (1960) 23. See William of Conches, *De philosophia mundi* 1, praef., PL 172. 43A and *Metalogicon* 1.1 (*initium*, and PL 199.827D), 1.4 (quoted Poole [n. 7 above] 311), 4.26 and *Policraticus* 7.12 (PL 199.662A).

cellor "vers 1150." Thus Thierry probably held the chancellorship from about 1140 until at least 1148 when he attended the Council of Rheims, and, in the following year, the diet of Frankfort in the company of Bishop Albero of Trier.[60]

The remainder of the evidence for Thierry's life can be set out briefly. In 1144 Hermann the Dalmatian sent him from Toulouse the Latin translation of Ptolemy's *Planisphere.* "To whom," Hermann says in his dedication, "should I have destined what is the beginning and root of all studies of the highest humanity rather than to you, most loving and painstaking of teachers, Theodoricus, you whom I clearly know and confess to be the first and highest and immovably fixed anchor in the throne of philosophy at this time, midst varying storm of fluctuating studies."[61]

In the forties, Thierry appears to have acquired the bulk of his fame: tributes pour in from all quarters, and continue on until the fifties.[62] Towards the end of the forties, Thierry seems to have published yet another commentary on Boethius's *De trinitate,* the "Aggreditur propositum," or the "Anonymus Berolinensis."[63] Thierry was probably, in his capacity as chancellor,

[60] That Thierry taught at Paris during the thirties is suggested by, among other things, the fact that John of Salisbury studied "rhetoric and certain other subjects" (presumably logic, cf. *Metalogicon* 4.24 and Haring, *Clarembald* [n. 1 above] 24, and perhaps the *quadrivium*) with him at Paris (Haring 27). Other information in this paragraph is drawn from Poole (n. 3 above) 236, 242-243; Hauréau (n. 51 above) 78, *Comptes rendus* (n. 19 above) 81-82; Klibansky (n. 46 above) 13; Clerval (n. 1 above) 171-172, (n. 44 above) 282; Vernet (n. 44 above) 661, 663 n. 2 (Bernard Silvester's dedication to Thierry of the *Cosmographia*). The diocese of Chartres comprised six archdeaconries, of which one was Dreux, and another the "Chief Archdeaconry," containing six deaneries (Épernon, Auneau, Rochefort, Perche, Brou, and Courville). The other archdeaconries were Dunois, Pinserais, Blois, and Vendôme. All the archdeacons were dignitaries of the Cathedral Chapter. The principal Archdeacon was the Archdeacon of Chartres, or the Grand Archdeacon. The cathedral city was administered by an Archpriest. See *Dictionnaire d'histoire et de géographie ecclésiastique,* vol. 12 s. v. Chartres 564 and cf. 554; A. H. Thompson, "Diocesan Organization in the Middle Ages: Archdeacons and Rural Deans," *Proceedings of the British Academy* 29 (1943) 153ff., esp. 173; *Cambridge Medieval History* 6.541, 547f.; F. L. Cross, *The Oxford Dictionary of the Christian Church,* (Oxford 1957) s. v. Thierry of Chartres. For Thierry at Rheims and the diet of Frankfort see *Archives* (1956) 259 and 264, and Appendix B.

[61] Paris, B. N. MS. lat. 7377B fol. 73, text in Clerval (n. 44 above) 295.

[62] These are all summarized in a number of publications: Clerval (n. 44 above) 280, 288-289 (n. 1 above) 171 (most of Walter of Mortagne's letters are, however, now dated before 1141, cf. N. Haring, *Clarembald* [n. 1 above] 16); Vernet (n. 44 above) 662; Haring *Archives* (n. 1 above) 183ff., *Med. St.* (1964) 271, *Clarembald* (n. 1 above) 24-25; Hauréau, *Comptes rendus* (n. 19 above) 80.

[63] The *glossa,* edited by Haring, *Archives* 23 (1956) 257ff. (264-265 for the date). The Reverend Haring's views on the dating and authorship of these commentaries have been disputed: Jeauneau, "Note sur l'école" (n. 1 above) 828-9. See Appendix B.

actively teaching theology in the years before 1148: the commentary "Tria sunt," from the school of Chartres, seems to have written before that date.[64]

By 1156 there is no evidence that Thierry was alive. It is likely that he became a Cistercian monk and in this capacity he may have lived on until the sixties.[65]

Three works have been omitted from the above summary. These are the *De sex dierum operibus*, the *Heptateuchon* and the Commentary on Cicero's *De inventione*. The first work[66] is not of immediate concern in the present context, but the latter two require further consideration.

The *Heptateuchon* has been dated by Clerval to circa 1141, when Thierry became too busy with his official duties to finish it. This does not necessarily follow: Thierry continued his teaching, it seems, well after 1141.[67] In view of the lack of precise evidence, it may be suggested that Thierry returned to Chartres in 1141, armed with the *Heptateuchon*, begun, or partly completed, took over the direction of the Cathedral sculptural programme as chancellor, and made a vigorous attempt to revive the prestige both of the *artes* and Chartres.[68]

[64] Cf. *Med. St.* (1956) 125ff.

[65] Vernet (n. 44 above) 668. Otto of Freising (n. 29 above) uses the perfect tense (*fuerunt*) in reference to Thierry and Bernard, suggesting that by 1157 Thierry was thought of as a scholar of the past.

[66] Ed. Haring, *Archives* 22 (1955) 137ff. It is discussed a little further in Appendix B.

[67] Cf. Clerval (n. 44 above) 281-282; Haskins, *Studies in the History of Medieval Science* (New York 1960 [1924]) 90. There is a summary of the *Heptateuchon* in Clerval (n. 1 above) 222-223. Cf. too Hofmeister (n. 52 above) 666ff., Manitius 3.200. On the MSS of the *Heptateuchon* see L. Minio-Paluello, *Rivista di filosofia neo-scolastica* 46 (1954) 211-233; *Catalogue général des MSS des bibliothèques publiques des départements* 11 (1890) 211-214; Y. Delaporte, *Les MSS enluminés de la bibliothèque de Chartres* (Chartres 1929) 34; *Corpus philosophorum medii aevi ... Aristoteles latinus*, cod. descr. G. Lacombe ... *pars prior* (Rome 1939) 467-468, *Cod. supp. altera* ed. L. Minio-Paluello (Bruges 1961) 25-42, 86 ... *pars posterior* (Cambridge 1955) 1245 ... 3.1-4; *Analecta priora*, ed. L. Minio-Paluello (Bruges 1962) 36-69, 83-123, 141-191; Jeauneau, "Note sur l'école" n. 1 above) 853-854.

[68] The main facade of the romanesque church had been damaged by fire in 1134. The Royal Portal sculptures of the gothic cathedral had been, it appears (Henderson, *Chartres* [Penguin Books 1968] 43), measured and carved for the inner end of the new narthex and entrance to the nave, the main processional entrance to the romanesque cathedral, before they were relocated by Bishop Geoffrey of Chartres, ca. 1144, under Suger's influence, in the position where they now stand.

"The Portail Royal ... owes its form and content to gifted original artists, to the well-informed and sensitive patronage of the Bishop and Chapter, and to the learning and intelligence of the personnel of the cathedral school who thought out the pictorial program and watched over its glorious materialization" (Henderson 60). A. Katzenellenbogen, *The Sculptural Programs of Chartres Cathedral* (New York 1964 [1959]) 19, O. von Simson, *The Gothic Cathedral* (New York 1964 [1956]) 153ff. and Klibansky (n. 46 above) 13 support the view that Thierry played an important role in the design of the Royal Portal.

W. S. Stoddard, *The West Portals of St. Denis and Chartres, Sculpture in the Île de France from 1140 to 1190, Theory of Origins* (Cambridge, Mass. 1952) 9-26, provides a detailed

The nature of the *Heptateuchon* suggests that it was intended as a stream-lined approach to the arts, containing the best of the old and the new learning. The prologue states: "Into the compass of one volume, with suitable modifi-cations, I have adapted the findings of the most outstanding thinkers on the seven liberal arts, and I have, as it were, married the *trivium* to the *qua-drivium* so that the race of philosophers might produce an abundant offspring.[69] The emphasis, it seems to me, is on the fact that Thierry has *adapted* the arts, compressed them into a small and efficient compass, so that they might fertilize the study of philosophy. The section on grammar contains selections only from the major authorities; that on rhetoric omits Quintilian, an ad-vanced author to whom Thierry himself refers his readers in his *De inventione* commentary; the *quadrivium* is similarly reduced to a fair minimum, with the exception, perhaps, of geometry, a subject with burgeoning prospects of practical employment at the time.[70] Dialectic comprises a reputable col-lection of authorities and is the largest section, perhaps because Thierry was endeavoring both to incorporate newly discovered treatises, and to satisfy the current thirst for dialectical instruction.

The *Heptateuchon* is not an elementary manual; but it does present the basic artistic texts of the mid-twelfth century in a manageable, balanced, yet scholarly manner. Had the Cathedral Library of Chartres made an effort to acquire a dozen or so copies of the collection, they could conceivably have been made the cornerstone of a thorough, yet shorter and more balanced, even more scholarly, course in the arts than would elsewhere have been avail-able.[71] It may even have been Thierry's aim to provide a short and succinct

---

review of scholarly opinion on the construction and dating of the Royal Portal sculptures. He concludes (25) that "all the ornament is homogeneous stylistically" and was probably put into its present position around the middle of the century, though the design and some of the actual sculpture must have been already complete by the later 1140s. See most re-cently A. Heimann, "The Capital Frieze and Pilasters of the Portail Royal, Chartres," *Journal of the Warburg and Courtauld Institutes* (JWCI) 31 (1968) 73ff., esp. 102, and J. Van der Meulen, "Recent Literature on the Chronology of Chartres Cathedral," *Art Bulle-tin* 49 (1967) 152ff. (on the date 1145-1150 for the west facade). For an interesting study of the relationship between the ideas of Chartrain thinkers and the Chartres stained glass windows, see the same author's "A Logos Creator at Chartres and its Copy," JWCI 29 (1966) 82ff.

[69] The prologue to the *Heptateuchon* has been edited most recently as an appendix to Jeauneau's "Note sur l'école" (n. 1 above). I have provided here a free translation.

[70] Thierry's stress on geometry underlines again the practical importance of the work of the translators of the early twelfth century. See the interesting remarks by Adelard of Bath cited in A. C. Crombie, *Medieval and Early Modern Science*, ed. 2, vol. 1 (New York, 1959) 50-51. Cf. too O. Von Simson (n. 68 above) 27ff. and J. H. Harvey, in *The Antiquaries Journal* 48 (1968) 92ff.

[71] Traditional study of the arts at the time, at its best, undoubtedly made use of a wider body of texts: cf. *Metalogicon* 1.19, 21, 2.16, 3.6, 8. The pioneering aspects of the *Hepta-teuchon* (dialectic) are discussed by Clerval (n. 44 above) and Haskins (n. 67 above) 226.

digest of previous and current commentation on each of his texts, for the guidance of both teachers and students. The *De inventione* commentary, the character of which cannot be discussed in the present context, is shorter, more streamlined, and better organized than any previous *De inventione* commentary known to us. There is a distinct attempt to concentrate on explanation of the *continuatio* of the text, and on clear understanding of the relationship between the *materia artis* and the *partes artis*, the rhetorical categories put forward in the *De inventione*. These "speculative" characteristics were to dominate northern rhetorical scholarship for many years, and there is clear evidence that Thierry's commentary shaped, if only in broad outline, the content and nature of the rhetorical commentaries of the immediately succeeding generations.[72]

If the *Heptateuchon* and the *De inventione* commentary are to be seen as part of Thierry's attempt to "revive the arts" in accordance with the drift of the *Metalogicon* 1.5, then why was the former collection left unfinished, and why has the commentary, in most manuscripts, the inflammatory preface *Ut ait Petronius* and the later expostulation *Invidia falso vultu dialetice* in the course of Book 1?[73]

The Reverend N. Haring concluded in 1964 that Thierry wrote the commentary as an "obviously elderly" and "already famous . . . man." He considered the personal elements in the commentary to be "the confessions of a man who once enjoyed and apparently still enjoyed a great name, but was no longer the object of universal admiration."[74] He therefore decided that the commentary was written circa 1150-1155. This would make the work Thierry's last gift to the learned world, shortly preceding his departure to a monastery, after, it appears, his tenure of the chancellorship at Chartres. Haring's arguments receive, it seems, valuable confirmation from the fact that Thierry appears to have borrowed large pieces of the *Circa artem* introduction to his commentary from Gundissalinus's *De divisione philosophiae*, a work which Haring takes to have been written about the middle of the twelfth century.[75]

Powerful as these arguments may be, it seems inconceivable that Thierry would have written such a work as this so late in life. The spirit of the two personal expostulations suggests the thirties, or the early forties as the most likely date of composition. If the expostulations are not later additions to

---

[72] I hope this will be clear from the material I am compiling for the article on the *De inventione* in the series *Catalogus translationum et commentariorum*, ed. P. O. Kristeller *et al.*

[73] Cf. Thomas (n. 2 above). The shortness of the second book of Thierry's *De inventione* commentary is not due to haste, but to his shrewd appreciation of the repetitive nature of the second book of the *De inventione* itself.

[74] Haring, *Med. St.* 26 (1964) 275, 277, 278.

[75] *Ibid.* 278.

the original commentary, I am tempted to integrate them with the chronology already suggested for William of Conches, whose Priscian glosses, in their revised form, become directly comparable with Thierry's *De inventione* glosses, as attempts to "revive the arts" after a period of concession to the "demands of the mob." The *Ut ait Petronius* preface, as has been seen, clearly states that Thierry, having "prostituted his educational wares," will write henceforth only for the dedicated few, the few in whose interests William of Conches apparently decided to write the revised Priscian glosses. Whether the *De inventione* commentary represents a partial return to the older method of instruction after the attempt to base arts teaching on an abbreviated balanced selection of authorities (the *Heptateuchon*) had seemed doomed to failure, or whether the *Heptateuchon* and the Commentary were part of the same educational drive, is difficult to tell. Certainly the note of bitterness in the Commentary is an easy explanation of the uncompleted nature of the *Heptateuchon*. It is also probable that Thierry became more exclusively concerned with administration and theological teaching as the forties wore on. This circumstance would help explain the abandonment of the *Heptateuchon* project.

Alternatively, R. W. Hunt's view that the Commentary is "in all probability (Thierry's) earliest work"[76] may be accepted, in which case the date may well be the early thirties (or late twenties?) when other sources indicate that the attacks of the Cornifician students were becoming pronounced. The *Ut ait Petronius* preface would then reflect Thierry's initial desire to resist the revisionist tendencies. Although I prefer a dating in the early forties, I do not think Hunt's dating may be objected to on the grounds that Thierry in the *De inventione* commentary is an old and famous man, indeed a man whose fame is on the wane. Thierry was even in the late twenties a notable scholar; he was perhaps as a youth a precocious student. *Invidia*, in the second personal reference in the Commentary, speaks to *fama* (rumor rather than, by itself, "fame"). "Envy," rivalry, loss, and acquisition of scholastic reputation are familiar features of the Parisian academic scene in Abelard's day: they are themes deeply woven into the fabric of Cornifician propaganda and counterpropaganda. They are preoccupations one would have hoped an elderly man, soon to retire into a monastery after an extraordinarily fruitful career devoted to God and man, would have counted as trivial.[77]

---

[76] R. W. Hunt, "The 'Introductions to the *artes*' in the Twelfth Century," *Studia Mediaevalia in honorem R. J. Martin* (Bruges 1948) 93.

[77] Cf. *fama* in Abelard's *Historia calamitatum*, trans. J. T. Muckle (Toronto 1954) 12,55. On the currency of "envy" as a topos in this period, see Klibansky (n. 33 above) 22; Clerval (n. 1 above) 167; Bernard of Cluny, *De contemptu mundi* 3.45, 50; *Metalogicon* 1.5; J. R. O'Donnell (n. 3 above) 34 (para. 6) "magnificos infamant"; 33 (para. 4) "et obliti." One "insult" Thierry may not have been able to digest was the assertion that he was a Boeotian,

If Hunt's chronology, or some variant of it, is to be accepted in preference to Haring's, then the relationship between the *Circa artem* preface to Thierry's *De inventione* commentary and the *De divisione philosophiae* of Gundissalinus must be sorted out. The peculiar form of *accessus ad artem* to be found in the *Circa artem* preface is a considerable innovation in the academic climate of northern France in the first half of the twelfth century, and the question of priority is therefore an important one, to which the rest of this investigation will be devoted. If it can be established that Thierry was the innovator, then his status as a pioneer in the fruitful study of the *artes* in the twelfth century is considerably enhanced, and his reputation as the master of masters in yet another respect justly deserved. If, however, he pillaged Gundissalinus's work, the *De inventione* commentary becomes, as Haring recognised, an unusual exception among Thierry's otherwise original works, and its author's status as a student of the *artes* is proportionately reduced. To this problem I now turn.

IV

The construction from earlier materials of a proper methodology for the comparative study of the *artes liberales*, law, and related subjects, was an important achievement of the twelfth century. Since secular studies were generally not thought of as ends in themselves, but as departments of knowledge leading to and constituting a total comprehension of creation, it was assumed that scholars would, in the course of their career, tackle all or many of them. Hence the relation between them, their individual role, and position in the framework of knowledge, was at least as important as their special content. These aspects of the art were made clear by the formalized "introduction to the art (or author)," the *accessus ad artem* (or *auctorem*), as it came to be developed in the scholastic writings of the twelfth century. At best, the *accessus* encouraged reflection on the nature and function of knowledge; at worst, it reminded the preoccupied scholar that a wider intellectual world lay beyond the field of his special discipline.

---

born in a land where the air was thick with stupidity (Thomas [n. 2 above] 42). William of Conches in his *Dragmaticon* (Poole [n. 7 above] 300) parodies his own detractors' use of the same line from Juvenal (*Sat.* 10.49f.). The jest undoubtedly refers to Brittany, where, according to Otto of Freising, the natives were "witless" in all things but the *artes* (n. 29 above) 1.49 (47) 83; a common Cornifician abuse was "duller than an (Arcadian) ass"; *Policraticus* 7.12, *Entheticus* 43, *Metalogicon* 1.3, 5, Hugh of Saint Victor, *Didascalicon* 6.3. Thierry was clearly no administrative fool: he held the office of Archdeacon and amassed a very considerable (for the time) library by the time of his death. He may well have remained incensed at Parisian attitudes towards the "provincialism" of Brittany which was, by Abelard's own account, a linguistic wilderness.

In the *Circa artem* preface to his *De inventione* commentary, Thierry tells us that to define, divide, and expound with reasons the ten heads into which the proper introductory treatment (*scientia introductoria*) of any art should be divided, was called by the *antiqui rhetores* the *ars extrinseca*, because it came before consideration of the details of the art.[78] Thierry also provides us with two heads under which the actual textbook of the art should first be considered: "quae sit in ipso auctoris intentio et quae libri utilitas" (Haring 281 sect. 3). Since the textbook deals with the details of the art, its rules, or the *ars intrinseca*, the introductory headings for the book later acquired the label "intrinsic"; at the same time the number of headings was expanded, from the logical writings of Boethius.[79]

Although the concept of an *accessus ad artem* or *auctorem* was over a thousand years old by Thierry's time,[80] the arrangement of extrinsic heads which he adopts, together with the division of the art into "extrinsic" and "intrinsic" aspects, struck R. W. Hunt in 1948 as novel.[81] Thierry tells us the origin of the scheme. He took it from the *antiqui rhetores*. As Hunt has shown, Thierry's reference is to Victorinus's commentary on the *De inventione* (C. Halm, *Rhetores latini minores* 170 line 25), where the distinction is attributed to Varro. Victorinus distinguished between *scientia sola* (that is, knowledge of what the art is and effects, *non exercere*), and knowledge of the art, how to put its precepts into action: *in actu*. Cicero, in the *De inventione*, had divided what Varro and Victorinus called the extrinsic aspects of the art (*scientia sola*) into *genus, officium, finis, materia*, and *partes* (*De inventione* 1.4.5). Boethius, in the fourth book of the *De differentiis topicis* (PL 64.1207A) provided a fuller list: *genus, species, materia, partes, instrumentum, partes*

---

[78] Haring, *Med. St.* (1964) 281 sect. 1. Compare the *antequam* of sect. 2 with *De inventione* 1.4.5 *sed antequam.*

[79] See Hunt (n. 76 above) 95. The intrinsic introduction came eventually to include the *modus tractandi* (*ordo, libri titulus, causa operis*, and *cui parti philosophiae supponitur*. Compare Paris B. N. MS lat. 2904 (*Catalogus trans. lat. et comm.* 1 [1960] 193-194) "There are some who think that it ought to be asked in connection with this and other authors to what part of philosophy they pertain. Master Bernard of Chartres used to say that this ought not be enquired into *in actoribus*, since they deal neither with the parts of philosophy nor with philosophy. Master William of Conches says that all authors, though they are not parts of philosophy, nor deal *de ipsa*, ought yet to be assigned to that part of philosophy of which they treat (i.e. ethics)." This passage recalls Hugh of Saint Victor's view of the *auctores* (*Didascalicon* 3.4). On Thierry's use of the *accessus* see also his *opuscula sacra*: *Archives* (1960) 67ff., (1958) 117-123. See also *Archives* (1954) 252 (prol. 6) and Abelard, PL 178.798.

[80] On the history of the *accessus* see Hunt (n. 76 above) 94ff. and E. A. Quain, "The Medieval Accessus ad auctores," *Traditio* 3 (1945) 215-264. See also H. Kantorowicz, *Studies in the Glossators of the Roman Law* (Cambridge 1938) 37, 38, 42; Conrad of Hirsau, *Dialogus Super Auctores*, ed. Schepss 20-21; Ellis, in *American Journal of Philology* 10.162; De Rijk, *Vivarium* (1966) 39 and 41.

[81] Cf. n. 76 above.

instrumenti, opus et officium actoris, finis, and (at 1208D and 1211D) *effector,* and *artifex;* (cf. too Quintilian, *Institutes of Oratory,* 2.14.5). Cicero, whilst he made no mention of the *ars extrinseca* and *intrinseca,* offered a distinction between *de arte loqui* (extrinsic knowledge) and *ex arte dicere* (*exercere artem*): *De inventione* 1.6.8. This distinction is mentioned by the author of the *Ad Herennium* in the following manner: "Tum quis est qui possit id quod de arte scripserit conprobare, nisi aliquid scribat ex arte?" (*Ad Herennium* 4.3.6). Victorinus, who appears to be the only ancient authority to have made an easily accessible reference to Varro's distinction between the intrinsic and extrinsic art, does not clarify the relationship between the terms *extrinsecus / intrinsecus* and *de arte / ex arte,* nor does he provide any other headings under which the art may be considered than those already used by Cicero (cf. Halm 170.41). He does, however, tentatively identify *extrinsecus* with *de ea arte,* calling the *ars intrinseca* "quae nobis ad actus praecepta dat," and he provides the following gloss: "Cum accipimus alicuius rei artem necesse est nos aliquid ex ea consequi. Quare id, quod ex arte conficitur ut supra docuimus, facultas dicitur; cuncta enim per artem facilius transiguntur" (Halm 174.17). Grillius elaborates in the same manner: to speak "de arte" is to teach the precepts of the art, as Cicero does in the *De inventione.* To speak "ex arte" is "ipsam dictionem per artis praecepta implere, ut facit Tullius in orationibus."[82] This is the distinction between the *orator* and the *rhetor.* Victorinus has the duty of the latter as "artem tradat dicendi," and of the former "ex arte dicat" (Halm 177.16ff). These materials Thierry appears to have built up into the following system: *Ars extrinseca:* "genus ipsius artis, quid ipsa ars sit, quae eius materia, quod officium, quis finis, quae partes, quae species, quod instrumentum, quis artifex, quare rhetorica vocetur." *Ars intrinseca* (to which the foregoing stands as *scientia introductoria*): "ipsam artem eloquendi." Considerations *circa librum*: "auctoris intentio et libri utilitas" (Haring 281 sections 1-3).

These distinctions were important in the intellectual context of the twelfth century. They enabled scholars to envisage and study human knowledge as an entire integrated corpus, directed towards a complete understanding of God and man. They formed one of the principal ways by which the heterogeneous didactic materials of Antiquity, at the time in receipt of renewed attention and study, were absorbed, analyzed, and placed into a useful context in the light of contemporary intellectual goals and influences. A proper appreciation of the extrinsic aspects of the arts, it was argued by John of Salisbury, Gerald of Wales, Thierry of Chartres, William of Conches, Peter of Blois, and other "humanists", would forestall that tendency to become lost in the practice of the art as an end in itself. In the case especially of dialectic and sophistic rhetoric, this represented a miscarriage of learning.

[82] J. Martin, *Grillius* (n. 46 above) 47.

Alexander Neckam and Peter of Blois, among others, complain that preoccupation with the practice of an art per se threatened even the *quadrivium*. Proper study of the extrinsic and intrinsic heads alone enforced the lesson that dialectic and rhetoric were parts of the instrument of philosophy, rather than goals in themselves. The lesson of the *proemium* to the *De inventione*, with its insistence upon a proper union of wisdom and eloquence, hammered home the same message. All the arts, insisted Thierry in the prologue to his *Heptateuchon*, made up an instrument for philosophy: they were not autonomous and unrelated disciplines.[83]

R. W. Hunt considered Thierry's *accessus*, which he shows to have been very influential in the later twelfth and thirteenth centuries, to be a combination of the heads of Boethius's *De differentiis topicis* 4 (Hunt's type "D," *Studia* 97), the heads of Boethius's logical works (type "C," *Studia* 95, and see Quain 263) and the distinction *extrinsecus / intrinsecus* (Victorinus) and *de arte agere / per artem agere*. Hunt, while admitting that *de / per* is far less common than *de / ex* in the twelfth century, ignores the classical origin of the latter distinction and attributes it to Hugh of Saint Victor (*Studia* 99, Hugh of Saint Victor, *Didascalicon*, 3.5, trans. J. Taylor 89-90).[84] That Hugh is simply borrowing (and slightly adjusting) the terminology of the rhetorical tradition, is made clear by two remarks of John of Salisbury. In a letter written in 1166, he says:

---

[83] Cf. Hugh of Saint Victor, *Didascalicon* 3.3. This "integrated" or "humanist" conception of the arts deserves a fuller analysis, but not in the present context. See G. Paré, A. Brunet, P. Tremblay, *La renaissance du XIIᵉ Siècle* (Paris 1933) 174ff. On twelfth century "humanism" see D. Knowles, in *The Historian* (n. 36 above): "The Humanism of the Twelfth Century" (now in B. Tierney, ed., *The Middle Ages* 2, *Readings*, [New York 1970]); J. Leclercq, "l'humanisme des moines au moyen âge," *St. Med.* 10 (1969) 69ff.; R. W. Southern (n. 1 above) 42ff. Definitions of humanism will vary and some may reject one that allocates any significant portion of man's thoughts and labors to the study of divinity. Thus Southern's essay in some ways does not make its point. Completely convincing, however, is Southern's concept of an increased preoccupation in the eleventh and twelfth centuries with the nature of man, his world, as God's creation, and his position in relation to God. This preoccupation on the part of western scholars was accompanied by the interpretation of divine mysteries in essentially human, sympathetic terms. In this respect the phenomenon Southern describes in *The Making of the Middle Ages* (London 1953) chap. 5 and *Medieval Humanism* 35ff. is comparable to the warmth and human interest inherent in early trecento Tuscan interpretations of divinity and the story of Christ: see Millard Meiss, *Painting in Florence and Siena after the Black Death* (Harper Torchbook edition, New York 1964) 60, 109, 127-129, 157 (where, as in the twelfth century, the new "humanism" is characterized by a renewed interest in antiquity), and *passim*. On the importance of the links between the arts in Chartrain thought, cf. John of Salisbury's remark about Gilbert of Poitiers (*Historia Pontificalis*, ed. Chibnall, 27), "Habebat enim connexas disciplinas easque theologie servire faciebat." On de / ex arte: *Metalogicon* 1.3 (*fin*).

[84] For the words *extrinsecus* and *intrinsecus* in Hugh's *De tribus maximis circumstanciis gestorum*, see *Speculum* 18 (1943) 490, lines 16, 26.

> Orator quoque in arte dicendi docet, quia in artem praecepta tradere, et de arte dicere facillimum est, sed ex arte difficillimum, id est quae praeceperis observare mandata. Nusquam vero difficilius quam in arte vivendi.

Six or so years earlier John had indicated the rhetorical link more explicitly:[85]

> Nam, sicut ait Cicero, in unamquamque rem dare praecepta facillimum est sed eam efficaciter exequi laboriosissimum. Quod vero in praeceptis eloquentiae ad Herennium scribens de arte dicendi asseruit eam scilicet inefficacem et inutilem esse sine usu et exercitatione dicendi, ad omnes artes arbitror transferendum quatenus non firmantur usu nec exercitio roborantur; adeo quidem ut, si artem usumque dissocies, utilior sit usus expers artis quam ars quae sui usum non habet.

The type 'D' *accessus*, continues Hunt, was first revived by the school of Chartres, "probably by Thierry of Chartres. It found favor with the glossators on the *artes* in the second half of the twelfth century, who combined it with the other type "C," derived from Boethius, by means of the distinction between the *ars extrinseca* and *intrinseca*, also revived, it seems by Thierry" (Hunt, *Studia* 109). Gundissalinus, says Hunt, did not actually copy Thierry's *De inventione* commentary when he came to incorporate the new *accessus* into his *De divisione philosophiae*; his source was ultimately a gloss on Priscian, but not the gloss by Peter Helias (ca. 1100-1170/80) in which the *accessus*, in one form, is also found (*Studia* 90-91).

Haring in his 1964 *Mediaeval Studies* article overturned these conclusions by proposing, implicitly, that Gundissalinus invented the *accessus* scheme that Thierry "copied with such complete abandon" (278) or at least provided its basic utilization in the West.[86] The remaining pages of this study will attempt to decide the issue between these two views.

It cannot, I think, be argued that the new *accessus* in the twelfth century was a discovery of the grammatical commentators, despite the fact that Victorinus uses a grammatical illustration to explain the difference between *extrinsecus* and *intrinsecus*, and despite the fact that the two terms appear

---

[85] *Ep.* 179, PL 199.175BC; I owe the reference to C. Brooke, *The Twelfth Century Renaissance* (London 1969) 69. The second reference is *Policraticus* 6.19, ed. Webb 2.57, 618a.

[86] L. Baur "Domenico Gundissalinus, De divisione philosophiae," *Beiträge zur Geschichte der Philosophie des Mittelalters* 4.2-3 (Münster 1903) 274ff. thought the distinction *extrinsecus/intrinsecus* was Arabic in origin (Haring, *Med. St.* [1964] 173-174). See A. G. Palencia's edition of Gerard of Cremona's translation of Alfarabi's *De scientiis* (*Alfarabi, Catálogo de las ciencias*, [Madrid 1932]) 94: "extrinsecus vero cum voce sunt ex pluribus dictionibus ligatis, ordinatis, significantibus illos intellectis."

in Gundissalinus's section on grammar, not his remarks on rhetoric. Aspects of the new *accessus* certainly appear in the grammatical glosses,[87] but Peter Helias, who has the *extrinsecus* heads in a form much closer to the later *Ad Herennium* commentator Alanus, who clearly followed Thierry,[88] than to Thierry himself,[89] does not mention the *extrinsecus / intrinsecus* division (Hunt 88, 91, Haring 274) and could well have acquired his knowledge of the *extrinsecus* heads from the rhetorical tradition. Thierry, after all, had been his teacher.

Gundissalinus's use of the new *accessus* is more sophisticated than Thierry's. He adopts a fuller (later?) version of it, especially its intrinsic or *circa librum* division, and makes use of it generally throughout his work.[90] Far from being an indication that Gundissalinus's utilization of the *accessus* was prior to that of Thierry (McKeon, *Speculum* [1942] 17 n. 2), this is, I think, evidence of the popularity and utility on a broad scale of Thierry's *accessus*, which, as it stands in his *De inventione* commentary, is clearly not completely worked out. The extrinsic and intrinsic heads, since they are intended principally to sum up the art in question, in the context of the divisions of philosophy, are clearly of great utility in a work like the *De divisione philosophiae*, which does not purport to expound the intrinsic detail of each art. Gundissalinus, who was aware of the current tendency to divorce wisdom and eloquence,[91] takes the *accessus* a step further and equates the *extrinsecus / intrinsecus* distinction with the two divisions of philosophy known as the Aristotelian scheme from Boethius's *De consolatione philosophiae*: theoretical (*ad intelligendum*) and practical (*ad agendum*).[92] These extensions of Thierry's *accessus*, to anticipate my theme, fall naturally into place if we suppose that Gundissalinus seized upon the potentialities of Thierry's *accessus* scheme as an organizing structure for an extensive treatise on the divisions of philosophy taking into account perspectives acquired from the newly discovered Arab

[87] Cf. the *tria sunt* gloss, cited in Hunt (n. 76 above) 101, where the "de" and "ex" *arte* distinction is included under the *officium artificis*; cf. below n. 111. See also R. B. C. Huygens, ed. *Accessus ad auctores*, Collection Latomus 17 (Brussels 1955) 43, the *accessus* to Priscian, "extrinsecam artem nuncupamus regulas que date sunt secundum placitum auctorum."

[88] See the first folios of London, B. M. MS Harley 6324. Professor Harry Caplan is preparing an edition of this commentary, and will no doubt include relevant passages in his *Ad Herennium* article for the *Catalogus trans. lat. et comm.* series.

[89] The order in which the heads appear in Peter Helias's gloss is closer to Thierry (and Alanus) than to Gundissalinus, but Peter has the eleventh head ("quo ordine etiam sit docenda et discenda") with Alanus and Gundissalinus.

[90] Gundissalinus (Baur [n. 86 above] 140-2, Hunt [n. 76 above] 97) has *intentio auctoris, utilitas libri, causa operis, titulus.* He uses the *accessus* heads at Baur 3, 5, 8, 9, 17, 19 etc.

[91] Baur 3.

[92] Baur 11-12, 44; on this division of philosophy cf. Taylor's translation of Hugh's *Didascalicon* 161-162.

and Greek writings. Gundissalinus was no doubt familiar with the researches of the northern schools and may even (Haring 280) have studied at Chartres. At the least he seems to have studied some of Thierry's writings. Haring (279) thinks that the fact that certain passages of a "general nature" in Gundissalinus's section on grammar are found also in the *Circa artem* preface of Thierry (281 sect. 2 = Baur 43.10-18, the *intrinsecus / extrinsecus* distinction) suggests that Thierry was copying Gundissalinus rather than that both were using a common source, in which case one would expect to find these passages of a "general nature" in the rhetorical section of Gundissalinus's *De divisione*. Yet Gundissalinus, in this same passage, has *antiqui* instead of the far more accurate *antiqui rhetores* as the source of the distinction in question, and it seems clear that he made mention of the distinction in his grammatical section rather than his rhetorical section for the simple reason that the grammatical section came first and since the *extrinsecus / intrinsecus* distinction was relevant to all the arts, he announced it in connection with the first art treated. Gundissalinus's reference to the distinction is also more fully worded to suit his *ad agendum / ad intelligendum* distinction; in Thierry's preface, the wording is, suitably, more concise. The other passages found in both the grammatical section of the *De divisione* and in the *Circa artem* preface are too stock to be of much significance as an indication of priority (as also is Baur 63.21-4). Some occur also in Peter Helias's gloss (Hunt, *Studia* 88).[93]

The most difficult aspect of Haring's theory, however, is the chronology it supposes. If Baeumker's assertion that the *De divisione* shows no knowledge of Avicebron's *Fons vitae*, which Gundissalinus translated, is correct, then it is clearly a fairly early work of the Spanish translator. Baur argues that since the section on geometry in the *De divisione* uses Gerard of Cremona's translation of Al-Nairizi's work, it must have been written at the earliest shortly after Gerard of Cremona's first efforts in the translating field (if Al-Nairizi was an author he tackled early in his career) and this could hardly have been before 1135, when Gerard was 21 years old. M.-T. d'Alverny, however, has pointed to evidence that Gundissalinus was still active and attesting cathedral documents as late as 1190.[94] This makes the year 1110 accepted by Hunt (91 n. 2) and Haring (280) as the date of Gundissalinus's birth probably unrealistic. D'Alverny, in fact, sees fit to place Gundissalinus's literary activity in the second half of the twelfth century. If indeed

[93] Note that in the body of his commentary, Thierry takes care not to duplicate points made in his preface: Brussels MS fol. 5ra-b etc.

[94] Haskins (n. 67 above) 15. D'Alverny: *Archives* 19 (1952) 343, B. Lawn (n. 1 above) 60. On earlier dating of Gundissalinus's work, see Haring *Med. St.* (1964) 278, Baur (n. 86 above) 162-164. Gundissalinus is cited in the *Actes* of a Mozarabic cartulary of Toledo Cathedral 1178-1181 and in an act of the archives of Burgos, 1190 (*Archives* [1961] 285). There is, of course, no definite proof that this Gundissalinus is the same man as the translator.

Gundissalinus was still active in the last decade of the twelfth century, it seems highly unlikely that he could have written the *De divisione* much before Thierry's death, let alone in time for Thierry to have pillaged it for the preface to his *De inventione* commentary.

The *extrinsecus / intrinsecus, de / ex arte* distinctions, because of their early appearance in the principal rhetorical texts of antiquity, the *De inventione*, and Victorinus's commentary[95] on it, were deeply imbedded in the medieval rhetorical tradition. Not only were the extrinsic aspects of the art a subject of concern in the Cassiodorus and Vadianus Quintilian extracts compiled in the early Middle Ages,[96] but the actual phraseology of the distinctions appears in the rhetorical sections of the work of the Italians Gunzo of Novara (who mentions the distinction *extrinsecus / intrinsecus*) and Anselm of Besate (who makes use of the distinction *de / ex* arte).[97] Attention might also be directed to the passage from Richer's description of Gerbert's teaching (*Histoire de France*, ed. and trans. R. Latouche [Paris 1964] 3.48) in which the *sophista* is described in language closely resembling Victorinus (ed. Halm 156.23-4) as the instructor "apud quem in controversiis exercerentur ac sic ex arte agerent ut praeter artem agere viderentur, quod oratoris maximum videtur." Gerbert took an exceptional interest in rhetoric, and his teacher Gerannus was an Italian. There is, therefore, reason to suppose that Thierry derived the materials for his new *accessus* from his study of the medieval rhetorical tradition. This suspicion is confirmed by a reading of the *De inventione* commentaries of the generation immediately preceding that of Thierry himself.

The introduction to the commentary by Menegaldus, written probably in the last quarter of the eleventh century in northern France, concerns itself with the relationship between eloquence and the other arts. The theme of the *proemium* to the *De inventione* and the references to the views of Plato and Aristotle in the introduction to Grillius's *De inventione* commentary must have suggested the distinction between eloquence considered per se, and *in agente*, which appears in Menegaldus's introduction. This is clearly a distinction between *scientia sola* and the art *in actu*, which we have already met with in Victorinus's commentary. Menegaldus's preface contains a ru-

---

[95] Quain (n. 80 above) shows the indebtedness of the Greek rhetoricians to the philosophers (256ff.), but curiously remarks (263) that "the Latin rhetoricians do not manifest any acquaintance with it (this stylized form of introduction) in its proper form."

[96] C. Halm, *Rhetores latini minores* xii and 501ff. (see R. A. B. Mynors *Cassiodori senatoris institutiones* [Oxford 1937; repr. 1961] ix, xxviii-xxxi) and A. Stückelberger, *Museum helveticum* (1965) 217ff. and (1966) 197ff. I owe this latter reference to the kindness of Dr. Michael Winterbottom. I hope to deal elsewhere with the significance of these extracts.

[97] See Karl Manitius's edition of the *Epistola ad Augienses* of Gunzo of Novara and of Anselm of Besate's *Rhetorimachia* in MGH Quellen zur Geistesgeschichte 2.2 (Weimar 1958) 53, 102-103.

dimentary *accessus* (*titulus, quid sit, intencio, modus intencionis,* Hunt's types "B" and "C"); more relevant to the present inquiry are the remarks on *De inventione* 1.4.5 at fol. 6v of Cologne, Dombibliothek manuscript 197:

> Quid sit genus et officium et finis et materia et partes huius artis. Et sciendum quia hec pertinet ad extrinsecam artem. Ars alia intrinseca, alia extrinseca. Intrinseca ars dicuntur illa precepta que valent ad agendum; hoc est, que oratorem quomodo causa agere debeat instruunt. Extrinseca vero ars sunt ea que tantum valent ad sciendum non etiam ad agendum.

On fol. 7v there is an allusion to Victorinus (Halm 177.16ff) and Boethius, *De differentiis topicis* 4 (PL 64.1208D): the *finis* is twofold, "scilicet et in oratore, et extrinsecus, i.e. in accidente." Here the term *extrinsecus* is not used in its technical *accessus* sense, but it does point up the tendency to divide *officium* and *finis artificis* in accordance with the *de / ex arte* distinction: the duty and aim of the *rhetor / orator* will be one thing in practice, another in theory.[98]

On *De Inventione* 1.6.8, Menegaldus makes explicit the link between the *de / ex arte* and the *extrinsecus / intrinsecus* distinction (fol. 9v):

> Quasi dicat, precepta quidem dedit, sed hec non multum fuit, quia dare precepta non multum est, uti vero eis permultum est, sicut dicere quid faciendum sit non multum est, facere autem quod expedit perfectum est. Et per hec aufert cum non potuisse esse oratorem. Notande autem sunt prepositiones "de" et "ex," quia "de" extrinsecam, "ex" intrinsecam habet significationem.

Hereford Cathedral Library manuscript P.1.iv contains a *De inventione* glossed probably in the decades following the composition of Menegaldus's commentary. In the Hereford manuscript *omnis ars, De inventione* 1.5.7, is glossed "ars exterius, i.e. preceptio," and *ea facultas* "ars interius, i.e. scientia que unde generatur." The expression "intrinsecus et extrinsecus" appears (fol. 2r) as a gloss on *vi et artificio* (*De inventione* 1.5.6) and at fol. 2v, on *De inventione* 1.6.8 the passage from Victorinus (ed. Halm 177 lines 16ff) describing the twofold *officium* of the *orator/rhetor* (to speak "ex arte" and to hand down the art, *officium accidens*) appears. The standard description of the extrinsic and intrinsic art is to be found, taken from Victorinus (Halm 170.38ff), at fol 3r.

---

[98] Cf. the *tria sunt* gloss, cited Hunt (n. 87 above) where the distinction *de / ex arte* is found in this context.

The glossator known as *In primis*, a follower of Menegaldus, and perhaps a scholar at Laon in the very early years of the twelfth century, adds little to these elements:[99]

> Fol. 5ra: Alia docilitas ubi se dicere promittit quedam promittenda que valent ad maiorem evidentiam sequentis negotii; sic faciunt boni tractatores. Tractatus alius extra artem alius in arte. Extra artem videtur qui est de extrinsecis, que predocentur ad evidentiam. In arte quando agitur de arte, quam proponit dicendo intrinseca precepta, i.e. ipsam artem docentia. Continuatio: videre debemus precepta intrinseca, sed prius extrinseca dicemus. Oratoria vocat precepta quia orator utitur illis.
> Fol. 7rb: *Verum*: precepta bene dedit, sed hoc est multum, uti vero bene preceptis permultum est. De arte loqui vocat dare precepta de arte. Ex arte loqui appellat agere secundum artem. Sicut difficilius est versificare quam dare precepta de versibus.

Durham Cathedral Library Manuscript C.IV.29 contains a fragmentary commentary on the *De inventione*, probably written a little later than the glosses cited above. It presents an elementary *accessus* of Hunt types "D" and "C," comprising *materia, modus tractandi, instrumentum, intentio, utilitas, cui parti philosophie supponitur*. Under the first head the commentary reads:[100]

> Materia Tullii est in hoc opere rethorica, id est artificiosa eloquentia non tamen in essentia sua accepta, hoc enim modo accepta non hominis sed dei est materia, utpote qualitas quedam in anima fundata, sed eo modo materia est Tulli quo exercetur, id est quo in agente, id est in oratione habetur. (fol. 196ra)

The commentator goes on to explain that by itself rhetoric cannot be considered good or evil. It is only when it is "embodied" in *materia* that it can become an influence for good or evil. Menegaldus's treatment of Cicero's *proemium* lies behind these remarks.

The Durham glossator approaches the distinction *de / ex arte* in conventional terms ("apparet quod illud quod orator intendit facere rethor intendit docere"), but introduces a novel distinction between those *accessus* heads that pertain to eloquence considered per se, and those that pertain to it *in agente*:

---

[99] York Minster, MS XVI.M.7, described in M. Dickey, "Some Commentaries on the *De inventione* and *Ad Herennium* of the Eleventh and early Twelfth Century," MRS 6 (1968) 1-41, esp. 5-7.

[100] This is the *incipit* of the work.

> Fol. 196va-b *nam ipsis rebus cognitis* etc. (*De inventione* 1.4.5):
> Per rationem artis, accipit essentiam artis, quam essentiam cog-
> noscimus, cognito genere ipsius artis, quod est civilis scientia, et par-
> tibus eius, que sunt inventio, dispositio, pronuntiatio, memoria, elo-
> cutio. . . . habet itaque quedam ex predictis ars ista in se ipsa, ut
> genus et partes, quedam autem extra se ipsam, i.e. extra suam es-
> sentiam, ut sunt materia, officium, finis, instrumentum, que om-
> nia in agente habet. Per se enim non movetur. Et notandum rethor,
> ut nobis videtur, esse equivocum. Potest enim rethorica et scien-
> tiam que est in oratore significare, i.e. ipsam artificiosam eloquen-
> tiam, et illam que est in rethore, i.e. in preceptore, secundum quam
> scit precepta eloquentie dare, i.e. oratorem instruere loqui apposite
> ad persuasionem.

There follows a reference to those who can teach but not perform an art,
alluding to the poet and the teacher of versification. The commentator does
not say so, but his remarks come close to dividing the *accessus* heads found
in Thierry's new scheme under *extrinsecus*, into *extrinsecus* and *intrinsecus*
heads.

That Thierry himself had absorbed this tradition of rhetorical commentation, is suggested by his own glosses on the relevant passages of the text of
the *De inventione*:

> Brussels, Bibliothèque Royale manuscript 10057-62 fols. 4vb-5ra:
> *sed antequam* etc.
> (*De inventione* 1.4.5). Postquam fecit Tullius benevolos lectores de-
> fendendo artem, attentos autem eandem commendando, nunc demum
> reddit lectores dociles prelibando ea de quibus tractaturus est. *Nam
> his rebus* etc. Reddit causam quare ista quibus ars extrinsecus
> docetur cognoscenda sint ante precepta quibus ars intrinsecus con-
> tinetur. Facile vero est quod sine magno labore potest fieri. Ex-
> peditum vero quod sine ullo. *Rationem* vero et *viam artis* appellat
> precepta artis rationabiliter ordinata.

On *De inventione* 1.6.8:

> "Ex arte" loqui est secundum artem vel causas tractare vel ali-
> quid aliud persuadere, quod Hermagoras non potuit. "De arte"
> vero loqui, est artem ipsam docere quod minimum est ad compara-
> tionem alterius. (MS Brussels fol. 5vb).

After an oblique reference to Cicero's *Topica* 2.6 (cf. Hugh of Saint Victor,
Didascalicon, 2.30, and MS Durham C.IV.29 fol. 196rb), Thierry dismisses
further discussion of the extrinsic aspects of the art "cum Tullius de arte
intrinsecus in hoc opere intendat . . . nam qui docet exercere partes artis

rethorice, quod est artem intrinsecus docere, oportet ut doceat in qua re exerceantur. Quod est materiam docere" (MS Brussels fol. 6ra).

I think it can be concluded, therefore, that Thierry of Chartres was not indebted to Gundissalinus for his new *accessus*. He discovered the elements of it in the rhetorical tradition, in the medieval study of the very text that stressed the union of *eloquentia* and *sapientia* so dear to thinkers of a literary or "humanistic" persuasion in the twelfth century. The individual passages of the *Circa artem* preface suggest this. The remarks on *genus* (Haring, *Mediaeval Studies* [1964] 281-282, sections 4 and 5) are appropriate to a student of the *De inventione*, rather than to an expositor of the divisions of philosophy.[101] The definition given of *sapientia* in section 4 does not conform to the definitions of *sapientia* or *philosophia* provided by Gundissalinus in his *De divisione*, (ed. Baur 7-9), and it is clear from the definition of *scientia practica* (16) that Gundissalinus does not consider *sapientia* and *rhetorica* to be the two divisions of civil science (although he will have it [4] that *eloquentia* + *sapientia* = *scientia*.)[102] *Practica* divides into politics (grammar, poetry, rhetoric, and law), domestic economy, and private economy or morals (16, and cf. also Baur 134). In addition Gundissalinus elsewhere places rhetoric under logic (cf. 71 and MS Durham C.IV.29 fol. 196ra). On page 77 *syllogismum* and *inductio* are said to be the instruments of logic, and "sunt alia dua secundaria que ab hiis descendunt per subtractionem unius partis vel plurium, que sunt entimema et exemplum." The *artifex* of logic is the *disputator* "qui . . . vel thopice, vel demonstrative, vel sophistice exercet ipsam artem circa generales questiones vel morales vel naturales vel racionales," and the *logicus* is he "qui docet artem logicam."[103]

---

[101] Cf. McKeon (p. 252 above) 17. C. Jourdain, *Notices et extraits des MSS de la Bibliothèque Impériale*, 20 (1862) 73 considers William of Conches's remarks on *sapientia* (*in contemplando*) and *eloquentia* (*in agendo*) at the beginning of his commentary on Boethius's *De consolatione philosophiae* to be drawn from the *De inventione*. The influence of the *sapientia eloquentia* theme on medieval thought has been dealt with by G. Nuchelmans, "Philologia et son marriage avec Mercure, jusqu'à la fin du xiie siècle," *Latomus*, 16 (1957) 84-107.

[102] Gundissalinus (47) says that rhetoric makes the student *facundum*, logic *disertum*, and the *disciplinales artes*, *sapientem*.

[103] Cf. also Baur (n. 86 above) 81, 193, 283, 375, 377. On Gundissalinus and Alfarabi see M. Bouyges, "Sur le *De scientiis* d'Alfarabi, et sur le *De divisione philosophiae* de Gundissalinus," *Mélanges de l'Université St. Joseph, Beyrouth*, 9 (1923-4) 49ff.; on Alfarabi, see M. Steinschneider, *Die europäischen Übersetzungen aus dem Arabischen bis Mitte des 17 J/h.* (Graz 1956 [repr. from *Sitzungsberichte der Akademie der Wissenschaften in Wien*, phil.-hist. Klasse, 149, 151, 1905-1906]) and St. Petersburg, *Academia scientiarum imperialis, Mémoires* etc. sér. 7, 13.4 (1859) 58ff., 82ff. In Gerard of Cremona's translation of Alfarabi's *De scientiis* (Palencia, 5.172), the third division of *scientia practica* (*politica*), with civil science and the science of law is the *ars elocutionis*, a virtue "qua homo potest defendere sententias et actiones determinatas qua secte positor propalavit et reicere totum quod diversificatur eis cum sermonibus." This is "la science du Kalam" (Bouyges, 93 n. 1, J. J.

Thierry (Haring 282 section 6, *non est autem*, etc.) specifically warns his readers not to consider rhetoric a part of logic, or logic itself, because it deals with hypotheses rather than theses. Gundissalinus has not copied this passage (though he liked the *eum efficit facundum* of the preceding paragraph well enough to include it also under Grammar, Baur 47 line 7). It cannot be supposed that Thierry therefore is copying Gundissalinus and diverting his reader from Gundissalinus's confusion. Gundissalinus gives no evidence of this confusion in his rhetorical section (which Thierry was allegedly copying) and the inclusion of rhetoric under logic was too widespread a practice in the twelfth century for Thierry's rebuttal of it to point to Gundissalinus. The writer of the *De divisione*, observing that the passage pointed up a contradiction in his own work, simply left it out.

In section 8 (Haring 282-283) of his *Circa artem* preface, Thierry states that the *materia* of rhetoric is the hypothesis. McKeon (*Speculum* [1942] 19) considers this to be "Hermagorean," since Aristotle and Cicero considered the *materia* to be the *tria genera dicendi*. This distinction is, however, as Thierry himself explains (Haring 283 sect. 12), more apparent than real, since the judicial, demonstrative, or deliberative "circumstances" determine the *causa / hypothesis*, and "haec igitur causa triplex artis rhetoricae materia est." Gundissalinus (Baur 71) denies that the thesis is the *materia* of logic, "sicut quidam putant." This would be an unusual statement if we were not to suppose that Gundissalinus copied, more or less unwittingly, Thierry's view that the hypothesis was the *materia* of rhetoric.

Other considerations arising out of an analysis of the text of Thierry's *Circa artem* preface may be left to a footnote.[104] It remains to indicate cer-

---

Murphy, *Quarterly Journal of Speech* [1966] 110), which Gundissalinus 134ff. omits. Why did he omit it, for the practical effect of the omission, as Murphy points out, was to leave rhetoric a part of logic? Bouyges says because it touches on *honesta scientia divina*, which Gundissalinus does not purport to deal with. Yet he does deal with theology. I suspect Gundissalinus omitted "Kalam" because he had already included rhetoric under logic and saw the potential contradiction. On the significance of poetry as a division of logic see R. McKeon, "Poetry and Philosophy in the Twelfth Century: the Renaissance of Rhetoric," *Modern Philology* 43 (1945-1946) 217-234, reprinted in R. S. Crane, ed., *Critics and Criticism, Ancient and Modern* (Chicago 1952) 313 etc.

[104] Haring, *Med. St.* (1964) 284 sect. 15: again Gundissalinus omits a passage that fits Thierry's rhetorical context much better than it does Gundissalinus's more generalized context: the fourth book of the *De differentis Topicis* of Boethius, PL 64.1208D-1209A (and compare *defuerit*, Thierry sect. 16 with Boethius 1208A), lies behind the discussion here, and this was a basic text for the rhetoricians. The conception of "integral" parts recalls aspects of northern academic discussion in the first decades of the twelfth century: cf. Hugh's *Didascalicon* 2.30, MS Durham C.IV.29 fol. 196rb, Brussels MS 10057-62 fol. 6ra and MS York XVI.M.7 fol. 1vb *et seqq.* Compare Quintilian, *Institutes* 3.3.14-15, 3.9.2-3.

Thierry sect.19: *sex partibus* = *De inventione* 1.14.19, whereas Gundissalinus has "five parts." The Arundel MS of Thierry's commentary, and London B. M. MS Harley 5060 (which, as I was able to ascertain in the summer of 1966, contains a version of the commentain other sources that suggest a link between Chartres, Thierry, the medieval tradition of rhetorical commentation, and the new *accessus*.

R. W. Hunt had been led to associate Alan of Lille with the new *accessus* developments, in view of a passage in the *Anticlaudianus*.[105] If the Alanus who wrote the important *Ad Herennium* commentary preserved in London, British Museum Manuscript Harley 6324, and elsewhere,[106] is Alan of Lille, then the influence of Thierry's *accessus* in the work of that thinker is even more pronounced. In his introduction to the *Ad Herennium* commentary, Alanus follows Thierry's *Circa artem* preface very closely.

The influence of the preface is even to be seen in the work of Giraldus Cambrensis, by his own admission a diligent student of rhetoric. In his *De invectionibus*, Giraldus uses a quotation from a work of Aristotle to suggest that the worth of a person's actions must not be judged by their success. Brewer gives Aristotle's *Rhetoric* 1.1.1 as the source for this quotation, but the correct reference should be the *Topica* 1.3 (101b). The full reference is, in fact, to be found in the *Circa artem* preface of Thierry (Haring 284, sect. 13).[107] Thierry was one of the pioneers who attempted to provide Aristotle's *Topics* with a wider audience in the twelfth century. He included extracts from a Latin translation of it in his *Heptateuchon*, and his student, John of Salisbury, spoke highly of the work.[108]

---

tary without the *Ut ait Petronius* preface), however, have "seven parts." Clearly, little can be made of this point. Baur (n. 86 above) 68 lines 5-10 is repetitive of 66 lines 11-16, and is not to be found in Thierry's text (Haring *Med. St.* [1964] 286). Since the passage is taken directly from Isidore, Halm (n. 96 above) 507.16ff., I consider it to be evidence that Gundissalinus was conflating his rhetorical section from a number of text books, one of which was Thierry's commentary. A last point: Haring says (275) that the placing of *genus* before *quid* lacks logic. However, if a rhetorical student were working from Boethius *De diff. top.* 4 and the *De inventione*, he would come upon the *genus* (*facultas*, or civil science) before he would the *species*, rhetoric. This may be seen then, as yet another indication that Thierry developed his *accessus* from his rhetorical studies rather than from a reading of Gundissalinus's *De divisione philosophiae*.

[105] 3.170-172, ed. R. Bossuat (Paris 1955) 94; Hunt (n. 76 above) 103.

[106] M. T. d'Alverny, *Alain de Lille, textes inédits* (Paris 1965) 52ff. Professor Caplan, in a paper delivered in 1964 and soon to appear in a volume of collected studies, describes the manuscripts of Alanus's commentary more fully.

[107] Giraldus Cambrensis, *Opera*, ed. Brewer (Rolls Series) 1.129, *De invectionibus* 5.4. The source has escaped Hultzén, who attributes the reference to Aristole's *Rhetoric*. See L. S. Hultzén, *Aristotle's Rhetoric in England to 1600*, dissertation (Cornell 1932) 55.

[108] *Metalogicon* 3.6. It is surely facile to suppose, with Webb and Hofmeister, that Thierry "derided" the *Topics* (*Metalogicon* 4.24, McGarry [n. 3 above] 240, n. 290). I consider the sense of *Metalogicon* 4.24 to be "I commend the *Topics* and so did Thierry—it was Drogo's *Topics* he derided." Would it be reasonable to suppose that Drogo's *Topics* clung to the Boethian rhetorically influenced treatises on topics (the *In top. cic.*, and *De diff. top.*, cf. *Metalogicon* 4.27), whereas, by the middle of the twelfth century, Aristotle's *Topics* provided a proper dialectical treatment of topics? Drogo's *Topics* would thus have seemed

If the new *accessus* was influential in rhetorical study after Thierry's death, it was clearly common property amongst scholars associated with the school of Chartres in Thierry's lifetime. Herman of Carinthia, whose connections with Chartres are well known,[109] writes: "apud Latinos artium principiis quedam ars extrinseca prescribi solet." William of Conches, in his gloss on Priscian,[110] mentions the distinction between *ars extrinseca* and *intrinseca* and considers the headings into which the former ought to be divided as "quid sit ars ipsa, quod nomen eius, quo causa nominis, quod genus, quod officium, quis finis, que materia, que partes, quod instrumentum, quis artifex, quis doctor, que auctoris intencio." William's Priscian gloss has already been linked, in time and circumstance, with Thierry's *De inventione* gloss.[111]

V

The conclusions warranted by the investigation I have conducted in these pages may be summarized thus. The appearance of Thierry's *Circa artem*

"old-fashioned." On Drogo see *Actes* (n. 2 above) 795 and McKeon (p. 252 above) 26. On Thierry and the "New Logic" of Aristotle, see Haskins (n. 67 above) 226ff.

[109] See Haskins 45.

[110] Ed. Jeauneau, RTAM (n. 1 above) 244.

[111] William's *Timaeus* gloss, ed. Jeauneau (Paris 1965) 58ff., has an elaborate "intrinsic" accessus: "causa compositionis, materia (ostendendo efficientem, formalem, finalem, materialem mundi causam) utilitas, cui parti philosophie supponitur, titulus." A logical gloss in the time Alberic of Paris, (De Rijk, *Vivarium* 4 [1966] 9) has "intentio, materia, finis et officium assignanda sunt secundum opificem agentem ex arte et secundum opificem agentem de arte" (cf. n. 87 above). See also *ibid.* 23 and De Rijk, *Logica modernorum*, 1. (Assen 1962) 265 (B. N. lat. 15,141, after 1155): "Tullius enim antequam artem rethoricam tractet, demonstrat quod sit genus rethorice, et que partes, que omnia dicuntur ars extrinseca." See too De Rijk, *Logica* (n. 2 above) 234-238, 426, 430-431, and for *in arte/ex arte* in Adam of the Little Bridge's *Ars disserendi*, MRS 3.117. Other references that ought to be added to those presented in Hunt (n. 76 above) 99ff., showing knowledge of different aspects of Thierry's *accessus* in the century following his death, are: Grabmann, *Med. St.* (1947) 60; N. Valois, *De arte scribendi epistolas apud gallicos medii aevi scriptores* (Paris 1880) 87; Ghisalberti, JWCI 9.50-51 (cf. Hunt 109, Gundissalinus ed. Baur 6ff., on the four Aristotelian causes in the *accessus*); Ghisalberti, *Mem. del Reale Ist. Lombardo di Scienze e Lettere*, Classe di Lettere, Scienze Morali e Storiche (1932) 167 (Arnulf of Orleans's gloss on Ovid, *Ars amandi*); L. Thorndike, *Michael Scot* (London 1965) 4; Giraldus Cambrensis, *Opera*, ed. Brewer, 2.351 (*instrumentum*) and 355-356 (*de / ex arte*); Robert of Melun (n. 2 above) 1.9 (*a materia ad instrumentum*); Wibald of Corvey, in a letter of 1148 to a canon of Paderborn, Manegold, has the phrase *de tua arte* (P. Jaffé, *Bibl. Rer. German.* 1.278); Gervase of Melkley, *Ars poetica* (ed. H. J. Gräbener [Münster 1965] 92, 126) works the distinction *ars extr./intr.* into the teaching and practice of the art of poetry; De Rijk, *Logica Modernorum* (n. 2 above) 2.1.234ff., 2.2.77, 417; Kristeller, *Iter Italicum*, 1.333 (*quedam extrinseca requirenda*). The "extrinsic and intrinsic" *accessus*, in fact, lived on well into the Renaissance, as the various volumes of the *Catalogus translationum* reveal, and will continue to reveal as they are published. For a hint of this material see Appendix D.

preface in the *De divisione philosophiae* of Gundissalinus is evidence of the importance and popularity of the new *accessus* form pioneered at Chartres, principally by Thierry himself. Gundissalinus became acquainted with the *accessus* when gathering materials for his *De divisione*. As one well acquainted with Thierry's work,[112] he must have known that the most up-to-date treatment of rhetoric in use in the schools of Paris was Thierry's commentary. He therefore made use of it for his rhetorical section, and organized his treatment of the various arts along the lines envisaged by the new *accessus*, to which he had access in a slightly more up-to-date or sophisticated form than that to be found in the *Circa artem* preface.

The essential ingredients of the new *accessus* form appear (simultaneously?) in William of Conches's *Glosses on Priscian*, and Thierry's glosses on the *De inventione*. Thierry's *accessus* is the more definitively organized, and there are signs of rhetorical influence in that of William of Conches.[113] Since the aim of the new *accessus* seems to have been to simplify and clarify contemporary understanding of the practice or operation of the art in question, and its relationship to the other divisions of *Philosophia*, and to forestall an exclusive concentration on the art as an end in itself, it does not seem too far-fetched to suppose that the *accessus* formed part of an attempt by the principal masters in the arts to revive the prestige of the arts after concessions to the "Cornifician" desire for briefer, more relevant instruction had led to a decline in teaching standards and the alienation of the better students. The dimensions of the "new" grammar and rhetoric expounded in the glosses by William and Thierry cannot be outlined here; in the case of rhetoric, the main stress seems to have been on the paring away of irrelevant material, a new concision, and a concentration on the relationship between the categories of the art and the *materia*, and between the categories themselves.

Thierry's "neuen gründlichen Kommentar . . . zu Ciceros Rhetorik,"[114] therefore, takes its place among the efforts of "those who were [real] lovers of letters" to revive the honor of the *artes*. John of Salisbury's words, with which this investigation began, can to this extent be documented, and in the process, a tentative date offered for the composition of the commentary: between the date of John of Salisbury's departure from Chartres (1141/42) and William of Conches's retirement from the world of the cathedral schools, shortly after 1144. Finality cannot be attained; it may, indeed, emerge that Hunt was right in suggesting that the commentary was Thierry's earliest work; nevertheless, in view of John of Salisbury's tantalizing attempts at a history of the "Cornifician Movement", scholars have an obligation to push

---

[112] Haring, *Med. St.* (1964) 280.

[113] Jeauneau, RTAM (n. 1 above) 246 lines 38ff.

[114] Berthe Widmer (n. 1 above) 567. Widmer dates the *De inventione* commentary to "the Cornifician crisis."

their conjectures as far as they may. The *De inventione* commentary is, in all probability, neither Thierry's first work nor his last.[115]

APPENDIXES

APPENDIX A. BERNARD AND THIERRY OF CHARTRES

In note 52 above will be found the evidence linking Bernard and Thierry as brothers. The currently accepted view of the relationship between the two men is not entirely satisfactory as the following résumé of the scholarly debate on their identity should make clear.

Scholars once supposed that Bernard was the younger brother on the grounds that the author of the anonymous *Metamorphosis Goliae* was thought to have seen him at Paris in 1141, following which it was asserted that he became Bishop of Quimper until his death in 1167. By contrast, Thierry was considered to have died circa 1155. This same Bernard was identified with Bernard Silvester, the commentator on the *Aeneid* and the author of the *Cosmographia*. This was roughly the position when Hauréau wrote his article in the *Comptes rendus* of the Académie des inscriptions et belles-lettres in 1873. His article in the *Mémoires* (MAIBL) of the same Academy, in 1876 (233f), made few advances on his earlier study. In the first edition of his *Illustrations* (1884), Poole followed Hauréau in all essentials, but in the same year the French scholar subjected his views to closer analysis and came up with a number of modifications: Bernard Silvester was centered on Tours and was therefore not the same person as Bernard of Chartres, who was based on Chartres. Two Bernards had been chancellor at Chartres, Bernard of Chartres and Bernard of Moëlan, who became Bishop of Quimper in 1159. The former Bernard was Thierry's brother and he must have died before John wrote his *Metalogicon*. John must have studied under Bernard, who is the recipient of the letter from Gilbert cited in n. 51 above, written in 1141. The obit in the *Cartulaire de Notre Dame de Chartres*, 3.148, of the fourth

---

[115] The emphasis on the extrinsic aspects of the art advocated at Chartres seems, by the end of the century, to have come to naught in the schools of Paris. Such at least could be inferred from the strictures of scholars like Alexander Neckam, Gerald of Wales, and Stephen of Tournai. See A. C. Crombie, *Robert Grosseteste and the Origins of Experimental Science* (Oxford 1961) 30-40; Lawn (n. 1 above) 68-69; Manitius 3.787; Alexander Neckam, *De naturis rerum*, ed. T. Wright (Rolls Series, London 1863) chap. 173.283ff; Giraldus Cambrensis (n. 111 above) 2.356, 4.3, 7 etc; L. Thorndike, *University Records and Life in the Middle Ages* (New York 1944) 23ff., Denifle and Chatelain, *Chart. Univ. Paris.*, 1.47ff., no. 48, etc. For further consideration of the date of Thierry's commentary on the *De inventione*, see Appendix B. Appendix C provides some indication of the special didactic qualities of the commentary which made it peculiarly suited to the task of simplifying the study of the *artes*.

of August refers to the second Bernard, and that of the second of June (J. A. Clerval and R. Merlet, *Un manuscrit chartrain du XIᵉ siècle* [Chartres 1893] 100ff., 140, 165) to the first Bernard (MAIBL [1884] 31 pt. 2). In 1893, Charles Langlois asserted again that Bernard of Chartres and Bernard Silvester were the same person (*Bibliothèque de l'École des chartes*, 54 [1893] 242-247, and for refutation, Poole [n. 3 above] 234-235). As mentioned in n. 5 above, Hauréau's ideas about the date of the *Metamorphosis Goliae* have undergone considerable revision at the hands of later scholars, as has his identification of the Bernard of line 198 of the poem. In the present state of our knowledge, this must be Bernard of Moëlan, a Breton, who became Bishop of Quimper (*Latomus* [1962] 825). The author of the *Metamorphosis Goliae* may have included the name of Bernard of Chartres in his poem to add lustre to his galaxy of *magistri*, though he would not have expected his readers to suppose that the old scholar was still alive at time of writing. This is Brinkmann's interpretation. Nevertheless, if this is so, it is strange that Bernard is not given a line or two of explanation in the poem, to indicate that it was in fact Bernard of Chartres whom the author had in mind. It is also difficult to see how the *senex Carnotensis* could have been a disciple of Abelard (line 200). The fact that the poet lists Ivo, Peter Helias, and Bernard in the one line, brings William of Tyre to mind, for William lists Bernardus Brito, Peter Helias, and Ivo together as the first of his *magistri*. The three seem to have been a well-known trio of *trivium* teachers at Paris. It seems reasonable, therefore, to suppose that the Bernard of the *Metamorphosis Goliae* 198, was Bernard of Brittany, who afterwards returned to his fatherland to become Bishop of Quimper (*Latomus* [1962] 822). This Bernard was the "bonum clericum tempore suo" (Poole, *Illustrations*, ed. 1, 117 n. 12). There is no evidence that he was connected with Chartres, for, despite Hauréau's opinion, the fourth of August obit in the Chartres necrology is now considered to have belonged to a fourteenth-century Bishop Bernard of Quimper (*Latomus* [1962] 825, Hauréau, *Comptes rendus* 75-76, MAIBL 31.2.86). Who the Bernardus decanus carnotensis of *Gallia christiana* 8.1199C (Poole, *Illustrations* 115) who signs a document around 1130 was, we do not know. It may have been Bernard of Moëlan in his early days, but there is no support for such a view. Clerval (n. 1 above) 145 seems to have thought that the chancellor took on the office of dean, but there was no Bernard chancellor at Chartres at the time. It has been suggested (*Actes* [n. 2 above] 154) that the *Bernardum* of *Metamorphosis Goliae* 198 is Everard of Béthune, on the grounds that a variant reading of *Bernardum* is *Erinardum*. The variant reading is, in fact, *Ernaldum*, which would make sense (*Latomus* [1962] 825). One could as well suggest that the reference was to Arnold of Brescia, as to Everard of Béthune, or to the *magister Ernaldus* to whom Peter of Blois addresses a letter (Denifle and Chatelain, *Chartularium Universitatis Parisiensis*, 1 [1889] 33 no. 28).

The second of June obit, mentioning chancellor Bernard at Chartres has yet to be dealt with: the consensus of paleographical opinion seems to indicate that this obit was entered some time between 1125 and 1135 (Clerval [n. 1 above] 161, Poole [n. 3 above] 230 arguing against Hauréau, MAIBL 31.2.98). It can only refer, therefore, to Thierry's brother, who seems to have been supplanted as chancellor by Gilbert from 1126 onwards. Clerval, who felt that a chancellorship would not have been vacated unless for a higher position, or death, had long argued that this was the case and that Bernard must thereafter have died. Thierry vacated a chancellorship without preferment to a higher position and without dying, and the same appears to have been the case, in the short term, for Gilbert of Poitiers, but the evidence does point to Bernard's death in the mid-twenties (cf. Clerval 160). In the *Policraticus* 7.13, John of Salisbury writes "senex Carnotensis paucis expressit" and the famous keys of learning follow (PL 199.666C). These are also quoted by Hugh of Saint Victor in his *Didascalicon* (3.12ff.) as the words of "a certain wise man." In 1127, then, Bernard's words had acquired a rather legendary authority, quite compatible with a man dead, or in old age. John always uses the imperfect when he talks of Bernard (*Policraticus* 2.22, PL 199.454C; *Metalogicon* 1.24, PL 199.854) which could imply that he is quoting common memory. The fact that Bernard is usually referred to by John as "the old man" indicates that he was remembered as such by John's own masters and contemporaries. John did not himself study under Bernard: he would have said so if he had; his own instructors in grammar were, however, William and Richard, not Bernard (PL 199.856A). Since Bernard appears to have been something of a "lengendary" figure, it is very peculiar, if he did, in fact, live on until the fifties of the twelfth century, that there is no mention of this in the sources. I have set forth at length the various scholarly views on Bernard's identity, because it still remains a puzzle that Thierry was, relatively, so long-lived: he appears in the sources as a *magister* not more than a few years after Bernard himself so appears, but lives on for a further thirty years. Was Thierry a precocious student, and Bernard a scholar who lay long in relative obscurity? Or were Thierry's brother and Bernard of Chartres different scholars (cf. the article by R. W. Southern, n. 1 above)? By the time of William of Tyre's education in Paris, it seems that Thierry was no longer a master himself: had he been a master, William would surely have sought instruction under him (William's opinion of Thierry is suitably lofty, "Theodorici senioris viri litteratissimi," *Latomus* [1962] 822). The author of the *Metamorphosis Goliae* depicts Thierry as taking part in the events attending the quarrel between Pallas and Venus. He appears to have studied under him (line 190, *cuius lingua*, etc.). This would support the idea that the author of the *Metamorphosis Goliae* belonged to an academic generation slightly anterior to that of William of Tyre. There is a hint of a similar case of brothers of very different ages in the Chartres

Letter-Book (if we ignore Poole's reasoning, [n. 3 above] 226-227). See Clerval 173-174, Manitius 3.196-198, and Savorelli, *Riv. Crit. di Stor. della Filos.* 14 (1959) 284, 20 (1965) 183. Note that John describes both Cornificius and Bernard as *senex.*

APPENDIX B. THIERRY'S COMMENTARIES ON BOETHIUS'S DE TRINITATE AND THEIR CHRONOLOGICAL IMPLICATIONS FOR THE DATING OF THE DE INVENTIONE COMMENTARY

The dates of the three *De trinitate* commentaries ascribed to Thierry of Chatres are difficult to ascertain, but important, since one of them appears to quote from the *De inventione* commentary. Haring suggested the following chronological sequence:

The *Commentum, Librum hunc* (ed. *Archives* 27 [1960]) can be dated ca. 1135 "or even earlier" (*ibid.* 75). Cf. *Archives* 25 (1958) 122 and 23 (1956) 262, "an earlier period in the author's life."

The *Lectiones, Quae sit* (ed. *Archives* 25 [1958]) can be dated relatively to a period "slightly earlier" than *Aggreditur propositum* (*ibid.* 122), close to *Aggreditur propositum*, but prior to it (*Archives* 23 [1956] 262).

The *Anonymus berolinensis, Glossa,* or *Aggreditur propositum* (ed. *Archives* 23 [1956]), without a preface, seems to date from the middle of the century. Probability suggests ca. 1145-1150 (*ibid.* 264-265).

This dating has been questioned by Jeauneau (n. 63 above), M.-T. d'Alverny and, lately, K. M. Fredborg. D'Alverny (*Alain de Lille*; *textes inédits* [Paris 1965] 176 n. 62, a reference I owe to the kindness of K. M. Fredborg) considers Peter Helias to be the author of *Librum hunc* which she feels was written after 1148 for the following reason: the prophecy of the *Hyspana Sybilla,* which appears in Thierry's *Librum hunc,* Clarenbald's *Tractatus super librum Boetii De trinitate* (cf. the edition of Haring [Toronto 1965] 122), the codex heidelbergensis 71 (discussed by Klibansky [n. 33 above] 3ff.) and elsewhere, is found in the prologue to Otto of Freising's *Gesta Frederici,* where its currency in France is ascribed to Gallic credulity. D'Alverny says the prophecy became common knowledge in France "vers 1148" but did not remain current for long because it was soon disproved by the outcome of the Second Crusade. Klibansky (4-5) says that the text of the prophecy has been erased from the Heidelberg manuscript, fol. 9r (-9v?), a collection of documents (1140-1146) made by a German scribe ca. 1150- 1175. Klibansky describes the prophecy as "a piece of skillful political propaganda of the year 1146" and promises a special study of the printed versions of the text, but this has not come to my attention.

In view of these observations, it may seem unusual that the *Librum hunc,* if it were written by Thierry in the mid-thirties of the twelfth century, should contain a reference to the prophecy. But, since the text is known principally from the *Librum hunc*, Clarenbald's *Tractatus*, and another work connected with the school of Chartres, the so-called *In titulo*, and since Thierry had long-standing connections with the Spanish translating movement, I cannot see why the prophecy could only have been known at Chartres, or even Paris, "after 1148." This debate is not, however, directly pertinent to the subject of this appendix, although it serves to indicate the difficulty of arriving at accepted dates for scholastic comentaries of this type.

The commentary *Quae sit* seems to be the most closely related in time of the three theological *opuscula* to the *De inventione* commentary. The commentary *Aggreditur propositum* (293-294) uses the terms *intrinsecus / extrinsecus* ("Hic vitanda est quorundam modernorum haeresis prava quae tota subversionis fidei plena est. Dicunt enim quod quia nihil extrinsecus accidit vel recedit intrinsecus non posse dici 'dii' sub plurali numero."), and *Librum hunc* (*ed. cit.* 117 sect. 6) refers to the art of grammar and mentions the term *modus significandi* ("habent significandi modum"). In geeral, however, *Quae sit* reveals a far greater concern with the secular arts of the *trivium*.

The prologue (*Archives* 25 [1958] 124-131, and cf. *ibid.* 27 [1960] 67ff.) presents an *accessus ad librum* based on the *intentio auctoris*, the *utilitas libri* (*Archives* 25 [1958] 124 sections 1-2 and cf. the *De inventione* commentary ed. Haring, *Med. St.* [1964] 286.22), *cui parti philosophiae* (*Archives* [1958] 124.3) and *causa* (*ibid.* 125-126). This *accessus ad librum* (cf. Gundissalinus, ed. Baur 140, Hunt Type 'C,' popular in early twelfth century glosses, [above n. 76] 95) is fuller than that contained in Thierry's other theological works: the commentary on Boethius's *De hebdomadibus* (ed. Haring *Archives* 27 [1960] 134-136) has the *intentio, utilitas,* and *causa* (together with the rhetorical notion of the necessity for rendering the auditors attentive, docile, and benevolent); the *De septem diebus* (*Archives* [1955] 184) has *intentio, utilitas,* and *titulus* and the *Librum hunc* has *utilitas* and *intentio* (*Archives* [1960] 69, 80). *Aggreditur propositum* lacks a preface. The inclusion of *cui parti philosophiae* in the *Quae sit accessus* reveals Thierry's interest in the totality of knowledge, an interest suggested in this instance, at least, by the text of the *De trinitate* (sect. 2, and cf. *Quae sit.* 124.3, 152-154 and *Aggreditur propositum* 285-287).

The *Quae sit* prologue makes considerable use of the rhetorical *reddit auditorem docilem, benevolum et attentum* theme (125.7, 8, 126.9, 11, 127.15, 17, 129.22, 129.23—on which see Thierry's remarks on the *De inventione* 1.16 at MS Brussels fol. 11ra). The *De inventione* commentary (Suringar 224) has only *benivolos reddit,* though there is a full treatment of the subject later in connection with the treatment of the *exordium,* MS Brussels fol. 10rb-va. *Librum hunc* deals with this topic (*ed. cit.* 80.2-5) but the Genesis commentary, *De septem diebus* does not; cf. Gundissalinus, ed. Baur 142.

Quae sit refers to the *instrumentum* (*ed. cit.* 127.13, see *Librum hunc ed. cit.* 91.3 and the *De inventione* commentary *ed. cit.* 285.19) and on 130.24-25 makes what appears to be a direct reference to the *De inventione* commentary:

> *Nam ceteris quoque artibus*, inquit. Sensus huius litterae hic est: sicut in aliis artibus non quaeritur ab auctore vel artifice, nisi id ad quod humana ratio valet ascendere, ita in hoc loco faciendum est, scilicet non est a me quaerendum ultra quam humana ratio valet comprehendere. *Ceteris*, inquit, a theologia scilicet.
> *Idem*, inquit, i.e. consimilis. *Quidam finis*, inquit.
> Finis cuiuslibet artis, sicut alibi dicitur, est id ad quod tendit artifex per officium, sicut finis rhetoricae est persuadere dictione, sicut in rhetorica dicitur. Finis logicae est veri et falsi discretio. Et eodem modo unaquaeque ars proprium finem habet. Sed in nulla arte quaeritur ab artifice eius ultra id quod humana ratio valeat comprehendere. Quare nec hic.

As K. M. Fredborg has recognized, this passage would appear to contain a reference to, and near-verbatim quotation from, the *De inventione* commentary, ed. Haring *Med. St.* [1964] 284 sect. 14.

In the following lines *Quae sit* (130.26) expands on Boethius's comparative reference to the medical art:

> *Neque enim medicina*, inquit. Simile est quod adducit.
> Quasi diceret: sicut non est plus quaerendum a medico nisi ut convenientia adhibeat ad sanandum, et si ea adhibeat, finem ad quem tendit consequitur eodem modo dicit auctor non est plus a me quaerendum, nisi ut convenientia ad id ad quod humana ratio possit ascendere, adhibeam. Quod si ea adhibuero et si quid perfecte exequor de eo, de quo loquor, tunc consecutus sum finem ad quem tendo: sicut medicus consequitur finem, ad quem tendit apponendo sufficientia ad sanandum etsi aliquando non sanat.

This too, is a staple of the rhetorical commentators. Cf. *De inventione* 1.5.6; Menegaldus, MS Cologne Dombibliothek 197 fols. 7v-8r; Boethius *De diff. top.* PL 64.1208D-1209A; and the like.

It is also interesting, in this connection, that at one point *Quae sit* seems to have in mind the language of the proem to the *De inventione*: "*hominum monstris* . . . (*ed. cit.* 128.19), ad hoc enim *homo* creatus est, ut *rationem* exerceat. Sed tales ad *modum* vivunt *bestiarum* et ventris voluptati dediti negligent exercitium rationis." The verbal resemblance is not very close (indicated by broken and continuous italics) but the parallelism of thought may be indicative; certainly *Aggreditur propositum* (*ed. cit.* 281.10) does not at this point suggest the language of the *De inventione* nearly as strongly.

There are hints that the author of *Quae sit* was familiar with the language of intellectual abuse found in certain theological writings of the time (e.g.

by Gilbert of Poitiers, in O'Donnell [n. 3 above] 33-34) and in the writings of those scholars who were opposed to the "Cornifician Movement": compare with the passages cited in footnote 2 above, *Quae sit* 127.15 on *famae iactantia* (and note the substitution of *sine iactatione* for the *De inventione's sine arrogantia* (*De inventione* 1.16.22) in Thierry's comment on the first way of winning benevolence in an audience, *Commentary on the De inventione* MS Brussels fol. 11ra); 128.17; 137.21, *quia temerarius* (cf. *De inventione* 1.3.4) *et imperitus*; 141.35, *garriant*. Neither this terminology, however, nor the occasional reference in the *Quae sit* to other *artes* links the work specifically with the *De inventione* gloss (see *Quae sit* 144.42 on arithmetic [cf. also 177.5 and *Aggreditur propositum* 277.38,293.3] and 139.30 and 148 on dialectic).

The most significant feature of the *Quae sit* commentary for our present purposes remains its greater interest in and knowledge of rhetorical theory than is the case with the other theological commentaries. One last quotation should serve to illustrate the interest the *Qae sit* commentator displays in rhetoric: "Et ita de ceteris, velut in rhetorica videri potest." Dicitur enim in rhetorica proprie: circumstantia est quis? Quid? Ubi? Et cetera" (*Quae sit* 185.4). At the comparable place in *Librum hunc* and *Aggreditur propositum* there is no reference at all to rhetoric.

It seems probable, therefore, that the writing of *Quae sit* took place closer in time to the writing of the *De inventione* commentary than to any other of Thierry's works (except, perhaps, the *Heptateuchon*). It is difficult, however, to say very much more than this since attempts to give approximate absolute dates to the theological *opuscula* have not been completely successful.

In *Quae sit* 1.21 (137), 2.55 (172) and 4.28 (194), Thierry writes, apparently, against the views entertained by Gilbert of Poitiers. Fredborg reasons that this dates the work after 1148, since the definition of *unitas=trinitas, trinitas=unitas* is a kind of theology which was confirmed by the Council of Rheims (letter to me 28/XII/70). She quotes *In titulo*, PL 95.403D (see Haring, *Archives* [1956] 264 n. 2, [1960] 75), and considers the lack of specific reference to Gilbert of Poitiers in keeping with Thierry's manner: "nec est credendum ei qui hoc deneget" ("nor should the man [or "one"] who would hold this view be believed"). Haring's remarks on this passage (*Archives* [1956] 264-265 and [1960] 74) seem to me to be entirely justified. The *In titulo* passage mentioning the fact that the Council of Rheims sanctioned the "intransitive" interpretation of the Boethian phrase *de Trinitatis unitate* applies to *Aggreditur propositum* 1.21 rather than to *Quae sit* 1.21, and even then, as Haring says (265), *Aggreditur propositum* does not necessarily postdate the 1148 decision: it may form part of the intellectual background from which that decision sprang. *Librum hunc* alludes to distinctions of a similar nature (*ed. cit.* 4.2.116, *Archives* [1960] 73) but it would seem a dubious procedure to use this as evidence that the commentary was written after 1148.

It seems to me that if the *nec est credendum* remark of Thierry's, quoted above, was intended to refer to Gilbert, it would have been phrased more explicitly and, as Haring (*Archives* 23 [1956] 264) has already suggested, *deneget* would not have been placed in the subjunctive mood. Thierry's conception of the relationship between faith and reason must in all essentials have been close to that of Gilbert: "de talibus locutionibus oportet nos in sequentibus ratiocinando multa dicere" (*Quae sit* 1.24.138), "non enim absurdum est philosophicas adducere rationes ad confirmandum et ad tenendum fidem. Quod si quaeratur, sub quo loco in *Topicis* sit argumentum sumptum ab indifferentia, dicimus quod sub loco a differentia" (*ibid.* 1.30.139). Thierry in an earlier day had supported Abelard and seems to have acquired a reputation for relatively left-wing theological doctrines (Haring, *Archives* [1955] 138). There is no doubt that he was present at Gilbert's trial at Rheims, and at the secret meeting held at Saint Bernard's residence after (?) the trial, but he is not listed by John of Salisbury as one of Gilbert's fiercest opponents (*Historia Pontificalis*, ed. Chibnall, 16, Haring in *Analecta cisterciensia* 22 [1966] 12; on grammatical differences between Thierry and the "porretani", see Haring, *Archives* 23 [1956] 272 n. 2, and references cited there).

In the circumstances, all that can with safety be concluded is that *Aggreditur propositum* and *Quae sit* both seem to have been written in the theologically disturbed atmosphere of the later forties of the twelfth century. The latter treatise seems to have been written by a scholar who was at the time thinking to some purpose about the nature and methodology of the *artes*, in particular the *trivium*, and perhaps especially, rhetoric. It may therefore, as Haring has asserted, be a little earlier in date then the *Aggreditur propositum* which does not show any unusual interest in the *trivium* and rhetoric, and seems closer in a number of ways to the events of 1148. Since the author of the *Quae sit* commentary seems at least to have had the *De inventione* gloss in mind, and may even be quoting from it, it is probable that the latter work was already written by the later forties of the century. Such a conclusion is not in conflict with the approximate date arrived at in the body of this article.

Appendix C

The following passage, taken from the Brussels manuscript (Bibliothèque Royale no. 10057-10062) of Thierry's commentary (on *De inventione* 1.24), illustrates the simple and kindly approach to complex problems adopted in the commentary. Thierry does not make very much use of analogies such as the following, but throughout his work he seems to be intent upon getting across an uncluttered understanding of his text. Variant readings from MS CLM 3565, saec. xv (M) and MS Heidelberg, Universitätsbibliothek Salem VII.103, saec. xii (H) are indicated in the notes.

Fol. 13vb: Nam sicut non in omni loco pisces nascuntur vel aves, sed unus locus naturalis sedes est piscibus, alius autem avibus, alius vero ceteris animantibus,[1] et horum locorum periti cito et facile inveniunt quod querunt, sicut, inquam, hoc est ita in ratione disserendi et in rethorica sunt quedam res ex quibus sunt origines probationum quasi sedes naturalis argumentorum et istarum rerum periti cito et facile probationem rei proposite inveniunt. Sunt autem in ratione disserendi[2] loci argumentorum maxime propositiones aut earum[3] differentie. Nam maxime propositiones prima sunt prelationum[4] principia. Differentias vero maximarum dico esse quod eorum[5] una[6] est[7] a diffinitione, alia vero a genere; et ita de aliis. Que differentie[8] idcirco loci argumentorum dicuntur quoniam ipsos locos argumentorum continent.[9] Nam plures maxime sunt quarum unaqueque a diffinitione est; et ita de aliis. Et hi quidem loci, quia generales sunt, ad questionem generalem, i.e. ad thesin pertinent. In rethorica vero quoniam ypotesis, i.e. particularis questio que est de certa persona, tractatur, idcirco particulares loci, i.e. circumstantie septem reputantur sedes esse argumentorum. Circumstantie vero sunt quedam particularia que personis aut negotiis insunt ex quibus argumenta fiunt in causa ut aliquod genus vel aliqua species vel aliqua diffinitio vel aliqua causa et consimilia quibus aliquid ostenditur aut de persona aut de negotio. In ratione ergo disserendi sedes argumentorum sunt hec, maxima propositio unde adest diffinitio, et quod diffinitur, et hec alia, cui adest species et genus et consimiles quarum una ad omnem diffinitionem pertinet alia vero ad omnem speciem et sic alie generaliter ad multa pertinent. In rethorica vero sedes argumentorum[10] est[11] hoc genus vel hec species vel hec diffinitio et consimilia que particularia esse quantum ad predictas maximas patet quilibet.[12] Non[13] de circumstantiis. Sunt igitur duo de quibus in rethorica questione agitur: persona scilicet, atque negotium. Persona est ille

---

1 H: "animalibus." The source of the analogy is Quintilian, *Inst.* 5.10.21 (Fredborg).

2 H: "discernendi."

3 MS M appears to jump from Brussels fol. 12va, "maxime pertinere videntur" (on *De Inventione* 1.20.28), to this point in the commentary.

4 H: "probationum."

5 M, H *om.*

6 H adds "earum."

7 M adds "eorum."

8 H omits these two words.

9 This is the reading of M and H.

10 H, M: "argumenti."

11 H, M add "vel."

12 H: "cuilibet."

13 H: "nunc."

vel illa qui vel que ducitur in causam. Negotium vero dictum est vel factum persone propter quod ipsa detinetur[14] in causa.[15]

APPENDIX D. THE ACCESSUS OF THIERRY OF CHARTRES IN THE MINOR RHETORICAL GLOSSES OF THE TWELFTH CENTURY

Since the present article was written, a number of lesser rhetorical glosses making use of Thierry's *accessus* have come to my attention. These glosses are noteworthy in that they make explicit reference not only to the distinction *ars intrinsecus / extrinsecus*, but also to all or the majority of the ten heads under which Thierry thought the extrinsic aspects of the art should be considered (*quid sit genus, quid ipsa sit*, etc.; see N. Haring, *Medieval Studies* [1964] 281 section 1). They are to be distinguished from glosses such as those in Hereford, Cathedral Library MS P.1.iv or Prague, Universitní Knihovna MS (Truhlář) 1634, which mention only the distinction *intrinsecus / extrinsecus*. Most of the glosses of the former group can be safely assigned to the second half of the twelfth century (for the grounds see my forthcoming article on the *De inventione* commentators in the series *Catalogus translationum et commentariorum*), the "immediate post-Thierry" generation of commentators ("Alanus," the author of the rhetorical gloss *Ut ait Quintilianus* in Oxford, Corpus Christi College MS 250, and others). Such glosses are those in the following manuscripts:

El Escorial f.IV.18 fol. 1r-v;

Venice, Biblioteca Nazionale Marciana, Appendice, Codici Latini, Classe XI, Cod. 23 (4686);

Cambridge, Pembroke College 85 ("Sicut ordo nostre doctrine," contained also in Brescia, Biblioteca Civica Queriniana A.V.4 [no. 4, fols. 69-113v]).

Perhaps the most interesting gloss in this group is the fragmentary *De inventione* commentary contained in the early folios of Oxford, Bodleian Library MS Canon. Class. Lat. 201 (S.C. 18,782). The first sentence of this gloss mentions the distinction *intrinsecus / extrinsecus*, while the second lists as the heads under which the extrinsic aspects of the art are to be considered nine of Thierry's ten heads (the order differing slightly from Thierry, Gundissalinus and "Alanus"). Dickey (*Mediaeval and Renaissance Studies* 6

---

[14] H: "devocatur."

[15] H: "causam."

The passage is a gloss on *De inventione* 1.24.34 (*de confirmatione*). Compare Victorinus *ad loc.* (Halm 213 and cf. 207); Boethius, *De differentiis topicis*, PL 64. 1176CD, 1185-1186, 1212; Menegaldus, MS. Cologne, Dombibliothek 197 fol. 18v and *In primis*, MS York XVI. M.7 fol. 14vaff. When I was a graduate student in Toronto, the Reverend Haring very kindly placed at my disposal his careful transcription of the Brussels manuscript and I was able to use it in conjunction with a (very poor) microfilm of the manuscript for an extended period. For his generosity in this and other matters I owe him great thanks.

[1968] 19-20) considers that the work was written in the first half of the twelfth century, by an Italian, or in Italy. This dating immediately raises the question of the relationship between Thierry's commentary and this fragment. The most plausible estimate of these relations would seem to me to be as follows (detailed demonstration must await my *Catalogus* article): the author was either a native Lombard, perhaps a canon or cleric attached to a bustling cathedral town in northern Italy (Milan?), or a German, attached to a German adminstrative unit in Lombardy, and possibly at some stage the court of Lothair, Conrad III, or even Frederick Barbarossa. There can be little doubt that the writer (like another famous German, Otto of Freising), was educated at Paris or Chartres, and possibly Laon, where he absorbed the tradition of rhetorical commentation represented by Menegaldus, *In primis*, the Laudian, Hereford, and Prague glosses. At some stage, presumably in the twenties and thirties of the century, he came into contact with the teaching of Thierry of Chartres and the new thinking about the ten-point extrinsic *accessus*. His own gloss seems to have been written without precise knowledge of Thierry's *De inventione* commentary. This could be explained either by assuming that its composition took place in northern France (or the Rhineland) in the early forties of the twelfth century, or in northern Italy within a decade of the writing of Thierry's commentary.

Department of History
University of Sydney
Sydney, New South Wales
Australia

THE LIFE AND WRITINGS OF ALFREDUS ANGLICUS

•

by James K. Otte

For more than half a century scholars have attempted to reconstruct the life, the writings, and the philosophy of Alfredus Anglicus, de Sareshel. While they have failed in their endeavor to achieve a complete account of Alfred, they have nevertheless established him as one of the most influential intellectual figures of the generation that flourished around the year 1200. The studies of Clemens Baeumker, Auguste Pelzer, Martin Grabmann, Miss S. Wingate, and George Lacombe have identified Alfred as a translator, commentator, and author of an independent treatise. These scholars have examined Alfred's work in part and have established his role in the intellectual stream of the thirteenth century. Yet, in spite of Alfred's eminence, scholars have not been able to discover definite dates, a translating center, or a school with which to connect him.

It is the purpose of this study to summarize the previous scholarship on Alfred of Sareshel and to complement the efforts of previous scholars with the findings of my recent edition of Alfred's commentary on the *Metheora* of Aristotle.[1] This study is, therefore, devoted to a discussion of the life and the literary activity of Alfred as translator from Arabic, as commentator on the new Aristotle, and as author of an independent treatise on the movement of the heart. It will incorporate my findings from the study of Alfred's commentary on the *Metheora,* and it will seek to establish the date and indicate the relationship of the commentary among the other writings of Alfred. The result of this study, it is hoped, will provide a meaningful addition in the quest for a *vita Alfredi* that in spite of Alfred's eminence in the dissemination of Aristotle is still very incomplete.

The outline of this paper first emerged while I was writing my dissertation under the direction of Professor Richard C. Dales and while I was Research Assistant to Professor Marshall Clagett. I would like to take this opportunity to express my gratitude for their kind assistance and their many valuable suggestions.

[1] James K. Otte, "Alfred of Sareshel's Commentary on the Metheora of Aristotle" (Ph. D. dissertation, University of Southern California 1969).

Biographical material relevant to Alfredus Anglicus[2] can be divided into some four categories: Dedications; Alfred in sources of the first half of the thirteenth century; Roger Bacon's testimony; some recent speculation.

DEDICATIONS

Two dedications by Alfred give conclusive evidence that he was active and flourished in the decades just preceding and following the year 1200. Alfred dedicated his translation of De plantis to Roger of Hereford,[3] whose only certain dates are based on a Computus of 1176, in which Roger refers to himself as "iuvenis," and on an astronomical table now at the British Museum and dated by Roger personally for the year 1178.[4] The second date is established by the dedication of De motu cordis[5] to Alexander Neckam who died in 1217. This date is confirmed by three independent annals.[6] Since the dedication was presumably made to a living friend, it can be concluded that De motu cordis was written not later than 1217.

The form and nature of the dedication provide additional information. The simplicity of the dedication of De plantis, "Alfredi ad Rogerium dedicatio,"[7] and the absence of a formal title for Roger suggest that the latter was not yet a magister. However, Miss Wingate observed that the "whole tone of the dedication [i.e., Alfred's preface to his translation of De plantis] suggests that Roger is a man of mature age, already familiar with the available Aristotelian and other philosophical works" and concluded that Alfred translated the work "about the year 1200 or soon after."[8] It is entirely possible

---

[2] S. D. Wingate, The Mediaeval Latin Versions of the Aristotelian Scientific Corpus, with Special Reference to the Biological Works (London 1931) 98 n. 7. In this very useful study Miss Wingate observes: "Alfredus is among the most elusive of mediaeval writers, if only because of the Protean forms under which his name appears. His surname is found as Sarchel, Sareshel, Sarewell, and in many other variations of spelling, and it has not yet been successfully identified with any known English place-name. The variations on 'Alfredus' are no less numerous, and were the cause of considerable confusion." Cf. 99 n. 10. Josiah C. Russell, Dictionary of Writers of Thirteenth Century England (London 1936) 19, seems to have solved this riddle; see below at n. 48.

[3] Eduard H. F. Meyer, ed., Nicolai Damasceni: De plantis (Leipzig 1841) 3.

[4] Charles Homer Haskins, Studies in the History of Mediaeval Science, ed. 2 (Cambridge, Mass. 1927) 125. Cf. Wingate (n. 2 above) 55.

[5] Clemens Baeumker, ed., Des Alfred von Sareshel (Alfredus Anglicus) Schrift De motu cordis, Beiträge zur Geschichte der Philosophie des Mittelalters, (Beiträge) 23 (Münster 1923) 11.

[6] Thomas Wright, ed., Alexandri Neckam: De naturis rerum (London 1863) xii. Cf. Baeumker, Die Stellung des Alfred von Sareshel (Alfredus Anglicus) und seiner Schrift De motu cordis in der Wissenschaft des beginnenden 13.Jahrhunderts. Sitzungsberichte der Königlich bayerischen Akademie der Wissenschaften (Sitzungsberichte) 9 (Munich 1913) 28.

[7] Meyer (n. 3 above) 3.

[8] Wingate (n. 2 above) 59.

that Alfred and Roger were close friends and for that reason Alfred refrained from using a formal title in his address. Roger, who was about thirty years of age in 1176 (for in that year he refers to himself as still "iuvenis," although he had already given many years to the "regimen scholarum"),[9] would have been too young to fit the description: "a man of mature age already familiar with the available Aristotelian and other philosophical works." Any extensive knowledge of the "new Aristotle" also makes unlikely a date much earlier than the year 1200. The evidence then points to the years 1185-1190 as the earliest likely date for the translation of *De plantis*.

An additional remark may be called for in regard to Roger of Hereford. Oxford, Bodleian Library MS Digby 40, fol. 21r, introduces Roger's work: "Prefatio magistri Rogeri Infantis in computum." "Infantis" has caused some confusion among later writers, especially since Roger's name also appears with "infans" and "yonge," and a gloss on Alfred called him "Rogerus Puer."[10] Possibly these are various forms of a surname; certainly a man of mature age would not have been called "boy" in the primary sense of the word. It seems very likely to me that "infans," "yonge," and "puer" are variants of a nickname for which Roger personally supplied the motive when early in his career he referred to himself as "iuvenis."

Alfred dedicated his own treatise, *De motu cordis*, to Alexander Neckam. The dedication reads: "Liber magistri Alfredi de Sareshel ad magistrum magnum Alexandrum Nequam de motu cordis."[11]

In contrast to the earlier dedication, Alfred now appears as *magister*, addressing another magister. Unlike Roger and Alfred, Alexander Neckam appears in several records which establish his career with considerable exactness. He was born at Saint Alban's in 1157 and became a distinguished professor at the school of Petit Pont by 1180. By 1186 he was back in England, resuming "his old position of director or master of the school at Dunstable,"[12] while during the last decade of the twelfth century he taught at Oxford.[13] In 1213 Alexander Neckam was elected abbot of Cirencester in which capacity he died in 1217.[14]

The period in which Alfred dedicated *De motu cordis* to Alexander could thus extend from about 1180 to 1217. However, at the earlier date Alexander would hardly have been a "magistrum magnum." Further, the wealth of

[9] Haskins (n. 4 above) 124.

[10] *Ibid.* 124-125, Wingate (n. 2 above) 98. Josiah C. Russell, "Hereford and Arabic Science in England about 1175-1200," *Isis* 18 (1932) 15. Antoine Thomas, "Roger Bacon et les étudiants espagnols," *Bulletin Hispanique* 6 (1904) 24-25, cites the gloss.

[11] Baeumker (n. 5 above) 1.

[12] Wright (n. 6 above) ix-xi.

[13] R. W. Hunt, "English Learning in the Late Twelfth Century," *Transactions of the Royal Historical Society* 19 (1936) 20.

[14] Wright (n. 6 above) xii.

Aristotelian citations employed in *De motu cordis*, which in Baeumker's words "im Anfang des 13 Jahrhunderts nirgendwo sich finde,"[15] motivated this great scholar to establish a date close to 1217, the year of Alexander's death.[16] In a subsequent study, Baeumker preferred 1210 as a more likely date.[17] On the basis of the documents, I suggest a date for the composition of *De motu cordis* no later than 1213, for in that year Alexander was elected abbot of Cirencester,[18] and it is highly unlikely that Alfred would address an abbot as *magister*. Since Neckam seems to have left Oxford by spring 1203 to become canon of Cirencester,[19] Alfred's dedication points to the last decade of the twelfth century, at the latest to 1203, when Neckam was a teacher at Oxford. However, the lower status of canon, as compared with *magister*, would not necessarily prevent Alfred from addressing Alexander as "magistrum magnum" and so a date later than 1203 for the dedication of *De motu cordis* is still possible.

ALFRED IN THE SOURCES OF THE FIRST HALF
OF THE THIRTEENTH CENTURY

Although no exact dates can be gleaned from references to Alfred by other writers of the first half of the thirteenth century, the testimony of several authors has helped establish Alfred's career and provides some measure of the rapid diffusion of his works. Alfred's name appears several times in the anonymous *Summa philosophiae*, which is sometimes attributed to Robert Grosseteste. In this work he is called a "modern" in one place, in another he is confused with Alfarabius (probably because of the paleographic similarity of the two names), and in a third place the author of the *Summa* cites Alfred's commentary on the *Metheora*.[20] Robert Grosseteste, in his *De natura locorum* (written ca. 1231)[21] not only cites Alfred's translation of *De plantis*, but also his commentary: "Aristoteles dicit secundo *De vegetabilibus* . . . et commentator dicit. . . ." The "commentator" of course is Alfred.[22] A citation from *De plantis* was also employed in Moneta of Cremona's *Summa contra Catharos et Waldenses* in 1244.[23] Alfred's own composition, *De motu cordis*

[15] Baeumker (n. 6 above) 33.

[16] *Ibid.* 48.

[17] Baeumker (n. 5 above) viii.

[18] Wright (n. 6 above) xii.

[19] Russell (n. 10 above) 18.

[20] Ludwig Baur, ed., *Die philosophischen Werke des Robert Grosseteste, Bischofs von Lincoln*, Beiträge 9 (Münster 1912) 280, 378, 599.

[21] Richard C. Dales, "Robert Grosseteste's Scientific Works," *Isis* 52 (1961) 382.

[22] Baur (n. 20 above) 68. Cf. Wingate (n. 2 above) 71.

[23] Martin Grabmann, *Forschungen über die lateinischen Aristotelesübersetzungen des 13. Jahrhunderts*, Beiträge 17 (Münster 1916) 48-49.

was used as a philosophic text by the Arts Faculty at Paris by 1250.[24] By the middle of the thirteenth century also, Adam of Buckfield made extensive use of Alfred's glosses on the *Metheora*.[25] Recently, Richard C. Dales has shown that R. de Staningtona, who taught at Oxford circa 1240-1255, employed some of Alfred's glosses in his own *expositio* on the *Metheora*.[26] Finally, Roger Bacon in many of his works referred to and made ample use of a "commentator: super librum metheororum, super capitulum de iride, super tertium metheororum," without ever giving his name. Upon closer investigation, Auguste Pelzer was able to identify this commentator as Alfred of Sareshel, "une source inconnue de Roger Bacon."[27]

BACON'S TESTIMONY

Some biographical material for Alfred of Sareshel is provided by Roger Bacon. Roger mentions Alfred several times along with Gerard of Cremona, Michael Scot, and Hermann the German,[28] to which list in a later work is added William of Moerbeke.[29] In his customary manner Roger finds only words of contempt for the efforts and abilities of these translators,[30] and concludes that "of all the translators Boethius alone possessed the languages, while Robert Grosseteste alone possessed the scientific training."[31] Incidentally,

[24] Grabmann, *Mittelalterliches Geistesleben*, 3 vols. (Munich 1926-1956) 2.192.

[25] Franz Pelster, "Neuere Forschungen über die Aristotelesübersetzungen des 12. und 13. Jahrhunderts," *Gregorianum* 30 (1949) 50-51. Cf. Grabmann, *Mittelalterliche lateinische Aristotelesübersetzungen und Aristoteleskommentare in Handschriften spanischer Bibliotheken*, Sitzungsberichte (Munich 1928) 56-41.

[26] Richard C. Dales, "R. de Staningtona: An Unknown Writer of the Thirteenth Century," *Journal of the History of Philosophy* 4 (1966) 206.

[27] Auguste Pelzer, "Une source inconnue de Roger Bacon: Alfred de Sareshel, commentateur des Météorologiques d'Aristote," *Archivum franciscanum historicum* 12 (1919) 44-67.

[28] J. S. Brewer, ed., *Fr. Rogeri Bacon: Opera quaedam hactenus inedita* (London 1859) 91. The text reads: "Alii vero qui infinita quasi converterunt in Latinum ut Gerardus Cremonensis, Michael Scotus, Aluredus Anglicus, Hermannus Alemannus, et translator Meinfredi nuper a domino rege Carolo devicti; hi praesumpserunt innumerabilia transferre, sed nec scientias nec linguas sciverunt, etiam non Latinum." Cf. 471.

[29] *Ibid.* 471. William's name first appears in the *Compendium studii philosophiae*.

[30] *Ibid.* 472. Roger Bacon's polemic runs as follows: "Unde Michaelus, sicut Heremannus, retulit, nec scivit scientias neque linguas. Et sic de aliis. Maxime iste Willielmus Flemingus, qui nunc floret. Cum tamen notum est omnibus Parisius literatis, quod nullam novit scientiam in lingua Graeca, de qua praesumit. Et ideo omnia transfert falsa et corrumpit sapientiam Latinorum . . . Omnes autem alii ignoraverunt linguas et scientias et maxime hic Willielmus Flemingus, qui nihil novit dignum neque in scientiis neque in linguis; tamen omnes translationes factas promisit immutare et novas cudere varias. Sed eas vidimus et scimus esse omnino erroneas et vitandas."

[31] *Opus majus*, ed. Bridges (Oxford 1897-1900) 1.67. "Solus Boethius primus interpres novit plenarie potestatem linguarum. Et solus dominus Robertus, dictus Grossum Caput, novit scientias."

the order in which Bacon gives the names of the translators has led Clemens Baeumker to speculate on a possible date of death for Alfred. Baeumker believes that Bacon listed their names in chronological order,[32] and since Bacon names Alfred between Michael (d. 1235) and Hermann (d. 1272) Alfred's life could span a considerable part of the thirteenth century. This theory raises at least three serious difficulties. First, speculation on the dates of Alfred's career must take into account the years 1178 and 1217 by which latter date he had already completed his crowning achievement.[33] Second, the literary period of the two translators certainly suggests the opposite of Baeumker's conjecture, because there can be very little doubt that Alfred completed his last work, *De motu cordis*, before 1217, the same year in which Michael Scot made his first translations from the Arabic.[34] Third, Roger Bacon may well have given the translators' names at random or in what he considered their decreasing order of eminence. The polemic with which Bacon assailed William of Moerbeke confirms the third objection to Baeumker's theory; it also reveals the detestable arrogance as well as the vicious disposition of its unkind author.[35]

Alfred of Sareshel also spent some time in Spain. His visit to the Iberian peninsula is attested by Roger Bacon[36] and confirmed by Castilianisms in Alfred's writings. In the translation of *De plantis* he uses the Spanish term *beleño* to render the Arabic word for "henbane" or "nightshade,"[37] while in the translation of *De mineralibus* he employs the Spanish word *arrova* to translate the Arabic term for a weight.[38] Although Bacon complained in the *Opus maius*: "Hoc vocabulum [i.e., belenum] non est scientiale sed laicorum hispanorum,"[39] he felt free to make it part of his vocabulary in the *Opus tertium*.[40] Alfred's translations of *De plantis* and *De mineralibus* from the Arabic immediately suggest Spain, Toledo, or Cordova, where much

[32] Baeumker (n. 6 above) 23-24.

[33] For the probable chronological order of Alfred's works see my discussion at n. 84ff. below.

[34] See Haskins (n. 4 above) 272-280 for an excellent discussion of the dates of Scot's writings and cf. the unsatisfactory attempt by Wingate to date his translation of *De animalibus* for 1200-1210 below (n. 2 above) 65, 76 and cf. my discussion at n. 73.

[35] See n. 30 above for Roger's vicious attack on William of Moerbeke.

[36] Brewer (n. 28 above) 472. Although Bacon claims that Saracens did all the work for the translators in Spain, the latter are nevertheless blamed for the poor quality of the translations.

[37] Meyer (n. 3 above) 23. Of course Alfred has Latinized *beleño* to *belenum*. Cf. E. S. Forster, tr., *De plantis*, in *The Works of Aristotle*, W. D. Ross, ed., 6 (Oxford 1913) 821ª33.

[38] E. J. Holmyard and D. C. Mandeville, eds., *Avicennae, De congelatione et conglutinatione lapidum*, being sections of the *Kitab al-Shifa* (Paris 1927) 47. The editors read the Latinized form as *arenorum* in the genitive, but Vatican MS Urb. lat. 206, fol. 254r has *aronarum* or *arovarum*, while Escorial MS F. 11, 4, fol. 311r has *aravarum*.

[39] Bridges (n. 31 above) 3.82.

[40] Brewer (n. 28 above) 91.

of Greek and Arabic learning was passed on to the Latin West during the twelfth century.

Alfred himself speaks of "certain other books of Aristotle on philosophy, of which I even have translated some from Arabic into Latin."[41] For such activities there was no better place than Spain. Also, his teacher seems to have been a Spanish Jew. Alfred calls him "Magister meus Salomon Avenraza, et Israelita celeberrimus, et modernorum philosophorum precipuus."[42] Avenraza is perhaps a Latinized form of ibn Ezra. But in spite of Salomon's prominence, as vouched for by Alfred, I have been unable to identify him. In spite of Alfred's superlatives, "celiberrimus" and "precipuus," and my searching, Salomon Avenraza, or ibn Ezra, remains an enigma for the present. Finally, the very form in which Alfred's name appears in the manuscripts —Alfredus Anglicus—proves that he was an Englishman. But, what is more important in our consideration, it proves conclusively that Alfred spent some time in a place other than England. This follows clearly from a quick consideration concerning the etymology of the names Gerardus Lombardus, Hermannus Alemannus, Willelmus Flemingus and others, who were sometimes or always identified by their homeland. This in itself does of course not necessarily prove Alfred's Spanish residence, but in conjunction with the other evidence, there can be little doubt that Alfred journeyed to Spain, following many of his contemporaries, to tap the rich sources of Greek and Arabic knowledge.

ALFRED IN RECENT SPECULATION

The scarcity of concrete facts concerning the *vita Alfredi*, rather than prevented, has produced some interesting speculative writing. It has been difficult for scholars to reconcile Alfred's eminent position as translator and expositor of Aristotle with his absence from a known center of Aristotelian or Arabic learning. Although Alfred's name appears in numerous manuscripts as "magister Alfredus," we can only with some reservation conclude that he was a teacher. In no instance is his name or title connected with an institution of learning. Daniel A. Callus writes: "Still more important [than Alexander Neckam] in introducing the new Aristotle into England is Alfred of Sareshel." He speculates on the supposition that Alfred's glosses on *De generatione et corruptione*, the *Metheora*, and *De plantis*[43] represent his lectures at Oxford but concludes that there is not the slightest evidence to support this presumption.[44] Alfred is not listed in the University Register, nor is he ever mentioned in connection with Oxford as a teacher.

---

[41] Durham, Chapter Library MS C. 15, fol. 14va.

[42] *Ibid.*

[43] See below, at n. 68ff.

[44] Daniel A. Callus, "The Introduction of Aristotelian Learning at Oxford," *Proceedings of the British Academy* 29 (1943) 236-237.

Another attempt to connect Alfred with a school, the "cathedral school" of Hereford, has been made by Josiah C. Russell.[45] On the basis of the rarity of the name Alfred among "thirteenth-century literary men" Russell suggests that the five Alfreds who appear in documents relating to Hereford for the period 1153-1207 are identical with the translator Alfredus Anglicus. This is highly unlikely for several reasons. The popularity of any given name may change rapidly within a few years, and the dates—1153 the earliest, 1207 the latest—simply lie outside the sphere of an argument for the rarity of the name Alfred among "thirteenth-century literary men." Perhaps the greatest shortcoming of this thesis is the premise that the five Alfreds mentioned in the documents belong to one person, and possibly to Alfred of Sareshel. For if they do not refer to the same person, which is highly probable, "the rarity of the name Alfred" argument would indeed prove the opposite. A similar comparison of names for the twelfth century may well establish the popularity of the name Alfred for that century. A son named after the Anglo-Saxon king Alfred would seem to have been a symbol of defiance toward the feudal hierarchy of the Normans, an expression that would diminish with time and cultural assimilation.

While Russell couches his statements in the language of "probable," "may have," "highly probable," he concludes, nevertheless, that Alfred of Sareshel was "canon of St. Peter of Exeter about 1205"[46] while in another account he appears as canon of Lichfield about 1220.[47] One feels somewhat uneasy about a life and career strung together from an occasional mentioning of the name Alfred in the records covering a period of seven decades. If one assumes the birthdate of Master Alfredus to antedate 1153-1155 by about thirty years, the time required to gain the distinction *magister*, and believes him to be the Alfred who in about 1220 is still canon of Lichfield, one would have reconstructed the life of one of the oldest Englishmen in the Middle Ages.

Yet, some of the Alfreds enumerated by Russell may well belong to the career of Alfredus Anglicus de Sareshel; but it is highly unlikely that all, especially the early references, pertain to him. Russell neglected to see the significance of one document he cites in his *Dictionary of Writers of Thirteenth Century England*. In a charter of about 1220, a certain "Magister Alueredus de Sarutehill or Sarntehill canonicus Lich" appears as a witness.[48] Interestingly, this is the only time in Russell's long lists of Alfreds that the name

[45] Russell (n. 10 above) 14-25.

[46] *Ibid.* 19.

[47] Russell (n. 2 above) 19.

[48] *Ibid.* 19. Professor Clagett who kindly checked this reference for me at the British Museum writes: "Professor Russell is quite correct, it reads 'magister Alvredus de Sarutehill or Sarntehill'; I have found both a 'u' and an 'n' that resemble the disputed letter."

Alfred is distinguished by some form of "de Sareshel," which according to Russell, is Shareshull, a village near Lichfield in the barony of Stafford which was held by the Purcell family.[49] In view of the fact that Sareshel had been so highly obscure and that so far no place had been found that even remotely suggested itself for identification with that name,[50] we can be reasonably sure that "Magister Alueredus de Sarutehill or Sarntehill canonicus Lich" is indeed Alfredus Anglicus, the translator, commentator, and author of *De motu cordis*. Certainly, the odds of finding another Alfredus de Sareshel, contemporary with and as elusive as our Alfred, seriously taxes credulity. Until more evidence elucidates these questions, we may conclude that Alfred retired from his scholarly activities by about 1217 to become canon of Lichfield.

ALFRED AS TRANSLATOR

Alfred tells us in the commentary to the *Metheora* that he translated some Aristotelian books on philosophy from Arabic into Latin:[51] "quosdam alios Aristotelis libros de philosophia, quorum etiam aliquos de arabico in latinum transtuli." Alfred does not give their titles, but these comprise the versions of *De plantis* and *De mineralibus*, since these are the only known translations by Alfred. Many of the *Metheora* manuscripts of the *translatio vetus* have the following colophon:[52] "Completus est liber metheororum cuius tres primos libros transtulit magister Gerardus Lumbardus summus philosophus de arabico in latinum. Quartum autem transtulit Henricus Aristippus de greco in latinum. Tria ultima capitula transtulit Aluredus Anglicus Sarelensis de arabico in latinum."

Actually the final three chapters that Alfred added to book 4 of the *Metheora* were not from the pen of Aristotle but represent the chemical and geological part of Avicenna's *Kitab al-Shifa*, which during the Middle Ages was sometimes called *De congelatione et conglutinatione lapidum*, or *De mineralibus*.[53] Whatever the reasons were for appending this treatise of Avicenna to book 4 of the *Metheora*, Alfred's choice was an intelligent one. The subject matter of the *De mineralibus* lends itself intrinsically to book 4 of the *Metheora*

---

[49] *Ibid*. 19.

[50] Wingate (n. 2 above) 98-99, nn. 7, 10. After listing the variations on the names "Alfred" and "Sareshel," Miss Wingate concluded that Sareshel is probably the old English surname, Saresell.

[51] Durham MS, fol. 14va.

[52] Among the MSS, Bibliothèque Nationale, lat. 6325, Reims, cod. 682, listed by Grabmann (n. 23 above) 179, Nuremberg, MS Cent. V, 59, listed by Baeumker (n. 6 above) 34, where this colophon is found, we can add MS Selden Supra, 24.

[53] Holmyard, Mandeville (n. 38 above). In their introduction to the edition there is a discussion of the reasons why this superb treatise was believed to have been of Aristotelan authorship.

and it is closer in substance to book 4 than the latter is to the first three books of the *Metheora*.[54] Most of all, Aristotle promises a treatise dealing specifically with minerals at the conclusion of book 3,[55] and when Alfred found the a-nonymous *De mineralibus*, he may well have considered it Aristotle's promised book.

This controversy has not yet been settled completely, and some recent scholars have held on to a tradition that considered at least large portions of the *De mineralibus* as genuine Aristotle.[56] There seems to have been no doubt in the mind of Albert the Great that the *De mineralibus* was from the pen of Avicenna, and not Aristotle. F. H. Fobes cites a note from Oxford, Bod-leian Library MS Digby 153, fol. 28, which reads:[57] "Et ultimum capitulum in antiqua translacione quod sic incipit 'terra pura lapis non fit' non est capitulum aristotelis sed additum ab alueredo, ut dicit bacun in sua naturali philosophia capitulo secundo secundum albertum 3 mineralium c. 9, et con-traria per totum librum suum patet quod illud capitulum est avicenne."

Actually the scribe of the Oxford note was very kind to Bacon, for Roger never quite solved the problem of authorship for *De mineralibus*: "In his *Breve breviarum* he quotes the passage 'Terra pura lapis' as Aristotle's, in the *Tractatus trium verborum* he ascribes it to Gerard of Cremona, and only in 1266 or thereabouts does he find that it was an addition of Alfred's, still apparently in ignorance of its Avicennian origin."[58]

The importance of the *De mineralibus* lay not in its authorship, but in its influence on medieval natural science. The great encyclopedist of science, George Sarton, found that the *De mineralibus* was used extensively by almost every Latin scholar who concerned himself with chemical and geological subjects[59] and that from this treatise they could derive some clear ideas on the nature of minerals and on the formation of mountains.[60] Clearly then,

---

[54] For a detailed analysis of the authenticity of book 4 of the *Metheora* see Victor C. B. Coutant, *Alexander of Aphrodisias*: *Commentary on Book IV of Aristotle's Metevrologica* (Ph. D. dissertation, Columbia University 1936) 7-24. Cf. H. D. P. Lee, ed., *Aristotle*: *Meteorologica* (London 1952) ix-xxv; and especially the masterfull discussion of Ingemar Düring, *Aristotle's Chemical Treatise Meteorologica*, Book IV (Göteborg 1944) 17-26. Alexander of Aphrodisias also believed that Book IV of the *Metheora* belonged more properly to the *De generatione et corruptione*: "Quartus inscriptus Aristotelis Meteorologicorum est quidem Aristotelis, non tamen meteorologici negotii: non enim illius propria quae dicuntur in ipso; magis autem, quantum ad ea quae dicuntur, esse utique consequens his quae De generatione et corruptione," Quoted from A. J. Smet, ed., *Alexandre d'Aphrodisias*: *Commentaire sur les Météores d'Aristote* (Louvain 1968) 281.

[55] Lee 289, 378ᵇ5.

[56] Holmyard, Mandeville (n. 38 above) 1-4.

[57] F. H. Fobes, "Medieval Versions of Aristotle's Meteorology," *Classical Philology* 10 (1915) 300.

[58] Holmyard, Mandeville (n. 38 above) 10.

[59] George Sarton, *Introduction to the History of Science* (Baltimore 1931) 2.2.511.

[60] *Ibid.* 515.

Alfred's translation of *De mineralibus* was a significant contribution to the history of mineralogy and geology.

Besides *De mineralibus*, Alfred translated from Arabic a treatise on botany, variously called *De vegetabilibus* or *De plantis*.[61] Miss Wingate in her excellent discussion of this work, which according to its editor Eduard Meyer was composed by Nicholas of Damascus, outlines its medieval Arabic and Latin traditions according to which Aristotle seems to be its ultimate source.[62] Nevertheless, most modern writers have accepted Meyer's judgment in treating *De plantis* as a composition by Nicholas.[63] This treatise was translated into Arabic by Hunain ibn Ishaq during the ninth century and later corrected by Thabit ibn Qurra.[64]

Miss Wingate examined over sixty copies of *De plantis*, which in every case were based on Alfred's version.[65] Some one hundred and fifty-seven copies of *De plantis* have been found,[66] and this translation constituted "the chief source of botanical theory down to the 16th century."[67] The *De plantis* is usually found in the codices that also contain the earliest translations of the "new Aristotle" and it belongs to the oldest *compilatio* of the *libri naturales*. The early translation, the great diffusion, and the extended use of *De plantis*, earned Alfred a significant place in the history of botany.

ALFRED AS COMMENTATOR

Besides translating *De mineralibus* and *De plantis*, Alfred wrote several commentaries of which none had been edited prior to my edition of the *Metheora*. Montfaucon mentions a Catalogue of Beauvais Cathedral, compiled in 1664, with the following entry: "Alfredus Anglicus in Aristotelem" *De mundo et celo, De generatione et corruptione, De anima, De sompno et vigilia, De morte et vita, De colore celi.*"[68] George Lacombe believes that by *De colore celi*, the *Metheora* is meant.[69]

Although this list has not been vindicated, because no commentary by Alfred on any of the items has so far been found, there is very good evidence

---

[61] Meyer (n. 3 above).

[62] Wingate (n. 2 above) 56.

[63] Grabmann (n. 23 above) 184. Baeumker (n. 6 above) 33, and Haskins (n. 4 above) 128, follow Meyer in calling *De plantis* pseudo-Aristotelian.

[64] Sarton (n. 59 above) 561. Cf. *Aristoteles Latinus* (Roma 1939) 1.91.

[65] Wingate (n. 2 above) 64.

[66] George Lacombe, "Alfredus in Metheora," *Beiträge zur Geschichte der Philosophie und Theologie des Mittelalters*, supp., 3 (Münster 1935).

[67] A. C. Crombie, *Medieval and Early Modern Science*, 2 vols. (Garden City, New York 1959) 1.147.

[68] H. Omont, "Recherches sur la bibliothèque de l'église cathédrale de Beauvais," *Mémoires de l'Academie des inscriptions et belles lettres* 40 (Paris 1916) 48, no. 134.

[69] Lacombe (n. 66 above) 464.

that Alfred wrote glosses on *De generatione et corruptione* and indeed commented on *De colore celi*, provided of course Lacombe's theory is correct about the latter's confusion with the *Metheora*. In an unmarked codex of Aristotelian manuscripts at the John Walters Library in Baltimore, the following note is found in the margin of a Greek-Latin version of *De generatione et corruptione*:[70] "Liber Aristotelis translatus ab Henrico Aristippo de greco in latinum, correctus et per capitula distinctus a magistro Alvredo de Sares(hel), secundum commentum Alkindi super eundem librum." On folio 14ra of Durham, Chapter Library MS C. III 15, is the following entry:[71] "Quare autem vapor et calor invisibiles flammam visibilem producant, in libro *De generatione et corruptione* discussimus." So far there is no trace of the other entries in the Beauvais Catalogue, but our account of Alfred is far from complete, and some or all of the listed items may well turn out to be of his authorship.

Fortunately, Alfred's authorship of a commentary on *De plantis* is well established. Miss Wingate examined this commentary in some detail and observed:[72]

> The first commentary written on the *De plantis* was that of Alfredus himself, written probably between 1210 and 1215. If, as we shall show below, there is reason to suppose that Alfredus used in this commentary the Arabic-Latin version of the *De animalibus* by Michael Scot, it can hardly have been composed earlier than 1210. Moreover, the number of Aristotelian natural works utilized by Alfredus in this commentary, a number only exceeded in his *De motu cordis*, suggests that the commentary of *De plantis* belongs to the last period of Alfred's literary activity. There is no work known to have been composed at this date which shows so wide an acquaintance with the biological and natural works. On the other hand, it is probable that this commentary was composed before the *De motu cordis*, which seems to have been the last of the extant works of Alfredus. The *De motu cordis* is certainly later than the version of the *De plantis*, which it cites, and its wider use of Aristotelian and other works makes it natural to suppose that it is also subsequent to the commentary on that work.

Actually Miss Wingate's argument for Alfred's utilization of Michael Scot's translation of *De animalibus* in his commentary on *De vegetabilibus* is quite weak. Alfred's gloss reads: "Animata enim sunt predicta corpora. Quid vero naturam disiungat ab anima ipse determinat in animalibus," while Scot's

---

[70] *Ibid.* 464. Cf. *Aristoteles Latinus* 1.238.
[71] Durham MS fol. 14ra.
[72] Wingate (n. 2 above) 65-66.

translation reads: "Et similiter natura graditur paulatim a non animato ad animalia . . . et hoc genus, quum confertur ad alia copora, videbitur magis simile animato, quum remotio inter ipsum et animal est continua."[73] A loose paraphrase of this kind by no means proves that Alfred used Scot's translation. Alfred was in Spain to translate Arabic works and he probably translated this section on his own, as he seems to have done elsewhere.[74] According to Miss Wingate, Alfred cites in his commentary on *De plantis* the following "Aristotelian works": *De generatione et corruptione, De metheoris, De anima, Analytica posteriora, De mineralibus* and *De animalibus.*[75]

ALFRED AND THE "DE MOTU CORDIS"

Beside the translations, and the commentaries, Alfred wrote a treatise on the heart, the *De motu cordis.* Clemens Baeumker edited this work in 1923,[76] but he had shown Alfred's position in the transmission and diffusion of Greco-Arabic natural philosophy a full decade earlier.[77] Baeumker observed that "Two lines of thought come together in Alfred's work—the neo-Platonic metaphysics and the natural philosophy and science of Aristotle."[78] Alfred's conception of the degrees of reality in being and their emanation from the absolute are Neoplatonic. In contrast to this, Aristotle's treatises represent a major part of *De motu cordis.* Alfred quotes extensively in this work from book 4 of the *Metheora, De anima, De somno et vigilia, Ethica Nicomachea, Metaphysica, Physica,* and *De vegetabilibus.*[79]

Alfred accepted Aristotle's view of the supremacy of the heart over the brain,[80] and maintained that the movement of the heart is caused by the soul as well as by heat—the soul as the *causa principalis,* and heat as the *causa instrumentalis.*[81] Following Avicenna, Alfred accepts the soul as an independent substance which gives the body its form and represents the function of the mind. By giving the soul an independent existence, he escaped the conclusion of some thinkers that the soul lives and dies with the body. Among those who quoted Alfred's definition of the soul were Philip the Chancellor, John de la Rochelle, Albert the Great, and Bartholemew the Englishman.[82] Although Alfred was a prominent translator whose own

---

[73] *Ibid.* 76.

[74] For a discussion of Alfred's use of unstranslated Arabic works see my "The Sources of Alfred of Sareshel's (Alfredus Anglicus) Commentary on the *Metheora* of Aristotle."

[75] Wingate (n. 2 above) 100 n. 33.

[76] Baeumker (n. 5 above).

[77] Baeumker (n. 6 above).

[78] *Ibid.* 48.

[79] *Ibid.* 33-34.

[80] Sarton (n. 59 above) 520.

[81] Baeumker (n. 5 above) xviii.

[82] Callus (n. 44 above) 238.

commentaries helped diffuse the "new Aristotle," his reputation rested principally on the *De motu cordis*, which as early as the first half of the thirteenth century, as I have mentioned, was used as a philosophical text by the Arts Faculty at Paris.[83]

THE DATE OF ALFRED'S COMMENTARY
ON THE "METHEORA" AND HIS OTHER WORKS

Alfred's glosses on the *Metheora* as a separate and complete commentary are extant in only one manuscript (Durham, Chapter Library C. III. 15, fols. 11v-18r) henceforth cited as *D*. A parallel account, limited to book 4, exists in *P* (Paris, Bibliothèque Nationale, Latin 7131 fols. 82v-85r). A third MS, *O* (Oxford, Bodleian Library, Selden Supra, 24, fols. 84r-109r), like *D* also provides glosses for all four books of the *Metheora*, but unlike *D* the glosses of *O* constitute only marginalia which are extensive but incomplete. Besides these three manuscripts, an impressive number of *Metheora* manuscripts exist in which glosses and marginalia are attributed to Alfred by other commentators.[84]

Prior to William of Moerbeke's translation of the *Metheora* from Greek, known as the "translatio nova," there existed an earlier version, known as the "translatio vetus." As we have seen, a frequently found colophon describes the *Metheora* of the old translation;[85] let us cite it again:

> Completus est liber metheororum cuius tres primos libros transtulit magister Gerardus Lumbardus summus philosophus de arabico in latinum. Quartum autem transtulit Henricus Aristippus de greco in latinum. Tria ultima capitula transtulit Aluredus Anglicus Sarelensis de arabico in latinum.

Henry Aristippus died in 1162 and Gerard of Cremona in 1187. These dates establish *termini ante quos* of 1162 for book 4 and 1187 for books 1-3 at the very latest. When did Alfred translate the "tria ultima capitula" (Avicenna's *De mineralibus*)?[86] Alfred's addition regularly follows book 4 in the oldest surviving manuscripts of the "translatio vetus" which date from the end of the twelfth century.[87] Moreover, in the five manuscripts that I have ex-

---

[83] Grabmann (n. 24 above) 192.

[84] Lacombe (n. 66 above) 465 n. 14. Cf. Grabmann (n. 24 above) 138-182; Dales (n. 26 above).

[85] For a list of manuscripts that have this colophon, see n. 52 above.

[86] For a detailed discussion of "tria ultima capitual" = *De mineralibus*, see above, at n. 53.

[87] *Aristoteles Latinus* 2.1330 lists over 100 Translatio vetus manuscripts of the *Metheora*, all of which contain Alfred's addition of *De mineralibus*.

amined, the incipit of *De mineralibus*: "Terra pura lapis non fit" follows the explicit of book 4 without a title or any other sign of division.[88] Clearly then, Alfred translated the "last three chapters," that is, *De mineralibus*, before the year 1200, and his addition was considered part of book 4 in the earliest tradition of the *Metheora*.

The translation of *De mineralibus* also provides some knowledge for Alfred's commentary on the *Metheora*. As I indicated above, the commentary accompanies MS Selden Supra 24 (*O*) in the form of marginal glosses, but what is more significant, the largest portion of the commentary is written in the same hand as the text itself. The commentary in *O* is therefore most likely as old as the text of the *Metheora* itself. In the *Aristoteles Latinus*,[89] MS Selden Supra 24 is dated: "Saec. XII ex. et XIII in.," giving clear evidence that Alfred's commentary, as well as his translation of *De mineralibus*, were in circulation by about 1200, certainly not much later. There are also several typical copying errors and short omissions in the commentary of *O*, slips that the scribe himself caught and then corrected below.[90] Obviously then, *O* is a copy from an earlier manuscript, but at present there is no way of knowing how much earlier. At the same time, the anonymity of the glosses in *O* seems to point to the holograph itself or a source very close to it. For, excepting the later manuscripts *D* and *P*, which are also anonymous, Alfred's glosses were frequently cited and identified by other writers. The fact that they are not identified in *O*, the early date of *O*, and the fact that *O* was copied from an earlier manuscript permit us to conclude with some certainty that Alfred wrote his commentary on the *Metheora* no later than 1200, and perhaps several years earlier.

As I indicated earlier, Alfred speaks of "quosdam alios Aristotelis libros de philosophia quorum etiam aliquos de Arabico in Latinum transtuli."[91] Since Alfred is not known to have translated any other works beyond *De vegetabilibus* (i.e., *De plantis*) and *De mineralibus* (i.e., "tria ultima capitula" of the *Metheora*), we may conclude that Alfred means these two treatises when he speaks of "quosdam alios Aristotelis libros." This is also confirmed by the commentary on the *Metheora* in which *De vegetabilibus* and *De mineralibus* are cited several times.[92] But without Alfred's explicit reference to his translations it would be impossible to say whether or not he cited them in translation or from the Arabic original. His little note permits us to conclude that Alfred had already made his translations before he commented on the

---

[88] MSS: Vatican, Urb. lat. 206, fol. 253r; Oxford, Corpus Christi College C. 114 fol. 110v and D. 111 fol. 227v; Bodleian, Selden Supra 24, fol. 113r Escorial, F. II, 4, fol. 309v.

[89] *Aristoteles Latinus*, 1.398.

[90] MS Selden Supra, 24, fols. 85v, 107v, and others.

[91] MS Durham, fol. 14va.

[92] Ibis. fols. 13ra; 13rb; 13va; 14vb.

Metheora. Further, since the commentary dates from at least 1200, we may conclude that his translations were made before 1200, and perhaps as much as fifteen or twenty years before the turn of the century. In regard to Alfred's dedication of *De plantis* to Roger of Hereford and the latter's known dates, I suggested the interval 1185-1190 as the most likely period for Alfred's translating activities in Spain.[93] The translation of *De mineralibus* also belongs to this period, but we cannot say whether or not it preceded the translation of *De plantis.*

As was stated earlier, Alfred in his commentary on the *Metheora* refers directly to a gloss on *De generatione et corruptione*:[94] "Quare autem vapor et calor invisibiles flammam visibilem producant, in libro *De generatione et corruptione* discussimus." This commentary too then is earlier than the commentary on the *Metheora*, and probably Alfred's first attempt at explaining the "new Aristotle." But beyond this gloss and a note indicating that Alfred corrected and arranged it into chapters, nothing is known.[95]

Up to this point it has been possible to place Alfred's works in chronological order by his occasional references to earlier works and by circumstantial evidence. This convenience is not provided regarding his two remaining works, the commentary on *De plantis* and his own composition, *De motu cordis.* The *De plantis* commentary cites *De mineralibus*, but it does not cite Alfred's commentary on the *Metheora* or *De motu cordis.*[96] In turn, the *Metheora* commentary does not cite the commentary on the *De plantis* or *De motu cordis.*[97] Finally *De motu cordis* cites Alfred's translations (i.e., *De mineralibus* and *De plantis*) but neither the commentary on the *Metheora* nor that on *De plantis.*[98] Closer examination of the unprinted commentary on *De plantis* may well reveal its chronological relationship to the commentary on the *Metheora* and to the *De motu cordis*, but that is beyond the scope of the present study.

The chronological relationship of the commentary on the *Metheora* to the *De motu cordis* also remains unsolved. I have compared these two works at some length but have found no direct evidence that would permit a sound answer pertinent to their sequential order of composition. Since there is

[93] For a discussion of Alfred's dedication of *De plantis* to Roger of Hereford, see above at n. 3.

[94] Durham MS fol. 14ra.

[95] A marginal note in an unmarked codex of Aristotelian manuscripts at the John Walters Library in Baltimore accompanies a Greek-Latin version of *De generatione corruptione*: "Liber Aristotelis translatus ab Henrico Aristippo de greco in latinum, correctus et per capitula distinctus a magistro Alvredo de Sares(hel), secundum commentum Alkindi super eundem librum." See above at n. 70.

[96] Baeumker (n. 6 above) 26; Wingate (n. 2 above) 58, 66.

[97] In the commentary on the *Metheora* there is no hint that Alfred commented upon *De plantis*, which may be subsequent to the *Metheora.*

[98] Baeumker (n. 5 above).

no explicit reference to Alfred's commentaries on *De generatione et corruptione De plantis*, or the *Metheora* in his *De motu cordis*, although all of these texts are cited,[99] one could be tempted to conclude that Alfred translated Aristotelian works and composed his independent treatise (*De motu cordis*) before he commented on his own translations. But the *argumentum ex silentio* can be equally well employed in establishing *De motu cordis* as Alfred's *opus ultimum*, simply because a reference to *De motu cordis* is conspiciously missing in any of his commentaries. All we can say then is that Alfred perhaps did not always refer to his earlier works.

It is clear, however, that Alfred's first literary endeavor was directed toward translating treatises on natural philosophy. The second logical undertaking would be commenting on these translations as well as on others. Last, after gaining intellectual maturity from an "iter hispanicum" that exposed him to the wealth of Greek and Arabic science, and after several volumes of translations and commentaries, Alfred would combine his experiences for composing an independent treatise like *De motu cordis*. The *De motu cordis* abounds in the natural science of the Greeks and Arabs and distinguishes its author by a wealth of Aristotelian citations unequaled by any Latin author of the time.[100] The importance of this treatise and the eminence of its author perhaps are gauged best by the adoption of *De motu cordis* as a philosophical text of the Arts Faculty at Paris during the first half of the thirteenth century.[101] All the evidence then suggests that *De motu cordis* was Alfred's last and crowning achievement.

As was mentioned earlier, *De motu cordis* was written no later than 1217 and possibly before 1203. On the basis of what has been demonstrated I would then suggest the following order and dates for Alfred's works: translations of *De mineralibus* and *De plantis* (1180-1190); commentaries on *De generatione et corruptione*, the *Metheora* and *De plantis* (1190-1200); composition of *De motu cordis* (ca. 1200). As the remaining commentaries by Alfred are edited, it is to be hoped that a definite order of his works and a more complete *vita* than the present one will emerge. Establishing that tradition will close a significant gap in the chain of transmission of Greek and Arabic thought in which Alfredus Anglicus was such an important link.

Department of History
University of Wisconsin—Eau Claire
Eau Claire, Wisconsin, U.S.A.

---

[99] *Ibid.*
[100] Baeumker (n. 6 above) 33; cf. Haskins (n. 4 above) 129.
[101] Grabmann (n. 24 above) 2.192.

THE "DE DIFFERENTIIS ET DERIVATIONIBUS GRECORUM" ATTRIBUTED TO WILLIAM OF CORBEIL

•

by John R. Williams

Most grammarians of the later Middle Ages believed that thorough mastery of Latin demanded knowledge of *ethimologia*. This word, explained Peter Helias, a French grammarian of the mid-twelfth century, is a compound of *ethimos*, true, and *logos*, word. He who etymologizes assigns a word its true, that is, its original, meaning.[1] From the twelfth century on *ethimologia* held an important place in grammatical instruction. In the classroom students were taught the supposedly original stems of simple and composite Latin words (*derivatio* and *compositio*). Inevitably the quest for original stems led grammarians from Latin to Greek vocabulary. From early times the works of Saint Jerome, Isidore of Seville, Remi of Auxerre, and Greco-Latin glossaries had provided westerners with many Greek words. From the eleventh century on, their numbers rapidly increased. The growing interest in Greek vocabulary can be traced through the great lexicons produced in this later period, from the *Elementarium doctrine erudimentum* of Papias (ca. 1053), through the *Catholicon* of John of Genoa (d. 1286).[2] The *Liber derivationum* of Hugutio of Pisa (ca. 1200) which enjoyed great popularity contains hundreds of Greek and supposedly Greek words. As Hugutio was convinced that Greek was the main font of Latin vocabulary, these gave him endless opportunity for the proliferation of etymological illustrations.[3]

Lexicons provided the grammarians with many Greek words, but bulky tomes were ill suited for ordinary use in the classroom. Teachers needed

---

[1] Cited from R. W. Hunt, "The 'lost' preface to the *Liber derivationum* of Osbern of Gloucester," *Mediaeval and Renaissance Studies* 4 (1958) 271. On *ethimologia*, see also C. Thurot, "Notices et extraits de divers manuscrits latins pour servir à l'histoire des doctrines grammaticales au moyen âge," *Notices et extraits des manuscrits de la Bibliothèque Impériale et autres bibliothèques* 22.2 (Paris 1868) 146f. This remarkable study has recently been reprinted as a separate work (Frankfurt am Main 1964).

[2] On the lexicographers, see G. Goetz, *Corpus glossariorum latinorum*, 7 vols. (Leipzig 1888-1923) 1.165ff. A convenient and up-to-date survey of the subject is given by K. Grubmüller, *Vocabularius ex quo* (Munich 1967) 13-44.

[3] C. Riessner, *Die "Magnae Derivationes" des Uguccione da Pisa und ihre Bedeutung für die romanische Philologie*, Temi e Testi 11 (Rome 1965) 44-45, 66.

texts of convenient format giving due attention to Greek words. Such a
manual was the very popular versified grammar of Eberhard of Bethune.[4]
From its eighth chapter, *De nominibus exortis a Greco*, Eberhard's text was
universally known as *Grecismus*. Specialized manuals devoted primarily to
Greek words also appeared. Such was the *Cornutus* (or *Distigium*) by John
of Garland (d. 1272) with its bizarre vocabulary, much of it Greek.[5] Another
was the recently published *Brito metricus*, a versified treatise on Hebrew
and Greek words by the lexicographer William Brito.[6] Still another was the
subject of this article, the *De differentiis et derivationibus Grecorum* attributed
to William of Corbeil.[7]

This treatise, to which it will be convenient to refer as the *Differentie*,
differs from the others mentioned by being in prose. Except for a letter of
dedication to a certain Gilbert and a selection from the beginning of the
text it remains unpublished.[8] It survives, however, in partial or complete
form in three manuscripts, of which I have been fortunate in securing microfilms. I shall comment on these manuscripts later. Before doing so it seems
advisable to inform the reader of the contents of the treatise and the author's method of presentation.

William's primary purpose is to warn Gilbert that like-appearing and like-
sounding Greek words differ in meaning and are not to be confused. To this
end he musters 115 pairs of such words, beginning with *alchos-archos*, and
concluding with *xenos-xanthos*. The pairs are arranged in the order of the
Latin alphabet, but no attempt is made to preserve the alphabetical sequence
within the main letter groupings, A, B, C, and so forth. Having emphasized
the difference between the components of a pair, William next gives the
Latin and sometimes the French equivalent of each word.[9] He next illustrates
at great length the use of his Greek stems in Latin words ordinary and rare
(*derivatio* and *compositio*). Most of the text is in fact devoted to this. There
are approximately 700 such illustrations, many of them farfetched or fan-

---

[4] *Eberhardi Bethuniensis Graecismus*, ed. J. Wrobel, Corpus grammaticorum medii aevi 1
(Breslau 1887). On the great popularity of this metrical grammar, see L. J. Paetow, *The
Arts Course at Medieval Universities* (Urbana 1910) 36-39.

[5] Published by E. Habel, *Der deutsche Cornutus* 1: *Der Cornutus des Johannes de Gar-
landia, ein Schulbuch des 13. Jahrhunderts in den deutschen Übersetzungen des Mittelalters*
(Berlin 1908) 23-28. For critical discussion of the work, see L. J. Paetow, *Morale scolarium
of John of Garland* (Berkeley 1927) 135-137.

[6] L. W. Daly, ed., *Brito metricus* (Philadelphia 1969).

[7] I take the title from a fourteenth-century manuscript of Rouen, to be described presently: *Summa magistri Guillelmi corballensis de differenciis et derivacionibus grecorum
secundum ordinem alphabeti*. All other titles are modern.

[8] See below, p. 297. *Gilberte* is the name in the two oldest manuscripts. The Rouen manuscript, the least reliable in spelling, gives it first as *Gillarde* and then as *Guillelme*.

[9] For example: "unde allodium . . . Gallice alleu;" "manthica . . . Gallice male"; "cu-
culus genus vestis . . . Gallice dicitur froc."

tastic. Some are conventional terms from medieval grammar and rhetoric, some are names from classical mythology, but most come from the routine of everyday life. Thus, his divisions abound in names for articles of dress, buildings, food, drink, utensils, diseases, plants, birds, animals, fish. Obviously a firm believer in verse as an aid to memory, he sums up his comments on each pair of terms with an *Unde versus*. So, *alchos-archos* concludes, "Est alchos fortis, sed princeps dicitur archos," and *machos-macros* is summarized, "Unde versus: Fertur pugna machos, sed longum sit tibi macros."

The three known manuscripts preserving complete or incomplete versions of the *Differentie* are:

1. Paris, Bibliothèque nationale, MS lat. 7100.[10] This manuscript, to which I shall refer as *P*, is a haphazard miscellany of six fragments. The fourth of these (fols. 27ra-38vb), contains two works. Neither has a title nor the name of its author. The arms and motto of Saint Victor of Paris decorate the right margin of the first folio.[11] Folios 27ra-32rb contain the metrical *Synonyma* usually attributed to John of Garland (1195-1272).[12] This is followed by the *Differentie*, unfortunately incomplete. It ends at the bottom of folio 38vb leaving the author differentiating between *grafos* and *grifos*. The folios that should follow are lost, or perhaps were never written. The script appears to be that of the late thirteenth century.

2. Wolfenbüttel, Gudiani lat. 326.[13] This manuscript, which I shall designate *W*, is also a compilation. The *Differentie* is the first work (fols. 1-19). A number of Latin and Gallo-Latin glossaries follow. The *Differentie* lacks the discussion of several pairs of supposedly Greek words beginning with the letters "O" and "P". At the end of the text, on folio 19, the scribe has very considerately noted that he finished his labors on the Tuesday that followed Ascension Day, 1308. Marquard Gude, founder of this important collection in the Ducal Library at Wolfenbüttel, has written on the inside cover, "Emi Andegavi MDCLXI."

3. Rouen, Bibliothèque municipale 1026 (O. 32).[14] I shall refer to this manuscript as *R*. The early folios contain works of John of Garland. Among

[10] The contents are listed in *Catalogus codicum manuscriptorum Bibliothecae Regiae*, 4 vols. (Paris 1739-1744) 4.313. The editors assign the compilation as a whole to the fourteenth century.

[11] The catalogue of Saint Victor manuscripts drawn up by Grandrue at the beginning of the sixteenth century lists this fragment as the first work in St. Victor MS JJJ23. For the works which followed it in the manuscript, see *The Bodleian Library Record* 4 (1952) 126. I am much indebted for this information to M. Gilbert Ouy of the *Centre national de la recherche scientifique*, Paris.

[12] On the *Synonyma*, see Paetow (n. 5 above) 134.

[13] For full description, see *Die Handschriften der Herzoglichen Bibliothek zu Wolfenbüttel*, ed. O. von Heinemann and others, 11 vols. (Wolfenbüttel 1884-1913) 4, *Die Gudischen Handschriften*.

them are his *Dictionarius* and the *Cornutus*. The *Differentie*, preceded
by the title I use in this article and the name of the author, begins on
folio 79 and ends on folio 105v. The hand is that of the late fourteenth
century. A note from the fifteenth century on the back cover informs
us that at that time the manuscript was at Saint Sulpice of Bourges.

The existence of the *Differentie* has long been known. To my knowledge
the first modern writer to mention it was the Benedictine, Jean Colomb,
a co-editor of early volumes of the *Histoire littéraire de la France*. Noting
the description of *P* in the catalogue of the Royal Library, "Guillermi Corborensis explicatio quorumdam vocabulorum graecorum ad Gillebertum Epis-
copum Pictaviensem," Colomb remarked in a letter of June 1758, "Ce doit
être Gilbert de la Porée, ou Poirée, car depuis lui il n'y a point d'évêques
à Poitiers de ce nom."[15] Well over a century later Colomb's words were noted
by the Abbé Clerval. He agreed that the Gilbert of the dedication must
have been the celebrated twelfth-century theologian and philosopher, Gilbert
de la Porrée (d. 1154). He conjectured that the author, Guillermus Corborensis, may have been one of Gilbert's many disciples, perhaps Guillaume
de Combourg, who was abbot of Marmoutier from 1105 to 1124.[16]

More recently (1924) the *Differentie* attracted the attention of Professor
Charles Haskins. In a chapter on "The Greek Element in the Renaissance
of the Twelfth Century" in his *Studies in the History of Mediaeval Science*
Haskins observed, "Some acquaintance with the language [that is, Greek]
was claimed by William of Corbeil, who in the early twelfth century dedicated
his *Differentie* to Gilbert de la Porrée."[17] In a later chapter, on North Italian
translators, he was somewhat more cautious, saying "Further interest in
the results of Greek studies is seen in the dedication to a Gilbert, apparently
Gilbert de la Porrée, of the *Differentie* of a certain Guillelmus Corborensis."[18]
In his footnote here he called attention to the hitherto unnoticed presence
of the treatise in the manuscript at Wolfenbüttel.

Haskins continued to be interested in this work. In 1930 he contributed
to a *Festschrift* honoring Paul Thomas a brief article on "The *Differentie
dictionum latinarum* of William of Corbeil."[19] In this he was able to add the

---

[14] *Catalogue général des manuscrits des bibliothèques publiques de France: Départements*, 1
(Paris 1886) 258.

[15] Colomb's letter was published by U. Robert, *Documents inédits concernant l'histoire
littéraire de la France* (Paris 1875) 121.

[16] Clerval, *Les écoles de Chartres au moyen âge* (Paris 1895) 187 and n. 5; 231.

[17] C. H. Haskins, *Studies in the History of Mediaeval Science* (Cambridge, Mass. 1924;
ed. 2, 1927) 150. The statement is repeated in his *Renaissance of the Twelfth Century* (Cambridge 1927) 133.

[18] Chap. 10, 213 and n. 119.

[19] Haskins, "The *Differentie dictionum latinarum* of William of Corbeil," in *Mélanges
Paul Thomas* (Bruges 1930) 417-421.

Rouen manuscript to the list of known manuscripts of the treatise. He also published the letter of dedication to Gilbert and the first distinction of the text, between *alchos* and *archos*. He was now less certain of the date of the treatise, but still favored the twelfth century. He was also less confident that Gilbert was Gilbert de la Porrée. Yet he did not eliminate him as a possibility. To him the author remained William "of Corbeil." The problem of William's sources and the extent of his knowledge of Greek he left to the investigation of others.

Since 1930 several scholars have found occasion to refer to the *Differentie*. Thus, Hans Walther, in 1959, cited the "Est alchos fortis, sed princeps dicitur archos" of the Wolfenbüttel manuscript as the first verse of a Latin poem,[20] which, of course, it is not. In 1965 Marie-Thérèse d'Alverny in her study of the life and works of Alan of Lille called attention to the treatise. Commenting on Alan's fondness for etymologies, she suggested that he may have used some "'jardin des racines grecques' comme l'ouvrage encore inédit, rédigé par un certain 'Guillelmus Corborensis.'"[21] She did not attempt to identify this author, and she cautioned against assuming that Gilbert de la Porrée was the Gilbert of the dedication. The following year, Nicholas Häring, in his edition of Gilbert de la Porrée's commentaries on Boethius, did, however, make this assumption, influenced by Haskins's early article.[22] Most recently, in 1967, Bernhard Bischoff, in a slightly revised version of an earlier article, has called attention to the *Differentie* in a footnote.[23]

Bischoff assumes that the treatise was a product of the twelfth century, and this has been the accepted opinion. In the light of this dating it is not remarkable that the Gilbert of the dedication has been identified as the eminent theologian and philosopher Gilbert de la Porrée. Aside from Clerval, who suggested that the author of the treatise may have been William of Combourg, scholars have persisted in calling him William "of Corbeil," despite a disconcerting inconsistency in the spelling of the name in the manuscripts. The only known William of Corbeil contemporary with Gilbert de la Porrée was archbishop of Canterbury from 1123 to 1136. There is nothing implausible in the view that this man might have dedicated a work to Gilbert. Both had studied at Laon under Master Anselm (d. 1117), and although

[20] Hans Walther, *Initia carminum et versuum medii aevi posterioris latinorum* (Göttingen 1959) 11.280, no. 5567.

[21] M. T. d'Alverny, *Alain de Lille: Textes inédits avec une introduction sur sa vie et ses œuvres* (Paris 1965) 97 and n. 6.

[22] N. M. Häring, *The Commentaries on Boethius by Gilbert of Poitiers*, Pontifical Institute of mediaeval Studies, Studies and Texts 13 (Toronto 1966) 45-46 and n. 7.

[23] The original article, Bernhard Bischoff, "Das griechische Element in der abendländischen Bildung des Mittelalters," appeared in *Byzantinische Zeitschrift* 44 (1951) 27-55. The revision is in his *Mittelalterliche Studien*, 2 vols. (Stuttgart 1966-67) 2.246-275. The reference to the *Differentie* is 271 n. 139.

Gilbert de la Porrée does not appear to have known the Greek language,
he was remarkably familiar with certain of the Greek Fathers.[24] It now remains to test the validity of these hypotheses by a reexamination of William's
treatise.

A careful reading of the *Differentie* quickly reveals that many of its Greek
words with their Latin equivalents also appear in Eberhard of Bethune's *Grecismus*.[25] The number of such duplications is large. Thus, of the 230 Greek
terms in William's alphabetical pairs, 116 also occur in Eberhard's chapter
8, *De nominibus exortis a Greco*. This is to say nothing of William's many
etymological examples identical with Eberhard's, not only in chapter 8 but
also in his other chapters.[26] Many such parallels might be given to illustrate
the point, but the following will suffice:[27]

Differentie	*Grecismus*
P fol. 33vb (*W* 3r; *R* 82r):	8.43:
Inde dicitur allobroga, ge, alie-natus a fide, et dicitur ab al-leos, quod est alienum et broge, quod est fides.	Quod fides broge sit comprobat Allobroga.
P fol. 35vb (*W* 6r; *R* 86r):	8.89:
Nota quod quando [romani] sal-utabant iulium cesarem ita di-cebant, cere cesar anichos, id est, salve cesar invictus.	Est chaere salve, hinc dic "Chae-re Caesar anicos !"
P fol. 37ra (*W* 7v; *R* 88v):	8.102-103:
Scribe per y grecum dyas et duo signabit. Scribe per i nostram de tibi signat.	Scribe per y Graecum dyas et duo significabit. Scribe per i nostrum, de tibi sig-nificat.

Such parallels are too numerous to be the result of chance. Clearly the
Differentie and the *Grecismus* are interdependent. The question is whether
William borrowed from Eberhard, or whether Eberhard drew on William.
In the light of preexisting opinion the latter would seem only logical, for

[24] Haskins (n. 17 above) 150.

[25] Haskins (n. 19 above) 421 n. 1 pointed out some of these parallels, but made no attempt
to account for them.

[26] K. Lohmeyer attributed the first eight chapters of the *Grecismus* to an unidentified
twelfth-century author, to whose work Eberhard's metrical grammar had been added after
Eberhard's death. See "Ebrard von Béthune: eine Untersuchung über den Verfasser des
Grecismus und Laborintus," *Romanische Forschungen* 11 (1901) 412-430. However this
may be, parallels between the *Differentie* and the *Grecismus* are not confined to any part
of the latter.

[27] I quote from *P*, apparently the oldest of the three manuscripts. There are slight but
insignificant variations in wording in *W* and *R*. The punctuation is mine.

this view assigns the *Differentie* to the twelfth century, while most modern scholars have accepted 1212 as the date of the *Grecismus*.[28] It seems appropriate, however, to examine at this point the evidence on which these conclusions have been based.

Discussion of the date of the *Grecismus* has centered on a distich that can be traced back as far as the fifteenth century:

> Anno milleno centeno bis duodeno
> Condidit Ebrardus Graecismum Betuniensis.[29]

Is the date intended here 1124 or 1212? As noted, most scholars for reasons which will become apparent have favored the latter. In an article of 1952, however, Giorgio Brugnoli challenged this conclusion and argued for the correctness of the earlier date.[30] He based this partly on the meter of the distich, but primarily on his discovery of verses from the *Grecismus* in Vat. lat. MS 625. As these are in a hand from the end of the twelfth century or beginning of the thirteenth, he reasoned that Eberhard must have written earlier than 1212. Hence, he argued, the *Grecismus* must be redated 1124. In support of this early date he noted what had been noted before, the presence of two verses from the *Grecismus* in the *Panormia* of Osbern of Gloucester who wrote in the third quarter of the twelfth century.[31] He admitted that this was not decisive, for Eberhard could have taken them from Osbern, or it might be a case of a common source. This it would indeed appear to have been.[32]

Brugnoli has at least succeeded in raising doubts as to the accuracy of 1212 as the date of the *Grecismus*. Actually he might have strengthened his argument had he noted the presence of the first verse of the distich in the

[28] *Das Doctrinale des Alexander de Villa-Dei*, ed. D. Reichling, Monumenta Germaniae paedagogica 12 (Berlin 1893) lxxxiii; Lohmeyer (n. 26 above) 427; Paetow (n. 4 above) 38; M. Manitius, *Geschichte der lateinischen Literatur des Mittelalters*, 3 vols. (Munich 1911-1931) 3.747.

[29] The distich has been traced back to the *Liber vaticanus* of Arnold of Rotterdam (d. 1442). See Reichling (n. 28 above) lxxx; A. Wauters in *Biographie nationale de Belgique* 6.748, and A. Rivier, *ibid.* 7.709. It appears as a scholia to Henry of Ghent's *De scriptoribus ecclesiasticis*, ed. A. Miraeus, Bibliotheca ecclesiastica 1 (Antwerp 1639) 173.

[30] "Di alcune 'differentiae' e 'sententiae' contenute nel cod. Vat. lat. 625," *Studi medievali* n.s. 18 (1952) 353-357.

[31] Osbern's lexicon (*Panormia*) was published by A. Mai, *Classicorum auctorum Vaticanis codicibus editorum* 8 (Rome 1836). The verses in question are:
    Grec. 10.166; Os. 218: Forfice fila, pilum cape forpice, forcipe ferrum.
    Grec. 10.168; Os. 259: Glis animal, glis terra tenax, glis lappa vocatur.
For Osbern's dates see Hunt (n. 1 above) 267. Manitius calls attention to these verses, 3.747.

[32] Both verses occur in a manuscript from circa 1175-1180. See A. Wilmart, "Le florilège de Saint-Gatien," *Revue bénédictine* 48 (1936) 31, no. 184; 32, no. 194.

twelfth-century *Vita Viscelini* by Helmold. Here it can mean only 1124.[33] Moreover, verses appearing in the *Grecismus* can be found in a number of works which antedate 1212, in Alan of Lille's *Distinctiones dictionum theologicarum* (1179-1195),[34] and in the *Corrogationes Promethei* of Alexander Neckam (late twelfth century).[35] There are also close parallels between verses in the *Grecismus* and Alexander of Villedieu's *Doctrinale* (ca. 1200).[36] As Reichling accepted 1212 as the date of the former, he naturally assumed that the *Doctrinale* was their source. If, however, 1212 is discarded, the opposite could have been the case. The verses in Alan and Neckam could, of course, have been interpolated. Those discovered by Brugnoli (in Vat. lat. MS 625) must be contemporary with the script. They consequently constitute a strong argument for rejecting 1212 as date for the *Grecismus*.

Yet, even if we do so, we are not justified in accepting 1124! It may well be that the author of the distich intended this date. He could, however, have been mistaken. We do not know who he was nor when he lived. The really troublesome point is that Brugnoli failed to observe certain facts that make 1124 incredible. Thus, he disregards Lohmeyer's data indicating that Eberhard drew on Peter Helias's commentary on Priscian.[37] As Helias flourished in the mid-twelfth century, a date as early as 1124 for the *Grecismus* seems highly improbable. Brugnoli's most serious fault, however, is failure to observe the chronology of other works attributed to Eberhard of Bethune.[38] The best known of these is a *Liber antiheresis*, which contains a chapter against the Waldensians.[39] Although scholars differ as to the precise date

---

[33] *Helmoldi presbyteri Bozoviensis cronica Slavorum*, ed. B. Schmeidler, Scriptores rerum Germanicarum in usum scholarum (Hannover 1909) 225 verses 8-9:

> Anno milleno centeno bis duodeno
> Completo, verbum quo subluxit caro factum.

[34] This was noted by F. Torraca, "A proposito del Graecismus di E. di Béthune," *Rivista critica della letteratura Italiana*, 5 (1888) 94. The verses are:

> Fur aurum, virgo flores, mare navita, libros
> Clericus: aequivoce singula quisque legit.

In *Grecismus* 17.56-57; Alan, PL 210.834D.

[35] P. Meyer, "Notice sur les *Corrogationes Promethei* d'Alexandre Neckam," *Notices et extraits* 35.2 (Paris 1897) 641-682. The verses are: *Grec.* 10:40, 50, 148, 213; 17:61. Neckam's *Corrogationes* antedates his *De naturis rerum* which was already well known by the end of the twelfth century. As Meyer was publishing from a thirteenth-century manuscript, the possibility of interpolation is not precluded.

[36] Reichling (n. 28 above) xxxvi-xxxvii gives convincing arguments for the date. As to the verses in *Grec.*, see lxxx n. 1.

[37] Lohmeyer (n. 26 above) 420 and n. 1.

[38] On works ascribed to Eberhard, see Daunou in *Histoire littéraire de la France* 17 (1832) 139.

[39] The *Antiheresis* has been published several times, first by J. Gretser, *Trias scriptorum adversus Waldensium sectam* (Ingolstadt 1614). Later it was republished in Gretser's *Opera omnia* (Ratisbon 1734-1741) 12.2.117-195. Chap. 25, against the Waldenses, has recently

of this tract, Waldensian history makes it unlikely that it could have been written much before 1185. There is, of course, a remote possibility that there were *two* Eberhards of Bethune. Yet Lohmeyer's comparison of the phraseology of the introduction to *Grecismus* with that in the introduction to the *Antiheresis* leaves little doubt of single authorship.[40] In short, Brugnoli has justifiably challenged 1212 as the date of the *Grecismus*, but has failed to prove that it was written in 1124. Present evidence seems to indicate a date between 1180 and 1200.

This conclusion does not eliminate the possibility that the *Differentie* was among Eberhard's sources. Close examination of William's text proves, however, that this could not have been so.[41] In addition to material common to him and to Eberhard, William's pages contain material from various sources. The identification of these sources is rather difficult, for William does not cite by name a single author of his own time. Moreover, he rarely follows his sources verbatim, preferring to give a rather free paraphrase. Despite this irritating habit, it is possible to identify with confidence certain of the works he had before him. Most valuable to him was Hugutio of Pisa's *Liber derivationum*. This huge lexicon, extant in many manuscripts, has never been published. Scattered excerpts from it have appeared, however, in several scholarly works.[42] It provided William with a virtually endless supply of supposedly Greek words for examples in *derivatio* and *compositio*. The following will illustrate the application he made of it:[43]

Differentie	*Hugutio*
P fol. 33rb (*W* 2v; *R* 81v):	Fol. 24rb (Riessner, p. 55):
Item actin, id est, portus vel lictus. Unde acteus, a, um, id est, lictoreus, a, um. Unde dicuntur athene, arum, quia mercatores ibi applicantes bonum portum invenerunt et ibi civitatem funda-[33va]verunt, vel dicuntur ab a quod est sine, et thanathos quod est mors, quasi immortales, quia ibi sapiencia	Unde athene quasi litorales (24va) quia in litore posite erant, vel dicuntur athene immortales propter studium quod olim ibi viguit in sapientia que immortalis est, sic dicte ab athanathos quod est immortale ab a quod est sine et tanathos quod est mortale.

---

been republished by G. Gonnet, *Enchiridion fontium Valdensium* (Torre Pellice 1958) 1.144-153.

[40] Lohmeyer (n. 26 above) 439.

[41] The presence of a few verses from the *Grecismus* in *P* and *W* does not prove the dependence of William on Eberhard. The two verses in *P* are absent from *W*, while the four in *W* are lacking in *P*. None of the verses appears in *R*. It is probable that the verses in *P* and *W* were interpolated.

[42] Riessner (n. 3 above) 12 estimates that 194 manuscripts of Hugutio are known.

[43] I am much indebted to the Houghton Library of Harvard University for permission to quote from its thirteenth-century manuscript of the *Liber derivationum*, MS Typ. 183H.

viget, que est immortalis.

P fol. 37vb (W 8v; R 90v):

Ethos, id est, tepidus. Unde
ethon, equus solis, quasi tepidus. Sol enim dicitur habere
 or   or
iiii equos propter iiii proprie-
tates quas habet. Primo rubet,
secundo splendet, postea fervet,
et ad ultimum tepit.

W fol. 13r (R 97v):

Item mene, id est, defficiens.
Unde eumenis, id est, furia infernalis, ab eu, bonum, et mene,
defficiens . . . [Unde menas, dis
vel dos, et dicuntur menades in
plurali sacerdotisse bachi, quasi
defficientes. Omitted in R].
Unde hec mena, ne, piscis qui
alio nomine dicitur ostrea, quia
crescit et decrescit secundum
augmentum vel decrescentiam
lune.

Fol. 29va (Riessner, p. 209):

Rubet [sol] enim mane, splendet
in tertia, claret in meridie, te-
pescit in nona, a quibus pro-
prietatibus iiij eius equi deno-
minantur. Primus dicitur ac-
teus . . . quartus eton, id est te-
pens, vel philogeus.

Fol. 176va:

Item a mene quod est defectus,
hec menas, dis, sacerdotissa bachi, quia deficiat a sensu. . . .
Item a mene, quod est luna vel
defectus, dicitur hec mena, quedam piscis, qui cum luna crescit
vel decrescit.
Mene quod est defectus componitur cum eu, quod est bonum,
et dicitur hec eumenis, dis, id est
furia infernalis, quasi in bono
deficiens.

The date of publication of the *Liber derivationum* is somewhat uncertain, but there is not the wide variation in opinion which has characterized the dating of the *Grecismus*. The evidence is strong that it saw the light while Hugutio was at Nonantula, between 1197 and 1201.[44] This does not preclude the probability that much of the gathering of material and actual writing had been done earlier. In any case it is impossible to believe that Hugutio's *magnum opus* was available to William until some time after 1200.

This is equally true of another source used by William. Alexander of Ville-dieu's *Doctrinale* appeared in 1199 or a little later.[45] William did not draw extensively on this metrical grammar, but the following passages strongly suggest his acquaintance with it:

---

[44] S. G. Mercati, "Sul luogo e sulla data della composizione delle 'Derivationes' di Uguccione da Pisa," *Aevum* 33 (1959) 490-494, argued that the task of compilation was so great and Hugutio so busy that the work could not possibly have been written in his four years at Nonantula. He considers 1192 the latest possible date for the completion of the work. Riessner (n. 3 above 7), agrees with Mercati as to the magnitude of the labor and time involved, but interprets Ricobald of Ferrara's statement that Hugutio *composuit* the work at Nonantula to mean that he "put it together" there.

[45] See n. 36 above.

Differentie	Doctrinale
W fol. 14v (R 99r):	Verses 2512-14:
anthonomasia . . . quando no-	antonomasia solet excellentia di-
men appellativum ponitur pro	ci, si proprius taceas ponens no-
proprio, ut cum dicitur propheta	men generale:
et interpretatur David, aposto-	sic David insinuas nomen dicen-
lus pro Paulo.	do prophetae.
W fol. 15v; (R 102r):	Verses 2634-35:
Unde anthropopatos, quando	si, quae sunt hominis, assignen-
humana passio attribuitur deo,	tur deitati,
ut irasci, errare.	anthropospathos est: sic saepe
	Dei legis iram.

William's use of Hugutio and Alexander proves that he wrote after 1200. As an interval must be allowed for the circulation of the works of these two authors, it must have been some years after the publication of the *Grecismus*. Unfortunately evidence is lacking for the establishment of the exact date. It was before 1308, for the scribe of the Wolfenbüttel manuscript tells us that he finished his chore in that year. Professor Haskins suggested that a gloss of "Guillelmus Continensis" used by Walter of Ascoli in his *Dedignomium* may have been the *Differentie*.[46] If so, the latter must have been in circulation before 1228-1229, the well-established date of the *Dedignomium*.[47] Haskins's suggestion actually has little to recommend its acceptance. It is much more probable that Walter of Ascoli's reference is to William of Conches's gloss on Priscian than to the *Differentie*.[48] No more helpful in determining a date is the recently published *Brito metricus* of the late thirteenth century.[49] Brito and William shared a concern for Greek vocabulary and their two works have much in common. Yet it is impossible to determine whether Brito used William or William used Brito. The parallels can almost always be traced to a common source. We are, then, left with the Paris fragment (*P*) as our principal indication of a limit ad quem. As noted, this manuscript appears to date from the late thirteenth century.[50] It cannot be an autograph so an earlier prototype must be assumed, taking us well

[46] Haskins, "Magister Gualterius Esculanus," *Mélanges d'histoire du moyen âge offerts à M. Ferdinand Lot par ses amis et ses élèves* (Paris 1925) 255.

[47] *Ibid.* 254.

[48] The *Differentie* is not a gloss. The interchangeability of *t* and *c* in manuscripts from this period makes it probable that Walter's *Continensis* is *Conches*, rather than any form of the place name given our William. It is gratifying to note that Édouard Jeanneau reaches this same conclusion in "Deux rédactions des gloses de Guillaume de Conches sur Priscien," *Recherches de théologie ancienne et médiévale* 27 (1960) 226 n. 56.

[49] For date, see Daly (n. 6 above) xi.

[50] See p. 295 above, and Haskins (n. 19 above) 417-418.

back into the thirteenth century. In the light of available evidence, then, the *Differentie* was written between 1220 and 1280.

This conclusion invalidates all previous speculation as to the date of the treatise. It does not come from the twelfth century. Consequently neither William of Combourg nor William of Corbeil, archbishop of Canterbury, could have been its author. The Gilbert of the dedication could not possibly have been Gilbert de la Porrée. It came too late to serve Alan of Lille as a "jardin des racines grecques."[51] The *Differentie* is a thirteenth-century schoolbook. Its purpose is to distinguish between like-sounding Greek words and to demonstrate their application in *ethimologia*. Actually the latter receives most of the author's attention.

It goes without saying that William's *ethimologia* is far removed from modern scientific etymology. If he may be said to have had a method, it was roughly analogous to that of Hugutio.[52] Like the Italian he was apparently convinced that most Latin words had Greek ancestors. If he does not know what they were, he does not hesitate to invent them. Thus for Latin *centum* he assumes a Greek original, *gentos*. Here he was differentiating between *gentos* and *gintos*, a pseudo-Greek word that Eberhard claimed meant *decem*. In many cases, as here, his illustrations are straight derivation. But he seems to delight especially in composite words. The elements in these may be words of Greek origin, partly Greek and partly Latin, or purely Latin. Thus, he analyzes *cronographia*, "a *cronos* tempus et *graphos* scriptio," *manubrium*, "a *manu* et *brios* mensura." Here Latin and Greek elements are combined. In a few cases he distinguishes more than two components. *Geralogodion*, he says, is "a *geral*, quod est sacrum, *logos*, quod est sermo, et *dyon*, confectio." *Kirieleison* combines *kirios*, deus, *eleys*, miserere, and *on*, omnem. This procedure is adhered to systematically through the Latin alphabet. Inevitably it becomes dull and monotonous. Perhaps William was aware of this, for occasionally he digresses at some length. For example, he gives a long account of the origin and significance of the kalends, most of it ap-

---

[51] There is, on the other hand, some indication that William may have known Alan's *Distinctiones dictionum theologicarum*, written between 1179 and 1195. Compare, for example, Alan, PL 210.964, with *P* fol. 34rb (*W* 4r; *R* 83v): "Item, bolon, id est mordeo, a quo dicitur bolus, id est morsellus, et habet componi hoc simbolum [*W* and *R*: escot Gallice. Et canticum apostolorum vocatur symbolum metaforice] Quia sicuti communicantes [*W* and *R*: convinantes; convinentes] ponunt particulas suas ad precium commissiorum [*W* and *R*: convinii] unusquisque apostolorum posuit particulam suam in testimonio fidei catholice. Dixit enim primus, Credo in deum patrem et cetera. secundus, et in ihesum christum filium eius, et sic deinceps. Et dicitur a sin quod est simul, et bolus morsellus."

Also, Alan PL 210.779-780, with *P* 38rb (*W* 9v; *R* 91v):

"Item dicitur yperphania cognitio illa quam habent superiores [*W* and *R*: angeli] de deo, ab yper, super, et phanes [*W* and *R* add, Ypofania est ista apparitio quam habent inferiores a deo, a hypos, sub, et fanes apparere."]

[52] Hugutio's methods are analyzed by Riessner (n. 3 above) 39-84.

parently from Hugutio. He describes in some detail the way in which tolls
are collected on the roads, and dwells at some length on various explanations
of the word *synod*. Some of these are rather cynical, for those "qui nugis
applaudunt."

Professor Haskins did not venture to pass judgment on the quality of William's Greek. It does not take long, however, to realize that it is a caricature
of the language of Homer. William's ignorance of Greek syntax and orthography appears to have been abysmal. Although he could have known the
Greek alphabet from Isidore of Seville, or even Eberhard, not a single Greek
letter appears in his text. He seems to have been unaware that the Greek
alphabet lacked some of the letters of the Latin, while the Latin lacked some
of those of the Greek. A few of his words, such as *saba, sada, sale*, and *rama*
are Hebrew, but William apparently took them to be Greek.[53] Most of the
words he uses as examples are in fact of genuine Greek origin, but they have
been badly mangled in transition. Some, which I have failed to find either
in Eberhard or Hugutio, have a deceptively Greek ring to them. Thus, William cites *amphisis* ("puer cuius pater vel mater ignoratur, sed latine dicitur
inveticus"); *polisamphia* ("processio facta circum civitatem"); *oenonemus*
("ille qui scit iudicare utrum vinum sit bonum vel malum"). None of these
words can be found in any Greek lexicon, ancient, medieval, or modern.
His *kiriarcha* ("ecclesia que dicitur casa domini"), however, appears in almost
identical words in a dictionary of medieval Greek.[54] William's *kiriasta* ("stab-
ulum porcorum") is not in this dictionary, but one of modern Greek does
give Χοιροστάσιον for pigsty.[55]

One wonders whether William may not at some time have listened to ver-
nacular Greek being spoken. Suspicion of this is arroused by two clumsy
attempts to quote Greek. Commenting on *dochi* (voluntas), he tells us, "Greci
dicunt *doxa en rama theos euphistius re. en. ge. salon entropiem dochi*, ubi
nos dicimus, gloria in excelsis deo et in terra pax hominibus bone voluntatis."[56]
It is difficult to believe that William found this bizarre version of Luke 2.14,
in a Greek New Testament. *Rama* and *salon* are not even Greek! It is more

---

[53] *Brito metricus* (n 6 above) 3-8, seeks to distinguish between Hebrew and Greek words
frequently confused, but does not cite any of these.

[54] E. A. Sophocles, *Greek lexicon of the Roman and Byzantine periods from B. C. 146 to
A. D. 1100* (Boston 1870) 698: "τὸ κυριακόν, the Lord's house, kirk, church . . . ἡ κυριακή,
in the same sense."

[55] *Dury's modern English-Greek and Greek-English Desk Dictionary* (New York 1964)
742: "χοιροστάσιον, χοιροτροφεῖον, τό, pigsty."

[56] This is as given in *P* 37rb. The italics, of course, are mine. The dots after *re, en*, and
ge probably represent letters indecipherable to the copyist. *W* 7v has: "greci dicunt *doxis rama
theos. empsulis Re ne Ge salos antropis eudochi*, ubi nos dicimus. . . ." In *R* 89r it is: "greci
dicunt, *doxa rama theos re en ge. salos antropis eudochi*, ubi nos dicimus. . . ." A modern
Greek New Testament gives the wording as follows: "Δόξα ἐν ὑψίστοις θεῷ καὶ ἐπὶ γῆς
εἰρήνη ἐν ἀνθρώποις εὐδοκίας."

probable that he was attempting to reproduce from memory words he had heard spoken at some time. Where memory slipped he inserted *rama* and *salon*, assuming that they were Greek. Still more puzzling is William's quotation of a Greek proverb on the dangers of wine drinking. "Item *nectem*," he writes, "id est venit, quod patet in hoc exemplo a grecis sumpto, sic, *apos calo crasim nectem chaos pros cephalim*, quod est dictum quia de bono vino venit malum ad caput."[57] This appears to be a badly mangled rendering of a genuine Greek proverb, picked up, perhaps, in some tavern. Yet William fails to betray the source of this "Greek." He could have heard it in France from the lips of crusaders or pilgrims returning from the east. There is, however, one tantalizing hint that he himself may have been in Italy, where the chances for hearing spoken Greek were more numerous than in his native land.[58]

Unfortunately the *Differentie* reveals little about the personality or life of its author. Modern writers have persisted in styling him William "of Corbeil." Yet it is questionable whether William was born in or lived at a place named *Corbeil*. Each of the three manuscripts spells the place name differently. *P* has *Corborensis*, *W Corbonensis*, while *R* permits a choice between *Corballensis* and *Corbellensis*. Either of these might be the French Corbeil. Yet *R* is the latest of the three manuscripts, and its scribe was the most careless in his spelling. From *P*, the oldest manuscript, one might judge the place name to be *Corberon*; from *W*, *Corbon*. There are five Corberons in France, the largest near Beaune in Burgundy, and two Corbons, both of them insignificant Norman villages.[59] The age of *P* and the fact that William displays throughout his treatise great familiarity with many aspects of the production of wine lead me to suspect that Corberon, rather than Corbon or Corbeil, is the correct place name.

It can be safely assumed that William was a "clerk." He demonstrates throughout great respect for the clergy. His Latin is adequate but lacking in literary grace. One feels that his education was mediocre. He displays little acquaintance with the Latin classics. Ovid is the only poet from whom

---

[57] This is as in *W* 14r. *R* 98v has: "Item nectem, id est venit, quod patet in exemplo hoc a grecis sumpto sic, *apo calo crassim nectem cacos pro chephalim*, quod est dictu de vino venit malum apud caput." *P*, breaking off in the letter *G*, lacks the passage.

[58] Like the lexicographers, William illustrates the use of *ancho* (Greek ἀγκών) by the name of the town of Ancona: "Unde anchona, bonus portus est in illa villa." Then he adds: "unde, unus deus, una roma, unus portus est anchona." This is as given in *W* 2r. *P* 33rb has: "unde, unus [word left out], una roma, unus est anchona portus." *R*, the latest manuscript, lacks the passage. This is an Italian proverb that William might have heard in Ancona itself. See H. Walther, *Proverbia sententiaeque latinitatis medii aevi*, 6 vols. (Göttingen 1963-1969) 5.489 (No. 32245).

[59] P. Joanne, *Dictionnaire géographique et administratif de la France*, 7 vols. (Paris 1890-1905) 2.1059, 1061.

he quotes directly.[60] A verse or two from Juvenal is obviously taken from Hugutio.[61] He refers to several standard texts used in the schools, the *Isagoge* of Porphyry, the *Disticha* of Cato, the *Topica* of Aristotle, but his interest here is in the titles rather than in the contents. He does sprinkle fairly liberally through his text allusions to figures from classical mythology, Hercules, Jason, Tiresias, the harpies, and the like. Unless we blame the scribes, William makes some peculiar blunders. Thus, he tells us that Ulysses spent ten years at sea and ten at Rome; Seneca was the master of Venus![62] Despite these deficiencies, William was a *magister*. Gilbert was his disciple.

William had high hopes for his *Differentie*. In his dedication he fervently prays God to deem it worthy of perpetuation.[63] In one sense his prayer was answered, for the treatise survives in our three manuscripts. The extent of its use by medieval writers is difficult to ascertain. By its very nature it would have been of service to a very small group of lexicographers, grammarians, and schoolboys. There is no convincing evidence that it was utilized by the lexicographers. As noted, it is improbable that Walter of Ascoli's "Guillelmus Continensis" was our William.[64] I have not seen Brito's *Expositiones difficiliorum verborum de biblia*, but the *Brito metricus*, written after this lexicon, is a reliable index to Brito's Greek vocabulary and its sources.[65] Although, as noted, parallels with the *Differentie* are many, I find none that can not be explained by common sources such as Isidore of Seville and Hugutio. This is equally true of John of Genoa's *Catholicon*, which has been available to me in an early printed edition.[66]

One would expect William's treatise to have made its greatest appeal to grammarians teaching *ethimologia*. It provides a handy and natural complement to Eberhard's *De nominibus exortis a greco*. While Eberhard tersely lists his Greek words, William analyzes them in considerable detail. In so doing he makes available in abbreviated form the etymological labors of Hugutio. To prove that the *Differentie* served this purpose would require careful examination of the glosses in the many manuscripts of the *Grecismus*.

---

[60] In his dedication he quotes without acknowledgment, *Amores*, 1.8.113-114. Later (*W* 17r; *R* 103v), citing Ovid by name, he quotes *Heroides* 2.131.

[61] *Satires* 3.157; 5.72.

[62] Thus in both *W* and *R*. *P* does not continue this far. In fairness to William it should be noted that a scribe could very easily have mistaken *neronis* for *veneris*. It is not as easy to see how Rome could have been taken for Troy.

[63] Haskins (n. 19 above) 419.

[64] See p. 303 above.

[65] In "Guillelmus Brito and his works," *The Library Chronicle* (University of Pennsylvania) 32 (1966) 1-17, Professor Lloyd Daly noted that he and Mrs. Daly are engaged in preparing a modern edition of Brito's lexicon. I should like to express here my gratitude to Professor Daly for his courtesy in answering various questions I have asked him.

[66] Printed about 1470 at Strasburg by Adolph Rusch of Ingweilen. Now in the Treasure Room of Baker Library at Dartmouth College.

I have had access to those published by Wrobel only. In them many of the explanations of terms are identical or nearly identical to those given by the *Differentie*. Although in most cases Hugutio was probably a direct source, in some the source appears to have been Hugutio as modified by William.[67] In a gloss on the word *tomos* the glossator seems to have used the *Differentie* dircctly, for Hugutio does not give his example of the use of the term, but William does.[68] Medieval schoolmasters would have been negligent indeed had they failed to recognize the practical utility of William's manual in teaching the *Grecismus*.

That it had a wider utility is probable. Thus it was listed among the books he had studied and appreciated by Richard de Bazoques, a Norman clerk of the time of the Great Schism.[69] Further evidence is provided by certain manuscripts of John of Garland's *Cornutus* or *Distigium*, a metrical work to which reference has already been made. This consisted originally of 21 almost unintelligible distichs. In a few extant manuscripts, however, a later versifier has added two distichs to the original text. In a version of the *Cornutus* published in 1481, the second of these distichs reads as follows:[70]

> Kyria chere geram cuius philantropos est bar,
> Per te doxa theos necten et uranicis ymas.

Fortunately John Drolshagen, the schoolmaster of Zwolle, who edited and commented on these distichs has translated for us. *Kyria*, he says, is the Virgin, *chere* is Latin *salve*, *geram* is *sacra*, *philantropos* is Christ, *bar* is *filius*, *necten* "in Greco est venire Latine," and *ymas* is nobis. Allen puts the distich into English as follows:

---

[67] For example:

Wrobel (n. 4 above) 38	*Differentie*
Gloss to *Grec.* 8.158: Pergama moenia troiana dicitur a pir quod est ignis et gamma mulier, quia per ignem et mulierem fuerunt combusta.	*P* fol. 38vb (*W* 10r; *R* 92v): Unde pergama, menia troiana, a gamos mulier et pyr ignis quia per ignem et mulierem destructa fuerunt.

The ultimate source here was probably Hugutio, fol. 120va: "pergama. orum. edificia troiana. que per ignem et mulierem destructa." Note that Wrobel's gloss and William agree in substituting *menia* for *edificia* in Hugutio.

[68] Thus:

Wrobel 314	*Differentie*
Gloss on *Grec.* 8.318: homo de getica regione dicta a tomos, divisio, quia ibi Medea fratrem suum membratim dilaceravit.	*W* fol. 18r; *R* 104v: thomis dicitur alia ratione quia ibi divisit asserim fratrem suum membratim Medea illa domina.
Hugutio discusses *tomos* on fol. 289vb.	

[69] See J. Bignami-Odier and A. Vernet, "Les livres de Richard de Bazoques," *Bibliothèque de l'École des chartes* 110 (1952) 133. I am much indebted to Professor Richard H. Rouse for this reference to the *Differentie*.

> Hail, sacred queen, whose son is the lover of men;
> through thee divine and heavenly glory comes to us.

The striking feature of the distich is the bizarre Greek. It is significant that except for *philantropos* and *uranicis* all of the Greek words occur in the *Differentie*. To be sure, William does not have *Kyrie*, but he does have *Kyrios*. *Bar* is not Greek, but William assumed that it was, as did the author of the distich. Most interesting is the presence here of *necten* (venire),[71] and *ymas* (nobis).[72] I have found neither of these outside the *Differentie*. This suggests to me that the author of the distich, whoever he may have been, was acquainted with William's treatise.

The emphasis placed by medieval schoolmasters on the mangled Greek of Eberhard, Hugutio, and William is difficult to explain.[73] It may in part have been the result of the increasing contacts of the West with the Byzantine Greeks. It may in part have been the product of the analytical habit of mind produced by the popularity of dialectic. While theologians, philosophers, and scientists analyzed ideas and theories, the grammarians analyzed words. Certainly the Greek of the schools does not indicate an interest in Greek as a vehicle of thought or literature. On the contrary, Eberhard, Hugutio, and William were primarily interested in the Latin language, convinced that mastery of that tongue required familiarity with the Greek roots from which its vocabulary had evolved. Unfortunately they pursued their goals with greater zeal and imagination than knowledge of philological principles. Consequently, later generations have found the products of their etymological ventures fantastic. In the light of the classical Greek literature recovered in the Renaissance, this modern verdict is entirely justified. Yet the historian in attempting to understand the intellectual climate of late medieval Europe can no more ignore *ethimologia* with its Pseudo-Greek than he can disregard

---

[70] I take the distich from P. S. Allen, *The Age of Erasmus* (Oxford 1914) 38f. Habel's text (n. 5 above, 28) varies slightly.

[71] This is apparently the *nectem* (venit) of William's Greek proverb. Commenting on the word, Drolshagen remarks, "unde dicit Pristianus in primo minoris, antropos nectin." According to H. Keil, *Grammatici latini* (Leipzig 1855-1880) 3.124, Priscian says, ἄνθρωπος ἦλθεν. Allen (n. 70 above) was understandably perplexed by *necten*. I suspect that it is a corruption of the third person singular, present tense, of the deponent νέεσθαι, which is frequently used with πρός, as it is in William's proverb.

[72] The word occurs in W fol. 11v-12r in a somewhat garbled analysis of *kirieleison*: "unde kirieleison quod interpretatur, domine miserere omnem ymas nostrum, quia kirios est deus, eleys, miserere, on, omnem, ymas, nostrum." R fol. 95v has simply: "kyrieleison quod interpretatur, domine miserere nobis, quia dicitur a kyrios, domine, et eleis, quod est miserere."

[73] Bernhard Bischoff has well described this Pseudo-Greek in "The Study of Foreign Languages in the Middle Ages," *Speculum* 36 (1961) 215. The article has been reprinted in his *Mittelalterliche Studien* (n. 23 above) 2.227-245.

astrology and alchemy. Rightly or wrongly most educated men were exposed to it and considered it both "relevant" and important.

This is puzzling because acquaintance with genuine Greek, although rare in the West, was by no means entirely lacking. During the twelfth and thirteenth centuries Westerners were able to make numerous translations of Greek theological, philosophical, and scientific works.[74] Sophisticated and critical minds must have been conscious of the errors of the grammarians. French and Italian writers do not appear to have been offended by this Pseudo-Greek.[75] In England, however, Robert Grosseteste and Roger Bacon clearly were and sought to revive the genuine Greek.[76] Bacon's strictures on Eberhard, Hugutio, and Brito are well known.[77] He nowhere mentions William "of Corbeil," but his reaction to the *Differentie* can be easily imagined. Unfortunately the efforts of Grosseteste and Bacon proved premature. Ironically the Pseudo-Greek of the *Differentie* continued to flourish, as Drolshagen's edition of the *Cornutus* in 1481 testifies. It was only eradicated by the Humanists in the sixteenth century.

Department of History
Dartmouth College
Hanover, New Hampshire, U.S.A.

[74] On twelfth-century translators from Greek to Latin, see Haskins (n. 17 above) chap. 8. The leading thirteenth-century translator from Greek was William of Moerbeke. Others were Bartholomew of Messina, John of Basingstoke, and Robert Grosseteste. See G. Sarton, *Introduction to the History of Science* (Baltimore 1927-48) 2.2.567-569; 829-831.

[75] John of Garland was English, although he spent most of his life in France. He was highly critical of Eberhard of Bethune and Alexander of Villedieu. See Paetow (n. 5 above) 103.

[76] On Greek in England, see R. Weiss, "The Study of Greek in England during the Fourteenth Century," *Rinascimento* 2 (1951) 209-239. Grosseteste's competence as a Greek scholar is discussed by D. A. Callus, "The Contribution to the Study of the Fathers made by the Thirteenth-century Oxford Schools," *Journal of Ecclesiastical History* 5 (1954) 139-148, and in *Robert Grosseteste Scholar and Bishop, Essays in Commemoration of the Seventh Centenary of his Death*, ed. D. A. Callus (Oxford 1955) chap. 1, esp. 33ff.

[77] *Compendium studii philosophiae*, ed. J. S. Brewer, in *Fr. Rogeri Bacon opera quaedam hactenus inedita*, Rolls Series 15 (London 1859) 1.466ff. Bacon has high praise for John of Garland's Greek. If the *Cornutus* is an authentic specimen, one wonders whether his eulogy is justified.

URBAN DEVELOPMENT AND THE "CURA MONIALIUM" IN THIRTEENTH-CENTURY GERMANY

●

by John B. Freed

I

According to a widely-accepted analysis of the religious currents of the twelfth and thirteenth centuries, first propounded in Joseph Greven's *Die Anfänge der Beginen*[1] and subsequently elaborated in Herbert Grundmann's *Religiöse Bewegungen im Mittelalter*,[2] a succession of male orders struggled with the task of providing for the spiritual welfare and discipline of large numbers of devout women in northern Europe who were determined to lead lives of evangelical perfection. The Cistercians are said to have assumed the *cura monialium* after the Premonstratensians in 1198 obtained papal confirmation of their decision not to receive any additional women into their fellowship. In 1228 the Cistercian General Chapter, in turn disturbed by the disruption of monastic discipline and contemplation arising from the excessive involvement of the monks with the care of nuns, decreed: "No nunnery of any sort is to be constructed under the name or under the jurisdiction of our order. If, however, a nunnery which has not yet been incorporated in our order or which may be constructed, wishes to copy our institutions, we do not prohibit it; but we will not receive the care of those nuns nor will we assume

[1] Joseph Greven, *Die Anfänge der Beginen*, Vorreformationsgeschichtliche Forschungen 8 (Münster 1912). I wish to thank Professor Joseph R. Strayer of Princeton and my colleagues, Lawrence Walker and Roy Austensen, for their criticism and advice. Needless to say, all errors are my own.

[2] Herbert Grundmann, *Religiöse Bewegungen im Mittelalter*, ed. 2 (Darmstadt 1961) pp. 170-354. The Greven-Grundmann analysis provides the theoretical framework for such diverse studies as: Ernest W. McDonnell, *The Beguines and Beghards in Medieval Culture* (New Brunswick 1954); Eva Gertrud Neumann, *Rheinisches Beginen- und Begardenwesen: Ein mainzer Beitrag zur religiösen Bewegung am Rhein*, in Mainzer Abhandlungen zur mittleren und neuren Geschichte 4 (Meisenheim am Glan 1960); Dayton Phillips, *Beguines in Medieval Strasburg* (sic): *A Study of the Social Aspects of Beguine Life* (Palo Alto 1941); and Simone Roisin, "L'efflorescence cistercienne et le courant féminin de piété au xiiie siècle," *Revue d'histoire ecclésiastique* 39 (1943) 342-378.

the duty of visitation."[3] The Cistercians thus served notice that they were limiting their responsibilities to previously incorporated nunneries and that they would not provide in the future spiritual guidance to any additional groups of women. Instead of forcing the Cistercians to rescind their decree, which threatened to deprive numerous women in northern Europe of spiritual supervision, the papacy, the women themselves, and their patrons turned to the recently founded and rapidly expanding mendicant orders, whose own life style and ideals more closely resembled the women's aspirations than had been the case with the more traditionally oriented Premonstratensians and Cistercians. In spite of considerable opposition to the adoption of the *cura monialium* within both the Dominican and Franciscan orders, there were by the beginning of the fourteenth century in Germany alone seventy-four Dominican nunneries and supposedly forty houses of Clarisses.[4] Nevertheless, the number of women who wished to follow the poor Christ far exceeded the available places in the numerous Cistercian and mendicant nunneries; those women who were unable to enter a cloister adopted instead the semireligious status of beguines, many of whom were likewise under the care and supervision of the friars.

This paper will try to show that the Dominicans and Franciscans did not, as Greven and Grundmann contended, replace the Cistercians in the exercise of the *cura monialium* on account of the 1228 decree which remained in fact unheeded; but rather that the Cistercians and mendicant orders labored at the same time among the devout women of northern Europe, but in distinctly different areas. The real problem, therefore, is to explain the actual geographic distribution of the German Cistercian and mendicant nunneries. Table 1[5] compares the number of Cistercian nunneries founded before and after the 1228 decision in the Rhine Valley and in the dioceses of Liège and Cambrai with the number of mendicant nunneries established in the same bishoprics by 1273. The year 1273, the end of the Interregnum, has been

---

[3] *Statuta capitulorum generalium ordinis cisterciensis ad anno 1116 ad annum 1786*, ed. Josephus-Maria Canivez, in Bibliothèque de la Revue d'histoire ecclésiastique 10 (Louvain 1934) 2.68. The translation is my own.

[4] Grundmann (n. 2 above) 313-314. As Grundmann points out (313 n. 260) only twenty-five of the forty houses of Clarisses allegedly in existence can actually be proven to have existed.

[5] The statistics in Table One are derived from Joseph-Marie Canivez, *L'ordre de Cîteaux en Belgique des origines (1132) au XXᵉ siècle* (Forges lez-Chimay, Belgium 1926); Albert Hauck, *Kirchengeschichte Deutschlands*, ed. 5 (Leipzig 1925) 4.975-1030; Blasius Huemer, "Verzeichnis der deutschen Cisterzienserinnenklöster," *Studien und Mitteilungen zur Geschichte des Benediktiner-Ordens und seiner Zweige* n.s. 6 (1916) 1-47; Edmund Wauer. *Entstehung und Ausbreitung des Klarissenordens besonders in den deutschen Minoritenprovinzen* (Leipzig 1906) chaps. 7, 9; and Hieronymus Wilms, *Das älteste Verzeichnis der deutschen Dominikanerinnenklöster*, in Quellen und Forschungen zur Geschichte des Dominikanerordens in Deutschland (QFGDD) (Leipzig 1928).

selected as a convenient terminal date since the friars had been active in northern Europe by the time Rudolph of Habsburg's accession for approximately half a century.

TABLE 1

Founding of Cistercian and Mendicant Nunneries

Diocese	Cistercians		Dominicans	Clarisses
	Before 1228	1229-1273	Before 1273	Before 1273
Basel	1	2	4	1
Cambrai	4	8	1	0
Cologne	8	21	2	0
Constance	4	14	14	3 to 6*
Liège	16	14	0	0
Mainz	14	34	0	1
Speyer	0	4	2	0
Strasbourg	1	0	8	1
Trier	4	7	3	1
Utrecht	3	2	0	0
Worms	3	6	0	0

If Greven and Grundmann are correct, it is in the dioceses of Cologne, Liège, and Mainz, where the Cistercians had been most active before 1228 and which would presumably have been most affected by the 1228 decision, that the friars should have received their most enthusiastic reception from women whom the Cistercians had suddenly deprived of the hope of affiliation with their order. Table 1 indicates, however, that only three mendicant nunneries were actually founded in these three bishoprics before 1273. The women in these three dioceses, apparently unperturbed by the 1228 decision, continued to adopt instead the Cistercian rule; sixty-nine Cistercian nunneries were in fact established in the three bishoprics between 1228 and 1273. At the same time there is every indication that the friars very quickly established close contacts with the women of these dioceses. Jordan of Saxony, the second master general of the Dominicans (1222-1237), mentioned, for instance, the great sorrow of the women of Cologne at the death in 1229 of his dearest friend, Prior Henry of Cologne.[6] In spite of this early contact between the Cologne Dominicans and the devout women of that city, the Dominican

---

* See n. 15 below.

[6] Jordan of Saxony, *Libellus de principiis ordinis Praedicatorum*, ed. Heribert Chr. Scheeben, Monumenta ordinis fratrum Praedicatorum historica 16 (Rome 1935) c. 79; and Berthold Altaner, *Die Briefe Jordans von Sachsen, des zweiten Dominikanergenerals (1222-37): Text und Untersuchungen*, QFGDD 20 (Leipzig 1925) letter 44.

nunnery of Saint Gertrude in Cologne was only begun in 1263.[7] Interestingly enough, many of the friars' patrons were also great benefactors of the Cistercian nuns. Guderadis Gir, the widow of Hartmann, who had given the Cologne Dominicans a house before 1232, founded and endowed, for instance, the Cistercian nunnery of Burbach in 1232.[8] To cite another example, Bruno Hardevust, who was the procurator of the Cologne Dominicans in the 1270s converted the ruined collegiate church of Mechtern into a Cistercian nunnery in 1277.[9] It apparently never occurred either to Guderadis or to Bruno to establish instead a Dominican nunnery.

The friars' activity among the women of the lower Rhine Valley and the Low Countries was confined mainly to the care of beguines. There were eventually, for instance, one hundred and sixty-nine houses of beguines in Cologne, most of which were founded between 1275 and 1350.[10] Eleven of these were definitely in existence by 1273. Seven of these eleven houses were situated in the vicinity of the Dominican convent; one was located near the site of the Franciscans' first convent in the district of Saint Severin; and one was located approximately three and one-half blocks from the Franciscan friary in the district of Saint Columba.[11] The physical proximity of these houses to the mendicant convents suggests by itself that the friars were closely associated with the beguines. Documentary evidence bears this out. Archbishop Conrad at some unspecified time during his episcopate (1238-1261) entrusted the Dominicans with the supervision of the Cologne beguines.[12] The founders of such houses often specifically placed their foundations under the care of the friars, again most frequently the Dominicans.[13] The evidence seems to indicate that in these three key bishoprics, contrary to Greven's and Grundmann's thesis, the 1228 decision did not stop the establishment of additional Cistercian nunneries, the mendicants did not replace the Cistercians in the exercise of the *cura monialium*, but the friars, particularly the Dominicans, did assume the responsibility of providing for the large numbers of beguines.

Rather, it was in southwestern Germany, particularly in the dioceses of Basel, Constance, and Strasbourg, that the friars were active not merely

[7] *Die Regesten der Erzbischöfe von Köln im Mittelalter*, ed. Richard Knipping, Publikationen der Gesellschaft für rheinische Geschichtskunde 21 (Bonn 1909-1913) 3, Doc. 2266.

[8] Gabriel M. Löhr, *Beiträge zur Geschichte des kölner Dominikanerklosters im Mittelalter*, QFGDD 16-17 (Leipzig 1922) Doc. 9; and Luise von Winterfeld, *Handel, Kapital und Patriziat in Köln bis 1400*, Pfingstblätter des hansischen Geschichtsvereins 16 (1925) 44.

[9] Löhr, Docs. 48, 54; and *Quellen zur Geschichte der Stadt Köln*, eds. Leonard Ennen and Gottfried Eckertz (Cologne 1867) 3, Doc. 149.

[10] Johannes Asen, "Die Beguinen in Köln," *Annalen des historischen Vereins für den Niederrhein* 111 (1927) 94.

[11] Hermann Keussen, *Topographie der Stadt Köln im Mittelalter* (Bonn 1910) 1.150*ff.

[12] *Die Regesten* (n. 7 above) Doc. 2161.

[13] Löhr (n. 8 above) Docs. 18, 21, 24, 39, and 40.

in caring for beguines, but also in actually establishing nunneries. The Dominicans had founded, for instance, in sharp contrast to the situation in Cologne, five nunneries in the city and immediate vicinity of Strasbourg by 1237, that is, within thirteen years of their arrival in that city.[14] It would hardly be accurate to say, however, that the Dominicans and Franciscans replaced the Cistercians in these bishoprics since the Cistercians themselves had founded only six nunneries in these dioceses before 1228. It would in fact be more accurate to state that the Cistercians and the friars were rivals in the bishopric of Constance, the only diocese in which there were numerous Cistercian and mendicant nunneries, most of which were established between 1228 and 1273. It is possible to conclude, therefore, that the area north of the Main was a region of Cistercian activity, while the region south of the Main was an area of mendicant endeavor. Finally, table 1 points out one other interesting fact. In spite of the supposed need of devout women for spiritual guidance after the Cistercians' alleged abandonment of the *cura monialium*, at most only ten, and more probably seven,[15] convents of Clarisses had been founded in eleven of the most populated and most religiously active dioceses in northern Europe after half a century of Franciscan labor.

This examination of the geographical distribution of the Cistercian and mendicant nunneries in the Rhine Valley and in imperial Belgium raises several questions. Most important, why is there such a distinct pattern in the distribution of the mendicant and Cistercian nunneries; why were the Cistercian nunneries primarily located north of the Main and the mendicant cloisters south of the Main? This is all the more intriguing since it is clear that the friars had ample contacts with the beguines, presumably likely candidates for claustration, and with possible founders of nunneries in the lower Rhine Valley and the Low Countries. Secondly, is the distribution of the Cistercian and mendicant nunneries in any way related to the 1228 decision; indeed what was the effect, if any, of that decision? Finally, if there really was such an enormous need for the religious to assume the *cura monialium*, as Greven and Grundmann maintained and the large number of Cistercian and Dominican nuns and beguines seems to bear out, why did the Franciscans not play a larger role in providing for that need?

II

The answers to these questions must be sought in the religious and social forces that spawned the great outburst of feminine piety in the twelfth and

[14] *Les Registres de Grégoire IX*, ed. Lucien Auvray (Paris 1907) 2, Doc. 3983.

[15] There is considerable doubt whether the nunneries of the Clarisses located in Esslingen and Freiburg im Breisgau were actually in existence by 1273 as some sources allege. Furthermore, there is no proof that a convent located in Reutlingen, which supposedly accepted the rule of Saint Clare in 1267, ever existed.

thirteenth centuries.[16] The desire to lead a life of evangelical perfection was one of the unforeseen byproducts of the investiture conflict, the revolutionary attempt by the Gregorians to restructure earthly society in accordance with their vision of a properly organized Christian world. They wished to free the Church from lay control, to subordinate the laity to the clergy, to strip kings of their sacramental character, and to establish the primacy of the pope in fact as well as in canonical theory. If their program was carried out, the Gregorians were convinced righteousness would reign on earth.[17] When Gregory VII tried to implement this revolutionary plan, he not only aroused bitter opposition, which in the end thwarted the complete realization of the Gregorians' original aspirations, but also ignited an outburst of religious fervor. The attempt to establish a more perfect Christian society on earth naturally made men think more seriously about what it meant to be a Christian. Most individuals naturally concluded, as medieval Christians always had, that the highest form of the Christian life was monastic devotion. Several new orders, most notably the Premonstratensians and the Cistercians, were born during the investiture conflict. But some clerics, like Saint Norbert, though not his followers, slowly perceived that Christ and the Apostles had not abandoned the world as the monks did, but rather had lived in the very midst of earthly society. The religious aspirations of such individuals could not be satisfied by the observance of a monastic rule, but only by the imitation of Christ's and the Apostles' earthly life, particularly their abject poverty

[16] The concentration of mendicant nunneries in southwestern Germany has not gone completely unnoticed. Wauer (n. 5 above) 114 attributed the concentration of the Clarisses in the province of Strasbourg, which encompassed southwestern Germany, to the division of the Franciscan province of the Rhine in 1239 into the separate provinces of Strasbourg and Cologne. The Clarisses, who had only begun their first German cloister in Ulm/Söfflingen in the future province of Strasbourg in 1237, thus lacked sufficient time to expand northward before the new provincial boundary blocked their further growth. There are several problems with Wauer's explanation. First of all, Hugolinus Lippens, "Circa divisionem Provinciae Rheni disquisito (1246-1264)," *Archivum franciscanum historicum* 48 (1955) 217-224, points out that the province of the Rhine was in existence until at least 1246. Since the first definite evidence for the existence of the two provinces appears in 1249 (*Les Registres d'Innocent IV*), ed. Élie Berger [Paris 1887] 2, Doc. 4265), it seems most probable that the 1247 general chapter of Lyons subdivided the province of the Rhine. This would have given the Clarisses a decade to spread northward from Ulm/Söfflingen. Second, it is hard to believe that an essentially artificial, administrative boundary, whenever established, could by itself have been such an insurmountable barrier to the spread of the Clarisses in a period of extreme religious enthusiasm. Most important, Wauer failed to observe that the German Dominican nunneries, which formed part of a single Dominican province throughout the thirteenth century, were likewise concentrated in the upper Rhine Valley. Wauer's explanation for the concentration of the Clarisses in southwestern Germany must, therefore, be rejected.

[17] Norman F. Cantor, *Church, Kingship, and Lay Investiture in England 1089-1135* (Princeton 1958) 6-9.

and their public preaching. The Gospels thus replaced the monastic rule as the standard for measuring the Christian life.[18] The Gregorian program for restructuring earthly society was thus subtly transformed into a summons to reshape men's lives in accordance with the life and commands of Christ.

This new religious ideal appealed most of all to the wealthier and more privileged members of medieval society.[19] The leaders in this search for evangelical perfection, men and women like Waldo of Lyons, Saints Dominic and Francis, Saints Clare and Mary of Oignies, were, as one might expect in medieval society, by birth members of the upper classes. More significantly, their ordinary followers also seem to have been recruited from the wealthier strata of medieval society. Medieval sources, at least those favorably inclined to the ideal of evangelical perfection, tend to portray the members of such movements as wealthy and well-born individuals who for the love of God gave up the false comforts of this world. Jacques de Vitry, the confessor of Mary of Oignies and a future cardinal, in 1213 described the devout women of Brabant in these words:

> You have seen (and you have rejoiced) in the gardens of the lilies of the Lord great crowds of holy women in diverse places, who despising fleshly charms for Christ, and who likewise scorning the riches of this world for love of the heavenly kingdom, cleaving in poverty and humility to their divine husband, are seeking by the labor of their hands their meager nourishment although their relatives abound in great wealth. They, nevertheless, forgetting their people and the home of their father, preferred to endure indigence and poverty than to abound in wealth wrongly acquired or to stay with danger among the proud men of this world.[20]

While it is generally agreed that Cistercian and mendicant nuns belonged, as Jacques de Vitry observed, to the upper strata of medieval society, it is sometimes suggested that there was, nevertheless, a distinct difference in the social composition of the Cistercian and mendicant nunneries. The Cistercian nunneries are said to have recruited primarily from the ranks of the lower nobility, that is the ministerial class, whereas the mendicant cloisters were filled with women of urban origin.[21] Several studies of the social composition of individual Cistercian and mendicant houses, based primarily on evidence taken from the late thirteenth and fourteenth and fifteenth centuries,

---

[18] Grundmann (n. 2 above) 507-508.

[19] *Ibid.* 157-169.

[20] *Vita B. Mariae Ogniacensis*, in AS Jun. 4.636. The translation is my own.

[21] Ernst G. Krenig, "Mittelalterliche Frauenklöster nach den Konstitutionen von Cîteaux unter besonderer Berücksichtigung fränkischer Nonnenkonvente," *Analecta sacri ordinis cisterciensis* 10 (1954) 10-14, 48-49.

seem to confirm this.[22] If the same social exclusiveness prevailed in fact throughout the thirteenth century, it would further complicate the question raised by the geographical distribution of the nunneries. It would then be necessary to explain not only the distribution of the nunneries, but also why north of the Main women of ministerial origin were primarily attracted to the pursuit of evangelical perfection, whereas in the upper Rhine Valley the new ideal appealed mainly to the urban classes. Did, however, the same social snobbery exist in the Cistercian and mendicant nunneries in the formative period of the thirteenth century, when the cloisters were presumably animated by their original religious fervor and were not yet as richly endowed?

Unfortunately, it is very difficult to ascertain the social origins of individual nuns in the thirteenth century. The evidence consists chiefly of random references to individual nuns in the fragmentary extant property deeds of individual nunneries. The published documents and chronicles of Cistercian and mendicant nunneries located in the dioceses of Basel, Cambrai, Cologne, Constance, Liège, Mainz, Speyer, Strasbourg, Trier, Utrecht, and Worms have been culled for such references. When the document itself does not indicate in some way the social status of the nun, an attempt has been made for the purposes of this research to discover the social origins of the family whose surname the nun bore, in the neighborhood of the nunnery. The nun is then arbitrarily assumed to have belonged to that family. While the possibilities of individual mistaken identification are enormous, table 2 is sufficiently accurate to provide, I believe, a rough idea of the social composition of the Cistercian and mendicant nunneries in the thirteenth century.

Table 2 [23] divides into five social groups (nobles, ministerials, knights, patricians, and burghers) the women who according to these documents entered Cistercian and mendicant nunneries before 1273 in these eleven dioceses. Only those women whose ancestors are definitely known to have belonged to the old free nobility have been classified as noble. The designation ministerial has been reserved for those nuns whose families are either specifically called ministerial in a document or whose families held a household office of a noble or prelate, such as the stewardship. Nuns whose families

---

[22] See, for instance, Klaus Conrad, *Die Geschichte des Dominikanerinnenklosters in Lambrecht*, in Heidelberger Veröffentlichungen zur Landesgeschichte und Landeskunde 5 (Heidelberg 1960) 77-92; Johannes Linneborn, "Die westfälischen Klöster des Cistercienserordens bis zum 15. Jahrh.," *Festgabe, enthaltend vornehmlich vorreformationsgeschichtliche Forschungen, Heinrich Finke* (Münster 1904) 335-337; Gabriel M. Löhr, "Das Necrologium des Dominikanerinnenklosters St. Gertrud in Köln," *Annalen des historischen Vereins für den Niederrhein* 110 (1927), 87-89; and Volquart Pauls, "Das Klosterrecht der schleswig-holsteinischen Ritterschaft, seine Entstehung, Entwicklung und rechtliche Bedeutung," *Zeitschrift der Gesellschaft für schleswig-holsteinische Geschichte* 73 (1949) 87-118.

[23] The appendix contains a list of the chronicles, collections of sources, and monographs that were used in compiling table 2.

held municipal office in the thirteenth century or whose relatives are called both knights and burghers of a city have been labeled patricians; all other women of urban origin have been designated burghers. Finally the term knight, which came into increasing vogue in the thirteenth century, has been applied to all women whose male relatives are called knights, but who cannot more specifically be categorized as nobles, ministerials, or patricians, all of whom could have been and were described in thirteenth-century documents as knights.

TABLE 2

Social Status Among Nuns

	Nobles	Ministerials	Knights	Patricians	Burghers	Total
Cistercians	23	27	22	16	47	135
Dominicans	6	13	7	4	9	39
Clarisses	3	7	1	0	0	11
Total	32	47	30	20	56	185

The fragmentary and accidental nature of the original evidence makes it impossible to draw any definitive conclusions from table 2, but certain tentative observations can at least be ventured. Probably it was exceptional for a woman of the old free nobility to join either a Cistercian or mendicant nunnery. Unless she was inspired by a fervent desire to lead a life of evangelical perfection, it is more likely that she would have entered a Benedictine nunnery or a foundation of secular canonesses, which were still in large part the exclusive preserve of her social class.[24] The presence of thirty-two women of this class in table 2 does not invalidate this conclusion if it is remembered that these women and their families had a far better chance to achieve a position of local prominence and thus to be mentioned in surviving documents than their less well-born sisters. No less than eleven of these noble-born women, one third of the women classified as nobles, are definitely known, for instance, to have served as the abbess or prioress of their house. Table 2 suggests rather that most of the nuns came from either the ministerial class or urban families of at least some means. The women of burgher origin are, after all, usually mentioned in property transactions. Moreover, it seems likely that most of the women who have been classified as belonging to the knightly class came either from a ministerial or patrician background since it was ministerial or patrician families who would have had the most com-

[24] For further information about the social origins of Benedictine nuns and secular canonesses, see Aloys Schulte, *Der Adel und die deutsche Kirche im Mittelalter*: *Studien zur Sozial-, Rechts- und Kirchengeschichte*, ed. 3 (Darmstadt 1958).

pelling reasons to conceal their nonnoble origins under the more glamorous term, *knight*. The evidence strongly suggests therefore that both the Cistercians and the Dominicans—the evidence for the Clarisses is too inconclusive —recruited in the thirteenth century from the same layers of society: the lower nobility, that is the ministerial class, and at least moderately wealthy urban families. Grundmann has described the search for evangelical perfection, therefore, as "eine Reaktion gegen den Reichtum und gegen die wirtschaftliche-kulturelle Entwicklung nicht von aussen her, von den dadurch Geschädigten, sondern aus den eigenen Kreisen derer, die an dieser Entwicklung zum Reichtum und irdischen Wohlergehen beteiligt sind."[25]

This religious reaction against the changes created in medieval society by several centuries of growing economic prosperity was strongest in the most economically-advanced and urbanized areas in Europe: Lombardy, southern France, Flanders-Brabant, and the lower Rhine Valley.[26] This does not mean that the search for evangelical perfection was born in the towns. The opposite appears in fact to be nearer the truth; the first bearers of the new ideal, like Saint Norbert, were clerics of aristocratic origin. It also does not mean that the desire to lead the apostolic life ever became an exclusively urban ideal. The large number of women of ministerial and noble origin indicated in table 2 argues forcefully against such a conclusion. There were even beguines, who are usually viewed as the most urban of medieval religious phenomenon, in rural communities.[27] It was, however, in the most urbanized areas of Europe that the basic contradiction was most acutely felt between the religious ideal set forth in the Gospels and the growing wealth of the High Middle Ages, which ultimately affected both the urban and the rural populations. It is also worth mentioning that many ministerial families, who supplied the nunneries with numerous sisters, had close ties to the German towns. As imperial, princely, episcopal, and abbatial officials, the ministerials often resided in the towns and frequently served as administrative officials. Thus the imperial ministerial, Rudolph of Praunheim, whose daughter Adelaide was a Cistercian nun in Thron in the 1260s, was *Schultheiss* of Frankfurt.[28] In fact families of ministerial origin, like the Praunheims, formed part of the urban patriciate in many Alsatian, Swabian, and Franconian cities, as well as in Liège.[29] Under these circumstances it is not very surprising that

[25] Grundmann (n. 2 above) 194.

[26] *Ibid.* 519-524.

[27] Neumann (n. 2 above) 60-71.

[28] *Codex Diplomaticus Nassoicus, Nassauisches Urkundenbuch,* ed. W. Sauer (Wiesbaden 1885-1887) 1, Doc. 783; and Karl Bosl, *Die Reichsministerialität der Salier und Staufer,* in MGH Schriften, 10 (Stuttgart 1950) 302-309.

[29] Philippe Dollinger, "Patriciat noble et patriciat bourgeois à Strasbourg au xive siècle," *Revue d'Alsace* 90 (1950-1951) 52-82; and Henri Pirenne, *Histoire de Belgique* (Brussels 1902) 1.266.

the desire to follow the poor Christ was strongest in the most urbanized areas of Europe.

This correlation between urban development and feminine piety provides the key for explaining the distribution of the German Cistercian and mendicant nunneries. The lower Rhine Valley and Brabant were among the most economically advanced areas in medieval Europe. Brabant, the homeland of Mary of Oignies, was by 1200 a highly urbanized area, at least by medieval standards. The Brabantine towns were the product of the growth of trade in the eleventh century along the rivers that flow through Brabant in a south-north direction; their growth was given a further impetus in the second half of the twelfth century by the development of an east-west overland trade route between the entrepôts of Bruges and Cologne.[30] The large number of Cistercian nunneries that were founded in Brabant and in the lower Rhine Valley in the first decades of the thirteenth century were part, therefore, of the religious reaction that tended to accompany urbanization. The close ties that had been established between the Cistercians, the women of this area, and their patrons were not easily shaken by the 1228 decision, which was simply circumvented. An examination of the minutes of the annual meetings of the Cistercian general chapter reveals that numerous nunneries were incorporated by the general chapter at the request of powerful patrons, whom the order did not wish to antagonize. Individual nunneries north of the Main were incorporated between 1228 and 1273 at the request of such individuals as Popes Gregory IX and Innocent IV, Empress Mary of Brabant, King Conrad IV, Archbishops Conrad and Engelbert II of Cologne, Bishops Otto of Utrecht, Nicholas of Cambrai, Baldwin of Zemgale, and John and Robert of Liège, the Cologne cathedral chapter, Duke Henry II and Duchess Sophia of Brabant, Countesses Margaret of Luxembourg, and Johanna and Margaret of Flanders, Count Arnold of Loos, and Archdeacon Henry of Liège.[31] Since the 1228 decision was a dead letter in the region north of the Main, there was no pressing need for devout women who wished to lead a cloistered life to turn to the mendicant orders. Dominican and Franciscan activity was confined to the care and supervision of beguines.

Rather different conditions prevailed, however, in the upper Rhine Valley. A Colmar Dominican, whose long life spanned most of the thirteenth century, described at the end of his life in the *De rebus alsaticis ineuntis saeculi XIII* his native Alsace, for instance, as an extremely backward area in 1200, which had undergone enormous changes, in the chronicler's opinion for the better, in the intervening century. He specifically mentioned that in 1200 the two most important Alsatian cities, Basel and Strasbourg, had been small, rather

---

[30] Paul Bonenfant, "L'origine des villes brabançonnes et la 'route' de Bruges à Cologne," *Revue belge de philologie et d'histoire* 31 (1953) 399-447.

[31] *Statuta capitulorum generalium ordinis cisterciensis* 2 and 3 (1935) *passim*.

insignificant towns with inadequate fortifications and that such towns as Colmar, Sélestat, Rouffach, Mulhouse, and many others had not existed at all.[32] The Alsatian and Swabian towns were in large part the creation of the Hohenstaufen monarchs, particularly of Frederick II and his ill-fated son Henry (VII) in the first half of the thirteenth century.[33] It is hardly surprising, therefore, that only a handful of Cistercian nunneries had been established in this economically backward region before 1228, which never attained the same level of development as the lower Rhine Valley and the Low Countries. It was only at the time when the friars themselves arrived in southwestern Germany in the 1220s that the upper Rhine Valley started to feel the first effects of the economic and social changes, which the Colmar Dominican described with such obvious local pride. Unlike the situation in the lower Rhine Valley, the Cistercians and the Dominicans began, therefore, in a basically similar position in Alsace and Swabia; there was no strong tradition, as there was further north, for women to turn for spiritual guidance to the well-established Cistercians. These conditions no doubt favored the Dominicans. As a result of the 1228 decision, the Cistercian monks were not permitted to initiate the foundation of a Cistercian nunnery. Those Cistercian nunneries that were founded and incorporated in southwestern Germany after 1228 were admitted to the order, as was the case further north, by the Cistercian general chapter at the request of powerful patrons who could not easily be denied. In southwestern Germany such patrons, according to the records of the Cistercian general chapter, included: Popes Gregory IX, Innocent IV, and Alexander IV, Bishops Henry of Speyer, Philip of Lausanne, and Eberhard of Constance, the Basel cathedral chapter, the Margravine Ermengarde of Baden, Count Hartmann of Kyburg, and Countess Sophia of Freiburg.[34] In spite of prohibitions by the Dominican general chapter, the newly arrived Dominicans, especially in Alsace, did not hesitate to organize into nunneries women whom they found living together near chapels.[35] They had thus organized five nunneries within thirteen years of their arrival in Strasbourg in 1224. Arriving in virgin territory, the Dominicans took charge.

It seems at first glance, therefore, all the more surprising that the Franciscans did not assume the *cura monialium* in southwestern Germany with the

---

[32] *De rebus alsaticis ineuntis saeculi xiii*, ed. Philipp Jaffé, MGH Scriptores 17 (Hanover 1861) 236; and Karl Köster, "Die Geschichtsschreibung der kolmarer Dominikaner im 13. Jahrhundert," *Elsass-lothringisches Jahrbuch* 22 (1952) 52-63, 81-88.

[33] Paul Kirn, "Die Verdienste der staufischen Kaiser um das deutsche Reich," *Historische Zeitschrift* 164 (1941) 272; Karl Otto Müller, *Die oberschwabischen Reichstädte : Ihre Entstehung und ältere Verfassung*, Darstellungen aus der württembergischen Geschichte 8 (Stuttgart 1912) *passim*; and Karl Weller, "Die staufische Städtegründung in Schwaben," *Württembergische Vierteljahrshefte für Landesgeschichte* n.s. 36 (1930) 195-249.

[34] *Statuta capitulorum* (n. 31 above) *passim*.

[35] *De rebus alsaticis* (n. 32 above) 234; and Grundmann (n. 2 above) 208-252.

same enthusiasm as the Dominicans. The problem was that the German Franciscans lacked the personnel, that is priests to serve as confessors and preachers, to compete at first with either the Dominicans or the Cistercians in southwestern Germany. Jordan of Giano's account of the beginnings of the Franciscan mission in Germany makes abundantly clear that the German Franciscans were greatly handicapped by a lack of clerical brothers in the 1220s and 1230s. The early Franciscan mission in Germany suffered in Jordan's own words from a "lack of priests."[36] The situation was so critical that Jordan himself served in the summer of 1223 as the sole priest for the friaries in Worms, Mainz, and Speyer; the attempt to establish a Franciscan house in Nordhausen had to be abandoned in 1225 because the new foundation was composed entirely of laymen.[37] The Franciscans, who had difficulties in providing adequately for their own spiritual needs in the 1220s and 1230s, were hardly in a position to assume the *cura monialium*. It was only when the Franciscan order had been transformed after the overthrow of Elias in 1239 into an organization of learned clerics, modeled after the Dominicans, that they were able to assume, at least in Germany, the care of nuns on a large scale.[38] By the 1240s it was already too late, however, for the Franciscans to challenge seriously the well-entrenched Dominicans in the exercise of the *cura monialium* in southwestern Germany.

The Franciscans adopted instead in southwestern Germany the same position vis-à-vis the Dominicans which the Dominicans held in regard to the Cistercians in the lower Rhine Valley and in Brabant. In Cologne the Cistercians cared for the nuns, while the Dominicans supervised the beguines; in Strasbourg the Dominicans exercised the *cura monialium*, while the Franciscans provided for the beguines.[39]. Both Greven and Grundmann contended, however, that the beguines were women who could not find a place in the overcrowded Cistercian and mendicant nunneries.[40] Yet quite clearly the Cologne Dominicans and the Strasbourg Franciscans never organized into nunneries the beguines for whom they cared. The cloistered life demanded of a Cistercian or a mendicant nun seems to have been the major obstacle to such a move. Cistercian and mendicant nunneries were expected to be adequately endowed in order to provide a secure existence for their cloistered inmates.[41] Such endowments could only be obtained from

---

[36] *Chronica fratris Jordani*, ed. H. Boehmer, in *Collection d'études et de documents sur l'histoire religieuse et littéraire du moyen âge* 6 (Paris 1908) chap. 28. Jordan used the phrase, "paucitatem haberet sacerdotum."

[37] *Ibid.* chaps. 30, 44.

[38] Rosalind B. Brooke, *Early Franciscan Government: Elias to Bonaventure* (Cambridge 1959) 243-245.

[39] Phillips (n. 2 above) 119-126.

[40] Greven (n. 1 above) 120-132; and Grundmann (n. 2 above) 319-320.

[41] See, for instance, *Statuta capitulorum* (n. 3 above) 36, 7; *Urkunden- und Quellenbuch*

two sources: the gifts of wealthy benefactors and the dowries of the nuns themselves. The Colmar Dominican stated rather bluntly that the Alsatian Dominican nunneries in the early days of their existence for this reason only accepted wealthy women.[42] Hermann of Minden, the Dominican prior provincial in the 1280s, explained in a letter written in about 1284 that membership in many German Dominican nunneries was in effect limited to women who could contribute upon their entry either one hundred marks in cash or real property worth one hundred and forty marks.[43] Hermann indicated in the same letter that three marks were more than adequate to support a nun for a year; the nuns were expected to contribute enough, in other words, to maintain themselves for thirty-three years in the unlikely eventuality that the money was not carefully invested. Only the wealthy could afford the poverty of the cloister. While some beguines belonged to patrician families who could have given their daughters such a sizeable dowry, most beguines came from respectable, but poorer families who could not have provided their daughters with such a large sum of money.[44] The cloistered life was simply not a viable economic alternative for most beguines. Another factor, however, ought to be taken into consideration. There may have been some wealthy women who sincerely believed that the life of a beguine, at its finest a life of service to others in the midst of the world supported by manual labor, came closer to the ideal of evangelical perfection than the severely restricted and more traditional life of the cloistered nun. These women became beguines for the same reason that their male counterparts entered the Franciscan and Dominican orders, rather than the Benedictines, Cistercians, or Premonstratensians. In either case it was more than a lack of space in a nunnery which made women become beguines rather than nuns. The Dominicans and Franciscans did not so much assume the *cura monialium*, as Greven and Grundmann believed, at that moment in time when the Cistercians supposedly abandoned it, but rather labored in those most recently urbanized areas in which their predecessors had hitherto not been needed and among women whose innermost aspirations could not be fulfilled by an older religious tradition.

---

zur Geschichte der altluxemburgischen Territorien, ed. Camillus Wampach (Luxembourg 1939) 3, Doc. 479; and Die Regesten (n. 7 above) Doc. 2266.

[42] De rebus alsaticis (n. 32 above) 234.

[43] Gabriel M. Löhr, "Drei Briefe Hermanns von Minden O. P. über die Seelsorge und die Leitung der deutschen Dominikanerinnenklöster," Römische Quartalschrift 33 (1925) 161-162.

[44] Neumann (n. 2 above) 105-111; and Phillips (n. 2 above) 27.

APPENDIX

This appendix contains the list of chronicles, collections of sources, and monographs, geographically arranged, which were used in compiling table 2.

Basel

Bosl, Karl. *Die Reichsministerialität der Salier und Staufer.* MGH, Schriften 10 (Stuttgart 1950),

Urkundenbuch der Stadt Basel, eds. Rudolph Wackernagel and Rudolph Thommen 1 (Basel 1890).

Cambrai

Goetstouwers, Adr. "De oorsprong der Abdij Roosendaal," *Bulletin de la commission royale d'histoire* 114 (1949) 257-298.

Inventaire des chartes et cartulaires des duchés de Brabant et de Limbourg et des Pays d'Outre-Meuse, ed. Alphonse Verkooren 1 (Brussels 1910).

Ryckman de Betz, Baron de, Georges Dansaert, and Thibaut de Maisières. *L'abbaye cistercienne de la Cambre* (Antwerp 1948).

Cologne

Lau, Friedrich, "Das kölner Patriziat bis zum Jahre 1325," *Mitteilungen aus dem Stadtarchiv von Köln* 9 (1894) 65-89, 358-381, and 10 (1895) 103-158.

Löhr, Gabriel M. *Beiträge zur Geschichte des kölner Dominikanerklosters im Mittelalter.* Quellen und Forschungen zur Geschichte des Dominikanerordens in Deutschland 16-17 (Leipzig 1922).

Planitz, Hans and Thea Buyken. *Die kölner Schreinsbücher des 13. und 14. Jahrhundert.* Publikationen der Gesellschaft für rheinische Geschichtskunde (PGRG) 46 (Weimar 1937).

Quellen zur Geschichte der Stadt Köln, eds. Leonard Ennen and Gottfried Eckertz, 2 (Cologne 1863).

Die Regesten der Erzbischöfe von Köln im Mittelalter, ed. Richard Knipping, 3, PGRG 21 (Bonn 1909-1913).

Regesten der Reichstadt Aachen, ed. Wilhelm Mummenhoff, 1, PGRG 47 (Bonn 1961).

Urkundenbuch für die Geschichte des Niederrheins, ed. Theod. Jos. Lacomblet, 2 (Düsseldorf 1846).

Wellstein, Gilbert. "Das Cisterzienserinnenkloster Herchen an der Sieg" 1, *Studien und Mitteilungen zur Geschichte des Benediktiner-Ordens und seiner Zweige* n.s. 8 (1918) 341-375.

Westfälisches Urkunden-Buch, no editor, 7 (Münster 1908-1919).

Constance

Bosl, Karl (s.v. Basel above).

Chronicon Colmariense, ed. Philipp Jaffé. MGH Scriptores 17 (Hanover 1861) 240-270.

Freiburger Urkundenbuch, ed. Friedrich Hefele, 1 (Freiburg 1940).

Hohenlohisches Urkundenbuch, ed. Karl Weller, 1 (Stuttgart 1899).

Monumenta Hohenbergica, Urkundenbuch zur Geschichte der Grafen von Zollern-Hohenberg und ihrer Graftschaft, ed. L. Schmid (Stuttgart 1862).

Regesta episcoporum constantiensum, eds. Paul Ladewig and Theodor Müller, 1 (Innsbruck 1895).

Ulmisches Urkundenbuch, ed. Friedrich Pressel, 1 (Stuttgart 1873).

Urkundenbuch der Stadt und Landschaft Zürich, eds. J. Escher and P. Schweizer, 2, 3, 4 (Zürich 1892-1898).

Wirtembergisches Urkundenbuch, no editor, 4, 5, 6, 7 (Stuttgart 1883-1900).

Liège

Actes des prince-évêques de Liège, Hugues de Pirrepont, 1200-1229, ed. Édouard Poncelet. Académie royale de Belgique, Commission royale d'histoire (ARBCRH) (Brussels 1941).

Brouette, Émile. "Chartes et documents de l'abbaye d'Argenton à Lonzée," *Bulletin de la commission royale d'histoire* 115 (1950) 297-381.

Cartulaire de l'abbaye du Val-Benoît, ed. J. Cuvelier, ARBCRH (Brussels 1906).

Cartulaire de l'église Saint-Lambert de Liège, eds. S. Bormans and E. Schoolmeesters, 1 (Brussels, 1893).

Catalogue des actes de Henri de Gueldre prince-évêque de Liège, eds. Alph. Delescluse and Dd. Brouwers, Bibliothèque de la faculté de philosophie et lettres de l'université de Liège 5 (Brussels 1900).

Inventaire analytique des chartes de la collégiale de Saint-Jean l'Évangéliste à Liège, ed. L. Lahaye, 1, ARBCRH (Brussels 1921).

Inventaire des chartes et cartulaires des duchés de Brabant et de Limbourg et des Pays d'Outre-Meuse, ed. Alphonse Verkooren (Brussels 1910).

Poncelet, Édouard. "L'abbaye de Vivegnis," *Bulletin de la Société d'art et d'histoire du diocèse de Liège* (BSAHDL) 10 (1896) 1-41.

Reusens, E. "Documents relatifs à l'abbaye norbertine de Heylissem," *Analectes pour servir à l'histoire ecclésiastique de la Belgique*, ser. 2, 11 (1898), 114-196.

Thomas of Cantimpré. *Bonum universale de apibus* (Douai 1627).

Yans, Maurice. "Quelques acts originaux de Henri de Gueldre," BSAHDL 34 (1948) 1-33.

Mainz

Bosl, Karl (s.v. Basel above).

Codex Diplomaticus Nassoicus, Nassauisches Urkundenbuch, ed. W. Sauer, 1 (Wiesbaden 1885-1887).

Mittelrheinische Regesten, ed. Ad. Goerz, 2, 3 (Koblenz 1879-1881).

Regesta diplomatica necnon epistolaria historiae Thuringiae, eds. Otto Dobenecker and Gustav Fischer, 2, 3, 4 (Jena 1900-1939).

Speyer

Bosl, Karl (s.v. Basel above).

Reiss, Lucia. "Studien zur Wirtschafts- und Verfassungsgeschichte des Zister-zienserinnen-Klosters Lichtenthal (1245-1803)," *Zeitschrift für die Geschichte des Oberrheins* 96 (1948) 230-306.

Wirtembergisches Urkundenbuch, no editor, 5 (Stuttgart 1889).

Strasbourg

Hessel, Alfred. *Elsässische Urkunden vornehmlich des 13. Jahrhunderts.* Schriften der wissenschaftlichen Gesellschaft in Strassburg 23 (Strasbourg 1915).

Urkundenbuch der Stadt Strassburg, eds. Wilhelm Wiegand and Aloys Schulte, 1, 4 (Strasbourg 1879-1898).

Trier

Mittelrheinische Regesten (s.v. Mainz above) 3.

Quellen zur Geschichte der Klöster und Stifte im Gebiet der mittleren Lahn bis zum Ausgang des Mittelalters, ed. Wolf Heino Struck, 1, 3, Veröffentlichungen der historischen Kommission für Nassau 12 (Wiesbaden 1956-1961).

Thomas of Cantimpré (s.v. Liège above).

Urkunden- und Quellenbuch zur Geschichte der altluxemburgischen Territorien, ed. Camillus Wampach, 2, 3, 4 (Luxembourg 1938-1940).

Department of History
Illinois State University
Normal, Illinois, U.S.A.

REPRESENTATION AND AGENCY LAW IN THE LATER MIDDLE AGES: THE THEORETICAL FOUNDATIONS AND THE EVOLUTION OF PRACTICE IN THE THIRTEENTH- AND FOURTEENTH- CENTURY MIDI

•

by Elizabeth A. R. Brown

In the thirteenth and fourteenth centuries the royal, papal, and imperial governments of Western Europe were acquiring power on a scale unprecedented since the time of Charlemagne. They were becoming involved in ventures that forced them to enlist the support of as many of their subjects as possible to pay the growing expenses associated with bureaucratic and territorial expansion and consolidation.[1] Happy as the rulers might have been to impose their demands autocratically, they found themselves obliged to gain their subjects' consent in order to obtain the help they required; to this end they marshaled propaganda and arguments from all likely sources. Whether their subjects' consent was obtained piecemeal, through local negotiation, or in large assemblies, the rulers had to deal with them through representatives elected to act for them. Thus they and their subjects were inevitably concerned with the intricacies of the representative relationship and with the principles of the law of agency which were pertinent to it.

Subjects who were naïvely unaware of the theoretical and practical problems posed by the agency relationship were in danger of being exploited by shrewd rulers and their officials, for their representatives might be persuaded

[1] This study could not have been written without the assistance of the many directors of departmental and local archives in France who helped me to secure copies of the documents which I used in preparing this essay. I am particularly grateful to Jean Sablou, director of the Archives départementales du Gard, who located for me and permitted me to use in Paris the documents housed in the communal archives of Alès. Professor Charles H. Taylor brought many of these documents to my attention; in addition, he permitted me to use his notes on and microfilm copies of procurations he had located in southern archives. Professors Thomas Bisson, Fredric Cheyette, Walter Goffart, and Helene Wieruszowski all gave me valuable advice and counsel.

The paper was first presented at the January 1970 meeting of the Columbia University Collegium on the History of Legal and Political Thought; I am indebted to the members of the collegium for their sympathetic questions and comments.

or compelled to make pledges committing them to actions to which they were fundamentally opposed. It has in fact been argued that the terminology of the mandates borne by agents attending assemblies convoked by the rulers made them participants in a special judicial situation, so that the consent they were called upon to give was "consultative and judicial, not voluntary and democratic." Under these circumstances, "the strong king, not the communities, was the interpreter of *plena potestas* and could thereby obtain consent to decisions which were supported by public law. . . . 'Full power' was consent to the decision of king and court and council, consent given before the assembly was held."[2] The theoretical and practical issues raised by these statements deserve consideration, for they suggest that the technicalities of the agency relationship were such as to produce a natural advantage for the sovereign and to place the subject automatically in an unfavorable position in dealing with his superiors.

As far as practice is concerned, it seems undeniable that, as the statement implies, those occupying positions of authority yearn inevitably for absolute power and would choose, if they could, to act as the final determiners and interpreters of the limits of the powers of consent possessed by their subjects' representatives. Such powers would ideally be unrestricted: the agents would be able to hear, accept, and act on the rulers' demands without debate, and the rulers would exercise pressure on the deputies once assembled to see that they performed the actions desired of them. The repercussions that attempts to implement such aims could have are well illustrated by the situation which developed in the northern French diocese of Reims in 1264. In that year a papal legate convoked a general council of all cathedral chapters in France, in hopes of obtaining a grant of a tenth, ostensibly for the defense of the faith but in fact to support the papal campaign against Manfred in Apulia. To achieve his purpose, he commanded the chapters to send to the council proctors with power to consent to the precise decrees to be issued at the assembly. He said nothing of what he intended to accomplish, presumably because he assumed that the chapters would trust his judgment unquestioningly.[3] Some chapters did as he asked and dispatched delegates with mandates giving them power "to consent and to do the will of the lord cardinal," which was precisely the unbounded authority the cardinal had sought.[4] Other chapters, however, refused to follow the legate's instructions

[2] Gaines Post, *Studies in Medieval Legal Thought: Public Law and the State, 1100-1322* (Princeton 1964) 117, 126-127, 156; cf. 117-123, 161.

[3] "Quia mandavit capitulis cathedralibus quod mitterent ad eum procuratores suos qui haberent potestatem consentiendi in sua voluntate facienda precise, nulla mentione facta de sua voluntate facienda, nec aliqua certitudine super hoc expressa": F. J. Varin, ed., *Archives législatives de la ville de Reims*, 1: *Coutumes des cours ecclésiastiques et civiles* (Paris 1840) 455, cf. 448.

[4] "Ad consentiendum et ad voluntatem domini cardinalis faciendum": *ibid.* 448.

and gave their proctors mandates that permitted them simply to hear and report to their chapters the cardinal's demands. Whereas these agents were unable to vote the tenth that the cardinal wanted, the fully empowered proctors could—and did—do so. After the meeting, the cathedral chapter of Reims, angered by the proceedings, drafted a lengthy portest. If they began by inveighing against the tenth and discussing the limits of obedience in some detail, most significant for our purposes is the violent attack on the form of the mandate prescribed by the legate, with which the protest ended. Rather than criticizing the proctors for utilizing to their principals' detriment the powers they had been granted—or blaming themselves for having issued the mandate in the first place—they turned on the legate, arguing that he had no right to request such broad authorization. Such a form, the chapter asserted, would be proper only if all clerics of the Gallican church were the cardinal's slaves; no lord, they said, could issue a more rigorous command to any slave, who possessed nothing of his own and was totally subject to his lord's will.[5] However defensive and farfetched the chapter's argument that the superior had no justification for ordering his free subjects to issue unlimited mandates, the chapter members learned a valuable lesson from the experience of 1264, and they put it to good use later, in negotiations with the king. Summoned to a royal assembly to provide for the defense of the realm, the chapter decided to dispatch proctors supplied with two mandates, one empowering them simply to hear and report back, the other, requested by the king, authorizing them to agree and consent. In a detailed memorandum the chapter instructed its agents to employ only the first mandate, if this was possible. If not, they were to oppose the king's demands for money and agree to no more than a small loan.[6]

[5] *Ibid.* 450, 455. Richard of Middleton argued in 1287 that while slaves, the property of their master, were bound to meet his every request, free men were obligated to pay only those taxes imposed for the common good, when the royal treasury could not cover expenses without fatally weakening the kingdom: Ricardus de Media Villa, *Tria recognita reconcinataque quodlibeta* (Venice 1509) 42v-43; cf. P. Glorieux, *La littérature quodlibétique de 1260 à 1320* (Le Saulchoir 1925-1935) 2.267, 271.

[6] Varin (n. 3 above) 79-80. It is not clear with what royal money-raising effort this memorandum should be linked, although the appeal to the defense of the realm suggests that it may have been prepared during the reign of Philip the Fair.

The chapter instructed its proctors to argue that even if the necessity of defense was admitted—and they conceded that it was the king's prerogative to determine this—there was still no need for them to contribute, since the king was bound to use his own property before calling on his subjects for assistance, and this he had not done. A small loan, the chapter maintained, was far less likely to prejudice the chapter's rights than was a subsidy; if it were arranged, the proctors were to try to obtain a letter of nonprejudice from the king, although, the chapter noted, the king's citation was so phrased that the chapter's privileges were effectively protected even without such a document.

The lessons learned by the Reims chapter—that subjects could resist and reinterpret their ruler's instructions, and, more important, that constituents could issue limited mandates and detailed instructions to their proctors to protect their own interests—were fundamentally important for subjects to master if they were not to find themselves mere ciphers, whose acquiescence was presumed before their actual consent was obtained. If the members of the chapter became fully aware of this only after experiencing the difficulties that artlessness could engender, their reactions cannot be considered typical of those that could be expected from their contemporaries in thirteenth-century France. Even in 1264 some of the chapters summoned to the cardinal's general council refused to carry out his orders and responded to his demands with strictly limited mandates. Such sophistication as they demonstrated testifies to the expertise that they and other ecclesiastics and laymen had been acquiring since the early thirteenth century.

The accelerated tempo of life in the thirteenth and fourteenth centuries brought increased involvement in projects necessitating cooperation between individuals and groups—in more complex business negotiations, in agreements to promote peaceful exploitation of natural resources, in compromises to terminate disputes, in pacts to eradicate hostilities—as well as in negotiations with governmental authorities on both a local and more centralized level. For all these purposes men found it expedient and necessary to employ agents to act for them, and in the second section of this paper I will trace the development of the use of representatives in the Midi, showing how the experience acquired in business dealings, judicial affairs, and other local negotiations proved valuable when towns and individuals were called upon to respond to the demands of their increasingly powerful kings.

The men who, in the thirteenth and fourteenth centuries, were becoming expert at manipulating the agency relationship, were not, however, operating in a conceptual void: they were not forced to improvise the documents they needed nor to deal on a makeshift, trial-and-error basis with the situations that arose. If experience alone could give them the refined skill and shrewdness they needed to manage their agents easily and surely, they possessed a solid theoretical foundation on which to build. Available to them was a wealth of sophistication and legal knowledge distilled in books of Roman and canon law, clarified and expounded by commentators and glossators, digested and simplified in the writings of notarial theorists. These books provided them with a wide range of forms, models, and instructions to guide them in structuring any sort of relationship they might wish to establish.

These books and treatises are not—and were not—easy to understand and use: they contain contradictory statements, and the complex and sophisticated principles that they set forth are expressed in a manner that is often vague and obscure. Still, it seems hard to believe that those who read and studied them could have inferred, as has been suggested,[7] that simply by employing certain general empowering formulas commonly used in agency documents—specifically the terms "full power" (*plena potestas*) or "free and general administration" (*libera et generalis administratio*)—they were necessarily abrogating their right to control their agents, giving them unrestricted power to agree to any demands, and leaving them—and themselves—potentially at the mercy of the parties with whom the agents were to deal. The manuals and digests that they had at their disposal showed how the agency relationship could be manipulated, not only by third parties for their own ends, but, more important, by constituents, to protect and guard their interests and their property. Careful study of these works might have spared the chapter of Reims the anguish and trouble experienced in 1264; as will be seen, the precepts they contain seem to have been utilized fruitfully by the consuls of many towns in the Midi.

Passages in the corpus of Roman law did demonstrate the possibility of constituting proctors with such general and unlimited authority that their acts would bind the principal and leave him recourse only against his agent. Several statements indicated that the agent with unlimited and unrestricted free and general administrative rights over his principal's posesssions (*libera et generalis administratio, procurator omnium rerum*) possessed virtually unbounded power.[8] Another, however, suggested that even with such broad authority, the power to negotiate settlements and reach compromises (*transigere*)[9]—involving the power to alienate the principal's property—had to be specifically granted.[10] Yet another text stated that a proctor of all property

---

[7] Post (n. 2 above) 92-102.

[8] "Procurator, cui generaliter libera administratio rerum commissa est, potest exigere, novare, aliud pro alio permutare. Sed et id quoque ei mandari videtur, ut solvat creditoribus": Digest (D) 3.3.58-59. These assertions by Paulus suggest that his position on the agency relationship was less cautious and restrictive than it actually was: cf. D 3.3.49 and D 3.3.60, quoted in notes 10 and 12 below. Ulpian taught than an agreement made by a proctor with authority over all his principal's property was just as valid as if he possessed a special mandate authorizing the action: "Nam et nocere constat, sive ei mandavi ut pacisceretur, sive omnium rerum mearum procurator fuit": D 2.14.12. Also important is a statement of Gaius: "Nihil autem interest, utrum ipse dominus per se tradat alicui rem an voluntate eius aliquis. Qua ratione, si cui libera negotiorum administratio ab eo qui peregre proficiscitur permissa fuerit et is ex negotiis rem vendiderit et tradiderit, facit eam accipientis": D 41.1.9.4. Cf. the similar text, Institutes (I) 2.1.42-43. On the significance of the principal's *voluntas*, see Alberto Burdese, *Autorizzazione ad alienare in diritto romano* (Turin 1950) 46-87, esp. 46-48, 52; he concludes that a proctor who, in bad faith (*malae fidei*), flouted the will of his principal was subject to prosecution.

[9] For the meaning of *transactio*, see Adolf Berger, *Encyclopedic Dictionary of Roman Law*, Transactions of the American Philosophical Society n.s. 43.2 (Philadelphia 1953) s.v.

[10] "Mandato generali non contineri etiam transactionem decidendi causa interpositam: et ideo si postea is qui mandavit transactionem ratam non habuit, non posse eum repelli

(*procurator totorum bonorum*), authorized to administer his constituent's possessions, could not alienate the movable or immovable property or the slaves of his constituent without a special mandate; he could only dispose of fruit and other perishables.[11]   In addition, various sections of the law indicated that, whatever the terms of his mandate, an agent was duty-bound to advance his constituent's interests and guard his property rights.[12]   Still, it was clear that broad empowering formulas were to be employed with care. Since the Roman law stressed that all proctors were bound to adhere to the terms of their mandates and could not obligate their principals if they exceeded them,[13] the cautious reader might well have elected to avoid the more gen-

---

ab actionibus exercendis": D 3.3.60.   On this problem, see Cesare Bertolini, *Della transazione secondo il diritto romano* (Naples 1900) 19, 124-125, 134; cf. Maria Emilia Peterlongo, *La transazione nel diritto romano* (Milan 1936) and also Alan Watson, *The Law of Obligations in the Later Roman Republic* (Oxford 1965) 196-197, 204-205, who concluded that a proctor with power over all his principal's property needed no special authorization to alienate.

[11] "Procurator totorum bonorum, cui res administrandae mandatae sunt, res domini neque mobiles vel immobiles neque servos sine speciali domini mandatu alienare potest, nisi fructus aut alias res, quae facile corrumpi possunt": D 3.3.63 (Modestinus).   Other statements concerning specialized agency relationships confirmed this conservative approach.   Ulpian, treating the authority of the *filius familias*, the son under paternal power, said that even if he had been given free administration of his property (*peculium*), he could not give it away.   In explanation, Ulpian noted that this broad authority was not given so that the son could waste the property; he thought it likely, however, that a donation made by the son for a just cause would hold, and he said that the son could alienate property if he had been specifically empowered to do so: "Filius familias donare non potest, neque si liberam peculii administrationem habeat: non enim ad hoc ei conceditur libera peculii administratio, ut perdat.   Quid ergo, si iusta ratione motus donet, numquid possit dici locum esse donationi? quod magis probabitur.   Item videamus, si quis filio familias liberam peculii administrationem concesserit, ut nominatim adiceret sic se ei concedere, ut donare quoque possit, an locum habeat donatio: et non dubito donare quoque eum posse": D 39.5.7.

In dealing with imperial proctors, Ulpian wrote that unless they possessed the explicit authorization of the emperor they could not transfer imperial property: they could not sell it, give it away, or make any settlement affecting it, since they were bound not to alienate imperial property but to care diligently for it: "Si rem Caesaris procurator eius quasi rem propriam tradat, non puto eum dominium transferre: tunc enim transfert, cum negotium Caesaris gerens consensu ipsius tradit.   Denique si venditionis vel donationis vel transactionis causa quid agat, nihil agit: non enim alienare ei rem Caesaris, sed diligenter gerere commissum est": D 1.19.1.1.   Later commentators lifted these restrictive principles from the specialized contexts in which they appear and applied them to the ordinary agency relationship.

[12] Paulus wrote that the condition of an ignorant principal should not be impaired by his proctor: "Ignorantis domini condicio deterior per procuratorem fieri non debet": D 3.3.49. Cf. also Paulus's statement, "Sed si tantum ad actionem procurator factus sit, conventio facta domino non nocet, quia nec solvi ei possit.   Sed si in rem suam datus sit procurator, loco domini habetur: et ideo servandum erit pactum conventum": D 2.14.13.   Cf. also the texts quoted in the preceding note.

[13] "Is qui exsequitur mandatum non debet excedere fines mandati": I 3.26.8; on this. passage, see Vincenzo Arangio-Ruiz, *Il mandato in diritto romano* (Naples 1949) 168-188.

eral phrases altogether and to issue precise mandates listing specifically the tasks the agent might perform. On the contrary, the law showed that the broad phrases could be controlled and limited. One passage in the Code— the only text in the corpus in which the expression *plena potestas* appears —refers to the proctor with full power to act or plead (*plena potestas agendi*), and the limitation to acting or pleading imposed on his full power suggested that while he could perform any action in court, he could not act in other situations.[14] The implication of this passage for actual practice was clear: if full power could be restricted by adding a word to define the boundaries within which it could be exercised, the power of free and general administration could be similarly modified.

The medieval commentators treated the problems of agency law in great detail, and, although they made contradictory and conflicting statements, they generally concurred that a grant of unrestricted free and general administration gave the agent extensive power over the principal's possessions.[15] Azo believed that the proctor with free and general administration might alienate his principal's possessions, but he seems to have held that alienation was proper only if it seemed expedient, and he warned that a proctor could

---

Various provisions of the Code also emphasize that the proctor must carefully observe the limits of the mandate: "Procuratorem vel actorem praedii, si non specialiter distrahendi mandatum accepit, ius rerum dominii vendendi non habere certum ac manifestum est" (Code [C] 2.12.16); "Si pretium, quod actoribus alienis fundum vel servum citra mandatum tibi distrahentibus dedisti et neque praecessisse neque secuta contractum domini declaretur voluntas, in rem autem eius id pretium cessisse provinciae praeses causa cognita perspexerit, hoc tibi restitui iubebit" (C 2.12.19); cf. n. 9 above on the *voluntas* of the principal. Paulus's similar statement appears in the Digest: "Diligenter igitur fines mandati custodiendi sunt: nam qui excessit, aliud quid facere videtur et, si susceptum non impleverit, tenetur": D 17.1.5.

[14] "Si procurator ad unam speciem constitutus officium mandati egressus est, id quod gessit nullum domino praeiudicium facere potuit. Quod si plenam potestatem agendi habuit, rem iudicatum rescindi non oportet, cum, si quid fraude vel dolo egit, convenire eum more iudiciorum non prohiberis": C 2.12.10, a decree of the emperor Alexander Severus. On the classical doctrine of liability for *dolus*, see Arangio-Ruiz (n. 13 above) 167; Alan Watson (n. 10 above) 152-154, and *Contract of Mandate in Roman Law* (Oxford 1961) 7-8; and W. M. Gordon, "The Liability of the Mandatary," in *Synteleia Vincenzo Arangio-Ruiz* (Naples 1964) 1.202-205.

[15] The early Bolognese master, Martinus, was evidently troubled by the restrictions placed by Modestinus (D 3.3.63; see n. 11 above) on the right of the proctor with power over all his principal's property to dispose of such property. Martinus suggested that these limitations would not exist if the agent were named *procurator universorum* rather than *totorum bonorum*. This artificial distinction was rejected by Johannes Bassianus, who maintained that the crucial question was whether or not the proctor had rights of free administration or a special mandate permitting him to alienate: see Accursius's comments on D 3.3.63, *Glossa ordinaria* (Lyon 1569). Rogerius, another Bolognese legist, stated flatly that with either a special mandate or a general mandate including free license to dispose of the constituent's belongings (*generale [mandatum] et liberam amministrationem*), the proctor could sell, alienate, and perform such acts as reaching compromises: *Summa Codicis*, ed. G. B. Palmieri, in A. Gaudenzi, ed., *Scripta anecdota glossatorum* (Bologna 1888-1901) 1. 27-29.

be prosecuted not only for fraud but also for negligence in failing to protect his constituent's interests.[16] The thirteenth-century glossators, Accursius and Odofredus, held that an agent with powers of free and general administration could not only improve but also damage his principal's condition,[17] although

[16] "Si ergo habet literam (sic) et generalem administrationem, servatur quod fecit, sed tamen tenetur de dolo et fraude, et de lata culpa et levi": Azo, *Ad singulas leges XII librorum Codicis Iustinianei commentarius et magnus apparatus* (Paris 1577, pub. as *Lectura super Codicem*, Turin 1966) 101, 28. Azo also held that a proctor could be prosecuted for collusion with his principal's adversary: cf. Azo, *Summa super Codicem instituta extraordinaria* (1506, repr. Turin 1966) 32, or *Summa Azonis locuples* (Venice 1566) 85. For the criterion of expediency, *Glossa ordinaria* (n. 15 above) to D 1.19.1: "Sed nonne bene potest gerere alienando . . . sed hoc loquitur cum non expediat alienare: alioquin contra . . . quia hic habet liberam administrationem . . . vnde videtur posse alienare. sed speciale est, ne in Caesaris praeiudicium alienet. Alias contra [cf. D 3.3.58]"; see n. 11 above. According to Accursius, Azo held that a proctor lacking free administrative rights could nonetheless pledge his principal's property if the principal was accustomed to taking such action: Accursius (n. 15 above).

[17] Accursius stated that a proctor could impair his principal's condition when he was acting as proctor in his own behalf (*procurator in rem suam*; cf. n. 12 above and Berger [n. 9 above] s.v. *procurator*), when he had a special mandate, and when he had a general mandate with rights of free administration: Accursius (n. 15 above) to D 3.3.49. In his gloss on the Code, Accursius said that the power to sell property could be given either by an express mandate or by a grant of free and general administration, and he rejected as meaningless Martinus's distinction between the *procurator universorum bonorum* and the *procurator totorum bonorum*: Accursius, *Glossa in Codicem* (1488, repr. Turin 1968) 50, *Specialiter*, to C 2,12.16; cf. n. 15 above. According to Accursius, the proctor with free and general administration could act and plead, make settlements, and alienate his constituent's possessions: Accursius (n. 15 above) on C 2.12.10, and on D 3.3.63, where he cited C 4.26.10 and D 6.1.41 to prove that the proctor with free administration could alienate.

The position of Odofredus is similar to Accursius's. He did not hesitate to expand the list of powers possessed by a proctor with free administration given in D 3.3.58-59 (see n. 8 above) to include the authority to alienate: Odofredus, *Lectura super Digesto veteri* (Lyon 1550, 1552, repr. Bologna 1968) 120v and cf. 121 for his comments on D 3.3.63. As his statements there show, he believed that the proctor with free administration could weaken his principal's condition by disposing of his possessions: cf. also his comments on D 3.3.58. His statement on D 3.3.49 is, however, not so clear, for, having said "sed certe nec tunc quando liberam et generalem administrationem habet procurator non potest facere conditionem domini deteriorem donando," citing D 39.5.7 and D 2.14.28.2, he quoted without further comment the general rule, "licet domini conditionem deteriorem facere non possit tamen meliorem potest facere": *ibid.* 119v. Odofredus held, following Azo, that if the proctor was suspected of collusion with an opposing party, the principal could take action against him: Odofredus, *Lectura super Codice* (Lyon 1552) 1.87v.

Vivianus, a contemporary of Accursius and Odofredus, held that the proctor with rights of free and general administration had full power to act, and he maintained that a judgment given against such a proctor held against his principal. The proctor with simple rights of general administration had, however, no authority to effect compromises unless his principal had ratified in advance anything whatsoever he might do: Vivianus, *Casus longi super Codice* (Basel? 1483?) 10, included, like Vivianus's other *casus*, in Accursius's *Glossa ordinaria* (n. 15 above); cf. *ibid.* on D 3.3.60.

neither commentator was prepared to admit that he could squander or give away the constituent's property.[18] Vivianus also stressed the central importance of the principal's intention or will (*voluntas*) and taught that either before or after the proctor acted, the principal must sanction his agent's deed to give it validity.[19] Another early thirteenth-century commentator, Rofredus of Benevento, insisted on the proctor's duty to exercise prudence in fulfilling his commission. It was not enough, he said, for the proctor to act in good faith: he must be skeptical and wary, and he could be prosecuted and convicted for failing to be sufficiently cautious.[20] Such theoretical safe-

---

[18] At the end of his discussion of D 3.3.58 Accursius commented that even with rights of free administration, the proctor could not give his principal's possessions away: see n. 8 above; see also n. 11 above, for the text of D 39.5.7, which Accursius cited as authority for his statement. See also Accursius's discussion of D 39.5.7 and of D 1.19.1, which forbade imperial proctors to alienate to the emperor's disadvantage: cf. n. 11 above. Accurius said that this rule held because such action was against the ruler's best interests, but the passages cited to support his assertion suggest that he believed the ruling had general applicability and that no proctor should dispose of his principal's property unless such action seemed beneficial, for he remarked that the proctor with rights of free administration should alienate only if it was expedient to do so. Of the authorities cited, D 49.14.46.7 applies to imperial agents and D 2.14.28 to sons and slaves, but D 2.15.8.17 has more general relevance, as does D 26.7.46.7, which states that guardians cannot "etiam donare vel etiam deminuendi causa cum [debitoribus pupilli] transigere." Dealing with D 3.3.49, Accursius noted that even with rights of free and general administration the proctor could not give property away.

For Odofredus's similar position, see his comments on D 3.3.58, (n. 17 above) 120v; on D 2.14.28, *ibid.* 85v; and on D 3.3.49, *ibid.* 119v. Commenting on D 39.5.7 (see n. 11 above), Odofredus remarked that to give away was equivalent to losing property, since the recipient of the gift incurred no civil but only a natural, and therefore unenforceable, obligation: Odofredus, *Lectura super Digesto novo* (Lyon 1552) 32.

[19] Vivianus (n. 17 above) 10v stated, commenting on C 2.12.16, "Procurator tuus vel actor predium tuum sine speciali mandato distraxit et tradidit: an tibi preiudicat queritur, et respondeo quod non; neque emptor audiendus est si velit in se transferri cum voluntate tua precedente vel subsequente distractum non fuerat." In a subsequent passage, a comment on C 2.12.19, he repeated this opinion: "Respondeo quod preses prouidebit vt mihi restituatur, si declaret voluntatem non precedentem vel subsequentem contractui interuenisse." Cf. n. 8 above.

[20] "Allegatum fuit in primis, quod bonam fidem habuit procurator: unde contra ius esset, si iste in aliquo teneretur, tenetur enim procurator si in culpa deprehendatur. vt insti. mandati, nam illa culpa imputatur, scilicet quod alium nuncium elegit. sed illa non est culpa: quia illum idoneum existimauit. . . . Respon. non excusatur procurator proptera quia deceptus fuit in cogitatione sua. malus enim est inuentus, et sic tenetur: et quia malus presumatur ex facto conuincitur": "Quaestiones Sabbatinae" in *Dni. Rofredi . . . Tractatus, in quo ordinis iudiciarii positiones libellique pertractantur . . .* (Lyon 1561) 769. See 770: "Et si eum procuratorem ponas: fines mandati excessit, quod sibi excedere non licuit: vt allegatum est . . . delictum enim procuratoris non nocet domino . . . imo procurator punitur. Cum enim elegisti alium, de fide ipsius debuisti querere diligenter . . . et si audiuisti de illo bonum aliquando, non debuisti temerarie credere: imputatur enim alicui, qui statim

guards were well and good, but *voluntas* and prudence are notoriously slippery qualities, and the risks associated with grants of unlimited powers of free and general administration were evident. Since all the legists insisted that the proctor was bound to abide by any limitations expressed in his mandate, there were clear advantages to issuing such documents.[21]

The notarial writers of the twelfth and thirteenth centuries dealt with theory and broad principles on occasion, but they were primarily concerned with the drafting of practical, workable documents. Having acknowledged the broad power that could be transferred by giving the right of free and general administration,[22] they filled their treatises with examples of specific mandates that enumerated in detail the various tasks the agent was expected to perform. This may reflect a belief on their part that the extensive authority conveyed by powers of free and general administration should be given only under special circumstances. They may, however, have been attempting to encourage the use of long, detailed mandates in hopes of increasing notarial income; they may have been responding to demand; they may simply have been displaying their own erudition and inventiveness. In any case, their manuals showed clearly that limited mandates were eminently safe. As the author of an *Ordo Judiciarius* written late in the twelfth century stated, the proctor was bound neither to exceed nor to fail to carry out the duties assigned in his mandate, and he had *plenariam potestatem* only to perform the acts described there.[23] Aegidius de Fuscarariis pointed

---

credulus fuit. . . . Praeterea tu mihi teneris in eo quod est amissa pecunia: et tu agas contra illum. et ideo ego contra te: quia illum imprudenter elegisti."

[21] See their comments on C 2.12.10 (n. 14 above). In his discussion of this passage, Accursius distinguished between the limited full power to act (*plena potestas agendi*) and the broader free and general administration, which included the authority to reach compromises and alienate property as well as the power to act and plead. For a different interpretation, Post (n. 2 above) 93-94. Later, Bartolus equated free administration and full power (*plena potestas*, not *plena potestas agendi*); for him, the full power that was interchangeable with free administration was not restricted by any specific duties to be performed: Bartolus, *Commentaria* (Venice 1602-1615) on C 2.12.10. Bartolus held that such broad authority as this had to be specifically granted and could not be transferred by any general statemnet cf. his comments on D 1.19.1.

[22] Aegidius de Fuscarariis, "Ordo iudiciarius," in L. Wahrmund, ed., *Quellen zur Geschichte des römisch-kanonischen Processes im Mittelalter* (Innsbruck 1905-1931) 3.1.20; William of Drogheda, "Summa Aurea," *ibid.* 2.2.97, 104. The discussion given by Rolandinus Passagerii was more sophisticated and took into account the qualifications expressed by the glossators. He taught that a proctor with free and general administration, whose principal authorized him to do everything that he himself could do, was still unable to give away or squander his principal's property: Rolandinus Passagerii, *Summa totius artis notariae* (Turin 1590) 442-443; on Rolandinus, Wahrmund 3.2.lii. For an excellent guide to the writings of the notarial theorists, Gino Masi, ed., *Formularium florentinum artis notariae (1220-1242)*, Orbis Romanus: Biblioteca di testi medievali 17 (Milan 1943), esp. xli-xlvii.

[23] J. F. Schulte, ed., "Der *Ordo judiciarius* des Codex bambergensis P. I.11," *Sitzungs-*

out that the proctor could do nothing that was not expressly mentioned in his procuration and cautioned that the principal should take care to see that the mandate listed all the actions he wished his proctor to perform. The procurations in his treatise demonstrated his conviction that the wording of any mandate should be strictly construed. A proctor with special mandate and free power (*liberam potestatem*) still had to receive specific authorization to name a substitute. The authority conveyed by the grant of general mandate and free administration (*generale mandatum et liberam administrationem*) in another procuration was evidently limited by the context in which the phrase appeared and was confined to pleading a single case.[24]

The procurations given in the formulary composed by Rainerius of Perugia in the early thirteenth century are also detailed and specific. Three of them simply catalogue the deeds to be performed without using any broad empowering formula; the fourth gives the proctor *plena potestas*, but it is full power simply to take various actions connected with a specific piece of property.[25] Similarly, a model procuration included in a manual written between 1251 and 1270 gave full power and special mandate (*totalem potestatem et speciale mandatum*) only for certain judicial actions and was specifically said to bestow no authority to make compromises or perform any other action requiring a special mandate. The author of this manual warned that one should beware of concluding settlements or compromises with proctors lacking the requisite special powers, since their acts would have no binding force whatsoever.[26]

John of Bologna, who composed a valuable notarial *Summa* at the end of the thirteenth or beginning of the fourteenth century, also preferred specific procurations to more general ones. Dividing procurations into three

---

berichte der Kaiserliche Akademie der Wissenschaften zu Wien, philosophisch-historische Klasse 70 (1872) 299-300. Cf. Aegidius de Fuscarariis (n. 22 above) 20, and 22-23, where Aegidius cited as authority a decree of the Fourth Lateran Council, Decretals of Gregory IX 1.3.28, which stipulated that an agent must have a special mandate to seek apostolic letters, and a bull of Innocent III, *ibid.* 1.43.9, which dealt with the case of a proctor claiming to have power to compromise, whose principal contended that he simply had a general mandate and therefore lacked this authority.

[24] Aegidius de Fuscarariis (n. 22 above) 20, 26. Note the careful limitations expressed in the document appointing a general and special proctor which is included in the thirteenth-century Florentine handbook edited by Gino Masi (n. 22 above) 23-24, cf. in general 21-26.

[25] Rainerius de Perusio, "Ars notaria," ed. Augusto Gaudenzi, in Gaudenzi, ed. (n. 15 above) 2.40-41, nos. 44-48, no. 48 for the procuration mentioning *plena potestas*. One of these procurations (40, no. 45) was a virtual contract, recording the agent's oath to perform his duties *bona fide et sine fraude*, under certain explicit conditions; cf. the proctor's oath recorded in 41, no. 48. On Rainerius and the relationship between this formulary and the notarial *summa* he later composed, Wahrmund (n. 22 above) 3.2, viii-xvi; the section in the *summa* devoted to proctors is far shorter than the corresponding portion of the formulary: *ibid.*, 45-46.

[26] Wahrmund (n. 22 above) 1.2.53-54, and cf. Post (n. 2 above) 99 n. 40.

general categories—*ad causas, ad negotia,* and *ad impetrandum litteras gra-
ciam seu justiciam continentes*—he counseled the notary to inquire carefully
into the principal's intentions and the situation for which the mandate was
being drawn before drafting it.[27] In the model procurations inserted in his
manual, John repeatedly employed the phrase full and free power (*plena
et libera potestas*), but it was always limited to the particular tasks the proctor
was instructed to perform: it gave the proctor no general control over his
principal's property.[28] John included one sample procuration in which the
agent was empowered to manage all affairs of the principal, and in this mandate the formula "free and general administration" appeared, but, to judge
from the many other procurations in the treatise, the phrase was rarely used.
One of John's procurations, however, like one of Aegidius's mandates, showed
that the formula could be so modified by the terms of the document in which
it appeared that its meaning would be narrowly restricted: a procuration
ad causas containing the power of general and free administration seems to
have been intended for use only in connection with the various actions
enumerated in the mandate.[29] Even more striking is a procuration in Salatiele's *Ars Notarie,* composed in Bologna in the mid-thirteenth century. After
setting forth different tasks to be done by the proctor and specifying that
he was to "maintain and faithfully preserve" all the principal's rights in
a certain district, the mandate gave him, "generally, free administration
in the aforesaid matters." Evidently he was being given authority over his
principal's possessions only to deal with the specific situations listed in the
procuration.[30]

Knowledge of the Roman principles of agency law and familiarity with
notarial practice was widespread in customary law areas by the end of the
thirteenth century.[31] The author of the *Établissements de Saint Louis,* draw-

---

[27] Ludwig Rockinger, ed., "Briefsteller und Formelbücher des eilften bis vierzehnten
Jahrhunderts. xii. Iohann von Bologna," *Quellen zur bayrischen und deutschen Geschichte*
9.2 (1864) 605-607. On the three categories of mandates, Donald E. Queller, *The Office
of Ambassador in the Middle Ages* (Princeton 1967) 34-35, and cf. Jane Sayers, "Canterbury
Proctors at the Court of 'Audiencia litterarum contradictarum,'" *Traditio* 22 (1966) 312.

[28] Rockinger 607, 611-614, and cf. the example cited by Post (n. 2 above) 101 n. 47. For
the date of the *Summa,* Rockinger 596-598.

[29] Rockinger, 615-616.

[30] "In predictis generaliter liberam administrationem": Salatiele, *Ars notarie,* ed. Gian-
franco Orlandelli (Milan 1961) 291-292: note too the detailed instructions for modifying
the form of a basic procuration to make it suitable for different situations, *ibid..* 289. On
Salatiele, Wahrmund (n. 22 above) 3.2.li.

[31] For a survey of the situation in England, F. Pollock and F. W. Maitland, *History of
English Law,* ed. 2 (Cambridge 1898) 1.212-215; see also G. D. H. Hall, ed., *The Treatise
on the Laws and Customs of the Realm of England commonly called Glanvill* (London 1965)
12, 192, and cf. the review by Gaines Post in *Speculum* 42 (1967) 162-165; in the phrase
sufficiens responsalis, sufficiens seems clearly to mean "sufficiently qualified to act," rather
than "sufficiently instructed"; cf. Post (n. 2 above) 136-137, which shows that the courts

ing on both Roman law and traditional usage, stressed that a proctor should never damage his principal without possessing a specific mandate to do so.[32] Avoiding the question of free and general administration, he pointed out that the proctor's powers were strictly limited to those expressed in his procuration; in contrast, he stated firmly, a proctor must diligently implement all his principal's commands.[33] Similar principles are expressed in a customal of Artois compiled in the late thirteenth century.[34] Beaumanoir, too, was primarily concerned with the limited rather than with the broadly phrased procuration. The example of a general procuration which he included in is treatise entitled its holder to represent his principal in all court cases: the agent was given full power and special mandate (*pleniere poeste et especial mandement*), but these were limited to specifically judicial actions. Beaumanoir noted that even more restricted procurations could easily be drawn if the principal preferred.[35] Beaumanoir's discussion indeed suggests that constituents may have been reluctant to give their agents broad enough powers to permit them to act effectively. He warned that "everyone must beware of pleading against a proctor lacking power to win or lose, since without it his principal can always revoke his acts." If his agent's procuration was insufficient, the adversary could claim immunity from the court's unfavorable decree, whereas a favorable decision could be accepted ex post facto.[36]

However helpful the theoretical writings might be, it was the principals and their advisers who had to draft the procurations that were actually em-

---

distinguished between a sufficiently instructed proctor and his sufficient mandate. See also Bracton, *De legibus et consuetudinibus Angliae*, ed. G. E. Woodbine (New Haven 1915-1942) 212b.

For northern France, Charles Bataillard, *Les origines de l'histoire des procureurs et des avoués* (Paris 1868) 63-68, 99-104; *Li livres de jostice et de plet*, ed. Rapetti (Paris 1850) 105.

[32] *Les Établissements de Saint Louis*, ed. Paul Viollet (Paris 1881-1886) 2.344-345. To support his position he cited neither C 2.12.10 nor D 3.3.49 (see nn. 12, 14 above), but instead C 2.4.7, which, if not as evidently germane as the other two texts, was still relevant to his conclusion: "Transactionis placitum ab eo interpositum, cui causae actionem, non decisionem litis mandasti, nihil petitioni tuae derogavit."

[33] *Ibid.* 346-347.

[34] Adolphe Tardif, ed., *Coutumier d'Artois* . . . (Paris 1883) 38, nos. 3-5, also xv.

[35] Philippe de Beaumanoir, *Coutumes de Beauvaisis*, ed. A. Salmon (Paris 1899-1900) sections 140-142. See section 54 for Beaumanoir's treatment of the powers of the bailiff. Like Bracton, he held that the bailiff could take no action that might threaten the lord's property rights; he could simply sell those things that his predecessors had been accustomed to sell. If the lord wished him to perform any other office, he must give him a special mandate for the purpose.

[36] *Ibid.*, section 156, and cf. section 150 for a more general statement. In sections 806-807 Beaumanoir dealt with the problem of the insufficient mandate from the viewpoint of the agent, demonstrating the vulnerability of the proctor's position if he acted without sufficient authorization.

ployed and to instruct agents in the proper use of the documents given them. The constituents had to assess the different situations they faced and decide how far they could trust their agents to abide by oral or written instructions supplementing their formal mandates.[37] They must determine how likely it was that aggressive third parties might try to persuade or force broadly empowered agents to disregard such instructions and commit their principals to actions that they, the constituents, neither intended nor desired. They must weigh this possible danger against the inconvenience and damage they might suffer if their proctors' mandates proved to be insufficient to permit them to perform actions benefiting the principal.

Acquaintance with the principles of agency law and expertise in using them was not confined to southern France and Italy. In customary law areas proctors could appear in court cases, although this was still a privilege restricted to certain definite categories of people;[38] mandates were also issued to empower agents to carry on other business,[39] and the royal and northern French archives contain scattered examples of detailed procurations containing specific instructions and limitations.[40] In the Midi, however, the use of Roman legal forms had developed in close conjunction with the precocious growth of independent municipal organizations and the consequent

[37] For a valuable and quite rare instance of the survival of both the written instructions and a record of the actions taken later by the proctors, Ernest Barker, *The Dominican Order and Convocation* (Oxford 1913) 28. While the agents were able to implement some of the instructions, other items were abandoned, probably because the agents found themselves isolated when other proctors took a less uncompromising stand. See also above at n. 5. Because of the nature of the evidence, it is impossible to know how effectively oral instructions limited proctors to whom they were given. It is difficult to believe, however, that they were not as binding in the thirteenth and fourteenth centuries as they are today. Beaumanoir considered the oral commission fully binding, although naturally less easy to substantiate than a written commission: Beaumanoir (n. 35 above) sections 806-807. Bracton also maintained that oral obligations were binding, and in taking this stand, he cited a statement of Azo, who had relied on the Institutes: S. E. Thorne, ed., *Bracton On the Laws and Customs of England* (Cambridge, Mass. 1968) 2.287; cf. F. W. Maitland, *Select Passages from the Works of Bracton and Azo* (London 1895) 155-157. Since Roman legal tradition as well as customary practice upheld the authority of oral commitments, it seems likely that instructions given orally were considered as binding between agent and principal as written ones.

[38] Bataillard (n. 31 above) 64-68, 122-128; Heinrich Brunner, *Forschungen zur Geschichte des deutschen und französischen Rechts* (Stuttgart 1894) 391-426, and cf. the partial translation of this section in *Illinois Law Review* 3 (1908) 257-279; Hans Würdinger, *Geschichte der Stellvertretung in England zugleich ein Beitrag zur Entwicklung des englischen Privatrechts* (Marburg in Hessen 1933) 44-54.

[39] Bataillard and *Li livres* as cited in n. 31 above; see also *Établissements* (n. 32 above) 348 and Beaumanoir (n. 35 above) section 137.

[40] For a remarkably precise procuration issued by the citizens of Angers in 1310, which includes specific instructions and limitations, Archives Nationales, J 179A no. 90. Cf. also n. 76 below.

spread of the notariate there,[41] and, if Roman legal terminology had its most striking impact on the words and phrases used to describe the administrative offices of the towns, it was perhaps in the field of agency law that the town officers found Roman legal concepts most pragmatically useful. Since many southern communities possessed consular forms of government from an early date, they could be adequately represented by their own officials,[42] but, as town affairs became increasingly complex, they tended to rely on special agents or proctors to carry on their dealings with other towns and with the government. The extraordinary richness of the muncipal archives of southern France makes it possible to study in some depth the knowledge of agency law possessed by the Midi townsmen and to trace the development of their ability to put this knowledge into practice and utilize the agency relationship for their own ends. The wider political implications of the experience the townsmen acquired in managing their local affairs will become evident, for, when the king, demanding their support, called upon them to send representatives to appear before him or his agents, they could and did employ the skills and techniques they had already learned to deal with his requests and protect their interests.

Although few early procurations survive, the city of Cahors is known to have dispatched formally constituted proctors to the papal court in 1216, and this suggests one avenue by which the technicalities of agency law were learned, since, thanks to the work of the canonists, ecclesiastics had ready access to information about the agency relationship.[43] In 1233 the consuls of Cahors were acting for their fellow citizens,[44] but in 1249 the town was represented before a papal legate by a proctor, who appeared before the legate at Lyon and there named two substitutes to act in his place.[45] In this case as well, ecclesiastical practice probably influenced the agency document that was drawn. If the procurations involved in this case were strictly judicial, the consuls were also capable of commissioning mandates empowering agents to reach settlements and to perform other taks. As the theorists suggested was advisable and proper, in these mandates they were careful to enumerate the special powers needed by their agents. In 1286 the consuls of Cahors named three men "to treat, arrange, ordain and manage for us and in the

---

[41] André Gouron, "Diffusion des consulats méridionaux et expansion du droit romain aux xiie et xiiie siècles," *Bibliothèque de l'École des chartes* 121 (1963) 26-76.

[42] Cf. the comments of Johannes Faber, quoted in J. Declareuil, *Histoire générale du droit français* (Paris 1925) 513-514, nn. 271-272.

[43] See the letter of Innocent III, dated 2 June 1216, preserved in the Archives municipales de Cahors, AA 58. For ecclesiastics' familiarity with the principals of agency law, see at n. 5 above, and nn. 23 and 37 above, as well as n. 48 below.

[44] A. M. Cahors, AA 1. See also Bibliothèque Nationale, Doat 118, fol. 180vff. and A. M. Cahors, DD 24 for acts showing that in 1282 the town was represented by three consuls and four proctors.

[45] Bibliothèque Nationale, Doat 118, fol. 72vff.

name of the said town, and to compromise, pacify, act and defend in the business of the navigation of the river Lot."[46] These men were given "full, free, and every sort of power, and special mandate" (*plenam & liberam potestatem & omnimodam & speciale mandatum*) to do many things; they were specifically empowered to obligate the property and goods of the consulate, but, as the mandate made clear, these powers were to be exercised only in connection with the question of how the Lot was to be navigated.[47]

The archives of Cahors are particularly rich in examples of relatively early procurations, but documents from other southern archives show that by the end of the thirteenth century the officials of other towns had become as expert as the consuls of Cahors in commissioning procurations explicitly defining the scope of their agents' powers and duties.[48] In 1290 a rather loosely worded but still perfectly workable mandate was drafted in the town of Alès. The consuls were anxious to hire a professor of canon law, and, to judge from the quality of the procuration their agent bore, he would have found an intelligent and appreciative audience at Alès. The consuls gave their proctor the task of arranging a *pensionem siue salarium* to be paid to a certain canon of Maguelonne, or, if he would not accept the post, to the person who could be hired. So that their agent could do this, the consuls bestowed on him "free administration and full power and also special mandate,"[49] but this broad authority was to be exercised only in fulfilling the duties outlined in the mandate.[50] Still, the agent was given considerable discretion, and it seems likely that he received more exact supplementary instructions, either orally or in writing. The contract, concluded a month and a half later, was detailed and precise: not only did it set the salary of

---

[46] "Ad tractandum, gerendum, ordinandum, et componendum pro nobis et nomine vniuersitatis predicte et compromittendum, pacificandum, agendum, et deffendendum super negotio transitus fluminis Olti": A. M. Cahors, DD 28.

[47] Cf. the similar procuration dated 1284, found in A. M. Cahors, DD 26. A more specific procuration connected with the question of the navigation of the Lot was issued in 1290, when men were appointed "ad petendum, recipiendum et obtinendum pro nobis et vice et loco et nomine nostro litteras, obligationes et instrumenta que nobis debent concedi et dari apud Lausertam super uenditione, solutione et quitatione nobis seu mandato nostro factis": A. M. Cahors, DD 29. They too received "plenam et liberam et omnimodam potestatem et speciale mandatum," but this power was restricted to the specific task described above, and they had only limited financial powers.

[48] The archives of Agen contain a simple but carefully worded procuration drawn up by Amanieu d'Albret in 1253: A. Magen and G. Tholin, eds., *Archives municipales d'Agen: Chartes, première série (1189-1328)* (Villeneuve-sur-Lot 1876) 72, no. 50. They also contain a technically impeccable general procuration drawn by a prior of St-Caprais d'Agen while he was at Viterbo in 1268 (78-79, no 56). Such a document, deposited in the municipal archives, could serve as a convenient form for the town's lawyers, providing them with a working model or legally acceptable formulas.

[49] "Administrationem liberam et potestatem plenariam ac mandatum etiam speciale": Archives communales d'Alès, I.S. 18, no. 8.

the prospective professor, but it also provided for various contingencies, such as the possibility that the king, the lord of Alès, or the bishop of Nîmes might forbid him to teach.[51] It is hard to believe that the proctor of Alès would have negotiated or accepted such an agreement without additional instructions or further consultation with his constituents.

The southern consulates seem to have been well aware of the theorists' admonitions that proctors needed special powers to bring about settlements and effect compromises involving the property rights of the constituents.[52] How important the granting of these powers could be is illustrated by the experiences of two southern communities in the first decade of the fourteenth century. The first case involved a property dispute between Philip IV's minister, Guillaume de Nogaret, and the town of Lunel, a struggle that dragged on for many years.[53] In 1302, after appearing in the seneschal's court, the two parties agreed to put their quarrel into the hands of three arbitrators.[54] Two syndics of Lunel appeared before the mediators on 24 November 1302, and they presented a *nota* drawn by a notary public on 2 August 1302, claiming that this gave them authority to act, defend, compromise, negotiate settlements, and reach agreements concerning the questions at issue between the town and Nogaret. The arbitrators, however, refused to admit that the *nota* bestowed these powers and therefore ordered the men to obtain from their fellow townsmen, as a precautionary measure,[55] advance ratification of the arbitrators' decision as well as a new mandate for themselves "to pursue

---

[50] *Ibid.*, dated 6 May 1290.

[51] A. C. Alès, I.S. 18, no. 9, dated 18 June 1290.

[52] See above, at nn. 10, 16, and cf. esp. nn. 11, 17. Particularly striking are the procurations employed in 1315 by the prior and consuls of Najac, who were engaged in litigation over the church of Najac. The prior's agent employed a general, quite extensive document, which had been issued on 26 June 1310 and which gave full and free power and special mandate to perform many acts, including the authority "componendi, transigendi, assensandi, census et acapita recipiendi, redditus suos et prouentus dicti prioratus et alios quoscumque uendendi et arrendandi, ad firmam concedendi": Archives départementales de l'Aveyron, 2E. 178. 10. The mandate did not grant the agents free adinistration, but the proctors were referred to as "administratores seu negociorum gestores" and they evidently possessed broad authority over their principal's possessions. The prior's opponent, the community of Najac, drafted a special procuration on 13 February 1315 for the agents who would be involved in the dispute with the prior. Although the powers it contained were chiefly judicial in nature, it did give the town's proctors full and free power and special mandate both "componendi" and "transigendi" and authorized them to appear and act not only before court officials but also before arbitrators.

[53] For a detailed discussion of the quarrel, see Louis Thomas, "La vie privée de Guillaume de Nogaret," *Annales du Midi* 16 (1904) 161ff.

[54] Pons d'Omelas and Guillaume de Plaisians were chosen to act with Raymond *de Mugolano*: A. C. Lunel, DD 2, no. 2106, series P; cf. Thomas 172-178. For their appearance in the seneschal's court, A. C. Lunel, II. 5, unnumbered document.

[55] "Ad maiorem cautelam et debitam securitatem": A. C. Lunel, DD 2, no. 2106, series P.

the said compromise and to compromise anew if such action seemed advisable to the mediators."[56] Therefore on the next day two-thirds of the men of Lunel, as a notarized instrument testified, assembled in a public meeting and accepted the form of the compromise; then, for safety's sake, they bestowed fresh power on the syndics, giving them explicit authority "to pursue the said compromise and any matters connected with it, and to reach an accord, come to a settlement, or to negotiate an agreement and agree to a pact," and to accept the decrees of the arbitrators.[57] The arbitrators were wise to obtain this confirmation from the town, for after many conferences, on 5 October 1303 the syndics of Lunel lodged a formal protest against the proceedings. Thanks to the arbitrators' foresight, the syndics could not deny that the town had approved the agreement nor could they claim that they lacked proper powers to negotiate a settlement. Their only recourse was to assert that they had been elected by a minority of the men of Lunel: asserting that four or five thousand adult males were commonly said to live in the *castrum*, they maintained that only four or five hundred men were listed in the document describing the creation of the proctors. In the ensuing confusion, the arbitrators were unable to agree about what should be done, although two of them insisted on pronouncing sentence against Lunel. The proctors of Lunel promptly appealed. The townsmen naturally refused to accept the arbitrators' decision, despite the fact that the king issued letters supporting Nogaret.[58] Finally Nogaret had the men of Lunel cited to the seneschal's assize at Aigues Mortes, and the town was ordered to name proctors to appear there. In view of the obstacles encountered in the first round of negotiations, it is not surprising that the seneschal's lieutenant gave them specific instructions concerning the form of the procuration, telling them to name agents "to act, defend, compromise, or negotiate a settlement concerning certain matters affecting the men of the said community."[59] Obediently, the men of Lunel issued a suitable mandate, and the case progressed to a new stage.[60]

The town of Aimargues faced a similar situation in December 1309. In this case, however, the difficulty stemmed not from any doubt about the

[56] "Ad prosequendum dictum compromissum et compromitendum de nouo si ipsis dominis arbitris videbitur faciendum": *ibid.*

[57] "Ad dictum compromissum et omnia ab eo dependentia prosequendum et super predictis cum dicto domino Guillelmo seu quocumque alio eius nomine conueniendum, concordandum seu transigendum et paciscendum": *ibid.*

[58] A. C. Lunel, II.5, unnumbered document.

[59] "Ad agendum, deffendendum, componendum, seu transigendum super quibusdam que homines dicte vniuersitatis videntur tangere, que vobis sub nostro sigillo mittimus interclusa": *ibid.*

[60] For later developments, Thomas (n. 53 above) 187-192, 206-207; also various documents relating to the quarrel, dated 1302 and 1314, in A. C. Lunel, DD 2, and A. C. Lunel, AA 5, nos. 104, 1761, series 9ʲ.

proper formulation of the mandate but from the townsmen's own recognition
that the procuration they had given their agents did not provide them with
sufficient power to perform the tasks they wished to see accomplished. To
judge from the other procurations existing in the archives of Aimargues,[61]
the men of this town insisted on issuing extremely detailed and explicit procurations, listing item by item the specific actions to be performed. This
caution may reflect the tensions that existed between the nobles and people
of the town, who were involved in continual struggles; the jealousies and
rivalries that split the town meant that the townsmen undoubtedly wanted
to keep close control over their representatives' actions. Therefore, they
gave them little freedom of action and forced them to return for fresh instructions and mandates when unexpected developments occurred.[62] Thus,
on 23 December 1309 the people of Aimargues had the nobles summoned
from their dwellings in order to bestow expanded powers on the town's five
proctors, who lacked the requisite authority to negotiate a compromise over
the many sources of difference existing between the town and the lord of
Aimargues. The nobles grudgingly agreed—and only for the good of the
town, they said—not only to accept Clement de Fraxino, the arbitrator who
had been chosen by the proctors, but also to grant the agents the new procuration they needed to compromise and arrange a settlement.[63] Their new
mandate gave them full and free power and authority and special mandate
to put the dispute into the arbitrator's hands and to reach an agreement
with the lord through his mediation.

Individuals and associations of different communities and groups were
no less able than single towns to commission procurations for their agents
which were precisely limited in scope. A mandate drawn up in 1316 by the
nobles and consuls of Foix could scarcely have been more carefully defined.[64]
These men, concerned by the disturbed state of the county since the death
of Gaston of Foix, had determined to take some action, and therefore they
appointed a number of agents, nobles, and experienced lawyers, to ascertain
whether the count had made a will and codicils naming guardians for his
son and heir, to try to see the relevant documents and bring them back to

[61] See particularly the procurations dated 3 January 1305 and 10 September 1307 which
are copied in A. C. Aimargues, FF 45, nos. 211ff.

[62] For the division, see the procuration of 1305 referred to in n. 61, and, for more detail,
the document of 1309, A. C. Aimargues, FF 3, no. 17 (cf. FF 6, no. 18), which will be discussed below.

[63] A. C. Aimargues, FF 3, no. 17 (cf. FF 6, no. 18). For the outcome see A. C. Aimargues,
FF 3, no. 20.

[64] Bibliothèque Nationale, Doat 181, fols. 65-71v, dated 18 August 1316, with additional
adherences secured between that date and 1 September appended to the procuration. For
a full discussion of these incidents, Pierre Timbal, "La tutelle dans la famille des comtes
de Foix au xiv⁰ siècle," *Recueil de mémoires et travaux publiés par la Société d'histoire du
droit et des institutions des anciens pays de droit écrit* 1 (1948) 69-76.

the county, to view and have broken the seal that the count had used, to attempt to have appointed as provisional guardians five leading nobles of Foix whom the nobles and communities of the county had selected, and, generally, to do anything in connection with these matters which seemed appropriate. The agents received full and free power and authority to say, seek, do, act, obtain, have, recover, contest, seek, swear, appeal, and take any suitable action to implement their commission. The duties were precisely described, and although the proctors received broad powers, they were all confined to the execution of the tasks assigned to them. An equally specific but potentially far more compromising procuration had been prepared two years earlier for an individual noble of Saintonge. In this case the knight's problem centered on property that the king had seized, and therefore, to insure that his agents could adequately represent him, he gave his four agents free and general mandate with free and general administration (*liberum et generale mandatum cum libera et generali administratione*), that broad authority over property which so concerned the theorists. Nevertheless, the specific tasks they were to perform were carefully enumerated. Not only were they to present the noble's requests to the king and his court and to ask for the removal of the royal hand from his property; they were also authorized to take an oath of fealty to the king on the lord's behalf and to receive investiture of the land; finally, they were empowered to sell the land for any price they agreed upon, or to alienate the land in any way and to anyone they wished.[65]

As the documents that have been examined clearly demonstrate, by the end of the thirteenth century towns and individuals had acquired considerable proficiency at commissioning mandates of all sorts—general procurations and mandates limiting the actions their agents could take. The documents they issued testify to their familiarity with the intricate principles of agency law and show that exposure to theory and hard experience had taught these men and their notaries to adapt their procurations to the specific situations in which they expected their agents to be involved and to distinguish circumstances in which restricted procurations for court action would be appropriate from those in which broader negotiating powers were needed. Men with such sophistication and expertise were unlikely to be any less astute than the knight of Saintonge in commissioning documents to be used in negotiations with the king. Although, by virtue of his supreme authority and prerogative, the monarch was evidently superior to his subjects,

---

[65] Archives Nationales, JJ 49, fols. 99v-100, no. 225; the quoted portion appears on fol. 100. Part of this procuration was published by Paul Guérin, "Documents relatifs à l'histoire de la Saintonge et de l'Aunis extraits des registres du Trésor des chartes," *Archives historiques de la Saintonge et de l'Aunis* 12 (1884) 132, no. lvii; he unfortunately omitted the empowering clause, which, he said, contained only conventional formulas.

they did not consider him their absolute master, and they were determined to guard and defend their rights against him as against all other men. Before 1300 townsmen and other subjects had had many opportunities for dealing with the king and his officials, in courtroom and extrajudicial situations. In these negotiations they learned to utilize mandates to limit their proctors' freedom of action and to protect them from the pressures to which they might be subjected, while still giving them adequate authority to represent their constituents effectively. The balance was delicate, but the communities and individuals who dealt with the king gradually acquired experience in designing documents through which it could be achieved.

In 1286 the citizens of Montpellier were involved in a struggle with the seneschal of Beaucaire over 10,000 l.t. which the town, obeying a command of the king of France, had placed in his hands, and which the seneschal had subsequently disposed of in response to royal orders, against the wishes and the express prohibition of the consuls of Montpellier. Therefore on 1 November 1286 the consuls appointed three proctors, two consuls and a syndic of the town as their *ambaxatores* to negotiate a settlement. Those men were given "full and free power to compromise and negotiate a settlement if they and their co-ambassadors judge it expedient to do so,"[66] but this extensive authority was limited to the question of the 10,000 l.t., and the consuls insisted that any arrangement that was made should free them of all obligations to the former seneschal of Beaucaire and should preserve all liberties granted to the town by the kings of Majorca and earlier lords of Montpellier. An even more strictly defined mandate was issued in December 1294 to two Montpellier proctors, a lawyer and a notary, who were to appear on the town's behalf before the royal seneschal. These men received "full and general power," which was to be exercised only in appearing before the seneschal at Nîmes to answer the charge that the town had refused to obey his mandate to serve the king by helping the seneschal suppress a rising in the district. The men were to present the town's "appropriate defenses, excuses and exceptions" and were given authority to appeal, but this was the extent of their powers, which were thus exclusively judicial in nature.[67] These procurations contrast sharply with another mandate, drafted at Montpellier in November 1295, which empowered two men to approach the king of France and his council "to act and defend, seek and obtain letters and favors for [the community] . . . and to appear and present themselves . . . and to say, propose, petition, require, demand, supplicate and accept" anything that might prove useful and advantageous to the town. They were also given authority to pursue

---

[66] "Plenam et liberam potestatem componendi et transigendi si discretioni ipsorum et aliorum cohambaxatorum eorum videbitur expedire": A. M. Montpellier, Louvet 1989.

[67] "Defentiones, Excusationes et exceptiones . . . competentes": A. M. Montpellier, Louvet 1996.

appeals lying before the king, to protect the town, its property, and rights, and to defend it from any threat. They were, finally, given the general right to take any action that the merits of the cases in which they became involved might require.[68] This procuration gave the town's agents a far wider range of powers and permitted them to deal with many more cases and situations than did the mandate empowering proctors to appear before the seneschal. In contrast, the proctors of 1295 did not receive the valuable discretionary powers of negotiating settlements, and, had a situation arisen in which they wished to take such action, they would presumably have had to apply to their principals for a new procuration. This of course gave the consuls greater control over their agents than they would have had, had these powers been included in the mandate. The consuls may have thought it safe to give such extensive authority to agents who were to be negotiating in the vicinity of Montpellier, as was true in the case of the proctors appointed in 1286; the situation may have seemed different when the agents would be dealing with the king's court far to the north.

Under similar circumstances in 1317, when royal reform commissioners summoned the consuls of Narbonne to appear before them at Carcassonne, the consuls and councilors of the town named two proctors with an impressive range of powers, despite the fact that the royal commissioners had not suggested what authority the representatives should possess. The men were given full and free power to appear before the commissioners and other officials to defend the town, to take necessary oaths, to present proofs, but also to choose arbitrators, to arrange compromises and settlements, to accept penalties imposed on the town, to agree to the amounts of the penalties, and to obligate the town to pay these sums.[69] Perhaps the consuls believed that the town would be more likely to receive favorable treatment and less likely to incur the commissioners' wrath if the agents possessed effective negotiating powers.

Such broad bargaining authority was also regularly given in cases when townsmen, far from fearing the authority of the crown, were so anxious to secure its protection for themselves that their desire to obtain royal favor

---

[68] "Ad agendum et defendum, impetrandum et optinendum litteras et fauores pro nobis ... et ad comparendum et se representandum . . . et ad dicendum, proponendum, petendum, requirendum, postulandum, supplicandum et recipiendum": A. M. Montpellier, Louvet 1998.

[69] A. M. Narbonne, BB 178, a document dated 1 May 1317, which includes the summons issued by the commissioners, Guillaume *Arrenardi*, *scholasticus* of Limoges, and Pons d'Ome-las, on 13 April 1317. Townsmen could be far warier than this in dealing with royal officials and commissioners, as was seen in the case of the Montpellier proctors of 1294. Similarly, in 1304, when the men of Riom were summoned to appear before royal commissioners sent "ad Emendandum grauamina facta per nobilem virum Bone memorie dominum Alfonsum quondam comitem Pictauensem et tholose," they simply gave their agents the appropriate judicial powers to seek "quod gravamina facta eidem ville per dominum quondam comitem supradictum aut eius gentes penitus emendentur": A. C. Riom, AA 15, no. 1383.

outweighed their fear of the possible damage their proctors might cause them. In 1306 the city of Carcassonne was in serious trouble with the king. Following a revolt against the crown, the seneschal had fined the town 60,000 l.t. and deprived it forever of its rights of self-government.[70] The townsmen were naturally eager to regain their rights and obtain remission of the fine, and in October 1306 the royally appointed consuls sent two proctors to plead with the king on the town's behalf. Under these circumstances, it was to the town's own interest to give its proctors the widest possible range of powers: the city's position could hardly have been made any worse than it already was. Therefore the city consuls and councilors named two of the consuls their agents in any and all cases involving Carcassonne; the proctors were authorized to appear before the king, the auditors of his court, or his commissioners, and they were given full and free power and special mandate to act for and defend the town and to seek and obtain privileges and letters containing grace or justice. They also received a number of powers that suggest that the town was more hopeful of gaining the king's favor by negotiating with him than by pursuing their case through ordinary legal channels. They were given authority to effect a reconciliation, negotiate a settlement, compromise, reach an agreement, offer the king a free subvention, and fine or make a financial arrangement with the king and his officials.[71] When the proctors appeared before the king they magnanimously acknowledged the heavy expenses that the king had had to bear because of his wars and they avowed the benevolence of the king and his predecessors to the city. Therefore they offered an unrestricted subsidy to the king, promising to give him 30,000 l.t. within little more than two years. Nothing was said of the penalties imposed by the seneschal, but it is probably no coincidence that in January 1307 a royal notary prepared a letter restoring Carcassonne's privileges and canceling the seneschal's fine. There is no evidence that the letter was actually issued, for the town did not obtain formal forgiveness until May 1307, and a notation on the reverse of the letter of January questions whether or not it was ever dispatched by the chancery.[72] Still, the terms of the procuration

---

[70] For the quarrel and its background, H. C. Lea, *A History of the Inquisition of the Middle Ages* (New York 1887) 2.63-90; Claude de Vic and J. J. Vaissete, *Histoire générale de Languedoc*, ed. A. Molinier *et al.* (Toulouse 1872-1893) 9.277-280, esp. 279, n. 2; 10, *preuves* 457-463; Karl Wenck, *Philipp der Schöne von Frankreich* (Marburg 1905) 44-47.

[71] "Componendi, transigendi, compromittendi, paciscendi et domino nostro Regi gratis per modum subuentionis offerendi et etiam cum dicto domino Rege uel gentibus suis pro ipso finandi et financiam faciendi": Archives Nationales, J 335, no. 5, printed in de Vic and Vaissete (n. 70 above) 9, *preuves* 457-458. The procuration is dated at Carcassonne on 24 October 1306; when the proctors actually appeared before Philip is unknown; I plan to discuss this episode more fully in the study of Philip the Fair's aid for the marriage of his daughter which I am now preparing.

[72] De Vic and Vaissete 10, *preuves* 459-460, and cf. *ibid.* 9.279 n. 2 for Molinier's interpretation of these events, which differs in some respects from my own.

and the negotations carried on by the mandataries show what broad discretionary powers a town was willing to grant agents when it seemed to the
town's advantage to do so.

This incident is not an isolated example, and other instances of similar
broad mandates granted by townsmen eager to obtain favors from the crown
can be cited. In February 1314 the inhabitants of the community of Lautrec[73] and its administrative district were anxious to regain the governmental
rights that had been taken into the king's hands, and therefore they had
approached the special royal commissioners who were dealing with crown
business in Toulouse. Their overtures were warmly received, for, since the
community had never paid the marriage aid imposed in 1308, the commissioners evidently decided that negotiations could be extremely profitable
for the royal treasury. They ordered the inhabitants of Lautrec to send
proctors to appear before them in Toulouse, and, emphasizing that they were
acting at the community's request, they bade and authorized the election
of agents with power to treat, compromise, come to a financial agreement,
and obligate the inhabitants and their property to pay a fine in order to regain their rights and liquidate their debt; the proctors were also to receive
power to make all necessary stipulations and renunciations. The men of
Lautrec duly issued such a mandate to their syndics. The authority they
granted was exceedingly broad, and it seems unlikely that they would have
complied so readily with the commissioners' instructions—and far less likely
that they would have indicated a willingness to give such powers—had
they not been determined to recover their autonomy.[74]

Four years later proctors of the neighboring community of Briatexte[75]
appeared before the lieutenant of the seneschal of Carcassonne and Béziers
on a mission that was also designed to protect the community's privileged
status. In this case, however, it was the king's special guardianship of the
town which was in question, for the townsmen wanted to prevent the king
from alienating their community to a local lord. Not only did the agents
claim to have special mandate and adequate power to act, but, in a spurt
of superfluous enthusiasm, they pledged that all their commitments would
be ratified and confirmed by their fellow citizens. Unfortunately the agents'
procuration has not survived, so the precise extent of the authority the town

---

[73] Tarn, arrondissement Castres, ch.1.c.

[74] "Ad veniendum, et comparendum coram nobis, et nobiscum nomine domini Regis,
de subsidio per nos ab eis petito ratione Maritagii filiae domini nostri Regis, et de facto
Consulatus Lautrici, et Lautrigesii, nunc in manu Regia existentis tractandum, et componendum finandum ac ipsos pro financia Regi Soluenda obligandum atque Sua, cum stipu-
lationibus, et renuntiationibus ad haec opportunis": Bibliothèque Nationale, Doat 248,
fols. 44v-45. I plan to treat this episode in greater detail in the monograph on the marriage
aid which I am now completing: cf. n. 71 above.

[75] Tarn, arrondissement Castres, c. Graulhet.

had actually given them is unknown. Still, they were able to offer, without referring back to their constituents, an annual payment of 20 l.t., which the lieutenant accepted. In return they were promised that the community would remain under the king's direct control.[76]

As was seen in the case of Montpellier, under ordinary circumstances men were unlikely to grant their agents such extensive powers when they were to be negotiating far from home and would not be subject to their constituents' immediate supervision. While this factor could be overblanced by an urgent desire for speedy action, in other situations it was likely to be important and to influence constituents to draft more limited procurations. This was particularly likely to be true when the principals had reason to suspect that their mandataries might be subjected to pressure to involve them in commitments, particularly financial, which they wished to avoid.[77] Thus, in 1282, when the community of Riom sent two proctors to the king to protest against the royal *bailli*'s attempt to levy a sum of money promised solely for the king's campaign in Spain, a project that had never materialized, they gave their agents full power and special mandate to seek the king's intervention against his official. Nothing was said of the possibility that a compromise

[76] Jean Guerout, ed., *Registres du Trésor des chartes* 2: *Règnes des fils de Philippe le Bel*, pt. 1, *Règnes de Louis X et de Philippe V le Long* (Paris 1966) no. 2043, but, for the full text, Archives Nationales, JJ 56, fols. 180v-181 no. 416: "Habentes ad infrascripta ut dixerunt speciale mandatum et ydoneum potestatem, promittentes nichilominus se facturos et curaturos ita et taliter quod uniuersitas hominum dicti loci omnia et singula infrascripta approbabit, ratificabit et confirmabit."

Such negotiations as these were not confined to the Midi. In 1323 the inhabitants of Jonvelle-sur-Saône (Haute-Saône, arrondissement Vesoul, c. Jussey), a town in the northeastern part of the kingdom, wanted to obtain a guarantee of perpetual royal safeguard and they granted their proctors, who were to negotiate with the king's officials, every conceivable power they might need to act in court; in addition, they gave them full power, authority, and special mandate to come to an agreement, accord, and compromise over the question of the royal safeguard, and to obligate the town to make an annual payment to the king each November in return for the privilege; they also empowered them to contract debts in the name of the town and obligate the property of the members of the community to carry out their mission. Under these circumstances the men quickly reached an agreement with the royal representatives and obtained the guarantee in return for the promise of an annual payment of four *muids* of oats: Archives Nationales, JJ 62, fol. 115, no. 204, a royal confirmation dated July 1324 of an agreement reached on 10 October 1323 before two sworn clerks of the king at Coiffy, the seat of a *prévôté* of the *bailliage* of Chaumont.

[77] After a proctor of the consuls of Najac had declared before a royal official that the consuls had no jurisdictional rights in the castle of Najac, the consuls experienced some difficulty in having his act canceled. First Philip the Fair issued two letters, on 3 and 22 September 1308, informing the seneschal of Rouergue that the consuls of Najac had his permission to revoke their agent's declaration. Then the consuls had to issue a formal revocation, in which they carefully inserted the privilege issued to them by Alfonse, count of Toulouse, on which they based their claims: see Bibliothèque Nationale MS n.a.f. 564 (an inventory of the archives of Najac completed in 1575) fol. 47v.

settlement on any terms might be arranged.[78] Similarly, a procuration drafted
by thirty-one towns of Quercy in June 1307, naming five emissaries to the
royal court, was quite limited. The proctors were authorized to seek and
obtain from the king and his court letters containing grace and justice concerning the assessment of taxable property recently made in the seneschalsy
of Périgord and Quercy; the men were given full and free power and special
mandate, but only to carry out the task described in their procuration. They
were not empowered to negotiate any settlement with the king.[79] Again,
in 1309, when forty-seven towns and nine churches of the same region banded
together in loose confederations to protest against the marriage aid and the
fines for the acquisition of fiefs that were being levied in their district, the
agents were not able to make any financial composition with the king's agents
when they were offered the opportunity to do so in Paris. Their constituents
had carefully prepared for them mandates limiting their authority to specific
judicial and petitionary actions connected with the levies. Therefore, lacking
the important power of reaching settlements, they had to refer back to their
constituents for further instructions.[80]

[78] "Plenam potestatem et speciale mandatum super predictis semel vel pluries suppli-
candi et requirendi in vestre regie celsitudinis curia et omnia alia faciendi, impetrandi et
audiendi que super predictis fuerint facienda et etiam impetranda et que nos super predictis
faceremus et facere possemus si presentes essemus." A. C. Riom, CC 7, no. 1411, dated
22 October 1282. In 1287, when Cahors, Figeac, and Montcuq sent a joint delegation to
the king to request his assistance, they provided their agents, the consuls of Cahors and
Figeac, with a similarly limited mandate. The agents were given full and free power and
special mandate, but their sphere of competence was restricted "ad supplicandum et os-
tendendum, significandum et demonstrandum vestre regie celsitudini et vestre curie ve-
nerande grauamina quae nobis et communitati nostrae et singulis de vniuersitate inferuntur
seu inferri poterunt infuturis occasione plurium statutorum vt dicitur nuper in Bituricensi
consilio, et ad impetrandum super praedictis et super omnia praedicta tangentibus a vestra
regia magestate et vestra curia veneranda remedium, consilium, gratiam, literas contra-
dictionis et inhibitionis contra statuta praedicta": Bibliothèque Nationale, Doat 118, fols.
229v-230. Despite the wide range of powers bestowed on the proctors to enable them to
implement their constituents' wishes, they obtained no authority whatsoever over the property of the consulates or of the towns' inhabitants.

[79] A. M. Cahors, BB 6; cf. Edmond Albe, "Inventaire raisonné et analytique des archives
municipales de Cahors," *Bulletin trimestriel de la Société des études littéraires, scientifiques
et artistiques du Lot* 41 (1920) 22-23 no. 229. This incident is discussed in fuller detail in
the monograph referred to in n. 71 above.

[80] These events will also be discussed in the monograph on the marriage aid; for a summary of the provisional conclusions I had reached in 1968, see my paper, "Philip the Fair,
Plena Potestas, and the *Aide pur fille marier* of 1308," *Studies Presented to the International
Commission for the History of Representative and Parliamentary Institutions* 39 (1970) 1-27.
A restricted mandate was issued in 1311 by forty-six towns of Quercy, including many of
those which had participated in the 1307 and 1309 protests. In it they empowered twenty-
one proctors to pursue an appeal lodged by the seneschal and royal proctor of Périgord
and Quercy against certain decisions of the bishop of Cahors. The appeal was addressed

Such limitations as those imposed in these mandates were generally effective, but no mandate, no matter how precisely defined, was foolproof. This the consuls of Montpellier learned in the years following 1310. In that year the city named four men as its proctors,[81] giving them free and general power to say, do, agree upon, and arrange everything of which the consuls and community of Montpellier would be capable if they were present; the consuls judged it unwise, however, to send their proctors to the royal court to negotiate a particularly ticklish issue with powers as broad as these. Therefore, on the same day on which they drafted the general procuration, they drew up another, far more limited one. This second mandate proclaimed that, despite the general mandate, the agents had power to offer the king of France only 15,000 l.t., to be paid over a five-year period by the community of Montpellier. This money was to be given on condition that the king of France would confirm the consulate of Montpellier and all the good usages and privileges of the city. He was also to grant remission to all citizens of Montpellier for any crimes of disobedience which they had committed in the past and to renew the royal safeguard over the city.[82] As if this were not explicit enough, the consuls of Montpellier went on to forbid their agents to offer any more than the stipulated sum and to warn them not to grant the 15,000 l.t. unless the king fulfilled the conditions outlined in the mandate. The consuls stated that if the proctors exceeded their mandate, the town would not consider itself bound by the commitments they made, and they announced that they would refuse to ratify them. Finally the proctors themselves promised to abide by the terms of the mandate, to refuse to obligate the town for more than 15,000 l.t., and to grant the king this sum only when he had confirmed the consulate and its liberties, remitted the citizens' offenses, renewed the safeguard, and given them letters and receipts testifying to his actions. The proctors were momentarily successful, and in August, September, and October Philip IV granted numerous privileges to Montpellier.[83] Soon, however, word of what was happening reached the court

---

to the pope, but the powers granted were essentially the same as those given to the agents who had been sent to the king: Bibliothèque Nationale, Doat 119, fols. 23-26v, and also A. M. Cahors, FF 15; cf. Albe 35-36.

[81] For a detailed analysis of these events, see L. J. Thomas, "Montpellier entre la France et l'Aragon pendant la première moitié du xive siècle," *Monspeliensia* 1.1 (1928-1929) 8-18; a number of the most important texts relating to the quarrel are printed in an appendix to the article. The men were appointed the town's "procuratores, syndicos, actores, et fauctores": *ibid.* 33. In another document drafted the same day the men were referred to as *ambaxatores*: *ibid.* 36.

[82] This document is printed in *ibid.* 33-35, but in place of *remitionem*, found in the original document in the Montpellier archives, Thomas read *renunciationem*. The same error appears in the document printed on 36-37.

[83] On the same day the consuls prepared a declaration, denying that they had any intention of prejudicing the rights, jurisdiction, and honor of the king of Majorca, who was

of the king of Majorca, who was also lord of Montpellier. Jealous of his own rights, the king's son protested to Philip the Fair. Philip ordered the case to be heard in Parlement and consigned the letters of safeguard to his own coffers. Therefore, naturally enough, the consuls of Montpellier felt under no obligation to pay the 15,000 l.t. The king's officials tried to secure payment, and, year after year they doggedly persevered, as the town appealed repeatedly to Paris. Despite the genuine misunderstanding that seems to have occurred, the consuls of Montpellier were furious at their proctor, and in 1317 both they and the king of Majorca were calling him "the faithless one" (*infidelis*).[84] The case was still being disputed in the spring of 1321, and the problem of proper mandates was still plaguing the agents of Montpellier who were representing the city in Paris. Even more wary than before, the consuls had not provided them with procurations enabling them to deal effectively with the case, and therefore the proctors asked the consuls to supply them with an instrument stating that they could obligate the property of the consulate for 15,000 l.t. if judgment should go against them. They warned that the document should be dispatched as quickly as possible, for without it they were powerless to act.[85]

Thanks to the writings of the theorists and their own experience, the king's subjects in the Midi were well aware of the wide range of powers and restrictions that could be included in procurations. They were familiar with limited judicial mandates to be used in court or before special judicial commissions and also with procurations appropriate for seeking grace and privileges and for arranging compromises and settlements. Although the instances that have been examined all involve protests or requests presented to the king or his agents by individual communities or groups of towns, the same options were available when the king's subjects were called upon to respond to requests or demands submitted to them by the king, whether separately or in local or central assemblies.

As I have tried to demonstrate in another study, the later Capetians were fully cognizant of the difference between the familiar attorney powers that bound the agent to hear and accomplish what the court decreed and those negotiating powers that obligated the proctor to accept nothing to which he had not voluntarily agreed. On only three occasions before 1322 did the

---

lord of Montpellier: A. M. Montpellier, Louvet 50, printed by Thomas (n. 81 above) 36-37, and A. M. Montpellier, Louvet 52, vidimuses dated 29 January 1322 and 24 October 1317. The Louvet analyses of these documents led me to believe that one of them was the general mandate issued on 6 August 1310, but this procuration has apparently disappeared: *Archives de la ville de Montpellier: Inventaires et documents* 1.2-3 *Inventaire du "Grand Chartrier," rédigé par P. Louvet en 1662-1663* (Montpellier 1896-1899) nos. 50-52; cf. Brown (n. 80 above) at n. 27.

[84] Thomas (n. 81 above) 14, 41.

[85] *Ibid.*, 46, where the document is quoted in full.

Capetians ask that deputies to central assemblies be given powers similar to those possessed by attorneys, enabling them to accept the king's ordinances without having participated in determining what these ordinances should be. In two of these instances, when Philip the Fair was attacking Boniface VIII, simple moral support was being solicited, and even then the king's officials did not hesitate to negotiate with agents who were hesitant to commit their constituents. On the third occasion the king did not attempt to exploit any advantage he might have hoped to gain from the broad mandates but rather asked the agents to deliberate and treat when they finally met.[86] It is true that in 1316 the king, Louis X, asked for deputies supplied with full and valid power to hear what the king wished to tell them and to give a response that he would find worthy and pleasing and which would demonstrate his subjects' affection and fealty. Still, even the representatives accorded such powers were not thereby bound or authorized to take any particular action determined by the king, and a grant made by deputies of Riom, a town in Auvergne, was carefully limited. The city of Toulouse cautiously refused to accord their deputies the extensive powers demanded by the king and gave them a far more restricted mandate.[87]

Long before the Capetians attempted to secure financial support from their lay subjects in national assemblies, townsmen and nobles had gained experience in negotiating financial and other matters in local meetings with royal officials. There they had learned how to bargain shrewdly, and rather than becoming habituated to accepting meekly the decrees of the king, they had developed techniques with which to defend their own interests—chief among them the limited mandate. If, at the beginning, they gave their agents rather broad powers, as time passed the procurations were more narrowly restricted and more carefully defined. Once again, the archives of southern France provide evidence of this development and show how the men of the Midi learned to utilize the abilities to direct and control agents acquired in their own local dealings and in encounters with the government initiated by them when they were called upon to respond to royal demands for support presented to them at the local level.

In February 1295 the consuls of Narbonne named two men their agents to appear before the constable of France or any other royal official. The town had had to deal with the constable in 1294 over the problem of financial support for the king's Gascon war,[88] and it seems to have anticipated similar

---

[86] See Brown (n. 80 above) at nn. 34, 37-41, 47-50.

[87] See my article, "Assemblies of French Towns in 1316: Some New Texts," *Speculum* 46 (1971) 282-301, in which I publish several documents unknown to me when I wrote the article cited in the preceding note.

[88] J. R. Strayer, "Consent to Taxation under Philip the Fair," in J. R. Strayer and C. H. Taylor, *Studies in Early French Taxation* (Cambridge, Mass. 1939) 45-46.

demands in 1295. The powers the town gave its proctors are both judicial and extrajudicial in character. Thus, the agents could have resisted the royal officials' requests if they chose or could have reached a compromise agreement with them, for they received "complete license, free power, permission and authority . . . to act, defend, propose, protest, take exception, demand, oppose, require, compromise, negotiate, reach an agreement, appeal, and pursue an appeal or several appeals."[89]

It seems likely that the consuls of Millau faced a similar situation when they prepared a procuration on 19 November 1295. They were, however, far more intent on resisting the king's demands for funds than the men of Narbonne had been, and their intransigence is reflected in the wording of the mandate they issued. Taking an aggressive stand, they ordered their two agents to recover 500 l.t. which the community had lent the king, as well as 303 l.t. owed to the town for the wages of troops sent to Gascony; they were also to attempt to recover an additional 3 d. per day due to each soldier. Thus, they optimistically empowered their proctors to give the king and his treasures "full and sufficient quittance" for any sums received, to cancel any letters of obligation, and even to take the matter before the masters of the royal court at Paris. The townsmen undoubtedly realized, however, that they stood little chance of recovering much of their money and might in fact have to offer more, for finally, having confirmed their agents' power to perform all the enumerated actions, they also authorized them to compromise, negotiate, and come to an agreement concerning the aforesaid matters.[90] It is clear, however, that the townsmen had no intention of submitting to a levy imposed on them by royal fiat, and the proctors may well have been told in advance how much they might grant the king.

In 1296 similar resistance was encountered by commissioners attempting to collect the fiftieth imposed by the king after consultation with selected prelates and barons. After reaching Beaucaire, the commissioners apparently decided to announce the king's decree in a meeting or series of meetings at Nîmes, for they flatly ordered the consuls of Montpellier to appear themselves or to send suitably instructed agents "to hear and receive the said ordinances and commands."[91] No description of these decrees was included in the summons, and therefore it would have been impossible for the consuls to provide their proctors with "suitable instructions." The wording of the summons was in any case alarming enough to rouse the consuls' suspicions, and when

---

[89] "Plenam licenciam et liberam potestatem et vocem ac actoritatem . . . agendi, deffendendi, proponendi, protestandi, exipiendi, impetrandi, contradicendi, requirendi, componendi, transingendi, pascissendi, apellandi, apellationem et apellationes prosequendi": A. M. Narbonne, BB 175.

[90] A. C. Millau, CC 510.

[91] "Pro audiendis et recipiendis ordinationibus et preceptis predictis": Bibliothèque Nationale lat. MS 9192, fol. 64v, dated at Nîmes, 26 February 1296.

they named a proctor, they did not give him the authority requested by the commissioners, but simply empowered him to appear before the royal officials, to hear the ordinances and anything else they said, and to do the other things that were to be done in the said matters.[92] Of receiving or accepting the ordinances nothing was said, and in fact a lengthy protest against the royal decree was later lodged by a representative of the king of Majorca and by the consuls of Montpellier, who claimed that they had not consented and did not intend to consent either tacitly or expressly to the injunctions or commands of the royal commissioners, and who said that they were prepared to send their solemn representatives (*nuntii*) to assert their immunity from the tax.[93]

The wariness demonstrated in these encounters[94] makes it easy to understand why the Capetians were unable to secure effective support from central assemblies, and under the last of the Capetians and his Valois successors such meetings were replaced by local assemblies and negotations. As had been true in earlier years, however, the limited mandate was still proving its usefulness as a defensive weapon, and the kings found it difficult and in many cases impossible to secure consent to and compliance with their orders.

Events remarkably similar to those of the 1290s occurred in the seneschalsy of Nîmes thirty years later, showing that, over the years, neither the dedication and zeal of the royal officers nor the cleverness of the king's subjects had diminished. Early in 1325 the king had commissioned agents to levy a war subsidy and investigate infractions of royal ordinances. By the spring of the year the commissioners had set to work. On 4 April 1325 the prior of La Charité, the royal delegate to the seneschalsy of Nîmes,[95] called a meeting of towns, ecclesiastics, and nobles of two bailiwicks for 29 April. In the summons he ordered that individuals should appear in person or send agents with full power to hear, say, and do what he chose to enjoin and command in accordance with the royal commission he had received. His suggestion that his commands would be reasonable did not allay the suspicions of the

---

[92] *Ibid.*; the mandate is quoted in Thomas N. Bisson, *Assemblies and Representation in Languedoc in the Thirteenth Century* (Princeton 1964) 279 n. 178; cf. Strayer (n. 88 above) 49.

[93] Bibliothèque Nationale lat. MS 9192, fol. 66.

[94] The extensive powers given in 1314 to proctors of the community of Lautrec (see above, at n. 73) who were to appear before royal commissioners to treat concerning the payment of a marriage aid were probably granted without difficulty because of the community's overwhelming desire to recover its governmental rights, about which the agents were also to negotiate.

[95] For other activities connected with Montpellier, see de Vic and Vaissete (n. 70 above) 10 *preuves* 646-648, 653-654. On the campaign of 1325 to secure revenue, see, in general, J. B. Henneman, "'Enquêteurs-réformateurs' and Fiscal Officers in Fourteenth-Century France," *Traditio* 24 (1968) 325-328.

men of one bailiwick who met to name proctors.[96] When the bailiff assembled the greater part of the men of the bailiwick, they proceeded to elect three proctors, but instead of giving them the powers requested by the prior, they granted them full, general, and free power to appear before the proctor or his deputy, to supplicate, seek, give notice of the poverty and sad condition of the land, fine and make such financial arrangements as seemed expedient to the proctors, and also to say, do, treat, and carry out according to the tenor of the prior's letter what the principals could do if they were present. With such a mandate as this, the agents of the bailiwick were not likely simply to obey the prior's dictates.[97]

The caution and apprehension reflected in this procuration were by no means universally felt, as a mandate issued by the men of the community of Lunel three years later testifies. This town, located between Nîmes and Montpellier in the seneschalsy of Beaucaire and Nîmes, was summoned in 1328 to appear before the seneschal's lieutenant at a large assembly of five *vigueries* of the seneschalsy. The lieutenant had been informed that the king was planning to attack the Flemings and intended to lead the advance from Arras himself. Full mobilization of the seneschalsy had been ordered. On 29 June the lieutenant commanded the *viguiers* to hold meetings to notify the inhabitants of each community to appear in or send two proctors to Nîmes on 2 July. The agents were to have sufficient power to hear the royal mandates that the lieutenant would transmit and to make a composition or financial arrangement, in accordance with the king's orders, to release them from their obligation to fight. The lieutenant closed his letter by threatening to impose the full penalties prescribed by law on any who failed to appear.[98]

[96] The text of the mandate of the prior of La Charité survives only in a garbled version included in the account of the nomination of proctors by the men of the bailiwick of Cendras: A. C. Alès, I.S. 3, no. 5. There the summons reads," ut prima die lune proxima post tres septimanas pasche apud nemausum in aula [episcopali] per compareant per se uel alios habentes plenariam potestatem coram nobis uel deputatis a nobis audituros, dicturos, et facturos quod eisdem Iniungendum precipiendum duxerimus ex parte regis super nobis comissis quod fuerit rationis."

[97] *Ibid.* The *viguerie* of Alès negotiated separately with the prior, granting 400 l. for the war. By the end of the month the prior found it necessary to issue mandates ordering the inhabitants of different communities of the *viguerie* to pay their fair shares of the sum: A. C. Alès, I.S. 12, nos. 7 and 8.

[98] "Cum a domino nostro rege receperimus in mandatis quod gentes dicte senescallie faciamus parari ad eundum ad exercitum Flandrie ad obviandum Rebellionibus Flamingorum qui contra jura regia venire non verentur, qui dominus noster rex pro jure regio et regnicolarum interesse proponit Personaliter apud attrabacium Pro premissis die dominica post octabam festi beate marie magdalene, idcirco vobis et vestrum cuilibet precipimus et mandamus ac committimus quatinus voce preconia vel alio modo quo melius fieri poterit et in similibus est consuetum universitatibus vestrarum vicariarum et ressortorum eorumdem et cuilibet eorumdem precipiatis sub pena corporis et bonorum, quod ipsi vel duo pro ipsis de quolibet loco, sufficientem Potestatem habentes, ut die sabbati proxima apud Ne-

Perhaps because the lieutenant provided them with such full information about the purpose of the forthcoming assembly, the community of Lunel was willing to grant its agents powers adequate to enable them to perform the acts described in the summons. Two proctors were instructed to appear before the seneschal or his lieutenant and were authorized to take the actions enumerated in the lieutenant's letter. Their powers were limited to some extent, for although they were given full and free power, license, and authority to do anything connected with the business at hand, they were to be guided by their assessment of the community's welfare and to take only those actions that they judged necessary and opportune and that they thought would advance the community's well-being. Still, the agents of Lunel could have acted as virtually free agents, since they could have defended any commitment they made by arguing that under the circumstances they had done the best they could to defend Lunel's interests.[99]

It is not clear that, even with a procuration as unrestricted as this, the proctors of the *viguerie* of Lunel actually committed their constituents to a definite payment at the meeting in Nîmes. Three weeks after the assembly, on 22 July 1328, the governors of Alès were still trying to decide what action to take. While the *viguerie* of Alès had not been summoned to the meeting of 2 July, the seneschal of Beaucaire and Nîmes had formally asked them to grant the king a subsidy for the Flemish campaign. In a town meeting held on 22 July the councilors of Alès advised the consuls to commit the town to pay only if the majority of the communities of the seneschalsy agreed to contribute to the campaign. If the consuls of Alès were forced to make an offer, they were to do so on the best terms possible.[100] Had the seneschal achieved any notable success with the southern *vigueries* of the seneschalsy at Nîmes, his efforts with the townsmen of Alès would probably have pro-

---

mausum, omni excusatione postposita, compareant coram nobis ad audiendum injunctionem quam eisdem facere intendimus virtute mandati regii, vel ad componendum seu finandum nobiscum pro redimendo laborem eorumdem, sic et prout mandatum regium ad hoc se extendit, jntimantes eisdem quod nisi dicta die venerint, ad penas predictas levandas et alias contra eos procedemus, prout justicia suadebit": Bibliothèque Nationale lat. MS 9174, fols. 78v-79, dated at Nîmes, 29 June 1328, a late and faulty transcription.

[99] "Dantes et concedentes dictis procuratoribus et sindicis presentibus plenam et liberam potestatem, licentiam et auctoritatem omnia et singula pro et nomine dicte universitatis faciendi in et super premissis et circa premissa et que eis fuerint necessaria seu etiam opportuna ex (*sic*) deppendentibus ex eisdem prout eis ad utilitatem dicte universitatis magis et utilius videbitur expedire": *ibid.* fol. 79. The procuration was prepared at Lunel on 1 July 1328; the assembly at Nîmes was scheduled for the following day.

[100] "Quod si maior pars vniuersitatum senescallie bellicadri et nemausi finat cum dicto domino Senescallo super dicto subsidio de eundo vel aliquam pecunie quantitatem dando domino nostro Regi predicto quod Iddem faciant dicti consules, et cum eodem conueniant vt melius et graciosius et vtilius poterunt ad maiorem vtilitatem vniuersitatis ville alesti predicte": A. C. Alès, I.S. 12, no. 10.

duced more impressive results before 22 July, for the men of Alès were clearly ready to respond—however grudgingly—to commitments made by their
neighbors in the seneschalsy.

If the townsmen of Alès were wily and prudent in answering the royal
appeal for funds in 1328, the experience they acquired in the course of the
next years did nothing to increase their readiness to demonstrate their trust
in the royal government by issuing broad mandates to their agents. Early
in 1357 the consuls of Alès received word that they, or one of them, should
appear in Béziers on 1 March before the count of Armagnac, the kings' lieutenant. They were being summoned to review certain accounts and "for
various other matters," they were informed. That the consuls were made
apprehensive by the vague phraseology of the citation is suggested by the
wording of the mandate they prepared for Bernard de Arbussio. His fellow
consuls and the councilors of the town had chosen him, they said, to appear
before the royal lieutenant and to hear the accounts and the other things
that the count or his deputy wished to say; they expressly denied him, however, any power to obligate the community to undertake any act or deed
and forbade him to make any pledge. If Bernard failed to follow their instructions, they announced, they would refuse to carry out any commitment
he made which prejudiced the town.[101] Despite the restricted mandate he
bore, Bernard apparently considered himself—and was considered by the
king's lieutenant—sufficiently empowered to be able to make certain agreements. Rumors that Bernard had exceeded his commission reached Alès,
but Bernard would not inform his fellow townsmen of what he had done.
When they learned that he had been named the count's deputy to make
certain investigations in various places, Bernard again refused to reveal to
them what the nature of his commission was. Then the consuls heard that
Bernard was due to appear before the count to report to him, and they made
a public declaration stating that they would not accept anything that he
did against the tenor of his mandate. They also forbade him, as a consul

---

[101] "Dicti consules et consiliarii certifficati quod consules dicte ville seu eorum alter fuerunt citati de mandato Magnifici et potentis viri domini Comitis armaniacii locumtenentis
domini nostri francorum Regis in partibus occitanis ad comparendum coram eo in loco de
Biterris ad primam diem Mensis martii proximum (*sic*) ad audiendum computa Receptarum
capagii et pro quibusdam aliis, dicti Bertrandus Boni, Symon Gobi et Johannes Meleti una
cum consiliariis eorum et dicte vniuersitatis elegerunt ad comparendum coram dicto domino locum tenente uel ab eo deputatis dictum Bernardum de arbussio conconsulem ad
eundum et comparendum coram dicto domino locumtenente nomine dicte vniuersitatis
et ad audiendum dicta computa et alia que dictus dominus Comes uel ab eo deputati ei
dicere uel explicare voluerit, ab dicando dicto Bernardo de arbussio quamcumque potestatem dictam vniuersitatem ad aliquem actum uel factum obligare, ymo predicta eidem ex-
presse Inhibuerint, que si contingat ipsum facere uel concentire illa Inquantum preiudicia-
lia essent eisdem uel eorum vniuersitati nunc ut ex tunc grata non habent ymo ipsa nunc
ut ex tunc reuocant et pro non factis haberi voluerunt": A. C. Alès, I.S. 3, no. 7.

of the town, to accept any commission or to execute any commission he had already received. Finally, he was prohibited from doing anything at his meeting with the count which might harm the town, and the consuls announced that they would not approve or agree to any such commitment.[102]

As the declaration of the consuls of Alès demonstrates, the experience that the men of France had had in formulating agency documents and in using them in their negotiations with the government had made them shrewd and careful overseers of their own interests. From the beginning, their impulses to defend their rights and privileges had been as strong as they ever became during the fourteenth century. They had not always, however, been as suspicious of the government's intentions as long-term exposure to the king's repeated demands had made them. Furthermore, over the course of a hundred and fifty years, they had become much more adept at manipulating the formulas of agency law in order to create documents that would accurately and precisely express their true intentions. Whatever inclination toward autocracy the rulers of France may have had, they were unable to exploit the intricacies of the agency relationship to obtain from their subjects blind obedience even in cases in which they could claim that the interests of the whole demanded it. Much as they might have liked to assume the role of judge and dictator of the common welfare, they did not possess the authority or the power to do so, for they ruled men who were as aware of their own rights and of the king's obligation to serve the kingdom as the ruler was of the kingdom's duty to serve him. For many reasons France did not produce a central assembly similar to the English Parliament, nor did any accepted customary formula for empowering delegates to royal assemblies evolve there, whereas in England after 1295 representatives to central assemblies regularly received full and sufficient power for themselves and their communities to do and consent to what would be ordained by common counsel.[103] Thus they were empowered, although they were not directed, to bind their principals, but only to decisions reached by common counsel. The various formulas used in France were similar in nature, for they required that agreement be given only after discussion and consultation, when consensus had been reached. In neither France nor England were representatives simply authorized to submit to the decrees of a sovereign court, and the different uses to which the similar formulas were put in the two countries resulted from variations in the climate of politics, which were not reflected in the terminology of the representatives' mandates.

---

[102] Achille Bardon, *Histoire de la ville d'Alais de 1250 à 1340* (Nîmes 1894-1896) 2. xv-xvi, *pièce justificative* 8, a partial and occasionally unreliable transcription of A. C. Alès, I. S. 3, no. 8.

[103] Brown (n. 80 above) at n. 29.

There was nothing in the theory of agency law to make such a development a foregone conclusion, for the legal and notarial writers, working with principles found in the Roman law, provided instructions and model procurations for all sorts of agency relationships, whether they involved appearance before a judge, negotiation, petition for grace, or a combination of these functions. In any of these cases, careful analysis and interpretation of the theorists' statements could produce documents which so restricted the agent's power that he remained necessarily dependent for guidance on his principal, or which gave him such broad discretion that an unscrupulous third party could lead him to bind his constituent to inappropriate and unacceptable undertakings. The rulers of France and England did not possess that absolute and final authority over their subjects which might have enabled them, in dealing with representatives convoked for the common welfare, to demand, obtain, and exploit procurations similar to those given to attorneys. The realities of political life in both countries had produced relationships between ruler and subjects which make it understandable that these representatives were provided with mandates empowering them not merely to witness their acceptance of decisions that were the king's alone, but rather to engage in genuine negotiation and meaningful consultation on the issues affecting the realm.

Department of History
Brooklyn College of the City University of New York
New York City, New York, U.S.A.

THE DEFENSE OF ENGLAND
AND THE PEASANTS' REVOLT

•

by Eleanor Searle and Robert Burghart

"This story of betrayal and steadfastness ... did not change the world, but it lent support to the questions that must be asked; it aroused mistrust of a regime ... and of its favorites, and increased sensibility for that moment when the scales tremble between loyalty and disloyalty towards the unknown."[1]

The Peasants' Revolt of 1381 in England has lacked neither fame nor interpreters. Yet in spite of the many enumerated "causes," the real marrow of the matter—the source of that explosive and regionally isolated fury—eludes us. Rising expectations frustrated by seignorial exploitation, egalitarian notions and heavy royal taxation were all known before and long after 1381. That the rising should have begun in the very region in which lordship was weakest has found, we think, no satisfactory explanation. Neither the sources of the region's articulate and radical questioning of the social order, nor the compulsiveness of its appeal as a motive for violence against some lords and not others, has been convincingly demonstrated.

It is not part of our purpose to survey the enormous literature devoted to the Peasants' Revolt; such a survey would require a long study in itself. What we wish to point out is that of all the "causes" that have been adduced, one circumstance has been entirely neglected—the Hundred Years' War, and in particular the defense of England from attacks by the French. From the 1330s until 1389 the English fought almost continuous, large-scale wars, until war had come to be the dominant climate politically, perhaps economically. Yet it has passed virtually unnoticed that during these years the

This paper arose out of research carried out by the senior author on the economy of Southeast England during the fourteenth century, and was developed in her seminar at the University of California in 1969-1970. Both authors would like to thank the other members of the seminar, and in particular Mr. John Merrill, for their contributions.

[1] From the text by Ernst Schnabel for the oratorio *The Raft of the Frigate Medusa* by Hans Werner Henze.

southeast—from which so many of the 1381 rebels were to come—was the
subject of serious raids, and that after 1369 it lay undefended while the raids
increased in frequency and destructiveness. Even the great modern historian
of the war, when writing of the Peasants' Revolt, can say that "Richard II's
island . . . was not directly affected by invasion and the pillaging of *rou-
tiers.*"[2] Yet the evidence of the agony of both is abundant. Seen in the light
of the war, much about 1381 becomes explicable that is otherwise baffling.
It is the object of this paper to investigate the evidence of attacks upon the
southeast and of the measures taken for home defense. We wish then to
argue that the war was as central to the growing self-awareness and radical
questioning of the endangered villagers as it was to the political development
of their betters in the commons and lords. For the war meant that generations of men and boys of a customarily exploited class would be trained
in arms and hardened in bivouacking and in real combat. It meant that
their tithings and hundreds would gradually be shaped into instruments
of rapid military communication and of rapid mobilization. Yet ultimately,
because the defensive measures of the society were inadequate to protect
the region, and because their rulers came to lack even the will to defend them,
while exploitation became increasingly crude as the war went badly, the
villagers of the southeast were reduced to insecurity, fear, and at last to
fury. As much as the Jacquerie rebellion of 1358 in France, though less
obviously, the Peasants' Revolt was the fruit of the Hundred Years' War.

I

War, as Edward III chose to fight it, relied upon large numbers of men-at-
arms and archers. As his tactics evolved, he came to rely heavily upon archers
dismounted for the battle and mounted for pursuit and transport, rather
than upon cavalry or the combination of cavalry and foot preferred by his
father and grandfather.[3] As he planned the campaigns that were to add the
crown of France to that of England, it was evident enough to the young
king and his councillors that war, first with Scotland and then with France,
would mean raids against the southeast ports of embarcation and sporadic
pillaging of coastal towns and villages. Both offense and defense therefore
relied upon a large available supply of trained and mobile troops, and an
organization that could quickly call out local levies at central government
command. The organization was at hand in the ancient communal arrangements for defense and peace-keeping as these had been revised in Edward I's
system of array and embodied in the Statute of Winchester of 1285. Edward

[2] Edouard Perroy, *The Hundred Years' War*, trans. W. B. Wells (New York 1965) 183.
[3] Michael Powicke, *Military Obligation in Medieval England* (Oxford 1962) 189.

III had inherited a militarily trained populace and an organization for their control which no king before him had possessed. Upon the great armies the statute put at his disposal, warfare on a quite new scale and duration could be based.

Michael Powicke has so convincingly analysed the refining of the system of compulsion on which Edward relied, and A. E. Prince has so thoroughly described its operation in the early years of the reign that here we need describe it only briefly and as it impinges upon the question of defense.[4] The Statute of Winchester had made compulsory the possession of, and skill in, specified weapons for the nonmilitary classes of the realm.[5] The statute was itself a revision in the arms requirements for the populace rather than a novel requirement, and it served without serious revision as the standard in the century to come. As it laid down, every man between the ages of fifteen and sixty was to be assessed in his lands and chattels and to be sworn to provide himself with weapons according to their value for the maintenance of public peace and the defense of the realm. Those with land to an assessed annual value of £10 and £15 were to have hauberk, sword, knife, and horse. Those with a £5 land assessment were to have a doublet, iron breastplate, sword, and knife. The 40s freeholder was to have sword, bow, arrows, and knife, while freeholders below that value were to have "gisarmes, knives, and other weapons". Those with less than twenty marks in chattels—a group newly included by Edward I—were to have swords, knives, and "other weapons", and "everyone else that can" was to have bows and arrows (outside the forest) and bows and bolts (within the forest). Their normal hundreds were the basic units of men thus armed. Every hundred was to have two constables chosen to view the armor twice yearly and to present defaults before the sheriff on his tourn or before commissioners.[6]

The units so formed were the raw material from whom the sheriff might choose men for the *posse comitatus*, to serve as he required for police purposes. They were, at the same time, units for local defense and potential conscriptees for overseas expeditionary forces. As such, they were assembled before arrayers, armed with royal letters patent and aided by the sheriff and local officials, who had themselves received writs ordering their help. The arrayers of Edward III's time, and generally in that of his grandfather, were themselves men of the county: gentlemen of substance who would know the district

---

[4] Powicke 48-133. A. E. Prince, "Army and Navy," *The English Government at Work* 1 (Cambridge, Mass. 1940) 355-393.

[5] *Statutes of the Realm* 1 (London 1810) 97-98; hereafter *Stat. Realm*.

[6] *Stat. Realm* 1.98. The statute of 1285 makes unspecified "justices" responsible for receiving the presentments, but within two years, commissioners from the county were appointed to oversee the system. *Calendar of Patent Rolls* (CPR) *1281-1292*, 264. The sheriffs were given responsibility shortly thereafter. *Calendar of Close Rolls* (CCR) *1288-1296*, 330.

and could be called upon either to assume command of the levies or deliver them to the royal muster. The arrayers were to view the assembled hundredors and from among them choose men to fill the quota required by the king himself or for the defense of an invaded area. At moments of acute local danger and for coastal defense the whole force was to turn out as a *levée en masse* under its arrayer or his lieutenant.

Upon this system Edward built his Scottish war, his invasion of the Continent, and his hopes for home defense. In 1334 the Statute of Westminster was formally reenacted, and an order in council in 1336 emphasized that the levies were to maintain themselves properly armed.[7] Until around 1360 the commissions of array were important in recruiting foot-archers, men-at-arms, and mounted archers for service in France.[8] As Powicke has so clearly demonstrated, such compulsion was increasingly unpopular with the commons, whose opposition at last led in 1352 to the statute limiting conscription of men-at-arms and archers to those who held land by such services, save "by common assent and grant in parliament."[9] From that time on indentured retinues came more and more to predominate over the county levies in the composition of the armies. Yet even so, neither before nor after 1352 is the line easily drawn between conscripted and freely contracting troops. Commissions of array were issued for the levy of troops to serve in the retinues of various lords both for defense and for campaigns in France, however the commons might complain.[10]

Unwilling troops thus levied from unwilling communities were noted for their indiscipline, their thefts and casual atrocities, and for their frequent desertions. Occasionally the array offered only a rabble of the poor for selection. In the Norfolk array of 1336 few men had so much as a spear, sword, and knife; most could provide themselves with no more than a staff or an axe and knife.[11] Once taken for the army, or to join the defense militia of a coastal county, such men were unconstrained by the potent pressures of their own village communities, often frightened, and always ill-provided for. As the government deteriorated after 1369, they ravaged western France, and as we shall see, they terrorized the coastal districts of England itself when they camped at the shore for embarcation. Outside his county, the medieval villager was in foreign territory he little valued and among foreigners towards whom he could summon no feelings of kinship. The militia levied from inland counties for coastal defense went unwillingly or not at all, and their

[7] *Foedera . . . et Acta Publica*, ed. T. Rymer (London 1816-25) 1.2.900.

[8] J. W. Sherborne, "Indentured Retinues and English Expeditions to France, 1369-1380," *English Historical Review* 79 (1964) 741. Conscripts were arrayed for Edward's expeditions of 1338, '40, '42, '46-'47, and '59.

[9] *Stat. Realm* 1.321. Powicke (n. 3 above) 182-212.

[10] Powicke 213-215.

[11] Powicke 193.

reluctance was increased by the reluctance of either the royal government or their own counties to pay them for their time and danger.[12] Ultimately only if the threatened counties could afford both provisions and pay would the men of other counties even consider coming to their aid. The royal government was thus not entirely to blame for the agony of the coastal counties. England was a realm that was not yet a community. Its government had developed a machinery for control and total mobilization before either it or its people had developed a sense of the realm as a single people. Edward could force the realm to war as a whole, but neither he nor the shire communities saw that defense was therefore a new, and equally national responsibility.

Even had the arrayed troops from outside the coastal counties been willing defenders of the southerners, it will be seen that land-based levies could hardly be as effective as strong coastal fortifications and, above all, protection from the sea. The former was the ancient responsibility of the magnates, who in their own fortresses and as royal castellans, had their justificatory role of society's protectors to play. Orders and licenses for strengthening and repair of coastal castles were issued in number as Edward prepared for war.[13] The aristocracy, too, assumed the responsibility of coordinating coastal defense. In 1337 William de Clynton, earl of Huntingdon, aided by the archbishop of Canterbury, was named coordinator, and in the following year the earl was named with John de Warenne, earl of Surrey, as supervisor of the array of men for defense in Kent, Surrey, Sussex, Hampshire, Berkshire, and Oxford. Hugh de Courtenay, earl of Devon, and Philip de Columbariis were named supervisors of the defense arrays of Dorset, Somerset, Devon, and Cornwall.[14]

The first and best line of defense was—or might have been—the sea. Edward III indeed claimed control of and even jurisdiction over the seas, yet the claim was propaganda and boast.[15] The navy was not, and did not come to be, a fighting fleet under Edward. The navy was a transport fleet for men and supplies. Its permanent core was some fifteen royal ships docked at Winchelsea, two or three cogs, and the same number of galleys and barges.[16]

---

[12] For the differing methods of paying the levies, see Powicke 199-209.

[13] CCR 1333-1337 *passim.*

[14] CCR 1337-1339, 255. CPR 1338-1340, 139.

[15] *Select Pleas in the Court of Admiralty,* ed. R. G. Marsden, Selden Society 2 (1892), xiv, xxxiv. N. H. Nicolas, *A History of the Royal Navy* (London 1847) 15ff. For a useful revision of the concept "command of the sea" and for naval operations after 1372, see J. W. Sherborne, "The Battle of La Rochelle and the War at Sea, 1372-1375," *Bulletin of the Institute of Historical Research* 42 (1969).

[16] Prince (n. 4 bove) 377-378. Nicolas 158. Fighting men could of course be carried on the ships. The royal ships, for example, were of approximately two hundred tons each and each could carry a complement of some 130 sailors, 35 men-at-arms and 35 archers. The barges could carry some 40 to 60 men-at-arms and archers.

This permanent navy was greatly enlarged in time of need by the ship service due from the Cinque Ports, Yarmouth, Bristol, and a few other maritime towns. By ancient custom the Cinque Ports were excused from other obligations by contributing to the Crown fifty-seven ships for a period of fifteen days at their own expense.[17] When hostilities appeared certain the fleet could be enlarged to include any shipping the Crown required. Orders were issued for the arrest of such ships as were wanted, either to provide transport or to prevent their capture by the enemy. Those chosen for duty were then provisioned and armed by the king's commissioners, and manned, as were all naval ships, by the impressment of men-at-arms and sailors. Thus by far the largest part of the fourteenth century navy depended upon the ships of merchants and fishermen. The ship service of the old ports was in fact a regularized version of the emergency arrest of merchant shipping: the warships of Yarmouth and Winchelsea were traders and herring boats in peace. Defense from the sea under these conditions relied upon there being many merchant ships at dock in English ports: ships to range the coastal waters, as the Cinque Ports were enjoined to do, and ships to transport levies from the north to the defense of the channel shores. Defense thus rested upon a prosperous trade, and the obvious answer of the enemy was to attack the merchant ports.

II

Edward III's Scottish wars presented the southern coasts with an opportunity to refine their defense arrangements under ideal conditions, for though the coast was vulnerable to Scottish raids mounted from France, yet the urgency that this situation created was not followed by any actual danger. In the mid-1330s the defenders of the coast were ordered to array the armed levies, to erect beacons on the coastline, and to establish regular watches.[18] Funds were allotted by the Crown for the repair of Channel Island castles, and the fortifications at Yarmouth, Cowes, Ryde, and the Abbey of Quarr were strengthened.[19] Because it was particularly susceptible to attack, the Isle of Wight received special consideration. A list was compiled of the 54 men-at-arms and 141 archers liable by their tenures for duty on the Isle. The local militia was divided into east and west districts and then separated into smaller units, each of which was placed under the command of the principal local landowner. Watches were set along the coast, beacons stacked on head-

[17] Montague Burrows, *The Cinque Ports* (London 1888) 385. The obligation was not always met, even at the beginning of the war, and rarely in the 1370s. Sherborne (n. 15 above) 26-27.

[18] CCR 1333-1337, 469-470, 715.

[19] *Ibid.* 434.

lands ready to be lit to warn the residents of attack, and light horsemen were to be kept ready to alert the vills.[20]

By 1337 the war with France had begun and along the southern coast the fear of a combined French and Scottish invasion grew acute. From his French sanctuary, David Bruce led a fleet of galleys to attack the English fleet anchored off the Isle of Wight. He succeeded in seizing several English vessels and returned to France with them. In March 1337 a French force raided Guernsey and then landed a large force under English banners near Portsmouth. After easily taking the town they plundered and set it afire. So extensive was the destruction that the burgesses were excused from the taxes of the following year.[21] Defense indeed became a theme in the government propaganda that preceded the tax. The king now exhorted the archbishop of Canterbury to preach the war effort in Kent: "to expound to the clergy and the people of that county the contents of a schedule which the king is sending to them, containing the endeavors which he has made to avoid war with the king of France, inducing them to aid the king to the extent of their ability, as it will be necessary for the king to incur great expense for the public defense."[22] The following year the king could at last lead his long-desired invasion of the continent.

With the invasion, the defenders of the coast were put on the alert against attack. The arrayers were to be carefully supervised by their magnate-overseers, and not only gentlemen but local churchmen were called to service. As early as June 1338, the abbot of Battle in Sussex was fortifying his abbey, and during the summer and autumn he had "caused all his servants and others to be arrayed, and retains them with him on the sea coast near Winchelsea . . . for the safety of those parts against invasion, by the king's order."[23] The abbot of Faversham and the priors of Christ Church, Canterbury, of Dover and of Rochester were at the same time told to arm themselves and their servants, and to stay at their manors near the sea for the defense of the realm.[24] From then on throughout the century the defense of their districts was a continual expense for such abbeys. The abbot of Battle, and no doubt monks of other houses, began of necessity to keep up the warrior state. In 1346-1347, for example, the central receiving accounts of Battle Abbey report expenditure on livery: *in pannis emptis pro sagittariis euntiis cum domino abbate pro custode maritima.*[25]

---

[20] *Victoria County History* (VCH) *of Hampshire* 5.312. For the defense of the Isle of Wight, see also S. J. Hockey, *Quarr Abbey and its Lands* (Leicester 1970) 131-155.

[21] Nicolas (n. 15 above) 27. CCR 1337-1339, 528.

[22] CCR 1337-1339, 255. *Foedera* (n. 7 above) 1.2.989-991.

[23] CCR 1337-1339, 542. CPR 1338-1340, 92.

[24] CCR 1337-1339, 414.

[25] San Marino, California, Henry E. Huntington Library, Battle Collection (HBA Coll.), Abbey Accounts.

The preparations were not enough. While Edward enjoyed the festivities and diplomacy that alone marked his campaign in 1338, the French, supported by their Scottish allies and Genoese mercenaries, landed at Southampton's West Quay on a midsummer Sunday morning, and sacked the town. After removing their booty, they put the town to the torch. The scandalous case with which a major port could be attacked showed up the actual mismanagement of the defense arrangements. It was reported to the king that "the keepers of the coast and the arrayers of the men in the county, knowing that the attack was to be made, not only neglected to provide for the defense of the ports threatened, but basely fled with the men of the said towns on sight of the enemy," and that "the said keepers and their deputies permitted the men appointed to stay to guard the coast at the charges of the said county . . . to go home, and did not find the men-at-arms, archers, and others for whom they had levied divers other sums of money on the said county."[26] In reponse to these alleged shortcomings of the keepers, letters patent were issued to the earl of Arundel and to two justices of Common Bench (justices Stonor and Inge), to conduct an inquiry into "how the keepers and arrayers bore themselves when the galleys came into sight." The commission was also directed to secure the town against any further incursions. Meanwhile a commission was appointed in Winchester to assess and levy there the funds sufficient to repair the walls and to "put the city into an effective state of defense" since another invasion was thought imminent.[27] Southampton's easy fall, and the evident ability of the enemy to negotiate the short crossing of the channel undetected, clearly frightened the government for the safety of London itself. Commands were now issued to the mayor and aldermen to prepare against invasion by enclosing and fortifying the city towards the river with stone and timber, and to fix piles across the Thames. All men with rents in the city, lay and cleric, were to assist in the city's defense.[28]

The earl of Arundel's inquiry into the debacle at Southampton had evidently made it clear that the arrayers and the levies of inland hundreds had not taken seriously their defense duties. John de Warenne, earl of Surrey, and others were rebuked in November following the raid for default of duty, and it was charged that "on account of the disobedience and rebellion of some in the said counties, loss of life, destruction of property, and other evils have occurred at Southampton, Portsmouth, and at other places in the said counties." The overseers were urged to charge their arrayers, "all bishops, earls, barons, knights, and others, by their faith and allegiance to the king, to go with all speed to avert the threatened dangers, and from time to time

---

[26] CPR 1338-1340, 180.

[27] *Ibid.* 180-181, 286.

[28] CCR 1337-1339, 612.

to return the names of such as neglect to obey them."[29] An inquiry was now made into the defects found at Winchester castle.[30]

The experience gained from the early failures in home defense did begin to have its effect. At Easter in the beginning of the next raiding season, the Normans, with twelve galleys, eight pinnaces, and four thousand men, again appeared at Southampton. They demanded that the town surrender to them. The town, properly defended on this occasion, countered with the sporting proposition that it would allow the enemy to disembark, refresh themselves for two days, and then do battle with the English, ten with ten, twenty with twenty, or in any manner the French desired. The story, whatever element of truth there is in it, indicates at least the high morale of the defenders, and whatever their real offer, it was declined by the Normans, who retired.[31] In May they were sighted once again, and again were discouraged from attacking by the defense preparations. Moving up the coast they landed at Hastings, burned some fishermen's huts, and sacked the decrepit Hastings castle. Presumably this is the same force of fiteen galleys that attempted to force a landing at Eastbourne, and was beaten back by a mass levy of Pevensey Rape commanded by Andrew Peverel.[32] They then sailed up the coast as far as the Isle of Thanet and threatened Dover and Folkestone, but with little success.

This French force had sailed along the coast from Southampton to the mouth of the Thames without encountering any sea defenses, but in such a year as 1339, when shipping was not required for the transport of armies, the Cinque Ports could aid the coastal defense and enjoy some agreeable looting of their own. The ports had been enjoined to organize sea defense, and they had furnished sixty ships for the purpose, armed and manned at their own expense. The ports had their own interest in protecting themselves and their merchant ships, as well as the coast, and the utility of their defense fleet was now proved when in June, 1339, a squadron of some seventy enemy vessels appeared off Rye. The English fleet hurried to the scene (probably from nearby Winchelsea) and the French withdrew, with the English in pursuit. The chase led to Boulogne, where the inferior French fleet was trapped; entering the port the English captured several vessels, hung twelve French shipmasters, and burned a section of the town.[33]

---

[29] CPR 1338-1340, 149-150.

[30] The sheriff of Southampton was ordered to garrison the castle at all times with ten men-at-arms and twenty archers. CCR 1339-1341, 7. The sheriff of Devon was also ordered to repair Exeter castle. *Ibid.* 166. In Sussex the earl of Arundel and two fellow-commissioners were ordered to strengthen the defenses of Chichester. *Ibid.* 620, 634.

[31] Nicolas (n. 15 above) 40.

[32] L. F. Salzman, "Political History," VCH, *Sussex* 1 (London 1905) 509.

[33] Nicholas 41-42.

Yet this was an isolated success, and followed by pillaging rather than by a renewed patrol of the English coast. The commons, meeting in October, expressed their dissatisfaction with naval defense, singling out for criticism the Cinque Ports, who in return for their privileges and exemptions were responsible for shore defense.[34] The dissatisfaction was reasonable enough. For the French had merely turned their attentions temporarily away from the seriously defended southeastern ports to easier targets. The channel islands were constantly vulnerable. In 1339 Jersey was overrun.[35] The Isle of Wight too was attacked and its warden, Sir Theobald Russell of Yaverland, was mortally wounded in its defense. In contrast, Bartholomew de Lisle, a man with "great possessions" on the isle, had retired to the safety of his mainland estates. The king was forced to call this warden back to the beseiged area where he held his great possessions in return for defending its people. Sharply the king reminded de Lisle that he "learns that (de Lisle) withdraws himself from the island with his men, to its great danger, and it is not becoming for belted knights to eloign themselves from places where deeds of war may take place, but rather to go to those places and stay there for their honor's sake."[36]

At about the same time, the French attacked landfalls and towns of the southwest, devastating Portland and attacking villages in Dorset.[37] To avoid the constant danger, the men of the coast now began to drift inland. Even in Southampton and Sandwich men began to leave, and there proclamations threatened with forfeiture all who did not immediately return.[38] The *Inquisitiones Nonarum* of 1340 show that, whether or not burgesses were persuaded to return to the aid of towns that had at least a hope of defense, villagers and peasants were leaving their indefensible fields uncultivated. Near Sussex landfalls men reported that they did not dare to cultivate their arable. In Hound parish, Hampshire, the jury reported that the tithes of fleeces and lambs among them were much reduced "because sailors and others coming to guard the shore stole both ewes and lambs from them." Much land in the hundred, they reported lay uncultivated out of dread of "foreigners and sailors." In Eling parish, Hampshire, they reported that much of the parish's arable lay uncultivated because the men of the parish carried timber for the defenses of Southampton, while those near the sea were threatened both at sowing and reaping season. They spent much time camping along the shore to withstand the foreigners, "to their great destruction and expense, and thus they have been destroyed."[39] Clearly there was much more small-

---

[34] *Rotuli Parliamentorum* (Rot. Parl.) 2.105, 108.
[35] CCR 1339-1341, 221, 499.
[36] *Ibid.* 444.
[37] *Ibid.* 74. *Inquisitiones Nonarum in Curia Scaccarii* (London 1807) 50.
[38] CCR 1339-1341, 101.

scale piracy and pillaging than are taken notice of in the royal writs to arrayers, and such small raids, together with the hostility of the levies from inland villages, was taking a toll of agricultural production, and thus of the capacity of the south to feed not only its own inhabitants, but the levies mustering at the shore for embarcation and the levies coming to the defense of that shore.

The great English naval victory at Sluys in 1340 clearly did much to lessen the possibility of large-scale raids, and the English intervention in the Breton ducal struggle after 1341 neutralized a portion of the coast from which raiders had come. The two decades that followed were years of victory for the English in the face of French civil war. The successful seige of Calais in 1341 showed well enough that Edward's navy could both transport reinforcements and blockade the city with little opposition from the French. Yet villagers could still suffer disaster. The villagers of Budleigh in Devon complained to the king in the late 1340s that they had been ruined by the enemy. Over the period of a year the French had taken three ships and twelve boats from their harbor and had killed or seized 140 men. Some had been able to purchase their freedom, but many languished in prison unable to pay their ransoms.[40] The war weariness of the coastal villagers is evident from a royal mandate in 1348 to the archdeacon of Cornwall instructing him that the people were to be stirred up to a greater activity in their own defense.[41]

The disorienting horror of the Black Death thus came upon an already strained society. Raids lessened during periods of truce and picked up once more during renewed hostilities, while during truces, deserters and returned soldiers roamed in bands through the southeast, only to be pardoned and the district relieved of them when war began anew. The patent rolls of the 1350s are unusually full of commissions of oyer and terminer to the southeast to investigate smuggling, threats, assaults, cattle theft, and terrorism. Even monks could not but be affected by the violence. The abbot of Battle in Sussex had been a continual arrayer of the district, and at least three monks of outstanding ability ran away.[42] Their names show them to be local men, and the pull of society, family, or adventure now proved stronger than their vows. One member of a local gang of the 1350s admitted to the murder of two men, to the theft of cattle and sheep from three others, and was convicted on the further charge "that he and others received and maintained other

---

[39] *Inq. Nonarum*, 125-126, 354-355.

[40] Nicolas (n. 15 above) 99.

[41] L. E. Elliott-Binns, *Medieval Cornwall* (London 1955) 91.

[42] The patent rolls imply that they had become vagabonds, but this is a formality and their stories do not appear in the calendars. One such monk, John Lose, later became prior of Battle's cell at Brecon, while another, William Merssh, who ran away later in the century was elected abbot a few years after his return. CPR 1354-1358, 296-297. CPR 1396-1399, 362.

common and notorious thieves, plundering in Slepersden and the pass at Alton, and were vagabonds with them at Battle and all over the county of Sussex, lying in wait to rob men so that none after sunset dared to go out of their houses." The convicted murderer was pardoned for service in France.[43]

Even the spectacular successes of the king and the Black Prince on the continent, culminating in the capture of the French king at Poitiers, did little to alleviate the war's toll on the southern coast and its inhabitants' economic condition. Shore manors were subject to fluctuations in their demesne crops so wild as to be explicable by nothing save destructive raids.[44] The king learned in 1356 that Seaford "used to find several ships of war for him and used to defend itself and its neighborhood, and pay eleven marks for the fifteenth. But recently [it] has been burned and so desolate by plague and chances of war that men living there do not suffice due to fewness and want, to bear charges."[45]

In 1360, French fortunes were at their lowest point. Yet even so the worst raid of the war could still be launched. In March 1360 came the warning of "the grave peril of invasions of the king's enemies now on the sea in a great fleet."[46] Intelligence reports had come in time for the defense to be organized and ready.[47] The government was ordering arrays nearly a fortnight before the landing. The danger, it emphasized, was very serious indeed, for the king had "sure intelligence that his enemies of France are actually at sea with a host of men-at-arms, archers and other, horses and foot, in a great navy, and purpose to invade the realm at Southampton, Sandwich, Portsmouth, or elsewhere." A general array of Hampshire and ten other counties was therefore ordered, and the levies were to go immediately to the coast. The Oxfordshire arrayers and men were ordered to Hampshire, the Gloucester and Worcestershire levies were to assist Cornwall, Devon, Somerset, and Dorset, while Kent and Sussex were to be aided by Surrey and London. The admiral of the Thames and the west was directed to arrest ships and equip them as strongly as possible, "ready to sail upon notice, and [to] certify the king in chancery of the number and equipment thereof."[48] The entire ma-

---

[43] CPR 1358-1361, 565-566.

[44] HBA Coll. Abbey Accounts. The demesne crops of the Battle manor of Barnhorn on the Pevensey Levels fluctuated between an estimated normal value of around £ 60 to less than £ 20 in some years of the 1350s.

[45] CCR 1354-1360, 269.

[46] CPR 1358-1361, 344. The abbots of Battle, Robertsbridge, Robert Belknap, and two others were sent commissions of array and were charged with compelling all with foodstuffs for sale to "bring their victuals to certain places by the sea and sell them for a reasonable price" to the arrayed levies. *Ibid.* 411.

[47] On February 10 the king had summoned two knights and two citizens of the shires to discuss the arraying of men, since the king had learned that an invasion was planned. CCR 1360-1364, 96-97.

[48] *Ibid.* 98.

chinery of home defense was thus alerted, supervised, and ready to repel the greatest threat yet offered, with all the experience gained in nearly thirty years.

Intelligence reports had been correct about the strength of the French force, but wrong about its probable destination. Yet the defense command had forseen this possibility in its general alert. Nevertheless, the French landed without difficulty. A report of mid-March described the attack tersely: the French "landed at Winchelsea on Sunday last in a great host of armed men with their horses, took the town, barbarously slew the men found therein, and are riding over the country, slaying, burning, destroying."[49] It was thus no lighting raid. The French remained, and the king was thoroughly alarmed at an emergency "whereon peril of the subversion or loss of the whole realm seemed to turn."[50] The attack showed up the complete inadequacy of the home defense arrangements. The arrayers of Essex were now to mobilize their men, to march them to London, and from there take ship to Winchelsea. The Londoners promised men-at-arms and archers with twenty ships. The council ordered the fleets from the north and the west to sail with all speed to the succor of the southeast. The bailiff of the earl of Richmond at Boston was commanded to arrest all ships fit for war, to furnish them with sailors and soldiers, and to dispatch them for Sandwhich where they would wait for the collection of the fleet.[51] Yet when the French left at last, it was not for fear of English home defense, but "for the collection of a greater fleet to commit therein worse mischiefs."[52] In July the government admitted that, despite its many mobilization orders, which should have filled the northern and western fleets with fighting men, "few men of the counties named came according to notice to the places appointed to sail therein, and because of the urgency of the need . . . the king could not send again to distant places to seek for men."[53] He fell back, very late indeed, on hiring what soldiers he could to furnish the collected ships. The hundreds were effective enough instruments of mobilization; their limitation for defense was that they could not be relied upon to send their men to other regions, and against a well-planned, well-manned attack the hundreds of a single locality were inadequate.

[49] *Ibid*. 107. When he heard that the invaders had brought horses, the king became alarmed for the security of his valuable French prisoners. *Ibid*. 15, 33-34, 100.

[50] *Ibid*. 51. This seems a hysterical overstatement, but we cannot assume that it was merely propaganda, for the alarm of the government was clearly very real.

[51] *Ibid*. 9, 10, 15-18. Merchant ships were to unload their cargoes with all haste and to sail against the raiders "at the king's wages of war, with promise of indemnification" (16). CPR 1358-1361, 100ff. 350, 411.

[52] CPR 1358-1361, 51.

[53] *Ibid*.

III

For the immediate future, the treaty of Brétigny, signed in October, 1360, gave the southeast nearly a decade to rebuild and to enjoy safety once more. Seen from the point of view of the English villagers, the famous command of Edward concerning archery practice is a moving testimony to the delight with which they exchanged their weapons for the pleasures of peace. But the king had not done with them. In 1363 he commanded that all able-bodied men on feast days and Sundays "shall in his sports use bows and arrows, pellets and bolts, and shall learn and practice the art of shooting, forbidding all and singular on pain of imprisonment to attend and meddle with the hurling of stones, loggets or quoits, handball, football, club ball, cambuc, cock fighting or other vain games of no value; as the people of the realm, noble and simple, used heretofore to practice the said art in their sports, whence by God's help came forth honor to the kingdom and advantage to the king in his actions of war, and now the said art is almost wholly disused, and the people indulge in the games aforesaid and other dishonest and unthrifty games, whereby the realm is like to be kept without archers."[54]

When hostilities began again, in 1369, it was quickly obvious that they had begun with the balance of power shifted to the French side. A new king of France, the great Charles V, had, during the truce, effected a complete military reorganization, had reformed his administrative and fiscal machinery, and above all had concluded a treaty with Castile which gave him access to its superb and professionally manned galleys. By 1372 they had destroyed the English fleet off La Rochelle.[55] By 1375 the Black Prince was dead and the English had been confined to Calais and to a strip of coast from Bordeaux to Bayonne.

The English navy, based on a commerce that was declining, found itself unable to cope with the powerful new alliance. The professionalism of the Castilians and the coordinated campaigns of the French and their new allies could not be equaled by the unwilling English merchant seamen and the Crown's bungling handling of the merchants on whose prosperity the navy relied. In 1371 the commons was complaining of the decrepit state of the realm's shipping. A third of the towns, boroughs, and ports that provided ships were ruined and shrunken, they complained, shipping was bankrupt, and the merchants were reduced to poverty. Responsibility lay with the Crown's policies, for ships were arrested long before they were actually needed and during the interim the owners had to pay for the maintenance and for

[54] CCR 1360-1364, 534-535. *Foedera* (n. 7 above) 3.2.704.

[55] P. E. Russell, *The English Intervention in Spain and Portugal in the Time of Edward III and Richard II* (Oxford 1955) 229-235. Sherborne (n. 15 above).

the crews' wages without any income. Many merchants had thus turned away from shipping. Idled, many sailors had abandoned the sea and changed their trades to support themselves. Furthermore, the merchants who had supported the naval campaigns were crippled by a variety of ordinances that prohibited the profitable employment of their ships. Lastly, the Crown impressed the masters of merchant ships and the best of their seamen to serve aboard the royal ships, leaving without competent crews the remaining merchant ships that were thus often lost at sea. The Crown promised that these faults would be corrrected.[56] Yet in 1377 the commons was still complaining bitterly that the advice of merchants, which once had made the navy strong, was never sought, and they demanded that the new king, Richard II, take into his council men of classes other than the aristocracy.[57]

The commons was perfectly correct about the desertion of merchants from their investments and their once-prosperous ports. Rentals, court records, and charters of the inland town of Battle in Sussex show clearly that Winchelsea and Hastings burgesses were moving into this nearby, but safe, market town and taking up holdings of demesne that were coming on the market since the late 1350s. The descriptions *de Wynchelsea* and *de Hastyngs* now commence to distinguish the newcomers from their Battle cousins, as was true of the Fynhaw and Padiham families. Vincent Finch of Winchelsea, wine merchant and former bailiff of the port, moved his residence to Netherfield manor near Battle, purchased further land from the monks, and, in the 1360s, a genteely located town house in Battle.[58] Refugees from the coast helped to keep up the price of land in the weald; for those who could afford it, cattle breeding and timbering had become a better investment than shipping. In 1371 the Crown was sufficiently concerned about the effect of refugees leaving the Isle of Wight that it was threatening confiscature of all lands and chattels if the refugees had not returned within the month.[59] In 1373 the king was attempting to compensate for the drying up of merchant shipping by commanding the wealthier citizens of certain towns to build ships "for defense of the realm against French and Spanish fleets."[60]

[56] Rot. Parl. 2.306-307. For the effect of the war on the wool trade, see Eileen Power, *The Medieval English Wool Trade* (Oxford 1941) 97-103, 118-119.

[57] Rot. Parl. 3.5-6: "Quant les Marchantz du Roialme furent Seigneurs et Maistres et avoient la disposition et ordinance de lours propres Niefs, si estoit la Navye de Roialme grande et pleintinouse." Their request was that Parliament choose "suffisantz persones de diverses estatz d'estre continuelment residentz du Conseil."

[58] HBA Coll. Rentals: Battle, 1367. Vincent already held a mortgaged land at Netherfield in the 1340s. VCH, *Sussex* 9.107. From this prudent bourgeois family were descended the great lawyer Sir Heneage Finch and the earls of Winchelsea.

[59] CCR 1369-1374, 276.

[60] Sherborne (n. 15 above) 25.

The entry of the Castilians into the conflict in 1372 signaled the commencement of the most terrible years the southern counties had ever known. Mobilization from other areas had proved ineffective during the first phase of the war, and it was rarely attempted at all now with the newer type of swift, deadly raid. So few were the English ships that the raiders sailed along the coast virtually unopposed save by a few local ships out of the southeastern ports—such ships as were left for defense after transport had been provided for the footling campaigns now mounted almost yearly by magnates and their indentured armies. These ports of embarcation and defense the enemy allies now proceeded to destroy. The dreaded Castilian galleys swept into port on the flood tide and landed armed parties who would sack and burn the town, and fire the immobile merchant ships. Usually they accomplished their task within three hours and left on the ebb tide, before the English could assemble the levies, but they did not hesitate to engage the local levies if necessary.

Yet Charles V did not leave the supply of ships to an ally, however faithful. In the mid-1370s measures were taken to build a strong French fleet, and Jean de Vienne was appointed admiral with sweeping powers of reform. The Rouen naval arsenal was converted into a naval dockyard, launching ten ships in 1376 and thirty-five in the following year.[61] The way was now open to take the war to England on a massive scale. In January of 1377 the French and Castilians laid plans for a combined campaign. By June the ships of France had rendezvoused with a squadron of eight Castilian galleys, five Portugese galleys, and a fleet of armed Castilian merchantmen. English intelligence had informed the Crown of the intention, but now the Crown was paralyzed before the threat, and little was done to put local defenses in a state of preparedness. Not until July—after the French and their allies had attacked—were commissions issued for a general array of Hampshire. Southampton was found to be in disrepair, and orders were sent hurriedly to its keeper to arrest workmen from the county to repair its defenses.[62] Rye, unwalled and virtually unprotected, was burned on June 29. The king's council, taking note of the town's plight, determined that the blame lay upon the townspeople and ordered some few executed.[63]

From Rye the enemy moved west to the Ouse and penetrated upriver towards Lewes. In a fight in the village of Rottingdean they met the local levies, led by two knights of the district and by the prior of Lewes. More than a hundred fell, and the three leaders were taken prisoner, but the attackers withdrew.[64] The flotilla then moved eastwards to Folkestone, which

[61] Perroy (n. 2 above) 168.
[62] CPR 1377-1381, 40.
[63] Burrows (n. 17 above) 150. See also J. Hatcher, *Duchy of Cornwall* (1970) 144-145.
[64] Thomas of Walsingham, *Historia Anglicana* ed. H. T. Riley, Rolls Series (RS) i.342.

was sacked on July 20. To keep the defense forces from concentrating, the attackers moved west again. After burning Portsmouth they sacked both Dartmouth and Plymouth. They then returned to Harfleur to refit and to land their booty and prisoners.[65]

The following month the enemy allies were back to repeat their successes. They descended upon the Isle of Wight, where they burned Yarmouth, Newton, and Newport. They then advanced on Carisbrooke castle, which was defended by a force led by Sir Hugh Tyrel. After their leader was killed by a defender's arrow, the attacking party agreed to retire from the island without further destruction upon the payment of a thousand marks. Returning to Sussex they landed at Winchelsea, and there offered the leader of the Sussex levies, Abbot Hamo de Offyngton of Battle, ransom terms that included the surrender of the town. The abbot refused, and became famous as a hero for his personal bravery in the ensuing fight.[66] He and his men fought off the invaders, but with the few men available, even the bravest defense of one place could mean disaster for another. While the battle for Winchelsea was going on, the French sent part of their fleet to Hastings, and finding it virtually undefended, they burned the town. They then withdrew towards Dover, but finding it too well defended for their tired fighters, the fleet quit the coast and sailed home.

The commons meeting in the autumn had much to complain of in both the general defense measures and the conduct of the aristocratic arrayers and overseers of defense. Just what defense measures would be most effective was no longer a matter of general agreement. Both inland and sea defense had their advocates, and a compromise was devised whereby money would be made available for the restoration and manning of coastal forts while the remainder of a subsidy now granted would be allocated for the preparation of a fleet. In the meantime nine Bayonnese ships were hired to protect the entire coast.[67]

John of Gaunt, duke of Lancaster, was the target of an extreme dislike that centered upon him as responsible for the paralysis of the government in organizing home defense during the six months between the planning of the enemy attack and its execution. The government had known of the plans, the government had done nothing, and Gaunt was the government. But Gaunt had other reason to complain, as he did to the new king, that *la Commune avoit malement parlez de luy*.[68] For the personal conduct of Gaunt as keeper of Pevensey castle in Sussex had become a quickly rumored scandal. The royal duke, it was said, had left Pevensey castle undefended and had

[65] Froissart, *Chronicles*, trans. Thomas Johnes (1762) 2.182.

[66] Walsingham 340-342. Abbot Hamo did fight, for his hauberk and crossbow (*balista*) are mentioned in the abbey central accounts. HBA Coll. Abbey Accounts 1381-1382.

[67] Russell (n. 55 above) 241.

[68] Rot. Parl. 3.5.

refused to garrison it at the appeal of the local villagers around the Pevensey Levels. He had answered that he could rebuild what the French had destroyed. The story may have been a political calumny, but certainly there is no evidence that the duke had bestirred himself about the defense of Sussex, and his alleged answer is indeed much to the point. Nonresident noblemen, who could still draw rents from, and retire to, their inland estates, could better afford to repair their castles than to defend town, countryside, and castle alike. A castle was lightly damaged—particularly if firmly shut and unmanned—in a pillaging raid. It was costly, dangerous, and without glory to fight in defense of burgess shops and peasant villages. It is thus no coincidence that effective defense came only from priories and abbeys of the district, from gentlemen whose estates were not dispersed, and above all from the fighting forces of the hundreds. Only those, both gentle and simple, who could not get away had stayed to be attacked. The earl of Arundel, the arrayer of Sussex jointly with the heroic Abbot Hamo of Battle, fled his post because of the raids and left Lewes castle undefended. When the townspeople applied for aid he refused to furnish any armed men unless the town would pay the price of four hundred lances.[69] It had been left for the prior of Lewes and the two local knights to make their tragic stand with the local levies at Rottingdean.

Their tragedy and that of the hundred villagers who died at Rottingdean was that such aristocrats as the earl of Arundel and the duke of Lancaster were, in the eyes of a government that looked at the matter through feudal theory, the natural defenders of the territory. The men left at the mercy of the terrible raids of the 1370s and 1380s were brought to look at their feudal betters and at the feudal ordering of society in a new, and very different way. By the flames of their undefended houses they saw their world revealed. They did not forget Arundel, nor John of Gaunt. The commons in parliament knew well enough what the temper of the ravaged districts was coming to be, for as the speaker warned, *le Roialme ad ore novellement suffert grantz damages et outrage de lours ditz Enemys de plusours partz, et est a douter que pluis soeffrera si Dieu n'y mette remede au gouvernaille d'ycell*[70].

---

[69] *Chronicon Angliae*, ed. E. M. Thompson (RS) 168-169. The chronicler ends his account of Lancaster and Arundel with an anger scarcely disguised: *Consideret, sapiens lector, hujus comitis atque ducis verba cum factis, et interpretur, si poterit, bono modo.*

[70] Rot. Parl. 3.5. The Speaker, Piers de la Mare (also speaker during the Good Parliament, a few months earlier) blamed the aristocracy: "Y dist, en compleignant que tant come le noble Chivalrie del Roialme estoit bien nurriz, encherriz, honores et noblement guerdonez pur lours grantz benefaitz, si estoit celle Chivalrie molt urgerouse et ardantment desirouse a faire grantz emprises et grantz faitz d'armes, chescun devant autre, per ont le Roialme fust grantement enrichez et pleintinouse de toute bien, et les habitantz en ycelle doutez de lours enemys. . . Mais ore, depuis que celle Chivalrie ad este rebuquiz et tenuz

The raids from the combined enemy allies slackened only slightly in the years immediately following the massive attacks of 1377. In the following year Cornwall was the target of the Castilian galleys. Its coastal towns were attacked, its shipping burned and the area forced to pay large ransoms.[71] Yet the southeast, as the location of the chief ports of embarcation, was the favored target. For the 1380 campaign Winchelsea and the Kentish and Sussex coast were singled out for attack by the French and Spanish. Once again Abbot Hamo of Battle led the defenders to the beleaguered town, but they were driven off and the town was sacked. Once again the earl of Arundel was castigated for his failure to render aid.[72] In 1384 it was reported that Winchelsea, "which was once well inhabited, but by being burned by the king's enemies and much more by the withdrawal of its inhabitants, is now so desolate and almost destroyed that proprietorship of vacant plots and tenements can scarcely be known."[73]

A long period of recurring inflations in the price of grain added to the misery of the people. For the better part of ten years in the late 1360s and 1370 the price of wheat in Sussex fluctuated to above 10s a quarter, with other grains nearly as inflated.[74] From the accounts of the almoner of Battle Abbey in Sussex, we have evidence of the plight of the poor that confirms the complaints in the commons and our deductions from the frequency of the French attacks. During the years between 1368 and 1384 the poor crowded to Battle for help from the monks.[75] In years of normal prices the almoner dispensed his abbey's old clothing and leftover food with little mention of his benefactions in his accounts. But during these years of inflation and attack he

---

en viletee et que pluis est, lour biens noblement gaignez de lours Enemys de Guerre lour tolluz sanz jouste cause, et auxint celle Chivalrie et toute autre vertu mys a derire et vice preisee, avancee et honouree et nullement puniz ou chasticee. . . de qoy le Roialme ad ore nouvellement suffert grantz damages et outrage de lours ditz Enemys des plusours partz et est a douter que pluis soeffrera."

[71] Rot. Parl. 3.42.

[72] *Chronicon* (n. 69 above) 167-169.

[73] CPR 1381-1385, 425. The king's answer to the burgesses' petition was to issue a proclamation that all owners must rebuild or sell to men who would rebuild, lest the royal farm of the town be diminished. *Ibid.* No royal proclamation could restore Winchelsea, however, and in 1414 the mayor and commonalty of the town were petitioning for permission to enclose the town with a new wall "of a lesser circuit than the former site of the town, to enclose which would be an unbearable burden." CPR 1413-1416, 263.

[74] J. E. Thorold Rogers, *A History of Agriculture and Prices*, (London 1866-1902) 2.442-55. Prices in the Winchelsea-Hastings-Battle district were higher than these recorded by Thorold Rogers. HBA Coll., Almoners Accounts.

[75] The years in which most was given to the poor were 1368-1373 and 1380-1384, years of the highest prices. Extra food was purchased in those years evidently because of the poor yield of the almoner's tithes and his few fields, for in normal years he kept aside a portion of his grain "for the schoolchildren and the poor." HBA Coll., Almoners Accounts.

purchased extra food to distribute among the needy. During those years he bought beans, peas, herrings, and even meat for the poor, and bought clothing and warm footwear (*socular' et calig'*) to distribute in addition to the monks' old clothes. He mentions too that he gave extra jobs to the poor who had taken to the road, the *extranei garciones*. The men were by no means laborers circumventing the wage legislation; they took the low-paying job of the down-and-out: manure pitching.

Staying to defend their homes from the raiders had become not only dangerous but financially impossible for the villagers of the shore, and indeed nearly so for the poor of the threatened counties as a whole. For as the coastal towns deteriorated and the more prosperous took their money elsewhere, the cost of the fortifications came to bear heavily on those who stayed. In the early 1380s a tax was levied upon all fish—the food of the poor—sold in coastal towns, to be applied to the rebuilding of the fortifications of Rye.[76] Such royal intervention as was now vouchsafed the area amounted to little more than attacks upon the villagers. For the fortifications of Rye the government ordered the arrest of "masons, carpenters, and other laborers . . . with power to imprison the disobedient."[77] Ar the height of the renewed raids, in 1378, the abbot of Battle had been given a commission behind which we can see clearly enough that for laborers, the enemy attacked from London as well as from France, and from this enemy the inland districts were not safe. The abbot was to inquire "of the trespass and contempt committed by John Wauter the younger, carpenter, when arrested at Bodiam (Kent) . . . by John de Neubolt acting under the king's commission empowering him to arrest workmen for the works at Calais, for breaking the arrest and along with John Wauter the elder, assaulting him."[78]

Indeed the lesson, that in this deteriorating military situation the control mechanisms of society would be used to exploit the men and resources of the coastal counties while vouchsafing them no protection, was further made clear by the conduct of the troops waiting to sail for France. The conduct of the magnates as defenders from 1377 on was irresponsible, but their conduct as disciplinarians of their retinues during this diastrous decades drove home a new lesson about them. Between 1369 and 1380 armies embarked from southern ports in every year save 1376. But the requisite shipping was no longer to hand, supplies in the ravaged districts were becoming scarce, and the morale of these troops was clearly very low. Discipline was exceedingly difficult at best in such conditions, and occasionally the retinues got completely out of hand. In 1372, Nevill's retinue was forced to wait for three

[76] CPR 1381-1385, 588.
[77] *Ibid.*
[78] CPR 1377-1381, 300.

months for transport after being mustered at Southampton.[79] In 1370 Sir
Robert Knolls billeted an army of four thousand around Rye and Winchelsea
for a month while they awaited transport. It was hardly surprising, then,
that the men plundered. A petition from the coastal counties in 1379-1380
charged that their houses had been robbed and destroyed by the armies *ve-
nantz et passantz . . . et par lour long demoer*. In one Hampshire village, the
complaint continued, the billeted troops had destroyed houses and chattels.
The commons of the coast (certainly themselves not villagers) now took
courage to address the king in a tone of unusual exasperation and to read
him a lesson he did not know: that burgesses and villagers alike were *si bien
gentz de Seinte Eglise come autres*.[80]

In early 1380 an atrocity scandal was widely circulated. Troops of Sir
John of Arundel, waiting transport to France in December, 1379, had rioted
and gone berserk in a nunnery. A night of rape and murder had followed,
and when the men left they had dragged nuns with them onto their ships,
where the women were raped and eventually thrown overboard. The expedition sailed into a December storm that scattered the ships and took
a heavy toll. Among others, Arundel was drowned, and the story of his ir-
responsibility, and of the atrocity that had finally been its consequence, was
told with the moral that God, at least, if tried enough, would wreak a violent
revenge.[81]

The campaigns for which such troops were mustered were of no use in
relieving the south coast. Year after year the expeditions sailed for France,
but the successful strategy of the 1340s and 1350s was now abandoned for
uncoordinated plundering expeditions that roamed the barren countryside
with little purpose and no accomplishment. The French king wisely refused
to do battle with such negligible foes. While they dissipated their energies
in their fruitless *chevauchées* he now began systematically to reduce the
English position in Aquitaine by beseiging strategic fortresses. For the English, the usual route came to be that between Calais and the duchy of their
ally, the duke of Brittany. But instead of striking through Normandy, the
strong region from which many of the attacks on England were launched,
they took instead the route via Champagne and thence through Anjou to
Brittany.

It was this route that, in the summer of 1380, the prince, Thomas, earl
of Buckingham, chose while the French raided the defenseless English coast.
While he marched to the aid of the duke of Brittany, that duke was negotiating
secretly with the French king, and by the spring of 1381, had been reconciled

---

[79] Sherborne (n. 8 above) 726-727, shows that Nevill's claim that he was forced to wait
sixteen weeks is an exaggeration. The army waited from mid-July to mid-October.

[80] Rot. Parl. 3.80.

[81] Walsingham (n. 64 above) 418-425. He claims to have had the story from a survivor.

with the king. By early May, Buckingham and his army were back in England. Reinforcements had been mustered at Dartmouth, and without a counter-command, they waited there until mid-June. For the government this mismanagement was fortunate. By then they were needed in London to put down their own people.[82] The earl of Buckingham's reinforcements may have been of the greatest use to the government, but the earl's expedition had helped to spark the rising his troops now helped put down. His 1380 adventure had not paid, and for this among other unpopular expenses, the royal treasury needed gold. A poll tax—the third in four years—was granted. The rest of the story is well known. The assessments showed evidence of extensive evasions, and so into the country, on the heels of raiders, refugees, arrayers, arresters, and armies, came royal commissioners to reassess and to collect the tax, just at the beginning of the raiding season. The south broke into violent rebellion.

It is not our purpose here to trace that rebellion, nor do we claim to have explained the many other complex tensions released in 1381. We would emphasize, however, that until one has become aware of the seriousness of the attacks and understood the working of the defense arrangements, one has not even begun to enter the world of those to whom murder and destruction seemed the only course in 1381. Further, we think it worth considering whether the age-old inequities of the villeins' world might not have been changed slowly and without violence—as in the end they were—had not the central government itself revolutionized the peasants' world by coupling its statal demands upon their lives and chattels with its traditional disregard of their welfare.

About the revolt itself, we would call attention to two aspects that underline our argument. First is the discrimination of the rebels in their attacks. It was neither all the rich nor all the powerful to whom they showed hostility. They searched for the duke of Lancaster, who had fled, and they burned his Savoy palace in London, just as their own houses had burned. They looted the shops of foreign merchants. In Sussex, where the violence flared up intermittently for several years, a crowd stormed Lewes castle, beat its keepers and burned the earl of Arundel's muniments and property.[83] But Battle Abbey, only a few miles away, escaped any such rising. During the first half of the 1380s, the accounts of Battle's almoners show that a most unusual number of the poor, as we have said, came to Battle in need of food and clothing. During those years, and those years only, the almoner introduced a distinction among those he helped: he gave to none save the "honest

---

[82] Sherborne (n. 8 above). Buckingham's reinforcements, about a thousand men, were ordered to London to deal with the revolt in mid-June.

[83] CPR 1381-1385, 259. The farm buildings of the abbot of Saint Albans' manor of Coombe in Sussex were also burned. *Gesta Abbatum* (RS) 3.363.

poor"—the *honestiores pauperes*.[84] In the face of peasants who a few miles away were looting and burning at Lewes castle, it is remarkable that the Battle almoner could maintain his prim distinction. At the height of the violence of 1381, Abbot Hamo, the hero of Winchelsea, went off for a holiday to his little manor of Maxfield. Nor was he afraid, when the hunting season came around, to entertain the new archbishop of Canterbury, William Courtenay, at Battle for the sport. Both men had a cool confidence, for the archbishop's predecessor had been murdered by the mob during the revolt.[85]

Secondly, we should now understand more clearly the rapid communications the rebels commanded, the disciplined competence of their successful assaults on London and on the very Tower itself, and the extraordinary cohesiveness of the rebels from Kent and Sussex. Their sense of "themselves as a natural community, distinct from their east Saxon neighbors," the ignoring of manorial divisions in their units, have aroused interest and comment.[86] These are indeed of the highest significance for understanding the rebels, but they should not surprise us. For, as we have seen, the peasants of Kent and Sussex had long been isolated, trained in military discipline and communications, hardened in fighting. They had simply been arrayed in their usual hundred levies for the march on London. And as to John Ball's great question—the ideological contribution of the southeast to the rebellion—however implicit in popular preaching against avarice, the question had been inescapable during the long watches on the downs, in the hand-to-hand fighting in the

[84] An example of the strain put upon the coastal counties by the war is found in the almoner's account of 1384. In that year the poor were joined by refugees *propter fflandranc' infortunium*. The "Flemish misfortune" was the ill-planned "crusade" of the bishop of Norwich, on which an army of nearly five thosand had sailed. The armies, abandoned without wages on the English coast, added their misery to that of the region. It is not unlikely that the army of the earl of Buckingham, similarly abandoned at Falmouth on May 2, 1381, swelled the numbers of the region's peasants whose revolt was even then being organized. The earl's reinforcements, still waiting to sail in June, were still on his wages. Thus part of the violence was perhaps Buckingham's two armies fighting one another, but one was newly armed.

[85] Archbishop Simon Sudbury, the chancellor, was murdered. His successor, William Courtenay, was provided in early September and received the temporalities in late October, 1381. Abbot Hamo did not merely organize defense, but actually fought, for the Abbey Acconts list his hauberk and *balista*, a heavy crossbow. HBA Coll. Abbey Accounts 1381-1382: the abbot went to Maxfield *circa recreandum*. The abbey did not escape hatred by being poor, since it was a prosperous house, with extensive East Sussex estates. Most of its land was at farm by the 1380s, however, and it was clearly filling an expected role in the life of the district with its benefactions and leadership in defense.

[86] May McKisack, *The Fourteenth Century* (Oxford 1959) 420. Professor McKisack suggests that the peasantry had retained the memory of an ancient, prefeudal Kentish "tribalism," and that manorial arrangements that "cut across or ignore this tribalism" had not affected it. Yet it is of course true that the hundredal organization, which was the instrument of mobilization during the long defense of the coast, also generally ignored manorial boundaries. See esp. *The Anonimalle Chronicle*, ed. V. H. Galbraith (1927) 136.

streets of the Cinque Ports, in the bivouacs along the estuaries. This was a new kind of fighting, where monks, gentry, peasants, and bourgeois on foot had fought off invaders: and "Wo was thanne a gentilman?"

The Peasants' Revolt in 1381 did not change the world. Taxes, arrests, and levies continued, as indeed they had to, for the raids continued, though with decreasing violence, until the treaty of 1389 brought peace. Having learned that their subordinate place in society was not justified by any reciprocal obligation whatsoever—having been forced to questions that their ancestors perhaps had never faced—their reaction had at last, in the worst of their sufferings, been to strike at an aristocratic government that upheld that society. It was, of course, ineffective and brief. But their experience during the war had, after all, been shared by other classes in the unsuccored counties. At the moment when the revolt of the poor and ignorant had been put down, the voice of those other classes spoke. When Sir Richard Waldegrave of Kent in parliament placed the blame for the revolt not on the peasants, but on those who mulcted them without defending them, he spoke for all those who had been forced to remain and fight.[87] Not merely the peasants but the bourgeois and gentry had been caused to realize by the conduct of the defense of England that the justifications of feudal theory did not correspond to the realities of their experience. This had prepared them to entertain notions of social change, and it was this change of attitude on the part of the bourgeois that was, perhaps, the significant consequence of the events whose most dramatic consequence was the Peasants' Revolt.

[87] Rot. Parl. 3.100: "Et sanz cella encores, combien que grant Tresor en continuelment grantez et levez de eux (the commons) pur le defens de Roialme, nientmeins il n'en sont le plus defenduz ne sucourez encontre les Enemys du Roialme a leur escient, einz de an en an sont ars, robbez, et pilez, par terre et par meer par les ditz Enemys, et par lours Barges et Galeys et autres Vesseulx, de quoy nulle remede lour ad este, ne encores est, purveuz." It is the sentiment voiced by Piers de la Mare in 1377 (see n. 70 above), but the speaking is blunter.

Department of History
University of California
Los Angeles, California, U.S.A.

MAN'S DIGNITY, GOD'S LOVE, AND THE DESTINY OF ROME
A TEXT OF GILES OF VITERBO

•

by John W. O'Malley, S.J.

Giles of Viterbo's (1469-1532) place in the ecclesiastical and intellectual life of the High Renaissance is gradually being clarified by recent studies.[1] He combined a central and effective position in ecclesiastical administration with an active role in the leading scholarly and literary circles of the Rome of Julius II and Leo X. Julius favored his election as prior general of the Augustinian friars in 1507, after having appointed him vicar general of the order in the previous year. Giles served as prior general until 1518. During his terms of office he launched a vigorous reform of the order. He was also

I should like to express my gratitude to the American Philosophical Society for a grant-in-aid that made possible the research necessary for the publication of this text. I should also like to express my gratitude to Professor Charles Trinkaus of the University of Michigan for his comments on my Introduction to the text. In a very special way I am indebted to the Rev. Edmund F. Miller, S.J., and the Rev. Norman G. McKendrick, S.J. of the University of Detroit for their critical reading of my transcription of the text.

[1] For an excellent survey of studies on Giles of Viterbo, see Francis X. Martin, O.S.A., "The Problem of Giles of Viterbo: A Historiographical Survey," *Augustiniana* 9 (1959) 357-379; 10 (1960) 43-60. Giuseppe Signorelli's biography of Giles is outdated and eulogistic, but still helpful, *Egidio da Viterbo: Agostiniano, umanista e riformatore* (Florence 1929). My own book contains a bibliography and a listing of the more important studies published since Father Martin's survey appeared, *Giles of Viterbo on Church and Reform: A Study in Renaissance Thought* (Leiden 1968) 11-12, 192-206. To this bibliography should now be added the following: Vincenzo Cilento, "Glosse di Egidio da Viterbo alla traduzione ficiniana delle Enneadi in un incunabulo del 1492" in *Studi di bibliografia e di storia in onore di Tammaro de Marinis*, 4 vols. (Verona 1964) 1.281-296; Marjorie Reeves, *The Influence of Prophecy in the Later Middle Ages: A Study in Joachimism* (Oxford 1969) 267-271; Nelson H. Minnich, S.J., "Concepts of Reform Proposed at the Fifth Lateran Council," *Archivum historiae pontificiae* 7 (1969) esp. 168-173; François Secret, "Notes sur Egidio da Viterbo," *Augustiniana* 18 (1968) 134-150; Jean Gribomont, "Gilles de Viterbe, le moine Elie, et l'influence de la littérature maronite sur la Rome érudite de 1515," *Oriens christianus* 54 (1970) 125-129; Charles Trinkaus, *In Our Image and Likeness: Humanity and Divinity in Italian Humanist Thought*, 2 vols. (Chicago 1970) 2.526-529; and my own article, "Fulfillment of the Christian Golden Age under Pope Julius II: Text of a Discourse of Giles of Viterbo, 1507," *Traditio* 25 (1969) 265-338. Father Martin is now preparing another survey of studies that have appeared since 1959.

a popular preacher. At the request of Julius II he delivered the opening oration at the Fifth Lateran Council (1512-1517), an insistent plea for the reform of the Church. In this inaugural sermon Giles enunciated his well known norm for authentic ecclesiastical renewal: "Men must be changed by religion, not religion by men."[2] During the council he and Cajetan (Thomas de Vio), the renowned Thomist theologian and master general of the Dominican order, fought side by side to defend the privileges of the mendicants from the attacks of the bishops. In 1517 Leo X created Giles a cardinal, and after the council he sent him for a year as papal legate to the court of the young King Charles I of Spain, the future Emperor Charles V. By virtue of his position as vicar and prior general of the Augustinians, Giles was Martin Luther's highest ecclesiastical superior for the crucial years 1506-1518. Clement VII nominated him bishop of Viterbo in 1523. He died on the night of November 11-12, 1532, in Rome, and he is buried there in the church of S. Agostino.

Giles moved with familiarity in the most advanced intellectual circles of Padua, Naples, Florence, and Rome. Early in his career he edited at Padua three works of Giles of Rome, and throughout his life he sustained a lively, but unsympathetic, interest in Paduan Aristotelianism.[3] He seemingly exercised a salutary influence upon Giovanni Pontano and his group at Naples, as Pontano's dialogue *Aegidius* indicates. Giles was enthusiastic about Marsilio Ficino's Platonic theology, and he undertook a commentary on the *Sententiarum libri* of Peter Lombard "according to the mind of Plato," which he laid aside incomplete about 1512.[4] During the pontificate of Leo X, he wrote his lengthy history of the Church and papacy, "Historia xx saeculorum."[5] Pico and Reuchlin stirred Giles's interest in the cabala, which after about 1517 seems to have almost completely absorbed his intellectual interest and which culminated in his undertaking in 1530 his *Scechina*, an elaborate Christian interpretation and adaptation of cabalistic doctrine.[6] Girolamo Seripando, the great Augustinian theologian of the Council of Trent, was a protégé of Giles, and there is reason to believe that Giles's influence upon him was considerable.

[2] Mansi 32.669.

[3] These three works were published in two volumes at Padua in 1493: (1) *Egidii Romani eremite de materia celi questio, Egidii Romani de intellectu possibili contra Averoim questio aurea.* See *Gesamtkatalog der Wiegendrucke* 6, no. 7213. (2) *Egidii Romani comentaria in VIII libros physicorum Aristotelis*, no. 7197 in the *Gesamtkatalog.*

[4] For critical comment on the different manuscript versions of this work, see Eugenio Massa, *I fondamenti metafisici della "dignitas hominis" e testi inediti di Egidio da Viterbo* (Turin 1954) 49-53.

[5] The autograph version of this text is in Naples, Biblioteca Nazionale MS IX.B.14. See O'Malley, *Giles of Viterbo* 16, 193.

[6] Egidio da Viterbo, *Scechina e Libellus de litteris Hebraicis*, ed. François Secret, 2 vols. (Rome 1959).

Some years ago Eugenio Massa called attention to Giles's importance for the development of the Renaissance theme of man's dignity, and he published a portion of the text of Giles's commentary on the *Sententiarum libri* relating to it.[7] Charles Trinkaus's recent book, which provides an excellent context in which to view Giles's contribution to the theme, once again highlighted the importance of the Lombard commentary.[8] Our present discourse, however, was not utilized by either of these scholars in their discussion of Giles's thought on man's dignity, and it is here published for the first time.

The text is edited from what seem to be the only two extant versions, found in manuscript in the Biblioteca Nazionale, Naples, and in the Biblioteca Angelica, Rome.[9] The Naples and Angelica codices are collections of Giles's correspondence, and the discourse on man's dignity is presented in the form of a letter, addressed to "Antonio Zoccoli and the Romans." In its structure and content, however, the discourse much more closely resembles a formal discourse or sermon than it does the other "epistolae familiares" among which it is found.

What is particularly distinctive about the present text is that it relates the theme of man's dignity to the dignity and destiny of the city of Rome. This relationship is missing from the texts of Giles discussed by Massa and Trinkaus, and I know of no other instance in Renaissance writing where it is found. Thus the abstract and almost commonplace theme of man's dignity is here invested with new meaning as it contributes to the sacral mystique of Rome, a mystique that only remotely relates to the more sober and secular "civic humanism" sometimes associated with the theme of man's dignity in humanist writings.[10] Elsewhere I have shown what a significant contribution Giles made to the Roman mystique, especially as it colors his ideas on reform.[11] I shall not elaborate upon that contribution here. It might be appropriate, however, to call attention to Donald Weinstein's recent book, *Savonarola and Florence*, and to suggest that a comparison between the mystiques of the two cities would be enlightening.[12] In any case, it is becoming ever more apparent that we shall never fully understand the Rome of the High Renaissance apart from the writings of Giles of Viterbo.

[7] Massa (n. 4 above).

[8] Trinkaus (n. 1 above). For the general theme of man's dignity in relationship to the patristic tradition, see also Eugenio Garin, "La 'dignitas hominis' e la letteratura patristica," *La Rinascita* 1.4 (1938) 102-146.

[9] Naples, Biblioteca Nazionale MS V.F.20 fols. 256r-281r (letter no. 216), and Rome, Biblioteca Angelica MS lat. 1001 fols. 11r-23v. These manuscripts will henceforth be cited simply as Naples MS and Ang. MS respectively.

[10] Trinkaus (n. 1 above) for example, 75-76, 282-283.

[11] *Giles of Viterbo* esp. 120-138, 179-191; "Fulfillment"; and "Giles of Viterbo: A Reformer's Thought on Renaissance Rome," *Renaissance Quarterly* 20 (1967) 1-11.

[12] Donald Weinstein, *Savonarola and Florence* (Princeton 1970).

Our text is differentiated from the discussion in the commentary on the *Sententiarum libri* in that it does not base man's dignity on the fact of his being created "in the image and likeness of God." This verse from Genesis (l. 26) dominates Giles's discussion in the commentary, where it would have been suggested to him in Augustinian terms by Lombard himself. Trinkaus has shown, moreover, how fundamentally important the "image-and-likeness" verse was in general for the Renaissance theme of man's dignity. But here Giles does not employ it. He bases his case for man's dignity especially on certain key verses from the Gospel of John. The focus is not on the dignity with which God endowed man in Creation, but in the dignity that results from the Incarnation and from the outpouring of love that the Incarnation effects and symbolizes. The Redemption or Atonement is looked upon as an extension of this mysterious outpouring of love, a love identified with the Holy Spirit dwelling in men's hearts. Through this love man is transformed into "God" and rendered immortal.

There was considerable stress on the Incarnation among the humanists. But Giles, unlike many of his humanist counterparts who considered the Incarnation as at least partially constitutive of humankind's dignity, does not here imply that man's transformation is a return to the original image of God in which he was created. Through love man becomes simply "God" or a "son of God."

As the recipient of God's transforming love, man has a mission to help transform others by means of it. This mission is especially incumbent upon the "Romans." In the commentary on Lombard, Giles attempts to locate man in the universe by dicussing his dignity in relationship to the dignity of the angels, a problematic that he inherited from scholastic commentaries on the *Sententiarum libri*. In our present discourse such metaphysical comparisons are absent. Man's dignity or, in this case, transformation is not looked upon as assigning him to a niche in a hierarchy of honors, but as imposing upon him a mission. It also imbues him with a holy dynamism that enables him to fulfill the mission. In this discourse, therefore, Giles substantiates for religious literature the emphasis on action and achievement which Burckhardt discovered in Renaissance secular literature and which Trinkaus sees as generally characteristic of humanist thought on man's dignity.[13]

The present discourse falls into three rather distinct parts. The first part (fols. 256r-270v) treats of man's divinization through the power of divine love, his responsibility to respond to God's love especially with love for his neighbor, and the evil consequences of living without love. The second part of the discourse (fols. 270v-275v) is a long transition from the theme of man's divinization to that of the destiny of Rome; Elisha is here presented as in-

---

[13] Trinkaus (n. 1 above) for example, xx-xxi, 163-170, 247-248, 463-464.

dicating man's divinization in his very name and as being a type of Saint Peter. The last part (fols. 276r-281r) deals with the destiny of Rome, particularly as this was providentially mediated by Peter and his successors, including Julius II. Giles relates the last part to the first by recalling that Rome was chosen by God in love and that Rome must respond with love. This last part is animated by a bold rhetoric, as the nuptials between humanity and divinity are specified in the form of the nuptials between Rome and Christ.

Without doubt the discourse contains a number of interesting and suggestive themes. Although the term "dignity of man" is not here explicitly used by Giles, it well describes the first theme of the discourse. Through the effects of the Incarnation man is raised to the dignity of a son of God. He is not thereby made divine in any pantheistic sense, but he certainly is "divinized." Man's "divinization" or "deification" was a dominant theme of certain patristic writings, and it was closely related to speculation on the Incarnation.[14] Saint Augustine himself expounded on the theme, as did some Renaissance humanists.[15]

In the forefront of Giles's theological consciousness, therefore, was not the excellence of man's creation in God's image, nor the deprivation and even depravity resulting from Original Sin, but the surpassing sublimation effected by the Word's becoming flesh. Thus further verification is given to Trinkaus's assertion that in the Renaissance theme of the dignity of man we discover "what is possibly the most affirmative view of human nature in the history of thought and expression."[16] Elsewhere, especially in the "Historia," Giles shows us that he was perfectly aware of the misery of human life when man failed to live up to his high calling. But in this "letter" to Zoccoli and the Romans he gives energetic expression to what he felt man's potential to be. In this way Giles again verifies one of Trinkaus's conclusions, namely, that the humanists were convinced that "divine force alone was capable of restructuring the naturally egotistical motivations of mankind towards higher ethical and religious goals."[17]

The Incarnation is seen as a work of love. Through the Holy Spirit it evokes from man a response in love. Thus love or charity is seen as the principal and central duty of the Christian life. Giles's exegesis of the Epistle to the

---

[14] See the article "Divinisation" in the *Dictionnaire de spiritualité* 3.1370-1459.

[15] For Augustine, see Victorino Capánaga, "La deificación en la soteriología agustiniana," in *Augustinus magister*, 3 vols. (Paris 1954?) 2.745-754, and the *Dictionnaire* 3.1390-1392, 1395-1397. For the humanists, see the index to Trinkaus (n. 1 above) under "deification" 963, as well as Garin (n. 8 above). For an interesting article related to medieval political theory, see Ernst H. Kantorowicz, "Deus per naturam, deus per gratiam: A Note on Medieval Political Theology," *The Harvard Theological Review* 45 (1952) 253-277.

[16] Trinkaus (n. 1 above) xiv.

[17] *Ibid.* xx.

Romans bypasses the theme of man's justification by faith and fastens upon the text asserting that the charity of God is poured into our hearts (Rom. 5.5), a text that was a favorite also of his father, Saint Augustine. Life without that charity is dead, unpleasing to God. It is without the savor of the salt about which the Gospel speaks (Matt. 5.13). Charity preserves and restores health, and it attaches Rome to Christ, its spouse.

The religious message of this "letter" to Zoccoli and the Romans thus coincides with Giles's general viewpoint on Christian reform. The purpose of reform is not to change religion in any of its practices or beliefs, but to transform the individual Christian. "Men must be changed by religion, not religion by men." Charity effects the transformation which Giles saw as central to reform. Giles seems specifically to relate this present "letter" to the question of reform in his final apostrophe to Julius II.[18]

As I mentioned earlier, the destiny and theological meaning of Rome was a frequent subject of Giles's writings. He was thoroughly convinced of Rome's providential mission and at the same time often repelled by Rome's sins. His negative feelings towards Rome were several times revealed in his correspondence with Zoccoli. In one letter, undated, he refers to Rome as "Babylon."[19] In another letter, dated May, 1505, he tells Zoccoli of his desire never to return there to preach because he did not know what effective words he could say, given the low morals of the city.[20]

In the present discourse are to be found not much more than the suggestion of several other themes which Giles would develop at greater length in his other writings. The mystical meaning of Scripture, especially as it is revealed through a study of names, would be one of these themes.[21] Another would be the role in history of the Etruscans.[22] Giles's invectives against "philosophy" intimates the opposition to Paduan Averroism which would become characteristic of him.[23] Several times in this "letter" to Zoccoli and the Romans, Giles alludes to the oak of Julius II's coat of arms. The symbolism of the della Rovere coat of arms would play a significant part in the "libellus," which he wrote at the request of Julius II in 1507-1508 and which I published several years ago.[24]

---

[18] Naples MS fols. 280v-281r.

[19] Naples MS fol. 293r. See also the letter to Zoccoli dated "viii Kalendas Novembris" (Oct. 25) 1505, *ibid.* fol. 106v, as well as the letter to Serafino Ferri, "die diui Antonii" (Jan. 17 or June 13) 1500, *ibid.* fol. 297v, where he again refers to Rome as "Babylon."

[20] Naples MS fol. 105v.

[21] O'Malley, *Giles of Viterbo* (n. 1 above) 67-99, esp. 91-92.

[22] *Ibid.* 30-31, 123-124.

[23] *Ibid.* 40-49.

[24] O'Malley, "Fulfillment" (n. 1 above). See also Naples MS fols. 286r-287r, undated letter of Giles to Zoccoli.

The discourse on man's dignity, and so forth, was ostensibly occasioned by two letters that Giles had received from Antonio Zoccoli.[25] Unfortunately, these two letters have not survived. In fact, although we possess a total of fifty-four letters from Giles to Zoccoli, we do not have a single one from Zoccoli to Giles, nor to my knowledge has any of Zoccoli's other correspondence survived.[26] Most of what we know about Zoccoli, therefore, is reconstructed from Giles's letters. Our problem is further complicated by the fact that only eight of Giles's fifty-one letters to him in the Naples-Angelica codices bear dates. These dates range from 1500 to 1506. On this rather unsatisfactory basis we infer that Giles probably met Zoccoli when he was called to Rome in 1497 to preach before Alexander VI and that the extensive correspondence between them probably slackened once Giles himself took up permanent residence in Rome after his appointment as vicar general of the Augustinian order in 1506.

Zoccoli was a layman and a Roman citizen.[27] He distinguished himself in his efforts for Rome against the French, probably during Charles VIII's occupation of the city in 1495, and he held important military and civil offices in Rome at least until 1515.[28] He performed a number of services for Giles and his Augustinian brethren both before and after Giles assumed the office of superior general of the order. In particular, he assisted Giles in 1502 in his efforts to join the Augustinian monastery at Viterbo to the Observant Congregation of Lecceto, and he at times acted as an intermediary

[25] Naples MS fol. 256r. In the manuscripts Zoccoli's name is variously given as Zoccolus, Zocholus, Zoccholus, and Zocchulus.

[26] The index to the Naples MS lists fifty-one letters according to their *incipit*, fols. 6r-7r, but the codex contains only twenty-eight of them. All fifty-one of these, on the other hand, are to be found in the Ang. MS. Two of them were published in part by Signorelli (n. 1 above) 220-221, 226. A further collection of Giles's correspondence, consisting principally of his official letters as prior general, is to be found in Siena, Biblioteca Comunale MS G.X.26. This collection contains three letters from Giles to Zoccoli, thus bringing the total up to fifty-four: (1) pp. 189-190, "ii Nonis Iulii" (July 6), 1508; (2) p. 200, August 18, 1508; (3) p. 173, July 29, 1510. The last two of these letters are printed in Signorelli 236, 239.

[27] See Naples MS fols. 253r-256r. Zoccoli's relationship to Spain still requires clarification. See, for example, Naples MS fols. 252v, 283v, undated letter of Giles to Zoccoli in which he speaks in terms of "Hispania illa tua" and "De Hispania tua." A portion of the second letter is quoted in L. G. Pélissier, "Pour la biographie du Cardinal Gilles de Viterbe," *Miscellanea di studi critici edita in onore di Arturo Graf* (Bergamo 1903) 805 n. 1. Signorelli thought he was a Spaniard and suggested he was attached to the Spanish embassy in Rome, 134 n. 51.

[28] In undated letters addressed to Zoccoli, Giles refers to him as "tribuni quoque et cohortis praefectus," Naples MS fol. 288v, as "consul," fols. 245v-246r, and as "optimum militem, optimum imperatorem, optimum oratorem," fol. 246r. On Zoccoli's resistence to the French, see fols. 245v-246r, 299v-300r. In 1515 he was elected to the office of *imbussolatore* for the city of Rome, as reported in Pio Pecchiai, *Roma nel Cinquecento*, Storia di Roma 13 (Bologna 1948) 249.

between Giles and Julius II.[29] Zoccoli, moreover, was one of the three persons who brought Giles news of his appointment by Julius II as vicar general of the Augustinian order on June 27, 1506.[30]

The present text is undated. Since it ends with an apostrophe to Julius II, however, it clearly was written no earlier than 1503, the year of Julius's accession to the papal throne. From external evidence it is highly probable that the letter was written no later than 1508. Serafino Ferri, Giles's friend and fellow Augustinian, had begun compiling a collection of Giles's letters. In January, 1508, he wrote to Zoccoli to request him to send him the letters he had received from Giles. This letter is contained in the Naples and Angelica codices.[31] It is likely, therefore, that whatever we possess of the correspondence between Giles and Zoccoli in these codices antedates this request. This conjecture is supported by the fact that of the almost one hundred letters in the Naples codex which are dated, only two are subsequent to 1508 (1509, 1514).

The discourse ends with a brief appeal to Julius II to fulfill the exalted duties of his office. This appeal can be interpreted as an early expression of Giles's concern for the reform of the Church under papal leadership. It also seems to indicate that Giles hoped the discourse would be brought to Julius's attention by Zoccoli. If this is the case, it helps explain why the discourse contains nothing personal to Zoccoli beyond the first two sentences, in contrast with Giles's other letters to Zoccoli, which are very personal and direct.

I have used the Naples version of the discourse as the basic text for my edition. This version differs from the Angelica version relatively little, but in every instance where there is a discrepancy in the readings, the Naples version is clearly preferable. I have some hesitation at this point in describing the Naples codex as the archetype for those portions of the Angelica codex

---

[29] See Francis X. Martin, O.S.A., "Giles of Viterbo and the Monastery of Lecceto: the Making of a Reformer," *Analecta Augustiniana* 25 (1962) 245; Naples MS, for example, fols. 69v, 285, 291, 292v.

[30] See Giles's letter, undated, to the Monastery of Lecceto, written shortly after he received the news, Naples MS fols. 121r-122v, 126r-127v, and Ang. MS fols. 102r-105v. The letter was printed in E. Martène and U. Durand, *Veterum scriptorum et monumentorum historicorum, dogmaticorum, moralium amplissima collectio*, 9 vols. (Paris 1724-1733) 3.1235-1238.

[31] For the letter from Serafino to Zoccoli, Jan. 22, 1508, see Naples MS fols. 208v-209v, or Ang. MS fols. 181v-182r. On the collection in general, see Naples MS fols. 19v-21v, 165v-166v; L. G. Pélissier, "Manuscrits de Gilles de Viterbe à la Bibliothèque Angélique (Rome)," *Revue des bibliothèques* 2 (1892) 237-238; E. Narducci, *Catalogus codicum manuscriptorum praeter graecos et orientales in Bibliotheca Angelica olim coenobii Sancti Augustini de Urbe* (Rome 1893) 416-418; Paul Oskar Kristeller, *Iter italicum*, 2 vols. (London 1965-1967) 1.419-420. On Ferri, see Martin (n. 29 above) 244, and David Aurelius Perini, *Bibliographia Augustiniana* (Florence 1931) 2.58.

which correspond to the contents of the Naples codex.[32] But the minimum that can be said is that, if the appropriate portions of the Angelica codex were not directly copied from the Naples codex, they at least were copied from the same parent codex, now lost. Unfortunately, the Naples codex in its present form is incomplete. The last section has been excised, so that it now contains only 242 letters instead of the 329 it should contain.[33]

The orthography of the Naples, as well as the Angelica, codex approximates that of classical Latin. In transcribing the text it seemed reasonable, therefore, to make it generally conform with this norm for the sake of consistency and readability. Simple vowels, for example, have been expanded whenever necessary into their appropriate diphthongs, and spellings like "charitas" and "cathena" have been replaced with "caritas" and "catena." The only exception to the norm of classical orthography is the spelling of certain proper names; in the present transcription the orthography of the Naples codex for these names has been faithfully reproduced. The consistent usage of the manuscripts indicates that the medial n should be preferred to m in such words as "tanquam," "unquam;" the medial c should be preferred to d in such words as "quicquid," "quicquam"; the initial and medial i should be preferred to j; and the initial and medial u should be preferred to v except for capital letters. Obvious scribal errors have been corrected without further indication, and no attempt has been made to preserve contractions and abbreviations. For punctuation, paragraphing, and the use of capital letters only modern requirements have been considered.

Giles, when quoting, often changes the tense, mood, and so on, of verbs, and he correspondingly adapts other parts of speech. Italics have been employed only for those words in quotations or allusions which precisely reproduce the source from which Giles drew them. In these instances no attempt has been made in the "apparatus fontium" to indicate the omission of words or the inversion of word order except where such indication would especially seem to be called for, as in the case of poetry. Scripture quotations are italicized only when they coincide with the text of the Vulgate unless the contrary is specifically noted in the "apparatus fontium." Angular brackets <> indicate any additions I have made to the text. The abbreviations for names of classical and scriptural authors and works are taken from Lewis

---

[32] For example, Giles's "De Ilicetana familia," published from Ang. MS lat. 1156 by Father Martin (n. 29 above) 248-253, is broken up and out of place in the Naples MS fols. 127v-131r, 123r-125v, whereas it is perfectly ordered in the Ang. MS fols. 105v-111v.

[33] The index (Naples MS fols. 2r-18v) lists with numbers 326 letters. To these letters must be added the two introductory letters between Serafino Ferri and Deodatus of Siena, which are listed but not numbered. Then there is a further letter (fol. 1), which precedes the index and is neither numbered nor listed. This brings the total that the codex should have contained to 329.

and Short's *Latin Dictionary* and from Liddell and Scott's *Greek-English Lexicon*.[34]

256r   AEGIDIUS ANTONIO ZOCHOLO ET ROMANIS

Allatae mihi duae sunt epistolae, quae, quanquam parum habent lit-
256v   terarum, lectae a me sunt / multum. Lucet enim in eis amoris multum.
Soleo ego amorem ipsum, nescio an inepte, rerum omnium salem appellare. Insulsa enim omnia sine eo. Dedit hunc heroicis discipulis Do-
5   minus et, nisi fallor, hunc solum illis dedit, uenitque ad incolendum
Cedar et terras nobiscum non alio consilio quam ut hunc e caelo ad nos
afferret. Magna amoris uis, quid mirum si in homines? In superos
uis habet. Ille Deus deduxit ex Olympo Dominum, hoc est, hominem
fecit unde homines dii facti sunt amore plane eodem et filii excelsi omnes,
10   *quotquot receperunt eum*, quoniam receperunt amore ipso dumtaxat, qui
non *ex uoluntate carnis*, ut Aristippici et filii matrimonio geniti, neque
rursus *uoluntate uiri*, ut Stoici et qui uirtute a uiris praestantibus in-
257r   stituuntur, *sed ex Deo / nati sunt*, amore geniti, *aqua et Spiritu sancto*
renati, mundati flumine uiuo, ubi Spiritus uitae, et Spiritu, qui amor
15   est diuinus, natique patrisque completi.

Dices, qui fieri potest ut homo Dei filius sit? Homo enim ex homine,
et qui e ceruo nascitur ceruus, qui ex pauone pauo. Qui igitur ex Deo
item Deus. Qui fit ut homo, sanguis et caro (ut nostri dicunt), in deum
transeat, hoc est, euadat deus deusque efficiatur? Sed quid id mireris
20   quod homo fiat deus? Nam Deus effectus est homo et *Verbum caro
factum*? Si enim Deus, qui optimum in se habet, homo fit, cur homo,
cuius optimum in Deo situm habet, non uertatur in deum? Quae enim
perfecta non sunt ad perfectum natura stimulante concitantur.

Ex Deo nati sunt, amore non natura. Qui <non> natura? Quia
257v   25   *Verbum / caro factum est et habitauit in nobis*, et in nostris conceptus
pectoribus nos genuit diuersa ratione quam liberi uulgo procreari con-
sueuerint. Illi ut gignantur concipiuntur, hic habitans *in nobis* ut nos

---

[34] *A Latin Dictionary*, eds. Charlton T. Lewis and Charles Short (New York 1962) vii-xi,
and *A Greek-English Lexicon*, eds. Henry George Liddell and Robert Scott (Oxford 1953)
xvi-xli.

A Bibl. Angelica, Rome, MS lat. 1001, fols. 11r-23v   N Bibl. Naz., Naples, MS V.F.20,
fols. 256r-281r.

18 sanguis *scripsi* : deus N A   19 id *om*. A   23 concitatur A
6 Cf. Psa. 119 (120).5.   10-13 Joan. 1.12-13.   11 Cf. Cic. Fin. 2.6.18.
13 Joan. 3.5.   14 Cf. Joan. 7.38.   20-21 Cf. Aug. Serm. 192.1, PL 38.1012;
Serm. 342.5, PL 39.1504.   20-21 Joan. 1.14.   25 Joan. 1.14.   27 Joan. 1.14.

gignat a nobis concipitur prius, intusque ipse latens ex se ipso disquirit
semina flammae. Est enim lapis et silex. Illa uero sunt, ut scis, *abstrusa*
30 *in uenis silicis,* unde scintillas excutiens animum accendit et cor flammis corripit. *Cor nostrum erat ardens in uia* dicebant qui Emaum pro-
ficiscebantur.

Qui igitur *Spiritu Dei aguntur,* quod ait Apostolus, *filii Dei sunt,*
hoc est, qui diuino amore flagrant *ex Deo nati sunt.* Sed qua id ratione?
35 Quia *Verbum caro factum.* Vides ideo factum ut habitans *in nobis* ignem
amoremque in nobis excitaret, quo absumpta mor/tali natura immortales ex Deo nasceremur. Horum uero omnium ratio amor est, cuius
gratia Deum hominem effectum praedicabam. Huius amoris osculum
petit puella in epithalamio, non Hymenaeum, non Talassionem Sabini
40 raptus, sed os patris aeterni, aeternumque Verbum ad humanas nuptias uocans, optansque atque obtestans ut, posteaquam parentes eiecti
a Deo sunt, patrata culpa, exulem humanam subolem factam quandoque
sponso iungi liceret.

Has nuptias Adae parenti spopondit Deus cum dixit feminam ser-
45 pentis caput oppressuram, uirginem intelligens quam Hieremias uidit
circumdare uirum cum littera Mem contra naturam clausa, hoc pacto
dicens hanc clausam in oriente portam qua unus ingrederetur Dominus.
Vidit Ezechiel hanc concipientem. Vidit Esaias. Qua pariente, *paruulus*
natus et / filius datus est nobis. Has nuptias Noae post mundi naufragia,
50 has Abrahae, has filio, has nepoti, has post Erithrea uada Mosi, has
denique pastori ab ouibus et caula in regnum et sceptra gentis uocato
spopondit, qui lepidissimis suae linguae fidibus nuptiarum et sponsi
gloriam lusit.

Multo sane suauius id filius, utpote cui liberius per otia feriari licuerit.
55 Hic Cantica cecinit, diuinum undique et arcanum opus, ubi multo suauior
uisus in sacris castisque amoribus Salomon quam in obscenis ac per-
ditis Catullus. Illic sponsi sponsaeque lusus celebrati sunt atque illa
connubia quae statim ab orbe condito sunt et a Deo optimo promissa
et ab hominibus desiderata, illic nuptae uirique deliciae, illic oscu/la,
60 suspiria, complexus, et puellarum atque adolescentularum castissimi simul
et ardentissimi amores, ut denique quicquid fit, amore fit. Fons enim
affectus omnis est amor.

41-42 a Deo eiecti *tr.* A   58 optimo *om.* A   59 considerata A

29-30 Verg. Aen. 6.6-7.   31 Luc. 24.32.   33 Rom. 8.14.   34 Joan. 1.13.
35 Joan. 1.14.   38 Cf. Cant. 1.1.   39 Cf. Liv. 1.9.   41-42 Cf. Gen. 3.24.
44-45 Cf. Gen. 3.15.   45-46 Cf. Jer. 31.22.   46-48 Cf. Ezech. 43.1-2; 44.1-2;
46.12. Cf. also "Libellus," in *Scechina e libellus de litteris Hebraicis* I 47-49; *Scechina* I
68-70; II 154-156.   48-49 Isa. 9.6.   49-51 Cf. Gen. 9.1-17; 17.15-22; 22.15-18;
35.11-12; Exod. 32.13; 19.3-6; 2 Reg. 7.8-16.

Ita ferme amore persuasa, diuina bonitas *creauit caelum et terram*, in caelo mentes nudas, in terris membris clausas obuolutasque. Amore
65 idem Deus optimus patres quosdam sibi conciliauit: diuina illos amicitia dignatus, hos allocutus, illos complexatus, nonnullis uentura aperuit, quibusdam leges dedit, nec quieuit unquam donec Filium demisit, mortalem fecit, cruci affixit, emori denique cruenta et foeda morte iussit, ut experrecti mortales intelligant quandoque quantus amor fuerit Deo
259v 70 maximo optimo, qui, uti mortales homines uitam inuenirent, / immortalem Filium neci dedit. Vides, quantum iuris in superos amor habet! Homo qui pro homine mori passus sit rarus memoriae proditus; amare tamen homines nemo dubitat. At diuinus amor tanto humano est maior quanto plura Deum pati compulit atque indigniora pro mortalibus quam
75 soleant mortalium causa mortales. Amore ille ad nos descendit, amore ad illum ascendendum est nobis. Amore ille a uiuentibus seiunctus moritur, ut ipsi amore iuncti uiueremus.

Sed tanta Deus pertulit nostra causa, quid mercedis exegit? Num fortassis ut sua nos causa moreremur inuicem? Non plane. Sed facili
80 mercede contentus praecepit dumtaxat unum, ut ipsi inter nos inuicem amaremus. Non multa iussit, non multa in euangelio sunt, non multa
260r faciunda sunt homini. *Porro unum est ne/cessarium*, uerbum Domini est. Non igitur multa, si unum. Sed quod tandem id unum? Non intelligo quod praecipias unum. Nolo mortalem interpretem. Ipse *canas*
85 *oro*. Dic quod unum praeceperis. Facillima enim lex quae unum iubet. Da, audiam quid id sit. Nemo tam impotens quin sit ad unum potens. Quodnam igitur est praeceptum illud?

Audite uocem Domini, si oues (id quod putemus) estis Domini. Vox eius est, mediusfidius! Audite obiter! *Hoc est praeceptum meum ut*
90 *diligatis inuicem sicut dilexi uos*. Si itaque gratus es, si acceptum referre uis, si uulnera, si crucem, si mortem non contemnis, cura ut adsit amor, non quiuis tamen amor, sed *diligatis inuicem sicut dilexi uos*. Aperta significatio amoris diuini, quo diuinum per se bonum et homines illius gratia adamamus!
260v 95 Hoc ubi praeceptum dedit Dominus bis / senis comitibus, ubi amantes, ubi amore accensos fecit, dixit statim, *Iam non dicam uos seruos*, sed *amicos*. Ac rursus, *Vos estis sal terrae*, uti diceret: Qui in uobis est

---

66 complexatos A   67 dimisit A   70 optimo maximo *tr.* A   72 perditus A   75-76 amore—nobis *om.* A   78 quod A   81 non multa in euangelio sunt *om.* A   85 praeceperis *scripsi* : praeceperit N   praecepit A

---

63 Gen. 1.1.   80-81 Cf. Joan. 13.34; 15.12; 1 Joan. 3.23.   82 Luc. 10.42.
84-85 Verg. Aen. 6.76.   88 Cf. Psa. 94 (95).7-8; Joan. 10.3.   89-90 Joan. 15.12.
92 Joan. 15.12. Cf. Joan. 13.34.   96-97 Joan. 15.15.   97 Matt. 5.13.

amor condiet seruabitque omnia, mundusque uniuersus, tot iam per
saecula inter uitia erroresque putrescens, iam bene per uos olebit; sal
100 uestrum faciet ut non modo tabescentia non sint omnia, uerum etiam
ut suauissima sapidissimaque rerum auctori uideantur. Ac iure quidem
optimo, ut quos inuisos fecerat odium, gratos iucundosque amor faceret,
et qui pennis odio amissis e caelo lapsi erant, in caelum amore pennas
restituente resurgerent, quae denique omnia odio subripiente iam perie-
105 rant, amore instaurante redderentur.

Sane ueluti uoluptatum sectatoribus animas pro sale fuisse sunt qui di-
cant, ita haud plane absurde dixerim amorem ad diuinam spem uocatis pro
261r   sale tributum. Vt enim opiparae, / ut lautae, ut, si uis, etiam pontificiae
cenae sint, modo sal non adsit, nihil cenis hisce insuauius, nihil ingratius,
110 nihil prorsus insulsius. Idem, Hercule, Apostolus de amore disserit. *Si
habuero*, inquit, *omnem uirtutem, fidem ut montes transferam*, benefi-
centiam ut dem omnia egentibus, patientiam fortitudinemque ut flammis
dem *corpus* et *ardeam*, ἀγάπην δὲ μὴ ἔχω, οὐθέν εἰμι, amorem *caritatem*ue *non habeam, sum* adeo *nihil*. Hic est amor ille rerum potens,
115 qui ueluti mortales cum absit facit nihil, ita rursus facit idem cum adsit
et immortales et deos. Dei enim filii dii dicendi sunt, cum a simili simile oriatur.

Sed accipe oraculum: *Diligite inimicos uestros ut sitis filii patris uestri*.
Ecce deus efficeris, et ne aut mortalem aut terrestrem suspicareris, adiecit
120 sane *qui in caelis est*, quasi dixerit, Suscipe amoris alam utranque. /
261v   Geminae tibi pennae sint, *geminae si forte columbae* affuerint. Agnoscat
aues si nata parentis, is Deus *aetherias* atque immortalis *ad auras*. Porro
hoc sal fuit quod tantam dedit cenae ultimae uim, ut qui mortales accu-
buerant, surrexerint immortales, *mortem non in aeternum*, ut Domini
125 uerbis utar, gustaturi.

Quid, quod seruatae etiam nunc reliquiae mortem propellunt iis qui
in amorem et gratiam per Eucharistiam redeunt? Non tacuit id, remota
mensa, Dominus quin semina aperuit iacta esse ac fundamenta unde
noua seges, noua aedificia surgerent—terra, ut ipse inquit, noua et *cae-*
130 *lum nouum*. Quod amabo semen iecit. Quod cum Graecus nescioquis
mandaret sulcis, stultus credi uoluit, cum stultus minime esset. Ita

104 resurgeret A   106-107 qui dixerim amore A   110 de amore *om*. A
112 gentibus A

108-109 Cf. Hor. C. 2.14.28.   110-114 1 Cor. 13.1-3.   118 Matt. 5.44-45. Cf.
Luc. 6.27, 35.   120 Matt. 5.45.   121 Verg. Aen. 6.190, geminae cum forte
columbae.   122 Cf. Verg. Aen. 6.193. Verg. Aen. 4.445-446, ad auras // aetherias.
124 Joan. 8.52.   129-130 Apoc. 21.1.   130-131 Vlixes. Cf. Serv. In Verg.
Aen. 2.81.

262r   Dominus stultitia arguendus, ut Apostolus scribit. / Sed nihil stultum
         minus. *Sal terrae* commisit, unde seges in uniuerso mundo mox ap-
         paruit et siderea horrea frugum ubertate laborarunt. Nec unquam ia-
135   cuit tellus tam reposta, unde messor plaustra arcasque non impleuerit,
         seminis tam fecundi expectans nomen, nouum nouis noualibus adinuen-
         tum semen. Positis itaque epulis, ut Iohannes rettulit, infit. Ego uobis
         dico modo ueluti diceret, *Audiat terra* et *audite, caeli, quae loquor*: Vos
         olim terra nunc *terrae sal* et *caeli* ennarraturi *gloriam Dei.*
140   Sequitur in euangelio, *Mandatum nouum do uobis.* Hoc est, sal in
         uobis sulcis meis sero, nouum semen. Sed quodnam sal illud? *Vt di-*
         ligatis inuicem, idque uos meos esse discipulos declarabit, ἐὰν ἀγάπην
         ἔχητε, si amorem quem seui conseruaueritis. Omnia sacra scriptorum
262v   diuinorum uolumina / ita undique caritatem attollunt, ut non aliam
145   ob causam scripta quam ob caritatem uideantur. *Vniuersa delicta,* in-
         quit Salomon, *operit caritas,* ac rursus, *Melius ad olera uocari cum cari-*
         tate quam cum odio ad uitulum saginatum. In Sapientia quoque a Philone
         scribitur, *O quam pulchra est casta generatio cum* caritate!
            Dic, puella, nuptiarum munus maximum. *Ordinauit,* inquit, *in me*
150   *caritatem.* Media uirtutum ciuilium nihil erant, sed sponsus, mundi faber
         sapientissimus, *media caritate construit.* Sed tu, puella fortunatissima,
         quem accepisti anulum? Referat Hieremias non nisi *caritatem despon-*
         sationis tuae. Sed quandiu is anulus? Is idem inquit, *In caritate per-*
         petua dilexi uos. O magnete multo potentiorem caritatem! Illa per tantos
263r 155 anulos anulos alios ui / arcana trahit. Haec uel inuitos animos quauis ex
         mundi plaga diuinis uti catenis rapit in caelum. *Traham eos,* inquit Do-
         minus per Oseam, *in uinculis caritatis.* Quid, quod ea uincula perfrangi
         non possunt? Nupta enim uim omnem experta testatur, *Aquae multae*
         non potuerunt exstinguere caritatem. Hac diis similes factos apostolos!
160   Ad uos Romanos scribit Paulus cum canit, *Caritas Dei diffusa est in*
         cordibus eorum. Hanc etiam a Deo commendari asserit. Paulo inferius
         ostendit nulli illam cedere fortunae. *Quis ergo,* inquit, o Quirites, *nos*
         separabit a caritate Christi? Quare hac clausula epistolam claudit, ut
         caritatem inuicem fraternam diligerent. Idem ad Timotheum, *Sectare*

---

154 magnetem A   163 haec A

---

132 Cf. 1 Cor. 1.17-25; 3.18-19.   133 Matt. 5.13.   134-135 Cf. Verg. Aen. 6.655.
137 Cf. Joan. 13.2.   138 Deut. 32.1.   139 Matt. 5.13; Psa. 18 (19).2.
140 Joan. 13.34.   141-142 Joan. 13.34. Cf. Joan. 13.35.   142-143 Joan. 13.35.
145-146 Prov. 10.12.   146-147 Prov. 15.17.   147-148 Cf. Hier. Praef. in libros
Salomonis, PL 28.1242.   148 Sap. 4.1. Vulg., cum claritate.   149-150 Cant. 2.4.
151 Cant. 3.10.   152-153 Jer. 2.2.   153-154 Jer. 31.3.   156-157 Os. 11.4.
158-159 Cant. 8.7.   160-161 Rom. 5.5.   161 Cf. Rom. 5.8.   162-163 Rom.
8.35.   163-164 Cf. Rom. 12.10.   164-165 1 Tim. 6.11.

165 *caritatem. Finis* enim, ut superius scripserat, *praecepti* sola *caritas est.*
Ad Philippenses, Crescat *caritas uestra magis ac magis.* Ad Colossenses,
263v / *Super omnia caritatem habete.* Epheseos iubet esse *in caritate* radica-
tos (liceat secum loqui) semperque in eadem augeri. Causam Galathis
insensatis ostendebat, dicens, Spiritus sanctus caritas. Hanc persuadebat
170 Hebraeis. Hanc Thessalonicensibus precabatur. Hanc tandem unam
demonstrabat Corinthiis esse eam qua nihil maius, nihil optabilius, nihil
demum diuinius sit a Deo mortalibus tributum. Qua sublata, sublata
omnia sint; qua posita, ponantur et omnia.

Diuum Petrum quid memorem, ter rogatum a Domino an amaret,
175 ter rursus se amare asseuerantem? Nonne, quanquam rusticus ac
piscator, scribit *caritatem continuam* haberi oportere, quod *caritas* una
operiat *multitudinem peccatorum?* Taceo Iohannis epistolam priorem,
ubi hanc nunquam satis laudasse uideri potest, sibi adeo omnia in ea
264r commendanda conquirit. Quid, quod / audet inibi non modo diuinam
180 illam appellare, sed Deum? *Deus,* inquit, *caritas est.* Ducunt uirtutes
aliae ad Deum, haec quo uirtutes inhiant est ille ipse Deus. Nihil itaque
potest tristius euenire quam cum haec una perditur, quod deflebat hic
idem. *Caritatem tuam,* inquit, *primam reliquisti.* Deflet Dominus ipse
in Luca. Deflet in Mattheo. *Praeteritis,* inquit apud Lucam, *iudicium*
185 *et caritatem.* At demum apud Mattheum nostrae tempestatis miseriam
praesagiens, Heu, heu, tempora, inquit, quis *refrigescet caritas multorum.*

Quid ego longius traho epistolam superuacanea nimietate redundan-
tem? Hac stante, stabit mundus. Hac abeunte, mundus interibit. *Terra*
enim *caelum*que *transibunt,* ut Mattheus, ut Marcus, ut multis ante sae-
190 culis Ageus et scribunt et praedicant. Iam uero ortum mari sal, mare
264v est amori consentaneum. Nam et a gentibus dicitur, / *Venus orta mari.*

Vnica ea res sacrificiis accommodata est. Sacrificia enim quae amor
non commendat et gratia Deum animos spectantem irritant, non pla-
cant. Verum enimuero prius animus an amans sit spectatur a numine,
195 ac deinde quae aris imponuntur. *Respexit* enim *Dominus ad Abel et*
ad munera eius; ad Chaym uero minime *respexit.* Respicit prius Abel
ac proinde munera. Hoc est, si munera mouent quicquam Deum, non
ipsa ex se mouent, sed si amoris flammis iuncta sint. Qui mane surgitis

190 mari sed A   192 eas A   193 et animos A

165 1 Tim. 1.5.   166 Phil. 1.9.   167 Coloss. 3.14. Eph. 3.17.   168 Cf.
Gal. 3.1; 5.22.   170 Cf. Heb. 13.1; 1 Thess. 3.12; 4.9.   170-172 Cf. 1 Cor. 13.
174-176 Cf. Joan. 21.15-17.   176-177 1 Petr. 4.8.   180 1 Joan. 4.16.
183 Apoc. 2.4.   184-185 Luc. 11.42.   186 Matt. 24.12.   188-189 Matt. 24.35.
189-190 Cf. Marc. 13.31; Luc. 21.33; Agg. 2.7, 22.   191 Ov. Ep. Sapphus 213 (bis).
195-196 Gen. 4.4-5.

boni sacerdotes uota et sacra Deo nostro operaturi—ardeat prius animo
200 amoris flamma oportet. Sin secus molam uittasue paratis, uanum opus
265r agitis. *Vanum est uobis ante lucem surgere.* / Molam quaeritis salsam
sine sale, insulsum sacrificium. Quis *poterit insulsum* comedere? inquit
Iob.

Sed mola ex sale et farre, dicitis. At *sal* illud *insulsum* est, ut Marcus
205 meminit, ex ea ductum statua in quam curiosa Loth *uxor uersa est.* Hoc
illorum sal est quibus cognitio est illustris, uita obscura. Intelligunt
optime, uiuunt autem pessime. Hi sal habent quidem, multa scribentes
ac disputantes sapiunt. Praeceptis sapientissimis multos mouent *ad bene
beateque uiuendum.* Sed quoniam praeceptis ipsi suis nunquam mouentur,
210 sal illud statua est immobilis. Hoc carpit cum Aaron in Cantico diuus
Moses, *Fiant,* inquit, *immobiles quasi lapis.*

Omnis enim mortalium actio iacet torpetque nec ad beatam se uitam
attollit, nisi quibus alas addit amor. Hinc faciunt amori geminas alas,
265v altera mor/talium uota ad superos, altera superum munera ad mortales
215 uehit. *Angelos* uidet Iacob *scalam ascendentes descendentes*que. Quid sibi
uult tam illustre somnium nisi patere hominibus iter ad caelum non alia
ratione quam per amoris gradus, quibus, donec exulat animus in terris,
ueluti per legatos ultro citroque missos humana ad Deum pietas, diuina
ad hominem bonitas perfertur? Per eos nostra in caelum, per eos in
220 nos caelestia transmittuntur.

Quod si quis exstincto obriguerit amore, licet sal quoddam habeat,
id tamen gelidum, graue, immotum, minime ut ascendat idoneum,
quin in onerosissimam uersum statuam, loco moueri aut sursum ferri
nulla ui prorsus potest, haud equidem commodius quam ingens ferri
225 uis. In Ecclesiastico est id inuenire. Cum enim res quae fieri non pos-
266r set exponeretur, *Facilius,* inquit, *salem et massam ferri* / *ferre est,* ubi
de oneroso sale et altis ascensionibus minime apto mentio manifesta
habetur. Est et in Sophonia, *Siccitas spinarum et acerui salis,* ubi diui-
tiarum sitis gelida, hoc est amoris uacuae notitiae iuncta, hominem ab
230 his morbis habitum et possessum ostenditur mirum in modum premere
ac deprimere.

Sed ad Colossenses Apostolus alterum esse habendum omni in actione
sal. Sal quid ni caritatis, amicitiae, gratiae? *Sermo,* inquit, *uester semper
in gratia sale sit conditus.* Quae uolunt, quicquid dicturi simus, nunquam
235 in oratione caritatem atque amorem desiderari; quo fit ut grata unicuique

---

206 illustris est *tr.* A   215 scala N A   221 si quid A   222 descendat A

201 Psa. 126 (127).2.   202 Job 6.6.   204 Marc. 9.49.   205 Gen. 19.26.
208-209 Cic. Off. 1.6.19.   211 Exod. 15.16.   215 Gen. 28.12.   226 Eccli. 22.18.
228 Soph. 2.9.   233-234 Coloss. 4.6.

sit, Deo inquam et hominibus. Sal sanctum a Mattheo *sal terrae* dice-
batur; alterum ab eodem uanum appellabatur. *Si*, inquit, *euanuerit,
in quo salietur*? Vana autem atque inanis philosophia et doctrina ho-
266v mi/num uestigatione comparata dicta est ab Apostolo, ciue Romano tuo,
240 cui non consentire inuidere est gloriae Romanae maiorumque tuorum.
Ad Colossenses enim ita scribit, quod legi a te uelim. Dixerat enim su-
periore capite nos e tenebris ereptos translatosque *in regnum Filii di-
lectionis* Dei. Addit sequenti capite id quod sanctae dilectioni aduersa-
tur. Prius sal primum dixerat, nunc sal secundum refert, aris ineptum,
245 Deo inimicum, religioni contrarium. *Videte*, inquit, *ne quis uos decipiat
per philosophiam et inanem fallaciam secundum traditionem hominum,
secundum elementa mundi, et non secundum Christum.*

Haec Apostolus. Dixerat Dominus, *Si sal euanuerit, in quo salietur*?
Aliquid ergo sal est quod uanum atque inane fit. Inanis, inquit Apostolus,
250 est philosophia, inanis scientia omnis quae finem non attingit humanum.
Finis Deus, Alpha et Omega, Christus Iesus. Quae Christum igitur non
267r sapit sa/pientia, sapientia ac uacuum sal est, nullis usibus accommo-
datur, nisi *ut foras* eiiciatur confuteturque *conculcetur*e *ab hominibus,*
ab his qui uere hominis nomen merentur nec sensui falacissimo credunt
255 omnia, ut philosophi nonnulli parum se ea sententia a brutis attollentes.
Qui qua homines ratione dici possint non uideo, cum diuina rationis ui
seposita nihil recipiunt quod non brutus illis sensus insusurret. Nos *quae
sursum sunt* quaerimus, *non quae super terram*. Nec adeo nos sensui addicti
esse uolumus, ut quod ocellus non aspicit, aures non accipiunt, id non
260 esse existimemus. Qui secus existimant, irrationalis sensus partibus
studentes, nec rationales esse uelle nec homines uidentur, beluis pecu-
dibusque propinquiores. Horum sal et brutum et uanum calcetur ab
hominibus oportet, atque ab his qui rationem audiunt exterminetur,
explodatur, exsibiletur.
267v 265 / Vtrunque sal in Marco, hoc bonum, id insulsum. *Bonum est*, inquit,
sal, quod si insulsum fuerit, in quo condietis? Omnis enim uictima sale
condietur. Haec Marcus habet, et Lucas multa addidit. Nam cum duo
sint peccantium genera, alii in corpus, alii extra corpus crimen habent.
Illi uoluptate et libidinibus putrescunt, hi gloriae aut potentiae seruiunt,
270 utrique Spiritum pietatemque contemnentes, utrique asciti sunt et carni,
ut Iesus ait, et sanguini, rebus sane quae facile intereant contabescant-

248 *euanuerat* A   266 sit A   270 utrique *om.* A

236 Matt. 5.13.   237-238 Matt. 5.13.   238-239 Cf. Coloss. 2.8.
242-243 Coloss. 1.13.   245-247 Coloss. 2.8.   248 Matt. 5.13.   249-250 Cf.
Coloss. 2.8.   251 Apoc. 1.8; 21.6; 22.13.   253 Matt. 5.13.   257-258 Coloss.
3.1-2.   265-266 Marc. 9.49.

que. Seruari tamen sale carnes solent ab utraque labe, eius quae in corpore et eius quae extra corpus. Hanc terrenam nostri, illam sterquilinii labem uocant. (Non me pudet uerbis uti euangelii mei.) Ita enim Lucas:
275 *Bonum est sal*, inquit. *Si autem id euanuerit, in quo salietur* aut, ut alter textus habet, *in quo condietur?*

268r   Nunc duo / carnis genera cognosce apostolico condienda sale. Ait enim, *Neque in terram neque in sterquilinium utile est.* Per hoc sunt obscena corporis peccata intelligenda, quae auctores conuertunt in bruta. Hos
280 ita sugillat Iobel, *Computruerunt iumenta in stercore suo.* Per illud alios accipi oportet, qui caeli obliti, terrae tum opes, tum fastum sectantur. Qua ex re non iniuria terra nominatur. *Quid* superbis, *terra et cinis?* Sed carnem sale carentem atque a sacris rebus abhorrentem ubique diuinus sermo detestatur. Illam ita alloquitur Ezechiel, *Aqua non es*
285 *lota in salutem, nec sale salita.* Et Iudicum item libro, *Ipsa destructa* est, inquit, *ita ut sal in ea dispergeret.* Iob etiam accusat *quod non est sale conditum.*

     Et apud Ecclesiasticum, *Gelu* uelut *salem* effundi legere est. Apte nanque salis atque amoris expertia gelu comparantur. Gelida enim
268v 290 sunt quae ab igne procul distant. Quae igitur ab amore / seiuncta sunt, gelida plane sunt, cum amor flamma atque ignis appelletur. *Est mollis flamma medullas*, inquit quidam, atque iterum, *Agnosco ueteris uestigia flammae.* Est et apud eundem, *Et caeco carpitur igni*, et *Meus ignis, Amynthas.*

295   Quid, quod et ardere, quae ignis est actio, plerumque pro eo quod amare est usurpatur? *Corydon ardebat Alexim*, et *Ardet amans Dido*, ac permulta passim id genus lectitantur. Verum enimuero quid umbras recipimus? Lucem ignemue adeamus, ut lucentem ardentemue animo ignem intelligamus. Quid tu, Paule, inquis? *Caritas Dei diffusa est*
300 *in cordibus* eorum, hoc est, Spiritus sanctus, parentis natique amor, eorum pectoribus illapsus est. Sed qua is imagine, cuius elementi forma? Dic, Luca medice, naturae consultissime. *Apparuerunt illis*, inquit,
269r   *dispertitae linguae tanquam ignis.* Quid / clarius expectes? Visus Spiritus ille prius columbae similis, quae amoris est auis, idem ignis naturam
305 induens, uti promissus fuerat, ad caelestis reipublicae senatum trans-

---

281 factum A   298 recipimus umbras *tr.* A   298-299 ut—intelligamus *om.* A

273-274 Cf. Luc. 14.35.   275-276 Luc. 14.34, Vulg., condietur; Matt. 5.13, Vulg., salietur. 278 Luc. 14.35.   280 Joel 1.17.   282 Eccli. 10.9.   284-285 Ezech. 16.4. 285-286 Judic. 9.45.   286-287 Job 6.6.   288 Eccli. 43.21.   291-292 Verg. Aen. 4.66.   292-293 Verg. Aen. 4.23.   293 Verg. Aen. 4.2.   293-294 Verg. Ecl. 3.66.   296 Verg. Ecl. 2.1.   Verg. Aen. 4.101.   299-300 Rom. 5.5. 302-303 Act. 2.3.   303-304 Cf. Matt. 3.16; Marc. 1.10; Luc. 3.22; Joan. 1.32. 304 Cf. Cant. 2.10; Ov. M. 15.386.

mittitur. Dominus denique apud Lucam dixit, *Ignem ueni mittere in terram*, de eo ipso Spiritu locutus quem erat olim senatus suscepturus.

Diximus hactenus amorem dici ignem. Sed lege Marci librum. *Omnis*, inquit, *igne salietur*. Videri mysterium! Appellatur ignis sanctus amor. 310 Ignis ergo est amor; igne *salietur uictima*; amore igitur salietur. Vnde et sequitur diuus euangelista, *Omnis igne salietur*, et se ipsum aperiens sequitur, *Et omnis uictima sale salietur*. Nonne quae saliuntur sale saliuntur? At saliuntur igne uictimae. Ignis igitur sal dicendus est. Porro ignis amor supra nominabatur, et Chrysostomus consentit, utrunque 269v 315 tribuens sali. Si igitur *ignem mittere* uenit *in terram*, salem / uenit mittere in terram.

Habeo quod tandiu laborauimus: tanti esse amorem (quem nunc sal, nunc ignem appellabat Dominus) ut illius immittendi, elargiendi, accendendi gratia uenerit in has terras Deus, eo ueluti sale intereuntia 320 ab interitu uindicaturus. Illud profecto portendebat uetus lex. Est in Leuitico, Ne auferas *sal foederis tui*. Et in Numeris, *Pactum*, scribitur, *salis sempiternum*. Quo sane et Messias et Spiritus mittendi proponebantur, tunc, inquam, cum populus quasi infans lacte pasceretur. Sal sero perfecta in lege datum est. Binae leges a Deo profectae, infirma 325 ueluti adolescens altera, altera matura ac constans; illi lac, huic sal necessarium, cibus is facilis teneris infantibus, hic legitimus uiris iam robustis exhibetur. Lege Ecclesiasticum. *Initium*, inquit, *necessariae* 270r *rei / sal* et *lac*; finem, cuius gratia anteposuit quod alterius gratia fit, secundo nominauit, et ne non intelligeres addit, panem *et mel*. Mel 330 quippe et lac illis uti pueris promisit Deus. Dabo, inquit, et *introducam* uos *in terram fluentem lacte et melle*.

Nostro Domino, successori Petro aliisque dictum scimus, *Tu es sacerdos in aeternum secundum ordinem Melchisedech*. Qui ordo Melchisedech cum sacra faceret non mel ille, non lac, sed panem obtulit. Mel 335 igitur prioris legis est, panis posterioris. Lac igitur et sal necessaria sunt saluti hominum. Aut enim circumcisione aut fide praeditum oportet esse eum qui sit spectaculis diuinis potiturus. Caue, si sapis ipse, quicquam Deo muneris pares ubi sal non adsit. Offeres uitulum atque

310 amore *scripsi*: amor N A   312 Homo ne A   313 Aut saliuntur A
320 protendebat A   322-323 proponebatur A   325 natura A

306-307 Luc. 12.49.   308-309 Marc. 9.48.   310 Marc. 9.48.   311-312 Marc. 9.48.   314 Cf. In Matt. Homil. 10 (Opus imperfectum), PG 56.685; In Matt. Homil. 15.7, 32.7 al. 33.7, PG 57.232, 386.   315 Luc. 12.49.   321 Lev. 2.13. 321-322 Num. 18.19.   323 Cf. Eccli. 39.31; Exod. 3.17; 13.5; etc.   327-329 Eccli. 39.31.   330-331 Exod. 3.17; 13.5; 33.3; Lev. 20.24; Deut. 31.20; etc.   332-333 Psa. 109 (110).4; Heb. 5.6; 7.17.   333-334 Cf. Gen. 14.18.

alia. Mittant, inquit Ezechiel, *super* ea *sacerdotes sal.* In Leuitico quo-
270v 340 que dicitur, *In omni sacrificio tuo | offeras sal.*

Restat ut tandem recenseam quid Heliseus egerit cum ea quae diximus esset miro etiam ostentu praemonstraturus. Venerat dies supremus quo uidendus erat Helyas inter mortales. Quaerebat is ab Heliseo
comite seiungi, ne dum raperetur in aera sublimis quisquam euntem
345 uideret. Videri enim dum tolleretur nolebat. Auelli cor nolebat bonus
comes ducis atque aurigae optimi, ut ipse dictitabat, discessu magnopere
perculsus. Ibat ille multa causatus, modo huc, modo illuc, si unquam
forte posset relinquere res humanas et subuehi in auras arbitris remotis.
Profectus itaque est in Bethel, profectus ad Iordanem, profectus in Hie-
350 rico. At obstinato alter animo, lateri affixus et pallium manu tenens,
illud inter lacrimas et singultus uerabat, *Viuit Dominus et uiuit anima*
271r   *tua* (qui iurandi mos Hebreae gentis fu/it), *quod non relinquam te.* Is
frustra tentatis omnibus artemque omnem expertus incassum—cum Ior-
danis amnis fluenta pallio iniecto secuisset, cum prophetarum filios in
355 Bethel atque Hierico deseruisset, cum signum duplicis spiritus dedisset
—substitit paululum utque iam iam a comite atque humo eripiendus.
Et ecce ex aethere lapsus subito *currus igneus* inter utrunque astitit,
correptumque mox ante stupentis clamantisque oculos uectabat per auras.

Quid ageret Heliseus? Relinqui nolebat, sectari non poterat. Reuer-
360 sus est ad prophetas, uix desiderium sustinens, qui bono illum esse animo
iubent, operam omnem spondent, quinquaginta deligunt uiros, explorari
ab iis omnia, quaeri, scrutari, perspicique montes, ualles, loca demum
omnia imperant, sicubi raptus a Deo collocatus fuisset. Denique hortan-
tur ut secum esse uelit, pro patre uno filios innumerabiles inuenturum,
271v 365 affu/tura necessaria omnia, nihil defuturum, eum denique patriae ciuita-
tisque illius minime paenitendae parentem futurum, ciuitatem proinde cla-
ram alioqui atque illustrem, humanisque usibus maxime accommodatam,
senatu insuper patribusque ornatam haud equidem contemnendis; unum
dumtaxat aut duo deesse gentis felicitati; aquas siquidem parum salu-
370 bres esse, humum parum fertilem; caetera esse eiuscemodi ut nihil uitae
mortalium desideraretur. Heliseus maerore pressus, etsi decreuerat nec
consolationem nec conditionem accipere, M*** gentis tamen humani-

---

360 animo esse *tr.* A   364 uelint, quod A   372 M. gentis N A. *Non potui*
M. *identificare. Fortasse per aliquam confusionem Aegidius assimilauit Jericho ad Moa-*
bitem gentem. Cf. Num. 26.3, 63; 31.12; 33.48; 35.1; 36.13; Judic. 3.12-13; Jos. AJ
13.15.4.

---

339 Ezech. 43.24.   340 Lev. 2.13. Vulg., in omni oblatione tua offeres sal.
341 Cf. 4 Reg. 2.   345-346 Cf. 4 Reg. 2.12.   351-352 4 Reg. 2.2, 4, 6. Vulg.,
quia non derelinquam te.   357 4 Reg. 2.11.

tate delectatus, ut grato omnia animo accepisse uideretur, id quoque ut
adderet quod loci felicitati deerat, animum iniecit, et *Afferte mihi*, inquit,
375 *uas nouum et immittite in illud sal.* Mox illi paruerunt. Ipse manu
272r   attollens stetit secundum marginem fontis / aquasque clara uoce allocutus
haec dixit, *Haec dicit Dominus* Deus: *Has* ego *aquas* saluas esse iubeo,
omnisque et lues et *sterilitas* facessat atque in posterum salubres, com-
modae, fecundae sunto. Curatae sunt statim aquae, ex eoque optimae
380 saluberrimaeque inuentae sunt.

Quae quidem res, etsi ita ut exposuimus acta est, rerum tamen Christianarum magnam et quidem minime obscuram habet significationem. Ag-
grediar uero illam ea spe ut ille adsit nobis qui ideo haec ipsa uoluit et
agi et scribi ut se nobis faceret per amicorum uatum actiones manifestum.
385 Principio nomina nobis interpretanda occurrunt. Cratilus nanque non
temere ea imponi docet, et in propheta Dominus inquit, *Ego uoco nomen
tuum.* Ac iterum ille idem Esaias, *Vocaui te nomine tuo*, rursus etiam,
Dominus ab utero uocauit me. Et Paulus apostolus, *Vocat ea quae non*
272v   *sunt ut ea quae / sunt*, dictumque est amicis Dei, *Vestri capilli capitis*
390 *omnes numerati sunt*, hoc est, accidentia omnia quae uobis contigere
me ea instituente contigere. Quod gaudendum est et exsultandum, *quod
nomina uestra scripta sunt in caelis.* Calamo non nouo scribuntur, sed
ante mundi constitutionem, ut Apostolus ait, nomina ea uocata sunt
et scripta. Nos igitur electis ad summum hominibus in eorum ortu
395 non imponimus nomina, sed ante ortum orbis posita uocamus.

Helyas praeceptor, Heliseus discipulus fuit. Helyas deus, dominus,
aut dominator interpretatur; Heliseus dominus, salutare, deus, dominator. Licet dici Trinitas possit uniuersa ac tota condidisse, tamen
ratione Filio id conuenit, tum quod *omnia* Verbo *facta* ac condita *sunt*,
400 ut arte atque idea rerum, tum quod ipsi prouincia tradita est ad de-
273r   bellandum fugandumque / iniustum occupatorem terrarum. De quo Imperator noster uirtutis ac uictoriae conscius dicebat, cum milites ad
strenue confligendum et certa spe decernendum hortaretur, audita e
caelo <uoce> et uisa in monte beatitudine uultus atque indumentorum,

374-375 4 Reg. 2.20. Vulg., mittite.   377-378 4 Reg. 2.21.   385-386 Cf. Pl.
Cra. 390d-e.   Cf. also *Scechina* I 23-24; *Giles of Viterbo* 91-92.   386-387 Isa. 45.3.
387 Isa. 43.1.   388 Isa. 49.1.   388-389 Rom. 4.17. Vulg., tanquam.   389-390
Matt. 10.30.   391-392 Luc. 10.20.   393 Eph. 1.4. Also 1 Petr. 1.20.   396-
398 Cf. Hier. Lib. Interp. Heb. Nom. III Reg., PL 23.865; Isid. Etym. 7.8, PL 82.283.
399 Joan. 1.3.   404-405 Cf. Matt. 17.1-13; Marc. 9.1-12; Luc. 9.28-36; 2 Petr. 1.17-18.

405 suscepto Mosis et Helyae testimonio. *Venit,* inquit Imperator illustris, *uenit hora* cum terrarum *princeps* expugnabitur ac *foras eiicietur.* Is ergo iure Dominus, qui et condidit orbem ac rursus ab iniusto inuasore occupatum recepit. Ipse olim Dominus, Rex, Imperator a prophetis dictus est. *Mitte agnum, Domine, dominatorem terrae,* orabat Esaias.

410 Itidem, *Paruulus natus est nobis et filius, cuius imperium super humerum eius.* Et rursus ipse idem, *Erubescet luna et confundetur sol, cum regnaue-rit Dominus exercituum in Syon,* hoc est, cum regnum cruce accipiet,

273v spinis coronatus, etiam impiorum testimonio, qui titu/lum currui triumphantis inscripsere, *Iesus Nazarenus, Rex Iudeorum.*

415 Quid, quod cum sint *dii multi et domini* item *multi,* id quod Corynthiis Paulus scribebat, at unus tantum est Deus super omnes deos, et Dominus dominorum, regum Rex, principumque Princeps? Hic enim unus, cum Dominus sit, dominum non habet. Uti enim in numeris nihil unitatem praecedit, nihil punctum incohantem in linea finita, nihil inter alas et

420 copias antecellit imperatorem ac ducem, ita ferme in ordinata rerum natura nihil est primo prius. Alii dicuntur quidem aut dii aut domini, cum nec domini sint nec dii. Vnus hic Deus Dominusque et nominatur et est.

At Helyas ea duo significat. Ipse igitur multo quam prior uerius cen-

274r 425 sendus eo nomine uidetur. Heliseus uero salutare Dei, / Helyas Deus erat. Hic autem non Deus, sed Dei ipsius salutare. Est salutare quoddam quod idem est et Deus. Est et salutare alterum Christum sequens, quod Deus quidem non est sed tantum Dei. Salutare etiam pro saluatore usurpari consueuit—dent ueniam Latini; nominum nouatores non sumus

430 sed fidi scripturarum imitatores; detestabilius maiorique periculo a diuinis quam a Latinis desciscimus—at saluatoris saluationisque nomen non modo Deo tribui, uerum etiam et Dei comitibus, qui uiuenti credidere, morienti affuere, discedenti demum a terris successerunt. *De Hierusalem,* inquit Esaias, *exibunt reliquiae,* id est, quos Dominus successores reliquit,

435 *et saluatio de monte Syon.* Et psalmo septimo supra uigesimum Dauid, *Protector saluationum Christi sui.* Esaiae quoque non absona Iohel et

274v Abdias. Nam cum Abacuch scribit, *Quadrigae / tuae saluatio,* quid sibi aliud uult quam quattuor euangelii scriptores ea dignatos appellatione?

---

417 Rex regum *tr.* A   430 uiatores A   432 Deo tribui comitibus A

405-406 Joan. 12.23.   406 Joan. 12.31.   409 Isa. 16.1. Vulg., Emitte. 410-411 Isa. 9.6. Vulg., et filius datus est nobis; et factus est principatus super humerum eius.   411-412 Isa. 24.23.   414 Joan. 19.19. Cf. Matt. 27.37; Marc. 15.26; Luc. 23.38.   415 1 Cor. 8.5.   433-435 Isa. 37.32.   436 Psa. 27 (28).8. 436-437 Cf. Joel 3.17-21; Abd. 15-21.   437 Hab. 3.8.

Saluatoris etiam nomen bifariam sortiti sunt alii atque alii. Aliquis
440 saluator est ut Deus et causa, alii ut organa Dei uiuentia. De priore
Oseas, *Saluator praeter me non est.* De aliis Abdias, *Ascendent saluatores
in montem Syon,* quamuis etiam Ioseph, quod suos fame liberauerit,
ditauerit, illustrauerit, saluatorem uocatum esse non me lateat. Quod
Heliseus salutare Dei dicitur non Deus pro Dei organis, ministris, disci-
445 pulis accipi oportebit—duodecim illi inter omnes, maxime inter duodecim princeps Simon Petrus. Tu cum Helyam audis, Deum concipe
terras incolentem, Petrum sanctumque senatum instituentem. Cum dici
Heliseum accipis, Helyae discipulum praeceptoris uestigia tam sedulo
sectantem, Petrum sacrumque collegium accipe Christum praeceptorem
275r 450 sectantes, omnia uti sequi pos/sent relinquentes. Helyas in aera tol-
lendus haerentem lateri discipulum habet; habet Dominus suos Heliseos
caelestem profectionem minime aequo animo ferentes. Raptus ille in
aethera est, discipulo spectante. Noster rursus Helyas, *illis cernentibus,
est eleuatus* in caelum. Reliquit ille pallium Heliseo; reliquit et hic pallium
455 pontificium apostolis, atque inprimis Petro.

Reuersus Heliseus uitia offendit tum aquae, tum terrae. Terrae uitium
supra exposuimus cum duo peccatorum genera enarraremus; alterum
corporis, quod illic sterquilinium, hic aqua nominatur. Vtrunque mollis
animi uitium in corpore foedumque significat. *Effusus es ut aqua,* dice-
460 bat Iacob incesto filio, qui paternum torum temerare ausus est. Vtrunque scelus repperit in Hierusalem, et quod in corpus patratur et quod
extra corpus, hoc est, uoluptas et potestatis cum opibus laudibusque
275v affectatio. Quid uero / egerit Heliseus ante curam diximus, uas sibi
nouum cum sale afferri imperasse.

465 Audite, Romani. Audite, colles septem. Tu inprimis audi, Pater sanc-
tissime. Tu, inquam, tu, magne Iuli. Tibi enim Heliseus, tibi Simon
Petrus elaborarunt. Aaron uterque gradum deturbauit, sacro ephod,
sacro rationali exspoliauit; templo abire, meo Iulio cedere imperauit.
Sed quid egerit Heliseus uideamus. *Afferte,* inquit, *mihi uas nouum.*
470 Idem meus effecit Heliseus, discipulorum caput, Simon Petrus. Nam
unctus a Domino in sacerdotem maximum, quia unxerat Iacob petram,
Petrus uocari iussus a Domino est, quasi nouae ecclesiae constans atque
immotum fundamentum. *Vnguentum* primo *in capite*—gratiae pleni-

441 *Descendent* A   446 principes A   469 *mihi,* inquit *tr.* A

441 Os. 13.4.   441-442 Abd. 21.   442-443 Cf. Gen. 41.45.   449-450 Cf.
Matt. 19.27; Luc. 5.11, 28.   450-453 Cf. 4 Reg. 2.   453-454 Act. 1.9. Vulg.,
uidentibus illis, eleuatus est.   459 Gen. 49.4. Vulg., sicut.   463-464 Cf. 4 Reg.
2.20.   469 4 Reg. 2.20.   471 Cf. Gen. 28.18.   472-473 Cf. Matt. 16.18.
473-475 Psa. 132 (133).2.

tudo in Christo—inde *descendit in barbam, barbam Aaron,* in introrsum
276r 475 Petrum summum sacerdotem, de/nique *in oram* uestimentorum ueluti
in ultima uasa gratiae. Petrus, *uas auri solidum, sacerdos magnus, uas,*
inquam, *ornatum omni lapide pretioso,* quod de summo sacerdote apud
Ecclesiasticum legimus!

Verum redundans ingenti gratiae ui quaerit Petrus populum qui tantae
480 rei suscipiendae uas dignum fieri posse uideretur. Circuit, praedicat,
disputat, hortatur, omnique ope nititur, si qua efficere possit ut Hierusalem, legis ueteris domicilium, nouae gratiae sedes institueretur et quae,
uelut antiquum uas thymiamata umbrarum acceperat, oleum effusum
nominis, quod super omne nomen est, et uerae lucis acciperet. At Hebrea
485 gens, *durae,* ut Moses dicebat, *ceruicis* et contumax, miro modo non
modo Petrum conscriptosque patres non recipit, sed persequitur saeuis
odiis, a Sinagoga arcet, tacere Christum iubet, et ni taceat, supplicia,
276v   carcerem, mortem commi/natur.

Quid faceret diui coetus princeps? Duodecim secum fontes habebat,
490 uiuis aquis mortalium animos irrigaturos mortalesque in deos commu-
taturos. Sed aquas quidem habebat, uasa tantis fortunis digna non habebat. Versus is ad patres, Audite, inquit, animae felices, quid Spiritus
moneat: non recipit sacrum imbrem tellus impia, tellus a qua Deus accepit pro honore ignominiam, pro laude dedecus, pro amore odia, pro
495 praemio mortem, tellus, inquam, parricidii <ir>religionisque atque im-
pietatis et sacrilegii conscia—uoces sanguinis audit noxae ac caedis ul-
tionem postulantis. Tellus ea est unde uenturi praescius patriarcha
uxorem ducere prohibuit nato de puellis iuuenculisue Canaan. *Male-*
dictus Canaan, dicebat Noe, qui dominum patremque nudauit, nudatum
500 cruci affixit, affixum suppliciis ac morte truculentissima confecit. Alio
277r   igitur quam primum commeemus. / Relinquamus ominosas oras, meliores
in terras commigremus. In porcorum haram quid margaritas et beatas
lancęs infundamus? Abiit tam immane dirumue piaculum. *Afferte mihi*
uas nouum. Vtribus putrescentibus quis noua uina conuectet? Pretio-
505 sus humor gemmas postulat et uasa pretiosa. Quaerite mihi noua im-
peria.

Ecce Spiritus loquitur: caput caeli Christus, caput terrarum Roma,
Roma princeps, Christus princeps. Si is sponsus caelestis sponsam in

496 sanguinis *scripsi* : sanguis N A   498 natus A iuuenculisque A   504 *in uas* A
505 in noua A   507 sponsus loquitur A

476-477 Eccli. 50.1, 10.   483 Cf. Exod. 25.6; 30.1, 8, 9, etc.   485 Exod. 32.9;
33.3, 5; 34.9; etc.   487-488 Cf. Act., e.g., 4.5-22.   489 Cf. Exod. 15.27.
496 Cf. Gen. 4.10.   497-498 Cf. Gen. 28.1.   498-499 Gen. 9.25.   502-503 Cf.
Matt. 7.6.   503-504 4 Reg. 2.20.   504 Cf. Matt. 9.17; Marc. 2.22; Luc. 5.37-38.

terris quaerit, principem princeps ducat, rex reginam, terrarum impera-
510 tricem caeli atque terrarum imperator. Mea es, mea, o septimontia Roma!
Salue, o felix sponsa! Salue, Tarpeia rupes! Saluete, colles sacri! Salue, Auentine! Nouus ad te Romulus, tanto Romulo potior quanto
homine Deus! Is in te uolucres duodecim accepit ut Romam uocaret,
hic duodecim ad te columbas ut Christianam uocent. Ramum oleae sacro
277v 515 rostro ferunt / ut pacifico unguento peruncta urbs aeterno Ianum clau-
dat. Salue, o Iani sedes, nunc uere Ianiculum! Ianua in te statim unde
iter in superos! Salue, Tyrrhene collis, qui Ianiculo iungeris. Vagientem
in te et quasi in cunis Ianus suscepit Italiam. Vagientem in te religionem
ego suscipiam. Hoc sibi uolebat Hetrusca religio, hoc Volturnae fanum,
520 hoc diuinarum rerum interpretes Lucumones: optima statim post mundi
naufragia et innundationem iacta semina falsis diis procurantibus re-
generauerunt. Id sibi templa, arae, luci, ritus, et a tuo Caerete caeri-
monia portendebant praesagiebantque.

Tu, Tybris, Vaticanum labens meum, tu uas eris religioso alueo. Nouas
525 apporto aquas. Tu sinum pandito et uas mihi quod quaero esto nouum.
Te igitur manu capio, te ascisco mihi, pueris, nepotibus posterisque meis,
278r teque unde *super niuem* dealbemur rursus Albulam facio, / Christo caelique ministeriis do, dico, dedico, Iordanisque uim, maiestatem, potestatem trado. Sed et iubeo te salem accipere et salsas Dei semper
530 fruges sapere. Amore Deus ductus est ut homo fieret, amore ut sese
traderet, amore ut moriens sanguinem atque aquam funderet, ut te
dextrumque latus tuum consecrarem. Sacro igitur ego te ac ter ap-
pello, uoco, nuncupo amoris fluentum, iubeoque saluum sospitem sos-
pitatoremque esse mortalium et sanctorum beatorumue amorum prae-
535 ceptorem.

Vos testes, stellae! Tu, luna! Tu, sol! Vos, aethereae sphaerae
omnium spectatrices! Ego aeternis praefectus imperiis, sponsa potitus
mea, aeternam illam faxo. Viuat illa ut semper! Ego iam mortem op-
petam mecumque heroes diui ac quattuor supra triginta heredes mei.
540 Vt te, mea sponsa, incestaret conditor, fratrem interemit, te nos ut ex-

524 Tybris *scripsi* : Tybri N A 540 et nos A

511-513 Cf. Enn. apud Cic. Div. 1.48.107-108. 514-515 Cf. Gen. 8.11. 517-523 Cf.
"Fulfillment" 272, 285-295; *Giles of Viterbo* 30-31. 517-518 Cf. Macr. Sat. 1.7.19-24;
Aug. Civ. Dei 4.8, 11, PL 41.118, 122; Annio da Viterbo, *De commentariis antiquitatum*
(Rome 1498) fols. 175r-176v. 519 Volturna: cf. "Fulfillment" 294.330; Annio fols.
165v, 189r, etc. 521 Cf. Aug. Civ. Dei 7.2-3, PL 41.194-197; Macr. Sat. 1.9.16.
527 Psa. 50 (51).9. 528 Cf. Naples MS fol. 297v, letter of Giles to Serafino Ferri,
"die diui Antonii," 1500. 531 Cf. Joan. 19.34. 539 Thirty-four refers to
the number of popes from St. Peter to St. Sylvester. Cf., e.g., Mansi 32.739-740.

278v   piemus interibimus; ille ream / mortis ut imperaret fecit, nos nostram
ut absoluta morte imperes faciemus. Imperato ergo non terrae mariue
modo sed et caelo; claues accipe. Pande cum lubet caelum, cum lubet
rursus occlude.

545   Cadent aliae adolescentulac tuae. Ipsa utpote princeps superstes omnium eris—modo fida sis, bona fide sis, innocens, iusta, casta, pia sis,
modo non aliena sed mea sis, sis integra, sis simplex, sis sine dolo malo,
sine luxu, sine ambitu, sine auri cupiditate, sponsi sis amans tui sponsi-
que amicorum amicarumque omnium. Apta itaque uti regiis nuptiis
550   sies laui iam te duodecim fluminibus. Lota nomen accipe.

Roma, hucusque a Romulo, Roma, in posterum ex eadem radice nomen
ducas unde et amor ducit. Scribit non unus ueterum te Romam, hoc
est ualentiam, uocatam ac diu ante Amulii pueros; nunc ualentiam,
279r   nunc robor sortita Dei consortio / iuncta es. Cum abeo Hierosolima,
555   illa solo aequatur ruitque aeternum Asia. Cum te peto, uas te diuinae
dicionis efficio, *sal terrae* indo, amore reddo terrae caelique potentem.
Robur Romuli, regum, consulum, Caesarum magnum id quidem fuit
estque toto terrarum orbe magnum. Occidet id continuo tamen. Robur
regnumque nostrum regnum esto omnium saeculorum, cuius *nec metas*
560   *rerum nec tempora pono.* Metas certas si habiturum est in terris, certe
inter sidera nullas!

Dixi uti ames robustissimoque amore ames. Id tibi nomen inditum
non uulturis augurio sed numinis et cura et prouidentia. Roma tibi est
nomen. ʼΑπʼ <αὐτῆς> τῆς ῥώμης ἔρως ἐκλήθη docet Platonicus Phae-
565   drus, hoc est, amor a robore nuncupetur. Habes in nomine utrunque
279v   rebus rursus geren/dis; utrunque complectaris et amorem et fortitudinem
ut quem sponsum diliges, uita uel ipsa ardentius diligas.

Audite, patres. Annuit puella, linquit riuales. Comit, pectit, lauat,
ungit. Occurrit obvia gratulabunda sibi. Canit epithalamium. Ardet
570   iam in complexus. Audite, adest, uocem agnosco. *Osculetur me osculo*
oris sui. Fortis enim *ut mors dilectio* tua. Oscula da tandem, uir felicis-
sime, nobis. Non sine te patitur uiuere noster amor. Valete, o Augusti,
ualete, Claudii, Flauii, Nerones! Moechi estis, non uiri. Ego ad uirum
<....> sed suapte natura Deum.
575   Ille, patria posthabita, me patriam statuit. Ego, pulsis gentium diis,
deorum me trado Deo. Ille, gentem Israelitico nomine tumentem de-

541 reum A   543 caelum—lubet *om.* A   547 non modo *tr.* A   552 et nomen ducit A
560 certet A   569 obuiam A   571 osculanda A   572-573 o Augusti, ualete
om. A   574 *Lacuna unius fere lineae* N A   576 Israeliticam eo nomine A

543 Cf. Matt. 16.19.   550 Cf. Exod. 15.27.   553 Cf. Sol. 1; Fest. 16.
556 Matt. 5.13.   559-560 Ver. Aen. 1.278.   564 Pl. Phdr. 238c. Cf. *Scechina* II 65.
570 Cf. Cant. 2.6; 5.2; 8.3, 13.   570-571 Cant. 1.1; 8.6.

clinans, ueros nos sustituit Israelitas. Nos uicissim, dimota errorum
280r caligine, Deum Deo natum accipimus. Ille ex o/riente reliquias agit
Israel. Nos in occiduis illis pandimus gentis Capitolia Iuliae. Semen
580 Dei, ager Iulii. Iulia domus diuinum habitatorem accipiet.

Sub *arbore opaca* iam sumus; *sub umbra* quam desiderabam iam *sedi*.
Sedeo haud equidem uidua, sed et assidet diuus angelus. Angelus et
Gedeoni sub arbore uisus est. Hic me saluam esse iubet, Romam esse
monet, ac proinde decere oportereque ut amori ac robori dem operam,
585 Madianitis indicam bellum, militem comparem, copias fundam, spolia
direptis castris eripiam. Certum, superato hoste uictoriam ac triumphum
repromittit.

At ego Roma olim, nunc Romula sum, nullae copiae, nulli manipli,
nullae in bella uires. *Ego*, inquit, *tecum ero*, feriesque *Madian quasi*
590 *uirum unum*. Audi, Gedeon, qui paleas a frumento seiungis. O quem
280v elegit Dominus Israelique praefecit, audi angelum *sub quer/cu* compel-
lantem: *hostis habet muros* sponsam uti diripiant. Vtrinque hostis im-
minet, domi culpa, foris trux tyrannus. Vterque mihi hostis formi-
datus, multo tamen magis domesticus. Hic templa, hic aras, hic aditum,
595 hic penetralia, hic sacras ualuas, hic pectora, mentes, animos inuasit;
sacri gregis strages agit, trophea erigit.

Flet puella, scissis ungue genis. Haec uirum lacrimabili uoce testatur.
Caelum, diuos omnes appellat. Petrum, Paulum tutores pulsat cla-
moribus. Suppetias undecunque licet petit. Non audiri a mortalibus!
600 Si ab immortalibus deseratur, nil nisi desperatio ac ruina superest.
Esse iam satis rerum satisque ac supra datum esse flagitiis!

Te, Iuli beatissime, inuocat, iubet aspici angelum, praecepto obtem-
perari, peculiarem arborem recognosci. Id tellus omnis, id omnes mor-
281r tales, id optimi quique postulant. Aer, caelum, sidera, De/usque ipse,
605 cuius haeres es, monet ut opus aggrediaris animo dignum tuo. Salem
adhibeas, putrescentia cures, collapsa instaures, errata castiges, corrigas
inuersa, reuoces antiquata, in hostem utrunque quanta potes manu moueas. Id Helyseus, id diuus Petrus, id sponsa agendum suadet, id denique
Dominus ipse in Mattheo, *Non ueni*, inquiens, *pacem mittere in terram,*

---

584 dicere A   587 repromittet A   592 Vtrinque hominis A   600 ab mortalibus A   nil *om.* A   602 inuocant A

579-580 Cf. "Fulfillment" 269 n. 13 and *Giles of Viterbo* 127 on Giles's juxtaposing
of Julius Caesar and Julius II.   581 Verg. Aen. 6.136. Cant. 2.3. Cf. Biblioteca
comunale, Siena, MS G.X.26 p. 189, letter of Giles to Zoccoli, "ii Nonis Iulii" (July 6),
1508.   582 Cf. Isa. 47.8.   582-583 Cf. Judic. 6.11.   585 Cf. Judic. 6.11, etc.
589-590 Judic. 6.16.   590 Cf. Judic. 6.11.   591 Judic. 6.11, 19.   592 Verg.
Aen. 2.290.   597 Cf. Ov. Am. 1.7.50; 2.6.4; etc.   609-610 Matt. 10.34. Vulg.,
Nolite arbitrari quia pacem uenerim mittere in terram, non ueni pacem mittere, sed gladium.

610 *sed gladium.* Sed haec ideo frui ea pace fas sit *quae exsuperat omnem sensum.* Velit caelestis pastor Deus ut eo duce arma moueas ac felicissimus triumphum reportes in domum Domini Dei nostri, qui perpetuo uiuit. Amen.

611 Velut A   611-612 felicissimum A   613 uiuit et A   Amen *om.* A

610-611 Phil. 4.7.

Department of History
University of Detroit
Detroit, Michigan, U.S.A.

THE PRIVATE LIBRARY OF JOHANN SCHEUBEL, SIXTEENTH-CENTURY MATHEMATICIAN

•

by Barnabas B. Hughes, O.F.M.

Any inquiry into the intellectual life of a mathematician does well to seek out the resources at his disposal. Assuming native genius, one may search for only some of the material from which this talent drew. What he obtained from classroom lectures and coffeeshop conversations, unless it were recorded, may only be surmised. The literary resources are easier to trace. The books at his disposal, books in libraries, borrowed from friends, in his own collection, tell the inquirer much of his subject. But the last set, the books a person has at hand, is an important source of information. This set, perhaps the select residue from meanderings through bookstalls, makes available what the scholar considers most important.

Today, when the proliferation of books is almost a pollution problem, it is comparatively easy to peruse the private collection of a scholar, given the proper entrée. The further the intellectual historian retrogrades, however, the more difficult it becomes to know what volumes were gathered by his subject. Thus the discovery of the inventory of the private library of a Renaissance mathematician becomes something to be shared.[1]

Johann Scheubel (1494-1570), eminent mathematician and professor at the University of Tübingen, willed his books and mathematical instruments to the university. This testamentary bequest has been noted by several

---

[1] Johannes Müller, Regiomontanus, (1436-1476) certainly one of Germany's foremost mathematicians, left such a list of books. A friend of Cardinal Bessarion, he was invited by Mathias Corvinus, king of Hungary, to be librarian of the new Royal Library at Buda. This had been stocked recently with booty from the war against the Turks. Regiomontanus held this position for several years; then he returned to Nuremberg. Here he set up a printing press and announced his intention to publish all the important works in natural philosophy: twenty-one volumes from the great writers ancient and contemporary and twenty-one of his own works. Unfortunately he died abruptly before he could do more than launch his publishing career with the *Astronomia* of Manilius. Since he listed by names the works he intended to publish, one may assume not only his knowledge but his access to them. See my *Regiomontanus on Triangles* (Madison, Wis. 1967) 14-17, for the list. Of these books Scheubel had [4b], [4d], [5], [14b], [38], [47a], [50], [51b], [53c], [53d], and [102].

historians[2] yet no list is ever described. During an afternoon visit to the University Library in November 1969, I inquired of the librarian if such a list existed. Upon searching the cataolgue of manuscripts, he found none mentioned. I supposed that it must exist and inquired further. I found it in the Archives of the Library.[3] It consists of three pages, paper of quarto size written on both sides in corrosive ink by several hands. At the top of each page is the heading *Libri M. Ioannis Scheubelii pie memorie*. The verso of the last page contains the same statement with this addition, *Bibliotheca 1571*. The list mentions only the books and manuscripts; nothing is said of the instruments. Perhaps there is a list of these in the archives also.

One may wonder if all the books were taken into the library. Two things suggest this query. The first is a gloss in the upper left hand corner of 12r: "Nota + *signific*at accipiendos e*sse*." This is repeated in the same place on 13r. (The plus signs are noted in the transcription in their proper places.) The glosses and the marks are in the same hand as the inventory. In an entirely different hand is the second indication. It is found in the lower right eighth of 14v. A very clear lateral crease across the middle of all the pages tells us that the inventory was folded once. On the lower half of 14v the contents of the three folded pages was identified in the (now) upper right hand corner with the notation "Libri M. Ioannis Scheubelii pie memorie." And in the space referred to is a poorly written note in the same hand: "17 Iulii anno [15]71 Senatus commentat facultati artium ut eligant utilia et quae antea non habent." If one hypothesizes that the second and third notations were written before the first mentioned about the plus sign, then he may conclude that the College of Arts decided to accept many of the books. Since I inspected book [111] there, and saw library references to [77c] and [80b], it is evident that some of Scheubel's collection was accepted by, and now remains in, the University Library.

Before presenting the transcription of the inventory, a few words about Scheubel himself, the general contents of the list, its form, and bibliographical notes, are in order.

Johann Scheubel has been described as an intellectually heavy scholar, balanced and poised, a man of dignity.[4] A native of Württemberg, he began his mathematical studies at Vienna prior to the winter semester of 1532 when he transferred to the University of Leipzig. In 1535 he was a student at Tübingen. Here he became *Magister* in 1540, *Dozent* in 1544, *Euclidis pro-*

---

[2] Andreas Christoph Zellern, *Merckwürdigkeiten der Universitaet und Stadt Tübingen* (Tübingen, 1743), 495: "(Scheubelius) instrumenta sua et scripta mathematica academiae legavit." See also, David Eugene Smith, *History of Mathematics* (New York 1958) 1.329 n.

[3] *Actus senatus bibliothek 1, 1556-1702*, fol. 12-14.

[4] Smith (n. 2 above) 1.329. For perhaps the most comprehensive analysis of Scheubel's life and works see H. Staigmüller, "Johannes Scheubel, ein deutscher Algebraiker des xvi Jahrhunderts," *Abhandlungen z. Geschichte d. Mathematik* 9 (1899) 431-469.

fessor ordinarius in 1550, and *Professor ordinarius Euclidis et arithmetice* by 1555. Among his printed works are a commercial arithmetic, *De numeris et diversis rationibus seu regulis computationum opusculum* (1545), a theoretical arithmetic, *Compendium arithmetice artis* (1549), an algebra, *Algebre compendiosa facilisque descriptio* (1551), and a commentary on Euclid, *In libros arithmeticos .7.8.9. Euclidis* (1555). A most important work was never published,[5] his revision and edition (the only such !) of the unique advanced algebra of the Middle Ages, *De numeris datis*[6] by Jordanus de Nemore (fl. 1225). A thorough scholar, he seems to have avoided the turbulence of the times.

The booklist reflects the description of Scheubel. As today, mathematicians of that time became involved in social and religious reform. This involvement jailed his more brilliant colleague, Michael Stifel, for his reformist convictions in religious matters. Scheubel avoided such commitment. While the booklist names not a single social or religious tract, it does provide considerable information about his intellectual tastes.

A topical index of the books would include the following subject-headings: algebra, almanach, architecture, arithmetic, astrolabe, astrology, astronomy, biology, catoptrics, compass (magnetic), computus, cosmography, dialectics, fortification (city), geometry, gnomon, horology, literature (Greek and Latin), medicine, music, natural philosophy, optics, tables, trigonometry, weights. The greater number of books are in the areas of arithmetic, geometry, and astronomy. Noteworthy in this last group is a copy of Copernicus's *De revolutionibus*. While Scheubel collected the classical authors, he included works of German mathematicians little known to us, such as Jodocus Willich (1501-1552). In short, there are forty-one volumes in folio, thirty-seven in quarto, thirty in octavo, and seven sets of manuscripts noted separately. As was not uncommon in the early days of printing, several books are bound in the same volume. Finally, the books and manuscripts are composed in Greek, Latin, and German.

The inventory gives every indication that Scheubel kept abreast of publications in his areas of specialty, geometry and arithmetic. He had a good collection of Euclid, Archimedes, and Proclus, together with recent commentaries thereon. Of equal importance, he possessed a copy of Johann Werner's *Conics* [77b] and Giambattista Benedetti's *Fixed Compass Geometry* [69]. Both of these were unique and influential contributions to sixteenth-century geometry. In arithmetic, he possessed works in both the theory of numbers and calculations (not to mention the critical Cardano *Algebra* !).

---

[5] I am presently preparing a paper on this work of Scheubel.

[6] For a thorough discussion of this work, see my *The DE NUMERATIS DATIS of Jordanus de Nemore: a critical edition, analysis, evaluation and translation* (Stanford University Ph. D. Dissertation 1970; University Microfilms).

Stifel's *Arithmetic* [55] was a major source book for writers of the sixteenth and seventeenth centuries. Noteworthy also is the *Arithmetic* of Peter Ramus [81]. For practical arithmetic, Scheubel could turn easily to the works of Christoph Rudolph [84] and Peter Apian [86], to mention two. In short, Scheubel had every opportunity to know the mathematical thinking of the times.

The format employed by the cataloger suggests that he was thorough. First of all, the books are classified according to size, a page each for the volumes in folio, quarto, and octavo. Secondly, he notes that certain books are written *grece et latine* or *teutsch*. Only rarely does he describe a book *latine* and this usually where the author is Greek. Thus the reader is left with the presumption that, except where noted, all the works are in Latin. Finally, the reader finds much information about the appearance of the volumes. This last item is worth some expansion.

Immediately beneath the inscription on the recto of the first page is the expression *In asserculis, oder pappen*. The cataloguer is telling the reader that all these books are bound with cardboard covers. Then on the same page and following item [26] is the classification, *In membrana, ut et sequentes*. These books, he says, have vellum covers, with several noted exceptions. Book [30] is described, *sine tegumento*, without a cover (and this expression recurs a number of times). Book [33] is bound *in pappen*; [38] is *ungebunden* or unbound. Since [24] and [36] are singled out as *manuscripti* and *manuscripta* respectively, I conclude that wherever one of these terms is not used, the volume is printed. Item [1] is crossed out.

The list of quarto volumes begins well enough on the second page of the inventory. Next to the first four entries in the left margin is the gloss *Als in Bretlin gebunden: nisi ubi membranam notavi*, an interesting mixture of German and Latin which identifies two kinds of binding: boards and vellum. Another term appears for the first time, *In Berment*. This seems to be another expression for parchment but suggests a quality different from *membranum*. Books [46] and [65] to [70] are all *in berment*. Volumes [58], [59] and [61] are *sine tegumento*. Volume [64] is *in bappen* (*sic!*), as are numbers [73] to [78]. There are no manuscripts in this section, and items [71] and [75] are crossed out.

The third page, on the recto of which is recorded the complete list of octavo-size books, contains no reference to bindings, but has one correction and several additions—each in a different hand. The correction is at item [80]. The additions are on the verso side and titled *Manuscripti libri*, although one volume is described as *impressa*. At the bottom of this same side is the annotation mentioned above. It begins just below a latitudinal crease and identifies again the contents of these pages. In a fourth hand is the word *Bibliotheca* and the date 1571. The pages had been folded together once, labeled with their contents and provenance, and filed. Only later were they bound in the *Actus Senatus Bibliothek* where they now rest.

The transcription of the list was made from xerographed copies of the manuscript, prepared for me by the University Library, Tübingen.[7] The orthography of the scribe has been retained. His abbreviations and contractions have been expanded and indicated by italics. Items crossed out have been reproduced thus ~~opera~~. In a very few cases the script could not be unraveled to my satisfaction, and each of these is followed by (?). Finally, a bibliographical reconstruction follows and complements my transcription.

Admittedly a presumptuous exercise, my attempt to reconstruct Scheubel's library in a bibliographical fashion was quite enjoyable. Useful clues were found in the titles, sometimes merely descriptive, contained in the inventory. Grouping of the titles by size (folio, quarto, octavo, libri manuscripti) provided additional clues. Scheubel's death in 1570 was an obvious terminus. With these aids,[8] I sought the possible imprints in the literature.[9]

All of the items in the inventory have been renumbered consecutively, within brackets. Also within some brackets are found small letters that are employed to distinguish separate imprints (not titles) grouped after one of the scribe's numbers in the inventory. Mention of a single edition indicates it as the only candidate I found. Where there were several editions before Scheubel's death, some of these may be cited. Titles are given at length wherever it seemed necessary to clarify the description in the inventory or to justify my conjecture. In some instances the available literature did not identify the printer. Insufficient information that precluded any reasonable guess is signaled by *n.e.i.* (*not enough information*). With regard to the authors, some biographical information is given for those I suspect may be less well known; regarding a few, I could obtain no information.

(12r)		Libri M. Ioannis Scheubelii pie memorie in folio.
		In asserculis, oder pappen.
[1]	1.	~~Opera mathematica Iaonnis Scheubelii~~.
[2a,b]	+ 2.	Guidonis Bonati, Opera Astronomica: Albohazen de iudiciis astro*rum*.
[3a,b]	3.	Sebast*ianus* Munsterus de Horologiis: Georg*ius* Agricola de Mensuris et Ponderi*bus*.
[4a,b,c, d]	+ 4.	Procli *C*ommentarii latine in Euclidis lib*rum primu*m. Commentaria in Archimedem Eutocii: O*r*ontius de reb*us* mathematicis: Archimedis op*era* q*ue*da*m* latine.

[7] I am particularly thankful to Dr. Schäfer, Staatsarchivrat, who not only supervised the xerographing but also upon a later request transcribed four passages that withstood my scrutiny.

[8] I gratefully include Anne Bobrow, bibliographer for Zeitlin and Ver Brugge, Booksellers, Los Angeles, California.

[9] These include the standard reference works whose citations here would extend these footnotes unreasonably. Corrections and additions to my reconstruction will be received with gratitude.

[5]   5. Vitellionis perspectiva.
[6]   6. Euclidis latine cum expositione Theonis.
[7a,b]   7. Cardanus de regula Algebrae: Schonerus de iudiciis
                    natiuitatum.
[8a,b]   +   8. Orontii Cosmographia, item Orontii Geometrica in
                    Euclidem.
[9a,b]   +   9. Jacobus Ziglerus in secundum Plinii: Martiani Capelle
                    uaria opuscula.
[10a,b]   +   10. Instrumentum primi mobilis Petri Apiani: Osualdi
                    Schreckebuchsii commentaria Theoricas Planetarum.
[11]   11. Archimedis opera grece et latine, adiuncto Eutocio.
[12a,b]   +   12. Boethi opera uaria mathematica: Arithmetica M. Cas-
                    paris Laxii.
[13a,b]   +   13. Verneri commentaria in geographiam Ptolemei, item
                    Almagestum Ptolemei latine.
[14a,b,c]   +   14. Tabule eclipsium Purbachii: Regiomontanus de Trian-
                    gulis, et quadratura circuli: Instrumentum primi mo-
                    bilis Petri Apiani, cum astronomia Gebri.
[15]   15. Euclides grece cum commentario.
[16a.b]   +   16. Ioannis Camers in Solinum: Pomponius Mela cum
                    Vadiani Scholiis.
[17a,b]   17. Iuuenalis cum commentariis uariorum: Lucanius cum
                    commentariis.
[18a,b,c]   18. Euclides latine cum commentario. Et quadratum
                    Geometricum Purbachii: et Albubater, et Centiloqui-
                    um Hermetis.
[19]   19. Vitruuius de Architectura, item.
[20]   20. Astrolobium Stoefleri.
[21]   +   21. Copernicus de Reuolutionibus.
[22]   +   22. Tabule Alfonsi.
[23]   +   23. Petri Ramus arithmetica et geometria. In magna
                    forma quarto.
[24]   24. Commentarii Scheubelii in sex libros Euclidis priores,
                    manuscripti, quod non excusi.
[25]   25. Horatius cum commentariis Landini.
[26]   +   26. Stoefleri commentaria in Proclum. In membrana, ut
                    et sequentes.
[27]   +   27. Gnomonice Schoneri.
[28]   +   28. Xylander in sex priores libros Euclidis, teutsch.
[29a,b] (12v) + 29. Sphera mundi commentariis uariorum Au-
                    torum: Geometria Alberti Dureri teutsch.
[30]   30. Philosophia naturalis compendium ex libris Thome
                    sine tegumento.
[31]   +   31. Organum Vranicum Munsteri:
[32a,b]   32. Practica Musica Frankini Gaffori: aliud opuscula mu-
                    sica, Ioannis Froschii.
[33]   +   33. Eclipsium descriptiones Cypriani Leouitii, in pappen.

[34a,b]   34. Perspectiua Ioannis Pisani, seu communis: proemium philosopiae naturalis Alberti Magni.

[35a,b]   + 35. Durerus ceon betestigung der Staat Cend schlosser. Instrumentbuch Petri Apiani.

[36a,b,c, + 36. Manuscriptus liber componens sphera materialis: et d]   compositis instrumenti primi mobilis a Scheubelio collecta. Quadrans Apiani getruckt, latine compositum instrumenti obseruatorii: et astrologica quedam (de natiuitatibus) manuscripta.

[37]   + 37. Manuscriptus liber de doctrina triangulorum, ex uariis autoribus.

[38]   + 38. Regiomontani demonstrationes in tabulis primi mobilis, ungebunden.

[39]   + 39. Opera Georgii Valle mathematica in magno folio.

[40]   + 40. Opera eiusdem geometrica, dialectica, medica, item eiusdem magnitudinis.

[41]   41. Terentius cum commentariis.

(13r)   Catalogus librorum M. Scheubelii pie memorie, in quarto.

[42]   + 1. Ephemerides Ioannis Stadii   ⎫ in quarto
[43]   + 2. Ephemerides Stoefleri   ⎭
[44]   + 3. Prutenice tabule, item in quarto, ut et sequentes.
[45a,b]   4. Aristotelis liber de anima, et physicorum octo.
[46a,b]   + 5. Geometria practica Orontii, Ioannis Taisnier de annulo spherico, in bremento.
[47a,b,c] + 6. Vsus instrumentorum aliquorum astronomicorum Regiomontani: tabule resolute Virdungi: Albahatus de natiuitatibus.
[48]   + 7. Tabule directionum Reinholdi.
[49a,b]   + 8. Tabule directionum Regiomontani, cum additionibus Leouitii Ephemerides Carelli.
[50]   + 9. Tabule directionum Regiomontani, Venetiis excuse.
[51a,b]   + 10. Albumasar de magnis coniunctionibus, et alia astrologica: item compilatio Leopoldi de Austria, astrologica.
[52a,b,c] + 11. Cardanus de supplementis almanach, et alia astrologica: et Almanach nouum Petri Pitati: et quinque annorum Ephemerides Stoefleri.
[53a,b,c, + 12. Arithmetica Boethi, et Rudolfus Spoletanus de proportione, et Theodosii spherica latine, et Iordanus de d,e,f]   Ponderibus, et geographia Glareani, et cosmographia Petri Apiani.
[54a,b]   + 13. Alfragani rudimenta Astronomica, cum Albategnio: item tabule resolute Schoneri.
[55]   14. Arithmetica Stifelii latine.
[56]   15. Albumasaris introductorium in Astronimicam.
[57a,b,c]   16. Cosmographice descriptiones Stoefleri: Horologiographia Munsteri annulus Dryandri.

[58]   17. Usus astrolabii Koebeli, sine tegumento.

[59]   18. Usus instrumenti luminarii solis et lune, Munsteri,
                sine tegumento.

[60a,b,c]   19. Computus Ecclesiasticus: et rursus idem, quod supra,
                exemplar Aristotelis de anima, ct librorum octo phy-
                sicorum: item Petrus de Eliaca in meteora.

[61]   + 20. Hispalensis astrologia, sine tegumento.

[62a,b]   + 21. Ephemerides noue Ioachim Rhetici: canon doctrine
                triangulorum in bermento.

[63]   + 22. Tabule positionum Leouitii.

[64]   + 23. Petri Peregini de magnete: in bappen.

[65a,b]   24. Libellus geographicus Siderocratis: tabule ascensio-
                num Abdie Wickeri.

[66a,b]   (13v) + 25. Euclidis catoptrica, grece et latine. Quadrans
                planispherium Valentini Engelharti in bermento.

[67]   + 26. Geometria Christopheri Bueler, teutsch.   ⎫
[68]   + 27. Geometria Wolfgangi Schmid, teutsch.   ⎪
[69]   + 28. Problemata Euclidis, per Ioannem   ⎬ in bermento.
                Baptistam.   ⎪
[70a,b]   + 29. Geometria Georgii Peischii: Orontii   ⎪
                de Horologiis.   ⎭

[71]   30. ~~Nicomachi Gerasini Arithmetica Grece, in Pappen.~~

[72a,b]   + 31. Perspectiua communis: Geometria corporum regula-
                rium, teutsch in pappen, ut et sequentes libri.

[73a,b]   + 32. Gemma Frisii de radio astronomico: Petri Pitati de
                calendario Romano.

[74a,b]   33. Rursus Euclidis catoptrica, grece et latine. Ptole-
                mei planispherium latine.

[75a,b]   34. ~~Euclidis musica grece, item optica et catoptrica eius-
                dem grece.~~

[76]   + 35. Synopsis mensurarum et ponderum Michaelis Neandri.

[77a,b,c] + 36. Almanch Stoefleri seu Ephemerides: Verneri de conici
                Elementis: item Vsus Ephemeridum Tansteteri (?).

[78]   37. Budei epistole, grece.

    (14r)   Libri M. Ioannis Scheubelii pie memorie, in octavo.

[79]   1. Euclidis liber primus grece et latine, cum Dasypodii
                Scholiis.

[80a,b]   +   2. Euclidis liber secundus grece et latine ~~cum Dasypodii
                Scholiis~~ item demonstratio Barlaam.

[81]   +   3. Arithmetica Petri Rami.

[82]   +   4. Reliqui libri Euclidis, grece et latine.

[83]   +   5. Arithmetica Tonstalli.

[84]   +   6. Arithmetica Christopheri Rudolfi, teutsch.

[85]   7. Arithmetica Scheubelii latine.

[86]   8. Arithmetica Petri Apiani teutsch.

[87]   9. Cardani practica Arithmetica.

[88]   10. Proclus, Cleomedes, Aratus, item grece et latine.

[89]   + 11. Rudolfus Battingis de Astrolobio.

[90a,b]   12. Sphera Ioannis de Sacro Busco: Cosmographia Hon-
                 teri.

[91]   13. Euclidis latine sine commentariis.

[92]   + 14. Ptolemei liber primus mathematice constructionis,
                 grece et latine.

[93]   + 15. Theorica Planetarum Nicolai Simi.

[94a,b,c] + 16. Arithmetica Glareani: Cosmographia et Sphera Dryan-
                 dri: Arithmetica Iodoci Willichii.

[95]   17. Sphera Ioannis de Sacro Busco.

[96a,b]   + 18. Arithmetica Strigelii: Meditationes in Spheram Mer-
                 catoris.

[97]   19. Priores sex libri Euclidis grece et latine sine demon-
                 strationibus.

[98]   20. Dionysii Afri de situ orbis, grece et latine.

[99a,b]   21. Arithmetica Fabri Stapulensis in Boethium: musica
                 practica Gregorii Fabri.

[100a,b] + 22. Principia Astronomica et Cosmographia Gemma Fri-
                 sii: Libellus sphere Cornelii Valerii.

[101]   23. Arithmetica Gemma Frisii.

[102]   24. Theorica Planetarum Purbachii.

[103]   25. Stereometria Buckhardi Mythobii.

[104]   26. Astrolobii usus Kobeli.

[105]   27. Astrologia Iudiciania Ioannis Taisnieri.

[106]   28. Taisnieri de natura Magnetis.

[107]   29. Compendium Arithmetica Scheubelii.

[108]   30. iterum compendium Arithmetica eiusdem.

                    (14v)   Manuscripti libri

[109]   + 1. Commentarius in decem librorum Euclidis teutsch
                Scheubelii imperfectus et latine bis.

[110]   + 2. Idem Scheubelius in libro Arithmeticos 7, 8, 9 Eu-
                clidis latine bis.

[111]   +   In $\begin{cases} 1 \\ 2 \\ 3 \\ \\ 4 \\ 5 \\ 6 \end{cases}$ $\begin{array}{l} \text{priores} \\ \text{in reliquos libros Euclidis elementorum Scheu-} \\ \text{belii iam impressa.} \end{array}$

[112]   +   Descriptio Regule Algebre bis anno et impressa.

[113]   +   In quinque posteriones de stereometria, demonstra-
                tiones bis latine.

[114]   Allerley Scartecken in folio et in quarto.

[115]   Annotationes in Homero, Horatio et alios scholasti-
                       cos autores in fol*io* & *quar*ta forma.

                       Bibliotheca   Libri M. Ioannis Scheubelli pie memorie
                       1571

                                       17 Iulii a*nno 15*71 Senatus
                                       commentat facultati artiu*m*
                                       ut eligant utilia et q*uae*
                                       antea non habent.

Bibliographical reconstruction

[1]   There is no such collection. Seemingly the scribe meant this for
         a subtitle and then changed his mind.
[2a]   (?-1297), Venezia: I. Leuceseus, 1506; Basel: [I. Parcus], 1550.
[2b]   (Abū-l-Ḥasan, fl. 1016-1040), many editions.
[3a]   Three quarto editions noted (Basel: H. Petrus, 1531, 1533, 1543)
         but none in folio.
[3b]   (Bauer, German physician, philosopher, and naturalist, 1494-1555),
         Paris: C. Wechleus, 1533; or, Basel: H. Froebenius and N. Episco-
         pius, 1550.
[4a]   Edited and translated by F. Barocius, Padua: Gratiosus Perchacinus,
         1560.
[4b]   (Byzantine mathematician, fl. c. A.D. 510), probably Basel: I. Herua-
         gius, 1544.
[4c]   Paris: M. Vascosanus, 1556.
[4d]   Commandino's translation (Venezia, 1558).
[5]   περὶ ὀπτικῆς, id est de natura, ratione, & proiectione radiorum uisus.
         Nuremberg: I. Petreius, 1535.
[6]   Several editions.
[7a]   (Italian physician, mathematician, and astrologer, 1501-1573), Nu-
         remberg: I. Petreius, 1545.
[7b]   (Professor of mathematics at the Nuremberg Gymnasium, 1477-1547),
         Nuremberg: I. Montanus and U. Neuber, 1545.
[8a]   No folio in Latin found, but French folio edition, Paris: Simon du
         Bois, 1528.
[8b]   Paris, 1536 and 1544.
[9a]   (Bavarian Landave, fl. 1530), Basel: H. Petrius, 1531; Cologne, 1550.
[9b]   Several folio imprints beginning with the edition of Bodianus (Vicen-
         za, 1499).
[10a]   (Bienewitz, German astronomer and mathematician at Ingolstadt, one
         of the few university professors of his time to give instruction in
         arithmetic in German, 1495-1552), probably Nuremberg: I. Petreius,
         1534.

[10b]   (Professor of mathematics, rhetoric and Hebrew at the Universities of Tübingen and Freiburg, 1511-1579), *Commentaria in novas theoricas planetarum G. Purbachii* . . . Basel: H. Petrus, 1553 and 1556.

[11]   Basel: I. Heruagius, 1544.

[12a]   G. Ruffus's edition (Paris: S. Colinaeus, 1521); or perhaps Le Fevre's *Epitome* of 1503.

[12b]   (Theologian at Universities of Paris and Saragossa, 1487-1560), Paris: N. de la barre, 1515.

[13a]   (Werner, priest in Nuremberg who wrote the first original tract on conics to appear in the sixteenth century, see [77b], 1468-1528), Nuremberg: F. Peypus, 1514.

[13b]   Either Valla's translation (Basel: H. Petrus, 1541) or Schrekhenfuch's edition (*ibidem*, 1551).

[14a]   Wien: I. Winterburger, 1514.

[14b]   Nuremberg: I. Petreius, 1533.

[14c]   Nuremberg: I. Petreius, 1534.

[15]   S. Grynaeus's edition (Basel: I. Hervagius, 1553).

[16a]   (Giovanni Ricuzzi Vellini, Italian philosopher and theologian, 1468-1546), either Vienna: I. Singrenius, 1520, or Basel: H. Petrus, 1557.

[16b]   Either Basel: A. Cratandrus, 1522, or Paris: C. Wechelus, 1540.

[17a]   Several editions beginning at Venice: J. De Rubeis, 1475.

[17b]   Venice: B. de Zanis de Portesio, 1492.

[18a]   Campanus with Pacioli's commentary (Venice: A. Paganius Paganius, 1509); or perhaps Le Fevre's edition of Campanus (Paris: H. Stephanus, 1516).

[18b]   Nuremberg: I. Stuchs, 1516.

[18c]   (Abū Bakr al-Rāzī, ?-937); if this is one imprint, then Venice: I. B. Sessa, 1501; if two, then for Abū Bakr, his *Liber genethliacus sive de nativitatibus*, Nuremberg: I. Petrius, 1540; for the *Centiloquium*, there are many editions.

[19]   Several editions.

[20]   (Professor of mathematics at University of Tübingen, 1452-1531), Oppenheim: I. Köbel, 1513 and 1524.

[21]   Two editions, Nuremberg: I. Petreius, 1543, and Basel: H. Petrus, 1565.

[22]   N. Prugner's edition of the work by I. Blanchinus, N. Prugner, and G. Peurbach (Basel: I. Heruagius, 1553).

[23]   Basel: E. Episcopius & Nicolai fratris haeredes, 1569.

[24]   Manuscript, unidentified.

[25]   Milan: L. Pachel, 1508.

[26]   Tübingen: T. Anshelmus, 1514.

[27]   (Andreas Schoener, ?-1547), Nuremberg: I. Montanus and U. Neuberus, 1551.

[28]   (Wilhelm Holtzmann, Professor of mathematics at Heidelberg, 1532-1576), Basel: I. Kündig, 1562.

[29a]   Several editions beginning at Venice: S. Papiensis, 1499.

[29b]   *Vnderweysung der messung, mit dem zirkel vñ richtscheyt, in linien ebnen vnnd gantzen corporen.* Nuremberg: 1525-1527, 1538.

[30]   Probably the *Opusculum beati Thome ad fratrum Reynaldum de iudicijs astrorum* which went through several editions before 1570.

[31]   Basel, 1531; Basel: H. Petrus, 1536.

[32a]   (Choirmaster at the cathedral in Milan, 1451-1522), several editions.

[32b]   Strassburg: P. Schoeffer & M. Apiarius, 1535.

[33]   (Leowitz, mathematician for the Count of Pfalz, 1524-1574), Augsburg, 1554, 1556.

[34a]   (John Peckham, archbishop of Canterbury), only the Leipzig (M. Herbipolensis, 1504) edition has the author as *Ioannis Pisani*.

[34b]   Basel: M. Furter, 1506.

[35a]   *Etliche Underricht zur Befestigung der Stett, Schloss u. Flecken.* Nuremberg, 1527 (two editions in same year).

[35b]   Ingolstadt: [P. Apian], 1533.

[36a,b]   Manuscripts, unidentified.

[36c]   Ingolstadt: P. Apian, 1532.

[36d]   Manuscripts, unidentified.

[37]   Manuscript, unidentified.

[38]   Vienna: I. Winterburger, 1514 (this may have been bound orginally with [14a]).

[39]   Not found.

[40]   *G. Valla Placentino Interprete. Hoc in volumine hec continentur: Nicephori logica . . . Euclidis quartus decimus elementorum . . . Galenus de bono corporis habitus . . .* Venice: S. Papiensis, 1498.

[41]   Several editions.

[42]   (Professor of mathematics at Royal College of France—Paris, 1527-1579), published four *Ephemerides* in Cologne between 1556 and 1560.

[43]   Probably the *Ephemerides* for 1532-1552, Tübingen: H. Morhard, 1531.

[44]   (*Preussische Tabeln* by E. Reinhold, d. 1553), several editions.

[45a]   (?) Venice: H. Scotus, 1540.

[45b]   Latin translations with and without commentaries were published Kracow: I. Haller, 1519 and Paris: G. Buon, 1560.

[46a]   Strasbourg, 1544, and Paris, 1555.

[46b]   Antwerp: I. Richard, 1560.

[47a]   Nuremberg: I. Montanus and U. Neuber, 1544.

[47b]   (Astronomer at Heidelberg, fl. 1520), Nuremberg, 1542.

[47c]   *Albohali Arabis Astrologi de ivdiciis nativitatum liber unus, ante hac non editus . . .* Nuremberg: I. Montanus and U. Neuber, 1546.

[48]   (Professor of mathematics at Wittenberg and early follower of Co-
        pernicus, ?-1553), Tübingen: U. Morhards Erben, 1554.
[49a]   Several editions beginning at Augsburg, 1552.
[49b]   Venice: V. Valgrisius, 1558.
[50]   Venice: P. Liechtensteyn Coloniensis, 1504.
[51a]   (Abū Naṣr Manṣūr, fl. 1007), Augsburg: E. Ratdolt, 1489.
[51b]   Augsburg: E. Ratdolt, 1489.
[52a]   Nuremberg: I. Petreius, 1543 and 1547.
[52b]   (Venetian astronomer, fl. 1550), several editions.
[52c]   Tübingen: Morhard, 1548 and 1549.
[53a]   Many editions.
[53b]   Rome: I. Mazochius, 1516.
[53c]   Vienna: I. Singriener, 1529.
[53d]   Edited by Peter Apian, Nuremberg: I. Petreius, 1533.
[53e]   (Loritus, Professor of mathematics and fine arts in several univer-
        sities, 1488-1563), several editions.
[53f]   Landish: I. Weissenberger, 1524.
[54a]   Nuremberg: I. Petreius, 1537.
[54b]   Nuremberg: I. Petreius, 1536.
[55]   (Professor of mathematics at Jena, 1487-1567), several editions all
        printed in Nuremberg.
[56]   Augsburg: E. Ratdolt, 1489.
[57a]   Edited by Dryander, Marburg: E. Ceruicornus, 1537.
[57b]   See [3a].
[57c]   (Eichmann, Professor of mathematics and medicine at the Univer-
        sity of Marburg, 1500-1560), Marburg: E. Cervicornus, 1536 and
        1537 (twice).
[58]   (Fellow student of Copernicus and teacher of arithmetic in Oppen-
        heim, 1470-1533), Mainz: P. Jordan, 1532.
[59]   *Canones svper novvm instrvmentvm lvminarivm, docentes; quo pacto*
        per illud inuieniantur Solis et Lunae medij et ueri motus. . . Basel:
        A. Cratander, 1534.
[60a]   *N.e.i.*
[60b]   See [45a].
[60c]   Many editions.
[61]   (The eminent translator John of Seville, fl. 1150), Nuremberg, 1548.
[62a]   Leipzig: W. Gunter, 1550.
[62b]   Also by Rheticus (Leipzig: W. Gunter, 1551).
[63]   *Loca stellarum fixarum ab ann. 1349 usque ad ann. 3029.* Augsburg,
        1557.
[64]   (French physicist and teacher of Roger Bacon, fl. 1270). Two pos-
        sible editions: one done by Achilles Gasser (Augsburg, 1558); the
        other by Johann Taisneir (Cologne, 1562).

[65a]   (Eisenmenger, Professor of mathematics at the University of Tü-
        bingen, 1534-1585), Tübingen, 1562.

[65b]   (Professor of mathematics at Rotenburg an der Tauber, ?-1564),
        Tübingen, 1561.

[66a]   Dasypodius's edition, Strasbourg: W. Rihelius, 1557.

[66b]   (Professor of mathematics at Erfurt, 1516-1562), Viterbo, 1559.

[67]   Not found.

[68]   (Rechenmeister of Bamberg, fl. 1535), Nuremberg, 1539.

[69]   (Giambattista Benedetti of Venice, philosopher and mathematician
        to the dukes of Savoy, 1530-1590), *Resolutio omnium Euclidis pro-
        blematum aliorumque ad hoc necessario inventorum una tantummodo
        circini data apertura, per ecc.* Venice: B. Caesano, 1553; a most im-
        portant work on the geometry of the circle of fixed radius.

[70a]   Not found.

[70b]   French edition (Paris, 1553) or Latin edition (Paris: G. Cauellat
        1560—twice).

[71]   Paris: C. Wechelus, 1538.

[72a]   The edition of L. Gauricus (Venezia: J. B. Sessa, 1504) or of G. Hart-
        mann (Nuremberg: I. Petreius, 1542).

[72b]   *N.e.i.*

[73a]   (Professor of medicine at Löwen, 1508-1555), Antwerp, 1545.

[73b]   Basel, 1562.

[74a]   See [66a].

[74b]   Venice: Aldus, 1558.

[75a]   Greek with Latin translation of the *Musica* by I. Pena, Paris: A.
        Wechelus, 1557.

[75b]   Both also translated by Pena and in one volume by same publisher,
        same year.

[76]   (Michael Neumann of Joachimstal, Professor of mathematics, Greek,
        and medicine at Jena, 1529-1581), Basel, 1555.

[77a]   See [43]. Ulm 1499 and Venice 1513 editions of *Ephemerides* for
        1482-1518 have word *Almanach* in subtitle.

[77b]   *In hoc opere haec continentur: Libellus Ioannis Verneri Nurembergen
        super vigintiduobus elementis conicis.—Eiusdem Commentarius seu pa-
        raphrastica ennaratio in undecim modos conficiendi eius Problematis,
        quod Cubi duplicatio dicitur.* Nuremberg: Fr. Pezpus, 1522.

[77c]   Vienna: Pannonia, 1518.

[78]   (French humanist who laid the foundations for what became the
        Bibliothèque Nationale, 1467-1540), Paris: C. Wechleus, 1540, or Pa-
        ris: A. Wechelus, 1556.

[79]   (Rauhfuss or Hassenfuss, Professor of mathematics at the Univer-
        sity of Strassbourg and canon of Saint Thomas's Church there, 1532-
        1600), Strassbourg: C. Mylius, 1564.

[80a]   This volume contains not only book 2 of the *Elements* but two others: the Barlaam *Arithmetic* and the *Eight Propositions of Stereometry*, all under the editorship of Dasypodius. Strassbourg: C. Mylius, 1564.

[80b]   (Bernardo di Seminara, theologian, humanist, logician, and mathematician, sometime abbot of the Monastery of the Savior in Constantinople, ?-ca. 1350), see [80a].

[81]   Paris: A. Wechelus, 1557.

[82]   *Propositiones reliquorum Librorum Geometriae Euclidis, Graece, & Latine, vsum eorum, qui volumine Euclidis carent. Per Cunradum Dasypodium, scholae Argentinensis professorem.* Paris: G. Cavellat, 1557 and 1558. Apparently this was a popular book since it was republished in Cologne (M. Cholinus, 1564) and in Strassbourg (C. Mylius) the same year.

[83]   (Educated at Oxford, Cambridge, and Padua, sometimes bishop of London and Durham, 1474-1559), many editions.

[84]   Many editions.

[85]   Leipzig, 1545.

[86]   Many editions.

[87]   Several editions—Milan: Bemontinus Caluscus, 1539; Nuremberg: 1541 and 1542.

[88]   *Procli de sphaera, liber I. Cleomedis de Mvndo siue circularis inspectionis meteorum Libri II. Arati Solensis phaenomena, siue Apparentia. Dionysii Afri descriptio Orbis habitabilis . . . Omnia Graece et Latine . . . J. Honteri Coronensis de Cosmographiae rudimentis.* Basel: H. Petrus, 1561. If this is the book, then Scheubel may have had it divided and rebound into three parts, [88], [98], and [90b]. A minor point: the "*item*" in the inventory should probably read "omnia" in view of the title above.

[89]   (Rudolfus Battingius Frisius, a physician who combined medicine with astrology, ?-1588), Paris: I. du Puys, 1557.

[90a]   The paragon for clarity and simplicity, the *Sphaera* of Sacrobosco was the most widely used textbook in astronomy and cosmography from the thirteenth to the seventeenth century; many editions.

[90b]   (A Dacian from Cronstad, fl. 1560), several editions.

[91]   This may be the translation by Joachim Camerarius (Leipzig: V. Bapst., 1549) or that by Peter Ramus (Paris: L. Grandin, 1545 or Paris: T. Richard, 1549).

[92]   Edited by E. Reinholt, Wittenberg: J. Lufft, 1549.

[93]   (Professor of astronomy at the University of Bologna, 1530-1564), Basel: I. Oporinus, 1555.

[94a]   Either *Arithmetica et musica operum Boethii demonstratibus et figuris auctior*, Basel, 1546, or *De vi arithmeticae practicae*, Freiburg, 1550.

[94b]   For the *Sphaera*: Marburg: [Egenolff], 1539; for the *Cosmographia*: not found in *octavo*.

[94c]   (Professor of Greek and medicine in the University of Frankfurt an der Oder, who identified a certain Arabic philosopher by the name of "algebra," ?-1552), Strassbourg: C. Mylius, 1540.

[95]   See [90a].

[96a]   (Professor of theology at several German Universities, 1524-1569), Leipzig, 1563.

[96b]   (Son of Gerhard, ca. 1540-1568), Cologne: A. Birckmanns Ehen, 1563.

[97]   Not mentioned in Thomas-Stanford's *Early Editions of Euclid's Elements* (London: Bibliographical Society, 1926).

[98]   See [88].

[99a]   Paris: H. Stephanus, 1507.

[99b]   Basel: H. Petrus, 1553.

[100a]   Paris, 1547; in this work was proposed for the first time the idea of distinguishing longitudes by means of a clock. Another edition, Antwerp, 1553.

[100b]   Antwerp: C. Plantinus, 1561 and 1568.

[101]   Several editions—Wittenberg, 1548; Antwerp, 1552; Paris, 1556.

[102]   Several editions—Ingolstadt: Apian, 1528; Wittenberg, 1542; Basel, 1565.

[103]   (Professor of mathematics and medicine at the University of Marburg, 1504-1565), Frankfurt, 1544.

[104]   Two editions in Paris, 1552.

[105]   Cologne, 1559.

[106]   Cologne: I. Birckmannus, 1562.

[107] and [108]   Basel: I. Parcus, 1549 and 1560.

[109] to [115]   Manuscripts, but note that [114] is miscellaneous sheets or broadsides.

Department of Secondary Education
School of Education
California State University
Northridge, California, U.S.A.

THE MIDDLE AGES IN AUSTRIAN TRADITION: PROBLEMS OF AN IMPERIAL AND PATERNALISTIC IDEOLOGY

•

by Gerhart B. Ladner

This paper will attempt to illustrate the fact that the high and late Middle Ages in Austria were closely linked to the imperial ideology[1] that the Middle Ages had inherited from the Christianized Roman Empire and its successor, the early medieval empire of the West, later known as the Holy Roman Empire. This is, of course, only one aspect of the Austrian medieval tradition, but an important one, especially since it continued far into modern times while remaining distinct from the other type of imperial ideology which in the postmedieval period evolved in conjunction with nationalism and colonialism and is more specifically called imperialism.

It is not possible on this occasion to enter upon the entire history of the ideas and the realities connected with the terms "empire" and "imperialism." Suffice it to say that all empires have passed through stages of expansion which may be called imperialistic, but that only some of them reached the point at which they set an end to limitless goals, though marginal expansion may at times have seemed to be indispensable, for the defense of the basic status quo, or the revindication of definite rights may have seemed to be warranted. The Roman Empire after Augustus, the medieval empire after Charlemagne, the Hapsburg Empire after Charles V, and the British Empire after Queen Victoria were such representatives of an imperial idea which at least on principle, if not always in practice, were nonexpansionist, were interested chiefly in maintaining peace within the imperial framework—a *pax romana, pax christiana, pax austriaca, pax britannica.* That they were

This paper is a revised, enlarged, and annotated version of the Faculty Research Lecture at the University of California, Los Angeles, delivered by the author in April, 1971. I am most grateful to Professor Herwig Wolfram of the University of Vienna for his help in obtaining the photographs for some of the illustrations of this paper—fig. 2 (Dom- und Diözesanmuseum, Vienna), fig. 3 (Kunsthistorisches Museum, Vienna), figs. 4, 5, and 7 (Bildarchiv der Österreichischen Nationalbibliothek, Vienna)—as well as for some pertinent suggestions.

[1] Throughout this paper, the term "ideology" is used simply to denote a complex of ideas, and the term "idea" is interchangeable with "concept" or "conception."

ultimately not successful in doing so was in part because of the continued interference of ethnic—later national—aspirations that were tending toward new cycles of expansion and imperialism, and also to the almost inevitable gradual slackening of any imperial ideology based upon maintenance and the desire for peace rather than upon war and conquest.

These preliminary remarks consciously omit pre-Roman and non-Western imperialisms. They are only aimed at establishing the existence of two different ideas of empire to which it will be possible to refer without further explanation in later sections of this paper: an "imperial" idea centered on maintenance of a status quo and of peace, if at all possible, and an "imperialistic" idea centered around expansion and much less averse to war.[2]

I shall deal with the Austrian medieval tradition and the development of its imperial ideology on two levels: first I shall attempt to characterize a few selected aspects of the three main stages of the Austrian Middle Ages themselves—the period around 1150, the last quarter of the thirteenth and first half of the fourteenth century, and the transitional century from 1450 to 1550—and second I shall try to demonstrate the persistence and the varieties of the medieval imperial tradition in Austria in some of the great literary

---

[2] One of the most intelligent studies ever written on imperialisms and empires in general is undoubtedly that of J. Schumpeter, "Zur Soziologie der Imperialismen," *Archiv für Sozialwissenschaft und Sozialpolitik* 46 (1918-1919) 1ff. and 275ff. (An English translation [not always accurate] appeared, together with that of another of Schumpeter's essays, under the title *Imperialism and Social Classes* in Oxford, 1951, and in New York, 1955). In criticizing Marxist tendencies to confuse modern imperialism with capitalism, Schumpeter rightly stresses the continued existence of precapitalist and prebourgeois expansionism even in modern, and a fortiori in older imperialisms. Yet he does not in my opinion sufficiently consider that the aggressive process of empire building was on several historical occasions terminated by broadly speaking "pacifist" ideas, and not merely by socioeconomic changes such as transformation of warrior classes into agricultural or commercial-industrial classes. (For a different kind of criticism of Schumpeter's theory of imperialism, cf. G. Lichtheim, *Imperialism* [New York 1971], esp. 126ff.) The "imperial ideology" at any rate which will be discussed in these pages is no longer that of Roman or Germanic, and not yet that of modern, expansionist imperialism: in this sense "imperialism" as a dynamic process and "empire" as a relatively saturated, self-limiting, and static order of peace can be contrasted with one another.

No up-to-date comprehensive book on the Western medieval and early modern empire, the so-called Holy Roman Empire—which was a Hapsburg Empire of the "House of Austria" without interruption from 1437 to 1806—exists. There is still the old and famous work of James Bryce, *The Holy Roman Empire* (first published 1864; enlarged and revised edition by Bryce himself, New York 1904). There is the excellent survey by R. Folz, *L'idée d'empire en occident du Ve au XIVe siècle* (Paris 1953), which reaches only to the mid-fourteenth century. The two important books by R. Koebner, *Empire* (Cambridge 1961), and *Imperialism*, edited by H. D. Schmidt from notes left by Koebner (Cambridge 1964), are centered in the ideology of the British Empire. The special literature on various aspects of the post-Roman Western empire, which is very voluminous, will de cited only when relevant for this paper.

works that emerged in that country from the mid-nineteenth to the mid-twentieth century. I mention in anticipation the names of Adalbert Stifter, Hugo von Hofmannsthal, and Robert Musil.

Austria first appears as a political entity of considerable stature in the mid-twelfth century.[3] It was still far from being an empire itself, but after having been an outpost against the Hungarians for almost two centuries it had by then become one of the most important principalities of the German Kingdom, which was also the main part of the Holy Roman Empire. The relatively exalted position that Austria had reached was legalized and built into the constitution of the German Kingdom and Empire during the reigns of the Emperor Frederick Barbarossa and of a member of Austria's first dynasty, the Babenberg, Henry II with the never truly explained surname Jasomirgott.[4] This was done in 1156 by the elevation of what so far had been a Danubian border county, the March of Austria, into a duchy. Henry Jasomirgott thus became the first duke of Austria. He was granted an imperial charter, the so-called *Privilegium Minus* or "Minor Privilege," which may be said to have inaugurated the development toward an Austrian state, since it contained far-reaching rights concerning hereditary succession of the dynasty and its supreme jurisdiction in its lands, which would finally lead to full sovereignty. The privilege furthermore exempted the duke from attendance at the emperor's court, except if held in neighboring Bavaria, and from participation in imperial wars, except if waged in territories adjacent to Austria.[5] This last stipulation clearly foreshadows Austrian expansion: it occurred first toward the south, that is to say, toward the territories lying in the direction of the Adriatic Sea and Italy—such as Styria, Carinthia, Carniola, and Tirol, all regions that reach from the Alps either to Slovenia and Trieste or to Venice and Verona; later there was to be added expansion to the east, that is to say, toward Bohemia and Hungary.

[3] For the main facts of Austrian political history here referred to, cf., for instance, E. Zöllner, *Geschichte Österreichs von den Anfängen bis zur Gegenwart*, ed. 3 (Vienna 1966), K. and M. Uhlirz, *Handbuch der Geschichte Österreich-Ungarns* 1, ed. 2 (Graz 1963), to 1526.

[4] For this surname cf. F. Eheim, "Zur Geschichte der Beinamen der Babenberger," *Unsere Heimat: Monatsblatt des Vereines für Landeskunde von Niederösterreich und Wien* 26 (1955) 153ff. Eheim refers to J. Karabacek, *Beiträge zur Geschichte der Mazjaditen* (Leipzig 1874) 119ff., who quotes the Arabic chronicle of Ibn-el-Furat, where in all probability Henry Jasomirgott is mentioned under the name Jasan el-Kund Harri. Dr. L. Richter-Bernburg kindly checked Karabacek's text. Both he and my late-lamented friend, Gustave von Grunebaum doubted the cogency of Karabacek's interpretation of "Jasan" as "mir Gott."

[5] Among the many old and new studies on the *Privilegium Minus*, the enlightening synthesis of H. (von) Fichtenau, *Von der Mark zum Herzogtum: Grundlagen und Sinn des "Privilegium Minus" für Österreich* (Munich 1958), is especially noteworthy. The most recent edition of the document is that in *Urkundenbuch zur Geschichte der Babenberger in Österreich* 4.1, ed. H. Fichtenau (Vienna 1968) 147ff., no. 803.

Research of the last quarter of a century has clearly shown how important the Byzantine marriage alliances of the Babenberg dynasty were in connection with Austria's growth.[6] They were initiated by Henry II, who married Theodora Comnena, a niece of Emperor Manuel I, and were continued by later dukes alongside of Bohemian and Hungarian marriages. The close contact with Byzantium, with its old imperial ideology and with its sophisticated civilization, was an incentive to world openness, which was later to be characteristic also for Hapsburg Austria in the best periods of its history.

Austria was thus intimately related to the imperial tradition of both East and West, a two-fold tradition that was ultimately derived from that of the Christianized Roman Empire. The greatest historian of this tradition, and perhaps of the Middle Ages as a whole, was Otto, bishop of Freising in Bavaria (fig. 1). It is perhaps not surprising that he was an Austrian prince. He was in fact a brother of Duke Henry II Jasomirgott, and both were grandsons of Emperor Henry IV and uncles of Emperor Frederick Barbarossa.

The study of ascending and descending family trees, of dynastic lineage, in short the science of historical genealogy, is not a popular subject today, though among medieval historians it has in recent years attained a new vogue,[7] and for good reasons. The fact is that for the Middle Ages we still lack a systematic prosopography and portrait-iconography, that is to say, thorough knowledge of medieval personalities through literary and pictorial sources; in this respect, not only modern but also ancient history is far ahead of the medieval period.[7a] History is after all primarily that of men and women. The neglect of personal history for any period in favor of too exclusive a proliferation of the history of ideas on the one hand and of quantitative history on the other—and I would in no way wish to deny the importance of these disciplines—would nevertheless seem to impoverish, if not to distort, history and in addition to undermine the factual basis of the potentialities that a new type of psychological history might have.

To return to Otto of Freising: in his case genealogy explains so much that it simply cannot be left aside. Otto was not only an Austrian prince through his father Leopold III, but through his mother Agnes also a member of two

---

[6] See above all K. J. Heilig, "Ostrom und das Deutsche Reich um die Mitte des 12. Jahrhunderts: Die Erhebung Österreichs zum Herzogtum 1156 und das Bündnis zwischen Byzanz und dem Westreich," in *Kaisertum und Herzogsgewalt im Zeitalter Friedrichs I.*, MGH Schriften 9 (Leipzig 1944) 1-220.

[7] This is particularly true for the recent works of G. Tellenbach and his school; cf., for instance, Tellenbach, *Zur Bedeutung der Personenforschung für die Erkenntnis des früheren Mittelalters* (Freiburger Universitätsreden, Neue Folge, 25 [Freiburg i. B. 1951]), with literature, also *idem*, "Der Liber Memorialis von Remiremont," *Deutsches Archiv* 25 (1969) 64ff.

[7a] For a deepened concept of prosopography, cf. the recent article by L. Stone, "Prosopography," *Daedalus* (Winter 1971): *Historical Studies Today* 46ff.

imperial families, and in addition, as bishop of Freising, a prince of the Holy Roman Empire in his own right.

On almost every page of both of Otto of Freising's two historical works,[8] the Roman Empire is explicitly propounded or implicitly presupposed as the framework within which, or at least in relation to which, God had meant the peoples of the earth to live since the Emperor Augustus, and even more so since Constantine the Great. Yet, this positive attitude toward empire was, as we shall soon see, modified by a different one and also was affected by a conflict of loyalties: for church and papacy demanded and willingly received Otto's foremost allegiance, even when they clashed with the empire, as they did in the time of his grandfather Henry IV, in the Investiture Struggle.

If in every creative work of historical writing the seminal idea that enlivens the whole comes from the center of strong and formative personal experiences, this is true to a singularly high degree in the case of the earlier of Otto's two histories, which he composed in the traditional form of a world chronicle, but which he called most often *On the Two Cities*. He thus expressed his dependence on Saint Augustine's conception of history in the latter's famous work *On the City of God*, which also deals with two cities or mystical societies, one of the elect of God, the other of those who, because of their complete absorption in this world, will ultimately have no share in the world to come. Now, just as the fall of Rome to the Visigoths in 410 had stimulated Augustine's work by confirming his sceptical or at best neutral attitude toward political structures, including even the Christianized Roman Empire, so the apparent ascendancy of the papacy over the German Kingdom and empire, ever since Gregory VII had condemned Henry IV, made Otto feel that the whole imperial idea was faced with a grave crisis, in which he found it impossible to distinguish right and wrong from one another with certainty. There exists, however, one principal and great difference between the North African bishop of Hippo around 400 and the Austrian-Bavarian bishop of Freising around 1150, if we look at them as historians. They both strove to see historical events in the light of eternity, yet only for Otto was world history also family history. The happenings in his own family most probably confirmed an Augustinian bent of mind and led him toward poignant realizations and ever-repeated assertions of the ineluctable mutability of all things and of the more or less guilty entanglements of the main actors in a great historical drama, among whom were those closest to him.[9]

---

[8] These are the *Chronica* or *Historia de duabus civitatibus*, ed. A. Hofmeister, *Scriptores rerum germanicarum* (1912), and the *Gesta Friderici I. Imperatoris*, ed. B. von Simson (G. Waitz), *Script. rer. germ.* (1912), of which only the first two books are by Otto, the last two by his chaplain Rahewin.

[9] The literature on Otto of Freising, his life, his works, and the relation of his thought to that of Saint Augustine is very rich. One of the best recent syntheses is the last chapter in A. Funkenstein, *Heilsplan und natürliche Entwicklung* (Munich 1965) 93ff. See also R.

Let us put ourselves into the place of an exceedingly intelligent and sensitive adolescent—the young Otto, first in the monastery of Canons at Klosterneuburg, which had been richly endowed by his father; a little later, when he was fifteen or sixteen years old, as a student at Paris, where he seems to have been influenced by the great Augustinian Canon Regular Hugh of Saint Victor; then, at the age of nineteen or twenty, entering the Cistercian monastery of Morimond; and in his mid-twenties elevated to the bishopric of Freising—let us imagine the state of mind of this youth and young man when confronted with the fact that his own father and lord, Leopold III, had at the moment of a crucial battle left the army of Otto's maternal grandfather, the old Emperor Henry IV, and thus helped to decide the success of the emperor's rebellious son, the young Henry V. Leopold's action was not simply an act of high treason; it was at least in part due to "reasons of state" and "reasons of church." Nevertheless, Otto himself tells us that Henry V won Leopold III over to his side by promising him the hand of his own sister Agnes, who indeed was to become Otto's mother.[10] It is thus not very surprising that in his book *On the Two Cities*, exactly in the middle between his lament about the civil and family war that pitted Henry IV and Henry V against one another and his dry and factual report about his own father's change of allegiance and the arrangement of the marriage out of which he himself was born, he inserts one of his lengthy considerations on contempt for this world, the *mundus* in Latin, which, he says, should with Augustine rather be called the *in-mundus*, meaning the impure.[11] With all due caution one might surmise here religious sublimation on Otto's part of a somewhat problematic father-son relationship—it is, of course, a commonplace of history and literature that such problems have often been closely connected with the realities of rulership. I shall have to return to this point.

Folz, "Sur les traces de saint Augustin: Otton de Freising, historien des deux cités," *Collectanea Ordinis Cisterciensium Reformatorum* 20 (1958) 327ff.; furthermore the introductions and bibliographies to the following translations of Otto's works: *The Two Cities*, trans. C. C. Mierow, Columbia Records of Civilization (CRC) 9 (New York 1928), *The Deeds of Frederick Barbarossa*, trans. Mierow, CRC 49 (New York 1953), *Chronik oder die Geschichte der zwei Staaten*, trans. A. Schmidt, intro. W. Lammers, Ausgewählte Quellen zur Geschichte des deutschen Mittelalters 16 (Darmstadt 1960). See also the articles on Otto of Freising by E. F. Otto, J. Spörl, and J. Koch collected in *Geschichtsdenken und Geschichtsbild im Mittelalter*, ed. W. Lammers, Wege der Forschung 21 (Darmstadt 1965), and by A. Lhotsky in his *Aufsätze und Vorträge*, ed. H. Wagner and H. Koller, 1 (Vienna 1970).

[10] *Chronica* 7.9 (n. 8 above) 321.

[11] *Ibid.* 320: "Nonne tam inauditum, tam inhumanum hoc mundi factum ad contemptum sui solum nos provocare posset? Numquid non ipse mundus—vel potius iuxta Augustinum [cf. *Sermones* 105.6(8), PL 38.622: Quid strepis, o munde immunde?] immundus—sic amatores suos falsis delectationibus pellectos decipit, huiusmodi commertia inherentibus sibi tribuit ac ad ultimum transeundo in interitum trahit?"

It is typical for Otto and his age that he withdrew from the world to become a Cistercian monk, and also induced his father to found the first Cistercian monastery in Austria, Heiligenkreuz;[12] it is equally typical that he could not for long avoid becoming a bishop and remained involved in the combined affairs of his family, of Austria, and of the Holy Roman Empire all through his life. Thus, we know from the bishop of Freising himself that in the complicated sequence of events which preceded the granting of the *Privilegium Minus*, he acted as a mediator between his brother Henry Jasomirgott and their nephew, Emperor Frederick Barbarossa,[13] who was the grandson of their mother Agnes through an earlier marriage of hers with the ancestor of the Hohenstaufen dynasty. This emperor, especially in the beginnings of his reign, brought about a spectacular recovery of imperial power and prestige; this change is reflected in the second of Otto's historical works, the *Deeds of the Emperor Frederick I*, which he did not live to complete, as well as in the letter to Barbarossa with which he prefaced the copy of the work *On the Two Cities*, which he dedicated to him. Nevertheless, a basic attitude is common to both works, as regards history in general, and in particular concerning the function of a Christian empire. The main function is for Otto the establishment, maintenance, and if necessary reestablishment of peace—a continuation on a higher level of the pre-Christian *pax romana*. But even when peace was achieved, as seemed to have been the case in the first years of Frederick Barbarossa's reign, such achievement does not seem to have changed Otto's deep conviction of the preliminary and provisional character of even the best moments of history. According to Otto, a good emperor's felicitous government can bring about a period of relative peace. Yet, he never took back the tragic and paradoxical view of empire and rulership which he had expressed in many parts of the *Chronica*: even if it is

[12] Founded in the last year of Leopold III's life (d. 1136). Leopold had also in 1133, shortly after Otto had become a Cistercian, replaced the secular canons of Klosterneuburg by canons regular of Saint Augustine. Otto had been educated at Klosterneuburg and had been nominal provost there, before in his mid-teens he had left for Paris. It is possible that the canons regular of Klosterneuburg, just as a little later the Cistercians of Heiligenkreuz, were introduced on the suggestion of the monastically oriented and reform-minded Otto; cf. L. Grill, S. O. Cist., "Bildung und Wissenschaft im Leben Bischof Ottos von Freising," *Analecta Sacri Ordinis Cisterciensis* 14 (1958), esp. 282ff., 306f. It is also possible that the first establishment of a collegiate church in Klosterneuburg, where Leopold III had established his residence shortly after his marriage to Agnes in 1106 (cf. K. Öttinger, "Die Babenbergerpfalz in Klosterneuburg," *Mitteilungen des Instituts für Österreichische Geschichtsforschung* [MIÖG] 55 [1944] 156ff.), had been intended as an act of reconciliation on behalf of the soul of Henry IV, who had died excommunicated by the pope, and also as an act of reparation for Leopold's breach of faith with the old emperor; thus H. Maschek, "Kaiser Heinrich IV. und die Gründung des Chorherrenstiftes Klosterneuburg," MIÖG 47 (1933) 186ff.

[13] Cf. *Gesta Friderici I.* 2.41 (n. 8 above) 151.

true that the Roman, and even more so the Christian Roman, Empire has brought peace, it has never lastingly separated itself from that "lust for power," that *libido dominandi*, which already Augustine had condemned as dehumanizing in the extreme.[14]

Otto of Freising's father Leopold III had after the death of his brother-in-law Henry V refused the German and imperial crown, and Leopold's son could hardly have foreseen that later on Austria would actually fall heir to the imperial dignity. Yet, as we shall observe presently, the very problems of imperial ideology which Otto recognized in a general way and applied to his understanding of the Holy Roman Empire were actualized within the further history of medieval and modern Austria itself. We must now turn to the planning stage of the Hapsburg Empire from Rudolf I in the late thirteenth century to his great-grandson Rudolf IV in the middle of the fourteenth.

I must be very brief about Rudolf I. By origin a count in southwestern Germany and Switzerland, he became the first German king and prospective emperor of the Hapsburg dynasty in 1273 and was able to win the Austrian lands for his house. Yet, whereas Hapsburg rule over Austria was to remain continuous, this was not immediately to be the case as far as the German kingship and imperial dignity were concerned, for already in the second generation after Rudolf I they were to be lost for more than a hundred years, first to

---

[14] For Otto of Freising's views at the end of his life on the relationship between peace and power it is useful to compare the following passages with one another: Prologue to the *Gesta Friderici I* (n. 8 above) 9: "Post turbulentiam praeteritorum non solum pacis inaudita reluxit serenitas, sed et . . . ob victoriosissimi principis virtutes tanta Romani imperii pollet auctoritas," and the letters of dedication and introduction addressed to Frederick Barbarossa and Rainald of Dassel which Otto placed before the *Chronica* when he sent it to the emperor: these letters attempt to explain the somber mood in which he had written the *Chronicle*, before the "peace" brought about by Frederick, "qui re et nomine pacificus" (*Chronica*, Letter to Frederick I [n. 8 above] 2); and yet, in spite of Otto's changed mood, he had in no way changed his view of the fragility of terrestial peace—cf. *Gesta Friderici I.*, Prologue, 10: "Firma quies, si tamen rebus caducis aliqua fides adhibenda est" (see also *ibid*. 1.5, 21f., the philosophical disquisition about the instability of the human composite)—and had never found reason to abandon his certainty about the ineluctable end of the Roman Empire—cf. the letter to Rainald, *Chronica* 6: "Ostendi hoc, quod de ipso [i.e., of the Roman Empire] dicitur, quia a lapide exciso de monte plenarie subvertendum sit [cf. Daniel 2.34], usque in finem temporum iuxta Methodium [cf. Ps.-Methodius, ed. E. Sackur, *Sibyllinische Texte und Forschungen* (Halle 1898) 60ff.] expectandum estimans." For the establishment of the *pax romana* first by terror and then by the *pax inaudita saeculis* of Augustus—in preparation for the coming of Christ, the *vere pacificus, qui omnia quae in coelo et quae in terra sunt pacificavit*—cf. *Chronica* 3, Prologue, and *ibid*. 3.6, 132ff. and 141ff., and 2.51, 129; the *libido dominandi* is mentioned in connection with the civil war between Henry IV and Henry V, *Chronica* 7.9, 328, line 28, cf. also Augustine, *De civitate Dei* 19.15: "Cum saevissimo dominatu vastet corda mortalium . . . libido ipsa dominandi." Cf. the old but still illuminating article by E. Bernheim, "Der Charakter Ottos von Freising und seiner Werke," MIÖG 6 (1886) 1ff.

the Wittelsbach of Bavaria, then to the Luxemburg who had established themselves in Bohemia.

Nevertheless, there was one descendant of Ruldolf I, his greatgrandson Rudolf IV (fig. 2), who refused to accept the seemingly irreversible eclipse of the imperial rank of the Hapsburg dynasty and lands, that is to say, of the House of Austria, as this familial-territorial complex was called from the mid-fourteenth century onward.[15] Rudolf IV is called "The Founder," chiefly because he laid the foundations of the Gothic choir of Saint Stephen's Cathedral in Vienna, also because in 1365 he founded the University of Vienna. This same ruler added Tirol to the combined territories of Austria, Styria, Carinthia, and Carniola, thus almost completing the extent of medieval Austria before circa 1500. In a deeper sense, Rudolf's surname is justified because this brilliant, short-lived young ruler was the true founder of an imperial mystique[16] that after another hundred years was to carry Hapsburg not only back to the throne of the Holy Roman Empire, but also forward to many another throne, was indeed to form the greater Austria that existed from the end of the Middle Ages to the cessation of its self-identification with the Hapsburg dynasty.

The Rudolfian mystique found its most spectacular, but by no means sole, expression in forgeries of considerable boldness which were perpetrated in the ducal chancery in the very year following Rudolf IV's accession and without any doubt under his personal inspiration. These are the five famous so-called Austrian "Charters of Liberty," among which two are of particular significance.[17] One is the *Privilegium Maius*, the "Major Privilege," supposedly of Frederick Barbarossa, a forgery by which Rudolf IV meant to replace the *Privilegium Minus* that I discussed earlier.[18] The content of this forged charter surpasses even the great concessions that had actually been made

[15] For the dynastic, and later also territorial, connotations of this concept, cf. A. Lhotsky, "Was heisst 'Haus Österreich,'" *Anzeiger der Österreichischen Akademie der Wissenschaften*, Phil.-Hist. Klasse 93 (1956) 155ff, reprinted in Lhotsky, *Aufsätze und Vorträge* (n. 9 above) 344ff.

[16] Cf. above all E. K. Winter, *Rudolph IV. von Österreich* 1 (Vienna 1934), especially 340ff., the chapter "Vorbarocke Staatsmystik."

[17] The modern scientific critique of these documents began with W. Wattenbach, "Die österreichischen Freiheitsbriefe," *Archiv für Kunde österreichischer Geschichts-Quellen* 8 (1852) 77ff., and A. Huber, "Über die Entstehungszeit der österreichischen Freiheitsbriefe," *Sitzungsberichte der Kaiserlichen Akademie der Wissenschaften*, Phil.-Hist. Klasse 34 (Vienna 1860) 17ff. Cf. A. Lhotsky, *Privilegium Maius* (Vienna 1957); see also *idem*, "Epilegomena zu den österreichischen Freiheitsbriefen," in *Aufsätze und Vorträge* (n. 9 above) 1.265ff. Lhotsky has shown how these formal forgeries to a considerable part represent legitimate rights or claims of mid-fourteenth century Austria; he has also some very instructive remarks on the mental and cultural background of late medieval forgeries and fictions.

[18] This very skillfully executed forgery is still preserved in the Vienna Haus-, Hof-, und Staatsarchiv. The most recent edition of the *Privilegium Maius* (just as of the *Minus*, see above) is to be found in *Urkundenbuch* (n. 5 above) 151ff., no. 804.

by Barbarossa to Henry Jasomirgott in the authentic "Minor Privilege." Among other things, we now find such important symbolical claims as that of equality with the Princes Electors of the empire: in terms of the *Maius* the duke was to be *unus de palatinis archiducibus*—this is the origin of the title "Archduke" which was finally to prevail as the designation of the rulers of the Austrian lands;[19] there is also the claim to wear a quasi-royal crown with points on the base and an arc with a cross on top over the ducal hat (cf. fig. 2);[20] furthermore, there are constitutional innovations or at least developments of earlier claims or rights, such as the indivisibility of the Hapsburg territories and dispensation of its ruler from attendance at the emperor's court as well as limitation of military aid to the token participation of twelve men in wars against Hungary.[21] All these claims and pretensions were governed by one idea, that of the imperial rank of the Hapsburg dynasty and through it of Austria, the "shield and heart of the Holy Roman Empire," as Rudolf IV called it in the *Privilegium Maius*.[22] Rudolf believed in an imperishable right of his house to the imperial crown, in spite of its temporary loss to other princes. This right he derived both from the king-emperorship of his ancestor Rudolf I and from a typical late medieval and early Renaissance way

[19] Cf. Lhotsky, *Privilegium Maius* (n. 17 above) 22ff. and 28, also for the connection of Rudolf's archducal claim with the traditional right of the Duke of Carinthia—united with Austria since 1335—to be "Hunting Master" of the Holy Roman Empire; Rudolf called himself *archymagister venatorum* on his great seal (cf. the following note) and thus established his claim to be of a rank comparable to that of the other highest dignitaries of the empire, the Princes Electors, who were the holders of the "arch-offices" (*Erzämter*), such as that of the Archchancellors, and the like.

[20] A crown with points and arc occurs on Rudolf IV's famous contemporary portrait in the Diocesan Museum of Saint Stephen's in Vienna (fig. 2); a similar crown can be seen on the reverse of Rudolf's double seal, where he is shown as Arch-Hunting Master (see the preceding note); this seal is discussed and illustrated by Winter (n. 16 above) 372ff. and fig. XIII. The arc is particularly significant since it is characteristic of the crown of the Holy Roman Empire itself; cf. P. E. Schramm and collaborators, *Herrschaftszeichen und Staatsymbolik* 2, MGH Schriften 13 (Stuttgart 1955) 564ff.; J. Deér, "Die abendländische Kaiserkrone des Hochmittelalters," *Schweizer Beiträge zur allgemeinen Geschichte* 7 (1949) esp. 75ff. That the crown of Rudolf IV has points is less surprising in view of certain thirteenth-century attempts to raise Austria to the status of a kingdom, in the age of Emperor Frederick II and of his contemporary and namesake, the last Babenberg Duke Frederick II (d. 1246); cf. Lhotsky, *Privilegium Maius* (n. 17 above) 23f. The archducal hat of Austria, preserved at Klosterneuburg, dates from the early seventeenth century, whereas the archducal hat of Styria at the Museum Joanneum in Graz dates from the mid-fifteenth century, the reign of Frederick III (Frederick V as duke and archduke, see about him below); cf. W. Pauker and E. Kris. "Der österreichische Herzogshut im Stifte Klosterneuburg," *Jahrbuch der Kunsthistorischen Sammlungen in Wien*, N. F. 7 (1933) 229ff.

[21] Cf. Lhotsky, *Privilegium Maius* (n. 17 above) 22f.

[22] Cf. *Privilegium Maius*, ed. Fichtenau (n. 5 above) 154: "Terram Austrie, que clippeus et cor sacri Romani imperii esse dinoscitur."

of dynastic thinking in terms of "mythological" genealogies that linked the origins of dynasties to the remotest past, especially to Jewish, Trojan, or Roman antiquity.[23] Other royal or princely houses, and even lesser nobility too, used such myths to enhance their dignity, but only Rudolf IV had the daring to transform fantasy into direct political action. This he did in another of his forged "charters of liberty," the so-called *Heinricianum*.[24] This purports to be a charter of Emperor Henry IV for one of the early Babenberg rulers of Austria, and into it Rudolf and his helpers did not hesitate to insert alleged privileges of Julius Caesar and of Nero for Austria. It is worthwhile to quote the beginning of the Caesar insert:

> We Julius, Imperator, we Caesar and worshipper of the gods, we supreme Augustus of the imperial land, we the sustainer of the entire universe, to the region of the eastern country [meaning Austria] and to its inhabitants, the grace of Rome and our peace.

Anybody who knows anything about ancient Rome and has read anything written by Julius Caesar will immediately see that the almost baroque style of the sentence quoted completely excludes the origin that it claims. The sequel is even more bizarre. The forger makes the great Julius command the Austrians to obey his own uncle, a senator. It is to him that quite anachronistically Caesar is supposed to have given Austria as a fief, or more exactly to him and his descendants, who are declared to be the most intimate counselors of Rome and Caesar, without whose advice nothing important may be done.[25]

---

[23] The fabulous genealogy of Austrian princes in Stainreuter's late fourteenth-century "Austrian Chronicle of the 95 Reigns" goes probably back to Rudolf IV—here Jewish and pagan ancestors are followed by Christian Romans and Germans; cf. K. J. Heilig, "Leopold Stainreuter von Wien, der Verfasser der sogenannten Österreichischen Chronik von den 95 Herrschaften," MIÖG 47 (1933) 225ff., especially 236ff. Yet, Rudolf IV also knew that other genealogical tradition according to which the Hapsburg had come from Rome and were related to the Colonna, who in turn had for centuries claimed descent from the Julian emperors; cf. A. Lhotsky, "Apis Colonna: Fabeln und Theorien über die Abkunft der Habsburger," MIÖG 55 (1944) 171ff., esp. 191f. reprinted in Lhotsky, *Aufsätze und Vorträge* (n. 9 above) 2 (1971) 7ff., esp. 32f. (with additions).

[24] This alleged charter of Henry IV for Margrave Ernst of Austria is likewise preserved in the Vienna Haus-, Hof-, und Staatsarchiv. K. Helleiner, "Ein Deperditum von Heinrich IV.," MIÖG 41 (1926) 412ff., has proved that the model for the forgery was a lost Diploma of Henry IV, which was probably a simple donation for the same Ernst of Austria, issued on the very date—October 4, 1058—which was used in the forgery. For the text of the *Heinricianum*, cf. again *Urkundenbuch* 1.4 (n. 5 above) 20ff., no. 576.

[25] Cf. *loc. cit.* 22: "Nos Iulius imperator, nos cesar et cultor deorum, nos supremus terre imperialis augustus, nos sustentator orbis universi plage Orientalis Terre suisque incolis Romanam veniam et nostram pacem. Vobis mandamus per nostrum triumphum, quod vos illi precelso senatori nostro avunculo pareatis, quoniam nos eidem et suis heredibus sueque domus descendentibus donavimus vos in feodotariam possessionem perpetue tenendum, sibi et suis posteris imperpetuum relinquentes, quod nullam potestatem super eos

The insert of Nero, who somewhat comically styles himself "friend of the gods,"[26] was an even worse insult to those beginnings of modern historical sense and criticism which accompanied the first phase of Renaissance humanism in the fourteenth century. It was easy for a Petrarch, whose expert judgment Rudolf IV's father-in-law, the Luxemburg king of Bohemia and Emperor Charles IV, had sought, to unmask these forgeries and to pour derision on the Roman inserts.[27] And yet, Rudolf's appeal to ancient Roman origins for Austria was obviously an expression of the same new Romanism that also animated Petrarch.

The mixture of medieval tradition and Renaissance innovation which in Austria had crystallized in the precocious personality of Rudolf IV, did not at first survive strongly and did not return in full force until that period of further transition to modern times which extended from the mid-fifteenth to the mid-sixteenth century, a period during which, as far as the House of Austria was concerned, Frederick III and his more immediate descendants were the imperial protagonists.

It is no accident that Frederick III confirmed the *Privilegium Maius* and other privileges forged by Rudolf IV.[28] Though that relatively inactive, but very durable, long-lived man could hardly have been more different in character from his adventuresome predecessor, he did take over a goodly part of Rudolf IV's political symbolism[29] and above all shared with him the quasi-religious conviction of Austria's predestination to imperial rulership which he had the good luck to see become a reality.

Along with serious shortcomings, Frederick III all through his life displayed certain remarkable qualities.[30] There can be no doubt that the e-

---

statuere debemus. Nos ei et dictis suis successoribus largimur omnes utilitates Terre Orientalis memorate, insuper nos eundem avunculum nostrum et omnes eius successores assumpmimus [sic] consiliarium in secretissimum consilium Romanum taliter, quod deinceps nullum perpetuum negocium sive causa fieri debet suo sine scitu. Datum Rome capitali mundi die Veneris, regni nostri anno primo et exaccionis auri anno primo."

[26] Cf. *ibid.* 22: "Nos Nero, amicus deorum et fidei eorum propalator, preceptor potestatis Romane, imperator et cesar et augustus . . ."

[27] Cf. Petrarch to Charles IV, March 21, 1361, *Epist. de rebus senilibus* 16 (15).5, ed. P. Piur, *Petrarcas Briefwechsel mit deutschen Zeitgenossen* = K. Burdach, *Vom Mittelalter zur Reformation* 7 (Berlin 1933) 114ff. Even before receiving Petrarch's letter, Charles IV had rejected the alleged letters of Julius Caesar and Nero and curtailed many of the other claims of his son-in-law's "charters of liberty;" cf. the protocol concerning them of December, 1360, published by S. Steinherz, "Karl IV. und die österreichischen Freiheitsbriefe," MIÖG 9 (1888) 63ff., esp. 79.

[28] Cf. Lhotsky, *Privilegium Maius* (n. 17 above) 33f.

[29] Cf. Lhotsky, "AEIOV" (n. 32 below) 174, n. 88.

[30] The best character sketch of Frederick III is still that of Leopold von Ranke, *Deutsche Geschichte im Zeitalter der Reformation* 1, in Ranke, *Historische Meisterwerke* 19-20 (Hamburg n.d.) 52f. See also A. Lhotsky, "Kaiser Friedrich III.," *Aufsätze und Vorträge* (n. 9 above) 2 (1971) 119ff.

quanimity, the dignity, and the steadfastness that he could muster under extremely adverse circumstances were animated by consciousness of his imperial as well as dynastic vocation. A case in point is his journey to Rome for his marriage to Eleanor of Portugal and for the imperial coronation itself, through which the Holy Roman Empire definitely returned to Hapsburg to remain with it to that empire's end in 1806; Frederick III needed much personal courage and sureness of himself and of a higher mission for his house to leave Austria at that time, when his rule there was very gravely endangered and almost all his counselors advised against his departure for Rome.[31]

It is now time to discuss briefly Frederick III's famous device AEIOV, the meaning of which was greatly clarified twenty years ago by Alphons Lhotsky in a fundamental study.[32] These five vowels appear on many buildings, works of art, and books that Frederick had ordered to be made or which simply belonged to him. I mention only two examples: the Burgundian cup in the Vienna Kunsthistorisches Museum, a gift of Charles the Bold to the emperor, where each of the five vowels is held by an angel (fig. 3),[33] and the tomb of Frederick III in Saint Stephen's at Vienna, where the AEIOV is placed on a scroll near the head of his reclining statue (fig. 4).[34] Frederick himself mentions this device at the very beginning of a notebook that he started as a young man in 1437, after his return from Jerusalem. The autograph of the notebook is still preserved in the National Library at Vienna (Cod. Vindob. Palat. 2674) and it can be seen (fig. 5) that Frederick on fol. 1*r has entered with his own hand a German and a Latin interpretation of the five vowels, each of which is taken to signify the first letter of a word. The German form reads as follows:

> Als erdreich ist osterrich vnderthan
> (meaning in English: All the earth is subject to Austria),

and the Latin form:

---

[31] Cf. Aeneas Silvius (Piccolomini), *Historia rerum Friderici III. Imperatoris* (= *Historia Australis*), ed. A. Kollár, *Analecta monumentorum omnis aevi Vindobonensia* 2 (Vienna 1762) 226f.; Thomas Ebendorfer, *Chronica Austriae*, ed. A. Lhotsky, *Scriptores rerum germanicarum*, N. S. 13 (Berlin 1967) 414. See also Fürst E. M. Lichnowsky, *Geschichte des Hauses Habsburg* 6 (Vienna 1842) 102, J. Chmel, *Geschichte Kaiser Friedrichs IV. und seines Sohnes Maximilian I.* 2 (Hamburg 1843) 662ff.

[32] Cf. A. Lhotsky, "AEIOV: Die 'Devise' Kaiser Friedrichs III. und sein Notizbuch," MIÖG 60 (1952) 155ff., reprinted in Lhotsky, *Aufsätze und Vorträge* (n. 30 above) 2.164ff.; an earlier, illustrated version of Lhotsky's study was published in *Jahrbuch der Kunsthistorischen Sammlungen in Wien*, N.F. 13 (1944) 71ff.

[33] Cf. Lhotsky in *Jahrbuch* (n. 32 above) 75.

[34] Cf. F. Wimmer and E. Klebel, *Das Grabmal Friedrichs III.* (Vienna 1924).

Austriae est imperare orbi vniuerso
(in English: Austria's mission is to rule over the whole earth).[35]

On another page of the notebook (fol 2r) Frederick entered another interpretation of AEIOV, as part of a Latin distich:

En, amor ellectis, iniustis ordinor ultor
   Sic Fridericus ego rengna (*sic*) mea rego
(in English:
Behold, by the elect I am loved, for the unjust, avenger ordained.
   Thus Frederick, I, over my realms do rule).[36]

There existed still other contemporary interpretations, for instance, one
on the above-mentioned Burgundian cup:

Aquila eius iuste omnia vincet
(His eagle will rightly conquer everything).[37]

It is uncertain if any of these interpretations was invented by Frederick
himself;[38] the five vowels originally may have had an even more esoteric
meaning for him.

It should also be noted that these vowels are almost always accompanied
by a vertical and a horizontal line with a loop—a particularly clear example
can be seen in a manuscript of the year 1446 in the Vienna Haus-, Hof-, und
Staatsarchiv, the so-called "Handregistratur" of Frederick III (fig. 6)[39]—the
vowels are thus visually tied together. In this connection it may not be without interest to recall that according to Dante's treatise *The Banquet* a linking
together of the five vowels symbolizes *auctoritas*.[40]

---

[35] Ed. Lhotsky, "AEIOV" (n. 32 above) 193, no. 101, 102; cf. *ibid*. 166.

[36] Ed. Lhotsky, *ibid*. 190, no. 61; cf. *ibid*. 167f.

[37] Cf. *ibid*. 169. I consider it possible that Frederick himself also used AEIOV as a crypto-
gram for AETOV or AIETOV, i.e., belonging to the eagle; on his tomb, for instance (see
above), the five vowels appear together with the "old-Austrian" five eagle shield and with
the eagle of the Holy Roman Empire.

[38] We also know of an ironical "graffito," which a detractor or enemy of Frederick III
wrote above the five vowels on or in the Castle (*purkh*) of Vienna:
               Aller erst ist Osterreich verdorben
            (Before all [other lands?] Austria is ruined).
Cf. Lhotsky, "AEIOV" (n. 32 above) 168.

[39] Fig. 6, after I. Zibermayr, *Das Oberösterreichische Landesarchiv in Linz*, ed. 3 (Linz
1950) plate before p. 1.

[40] The reference to Dante I again owe to Lhotsky's study, "AEIOV" 171. Cf. Dante,
Convicio 4.6: "È dunque da sapere che 'autoritade' non è altro che 'atto d'autore.' Questo
vocabulo, cioè 'autore' . . . può discendere da due principii: l'uno si è d'uno verbo molto
lasciato da l'uso in gramatica, che significa tanto quanto 'legare parole,' cioè 'auieo.'
E chi ben guarda lui, ne la sua prima voce, apertamente vedrà che elli stesso lo dimostra,

Whether or not Frederick III knew the Dante text or other sources and adapted earlier meanings for his own purpose, it is certain that the AEIOV, in a way that we can no longer exactly ascertain,[41] served as a kind of shorthand signature in which the emperor's conception of himself and his vocation found expression.

Yet it was only from the Baroque period onward that the symbolism of the five vowels as denoting an imperishable and unique mission of the House and Empire of Austria played the role of a popular political prophecy that claimed a deceptive certainty.[42] Even at the end of old Austria when it was only half believed, the device lived on in that half-real way that was so characteristic of the last phase of the Hapsburg Empire.

We shall return to these matters later. At present I can only refer in most general and abbreviated terms to the almost incredible widening that the medieval idea of empire experienced in the three quarters of a century that comprise the end of Frederick III's reign and the reigns of his son Maximilian I and of the latter's grandsons Charles V and Ferdinand I. Let me simply recall a few basic facts and events. In the late seventies of the fifteenth century Maximilian married Maria, the heiress of Burgundy and the Netherlands; this marriage had been arranged by his father Frederick III, but only through his own youthful impetus and knightly enterprise could Maximilian after Maria's early death secure for their son Philip what is today Belgium, Holland, and Luxembourg. This Philip, surnamed the Handsome, died before

---

che solo di legame di parole è fatto, cioè di sole cinque vocali, che sono anima e legame d'ogni parole, e composto d'esse per modo volubile, a figurare imagine di legame. Chè, cominciando da l'A, ne l'U quindi si rivolve, e viene diritto per I ne l'E, quindi si rivolve e torna ne l'O; sì che veramente imagina questa figura: A, E, I, O, U, la quale è figura di legame. E in quanto 'autore' viene e discende da questo verbo, si prende solo per li poeti, che con l'arte musaica le loro parole hanno legate. . . ." As can be seen, Dante in this passage speaks of literary authorship; nevertheless, he does so in a context of both imperial and philosophical authority. The explicit mention of the AEIOV makes it seem not impossible that Frederick III knew this Dante text, though one can in no way be certain. Already in John of Salisbury's times, the five vowels seem to have been linked to rulership, according to what the great twelfth-century humanist ironically calls a spiritual sense. Cf. *Metalogicon* 1.3, ed. C. C. I. Webb (Oxford 1929) 10, esp. line 18: "potestates uocalium quinque iura regnorum"; Webb in a note raises the possibility that the second vowel in each of the then current terms for the "regalia": *pedaticum, moneta, comitatus, theloneus, portus* (cf., for instance, Otto of Freising's continuator Rahewin, *Gesta Friderici I.* 3.47 [n. 8 above] 223) may have served such artificial speculations.

[41] For various cryptographic, arithmological, and magic propensities of Frederick III and his age, which may have played a role, cf. Lhotsky, "AEIOV" (n. 32 above) passim.

[42] This conception goes back to the years after the middle of the seventeenth century, when the above-mentioned notebook of Frederick III—which he had apparently lost— was recovered and became part of the Imperial Library; the Prefect of the library, Peter Lambeck, and many others after him were convinced that Frederick III's insertions, which connect the AEIOV to Austria's destiny (cf. above), give the original and only meaning of the device; cf. Lhotsky, "AEIOV."

his father did, but not before Maximilian had married him to Joan, daughter
of the so-called Catholic kings, Ferdinand of Aragon and Isabel of Castile,
thus acquiring for his older grandson and successor as emperor, Charles V,
the Spanish kingdoms and their European and overseas dependencies. Maximilian's younger grandson from this same Spanish marriage was Ferdinand I;
Ferdinand was later to inherit territories situated almost at the opposite
end of Europe, Bohemia and Hungary—and this was the result of a marriage
contract that goes back to the last years of Frederick III.

No wonder that Maximilian I was deeply interested in his familial ties,
past and present, and in all they could mean to him and his house. Many
of the vast literary and pictorial enterprises that were undertaken under
his auspices[43] were animated by a characteristic mixture of medieval feudal
ideals and the Renaissance cult of fame.[44] Maximilian had his humanists
compose elaborate genealogies that were then translated into pictorial family
trees—for instance, the monumental one in Castle Tratzberg in Tirol (fig. 7),
which was copied soon after 1520 from a Hapsburg family tree of the time
of Maximilian—or incorporated into graphic works, for which he enlisted
some of the great artists of the time such as Albrecht Dürer and Hans Burgkmair. In general, the emperor made the woodcutter and the printer cooperate
in his political and at the same time somewhat fantastic propaganda for
the House of the Hapsburg, who he was convinced were descendants of the
ancient Trojans via the Franks. Maximilian rejected earlier beliefs according
to which the Hapsburg originated in Rome (see above 443f.); therefore, the
woodcuts of his genealogy, which he made Burgkmair execute for him, begin
with Hector of Troy (fig. 8).[45]

---

[43] In general cf. L. Baldass, *Der Künstlerkreis Kaiser Maximilians* (Vienna 1923).

[44] Cf., for instance. E. Chmelarz, "Die Ehrenpforte des Kaisers Maximilian I.," *Jahrbuch der Kunsthistorischen Sammlungen des Allerhöchsten Kaiserhauses* 4 (1886) 289. The
same mixture of cultural trends still inspired the artistic and literary activities of Maximilian's great-grandson, Archduke Ferdinand of Tirol, the founder of the collections of
Ambras; cf. G. Ladner, "Zur Porträtsammlung des Erzherzogs Ferdinand von Tirol,"
MIÖG 47 (1933) 471ff. and 49 (1936) 367ff.

[45] For Maximilian's humanists, and especially his historians, such as Sunthaim, Cus-
pinianus, Mennel (Manlius), Stabius, and others, cf. A. Lhotsky, *Quellenkunde zur mittelalterlichen Geschichte Österreichs* = MIÖG, Erg. Bd. 19 (Vienna 1963) 493ff. For the still
extant Maximilianean family trees and later derivations from them, cf. Lhotsky, *ibid.* 94;
F. Kenner, "Die Porträtsammlung des Erzherzogs Ferdinand von Tirol," *Jahrb. d. Kunsthist.
Samml. d. Allerhöchsten Kaiserhauses* 14 (1893) 61ff.; Ladner (n. 44 above) 47.478; Anna
(Gräfin) Coréth, "Ein Wappenbuch Maximilians I." in *Festschrift zur Feier des zweihundert-
jährigen Bestandes des Haus-, Hof- und Staatsarchivs* 1 (Vienna 1949) 293, n. 8; see also
the last named author's "Dynastisch-politische Ideen Kaiser Maximilians I.: 1. Die Bedeutung der fränkisch-trojanischen Abstammungstheorie für Kaiser Maximilian I.," *Mitteilungen des Österreichischen Staatsarchivs* 3 (1950) 81ff. For the great graphic sequence
on the genealogy of Maximilian I in woodcuts after drawings by Hans Burgkmair cf. S.
Laschitzer, "Die Genealogie des Kaisers Maximilian I.," *Jahrb. d. Kunsthist. Samml. d.*

The dazzling prospect of a Hapsburg world empire—which because of its overseas possessions would be immeasurably greater than even that of Charlemagne—found expression in the device that a humanist invented for Charles V. It consists of the words *Plus ultra* or *Plus outre*, and an image of the columns of Hercules, those ancient symbols of Gibraltar, which were now being transcended by far (figs. 9 and 10).[46]

It is often assumed that still another well-known device of Hapsburg imperial ideology was also created as a by-product of that family's rise to hegemonial power and prestige in the period around 1500. This is the famous sentence

Let others wage war, you, lucky Austria, marry
(Bella gerant alii, tu felix Austria nube).

Regardless of whether this adage, which politically adapts a verse from the erotic poetry of Ovid, really dates from the transitional period between Middle Ages and Renaissance or only from the Baroque era,[47] it is akin to many another adage in that it contains truth and falsehood mixed.[48] On the one hand Austria, and Hapsburg, have waged many wars successfully and unsuccessfully—though it may be said, in conformity with the terminological distinction introduced at the beginning of this paper, that at least from Frederick III onward their wars were on the whole imperial in the Roman and medieval sense rather than imperialistic. At least in Europe these wars were meant to preserve an imperial status quo, which was conceived as a Christian order of peace, a *pax austriaca*, as it were, in the sense of a renewed *pax romana* and *christiana*: *paz con todos los principes cristianos*, to be free

---

Allerhöchsten Kaiserhauses 7 (1888) 1ff.; see also the study by Chmelarz, cited in the preceding note, about the great woodcut of Maximilian's "Gate of Honor," (*Ehrenpforte*), a sort of triumphal arch structure, which also includes a pictorial genealogy.

[46] For this device cf. K. Brandi, *Kaiser Karl V.*, ed. 7 (Munich 1964) 46, 68, 94. Fig. 9 is taken from the frontispiece of the color prints illustrating Charles V's funeral published with French text in Antwerp, 1559, as reproduced in Vicomte Charles Terlinden, *Charles Quint, Empereur des Deux Mondes* (Bruxelles, 1965). Fig. 10 from an engraved apotheosis of the emperor of the year 1556, after Martin van Heemskerck, is likewise reproduced after Terlinden's fig. 157. In 1548, Hans Bolsterer had coined a medal, which on the reverse shows the imperial double eagle with the *Plus Ultra* and the columns of Hercules, and the additional legend: "Quod in celis sol, hoc in terra Caesar est;" cf. Brandi, Front of book cover and back of title page. For the origin and subsequent history of the device, see the important article by E. Rosenthal, "*Plus ultra, Non plus ultra*, and the Columnar Device of Emperor Charles V," *Journal of the Warburg and Courtauld Institutes* xxxiv (1971) 204ff.

[47] Cf. Lhotsky (n. 45 above) 71. The Ovidian model: *Heroides* 13.84.

[48] See also A. (von) Wandruszka, *The House of Habsburg*, trans. from the German (Garden City, N. Y. 1965) 62f.

for the defense of Christanity against the infidels,[49] a conception that was dominated by the Turkish danger, but no doubt also related to the recent Spanish exploits in America.[50] At least in one of Charles V's mentors, his Grand Chancellor, the Piedmontese Gattinara, the ideas of Dante's treatise on monarchy as a guarantee for peace were very much alive; Gattinara went even beyond the emperor in his advocation of universal world monarchy.[51] Already Frederick III had been under the influence of similar ideas, expressed by the most eminent among his advisors, Enea Silvio Piccolomini, later Pope Pius II, whose historical-political thinking on the function of empire had owed much to Otto of Freising, Dante, and more recent imperial theorists such as Antonio de Rosellis.[52] Meanwhile, Frederick III's son Maximilian I had considered toward the end of his life even the possibility of assuming the papal dignity,[53] not to mention his intention to wrest Constantinople from the Turks and to unite its renewed empire with his own.[54] Frederick, who would never have dreamt of such things, differed from his son also in his profoundly sceptical attitude toward the fortunes of war, which is typical of many Hapsburg rulers. In his notebook he entered as a sort of memento the remark "the banner of Austria is not victorious," and he recalled that in the preceding century his ancestors had suffered three formidable defeats[55]— probably he was referring to the battles of Morgarten (1315) and Sempach (1386) against the Swiss and of Mühldorf (1322), where Frederick the Fair was defeated by Lewis the Barbarian—one is reminded here of Emperor

[49] Cf. *Cortes de los antiguos reinos de León y de Castilla* 4 (Madrid 1882) 313 and 295, quoted by R. Menéndez Pidal, "Formación del fundamental pensamiento de Carlos V," *Karl V.: Der Kaiser und seine Zeit*, Kölner Colloquium 26.-29. November 1958 (Cologne 1960) 158f. For the imperial idea of Charles V, cf. also J. A. Maravall, *Carlos V y el pensamiento politico del Renacimento de base Hispanica* (Madrid 1960), esp. 97ff., "La concepción de un impero universal."

[50] Cf. R. Konetzke, "Amerika und Europa in der Zeit Karls V.," in *Karl V.* (n. 49 above) 138ff., esp. 143.

[51] Cf. Menéndez Pidal (n. 49 above) 158, 160f.

[52] The *Monarchia* of Enea Silvia's contemporary Antonio de Rosellis (printed Lyon 1535) largely constitutes an "updating" of Dante's *De Monarchia*. For Enea's imperial ideology and its sources, cf., for instance, Berthe Widmer, *Enea Silvio Piccolomini in der sittlichen und politischen Entscheidung* (Basel 1963) 137, 150f.; A. Lhotsky, *Aeneas Silvius und Österreich*, Vorträge der Aeneas-Silvius-Stiftung an der Universität Basel 5, (Basel 1965) 36ff., 40; see also J. B. Toews, "The View of Empire in Aeneas Sylvius Piccolomini (Pope Pius II)," *Traditio* 24 (1968) 471ff., and Karla Eckermann, *Studien zur Geschichte des monarchischen Gedankens im 15. Jahrhundert* (Berlin 1933).

[53] Cf. H. Ulmann, *Kaiser Maximilian's I. Absichten auf das Papstthum in den Jahren 1507-1511* (Greifswald 1888).

[54] Cf. Coreth (n. 45 above) 294; A. Lhotsky, "Der österreichische Staatsgedanke," *Aufsätze und Vorträge* (n. 9 above) 376.

[55] Cf. the edition of the notebook by Lhotsky, "AEIOV" (n. 32 above) 179, no. 13: "Das wainir von Österreich ist nit sigleich und mein vordern habent 3 streit darunder nidergelegen."

Francis Joseph, of whom it was said that he did not love wars because he knew that one loses them.[56]

If, then, the first part of the adage, "Let others wage wars," is not unproblematic, the second, "You, lucky Austria, marry" is even more of a simplification. If, as I tried to point out earlier, unusually strong concentration on the "house" in the sense of family or dynasty, led the Hapsburg to their enormous successes, it carried in itself also considerable weaknesses not only of a political nature, but probably also of a general anthropological as well as a more specifically psychological and genetic character. To apply the findings of structural anthropology à la Lévi-Strauss[57] to these matters might be promising, but perhaps premature. One thing of relevance in this context, however, can be said: from the fifteenth century onward, at the latest, we find in Hapsburg history a recurrent phenomenon that for lack of a better word might be called premature aging, and this is true not only of the rulers, but increasingly also of the institutions of their government. The beginnings of this process can be seen in the history of Frederick III and can be detected most clearly on the personal level in the portrait-iconography of Charles V, if, for instance, we compare the vibrantly alive Burgundian youth in his late teens (fig. 11)[58] with the emperor and Spanish king painted by Titian in 1548 at only forty-eight years of age (fig. 12):[59] in this painting we see the noble and still alert, but anxious and careworn figure of an old man.

If dynastic concentration formed the basis of the imperial ideology of the "House of Austria," it will not come as a surprise that the father-son relationship is of its essence. Again I can only briefly touch upon relevant phenomena such as the slow and often painful development toward primogeniture— that is to say, the succession of the firstborn (normally the firstborn son) to rulership.[60] On the whole, the relationship between fathers and sons—even younger sons—seems to have been close and affectionate.[61] There are, however, a number of extraordinary and spectacular cases in which members of the dynasty for various reasons, pathological or otherwise, broke out of the charmed paternalistic circle in acts of exasperation against fathers, uncles, or older brothers. The most famous examples were the murder of the second Hapsburg king of Germany and prospective emperor, Albert I, by his nephew

---

[56] Cf. Wandruszka (n. 48 above) 88.

[57] Cf. C. Lévi-Strauss, Les structures élémentaires de la parenté (Paris 1967).

[58] This terracotta bust in the Gruuthuse Museum in Brugge is probably a work of Konrad Meit. Cf. G. Tröscher, Conrat Meit von Worms (Freiburg 1927) 22.

[59] Titian's famous portrait is in the Alte Pinakothek at Munich.

[60] Cf. G. Turba, Geschichte des Thronfolgerechtes in allen Habsburgischen Ländern bis zur Pragmatischen Sanktion Kaiser Karls VI. (Vienna 1903) 101ff.

[61] For the "House of Hapsburg" as a dynasty of exceptional familial coherence, cf. E. von Kahler, Das Geschlecht Habsburg (Munich 1919).

in 1308; then the long and perfidious struggle of Frederick III's younger
brother Albert VI against his senior; the rebellion of Don Carlos against his
father Philip II;[62] the fraternal conflict around Emperor Rudolf II in the
early seventeenth century, which is the subject matter of the best Austrian
drama of the nineteenth century, Grillparzer's *Bruderzwist*. In more recent
times we find the tragedy of Francis Joseph's son Rudolf in Mayerling and
the mutual dislike between the patriarchal Francis Joseph and his nephew,
the substitute heir Francis Ferdinand, a potential autocrat, it is true, but
with innovating propensities, the victim not only of the revolver shots of
Sarajevo, but also of the dead-end situation in the terminal phase of the
Austrian Empire.

Prior to the late nineteenth century, however, such events and situations
had remained exceptional, and it may even be said that in the Hapsburg
ambiance, and only in it, imperialism and paternalistic dynasticism were
one and the same thing and that this combination functioned well for centuries. The *Haus Österreich*, the *Casa de Austria*, was the encompassing concept that under Charles V and his descendants could include the old *Sacrum
Imperium Romanum* and Austria, the Netherlands, Spain, and large parts
of Italy, Bohemia, and Hungary. It is extremely important for an understanding of Hapsburg imperial ideology to realize that it did not identify
istelf with an ethnic or national substratum, as did that, for instance, of
France or England. Nor was it simply identical with the quasi-religious
ideology of the earlier medieval empire, as it had appeared, for instance,
in Otto of Freising, though it did become blended with that earlier ideology
in the age of Frederick III, Maximilian I, and Charles V. The imperial idea
of the Hapsburg, even after the division of the Spanish and Austrian lines,
which had become effective with the abdication of Charles V in 1556, remained
above all a supranational dynastic idea, now increasingly focused in Austria.[63]
The Hapsburg ruler of Austria especially stressed his function as *pater familias*, as "patriarch" of his people, or in the exceptional case of Maria The-
resa, as "matriarch." The earlier medieval idea of the king or emperor as
place-holder of God on earth was not lost sight of, but it now operated through
the medium of the "illustrious house," the dynasty, and only through it.
While it is beyond the scope of this paper to investigate the relationship
between the general phenomenon of early absolutism and the Hapsburg dy-
nastic-imperial idea, it cannot be overlooked that the largely dynastic-pater-

---

[62] Cf. C. D. O'Malley, *Don Carlos of Spain*: *A Medical Portrait*, Faculty Research Lecture, University of California, Los Angeles, 15 April, 1969 (Berkeley 1970).

[63] Besides the essay by von Kahler (n. 61 above), cf. above all A. Lhotsky (n. 54 above)
365ff., with excellent distinctions of medieval ideas concerning *dominium* (*Herrschaft*),
dynasty, and empire, and the ideas of early modern times—though his conceptual separation of dynasty and "state" is less than convincing to me, as far as the history of Austria
and Hapsburg before the eightheenth century is concerned.

nalistic conception of empire in the last stages of the Holy Roman Empire, especially between 1780 and 1806, and in the Austrian and Austro-Hungarian Empire from 1804 to 1918 had certain adverse consequences. Dynastic paternalism proved impermeable to timely reform and ended in revolution of the "subject-children," who belonged to many ethnic groups, against the supranational "emperor-father." I do not wish to simplify very complex matters, which would require extensive and probing historical and psychological studies, but only to note by way of a reminder that Sigmund Freud was a son of old Austria, which gave him much of the raw material for his criticism of what might be called every family's private dynasticism. The life of an Austrian family, at least before 1918, was to some degree molded by the paternalistic model of the "all-highest," the imperial house—which even in its decline possessed more charisma than other Western dynasties.

I shall now try to characterize, in a manner that on this occasion must again remain highly selective, a few manifestations of old Austrian traditions with medieval connotations, which expressed themselves in some of the most significant works of Austrian poetic literature of the mid-nineteenth and early twentieth century.

The greatest example of medieval influences on modern Austrian literature is undoubtedly the *Witiko* of Adalbert Stifter, conventionally called a historical novel, which this greatest of all Austrian prose writers completed one year before his death in 1868.[64] It is, however, quite insufficient to call this work a novel. It is in reality the only modern epic in the German language which evokes the life of the Middle Ages in a manner that makes the period come alive.

The specific subject matter of this epic prose poem is the destiny of Witiko, the ancestor of the great Bohemian family of the Rosenberg. His life is shown in the midst of the much-agitated history of Bohemia, Austria, and the Holy Roman Empire around the middle of the twelfth century. This is the very same period that was discussed at the beginning of this paper: the era of Henry Jasomirgott of Austria, of Otto of Freising, of Agnes, daughter of Emperor Henry IV, and of Emperor Frederick Barbarossa; it is also the era of the duke, later king, of Bohemia, Vladislav II Przemysl, who after difficult beginnings was to become one of the country's better rulers.

Stifter assiduously studied much of the historical literature available at the time for medieval Bohemia and its adjacent regions—such as the then just published history of Bohemia by Palacký,[65] which had rightly become

---

[64] The *Witiko* will be cited after the standard edition, *Adalbert Stifters Sämmtliche Werke*, Bibliothek Deutscher Schriftsteller aus Böhmen, Mähren und Schlesien 9-11 (Reichenberg 1932), so also other works of Stifter's mentioned in this paper.

[65] E. Palacký, *Geschichte von Böhmen* 1 (Prague 1844). Palacký is also Stifter's main source for the family history of the Witkowici, ancestors of the Rosenberg; the latter derived their origin from the Orsini of Rome, who had the five-leaved rose in their coat of

famous; according to his repeated assertions, he also spent much time and
effort on the medieval sources themselves (see below).[66] Having thus acquired
very considerable knowledge of his historical subject, the poet achieved something that always must remain one of the highest ambitions of writers of historical poems and novels, and of historians as well: the reconstruction of
what Stifter called "the body" of a past epoch, in this case the Middle Ages,
so that "poet and reader breathe in the air of those past times," and for this,
he says, historical knowledge alone is not enough, for it would produce only
a "wooden skeleton"; historical *Mitleben*—empathy—is necessary, only thus
will the characters receive flesh and blood.[67]

Stifter amply used an artistic means that ancient and medieval historians
as well as poets had regularly employed to good effect. I am referring to
the insertion of long speeches into the narrative. Since it is not possible in
this paper to analyze the entire novel with regard to its relationship to the
Middle Ages, I shall concentrate on a brief discussion of the structure or general
character of the speeches. They are often part of very lively descriptions
of public assemblies and ceremonies which greatly contribute to the poetic
evocation of the men and women of that time, whose simple nobility and

---

arms. Cf. Palacký's genealogical remarks in J. G. Sommer, *Das Königreich Böhmen* 9
(Prague 1841) 60ff. Stifter also knew the late seventeenth-century *Rosenbergsche Chronik*
by Norbert Heermann, ed. M. Klimesch (Prague 1898), whence the poet took the legendary
derivation of Witiko's family from the Orsini, which in his novel is connected with the
important symbolic role that the five-leaved wild rose plays in Witiko's life. Cf. also Flöring, (n. 66 below) 50ff. For general up-to-date orientation on Bohemia and its relation
to Germany in the age of Vladislav II, I may refer to P. E. Schramm, "Böhmen und das
Regnum: Die Verleihungen der Königswürde an die Herzöge von Böhmen," *Adel und Kirche:
Gerd Tellenbach zum 65. Geburtstag dargebracht* (Freiburg 1968) 356ff., reprinted in
Schramm, *Kaiser, Könige und Päpste* 4, 2 (Stuttgart 1971) 517ff.; H. Hoffmann, "Böhmen
und das Deutsche Reich im Hohen Mittelalter," *Jahrbuch für die Geschichte Mittel- und
Ostdeutschlands* 18 (1969), esp. 40ff., with ample literature; also W. Wegener, *Böhmen/Mähren
und das Reich im Hochmittelalter* (Cologne 1959) and P. Hilsch, *Die Bischöfe von Prag
in der frühen Stauferzeit* (Munich 1969).

[66] Cf. K. Flöring, *Die historischen Elemente in Adalbert Stifters "Witiko"*, Giessener
Beiträge zur Deutschen Philologie 5 (Giessen 1922).

[67] Cf. Stifter (n. 64 above) *Briefwechsel, Sämmtliche Werke* 17 (Prague 1916) 302: Letter
to his publisher, Gustav Heckenast, September 8, 1848: "Wenn Sie wüssten, welche Ar-
beit es ist, aus den alten Urkunden und Documenten den Körper des Mittelalters zu con-
struieren . . . wie man oft tagelang in den widerstrebendsten Sprachen lesen muss (in einer
oft verzweifelten Weitschweifigkeit), um nur ein paar Züge für sich zu erhaschen"; furthermore, Stifter's letter to the same of June 9, 1853, *Briefwechsel, Sämmtliche Werke* 18
(Prague 1918) 152: "Der Roman hat eine wissenschaftliche Seite, die von vornherein in
keines Menschen Seele liegt, sondern die er sich erwerben muss, das Geschichtliche. Dieses
muss so treu angeeignet werden, dass Dichter und Leser in der Luft jener vergangenen
Zeiten athmen, und die Gegenwart für sie nicht ist, dies allein gibt Wahrheit. Aber zu
dem ist nicht das historische Wissen allein genug, dies gäbe nur ein hölzernes Geripppe,
sondern das historische Mitleben, dieses gibt den Gestalten Fleisch und Blut."

dignity Stifter emphasizes.[68] It is true that only a few instances have been found in which Stifter used a speech from a medieval source as a model for a speech on the same subject in the *Witiko*. The clearest example is Vincent of Prague's Annals—one of Stifter's principal sources for the novel. According to Stifter as well as Vincent, Vladislav II of Bohemia allegedly tipped the scales in favor of his people's participation in the first Milanese campaign of Frederick Barbarossa (1158) by telling them that those who were satisfied with "womanly play" might with his permission stay at home.[69] Regardless of how many more telling instances of this kind might still be discovered, it is more important in our context that many speeches in the *Witiko*—though not dependent upon a specific source dealing with an identical historical incident—nevertheless are thoroughly permeated by the tone and ethos of the twelfth century, and often close to that period even in language and style.

In this connection it is not without interest that Stifter himself in the narrative of the *Witiko* introduces Vincent of Prague[70] and Otto of Freising[71] as chroniclers. It seems very probable that he was familiar not only with their works, but also with Otto's continuator Rahewin and with Vincent's Bohemian predecessors, Cosmas of Prague and his continuators. Cosmas's *Chronicle*[72] and Otto-Rahewin's *Gesta Friederici I* contain speeches that are similar to the speeches in the *Witiko* in two obvious respects, which are characteristic for many historiographical sources of the High Middle Ages: solemn invocations of the person or persons to whom the speeches are addressed and acclamations of approval and praise. A more subtle and general sim-

---

[68] Cf., for instance, *Witiko* 1 (n. 64 above) 101ff., the impressive description of the assembly on the Vyšehrad, the royal residence in Prague, where Witiko as messenger of the dying Duke Sobieslav confronts the Bohemian nobles—the speeches held on that occasion go far in revealing the character of Witiko as well as of the other participants in the assembly and the historical climate in which it took place. Many similar examples could be given.

[69] Cf. Vincent of Prague, *Annales*, to the year 1158, MGH Scriptores 17 (Hannover 1861) 668: "Qui me in hoc negotio iuvare intendit, hunc honore debito et pecunia ad hec necessaria, ut decet, exorno; qui vero negligit, mulierum ludis contentus et ocio, mea pace securus propria sedeat in domo." (This may have been a *topos*, perhaps of classical origin; it occurs again a little later in Vincent's *Annals*, to the year 1164, *loc. cit.* 681). Compare with the Vincentian text, just quoted, Stifter's elaboration in the *Witiko* 3, (n. 64 above) 11.284: "Und wenn manche mit mir ziehen, so sind sie in ihrem Rechte, wie ich in meinem Rechte bin, und ich verleihe ihnen aus meinem Eigentume jede Zier der Ehre und Mittel. Und die in der Heimat bleiben, tun auch nach ihrem Rechte und ihrer Pflicht. Es werden auch solche sein, die mit Frauentändeleien und Musse zufrieden sind, diese mögen sicher unter meinem Frieden in ihrem Hause sitzen." Flöring (n. 66 above) 21 has shown that Stifter is here closer to Vincent than to the secondary literature that he knew.

[70] *Witiko* 3 (n. 64 above) 11.312.

[71] *Witiko* 2, 10.71.

[72] Cosmas of Prague, *Chronica Boemorum*, ed. B. Bretholz, *Scriptores rerum germanicarum*, N. S. 2 (Berlin 1923).

ilarity can be found between the *Witiko* and medieval chronicles or histories with regard to the deliberately slow and equanimous pace, the sober and reasoned exposition, the strong and yet measured spirit that is typical for most of the speeches in the *Witiko* even when matters of great concern to the speaker and listeners are at stake. I have already mentioned the assembly on the Vyšehrad as described in *Witiko* (cf. note 68), and we have only to open Otto of Freising's *Gesta Frederici I*, to find instances of a similar mood. I may refer to the confrontation between Frederick Barbarossa, who was bent on reestablishing imperial rights, and the ambassadors of the city of Rome, who were attempting to defend the prerogative of the eternal city in a "Roman Empire."[73] The mood expressed here, and also in Otto's and Rahewin's accounts of Barbarossa's conflict with Milan, is echoed in Stifter's description of the emperor's dealings with the Milanese in the *Witiko*,[74] and also in the great reckoning of Vladislav II of Bohemia with his relatives from the House of Przemysl, who had first elected him and later had rebelled.[75]

In addition to historical sources in the strict sense of the term, Stifter also read Middle High German poetry. He quotes a song of the Kürenberger[76] and also the *Nibelungenlied* which he calls "a great song that will emerge soon."[77] In calling it a great song, he no doubt compared it mentally to Homer, whose *Odyssey* he calls so great that no modern poet can stand beside him.[78] It is not far-fetched to call the epic spirit of Stifter's *Witiko* Homeric[79]— at least with regard to the immediacy with which the persons of the novel express their thoughts and feelings. Stifter indeed seems closer to Homer than to the often self-consciously reflective and sententious manner of speech of the *Nibelungenlied*.

What has been said about Stifter's use of medieval historiographical and poetic works must now be somewhat qualified by the undeniable fact that he seems to have depended to a very large degree on secondary sources, even

[73] Cf. Otto of Freising, *Gesta Friderici I*. 2.29f. (n. 8 above) 135ff.

[74] Cf. *Witiko* 3 (n. 64 above) 11.314ff.

[75] *Witiko* 1, 9.287ff., and 3, 11.142ff. For Stifter's style in the *Witiko* and its relation to a medieval tradition which had not yet been completely lost, cf. also G. Weippert, *Stifters Witiko* (Vienna 1967) 243ff.

[76] *Witiko* 2 (n. 64 above) 10.257.

[77] *Witiko* 3, 11.357.

[78] *Briefwechsel* (n. 67 above) 18.174ff., Letter to Gustav Heckenast of December 11, 1853: "Was bin ich gegen Homer, dessen Odysseus [*sic*] ich eben gelesen habe. . . . [176] Die grosse unglaubliche Kraft und Gewalt Homers . . . so gross, dass alle neueren Dichter nicht davor bestehen können. Die Alten hiessen ihn darum auch den göttlichen Homer." In 1857, Stifter had the plan to write a "Nausikae," cf. *ibid.* 19.27, Letter to Louise von Eichendorff, June 2, 1857.

[79] For Stifter's Homeric style, see also F. Hüller, *Adalbert Stifters Witiko* (Graz 1953) 105ff.

to a greater degree than on the primary ones;[80] the most important modern histories that he studied beside Palacký's "History of Bohemia" were Tomek's "History of Prague,"[81] Raumer's "History of the Hohenstaufen,"[82] and Tourtual's "The Share of Bohemia in the Italian Wars of the Emperor Frederick I."[83] It is all the more remarkable that the late Romantic style and spirit of these nineteenth-century authors interfered so little with Stifter's intuition of the Middle Ages, which remained much closer to the original sources.

Here it must not be forgotten that Stifter was not dependent upon literary sources alone. His intuition of the medieval past came from a natural affinity to it, which was founded on, and constantly reinforced by, his origin from, and life in, the borderlands between Bavaria, Austria, and Bohemia, and by his contact with the rural people, who in the middle of the nineteenth century had still preserved many medieval forms of life. They lived in an external landscape that had not changed much for centuries and which is exceedingly well described in Stifter's writings and to some extent reproduced also in his paintings.[84] It is the landscape that reaches from the darkly massed trees and bright clearings of the South Bohemian forests to the blue and ethereal outline of the Alps, as they rise distantly behind the valleys and plains of the Danube and its tributaries.

This quiet rather than spectacular country, and the people in it, were for Stifter a part and a symbol of that universal, and therefore also human, force that he called *das sanfte Gesetz*, "the gentle law": it is to him the most profound, the most important manifestation of the divine in the earthly. In the human sphere, "the gentle law" excludes all violence. It expresses itself in good government, which Stifter sees very much in those paternalistic and imperial terms with which we are by now familiar. As far as the old Austria is concerned, Stifter's *Witiko* may be regarded as the apotheosis of a political order that was imperial but not in any modern sense imperialistic.[85]

---

[80] Cf. Flöring (nn. 66 above) 20ff. and 24ff.

[81] W. W. T. Tomek, *Geschichte der Stadt Prag* 1 (Prague 1856).

[82] F. von Raumer, *Geschichte der Hohenstaufen* 1 and 2 (Leipzig 1823, later editions 1840f., 1857).

[83] F. Tourtual, *Böhmens Antheil an den Kämpfen Kaiser Friedrichs I. in Italien* (Göttingen 1865).

[84] For the latter, cf. F. Novotny, *Adalbert Stifter als Maler* (Vienna 1941).

[85] For Stifter's "gentle law" see the often-quoted formulation in the prologue (1852) to his *Bunte Steine, Sämmtliche Werke* 5.1 (Prague 1908) 6ff., of which I can cite only the main passage: "Wir wollen das sanfte Gesetz zu erblicken suchen, wodurch das menschliche Geschlecht geleitet wird ... Es ist ... das Gesetz der Gerechtigkeit, das Gesetz der Sitte, das Gesetz, das will, dass jeder geachtet, geehrt, ungefährdet neben dem anderen bestehe." For Stifter's "medieval" affirmation of law and lawful (even though possibly evil) authority, his opposition to disorder and lawless violence in internal and external policy, his paternalistic, antiimperialistic idea of empire, cf. Weippert (n. 75 above) 111ff., 145ff., also H. Augustin, *Adalbert Stifter und das christliche Weltbild* (Basel 1959) esp. 86ff.: "Die

For Stifter, the fundamental form of all political life was the house—a point of view, incidentally, which today is again very central to the study of the constitutional history of Europe.[86] Not by accident is the castle that Witiko builds, after he has, as he says, found his destiny, simply called the "Witiko House" by Stifter and identified with Wittinghausen.[87] Yet, the novel is the story also of the Houses of Bohemia under the Przemysl, of Austria under the Babenberg, and even of the imperial House of Hohenstaufen.

One may doubt if such a novel or epic story could at that time have been written anywhere but in Austria, where the framework of political life and thought was still—though not for much longer—dynastic in the special sense that I tried to describe earlier: a sense in which the idea of family and the idea of state were close to one another and were elevated together to the sacredness of an imperial house.

Like all human constructions, so that of the imperial-paternalistic tradition, too, had its built-in, unsettling problems, among which—as we already had the opportunity of observing—the father-son relationship was one, and certainly not the least important.

Hofmannsthal's *Der Turm*, completed in the mid-twenties of this century,[88] is a great modern tragedy in which the paternalistic-imperial idea is shown in a crisis. In this drama, rulership is linked to a fateful and mysterious old prophecy; there is disaster, but there is also hope in prophecy of a new kind which foretells the coming of a new order.

In "The Tower," Hofmannsthal has taken over and wholly transformed the plot of Calderon's *La vida es sueño*,[89] "Life is a Dream." The hero is Prince Sigismund, whom his father, King Basil, had condemned to languish in a dark tower, a symbol of concentrated and closed power. The reason for this

---

Kaiseridee." Stifter's ethical attitude is not simply identical with contemporary political conservatism, though it is true that he had been disappointed in his short-lived hopes for political improvement raised by the Revolution of 1848/49. Cf. W. Oberle, *Der adelige Mensch in der Dichtung: Eichendorff, Gotthelf, Stifter, Fontane* (Basel 1950) 88f., for Stifter's ideas on revolution and liberty, monarchy and democracy. There is no doubt that the failures of 1848 confirmed his paternalistic idea of a (constitutional) monarchy.

[86] Cf. above all the pioneer work by O. Brunner, *Land und Herrschaft*, ed. 5 (Vienna 1965); also the same author's *Adeliges Landleben und Europäischer Geist: Leben und Werk Wolf Helmhards von Hohberg 1612-1688* (Salzburg 1949).

[87] For the building of the castle "Witiko House" or Wittinghausen—the ruins of which Stifter himself painted, cf. Novotny (n. 84 above) figs. 12, 13, 17, 38, 40—see *Witiko* 3 (n. 64 above) 11.129ff., 211ff. The castle ruin is situated near Ober-Plan, Stifter's birthplace, in Southern Bohemia, in the "Bohemian Forest" (*Böhmerwald*).

[88] Hugo von Hofmannsthal, *Gesammelte Werke in Einzelausgaben*, ed. H. Steiner, *Dramen* 4 (Frankfurt 1958) 7ff., *Der Turm*, first version (1925); 321ff., *Der Turm*, new version (1927).

[89] For the relationship between the two dramas cf. E. R. Curtius, "George, Hofmannsthal und Calderon," *Kritische Essays zur europäischen Literatur* (Bern 1950) 158ff., especially 184ff.; Egon Schwarz, *Hofmannsthal und Calderon* (Cambridge, Mass. 1962) 91ff.

inhumanity is the father's inability to overcome his fear of the prediction that he will be overthrown by this son. This is not the time and place to explain why and how Sigismund survives as a human being and is freed. Even the tower had been unable to smother the innate nobility of his nature which prevails against the corrupt and tyrannical paternal regime. Sigismund triumphs with the help of the little people who see in him their savior. But immediately there arises the specter of mob rule under a demonic leader, Olivier, who understands how to use all the baser instincts awakened by a revolt of the masses and how to put them to the service of his very real genius for expediency and temporary success. When he sees that Sigismund will not be a figurehead in a dehumanized world, Olivier has him killed. But this need not be the end, for Sigismund was only an inter-rex, a forerunner. In one of the versions of the drama, Sigismund, dying, hands over his rule to a messianic young king, who has no longer any tie with the old imperial traditions. He is called the Children's King and comes out of the woods with his singing unarmed companions.[90] He will found a new community over the tomb of Sigismund, who was the link between the old and the new order. In the last version, however, the Children's King no longer appears. Sigismund himself has the last word:

Give witness that I was here, though no one knew me.[91]

Even this, the poet seems to say, will some day renew the face of the earth.

Der Turm is Hofmannsthal's last reckoning with the old imperial-paternalistic ideology, which had failed in the era of World War I—and not only in Austria. He finished this drama in the years that followed that war and after the revolutions that accompanied it. Whereas it is hard to say whether or not the figure of the fictitious Olivier is a divinatory anticipation of the role of the real Hitler, there can, I believe, be no doubt that Sigismund and the Children's King are mythical expressions of Hofmannsthal's hopes for a new and better world. These hopes have ancient and medieval roots in millenarian expectations of a savior-king at the end of history, but they also reflect, I think, the poetic-political youth movement of the early twentieth century. Furthermore, and in ultimate analysis, the "Tower" drama may be Hofmannsthal's final answer to Stefan George and thus a part of the ambivalent dialogue between these two protagonists of the Austrian and of the German spirit.[92]

[90] First version (n. 88 above) 203ff.

[91] New version (n. 88 above) 463: "Gebet Zeugnis, ich war da, wenngleich mich niemand gekannt hat."

[92] The attempt of Stefan George to renew Germany intrinsically by a new human elite might have been successful had it not been routed by the Nazis, who unsuccessfully tried to use George as their own symbolic puppet. Instead, he chose to leave Germany and died

Der Turm is at any rate unique in Hofmannsthal's *œuvre*. Stifter's *Witiko* had been the last epic celebration of the Austrian medieval tradition—still joyful as well as serious; Hofmannsthal's *Turm* evoked the tragedy of the imperial-paternalistic idea to which this poet had clung almost all his life, but which in the end he symbolically transcended.[93]

The necessity of modifying the old traditions, not only of Austria, but of Western civilization as a whole, had become clear to the best minds of Europe and America long before the general collapse of World War I, a collapse of which the disintegration of the Austrian Empire was only an especially significant part. One of Austria's special problems could be subsumed under the heading: discrepancy between an imperial ideology of medieval origins and modern nationalism, be it imperialistic or democratic or both. As far as democracy is concerned, it was the Athenian democrat and imperialist Cleon who, according to Thucydides's *History of the Peloponnesian War*, had said that democracy is incapable of empire.[94] Conversely, it might perhaps be said of old Austria—pulled, as it was, in many different directions by its nationalities problem and eclipsed by dynamically expansionist rather than traditionalist imperialisms—that it could not become democratic and remain an empire.

This was a tragic dilemma that, like all historical tragedies, was also one of human failures. There are few writers who have illuminated the relationship between personal and political-cultural disintegration as penetratingly as Robert Musil, who died in most miserable exile from Austria in 1942 in Geneva. Let me then terminate this paper with a few remarks on Musil's

---

in Switzerland in the very year of the Nazi power seizure. To return from reality to fiction, Hofmannsthal's Sigismund had to disappear when he refused to become Olivier's puppet. It may be that the name of the dictatorial Olivier is a reminder of Oliver Cromwell; but it is noteworthy that Olivier is a noncommissioned officer, just as Hitler was, of whose first exploits in 1923 Hofmannsthal must have had knowledge. As to George's belief in, and Hofmannsthal's fiction of, a youthful savior, much more could be said, but not on this occasion.

[93] From a somewhat different point of view, this evolution is described by C. E. Schorske, "The Transformation of the Garden: Ideal and Society in Austrian Literature," *XIIe Congrès international des sciences historiques*, *Vienne, 29.8.-5.9.1965*, section 1.5 (published by the Institute of International Studies, University of California, Berkely); cf. also Schorske's "Politics and the Psyche in *fin du siècle* Vienna: Schnitzler and Hofmannsthal," *American Historical Review* 66 (1961) 945f. What Austria and its symbolization by the emperor meant to Hofmannsthal, is well described by Hermann Broch, "Hofmannsthal und seine Zeit," *Gesammelte Werke*: *Essays 1* (Zurich 1955), esp. 139ff. Some good remarks on "The Tower" are found also in the recent essay by Egon Schwarz, "Hugo von Hofmannsthal as a Critic," in *On Four Modern Humanists*: *Hofmannsthal, Gundolf, Curtius, Kantorowicz* (Princeton 1970) 3ff., esp. 33, 46.

[94] Cf. Thucydides 3.37f., a passage kindly drawn to my attention by Professor T. S. Brown.

Mann ohne Eigenschaften,[95] a novel of extraordinary satirical and utopian range and depth, practically unknown in the author's lifetime, but now recognized as ranking with the works of Kafka, Broch, and Thomas Mann.

The explanation of the title of Musil's novel, "The Man without Qualities," is simply that Ulrich, the hero, tries to live an essential, not merely an accidental, existence. To his misfortune, and to our enlightenment, this existence takes place in a state called *Kakania*. This strange name signifies of course Austria, for it is formed from the repetition of the letter "K," or more exactly "k" and "k," meaning *kaiserlich* and *königlich*, that is to say, "imperial" and "royal." Since the early nineteenth century, and especially since 1867, the date of the settlement between the Empire Austria and the Kingdom Hungary, these letters "k" and "k" were encountered on practically all official documents. The mechanical proliferation of the combinations "k" and "k" or simply "k.k."—for there was since 1867 a significant difference between these two forms—may be considered as symbolic of the last phase of imperial Austria, when the old imperial idea had largely become a dead letter, both literally and substantially. Even in that last phase it still remained true for Musil and many others that, as Schiller had said in his *Wallenstein*:

> . . . Austrians possess a fatherland
> They love it and to love it have good reason.[96]

Yet, Musil and others of his generation and of the following generation felt the necessity to tear off the masks with which Austria—a peculiarly impressive paradigm of the state of the world in the early twentieth century—had overlaid its human essence and existence.[97] Musil, fictionally and yet very realistically, isolated and analyzed one section of an incredibly complicated situation of which perhaps the most characteristic aspect was the illusion and pretense that everything could be improved without anything having to change. The so-called "Parallel Action," which runs like a red thread through the whole enormous torso of Musil's work, is a bizarre attempt to imitate the Wilhelmian German Reich and thus constitutes a particular perversion of the old Austrian imperial ideology. In Musil's novel this action leads inevitably into the First World War and generally into troubles of unprecedented magnitude. And this, at least for Austria, corresponded to the actual facts because the inner core of the old imperial ideology—the *pax austriaca*, as

---

[95] Robert Musil, *Mann ohne Eigenschaften*, ed. A. Frisé (Hamburg 1952); English translation by E. Wilkins and E. Kaiser (London 1953).

[96] Friedrich Schiller, *Wallensteins Tod* 1.5:
> Der Österreicher hat ein Vaterland
> Und liebt's und hat auch Ursach, es zu lieben.

[97] Cf. L. G. Seeger, *Die Demaskierung der Lebenslüge: Eine Untersuchung zur Krise der Gesellschaft in Robert Musils Der Mann ohne Eigenschaften* (Bern 1969).

heir of the *pax romana* and *christiana*—had lost much of its credibility, often becoming a mere travesty of its original meaning. And yet, with the exception of the rather different traditionalism of England, it was Austria alone which among the European states had carried those great imperial traditions from the Middle Ages into the modern world with at least a modicum of dignity. Musil loved Austria for it, but nevertheless recognized that with or without the ingredients of modern nationalism the imperial idea was no longer viable.

In the last sentence of his essay "The Nation as Ideal and Reality," written in 1921, Musil said:

> The people which will be the first to find its way out of the dead-end street of imperial nationalism toward a new possible world order . . . will . . . have the leadership of the world . . . . Today nobody can yet outline the path to this aim in any detail; but it is necessary to create the thinking and feeling which will lead toward this path.[98]

This may be supplemented from Stifter's *Witiko*, where Vladislav of Bohemia expresses his hope that

> times will come, when peoples will no longer be alone, when they will be as man to man, as neighbor to neighbor, as friend to friend,[99]

and from the words of the Children's King in Hofmannsthal's *Turm*:

> We have built huts and keep fire on the hearth and forge the swords into plowshares. We have given new laws, for the laws must always come from the young. And beside the dead we set up lights.[100]

---

[98] Robert Musil, *Gesammelte Werke in Einzelausgaben*, ed. A. Frisé: *Tagebücher, Aphorismen, Essays und Reden* (Hamburg 1955) 622: "Das Volk, welches am frühsten beginnt, aus der Sackgasse des Imperial-Nationalismus herauszufinden zu einer neuen möglichen Weltordnung und allen seinen Massnahmen diesen Atem der Zukunft zu verleihen vermag, wird bald die Führung de Welt haben und seine berechtigten Wünsche durchsetzen können. Heute kann niemand noch den Weg dahin im einzelnen vorzeichnen; wohl aber gilt es, die Gesinnung zu schaffen, die auf den Weg führt."

[99] Witiko 2 (n. 64 above) 10.36: "Und es werden die Zeiten kommen, dass die Völker nicht mehr allein sind, dass sie sind, wie Mensch und Mensch, wie Nachbar und Nachbar, wie Freund und Freund."

[100] First version (n. 88 above) 206: "Wir haben Hütten gebaut und halten Feuer auf der Esse und schmieden die Schwerter zu Pflugscharen um. Wir haben neue Gesetze gegeben, denn die Gesetze müssen immer von den Jungen kommen. Und bei den Toten stellen wir Lichter auf."

Department of History
University of California
Los Angeles, California, U.S.A.

FIG. 1. Seal of Otto of Freising as Bishop

FIG. 2. Rudolf IV: Vienna, Dom und Diözesanmuseum

FIG. 3. "Burgundian Cup," Vienna, Kunsthistorisches Museum

FIG. 4. Tomb Statue of Frederick III: Vienna, Saint Stephen's

FIG. 5. Notebook of Frederick III: Vienna, Nationalbibliothek, Cod. Vindob. Palat. 2674, fol. l*r

FIG. 6. "Handregistratur" of Frederick III: Vienna, Haus-, Hof-, und Staatsarchiv

FIG. 7. Tratzberg,
Hapsburg Family Tree
(Detail)

HECTOR PRIAMI MAGNI
REGIS TROIANORVM FIL

FIG. 8. Burgkmair,
Genealogy of Maxi
Hector of Troy

FIG. 9. Frontispiece of *Pompe funèbre* of Charles V

FIG. 10. Print after Martin van Heemskerck, Apotheosis of Charles V

FIG. 11. Konrad Meit (?), Charles V: Brugge,
Grunthuse Museum

FIG. 12. Titian, Charles V: Munich, Alte Pinakothek

VIATOR Style Sheet

1. All contributions must be typewritten in double space, with ample margins. This applies to text, quoted material, and footnotes. Please do *not* use corrasible paper.

2. Footnotes should be typed in double space on separate sheets at the end of the article and numbered consecutively.

3. Bibliographical references ordinarily belong in the notes rather than in the text; the first reference to an item should contain the complete data:

Book: J. K. Brown, *Book Title* (City 1879) 234-236.

Title, 3 vols. (City 1870) 2.45ff.

Title [Translation of title] (City 1877) 34.

Title, ed. John Doe and Jane Doe (City [etc.].

ed. 2 (City [etc.].

trans. John Doe (City 1876) fol. 15v.

Monograph: John G. Black, *Monograph Title*, Title of Series (ABBRV) 21 (1786) 34.

C. J. Smith, *Monograph in Same Series*, ABBRV 22 (1787) 345-346.

Article: John Doe, "Article," *Journal* 76 (1879) 1-22, 34ff., 50.

Undated Journal 76.1-22.

Manuscript: Augustine, *De musica* 3.4, Paris, Bibliothèque Nationale lat. MS 9320, fols. 4, 5v, 6rv.

4. Subsequent references may be shortened as follows, always with a view to brevity without ambiguity.

    a. Smith 24-25.   (Only one Smith is cited, in a recent footnote, and there can be no possible ambiguity.)

    b. Jones (n. 2 above) 245-246.   (Complete reference is in n. 2 above.)

    c. Jones, "The Blue Book" (n. 2 above) 34.   (Jones has more than one reference in n. 2, so short title is necessary.)

    d. Augustine 3.6 (7v).

5. Sigla: *Acta sanctorum*: AS Apr. 3.420.

    Patrologia graeca: PG 37.96A.

    Patrologia latina: PL 129.432.

    Monumenta Germaniae historica: MGH Auctores antiquiores 5.1 (Berlin 1882) 130.

6. Titles of foreign books and articles should be capitalized according to the usages of the respective languages. In Latin and the Romance languages, only the first word and proper nouns should be capitalized.